Education

and Political Development

STUDIES IN
POLITICAL DEVELOPMENT

Sponsored by the Committee on
Comparative Politics of the Social
Science Research Council

Education
and
Political Development

Edited by James S. Coleman

CONTRIBUTORS

JEREMY R. AZRAEL	ANTHONY H. M. KIRK-GREENE
FRANK BONILLA	CARL H. LANDÉ
LEON CARL BROWN	JOHN WILSON LEWIS
MICHEL DEBEAUVAIS	DWAINE MARVICK
JOSEPH FISCHER	AYO OGUNSHEYE
WILLIAM F. GUTTERIDGE	HERBERT PASSIN
BERT F. HOSELITZ	WILLIAM J. PLATT
MALCOLM H. KERR	EDWARD A. SHILS
FRANCIS X. SUTTON	

PRINCETON, NEW JERSEY
PRINCETON UNIVERSITY PRESS

FOREWORD

~~~~~~

IN SPONSORING this fourth volume in the "Studies in Political Development" the Committee on Comparative Politics of the Social Science Research Council seeks to direct attention to the gap that exists between the broadly accepted assumptions about the paramount importance of education in national development and the limited amount of research which has been done on this subject. One out of every five American dollars in technical aid is now being channelled into assisting education, and in a majority of the developing countries education receives a higher proportion of the national budget than is common in Europe. Yet this heavy investment in education is inspired more by clichés and truisms—"Learning must proceed doing"—than by a systematic examination of the precise role that educational systems can play in facilitating development.

The few pioneering studies of education in the developing countries have concentrated mainly on manpower needs and the requirements of education for producing the array of skills essential for economic and industrial development. The relationship of education to political development has been almost entirely neglected, although the folklore of development contains many ambiguous sentiments about both the positive and the disruptive effects of the diffusion of education. This neglect is odd because in the history of the West public schools grew out of the ideals of citizenship training, and higher education was always linked to the need for responsible and capable public leaders. In contrast to this positive view of the relationship of education and politics in the West, in many of the new states, there has been anxiety over the political consequences of expanding education, and consequently a greater reliance upon economic development considerations to justify increasing support for school systems.

As Professor Coleman indicates in his provocative introduction to this book, the fault for neglecting to analyze the relationship between education and political development lies equally with professional educators and political scientists. In accepting as self-evident the inherent social value of education, the schoolmen have felt free to concentrate on education as though it were a self-contained system and to avoid any explicit treatment of the interrelationships of poli-

[v]

tics and education. This accords to the tradition of American educators, who have long recognized that while they must be sensitive to the nuances of politics they can best advance the interest of education by strictly adhering to the ethic of professionalism. The neglect of the subject by political scientists is harder to explain and justify; but it seems likely that the current interest in political socialization and citizenship attitudes may stimulate a renewed interest in the relationships between education and the polity.

Basic to the philosophy which informs the "Studies in Political Development" is the belief that the pressing problems of modernization in the new states call for the combined insights of representatives of all the social science disciplines. It was in this spirit that James S. Coleman organized this volume by bringing together educators, political scientists, and other social scientists. The seminar out of which this volume emerged was held at the Lake Arrowhead Conference Center (of the University of California, Los Angeles) on June 25-29, 1962. The participants in addition to the authors of this study and the members of the Committee on Comparative Politics included: C. Arnold Anderson, University of Chicago; David E. Apter, University of California, Berkeley; Robert E. Baldwin, Edouard Bustin, Charles R. Nixon, M. G. Smith, and Howard R. Swearer, University of California, Los Angeles; Robert D. Barendson and Kenneth L. Neff, U.S. Office of Education; Saburi Biobaku, University of Ife, Nigeria; William J. Foltz, Yale University; Eduardo Hamuy, University of Chile; H. Field Haviland, Jr., Brookings Institution; Pendleton Herring, Social Science Research Council; Benjamin Núñez, Interamerican Institute of Political Education, San José, Costa Rica; John Howard, Ford Foundation; C. Kenneth Snyder, U.S. Department of State; and Clarence E. Thurber, Pennsylvania State University.

The result of this collective effort is an impressive demonstration of the complex and subtle interrelationships between education and modernization, and our understanding has been significantly advanced beyond the level of the plausible but untested generalizations which have so long influenced thinking on this subject. In both the regional studies and the analytical chapters we are given disciplined interpretations as to the conditions under which different forms of education can have politically stabilizing or disruptive consequences.

Above all, this study adds to our knowledge of the general process of development by vividly accentuating a fundamental contradiction which lies at the heart of the modernization process and which must be satisfactorily resolved if national advancement is to occur. This is the contradiction between the universalistic aspects of modernization, on the one hand, and the need to give expression to the uniqueness of the particular culture, on the other hand. In the realm of education this dilemma takes the form of a sharp confrontation between generalized standards which reflect the universalistic nature of scientific knowledge and the equally mandatory requirement that education systems give coherence to the distinctive spirit of the parochial national culture. For education must encompass both the tested wisdom of mankind and training for life in a particular community and culture. In observing the problems of fusing the universal and the parochial in educational systems, we are presented with a magnified dramatization of the basic struggle that lies behind all aspects of national development and modernization.

Thus, although the editor and authors have concentrated on the apparently limited field of educational policy and practice in the new states, they have in fact produced a study of general value to students of all aspects of development.

LUCIAN W. PYE

ACKNOWLEDGMENTS

THIS VOLUME, like the earlier volumes in this series, is the product of the collaborative work of the Committee on Comparative Politics of the Social Science Research Council. All members of the Committee, fortified with the wise counsel of Pendleton Herring and Bryce Wood, contributed to the planning of the Lake Arrowhead Conference at which chapters of this book were initially presented as background papers. The comments of the members of the Committee and other participants during the discussions at the Conference were very helpful in subsequent revision and in the preparation of the introductory essays. It is a pleasure to acknowledge their contribution as well as the very useful suggestions and criticisms subsequently made by the following persons: David Abernethy, Gabriel A. Almond, C. Arnold Anderson, Lee J. Cronbach, Joshua A. Fishman, Philip J. Foster, I. L. Kandel, Leo Kuper, Joseph La Palombara, Juan Linz, Anthony Oberschall, Lucian W. Pye, Charles Wolf, Jr., and Sidney Verba.

Special thanks are also due Douglas E. Ferguson for his help in organizing the Lake Arrowhead Conference; to Kenneth I. Rothman for his excellent report of the conference discussions and for his preparation of the annotated bibliography which appears at the end of the book; to Dennis Beller for research assistance, to Dr. Grace Stimson for her editorial advice, to Dr. Gulgun Karal for her invaluable assistance at various stages, including her preparation of the index, and to Mrs. Ailene Benson for the final typing of the manuscript. My own contribution was made possible by a fellowship year at the Center for Advanced Study in the Behavioral Sciences, as well as by assistance received from the Political Change Committee and the African Studies Center, University of California, Los Angeles—all of which are gratefully acknowledged.

JAMES S. COLEMAN

CONTENTS

Education

and Political Development

INTRODUCTION:

EDUCATION AND POLITICAL DEVELOPMENT

JAMES S. COLEMAN

The Educational Revolution

"EDUCATION is the key that unlocks the door to modernization."[1] Statements like this recent one are gaining acceptance as truisms by many nation builders, policy planners, and scholars interested in the modernization process. Once regarded as an essentially conservative, culture-preserving, culture-transmitting institution, the educational system now tends to be viewed as the master determinant of all aspects of change.

Two major developments of the past two decades largely account for this new valuation of education and for the shift in perspectives regarding its relationship to society, the economy, and the polity. One is the large-scale entry onto the world stage of former colonies and developing countries—areas inhabited by more than half of mankind impatiently clamoring for rapid social and economic progress. The other is an increasingly acute awareness in the advanced industrialized countries, as they move into the technological age, that education is the kingpin in their own continued development. The combined impact of these two developments has brought high esteem to education, and it compels us to focus closer attention upon the character of its relationship to the processes of development.

The manifold implications of the "Great Awakening" in the developing countries are at once so vivid and obvious, and yet so complex and indeterminate, that we will not tarry here to discuss them. In at least three respects, however, the emergence of these countries, coupled with our strong concern for them, has heightened our consciousness of the role of education in the development process. This historical transformation is largely the product of the "educated minority," just as in other places and at other times in history educated minorities have played a similar vanguard role. The arrestingly distinctive feature about the educated minorities in most of the new states

[1] Frederick Harbison and Charles A. Myers, *Education, Manpower, and Economic Growth: Strategies of Human Resource Development*, New York, McGraw-Hill, 1964, p. 181.

emerging from colonialism is the cultural gap between them and the mass of their uneducated compatriots. Whether they were activists, organization builders, ideologists, or members of the literati, the leaders of the nationalist movements that brought about the sweeping structural and psychological changes in the non-Western world are the products of formal educational institutions, usually of the Western variety.

The relationship between formal education and the formation of the *new* political elite in these countries is so clear-cut, and is documented by so substantial a number of empirical studies, that the point needs no elaboration here. For political scientists the educated political elites in these countries have been a demographic category meriting particularly intensive study. Indeed, because formal education has come to be viewed as presumptively determinative of political elite status, students now in school are uncritically regarded as preordained members of the second- or third-generation successor elites. This highly visible correlation, actual or presumed, between education and political elite status has thrust education to the top of the list of variables commanding the special attention of social scientists interested in the new countries.

An equally simple relationship, also regarded as universally valid by an increasing number of persons, is that education is a prerequisite of economic growth.[2] So firm is this belief in a causal relationship between education and economic growth, and so uncritical has been its acceptance, that the United States has, as an official policy, given primacy to educational development.[3] The education-economy relationship will be examined in greater detail in Part IV. Here it should be noted that the acceptance of education as the master determinant

---

[2] Illustrative of this widely held view is the following: "Deeper understanding of the forces affecting long-term economic and social progress is leading to recognition of the fact that investment in education is an indispensable prerequisite of future economic growth." (*Policy Conference on Economic Growth and Investment in Education: Summary Report,* Organization for Economic Cooperation and Development, Washington, D.C., OECD, October, 1961, p. 1.)

[3] The Act for International Development of 1961 made this policy explicit: "In countries and areas which are in the earlier stages of economic development, programs of development of education and human resources through such means as technical cooperation shall be emphasized, and the furnishing of capital facilities for purposes other than the development of educational and human resources shall be given a lower priority until the requisite knowledge and skills have been developed." (Quoted in *Education and the Development of Human Technology,* U.S. Department of Health, Education and Welfare, Washington, D.C., GPO, 1962, p. 1.)

[4]

of long-term economic growth, apart from all its other effects in the development process, has become for many persons almost an article of faith. Of special concern is the related proposition that economic growth is indispensable for the creation of the minimal conditions requisite for any meaningful political development.

Education has acquired such high visibility in the developing countries not only because it has been an important criterion for political elite recruitment of the present generation, and is regarded as the prime mover in economic growth, but also because it is, quite tautologically, highly visible. In most of these countries the formal educational system is an exotic import, its higher reaches, in many instances, still being manned by foreign scholars. Although "Western-type schooling is one of the institutions most easily grafted into a non-Western society"[4] (in contrast, for example, to Western political institutions or economic organizations), it is nevertheless far more isolable in its non-Western cultural setting than in the cultural context of the exporting country. The greater isolability of Western education in non-Western countries enables us to see with greater clarity, at least at this stage, its relationship to economic, social, and political development. This point is made quite persuasively by Francis Sutton in Chapter 1. He also rightly stresses the possibility that in studying these relationships in non-Western milieus we will gain "fresh perspectives on the tangled web of interrelations in Western history."

In the West itself the relationship of education to the stratification systems, both social and political, as well as to the economy and the polity, is far from being a subject solely for retrospective contemplation. Indeed, impressive evidence points to the contrary: "Under conditions of advanced industrialism . . . the economy becomes increasingly dominated by institutions of research and technological innovation, with the result that the differentiation of educational institutions and functions assumes new proportions. So much is this so that the educational system comes to occupy a strategic place as a

[4] C. Arnold Anderson, "Education and Political Development: Reactions to a Conference," memorandum circulated to the participants in the Conference on Education and Political Development held at Lake Arrowhead, California, June 24-29, 1962, under the auspices of the Committee on Comparative Politics of the Social Science Research Council, p. 1. This comprehensive summary and commentary on the many issues raised in the conference discussion will hereafter be referred to as "Reactions to a Conference."

central determinant of the economic, political, social, and cultural character of society, and we propose using the term 'technological society' to distinguish the stage of industrialization in which these processes have developed."[5] In addition to the insatiable demands for the new skills and the human capacities required to cope with technological societies expanding according to their own logic and dynamic, enormous pressures are generated by the imperative of equality. These pressures operate not only within most nations in the form of individual strivings, but also between developing countries and industrially and technologically advanced nations, the former seeking to narrow the ever-widening gap that divides them from the latter. Additional pressures are created by the tensions of the cold war, the belief that education is a prime requisite for national prepared-ness and enhanced military capability, and the competition for techno-logical superiority among the great powers. Reflection on these and other evidences reminds us of the ubiquity and the strength of the forces behind what has become a world educational revolution.[6]

Education and the Political Scientist

Scholarly concern with the relationship between education and the polity is not new. Since Plato and Aristotle, political philosophers have affirmed principles embodied in the phrases, "As is the state, so is the school," or "What you want in the state, you must put into the school."[7] A prominent strand in democratic theory is the assumption that education is a correlate, if not a requisite, of a democratic order.[8]

[5] Jean Floud and A. H. Halsey, "Education and Social Structure: Theories and Methods," *Harvard Educational Review*, fall 1959, p. 290. Lee Cronbach has suggested in a personal communication that we are witnessing innovation separated institution-ally from education, so that it consumes education but its locus is no longer in educational institutions.

[6] Peter F. Drucker, "The Educational Revolution," in A. H. Halsey, Jean Floud, and C. Arnold Anderson, eds., *Education, Economy and Society*, New York, Free Press of Glencoe, 1961, pp. 15-21. John Vaizey reviews the many reasons for the heightened interest in education in his introduction to "Economics of Education," *International Social Science Journal*, Vol. XIV, 1962, pp. 610-632.

[7] I. L. Kandel, "The Methodology of Comparative Education," *International Re-view of Education*, Vol. V, 1959, p. 274. Cf. M. J. A. N. C. Marquis de Condorcet, *Sketch for a Historical Picture of the Progress of the Human Mind*, trans. by June Barraclough, London, Weidenfeld and Nicolson, 1955; Ernest Barker, *Church, State and Education*, Ann Arbor, University of Michigan Press, 1957.

[8] James Mill, *Essay on Government, Jurisprudence, Liberty of the Press and Law of Nations*, Garden City, N.Y., Doubleday, 1935; John Dewey, *Democracy and Educa-tion*, New York, 1916; Seymour M. Lipset, "Some Social Requisites of Democracy: Economic Development and Political Legitimacy," *American Political Science Review*, Vol. LIII, March 1959, pp. 69-105; Daniel Lerner, *The Passing of Traditional Society*, Glencoe, Free Press, 1958; James Bryant Conant, *Education and Liberty:*

The relationship between education and authoritarian and ethnocen-tric attitudes has commanded increased attention by political scientists.[9] There is a sizeable body of literature on the role of education in the growth of modern nationalism, and on its instrumental use by revolutionary totalitarian regimes.[10] The politics of the church-state struggle over education have been a significant feature of the political history of the Western world.[11] Studies of the political objectives and consequences of postwar educational reorganization in occupied Germany and Japan are also noteworthy.[12] Finally, educational issues have bulked large in studies of politics at the local level.[13] Yet,

The Role of the Schools in a Modern Democracy, Cambridge, Harvard University Press, 1953.

[9] Morris Janowitz and Dwaine Marvick, "Authoritarianism and Political Behavior," *Public Opinion Quarterly*, Vol. xvii, summer 1954, pp. 185-201; Herbert McClosky, "Conservatism and Personality," *American Political Science Review*, Vol. lii, March 1958, pp. 27-45; Angus Campbell, Philip E. Converse, Warren E. Miller, Donald E. Stokes, *The American Voter*, New York, John Wiley and Sons, 1960, pp. 512-515. See also T. W. Adorno et al., *The Authoritarian Personality*, New York, Harper and Brothers, 1950, pp. 281, 285-288. Richard Christie and Marie Jahoda, eds., *Studies in the Scope and Method of the Authoritarian Personality*, Glencoe, Free Press, 1954; Ralph K. White and Ronald Lippitt, *Autocracy and Democracy*, New York, Harper and Brothers, 1960.

[10] Edward H. Reisner, *Nationalism and Education since 1789*, New York, Macmillan, 1922; Bruce T. McCully, *English Education and the Origins of Indian Nationalism*, New York, Columbia University Press, 1950; J. L. Talmon, *The Rise of Totalitarian Democracy*, Boston, Beacon Press, 1952; Alfred Cobban, *Dictatorship*, London, Macmillan, 1938; Franz Neumann, *Behemoth*, New York, Macmillan, 1946; Kurt London, *Backgrounds of Conflict*, New York, Macmillan, 1945.

[11] David Thomson, *Democracy in France*, New York, Macmillan, 1947; Charles E. Bidwell and Andreas M. Kazamias, "Religion, Politics, and Popular Education: An Historical Comparison of England and America," *Comparative Education Review*, October 1962, pp. 97-110.

[12] Helen Liddell, "Education in Occupied Germany," *International Affairs*, January, 1948, pp. 30-62; Helen Liddell, ed., *Education in Occupied Germany*, Paris, M. Rivière, 1949; G. N. Shuster, "The American Occupation and German Education," *Proceedings of the American Philosophical Society*, Vol. 97, No. 2, 1953, pp. 159-162; H. Schelsky, *Die Skeptische Generation*, Dusseldorf, Diedrichs, 1957; Daishiro Hidaka, "The Aftermath of Educational Reform," in Kenneth E. Colton, Hattie Kawahara Colton, and George O. Totten, eds., "Japan since the Recovery of Independence," *The Annals*, Vol. 308, November 1956, pp. 140-155; Marius B. Jansen, "Education, Values and Politics in Japan," *Foreign Affairs*, Vol. 35, July 1957, pp. 666-678; R. P. Dore, "Education: Japan," in Robert E. Ward and Dankwart A. Rustow, eds., *Political Modernization in Japan and Turkey*, Princeton, Princeton University Press, 1964, pp. 176-204.

[13] For example, John A. Vieg, *The Government of Education in Metropolitan Chicago*, Chicago, University of Chicago Press, 1937; Vincent Ostrom, "Education and Politics," in *Forces Influencing American Education*, Chicago, National Society for the Study of Education, 1960; and Bruce Raup, *Education and Organized Interests in America*, New York, G. P. Putnam's Sons, 1936. Two recent works on the same theme are Jesse Burkhead, *Public School Finance: Economics and Politics*, Syracuse, Syracuse University Press, 1964; Nicholas A. Masters et al., *State Politics and the Public Schools*, New York, Alfred A. Knopf, 1964.

as David Easton observed a few years ago, "In political science as a whole, attention to problems of education has all but disappeared."[14] The fact is that despite certain notable exceptions, and the recent and current work that is beginning to fill the void,[15] political scientists in general have paid very little attention to the over-all character of the education-polity nexus, and very few empirical studies have been made which focus explicitly upon the specific ways in which educational systems affect the functioning of political systems.

This neglect of what today seems so manifestly critical a relationship is not a peculiarity of political science. Only recently have educators and other social scientists concerned themselves with the links between education, on the one hand, and the economy, polity, society, or culture on the other. Educators, Fred Eggan notes, have been so busy keeping educational operations under way that they have had "little time or opportunity to step outside their educational institutions and see them as a system in the society as a whole." Eggan graciously adds that he and his fellow anthropologists have been equally inattentive, mainly because in their quest to study and comprehend societies as wholes they have been "reluctant students of our society and culture," tending, quite understandably, to gravitate to simpler, smaller-scale preliterate societies.[16]

[14] David Easton, "The Function of Formal Education in a Political System," *School Review*, Vol. LXV, 1957, p. 304.

[15] Charles Merriam, *The Making of Citizens: A Comparative Study of Methods of Civic Training*, Chicago, University of Chicago Press, 1931; Herbert H. Hyman, *Political Socialization*, Glencoe, Free Press, 1959; V. O. Key, Jr., *Public Opinion and American Democracy*, New York, Alfred A. Knopf, 1961; York Willbern, "Education and the American Political System," *Teachers College Record*, February 1958, pp. 292-298; David Easton and Robert D. Hess, "Youth and the Political System," in Seymour Martin Lipset and Leo Lowenthal, eds., *Culture and Social Character*, New York, Free Press of Glencoe, 1961, pp. 220-251; and Gabriel Almond and Sidney Verba, *The Civic Culture*, Princeton, Princeton University Press, 1963; Don C. Piper and Taylor Cole, eds., *Post-Primary Education and Political and Economic Development*, Durham, N.C., Duke University Press, 1964; and Hans N. Weiler, ed., *Education and Politics in Nigeria*, Freiburg im Breisgau, Rombach, 1964.

[16] Fred Eggan, "Social Anthropology and the Educational System," *School Review*, Vol. LXV, Autumn 1957, p. 247. The presumptive link between anthropology and education is that both disciplines are "concerned with the transmission of the social heritage from one generation to the next and with the processes by which that transmission is achieved" (p. 247). The extent to which anthropology can contribute to the field of education has been discussed in several conferences (see George D. Spindler, ed., *Education and Anthropology*, Stanford, Stanford University Press, 1955). Some inherent limitations, apart from the predilection of anthropologists for preliterate societies, and the questionable relevance of educational processes of the latter for highly differentiated modern educational systems, are examined in Margaret Mead, "Our Educational Emphases in Primitive Perspective," *American Journal of Sociology*, Vol. XLVII, 1943, p. 637, and Jack Goody and Ian Watt, "The Consequences of Literacy," *Comparative Studies in Society and History*, Vol. V, April 1963, pp. 304-345.

When educators turned to comparative cross-cultural studies, their main initial concern was what C. Arnold Anderson has called "intra-educational analysis"; that is, they confined their attention exclusively to educational data, "treating education as if it were an autonomous social system."[17] The primary motivation of educators was not to seek generalization, but rather to discover practices and experiences that could be borrowed and adapted to advance reforms in their own educational systems. Here the earlier focus of political scientists upon the formal political institutions of foreign governments provides an interesting parallel. Only recently have some educators developed an explicit scholarly concern with the extra-educational determinants of educational systems and the broader relationships between education and other functions and institutional sectors of society.[18]

This expansion in the horizon of the educator is the end product of a period of intense self-criticism. The most striking aspect of the development is that the pattern of initial stocktaking, the poaching on the insights of other disciplines, the conceptual and methodological innovations, and the enlargement of the universe of discourse, polemic, and inquiry have closely paralleled the self-appraisal undertaken by students of comparative politics during the past tempestuous decade.

The traditional parochialism of educators has been under attack by pioneering self-critics within their profession and, as well, by an in-

[17] C. Arnold Anderson, "Methodology of Comparative Education," *International Review of Education*, Vol. VII, 1961, p. 2. For a recent bibliographical review of the literature of comparative education specialists useful to the political scientist see William W. Brickman, "Comparative Education," in *Review of Educational Research*, Vol. XXXIV, February 1964, pp. 44–61.

[18] There are certain exceptions to this generalization, however, as exemplified by the work of a few distinguished scholars who did view education in relation to the broad social order, such as John Dewey, *The School and Society*, rev. ed., Chicago, University of Chicago Press, 1915, particularly chap. III; and Newton Edwards and Herman G. Richey, *The School in the American Social Order*, Boston, Houghton Mifflin, 1947.

Educators have long had, of course, a consuming practical concern with the political system. Indeed, because "education must compete with other governmental functions for limited resources," educators and civic groups in Western democratic societies have had to exert powerful pressure in support of the educational component of public expenditures. See Michael D. Usdan, *The Political Power of Education in New York State*, Institute of Administrative Research, Teachers College, Columbia University, New York, Columbia University Press, 1964.

A. H. Halsey has noted: "Previously, neither the skeletal remarks of Weber on educational forms, nor the brilliant occupancy of a chair of education at the Sorbonne by Durkheim, nor the powerful if brief stimulus of Mannheim's sojourn at the London Institute of Education has been sufficient to generate continuing traditions of research or to rouse educational sociology from a position of dubious intellectual quality. A vigorous impulse of competent research did not emerge until the 1950's." (*The American Journal of Sociology*, Vol. XXX, Jan. 1959, p. 209.)

creasing number of educational sociologists. Similar shortcomings in political science have been subjected to critical examination by a group of restless practitioners in the field, stimulated in no small degree by the fresh approaches and the intellectual vigor of political sociologists. The influence of sociology, as well as of psychology, has sensitized both educators and political scientists to the relevance of the socialization process, the stratification system, and the nature of formal organizations.[19] Although the central focus of educators will continue to be the educational system and its determinants, and that of political scientists the political system and the factors affecting it, there is now a vastly broadened basis for a fruitful dialogue regarding the education-polity relationship on such questions as the role of education in the formation of attitudes, values, and personality; in the recruitment of elites; and in sociopolitical change.[20]

The lack of scholarly attention to the polity by educators is somewhat easier to explain than is the neglect of education by political scientists. David Easton has suggested that a minor contributory reason for such neglect is that somehow, in the increasing specialization of scholarly disciplines and research (and, impliedly, in the even more pronounced differentiation in the autonomy of educational institutions), the study of the role of education was relegated, by default, to educators. This indifference might also be explained by the low intellectual and professional status of education. Easton's main point,

---

[19] Kandel, op.cit., pp. 270-278; C. Arnold Anderson, "Sociology in the Service of Comparative Education," International Review of Education, Vol. V, 1959, pp. 310-318; Neal Gross, "Some Contributions of Sociology to the Field of Education," Harvard Educational Review, Vol. XXIX, 1959, pp. 275-283; Jean Floud and A. H. Halsey, "Trend Report on the Sociology of Education," Current Sociology, Vol. VII, 1959; and Burton R. Clark, Educating the Expert Society, San Francisco, Chandler, 1962.

[20] The "Great Debate" among comparative educators was launched by a conference on comparative education at the UNESCO Institute for Education in Hamburg in 1955. Its main themes and issues may be traced through the issues of the Comparative Education Review, organ of the Comparative Education Society, inaugurated in 1957. Early issues reflected a single-system, less explicitly comparative, orientation. More recent issues, however, demonstrate a marked shift toward the comparative study of the relationships between education and other variables, including those of a clearly political character (for example, George Z. F. Bereday and Bonnie B. Stretch, "Political Education in the U.S.A. and the U.S.S.R.," Comparative Education Review, Vol. VII, June 1963, pp. 9-16). The dialogue among scholars regarding the relationship between their world and society has been raised to a new plane in the recently inaugurated journal Minerva. Its editor (Edward Shils) notes that it "aims to improve our understanding of what contemporary developments in every sphere of life are doing to the pursuit of truth through science and scholarship, and of what science and scholarship are doing to themselves and to the rest of their society and the world beyond it." (Minerva, autumn 1962, p. 5.)

however, concerns the way in which political science came to be conceptualized as a discipline: empirical political scientists have been concerned primarily with the use of education in the competition for power both within and between states, whereas political philosophy has sought to discover the type of educational system "best calculated to promote the philosopher's conception of the good political society or the right social order."[21] In short, our notion of the political relevance of education has been too constricted because of our overriding concern either with power or with normative political theory —or with "Americanization."

Another explanation concerns the structure and the role of education in American society. In his study on public opinion, the late V. O. Key, Jr. provides us with a clue: "Usually the schools are regarded as apart from politics. They are thought of as agencies to equip young persons with those basic skills of literacy essential for the practice of even the simplest vocations of an industrial society. Or at the upper levels the schools transmit the skills and information necessary to practice the professions or provide a grounding for young men who, properly trained on the job, may become junior executives and, perhaps eventually, useful citizens."[22] Because the educational system in the United States is one of the most highly decentralized in the world, American schools "are not so obviously seen as arms of governance."[23] This consideration acquires added significance in the light of both the heavy preoccupation of political scientists with the study of the formal institutions of government, and the determination to "keep politics, as well as religion, out of the schools." True, educational issues frequently bulk large in political controversy at the local government level, having activated both enlightened and "lunatic fringe" groups of political significance, but political scientists have tended primarily to focus their intellectual endeavors upon politics at the national level. The same macro-politi-

[21] *Op.cit.*, pp. 304-306.
[22] Key, *op.cit.*, p. 315.
[23] *Ibid.*, p. 316. Paradoxically, the education-polity relationship either is considered insignificant or irrelevant because the link is seemingly so remote, as in America, or it cannot be brought effectively into sharp focus because the relationship is so close as to be extinguished, as in France, where the educational system is viewed as part of the governmental system. Kandel (*op.cit.*, p. 272) has noted that the famous Langevin Commission, which planned the postwar reform of education in France, listed all the factors educational planners must take into account (sociological, economic, technological, status of women, changing social stratification), but explicitly excluded political factors. Since the commission was a government body, its omission is understandable, but it underscores the different ways in which the polity is ignored as a variable.

cal orientation has characterized most American political scientists concerned with the comparison of foreign political systems.

These several aspects of the American scene—the decentralization of the educational system, the resultant absence of a highly visible link between that system and the national power structure or formal institutions of government, and the tendency of political scientists in the past to concentrate on the latter—all help to explain the limited attention given by American students of government to the role of education in political systems. Because political science as a specialized academic discipline has been most highly developed in the United States, the definition of its scope has reflected, to an unbalanced degree, an American imprimatur. Thus, in seeking to explain past indifference to the education-polity relationship, we should not overlook the fact that the changing fashions and focuses of academic inquiry usually reflect the situational or cultural conditioning, as well as the ethnocentrism, of the inquirers.

But this discussion merely explains the past. We have already noted that massive changes in human societies everywhere have greatly heightened the sensitivity of all persons concerned (educators, economists, sociologists, government leaders, as well as political scientists) to the crucial role of education in economic, social, and political development. Moreover, the magnitude of the changes that are occurring in all institutional spheres has served to illuminate their interrelatedness and mutual dependence.[24]

Increased awareness of this functional interdependence has stimulated social scientists and educators to concern themselves with a more comprehensive array of variables. Such broadening is essential if we are fully to understand and interpret the particular facet of the multi-dimensional development complex which engages our specialized training. As holists, conscious of this interdependence and interested in the maintenance, integration, and transformation of total societies, political scientists are particularly affected by this new challenge. It is the holistic imperative that enjoins political scientists to search for what has been termed "a more complete and systematic conception of the political process as a whole."[25] The same impera-

---

[24] Lerner, *op.cit.*, p. 438.

[25] Gabriel A. Almond, "A Comparative Study of Interest Groups and the Political Process," *American Political Science Review*, Vol. LII, March 1958, p. 270. Almond is here arguing for the importance of studying interest groups and public opinion systematically and comparatively, but his thesis is equally valid for the study of education, communications, or any other processes or parametric variables which might be fruitful for political analysis.

tive directs our attention to the study of the role of education in the political process and in political change.

Even without the major changes in the external world, however, political scientists, in the development of their own discipline, would inevitably have been drawn into an increased concern with education. Political science has always had within its fold, and continues to attract, a plentiful supply of scholars committed to the imperatives of holism and science, ceaselessly searching for fresh approaches to fill the lacunae in that very complex jigsaw puzzle called the political system.[26] The recent contributions of V. O. Key, David Easton, and Gabriel Almond and Sidney Verba found their inspiration and drew their strength from sources and influences already present in the discipline, fortified and stimulated by related ongoing work in sociology and psychology. In short, there is an autonomy and an inner logic of cumulation in the evolution of political science as a discipline.

The Concepts of Education and Political Development

The concept of education as used here is limited to teaching and related activities in schools and universities. This focus creates intellectual problems of considerable magnitude. It is at once too narrow and too broad. It is too narrow because the formal educational system is only one among the many agencies and processes involved in the formation of political culture, in the recruitment of political elites, in the inculcation of a sense of national identity, and in the performance of a variety of other politically relevant functions. Education as a process takes place in family, church, peer group, army, professional associations, and numerous other groups and contexts. In other respects the focus on education is too broad because the formal educational system is multi-purpose. It performs many non-political functions; indeed, beyond its use as an instrument for manifest political socialization, its re-

---

[26] The holistic imperative is a constant reminder that we are concerned with whole systems, and that their parts are interrelated; the scientific imperative is a diligent monitor pressing for rigor and respect for the recognized canons of scientific inquiry. Realization of these twin imperatives creates a dilemma when the "wholes" concerned are large-scale, complex, modern national states. So-called "traditional" political science largely ignored the scientific imperative, but satisfied the holistic principle in its concentration upon the state and its central institutions. Anthropology, the most holistic and scientifically committed of the disciplines, could resolve the dilemma only by turning to small-scale preliterate societies. Sociology prudently focused the major share of its attention upon "small groups," although its more daring practitioners turned to speculation regarding general theories of society; Edward Shils has recently argued for a more emphatic macro-sociological approach in the discipline. It is the pressure of the twin imperatives of holism and science which creates the "macro-micro" gap.

lationship to the polity is only indirect. There are many and varied demands made on it, and among these the political may be, in certain contexts, the least obvious or important.

Despite these limitations there are certain aspects of formal educational systems that facilitate focused inquiry into the ways in which they affect, and are in turn affected by, other structures and processes in society. In modern societies educational systems tend to be rather clearly differentiated from other societal elements, and there is a strong strain within an educational system toward the maximization of its autonomy within the society of which it is a part. Furthermore, these systems engage the lives of large numbers of persons during formative and impressionable years, in a singularly concentrated way, and for a prolonged period. For our purposes there is, in short, a solid rationale for concentrating upon formal education as defined above.

Just as multiple causality and the interrelatedness of social processes render difficult the abstraction and analysis of "education" as a variable, so do ethnocentrism, teleological bias, and the absence of a single objective measuring rod complicate the conceptualization of "political development." In the first three volumes of the "Studies in Political Development," the editors grapple rather extensively with this knotty definitional problem.[27] We need not repeat their arguments here. What we are collectively seeking is a conception of a generic open-end process which draws together the explicitly political components or aspects of what Pye terms an emerging "world culture." The trait list of this world culture is derived from "modern life," a concept including the prevalence of a scientific and rational outlook, the primacy of secularity in human relations, "at least a formal acknowledgment of humane values," the "acceptance of rational-legal norms for governmental behavior," and "deference to democratic values . . . at least in the minimum sense of encouraging mass involvement in political activities."[28] The quintessence of

[27] Lucian W. Pye, ed., *Communications and Political Development*, Princeton, Princeton University Press, 1963, pp. 14-20; Joseph LaPalombara, ed., *Bureaucracy and Political Development*, Princeton, Princeton University Press, 1963, pp. 9-14; and Robert E. Ward and Dankwart A. Rustow, *op.cit.*, pp. 3-7.

[28] Pye, *op.cit.*, p. 19. In a private communication Pye has pointed out the potential consequences for a world culture of the spread of school systems throughout the world. ". . . we are very shortly moving to a state of affairs in which the vast majority of mankind will have gone through a remarkably similar early experience in socialization. School children all over the world will be learning their arithmetic, learning the discipline of a classroom, learning from roughly the same kind of textbooks."

For another approach to the concept of a world culture see Pitirim A. Sorokin, "Mutual Convergence of the United States and the U.S.S.R. to the Mixed Sociocul-

the political character of this emerging world culture is a "political culture of participation" which leads to the concept of the "modern participatory state." There are two models of the latter: the totalitarian, with its subject political culture, and the democratic, with its civic political culture.[29] Ward and Rustow have suggested a list of eight traits of a "modern polity" which embraces several of these same notions and specifies others.[30]

Further efforts to identify and colligate the various traits that persistently recur in our search for a clearer working conception of the political development process have suggested the notion of a development syndrome, consisting of three major subsuming principles: (1) *differentiation*, as the dominant empirical trend in the historic evolution of human society; (2) *equality*, as the core ethos and ethical imperative pervading the operative ideals of all aspects of modern life; and (3) *capacity*, as not only the logical imperative of system maintenance, but also the enhanced adaptive and innovative potentialities possessed by man for the management of his environment (human and non-human) through increasing rationality, applied science, and organizational technology. The political development process is thus seen as an interminable contrapuntal interplay among the processes of differentiation, the imperatives of equality and the integrative and adaptive capacity of a political system. In this interplay, for example, excessive egalitarian pressures may put unbearable strains on system capacity; increased capacity may lead to or require greater differentiation; and so on. In these terms, *political development* can be regarded as the acquisition by a political system of a consciously-sought, and qualitatively new and enhanced, political capacity as manifested in the successful institutionalization of (1) new patterns of integration regulating and containing the tensions and conflicts produced by increased differentiation, and (2) new patterns of participation and resource distribution adequately responsive to the demands generated by the imperatives of equality.[31]

tural Type," *International Journal of Comparative Sociology*, Vol. I, October 1960, pp. 143-176.

[29] Almond and Verba, *op.cit.*, p. 4. See also Lerner, *op.cit.*, pp. 6off.

[30] *Op.cit.*, p. 7.

[31] These concepts will be developed further in a forthcoming volume in the "Studies in Political Development" which is to be entitled "Dilemmas of Political Development." On the concept of *differentiation* as an element in development see Dale B. Harris, ed., *The Concept of Development*, Minneapolis, University of Minnesota Press, 1957; Talcott Parsons, "Some Considerations on the Theory of Social Change," *Rural Sociology*, XXVI, 1961, No. 3, pp. 219-239; Neil J. Smelser, "Mechanisms of

This cluster of subsuming principles does not constitute the trait list of a fixed model of a modern polity. Indeed, we are concerned only with the political aspects of the major structural, aspirational, and capability *trends* discernible in the ongoing evolution of a *world* culture.[32] These trends are most clearly visible and most advanced in those countries generally regarded as the most developed and modern at this point in human history. It is assumed, however, that these are the dominant trends in all societies launched upon a path of modernization. For present purposes they provide us with a working concept of political development, to which we may relate the educational system.

At first view, education would seem to be the prime determinant of political development as defined above. Only a formal, institutionalized system of modern education can provide the specialized skills and training requisite for effective societal adaptation to the process of continuing structural differentiation in all sectors of a modern society, and to the concomitant increase in specialization. Moreover, political capacity is manifestly dependent upon modern education. A certain level of formal mass education is indispensable for the development of a modern communications system, which is critically important in resolving the "two most general and most fundamental problems in political modernization," namely, the "changing of attitudes and reducing the gap between the ruling elites and the less modernized masses."[33] Not only must mass literacy, which makes a

Change and Adjustment to Change," in Bert F. Hoselitz and Wilbert E. Moore, eds., *Industrialization and Society*, Paris, Mouton, 1963, pp. 32-56; Fred W. Riggs, "Bureaucrats and Political Development: A Paradoxical View," in Joseph LaPalombara, *op.cit.*, pp. 96-119; and S. N. Eisenstadt, "Social Change, Differentiation and Evolution," *American Sociological Review*, Vol. 29, June 1964, pp. 375-386. On the concept of *equality* as used in the present context see T. H. Marshall, *Class, Citizenship, and Social Development*, Garden City, Doubleday & Company, Inc., 1964, pp. 65-143; and Lloyd Fallers, "Equality, Modernity, and Democracy in the New States," in Clifford Geertz, ed., *Old Societies and New States*, New York, The Free Press of Glencoe, 1963, pp. 158-219. On the concept of *capacity* as an aspect of development see Marshall D. Sahlins and Elman R. Service, eds., *Evolution and Culture*, Ann Arbor, The University of Michigan Press, 1960; Gabriel Almond, "Political Systems and Political Change," *The American Behavioral Scientist*, Vol. VI, June 1963, pp. 3-10; and Talcott Parsons, "Evolutionary Universals in Society," *American Sociological Review*, Vol. 29, June 1964, pp. 339-357.

[32] The notion of an ongoing evolution of a world culture is similar to Marshall D. Sahlins' formulation of "general cultural evolution." He defines the latter as "passage from less to greater energy transformation, lower to higher levels of integration, and less to greater all-round adaptability," distinguishing it from "specific" cultural evolution, which is the "adaptive modification of particular cultures." Marshall D. Sahlins and Elman R. Service, *op.cit.*, p. 38.

[33] Pye, *op.cit.*, p. 13.

modern communications system possible, be developed, but so also must the rational-secular component in attitudes which are essential for individual participation in the modernization process.[34] Literacy, as well as attitudes congruent with modernization, is crucial for effective political "penetration" by government as well as for meaningful citizenship. Education, particularly in its higher reaches, alone makes possible the "modern intellectual system" which Edward Shils in Chapter 15 has persuasively postulated to be a component of developmental capacity. Formal education has a cardinal role in producing the bureaucratic, managerial, technical, and professional cadres required for modernization.[35] Finally, education is unquestionably the master determinant in the realization of equality in a modernizing society dominated by achievement and universalist norms.[36] In short, an impressive array of prima facie evidence points to the critical role of education in societal adaptation to increasing role specialization and structural differentiation, in the achievement of political capacity, and in the progressive attainment of equality.

The effect of education upon those major secular changes in the political evolution of a society is more or less self-evident. The relationship between education and the political system, as a whole, however, is far less clear. It is not a relationship readily amenable to analytical rigor, partly because of the limitations to education previously discussed, and partly because in many instances there are intervening variables between education and the polity which are themselves subject to multiple determinants. For our purposes, however, at least three processes or functions of the political system can be identi-

[34] See *From Max Weber: Essays in Sociology,* trans. H. H. Gerth and C. Wright Mills, New York, 1946, pp. 298-299; Goody and Watt, *op cit.,* pp. 332-345; Hilda Hertz Golden, "Literacy and Social Change in Underdeveloped Countries," *Rural Sociology,* Vol. xx, March 1955, pp. 1-7; and Lerner, *op. cit.,* p. 60. One of the more recent systematic efforts to identify the correlates of political development is that of Phillipps Cutright, "National Political Development: Measurement and Analysis," *American Sociological Review,* Vol. xxviii, April 1963, pp. 253-264. He finds (p. 260) that communications "best accounts for the political development of a nation," but the communication index is highly correlated with the education index.

[35] LaPalombara, *op.cit.* and Harbison and Myers, *op.cit.*

[36] Adam Curle has argued that the greatest contribution of education to development was in the eventual creation of a class which owes its position to its competence, training and usefulness rather than to any ascribed quality. Despite initial, sometimes very protracted, problems of unemployment and politically destabilizing situations, in time the social system of a modernizing country becomes dominated by a very mobile middle group of people whose contribution is very largely determined by their skill. In this sense education establishes the potentiality of an "egalitarian" society rather than necessarily a democratic one. See his "Education, Administration and Development" in *Comparative Education Review,* Vol. 7, April 1964. " meritocracy"

fied which have a fairly clear relationship to education. These are political socialization, political recruitment, and political integration. In the following sections these aspects of the polity, together with the relationship of education to them, will be briefly examined.

Education and Political Socialization

The concept of political socialization is now an accepted part of the vocabulary of political science. It refers to that process by which individuals acquire attitudes and feelings toward the political system and toward their role in it, including cognition (what one knows or believes about the system, its existence as well as its modus operandi), feeling (how one feels toward the system, including loyalty and a sense of civic obligation), and one's sense of political competence (what one's role is or can be in the system). As Almond has put it, "political socialization is the process of induction into the political culture."[37] The educational system is one of the agencies involved in this process, which begins at birth and, although its imprint is most pronounced during the impressionable formative years, continues well into adulthood.

Statistical correlations of American data, fortified recently by the five-nation comparative study by Almond and Verba, show that formal education has been a decisive factor in the political socialization process. Almond and Verba, finding a positive correlation between education and political cognition and participation ("awareness of governmental impact, exposure to politics, political information, range of political opinions, subjective political competence, political participation"), have reached the following conclusion: "Educational attainment appears to have the most important demographic effect on political attitudes. . . . [None of the other variables] compares with the educational variable in the extent to which it seems to determine political attitudes. The uneducated man or the man with limited education is a different political actor from the man who has achieved a higher level of education."[38] These data confirm and strengthen similar findings in earlier studies on the relationship between education and political attitudes.[39] But here the agreement

---

[37] Gabriel A. Almond and James S. Coleman, eds., *The Politics of the Developing Areas*, Princeton, Princeton University Press, 1960, p. 27. These concepts are developed extensively in Almond and Verba, *op.cit.* See also Key, *op.cit.*, pp. 323-343; Easton, *op.cit.*, pp. 311-316.

[38] *Op.cit.*, p. 379; see also pp. 380-387, *passim.*

[39] "High levels of political participation, a high sense of citizen efficacy, and a high sense of citizen duty occur far more frequently among persons with college

ends; on several rather crucial issues the data are inconclusive or contradictory. At least four of these issues require identification and brief discussion: (1) the *direction* of political orientation imparted by formal education; (2) the implications of *congruence* among the educational system and other socializing agencies or processes; (3) the consequences of manifest political socialization (that is, the inclusion of an explicitly *political content in the educational curriculum*); and (4) the significance of the *school environment* in the political socialization process. Crosscutting and pervading all these questions, of course, is the larger issue of the relevance of the findings of studies made in advanced industrial, democratically oriented countries to less-developed countries, which are our main concern here.[40]

The question of the direction of political orientation produced by education takes us once again to the heart of the great debate over the link between education and democracy. The evidence in support of the presumed positive correlation between the two has been reviewed by Lipset elsewhere and need not be repeated here.[41] In balance, the findings of the most recent studies indicate that the influence of education upon political attitudes is more complicated, uncertain, and variable than it was originally thought to be. It may reinforce or

---

training than among those whose formal education ended at the elementary state." (Key, *op. cit.*, p. 342; see also Hyman, *op. cit.*, p. 133.)

Both the Key and the Almond-Verba findings suggest that the higher the level reached, the more pronounced are the qualities characteristic of the educated category, if only because the impact of the socializing agency is more protracted. These conclusions are reinforced by another recent study reported in Harold Webster, Mervin Freedman, and Paul Heist, "Personality Change in College Students," in Nevitt Sanford, ed., *The American College*, New York, John Wiley and Sons, 1962. On the other hand, Robert E. Lane has warned that "the longer a student stays in college the more he expresses [while in college] cynical views on politics and a disinclination to take part in civic or political affairs." (*Political Life*, Glencoe, Free Press, 1959, p. 352. See also Rose K. Goldsen et al., *What College Students Think*, New York, Van Nostrand, 1960, pp. 97-124). Moreover, other studies have found that seniors do not differ from freshmen in terms of political knowledge, involvement, or ideology (Philip E. Jacob, *Changing Values in College*, New York, Harper and Brothers, 1957, pp. 38-54; and Charles G. McClintock and Henry A. Turner, "The Impact of College upon Political Knowledge, Participation and Values," *Human Relations*, Vol. xv, May 1962, pp. 163-176).

[40] "A major difficulty in identifying the impact of schools in new settings lies in the scarcity of information about how education operated in earlier stages of our own countries" (Anderson, "Reactions to a Conference," p. 2). On the limited relevance of Western experience for the present developing countries, see Alexander Gerschenkron, *Economic Backwardness in Historical Perspective*, Cambridge, Mass., The Belknap Press, 1962, pp. 5-71.

[41] *Op.cit.*, pp. 79ff. "Education presumably broadens men's outlooks, enables them to understand the need for norms of tolerance, restrains them from adhering to extremist and monistic doctrines, and increases their capacity to make rational electoral choice" (p. 79). (See also Harbison and Myers, *op.cit.*, pp. 181-182.)

weaken prejudice; it may lead either to radicalism or to conservatism; and it certainly does not ensure rationality in political orientation or behavior. The impact of education "varies in direction and strength with specific issues, with time periods and forms of measurement."[42]

This conclusion obviously does not mean that education is irrelevant; it simply is a corrective to the simplistic belief in a necessarily unidirectional and positive relationship between education and democratic political orientation. The most that can be said at this stage has been succinctly summarized by Almond and Verba: ". . . the orientations that distinguish the educated from the relatively uneducated tend . . . to be affectively neutral. . . . The educated individual is, in a sense, available for political participation. Education, however, does not determine the content of that participation."[43] This finding is consonant with our working definition of political development, which we deliberately sought to make affectively neutral, that is, not loaded in favor of either a democratic or a non-democratic direction. Once this point is made, however, the observation of Lord Bryce, speaking of Latin America, that "education, if it does not make men good citizens, makes it at least easier for them to become so,"[44] is still not invalidated.

The second major issue concerns the congruence of the variant socializing agencies and influences acting upon an individual, and, in particular, the relative position of the school among them. We are unable to establish more firmly the relationship between education and democracy chiefly because there are so many sources of political attitudes. Even if formal education were to leave a democratic imprint, its influence could be negated by other socializing experiences. It could also, of course, be reinforced. A complicating factor is that primacy and congruence among the several impinging experiences

[42] Charles Herbert Stember, *Education and Attitude Change*, New York, Institute of Human Relations Press, 1961, p. 179. In his pioneering study (*op.cit.*, p. 332), Key reaches a similar conclusion: "One proposition is incontrovertible: namely, extent of education has a good deal to do with the probability that a person has an opinion. Its bearing on the direction of opinion is far less clear. The best guess is that education makes a difference for the direction of opinion on some topics, but on other issues direction of opinion may be more nearly independent of level of education." (See also George S. Counts, "A Rational Faith in Education," *Teachers College Record*, Vol. 59, Feb. 1958, pp. 249-257.)

[43] *Op.cit.*, p. 382.

[44] Quoted in Lipset, *op.cit.*, p. 79. Lipset (p. 80) reformulates the conclusion: "If we cannot say that a 'high' level of education is a sufficient condition for democracy, the available evidence does suggest that it comes close to being a necessary condition in the modern world."

may be partly, or even exclusively, a function of their sequence, phasing, or spatial distribution. Despite this perplexing indeterminacy, however, the findings of various studies do establish certain exploratory hypotheses. Among other things, Almond and Verba have found that (1) there is a generalization from non-political experiences (family or school) to the polity, but the relationship is not unambiguous; (2) the attitudinal or orientational impact of the earlier experiences may be only predispositional in character; (3) if experiences are congruent, there is a cumulative effect, later ones reinforcing earlier ones; (4) educational experiences on the secondary level or above may suppress, substitute for, or transcend earlier familial experiences; and (5) there is a "strain toward congruence" when the authority pattern (i.e., the degree of formality and explicit hierarchism, as well as the criteria for authority positions) of a particular socializing agency is close in time and in structure to the polity.[45]

Political socialization in most of the developing countries is characterized by two gross features. One is the continued primacy of the family in socializing the vast mass of the population residing in rural areas, a fact brought out clearly in the several country chapters in this book. And, as Robert LeVine points out, "parents socialize their children for participation in the local authority systems of the rural areas rather than for roles in the national citizenry."[46] Limited social mobilization, weak penetration by the national government, discontinuities in the communications system, and the absence of mass education are among the many explanations of the continuing preeminence of the family in the socialization process. Also part of this syndrome of underdevelopment is a very high degree of cultural fragmentation. By cultural fragmentation we do not mean pronounced regional variations or local parochialisms within a larger cultural matrix. Rather, it is a fragmentation reflecting major, even total, political culture discontinuities among the traditional authority systems of the different ethnic groups of the new states. These systems may vary from the most extreme forms of centralized authoritarianism to equally pronounced egalitarianism. As a consequence, LeVine observes, "variation in authority systems among the [local subnational] ethnic groups of the new nations means that there

[45] *Op. cit.*, pp. 368-374. The earlier literature concerning the relative influence of and congruence among various socializing experiences is reviewed in Hyman, *op.cit.*
[46] Robert LeVine, "Political Socialization and Culture Change," in Clifford Geertz, ed., *Old Societies and New States*, New York, Free Press of Glencoe, 1963, p. 282.

should be concomitant variations in the socialization patterns of the groups."[47] The question of the significance of congruence between familial authority patterns and the new national polity then becomes very complex.

Paradoxically, the second striking feature of the political socialization process in most of the developing countries is that the formal educational system bears a much heavier load of socialization than it does in older countries. There are two reasons for this load imbalance. One, quite obviously, is the imperative of nation building, which dictates that the national government counter the continued primacy of the family as socializer for the bulk of the population. As LeVine argues, the political leaders seeking change in the new states "attempt to create national institutions for the counter-socialization of individuals whose orientations have already been formed to some extent along traditional lines."[48] The authors of chapters in this book on various countries have emphasized, several quite explicitly, the heavy burden carried by the educational system in the inculcation of a sense of larger nationhood. The formal educational system is given this load because it is obviously among the most effective and potentially manipulable resocializing institutions.

The burden of socialization of schools in new states is also heavy because of the absence or underdevelopment of other "cultural agencies." In Western countries ". . . the school had only a modest socialization task to perform; it mainly supplemented or embodied influences plentifully available outside school . . . in developing countries today schools are expected to carry a much heavier load of socialization . . . whatever they accomplish, they will make a proportionately larger marginal effect upon the lives of the residents—compared to the impact of the aggregate of other agencies—than do most schools in the West."[49] Both points underscore the wide gap between the modern and traditional sectors of the developing countries. Yet it is the very existence of this gap which, for quite another reason, elevates the formal educational system to a more determinative role in the political socialization process, and diminishes, if it does not extinguish, the role of the family, the prime socializer. The Almond-Verba study finds that, when the gap between the family and the polity is very wide, other social experiences "closer in time

[47] *Ibid.*, p. 283.
[48] *Ibid.*, p. 301.
[49] Anderson, "Reactions to a Conference," p. 6.

and in structure to the political system, may play a larger role."

The third issue raised by the foregoing discussion concerns the effects of manifest political socialization, that is, the deliberate effort to inculcate particular political attitudes and behavioral dispositions through the injection of a specific political content into the educational curriculum. Whether termed citizenship training, indoctrination, or, even more crudely, brainwashing, the objective of the educational system in all societies is to produce among the youth attitudes and dispositions that will support the society in which they live.[51] Societies differ markedly in the degree to which the political manipulation of the curriculum is self-conscious and explicit, as well as in the actual content injected into it.[52] The wide range of differences are illuminated by the several contrasting studies in this book.

The results of the very few systematic empirical studies which have been made on the effects of manifest political socialization in the schools in the more developed countries are inconclusive. Almond and Verba found that manifest teaching about politics may heighten an individual's sense of political competence, but that this depends very much upon the content and general political setting of the teaching. They note, for example, that "civic culture," the political culture most closely approximated by the United States and Great Britain, is in only a minor way the product of explicit training in the schools. In Great Britain there is little, if any, manifest political socialization comparable to civic training in American schools.[53] Again, a recent comparative study of moral and character education in several Western countries suggests that explicit indoctrination of this type has had no noticeable effect.[54] Thus, at this stage of our knowledge we may say only that the impact of manifest political socialization in schools is highly variable, and depends not only upon the content but also upon the particular context and the strength of reinforcing or negating experiences and influences in the larger environment outside the school.[55] The fact that schools in the

[50] *Op.cit.*, p. 373.
[51] Bereday and Stretch, *op.cit.*, p. 9.
[52] Charles Merriam, *op.cit.* See also Zbigniew Brzezinski and Samuel P. Huntington, *Political Power: USA/USSR*, New York, The Viking Press, 1963, pp. 76-89.
[53] *Op.cit.*, pp. 361-363, 498-499.
[54] Anderson, "Reactions to a Conference," p. 5.
[55] The serendipitous effects of a curriculum content that is not explicitly political raise an issue of great importance, and also elusiveness. At the Lake Arrowhead Conference, several participants stressed the importance of liberal education for development, because "liberally trained persons can be trained and retrained more flexibly, quickly and dependably" (Kenneth I. Rothman, "Report of Lake Arrowhead Conference on Education and Political Development," mimeographed, pp. 21-22).

newly developing countries have a presumptively larger role in political socialization may provide us with a clearer picture of the potentialities and limitations of the manipulation of curriculum content. This question will be examined at greater length in the introductions to the studies in Parts I and II of this book.

The fourth issue in this overview concerns the effect of the environment or "culture" of the school itself in the formulation of political attitudes and orientations. The Almond-Verba proposition that the school is potentially more influential than the family or other agencies because its authority is explicit and formal, and therefore closer to the polity,[56] immediately raises another question: What are the variant effects of different types of school authority systems? A study on the effects of democratic and authoritarian "group atmospheres" suggests that democratic leadership induces attitudes more consonant with democratic values.[57] The findings of Almond and Verba, which relate essentially to the latent effects of participatory experiences in school, are, however, inconclusive.[58] In short, we need a vastly larger array of comparative data before we can even begin to generalize about the political attitudinal consequences of school authority systems.

Irrespective of the type of authority system, however, the culture of the school itself produces effects that may contribute significantly to latent or analogous political socialization in at least two respects, namely, achievement orientation and elitism. Moreover, these effects are particularly likely to be marked in the developing countries, where ". . . school lessons are formal, abstract, and rather strictly cognitive. Certainly they contribute to giving pupils a sense of achievement represented by mastery of lessons. And they demon-

[56] In a private communication Philip Foster states that specialists in comparative education would be disinclined to accept this proposition because the school lacks the high affectivity of the family learning environment. In his view it is the emotional context in which learning takes place which is probably far more important than the explicitness and formality of the system.

[57] R. Lippitt, "An Experimental Study of the Effect of Democratic and Authoritarian Group Atmospheres." *University of Iowa Studies in Child Welfare*, Vol. 16, no. 3, 1940. Cf. Leonore Boehm, "The Development of Independence: A Comparative Study," *Child Development*, No. XXVII, March 1957, pp. 85-92; W. Haythorn et al., "The Effects of Varying Conditions of Authoritarian and Equalitarian Leaders and Followers," *Journal of Abnormal and Social Psychology*, Vol. 53, 1956, pp. 210-219; David Easton and Robert D. Hess, "Youth and the Political System," in Lipset and Lowenthal, eds., *op.cit.*, pp. 226-251.

[58] *Op. cit.*, pp. 355-373. "At best . . . there is some connection. But how strong the connection is, under what circumstances it is more or less close, and the process by which the connection is made are questions that cannot yet be answered" (p. 361).

strate how to cope with activities in which there are definite and objective standards of success or failure. . . . The simple fact of being an obviously pioneering or privileged cohort in the schools will focus pupils' attention on the advantages of effort and achievement. . . . This can be a major influence strengthening the forces that build an aloof elite and can contribute toward the life-views widely shared among the elites."[59] In this respect the schools tend to reinforce the prevalent assumption by members of the educated class that they have a "natural" right to rule.

A second aspect of school culture of potentially transcendent importance concerns the degree to which the school is isolated from other influences. Many sources supply impressive evidence that the effects of education upon attitude formation and change are most marked when the school is set off rather sharply from its environment.[60] Most formal educational institutions in developing countries tend to be far more isolated from other agencies or institutions than in developed countries. This separation has resulted from several factors: the inherent tendency for Western-type educational institutions to create a distinct subcultural milieu; the fact that most secondary and higher institutions are boarding schools, and therefore are usually physically separated from the home environment of most students; and the enormous gap, in many instances, between the indigenous traditional culture and the one of which the school is the carrier. This characteristic isolation presumably gives the schools a more powerful role as political socializers. From the standpoint of broader societal interests, however, what may be gained by more concentrated and undistracted—and therefore effective—socialization of the educated few may be lost by a deepening of the gap between the elite and the mass.

Education and Political Recruitment

Any discussion of the relationship of education to the recruitment of political elites in a particular society inevitably focuses on its social stratification system and on the degree of upward mobility within that system. Contemporary stratification theory suggests (1) that the life chances of an individual for achieving political elite status are

[59] Anderson, "Reactions to a Conference," pp. 5, 23.
[60] Stember, *op.cit.*, p. 180; Theodore Newcomb, *Personality and Social Change*, New York; Dryden, 1943; Sanford M. Dornbusch, "The Military Academy as an Assimilating Institution," *Social Forces*, Vol. XXXIII, May 1955, pp. 316-321; LeVine, *op.cit.*, pp. 301-302.

enormously enhanced if he belongs to, or can rise into, the upper levels of the stratification system; (2) that in modern achievement-oriented societies education tends to become the master determinant of social mobility because it alone leads to higher occupational achievement and consequently to higher income, upper social status, and higher prestige positions; and (3) that education is therefore the main, if not the sole, key to political mobility into elite status. This gross summation, undoubtedly so exaggerated that stratification theorists would reject it, is stated in bald and simplistic terms in order to dramatize the tendency toward reductionist thinking with regard to the impact of education upon the society-polity relationship via the stratification system.[61]

It is precisely in regard to the developing areas that this tendency is most pronounced, and not without reason. A modernizing society is *presumed* to be heavily committed to achievement criteria and therefore to place a high value upon education. As already noted, the fact that pre-independence political leadership was in the hands of a highly visible educated minority fostered the assumption that there is a close link between education, upward mobility, and political elite status. The most compelling support for this assumption, however, derives from the fact that in most developing countries there tends to be a tight fit between education and occupational mobility. This is the consequence of the weakness of the private sector, the fact that most opportunities for salaried employment are in the government service, and the fact that recruitment into that service emphasizes educational qualifications. This is brought out vividly in a recent study by Philip Foster, who concludes that the association of limited employment opportunities in the modern sector of the economy, the domination of these opportunities by government agencies, with the lack of ancillary mobil-

[61] Although exaggerated, this formulation does reflect a widely shared assumption "that in complex societies vertical mobility is closely dependent upon formal education," which C. Arnold Anderson notes is a proposition central in theories concerning education as well as in those concerning mobility. See his "A Skeptical Note on the Relation of Vertical Mobility to Education," *American Journal of Sociology*, Vol. LXVI, May 1961, pp. 560-569. In examining data from England, Sweden, and the United States he found that circumstances other than formal education played a major part in mobility. This conclusion regarding determinants of past mobility in complex societies do not invalidate the proposition that education will increasingly become the master determinant of high status in a technological society. Cf. Seymour Martin Lipset, "Research Problems in the Comparative Analysis of Mobility and Development," *International Social Science Journal*, Vol. XVI, 1964, pp. 35-48; Wilbert E. Moore, *Social Change*, Englewood Cliffs, Prentice-Hall, 1963, pp. 82-84; T. H. Marshall, *op.cit.*, pp. 65-199; and Lloyd Fallers, *op.cit.*, pp. 190-194, 206.

ity mechanisms, places a far greater premium upon the possession of formal education than characterized Western economies at earlier stages of their economic development."[62] While this serves to validate the assumption that there is a close empirical relationship between education and occupational mobility, it leaves unresolved the issue of whether high occupational status necessarily leads to political power.

We will not dwell here on the many interesting facets of this issue. Four problems raised by the foregoing discussion, however, seem to have fairly general applicability in most new states: (1) post-independence anti-intellectualism; (2) the tension between incumbent political elites and new bureaucratic and technical cadres; (3) the restricted political mobility of second-generation aspirants; and (4) the anomic potential of unemployed school leavers. All are problems of no little import in the relationship between education and political development. They are obviously related problems; that is, a school leaver may be a frustrated second-generation aspirant who is disesteemed by the politicians. The problems are, however, analytically separable. Each represents a different analytical dimension of the pervasive and bewildering paradox created by the coexistence of both a high and a low valuation on education, by both a shortage and a surfeit of high-level educated manpower.

We are indebted to Shils and Lipset for their insight into the first problem, summed up succinctly in Lipset's bold assertion that "the leadership of the intellectuals in new states does not survive the first revolutionary generation."[63] This statement dramatizes an important truth; but it can, unless qualified, convey a wrong impression. The truth is that the intellectuals (i.e., all those with an advanced modern education)—the ideologues and political figures who led in the agitation for independence—have been rejected "as a major political stratum who wield influence as a 'class.'"[64] The incorrect impression the generalization might leave is that the "educated," as a

[62] Philip J. Foster, "Secondary Schooling and Social Mobility in a West African Nation," *Sociology of Education*, Vol. 37, winter 1963, p. 153.

[63] Seymour Martin Lipset, *The First New Nation: The United States in Historical and Comparative Perspective*, New York, Basic Books, Inc., 1963, pp. 72-73. Edward Shils' ideas on this phenomenon have been expressed in numerous articles on the dilemma of intellectuals in developing areas, including, in particular, "The Intellectuals and the Powers: Some Perspectives for Comparative Analysis," *Comparative Studies in Society and History*, Vol. I, October 1958, pp. 5-22; "Influence and Withdrawal: The Intellectuals in Indian Political Development," in Dwaine Marvick, ed., *Political Decision-Makers*, New York, Free Press of Glencoe, 1961, pp. 29-56; and his article in this book.

[64] *The First New Nation*, p. 73.

※ any relevance for emigration here? Is emigration desirable under such conditions? If it more conducive to social harmony to have the unemployed leave the country than to stay? Can some of the serial unrest in e.g. Quebec be attributed to the limitations imposed by language on the migration of French Canadians?

demographic category, have been displaced in the power structure by the "uneducated," or even by the less educated, which is only partly true. The fact is, of course, that the "educated" are very much entrenched in the bureaucracy, as Lipset agrees, and that in most of the developing societies the bureaucracy remains overwhelmingly dominant. But two things have happened. One is that the original presumptive monopoly, and the *de facto* primacy and high visibility, of the educated minority in the political arena have been substantially reduced because political power has in many instances gravitated toward persons of lower educational attainments who command local power hierarchies. In this sense many of the new states have entered their own "Jacksonian Era." The second development, that the "educated" incumbents in the bureaucracy feel increasingly threatened by a younger, better-educated generation, is more subtle, but equally significant. Even though their own elite status has been rationalized in terms of their education, they display, paradoxically, a form of anti-intellectualism: ". . . those who have been exposed to modern forms of knowledge are often precisely the ones who are most anxious to obstruct the continued diffusion of the effects of that knowledge; they desperately need to hold on to what they have and avoid all risks."[65] At the core of both of these developments is distrust, fear, or envy of the better "educated." Thus education comes to be ambivalently valued: it is not disesteemed; it is feared.

The second, and closely related, problem concerns the emergence of new bureaucratic and technical elites who are increasingly at odds with incumbent political elites. As Foltz points out, if rapid modernization is given top priority in new states, it both requires and begets new managerial and technical elites—products of advanced professional and technical training—who are bound, through the progressive bureaucratization of society, to become ever more powerful, assertive, and even competitive with existing political leadership.[66] This cleavage, which is analyzed in greater detail in Part III, tends to become particularly pronounced in statist societies. In Eastern Bloc countries the link between bureaucratic and political elites has been a

---

[65] Lucian W. Pye, *Politics, Personality and Nation Building: Burma's Search for Identity*, New Haven, Yale University Press, 1962, p. 220.

[66] William J. Foltz, "Building the Newest Nations: Short-Run Strategies and Long-Run Problems," in Karl W. Deutsch and William J. Foltz, eds., *Nation-building*, New York, Atherton Press, 1963, pp. 124ff. See also James S. Coleman and Carl G. Rosberg, Jr., eds., *Political Parties and National Integration in Tropical Africa*, Berkeley and Los Angeles, University of California Press, 1964, pp. 674-679.

source of tension, although party leaders have thus far been successful in bringing about a fusional rather than an isolative relationship. In developing countries where members of the bureaucracy and party elites are recruited from different social strata, an isolative and politically dysfunctional relationship, such as exists in Ghana, is likely to develop.

The third problem—the restricted mobility of second-generation aspirants—arises in those instances where rapid development has not yet occurred. Rather, the channels for upward social and political mobility have been drastically contricted as a consequence of the preëmption of political and bureaucratic structures by the incumbent groups. The bureaucratic-authoritarian trend which has progressively diminished competitive politics as a vehicle for political mobility has further aggravated the situation. The frustrations of the second-and third-generation aspiring elites are particularly acute because the incredibly high rate of upward mobility of the preceding generation has created extravagant expectations. Many of the aspirants began their schooling when education was still the prime—certainly the most visible—determinant of high political status; when they finished they found their chances for political advancement drastically curtailed. This marked devaluation of education, coupled with a steady reduction in high-status career opportunities, has unquestionably sharpened the generational tensions between incumbents and aspirants.

The fourth problem, that of unemployed school leavers, is essentially nothing more than an extension of the above phenomenon downward into the mass stratum of the population. It is analytically separable, however, that in the important sense the problem is often created by the introduction of mass primary education, mainly for political considerations. Whether the reasons for the introduction of primary education on a large scale derive from the populist preconceptions of the elite or from a genuine mass demand for increased educational opportunity, a gross imbalance has tended to develop between the great expansion in the educational system and the comparatively limited growth in the economy and in the occupational structure. The result, now a commonplace, is a vast and nearly uncontrollable increase in the number of unemployed and under-employed school leavers, whose political orientation toward the polity is marked by disaffection and alienation, and whose behavioral disposition is basically anomic. Indeed, it is a category strikingly like the urban, underemployed, semieducated "masses" of the pre-independence agitational period, who helped to catapult the present governing elites into power. The latter, in a very ironical way, confront the progeny of their own populist agitation.

Education and Political Integration

The integrative role of education in nation building and political development is more or less self-evident. If political socialization into the national polity has been and is effective, and if the processes of recruitment to bureaucratic and political roles have become regularized and legitimated, it is reasonable to assume that the society concerned is effectively integrated.[67] Here we will concern ourselves only with two major respects in which educational development may be malintegrative in the modernization process: (1) it may perpetuate the *elite-mass gap*, a phenomenon widely regarded as the most striking characteristic of the social structure in most, but not all, developing countries;[68] and (2) it may perpetuate, and even intensify, divisions among different ethnic, regional, and parochial groups out of which nationbuilders, partly through education, must forge a larger sense of national identity. In the long run it will be education and the changes it stimulates which will bridge or reduce these gaps; in the initial stages, and for the short run (which Philip Foster reminds us may indeed be a very long time)[69] education may be dysfunctional to political unification.

[67] The concept of integration is rather amorphous. At least two dimensions should be distinguished: the vertical dimension, which refers to the bridging of the elite-mass gap and the development of an "integrated" political process; and the horizontal dimension, which refers to the welding together of previously separate political communities into a larger, more all-embracing polity. See James S. Coleman and Carl G. Rosberg, *op.cit.*, pp. 8-9.

[68] Philip Foster has rightly noted that the elite-mass gap in new African states can be exaggerated, particularly when contrasted to other former colonial areas, as well as 18th-century Europe. There are persisting ties and relationships which are meaningful and ameliorate what otherwise could be a serious discontinuity. *Op.cit.*, p. 152. On the elite-mass gap see Edward Shils, *Political Development in the New States*, The Hague, Mouton & Co., 1962, and Leonard Binder, "National Integration and Political Development," *American Political Science Review*, Vol. LVIII, September 1964, pp. 622-631.

[69] Philip J. Foster, "Ethnicity and the Schools in Ghana," *Comparative Education Review*, Vol. VI, Oct. 1962, p. 128. The effect of education upon integration is also a function of the physical location of educational establishments. The centrality of institutions of higher education, and their concentration in an actual or presumptive "national" capital (e.g., Manila, Dakar, etc.) further the creation of a nationally minded, integrative elite stratum. The dispersion of educational facilities, particularly secondary and higher, may strengthen ethnicity and regional parochialism. On policies designed to cope with ethnic pluralism see McKim Marriott, "Cultural Policy in the New States," in Geertz, *op.cit.*, pp. 27-56.

Education does not, in most instances, create these two dimensions of discontinuity; it merely serves to perpetuate or to exacerbate them. There are two explanations for its operating in this way. One is the empirical fact that individuals or groups or areas that are already more developed have an inherent advantage over those that are less developed: "It is a sad fact that, once the process of development starts in one sector of a society, the inequalities within that society tend to increase. . . . Trade, labour and enterprise are apt to move towards the progressive areas, leaving the poor zones still poorer. [Moreover,] . . . just as variations between localities have become more pronounced, so has the gap between the individuals who are rich, powerful, and highly educated, and those who are poor, impotent and illiterate."[70] Education is particularly likely to fortify this self-perpetuative propensity among preëxisting inequalities. This propensity is not necessarily the outcome of a Machiavellian effort by the more developed to stay on "top of the heap," although such a desire is probably a universal phenomenon; rather, it reflects the operation of what we might call the law of unequal development advantage (or disadvantage). Children of persons in the upper social stratum everywhere have greater access to higher education; areas more richly endowed by nature or possessing more development potential everywhere tend to attract investment, both public and private, more readily; and demographic groups whose members already have more skills, talents, and education everywhere have a differential advantage in further development. The process of uneven development tends to continue according to its own logic and dynamic unless countervailing influences, such as egalitarian political policies, provide for equal access to education, or deliberately allocate resources not only to ensure regional equality, but also to "level up" the less developed areas. .l." Robin Hood "policy .

There is a second explanation for the skewing of unequal advantage in favor of already better-developed demographic groups or geographical regions. It brings us once again to the heart of the equality-capacity dilemma. The capacity of a polity to launch and sustain a program of social and economic development is greatly enhanced in the short run if it can concentrate its resources on both human and physical "centers of strength." Short-run inequality maximizes capacity, whether as emphasis upon an elite versus a mass

[70] Adam Curle, *The Role of Education in Developing Societies*, Accra, Ghana University Press, 1961, pp. 7-8.

educational expansion in order to provide high-level manpower, upon preferential recruitment from groups or areas having the skills required, or upon preferential allocation of development funds for quicker and more substantial returns. On the other hand, a premature and excessive effort to impose or to realize equality may so disperse meager resources that system capacity is gravely weakened, if not destroyed. Ironically, governments of most developing societies are under populist pressures both to broaden the educational base and to achieve rapid economic development. In any event, both dimensions of discontinuity (the elite-mass gap and intranational ethnic and regional divisions) are significantly affected by whether the ultimate political decisions emphasize equality or capacity.

These and other problems will be examined in greater detail in the several chapters in this book. The chapters are divided into four parts, at the beginning of which there is an introduction specifying the general theme and some of the main issues raised by it. Each of the parts is concerned with a major analytical aspect of the relationship between education and political development. In the seven chapters of Part I we will be primarily concerned with variant patterns of educational underdevelopment, with special reference to the educational implications of different colonial experiences. In Part II we focus upon three countries (the Soviet Union, Japan and the Philippines) which have achieved a much higher level of educational development than those described in Part I. In these three countries, manifest political socialization has been far more intensive and protracted, and thus far many of the tensions and discontinuities prevalent in the former group of countries are either absent or have been successfully avoided or contained. The chapters in Part III focus upon the education of modern elites and the resultant problems of intra- and inter-elite relationships. Finally, in Part IV we turn to the problem of educational planning for political development.

Part I:

Patterns and Problems of Educational

Underdevelopment

INTRODUCTION TO PART I

JAMES S. COLEMAN

THE seven chapters in Part I illuminate some of the variant patterns and general aspects of the relationship between education and politics in those countries of the world educationally most underdeveloped. The overwhelming majority of these countries have been dependencies in the modern Western colonial system.[1] This common status, however, is not the sole or, indeed, the main explanation for their educational underdevelopment. Countries that missed both the stimulation and the humiliation of modern colonial rule, such as Afghanistan, Ethiopia, Liberia, and Haiti, also rank very low educationally, and the educational stagnation in many countries of Latin America is the legacy of pre-modern colonialism. In this category Brazil is a particularly outstanding example. Once these exceptions are noted, however, it is a fact that most of the countries least developed, both educationally and politically, have experienced recent colonial rule. That experience has had an impact of great significance, and it continues to wield a pervasive influence in the development of such countries. For this reason we are concerned with both the nature and the consequences of the educational legacy of modern Western colonialism.

One of the major indictments made by critics of Western colonialism has been its alleged neglect of education. Quantitatively, the charge is rather convincingly documented by the several studies in this book and by statistical comparisons of figures showing school enrollment and governmental support for education in the pre-colonial and post-colonial periods. Qualitatively, colonial education is criticized for having been inappropriate for the roles students were des-

[1] The relevant data are set forth in three distribution profiles which rank all countries of the world according to the indices of (a) students enrolled in higher education per 100,000 population; (b) primary- and secondary-school pupils as a percentage of total population between the ages of five and nineteen; and (c) percentage literate of the total population of age 15 and above. Bruce M. Russet, *Handbook of Basic Population and Social Data for Cross-National Comparisons*, New Haven, Yale University Political Data Program, September 1, 1963. These data show that more than 80 per cent of the countries of lesser educational development have had a recent colonial experience or are still in colonial status.

tined, or were allowed by colonial policy, to play,[2] and, as well, for having denationalized the colonial student, denigrated his culture, and socialized him into the political culture of the imperial country. The crux of the criticism is that education under colonialism did not prepare students to be productive and participant citizens in independent modern states of their own.

The educational policies of imperial powers undoubtedly were mainly self-serving. The actual patterns of educational development during the colonial period do not, however, seem to have resulted solely from calculated imperial self-interest. Indeed, some aspects of colonial education had radically dysfunctional consequences, many of which could have been foreseen. Both the amount and the type of education under colonialism mirrored the markedly different assumptions regarding the role of education which prevailed at the time in the imperial countries themselves. Colonial educational systems usually represented an uncritical transfer of the educational philosophy and structure of metropolitan countries to their colonies. This pattern is vividly illustrated in the studies of different countries in this book. In no other sphere did institutional transfer occur with so little alteration and adaptation; the reason was just as much colonial nationalist resistance to modification of the imported system as it was the cultural nationalism of the exporting imperial countries.[3]

The introduction of a modern educational system in colonial areas had significant political consequences. It was the single most important factor in the rise and spread of nationalist sentiment and activity. From the modern educational system emerged an indigenous elite which demanded the transfer of political power to itself on the basis of the political values of the Western liberal tradition or the ethical imperatives of Christianity, both of which had been learned in the schools. The educational system was also the medium for the devel-

[2] Sir Eric Ashby has noted that the "humiliations of colonialism cut deep, especially the implicit, if not explicit, job-reservation which used to be practiced in the colonies, whereby Africans were eligible only for posts in the lower ranks of the professions." (*African Universities and African Nationalism*, Cambridge, Harvard University Press, 1964, pp. 52-53.)

[3] The fact that British educational policy in the colonies subsequently became more pragmatic and sought local adaptation should not obscure the fact that English cultural nationalism animated that policy in earlier stages of imperial rule. As Ashby (*ibid.*, p. 2) observed in his Godkin Lectures: "In the past one of the symptoms of British cultural nationalism has been an invincible confidence in the efficacy of British education, not only for consumption but for export; not only for Englishmen but for Indians, Africans, Malayans and—for that matter—Americans. It was Macaulay who wanted to create in India 'a class of persons Indian in blood and colour, but English in tastes, in opinions, in morals and in intellect.' "

opment of a common territorial (national) language which alone made possible effective political communication and the political mobilization of a mass following. Designed essentially to serve only evangelizing or imperial purposes, Western education became a prime contributor to the emergence of new independent nations. Intended not to be a structure for political recruitment, it in fact called forth and activated some of the most upwardly mobile and aggressively ambitious elements of the population—elements most determined to acquire political power, most confident in the rightness of their claim, and most convinced of their capacity to govern. The serendipital effects of colonial education are among the great ironies of the historic encounter between the West and the non-West.

Western education not only hastened the collapse of colonial rule; it also left a legacy that continues to have relevance in many of the developing areas. At least two elements in this legacy should be noted. One is the instrumentalist attitude toward education which developed as a consequence of the high valuation it acquired under colonial conditions. European colonial rule was rationalized and justified in terms of the special grace that education purportedly bestowed upon the alien governing class, a class composed mainly of persons with higher education. Upward mobility into the more prestigious and remunerative roles available to the indigenous inhabitants in the modern sector of colonial society was usually determined by educational achievement alone. Education was also highly valued, and its legitimation of elite status was espoused, because so substantial a number of the upwardly mobile elements in the emerging indigenous elite in colonial society came from the lower strata of traditional societies. Members of this elite obviously had strong vested interests in the primacy of achievement criteria in recruitment to high occupational and political status. These and other factors furthered the belief that there was a close connection between educational achievement and elite status. The resultant instrumentalist conception of education has tended to persist in the post-colonial period.

There are, of course, exceptions to this trend, one of the most interesting of which is Guinea. During the critical formative years of organization building in Guinea, political leadership was largely in the hands of men who had had little more than a primary education. Sékou Touré, leader of the governing party and now president of the Republic, has consistently attacked the assumption that there is a necessary link between education and upward political mobility. "The

African elite," he declared, "is not to be recognized by its diplomas, or by its theoretical or practical knowledge, or by its wealth, but only by its devotion to the evolution of Africa."[4] Only to a very limited extent have university graduates in Guinea been allowed to occupy authoritative roles. As Cowan notes, "The intellectuals made good civil servants, but the party cadres remained in the hands of those with lesser education."[5] This explicit devaluation of education by the dominant political leadership in Guinea demonstrates the strong strain toward anti-intellectualism in many of the developing countries. This phenomenon, of course, is bound to be manifest wherever incumbent political elites are composed of persons of lesser educational attainment than claimant or potential successor elites.

A second aspect of the colonial legacy is the uneven acquisition of education by different ethnic or status groups, or in different regions of a country, during the colonial era. This unevenness in the impact of education was sometimes owing to colonial policies favoring or "protecting" one group or section against another. At other times it reflected the differential adaptive capacity, or receptivity, to education on the part of indigenous cultural groups. In many instances it was solely the consequence of the fortuity of the impingement of modernizing influences. Whatever the cause of the unevenness, at the time of independence gross imbalances frequently characterized the representation of ethnic groups or sections of the country in party leadership, the bureaucracy, the army, the police force, and other authoritative spheres of the polity. The struggle to counter or correct or to maintain such imbalances is often at the heart of post-colonial politics in the new states.

The attainment of independence and the transfer of power provided the opportunity for indigenous successor elites to make fundamental changes in educational systems. At least three types of change have been sought. Characteristically there has been a marked expansion in educational facilities, in the proportion of the national budget allocated to education, and in the number of students enrolled at all levels. A second pronounced tendency has been the secularization of both the structure and the content of education as manifested in the state's assumption of primary responsibility for the school system and the consequent atrophying and eclipse of traditional and religious

---

[4] Cited in L. Gray Cowan, "Guinea," in Gwendolen M. Carter, ed., *African One-Party States*, Ithaca, Cornell University Press, 1962, p. 196.
[5] *Ibid.*

educational institutions. Third, there has been pressure for a revision of the educational curriculum in the direction of "practicality," "indigenization," and "politicization."

The high valuation education acquired in the terminal stages of colonial rule resulted in strong political pressure for an expansion in educational opportunity. Among the commonalty there was a widespread conviction that only education could bring higher status and a better standard of living. Moreover, political elites tended to assume that increased educational opportunity was the sine qua non of their own continued popular support. Added to these influences has been the feeling that expanded education is the prime requisite not only for economic development, but also for the badge of modernity which will extinguish the stigma of backwardness, and secure for peoples in the developing areas, individually and collectively, full acceptance in the modern world community.[6]

The consequences of this great expansion in the educational system have been varied. An immediate result has been (or predictably will be, depending on the rate of economic growth and the expansion of occupational roles in the modern sector of the societies) the devaluation of education as the principal channel for upward mobility into political elite status. This point has been discussed in the general introduction to this book, and it is further illuminated by Joseph Fischer in his chapter on Indonesia.

Rapid educational expansion may also have disunifying consequences which, in the short run, may outweigh the integrative expectations on which such expansion has been predicated. Fischer shows how the expansion of schools in Indonesia has shifted the central focus of secondary education from the urban centers of the island of Java to the new outlying schools. During the colonial period the very limited extent of educational development and the centrality of institutions of higher education contributed immeasurably to elite integration in many instances. The existence of a single institution of higher learning in a country or region, particularly when it was a boarding

---

[6] Grant McConnell makes the point thus: "To newly independent nations, education, particularly in its higher levels, is a symbol of national prestige in much the same manner as a steel mill." ("The Political Aims of Education in Developing Countries," in Hobert W. Burns, ed., *Education and the Development of Nations,* Syracuse, Syracuse University Press, 1963, p. 40.) The pressures for expansion of educational facilities during the transition to independence in one country and the consequences of expansion are surveyed by James O'Connell, "The State and the Organisation of Elementary Education in Nigeria: 1945-1960," in Hans N. Weiler, ed., *Education and Politics in Nigeria,* Freiburg im Breisgau, Rombach, 1964, pp. 81-112.

school (as most of them were), provided an institutional setting for the homogenization, to a degree, of values and perspectives of diverse peoples drawn from an extremely heterogeneous milieu. The powerful role played by a single institution in socializing and homogenizing a generation of political leaders in former French West Africa, as described by Michel Debeauvais, is a particularly striking example of this phenomenon.[7] The characteristic result of the expansion of an educational system, however, is proliferation into an ever-increasing number of separate units. In culturally fragmented societies, where primordial ties tend to remain transcendent, expansion and proliferation of the system will at least perpetuate, and very likely intensify and exacerbate, local parochialisms. This accentuation of fragmentation is particularly to be expected where the central government's control over the educational system is weak and fragile, as Fischer points out is true of Indonesia.

The third consequence of educational expansion is, of course, the aggravation of the problems of unemployed school leavers and second-generation aspirants, discussed in the general introduction. Of variable internal political significance in the developing countries, these problems are bound to be most acute in countries that have experienced a rapid expansion of education, that have enjoyed only limited economic growth, and that have been burdened with fragile and unresponsive governments.

Politically dysfunctional situations of this type within one developing country frequently create or aggravate similar situations in other developing countries, because one of the first actions taken, or encouraged, by a government faced with mounting pressure from its own unemployed educated nationals is "localization." As used here, this term refers to the process of displacement of non-local by local per-

---

[7] Immanuel Wallerstein has also stressed the importance of this same central institution: "The coherence of this [educational] system was reinforced by the fact that the structure of education was centralized with AOF reaching an apex in the secondary school at Dakar known as the *Ecole William-Ponty*." ("Values of Elites in French-Speaking West Africa," unpublished manuscript, p. 4. Also see Gabriel A. Almond and James S. Coleman, eds., *The Politics of the Developing Areas*, Princeton, Princeton University Press, 1960, pp. 353-354.) This elite-unifying function at the national level has also been performed by the *grandes écoles* in France and by the public schools in England. Robert Wilkenson has pointed out that the "boarding school system, forcing one environment and culture upon boys from all over the country, helped to cut off middle-class pupils from their local roots and graft them into the single ruling group with common attitudes and a common accent." (See review of Robert Wilkenson, *Gentlemanly Powers: British Leadership in the Public School System*, Oxford, Oxford University Press, 1964, by Neal Ascherson, "The Playing Fields," in *The New York Review of Books*, May 14, 1964, p. 14.)

sons in all but the most menial jobs. The circumstances associated with localization campaigns are largely the product of the uneven spread of Western education during the colonial period. Certain groups, regions or countries became exporters of educated manpower to meet the needs of Western colonial enterprise in other areas. Jamaica, the former colony of Sierra Leone, southern Togo and Dahomey, eastern Nigeria, Uganda, Nyasaland, Egypt, Lebanon, and India, among others, sent educated persons to other less educationally developed areas during the colonial period. The post-colonial expansion of educational facilities in the less developed host countries has inevitably produced ever more "local" job aspirants asserting a higher and more rightful claim as "sons of the soil." Thus a process that commenced with the nationalist demand for the displacement of alien European colonists by non-Europeans in the power structure inexorably persists to its logical end of total localization, leaving in its wake a succession of displaced elements. Some become pariahs in the host country; others return to their country or region of origin, where they further aggravate an already acute problem of unemployment among educated persons. The process can be politically explosive in many developing countries in the years of sorting-out following independence.

The second post-colonial phenomenon of concern to us here is the pressure for the secularization of both the structure and the content of education. This process characteristically involves the assertion of the supremacy, if not the monopoly, of the state over the educational system, at the expense of religious schools or traditional educational institutions. It also reflects the triumph of secular values and the primacy of the technical and utilitarian imperatives of modernization, and, where foreign missionary societies are involved, becomes an assertion of nationalism. The impulse for secularization varies according to the character and the strength of traditional educational systems, the degree of penetration and control of the educational system by foreign missionary enterprise, and the strength of the commitment to secularism or ideological purity on the part of the new state builders. In Indonesia, as Fischer points out, the weakness or the hesitation of the central government, coupled with the decentralized character of the educational system, has moderated or dissipated the impulse toward secularization. In Egypt, however, as Kerr notes, the Nasser regime has established its control over both private Egyptian schools and foreign schools. In Guinea the strong commitment of the governing elite to a national education system has resulted in the progressive assertion of state control over mission-run schools, which under colonialism included most of the country's educational institutions. In mid-1961 the government finally ordered the closing of all such schools. The purpose has been not only to extinguish foreign influences, but also to consolidate a purely secular state-run educational system in the interest of a more effective political socialization of the new generation of Guinean citizens.

Drastic action like that taken in Guinea, particularly in developing countries where missionary societies have provided most of the teachers, can have profound short-run staffing and financial implications of no little political relevance. The state-church educational struggle will be most acute in sub-Saharan Africa where Christian missions have carried the main burden of education. The problem will not everywhere be solved so neatly, and with such finality, as it has been in Guinea. A similar effort at radical secularization in the Eastern Region of Nigeria or in Uganda, where Catholics are politically powerful, for example, would produce political strife of possibly serious proportions.[8]

In areas where traditional indigenous educational institutions have a longer history, and are more integrally a part of the local culture, the drive for secularization by modernizing elites has been pursued more cautiously. In his chapter on Tunisia, for example, Carl Brown has analyzed the problem of adapting a traditional system of theological training, the Zitouna mosque-university, to a modern secular system. In the accommodation apparently worked out, the mosque-university has become an integral part of the national educational system.[9]

---

[8] The political implications may be of the sort encountered by France during much of the period of the Third Republic, when the state tried to establish the *école laïque* and disestablish religious control. See Michalina Clifford-Vaughan, "Enlightenment and Education," *British Journal of Sociology*, Vol. XIV, June 1963, pp. 135-143.

[9] David Abernethy and Trevor Coombe, in a manuscript entitled "Education and Politics in Developing Countries" (Harvard University, Center for Studies in Education and Development, April 1964), have observed that modernizing elites in countries where traditional educational systems are rooted in a strong indigenous religious tradition tend to be sensitive to the political power of traditional religious leadership and the political hazards of an assault upon them. They note that "It is rare for a ban on traditional religious schools to be declared; it is more usual for the government to suggest or sponsor some means by which the traditional system may be integrated in the modern system without detriment to religious values" (p. 22). Leon Carl Brown notes in his chapter in this book, however, in reference to the Zitouna experience in Tunisia, that "the problem of introducing modern studies without impinging upon requisites of an essentially theological training was never resolved."

When a traditional educational system that has acquired high visibility and great respect has at its apex an ancient institution of renown such as Al-Azhar in Egypt, a dual pattern tends to evolve. As Kerr points out, there are limits to the adaptability of such an institution to a modern national educational system. The cultural gap between the educational patterns in the different spheres of the dual system inevitably means that the graduates of the traditional institution have a competitive disadvantage in the modern sector of society. In sub-Saharan Africa, however, the problem of integrating traditional indigenous educational patterns with modern secular structures has been and will continue to be much less of a problem, for the reasons Francis Sutton brings out in Chapter 1.

The third general post-colonial trend in educational development is curriculum revision. At least three aspects of the efforts to change the content of formal instruction are relevant: the move toward greater "practicality" in subject matter, the pressure for "indigenization," and "politicization." These trends, like educational expansion and secularization, are a reflection of both utilitarianism and nationalism. They show a determination to harness the educational system to the task of economic and social modernization and to the creation of a new viable political community of allegiant citizens.

The move toward greater "practicality" in the curriculum, a trend discussed with special reference to Africa by Francis Sutton, is also evident in many other developing areas. The impetus for change comes from a variety of sources; from governing elites alarmed over the ever-increasing number of unemployable graduates with literary or legal training; from those concerned over the high cost and the political undesirability of filling manpower shortages in the technical fields with foreigners; from nationalist leaders and development planners, who see the urgent need for a tighter fit between the content of instruction and the manpower needs and occupational structure of a developing society;[10] from educators who increasingly sense the need for a curriculum stressing applied science and technology; and from the students themselves, who perceive that a more technical and practical education offers brighter career prospects.

There are, nevertheless, obstacles and even resistance to the shift in

[10] At his installation as chancellor of the Kwame Nkrumah University of Science and Technology, the President of Ghana declared: "The ivory tower concept of the University is dead (and may it rest in peace). . . . Everything will be done to place a premium on the study of science and technology." (Quoted in Ashby, *op.cit.*, p. 64.)

emphasis. As Fischer notes regarding Indonesia, and as Kerr emphasizes for Egypt, legal degrees continue to have high prestige as a legacy from the past. The resistance to change also exists among some African intellectuals, who, writes Sir Eric Ashby, "confuse such changes with a lowering of standards. They are accordingly suspicious of any divergence from the British pattern."[11]

Several factors will operate to overcome such survivals from the colonial period. One is the emergence of a new occupational structure in which practical and technical education will provide the most visible means for higher status and upward mobility. Another is prospective changes in the curricula of European institutions of higher learning, which have heretofore served as models for most of the developing countries.[12] A third factor is the multilateralization of external educational assistance as a result of a conscious shift from a single-dependency relationship with the former metropolitan country (or the country whose institutions were emulated) to a multiple-dependency relationship with many countries having radically different educational traditions. The major foreign countries that have been added to the widened spectrum of post-colonial overseas educational dependence are the United States and the Soviet Union, countries in which the tradition of technical and practical education has always held a commanding position.

Students from developing countries who undertake training in institutions abroad will also enjoy an increasing diversity of foreign educational experiences. In the past the enormous resistance to any alteration or adaptation of the imported educational system came from its product, the indigenous educated elites. Their own sense of self-esteem, as well as their perception of how others esteemed them, was based upon the maintenance of the purity and the primacy of the system that had endowed them with actual or presumptive high sta-

---

[11] *Ibid.*, p. 61.
[12] See Frank Bowles, "Education in the New Europe," *Daedalus*, winter 1964, pp. 373-393. Bowles cites (p. 391) the report of a conference of ministers of education of European countries which stated that, in regard to secondary education, "until quite recently the humanities [classical secondary studies] had a prestige value stemming from the fact that they were the sole means of access to liberal professions or to posts of leadership. Today, as a direct result of the progress of science and technology [secondary] education in these branches holds an equally, if not more, esteemed place." A number of European countries are also experimenting with comprehensive secondary schools along the American model. The change in the curriculum in institutions of higher education, however, is less visible. Indeed, one report cited by Bowles (p. 391) observes that "a survey of all these plans [for the development of higher education] gives the impression that expansion is more stressed than reform."

tus. As new generations of persons return from abroad with more varied educational experiences, and with degrees from a variety of foreign educational systems, standards of evaluation and prestige ranking will be keenly debated. Those derived from the colonial period will be increasingly challenged. What sort of amalgam, if any, will finally emerge is still unclear. It is unlikely that the unbalanced legal, humanistic, and literary form of education will continue to prevail.

The pressure for "indigenization"[13] of the content of education, the second type of curriculum revision, is in some respects nothing more than characteristic nationalist assertiveness, frequently tinged with a heavy dose of romanticism. It also reflects an understandable effort to correct the neglect or underemphasis of local history and culture which everywhere resulted from the uncritical importation of the school curriculum of the imperial country. The injection of local or national content into the curriculum helps to develop a sense of national identity; it also enhances the students' understanding of their own human and natural environment. As Shils notes below, educational institutions everywhere must teach not only what is of universal validity, but also "what is of parochial value, either because it is practical or because it cultivates the parochial [or national] cultural tradition."[14]

Post-colonial political elites have shown surprising restraint on the issue of indigenization of the school curriculum. Pressure for radical changes in curriculum content has been strong among university students, as Dwaine Marvick notes in his chapter in Part III. It is most marked, however, in the revolutionary-centralizing regimes compulsively preoccupied with what David Apter calls "political religion."[15] Among the new states, Guinea, Ghana, Mali, Algeria, Egypt, and Indonesia represent an orientation toward this type of regime. Other

[13] "Indigenization" is a neologism used here to refer to the generic process of replacing foreign with indigenous content, symbols, meaning, or personnel. It subsumes such common terms as "Africanization," "Indianization," "Arabization," and the like.

[14] Long ago when he was president of Harvard, C. W. Eliot made the case for indigenization: "A university . . . must grow from seed. It cannot be transplanted from England or Germany in full leaf and bearing. . . . When the American university appears, it will not be a copy of foreign institutions . . . but the slow and natural outgrowth of American social and political habits." (Quoted in Ashby, *op.cit.*, p. 4.)

[15] David E. Apter, "Political Religion in the New Nations," in Clifford Geertz, ed., *Old Societies and New States*, New York, Free Press of Glencoe, 1963, pp. 57-104.

new states like Nigeria and Tunisia—in fact, most states recently removed from a colonial experience—tend to be more relaxed, less ideological, and more inclined to pragmatism in defining their relationships with the external world and in adapting imported institutions.[16]

There are several explanations for the limited degree of post-colonial tampering with the curriculum. One is illuminated by the Tunisian experience described by Brown. Tunisians have been able to draw a clear distinction between emphatic rejection of French political control and their continued acceptance—with no feeling of affront to their new sense of national identity—of the essentials of the French educational system. This phenomenon is not unique to Tunisia; indeed, most of the former French colonies display a virtually uncritical adherence to the French school curriculum.[17] To be sure, the French policy of cultural assimilation has meant that all but a few members of the educated class in former French colonies have been educated entirely in the French system; they know no other, and as a product of that system, they have a vested interest in it. Yet they also recognize that it is a good system; that, although distinctively French in certain respects, it is generically modern; and that, above all, it commands world respect. And, as we have noted before, international acceptance is a particularly strong imperative in post-colonial nationalist psychology.[18]

Several practical considerations also operate to restrain or thwart

[16] These two types of regimes are discussed in James S. Coleman and Carl G. Rosberg, eds., *Political Parties and National Integration in Tropical Africa*, Berkeley and Los Angeles, University of California Press, 1964, pp. 5-8.

[17] That this phenomenon is not peculiar to Tunisia is brought out vividly in a study of the attitudes of African students in French universities, who, despite their intense nationalism, unanimously wanted to continue strong cultural relations with France: J. P. N'Diaye, *Enquête sur les étudiants noirs en France*, Paris, Editions Réalités Africaines, 1962. The fact that Guinea and France have retreated since 1958 from their initial postures of defiance, as evidenced by the restoration of cultural and educational relations, is a further manifestation of the strength of the links that continue to persist between France and her former overseas dependencies. It also suggests that the French policy of cultural assimilation has had a far more pervasive impact than its critics have been willing to admit.

[18] Nationalism in non-Western countries may retard indigenization and preserve close ties with universities in the former imperial country because the latter implies the maintenance of high standards, and therefore international respectability. Sir Eric Ashby notes that upon the occasion of President Kwame Nkrumah's installation as chancellor of the University of Ghana, the latter spoke approvingly of the special relationship that had existed for more than a decade with the University of London, and charged lecturers and students "to maintain the high academic standards already set" because those standards were "acceptable anywhere in the world." (*Op.cit.*, p. 47.)

pressures to change the curriculum. One of the most overpowering factors is that many of the new states continue to be heavily dependent upon the external world for teachers. Such dependence, particularly at post-primary levels, is primarily placed upon the former metropolitan country. In many former French dependencies, for example, a majority of the secondary-school teachers are French nationals, provided by France under various forms of technical assistance.[19] The continuation of this single-dependency relationship is fostered by the very practical need to continue instruction in the language of the former metropolitan country. In all but a few instances—Indonesia is one of the striking and interesting exceptions—the national language, and consequently the medium of instruction in post-primary educational institutions, is the language of the former metropolitan country. Despite strong and persistent nationalist resentment over this degrading continuation of dependence, the imperatives of political unity and national integration, as well as the other obvious advantages derived from the continued primacy of the European language concerned, are very compelling. This fact is now well known; the important point here is that the heavy dependence for teaching staff upon the former metropolitan country is perpetuated. As a result, changes in the curriculum become less feasible. To the extent that the dependency relationships can be diversified—a situation rapidly being realized through the expansion of both American and Soviet bloc programs of educational assistance—the limitations to curricular innovation will be progressively eliminated.

One would expect that the politicization of educational content, the third form of curriculum revision examined here, would be actively sought by modernizing elites endeavoring to create new political communities and national identities. The remarkable fact is that in only a few instances have schools been made agencies for manifest political socialization by governing elites. Indeed, only the revolutionary-centralizing states—which have what David Apter calls "mobilization systems"—have taken explicit steps to politicize the school curriculum. One of the more eloquent proponents of this orientation is President Sékou Touré of Guinea. A key feature of the revised curriculum in the schools of independent Guinea is instruction in party history and doctrine. Touré has repeatedly criticized teachers

---

[19] France provides 6,000 French teachers in Morocco, 3,000 in Tunisia, and 3,000 in other parts of the world to new states previously under French control. See Charles F. Gallagher, "Tunisia," in Carter, *op.cit.*, p. 71.

for objecting to "teaching politics" in the schools, "as if," he adds, "the facts of politics were not the condensation of economic, social, and cultural facts!"[20]

How can one explain the fact that, except for such states as Guinea and Indonesia, the developing countries have not pursued the politicization of school curricula more vigorously? Most of the explanations are explicit or implicit in the previous discussion. Where there continues to be a marked dependence for teaching staff upon the former metropolitan country, overt ideological indoctrination in the schools would obviously be difficult, if not impossible. Moreover, in many instances, indigenous members of the teaching staff tend to be either to the left or to the right of the government of the day; they are, therefore, unreliable agents for political indoctrination in the ideological line of the regime.[21] Furthermore, despite a strong conviction that a national ideology is necessary, efforts thus far made by governing elites to develop an indigenous political ideology have been generally unimpressive. The reasons lie partly in the nature of the historical situation these elites confront and partly in the culturally fragmented societies they rule. In addition to these disabilities, the ruling elites in most new states also lack the necessary organizational capacity, and the supporting cadres which, among other things, would make possible more effective politicization in the schools.

It is against the backdrop of the similarities in experience and situation of the new states that Brazil, an educationally underdeveloped "old state," stands out with sharper clarity. Despite nearly a century and a half of independence, Brazil, like most other Latin American countries (Argentina excepted), falls into the lower levels of human resource development.[22] It reflects a pattern of virtual educational

[20] Cited in Cowan, op.cit., pp. 212-213.

[21] In a few instances indigenous and expatriate members of the faculty of a university in a new state have risen to the defense of the principles of academic freedom and university autonomy, and have successfully thwarted or restrained governmental intervention. Such action, too, is part of the colonial legacy. For one case study of a country in which the survival of these principles remains in the balance, see Adam Curle, "Nationalism and Higher Education in Ghana," *Universities Quarterly*, Vol. XVI, 1961-1962, pp. 229-242. Ashby (*op. cit.*, pp. 95-96) concludes his survey of the new African universities with the observation that "there is no sign whatever that Africans . . . will destroy the patterns of higher education which have been established in their countries. They acknowledge that universities are supranational. This concept of the catholicity of universities has taken root in Africa."

[22] Brazil is among the countries falling within the three lower levels of human resource development according to the four-level classificatory scheme of Harbison and Myers. Of the countries discussed in Part I of this book, Nigeria and other countries of Tropical Africa are in Level 1 ("the underdeveloped countries"); Indonesia,

stagnation, the legacy of an earlier pre-modern European colonialism, possibly accentuated by the fact that Portugal, the carrier of the European educational tradition Brazil inherited, was and remains one of the least educationally developed countries of the Western world.[23] In that tradition, education was for a small elite. Moreover, the circumstances under which the tradition was transmitted to Brazil were not, as Wagley observes, "conducive to providing an educational system for the mass of the people." Furthermore, the extreme conservatism and the aristocratic character of the Brazilian "slavocracy" tradition were not subjected to the populist onslaught that was so integral a part of the drive for independence against modern Western colonialism. Indeed, the contrast between modern and pre-modern colonialism, and between the circumstances under which they were extinguished, is one of the principal explanations for the different patterns of educational and political development among their respective legatees. As has been noted elsewhere, "most of the countries of Latin America achieved their independence in a pre-demo-

---

Tunisia, and Brazil are in Level 2 ("the partially developed countries"); and Egypt is in Level 3 ("the semi-advanced countries"). See Frederick Harbison and Charles A. Myers, *Education, Manpower, and Economic Growth*, New York, McGraw-Hill, 1964, pp. 45-48.

[23] The similarity in rank of Portugal and Brazil, after 150 years of separation, is quite striking, as the following figures show:

	Number of Countries Ranked	Rank of Portugal	Rank of Brazil
Per cent of population literate	136	54	59
Primary-school enrollment	112	54	68.5
Post-primary-school enrollment	134	58	56
Expenditure on education as per cent of National Income	—	2.0	2.6

See Norton Ginsburg, *Atlas of Economic Development*, Chicago, University of Chicago Press, 1962, pp. 38, 42, 44, and Harbison and Myers, *op.cit.*, pp. 46-47.

It is not solely the Portuguese colonial experience, nor the fact that Brazil was the legatee of a distinctive Portuguese educational system, which provides the main explanation of this similarity in level of educational development. Other factors, including particularly Brazil's own development, are significant. What Brazil inherited from Portugal formed part of what Wagley has called the "Brazilian Great Tradition." Although mainly Portuguese in origin, most of its essential features reflected a broader European tradition made up of the ensemble of "art and learning of the Western world developed in Europe and continued in the New World." (Charles Wagley, *An Introduction to Brazil*, New York, Columbia University Press, 1963, p. 5.) Wagley notes (p. 205), however, that the "mercantile policy of Portugal was perhaps even more strict than that of other European powers: it denied the Brazilian colony even the printing press and any form of university education. Unlike the Spanish who early established some form of university in their American colonies, there was no form of university in Brazil during the colonial period."

cratic period, and largely as a consequence of diplomatic events in Europe. By contrast, many of the countries of Africa-Asia secured their independence as a result of the progressive mobilization of the populations in nationalist movements of a populist character inspired by mid-twentieth century ideals of democracy, equality, and the social welfare state."[24]

Each chapter in Part I includes a general survey of the historical and situational context of education and political development, and, as well, examines more sharply a particular aspect of the education-polity relationship not only characteristic of the country concerned, but also generic to most of the developing countries in the lower levels of human resource development. The first two chapters provide a broad historical and comparative perspective of the educational legacy of modern Western colonialism, with special reference to Africa. The next four chapters are individual studies of selected new states in Africa and Asia. The last chapter, by Frank Bonilla, concerns Brazil. Its juxtaposition with the earlier chapters serves to illuminate the basic contrast between the two colonial legacies and subsequent patterns of evolution, and their significance for educational and political development in the countries concerned.

[24] James S. Coleman, "The Political Systems of the Developing Areas," in Almond and Coleman, *op.cit.*, p. 552.

CHAPTER 1

EDUCATION AND THE MAKING
OF MODERN NATIONS

FRANCIS X. SUTTON

THIS essay traces out some general ideas on the relations of education and modern political development, and illustrates them in the recent history of Africa. The principal lines of thought arose from contemplating the revolutionary consequences Western education has had in Africa. Western education seems to have had these consequences because it did not "fit" traditional African societies and because it created a new elite. Such observations set one to reflecting on the way educational institutions fit into the general functioning of society, and they direct particular attention to the way they relate to systems of social stratification. The general ideas in this essay deal with these questions, linking them to political institutions and movements.

I. Socialization, Social Integration, and Political Systems

"Socialization" is a social scientist's word that has now taken pride of generality, overtopping "education." It describes how societies cope with their "constant influx of barbarians," and we strive by neologism to extend our perceptions of the modes through which this difficult task is carried out. New generality of perception stimulates a useful self-consciousness about the word "education," which now connotes the more deliberate and functionally specialized forms of socialization. It is education in this restricted sense that will be discussed here, remembering that it does only part of the job of socialization and that it must fit in with the other agencies serving this end.

Three tasks of socialization may be distinguished in any society. They are: (1) the definition of memberships and affiliations; (2) the inculcation of ideas, symbols, and disciplines that are part of the general culture and transcend particular relationships or affiliations; and (3) a differential instruction in the accomplishments and expectations that go with different statuses in the society. These functions are only analytically distinguishable, since they are fulfilled in activities that serve more than one function. Teaching a child that he or she is French, or Japanese, or an Irish Catholic involves instruction in language and ideas that are essential to meaningful and proper behavior in the societies to which the child is taught he belongs. Some of this teaching is done in schools, some at home, some in the local community, or in other social institutions. And it is usually closely related with that differential teaching which directs people not merely into membership in a society but to some presumed station in it. All of these teachings have relevance to the integration of societies.

The role of political institutions as representing total societies and regulating their functioning is of major importance. Any disturbance of the integration of a society is likely to find its repercussion in political institutions and the political process. Proper socialization of the members of a society is essential to that social unity on which political institutions must rest. In a world crowded with new and uncertainly established nations we need hardly be reminded of this basic task. There are some tasks of socialization which relate directly to political loyalties. Learning to be a Frenchman or a Ghanaian in the political sense involves not only a national identification but considerable acquisitions of knowledge and attitudes about the institutions of the French or Ghanaian state. But there are more diffuse and scarcely less important links of socialization and politics.

Any political system rests on a system of social stratification. The people wielding political power must have high status and the political institutions must reflect the values, aristocratic or egalitarian, which infuse the stratification system. The Marxian doctrine of class struggle catches one facet in the complex of potential difficulties, but many others can be seen. In the modern world we are very conscious of the strains in competition for status through educational achievement, the frustrations of those who are denied access to educational opportunity, or the disillusionment of the intellectual unemployed. It is a maxim of sociology that no stratification system works perfectly. There are always misfits between the expectations which people are induced to have and the statuses they attain to. This seems to be true in societies where status is ascriptively fixed by birth as well as in societies like our own which emphasize achievement and strive toward a "meritocracy." The political implications of these strains and malfunctions in the stratification system of a society are various and we will attempt to work out these implications in some important contemporary cases later in this chapter.

Socialization aims toward the future and thus has intimate connections with continuity and change. The construction or preservation of a nation, a cultural group, a religion, or an aristocracy, depends on effective measures of socialization. A change in socialization means a change in the future character of a society, willed or not. The effects on political development may lie through a modification of any of the three socialization functions described above; they move through intricate pathways and are thus very difficult to control, but this does not deter governments from trying to control them. Statesmen have long talked of battles won on Eton playing fields or in Prussian schoolrooms, and education has been a major subject of national policy. The urgency and extensiveness of educational planning has been growing markedly in the recent past and will increasingly engage our attention, as a major aspect of the interaction of education and politics.

II. Educational Systems and Their Western Forms

Educational systems stand out in clearly differentiated forms in literate societies, much less clearly in pre-literate ones. Learning to read, write, and calculate has been the first business of schools in the West, as it was in India or China. These are activities that take continuous application and a measure of special competence in teachers. The separation of proper schools from tuition at home or in the families of teachers has been sometimes unclear (we find the historians of Indian indigenous education quarreling over what was really a school),[1] or surprisingly slow to develop (still in 1894 about a sixth of the students at Oxford and Cambridge came from private study or home tuition).[2] Still, literate societies can hardly dispense with schools to assure their staying literate, and the existence of schools means a complication of social structure that poses problems avoided by simpler societies. What schools do must somehow be related to socialization carried out by other groups and institutions.

Modern Africans like to argue that traditional African societies had educational systems that deserve more respectful recognition as such and that should be preserved (with suitable adaptation) to buttress

---

[1] Syed Nurullah and J. P. Naik, *A History of Education in India*, Bombay, Macmillan, 1951, p. 21.

[2] *15 to 18* (The Crowther Report), HMSO, 1959, Vol. I, p. 11.

or complement the modern educational systems of African nations. Such claims have often been made for the "bush schools" that exist among various tribes in West African countries.[3] However, most of the traditional education in African societies has not been carried out in schools. The basic reason lies in the possibility in these non-literate societies of carrying out most of the socialization needed within the frame of kinship and local groups. A great part of the general culture could be taught there, and with special statuses depending on birth, the young could be appropriately prepared for them in their kin groups. Relative continuity of status and style of life across the generations meant that general modes of behavior and their meaning could be confidently taught by parents. Everyday socialization has been reinforced by religious beliefs and ceremonies, with a typical culmination in initiation rites that solemnize the transition to adult privileges and responsibilities. Learning the traditions, myths, and symbols which interpret and express the social life of the tribe occurs in acting out the life of the tribe, with relatively little scope for the critical reflection and detachment we associate with schools and learning.

Even where a differentiated institution like the "bush school" occurs, a close correspondence between what goes on in the school and the traditional structure of the society is preserved. The bush school seems basically to be an unusually elaborated and extended initiation procedure. As Harley describes its traditional form among the Mano of Liberia, it set up a partial replica of the normal life the initiates

---

[3] For accounts of the "bush schools" see George Harley, "Notes on the Poro in Liberia," *Peabody Museum Papers*, Vol. 19, No. 2, Cambridge, Mass., 1941 (reprinted in large part in C. Coon, *A Reader in General Anthropology*, New York, Holt, 1948, pp. 347ff.), and, "Masks as Agencies of Social Control in Liberia," *Peabody Museum Papers*, Vol. 23, No. 2, Cambridge, Mass., 1950; K. L. Little, "The Role of the Secret Society in Cultural Specialization," *American Anthropologist*, Vol. 51, No. 2, 1949.

Why the bush school has assumed such special importance and elaborated educational functions in West Africa is an intriguing problem in the dynamics of social structures. The reasons appear to have something to do with the very imperfect security system among the numerous and rather isolated tribal groups in the West African forest belt. Here the weakness of political structures and the importance of some system in inter-tribal relations favored the elaboration of inter-tribal secret societies into which the bush schools provided initiation. The bush schools also provided occasions for the periodic reconstitution of local groups. Harley tells us that all of the members of a local community were called back from other areas when a bush school was to be held. A general war could not in principle be held during the time of a bush school. The bush school thus provided extended periods of peace in which there was a kind of climax in affirmation of the solidarity of a tribal group, its traditions, and the supernatural meaning of life in it.

would be expected to live as adults. Great emphasis was placed on what we would call character-building, with harsh punishments prescribed for indiscipline or ritual transgression.[4] The initiates were circumcised and scarified; in pain and fear they acquired the marks that made them indelibly members of their group. And they were instructed in a great variety of practical, magical, and religious matters. Common, awesome, and rigorous experiences in a common setting provided a bond among the future men of the society. But the school also conformed to the differentiations that mark adult statuses. Harley tells us that the sons of chiefs typically became the leaders of their age groups in the bush schools, and the sons of priests had a preliminary schooling in the religious and ritual aspects of the *poro* (secret society) which set them apart.

The bush school and the less clearly differentiated forms of education in traditional African societies seem to have discharged effectively the functions of socialization enumerated earlier. It is not surprising that contemporary Africans, dismayed by the disorientation, moral decay, and confusion that seem to have come with Western education, should look back, sometimes only in wistful regret, sometimes with a more bitter sense of loss, at the declining hold of their traditional ways of educating for adult life. But the demand that Western education be joined with African traditional education would not be easy to satisfy; the efficacy of the old ways depended on an intimate intertwining with the structure of the traditional life they served; to dissect them out and graft them onto a school system would be a very delicate operation indeed.

Any differentiated educational system poses problems in making it serve the basic tasks of socialization. Western education shares these difficulties with other sorts of education. If we consider first its functions in defining memberships and affiliations, Western education has displayed a dual nature. It is concerned on the one hand with children and young people as future citizens of modern states. It has also been very strongly concerned with their training as Christians of one persuasion or another. Historically, the use of the school as a path of induction into a religious community came first, a characteristic

[4] In the Mende bush schools of Sierra Leone, Little tells that "The boys are expected to bear hardships without complaint and grow accustomed to it. They sleep at night on a bed of sticks under covering cloths, which have been soaked in water, and they remain out-of-doors if it rains. The singing and drumming lasts until one or two o'clock in the morning, and the boys are wakened again at dawn. They are expected to get up and sing anytime they are called." (*Op.cit.*, p. 202.)

shared with many other cultures. Max Weber has treated the historical linkage between education and religion with characteristic brilliance. He writes:

". . . prophetic as well as priestly religions have repeatedly stood in intimate relation with rational intellectualism. The less magic or merely contemplative mysticism and the more 'doctrine' religion contains, the greater is its need of rational apologetics. Sorcerers everywhere have been the typical keepers of myths and heroic sagas, because they have participated in educating and training young warriors in order to waken them to heroic excitement and regeneration. From them the priesthood, as the only agents capable of conserving tradition, took over the training of youth in the law and often also in purely administrative technologies, and, above all, in writing and in calculation. The more religion became book-religion and doctrine, the more literary it became and the more effective in provoking rational lay-thinking, free from priestly control. From the thinking layman, however, emerged the prophets who were hostile to priests; as well as mystics, who searched for salvation independently of priests and sectarians; and finally skeptics and philosophers, who were hostile to any faith.

"Priestly apologetics reacted against all of these developments. Anti-religious skepticism was to be found in China, in Egypt, in the Vedas, in post-exilic Jewish literature. In principle, it was the same as it is today; almost no new arguments have been added. Therefore, a central question of power for the priesthood became the monopolization of the education of the youth.

"With the increasing rationality of political administration, the power of priesthoods could grow. Just as initially the priesthoods alone were able to supply scribes for Egypt and Babylonia, so did the Western Church for the medieval princes whose administration depended on writing. Of the great systems of pedagogy, only Confucianism and that of Mediterranean antiquity have known how to escape from the power of priesthoods. The former by virtue of its powerful state bureaucracy; the latter, conversely, through the absolute lack of bureaucratic administration. Escaping the power of priests, these societies also excluded the priestly religions. With these exceptions, priesthoods regularly managed the schools."[5]

[5] Max Weber, *Gesammelte Aufsätze zur Religionssoziologie*, Vol I, pp. 564-565, my translation. Compare Gerth-Mills, *From Max Weber*, pp. 351-352. Weber gives a broad discussion of types of education, *ibid.*, pp. 408ff.; Gerth-Mills, pp. 426ff.

The concern of priesthoods to monopolize the education of youth that Weber emphasizes seems to arise naturally from the need for a standard and unequivocal set of doctrines that will interpret the world and state the moral obligations of individuals in society. This is what the system of beliefs in spirits and the moral lessons of the bush school provided in less rationalized form in West Africa and what similar means provided in well-integrated primitive societies throughout the world. The fact that the West has been one of the major historical examples of this effort to hold societies together by intimately linking religion and education has been of enormous consequence both within the West and outside it. The long struggle of state and church over control of schools stemmed from it and a great part of the spread of Western education was left to missionaries, not simply because education was a natural adjunct to their proselytizing efforts, but also because statesmen and colonizers took it as normal that educational responsibilities should devolve on them.

While there has been a stubborn persistence in places like the Iberian peninsula of the ideal of religious uniformity, the emergence of the modern Western state has everywhere produced a conflict of church and state loyalties. Ultimately a conception of citizenship shorn of religious qualifications has emerged, and in this process education has figured largely.

From a general sociological point of view, the emergence of the modern state rested essentially on the universalization of citizenship and the corresponding attack on privileged statuses that this universalization implied. The demand that all men, however humble, be members of the state could not be separated from concern for their instruction. Indeed, the same eighteenth century intellectual currents which prepared the American and French Revolutions prepared for modern universal education. The universalizing of education responded to a demand that some basic enlightenment be brought to all the people. It gave reassurances about the loyalty, orderliness, and morality of the whole community in the modern state.

But there is another side to the matter. If to conservatives, universal education was prudent social insurance, to liberals it was social justice. It opened up a basic equality of opportunity, and was linked with the assault on educational privilege that has been a concomitant of the class structure of the West. Conservatives of course saw dangers in the "restless striving that equality begets." Fears that education brings expectations beyond the station which people ought to accept, such as we now hear about Indian and Egyptian universities or African primary schools, have had abundant precedents in the West itself. This is a real problem in the functional adaptation of education to social systems, and there is no straightforward, "correct" solution to this problem. The whole course of modern educational development in the West has been an integral part of the vast shift of our stratification systems toward a basis in occupational achievement, with the thrusts of assertive demand and the spasms of resistance that such a process inevitably displays. A great many of the phenomena we now see in the development of educational systems in the non-Western countries can be traced in the Western record. For this reason and because of the direct transfer of Western educational models elsewhere, a brief glance at the "democratization" of Western education appears useful.

A correspondence between education and social status has been a traditional feature of Western education. Secondary and higher education has traditionally been largely confined to the more affluent and higher placed strata of society. Professions like the ministry, law, and medicine have required specialized education, but this has been sought on top of general cultural attainments characteristic of the more elevated classes in society. The long persistence of Euclid and the classical languages as the core of secondary education marked educated men with attainments lacking to ordinary people and not directly relevant to their performance of occupational roles. Since it was presumed that such attainments would be the sole prerogative of the upper and middle classes, there was a certain inertia or stability in control of the higher statuses in society which assumed such accomplishments. Adam Smith tells us that in his day the professional schools were "lotteries." He means that there was a kind of competition and that schooling did not assure professional success. But the kind of competition he knew was not a fully open competition and the failures did not face dizzy falls to poverty in the lower depths of society. They could fall back on the resources and alternatives that had given them a chance to enter the competition in the first place.

When Czar Nicholas I of Russia asked his ministers of education to cope with the dangerous intrusion of Western education, they proposed schemes which rigidly denied the lower orders access to secondary schools and universities.[6] Such principled rigidity could not

[6] Cf. G. Z. F. Bereday, William H. Brickman, and Gerald H. Read, eds., *The Changing Soviet School*, Boston, Houghton Mifflin, 1960, pp. 37-40.

be maintained throughout the Western world, which has increasingly demanded careers open to talent of whatever origin. However, considerable differences in educational opportunity by class origin persist to the present day. We are now coming to a heightened awareness of the class-determined influences which affect school performance and put children from the lower classes at a competitive disadvantage even where they are not handicapped by want of money. Universal education has not meant uniform expectations, and we have undoubtedly been spared some sharpness of social tension thereby, though at a price in loss of potential talent of which we are increasingly conscious. Since World War II, with the new search for talent and more acutely felt demands for equal opportunity, there has been mounting pressure to eliminate these differential class advantages.

This movement toward equal educational opportunity has been concurrent with a movement to change the character of education. Radical democratic ideas have characteristically emphasized that education should be "practical." This was the bias of French revolutionary legislation,[7] and it has influenced a great deal of American educational thinking. The demand that education be directed to practical ends, either of a general sort or as preparation for a particular trade or profession, strikes against the character and pretensions of traditional liberal education. It has challenged the worth of diffuse accomplishments that have been associated with high social status and opens the way for a new egalitarianism. In the main European traditions, secondary education, as presented in the public school, the *lycée* or the Gymnasium, has been the stage at which the liberal educational tradition clearly affirmed itself. It is here that liberally educated men have been set off against those merely usefully educated and as such it has been a narrow gateway to the higher social statuses. Hence a critical phase of the democratization of educational systems has been the struggle to alter the character of secondary education.

It is important to realize how recent serious concern about full utilization of the talent of a nation and the resulting impetus to expanding secondary and higher education have been. We now live with

[7] Under the Convention, a bill presented by Rabaut-Saint-Etienne sought to deny the rights of citizenship, public office, or service in the army to anyone who had not learned a practical *métier* by the age of 21. The legislation of 1793 (projets Lepeletier and Romme) remind one strongly of current African educational proposals with their emphases on realism and practicality, and their demands for manual work, especially agricultural. Cf. Antoine Léon, *Histoire de l'Education Technique*, Presses Univ. de France, 1961, pp. 42-46.

manpower surveys, schemes for identification of talent and its encouragement in those disadvantaged by class background. The notion that men of whatever origin should have the chance to carry their talents to full realization was not strongly buttressed by the related notion that a nation needs all the talent it could possibly realize from its population until the Second World War. There was, of course, the pioneering development in nineteenth century Germany in promoting higher education and technical schools for the benefit of the nation-state. But this was a relatively small and limited effort in comparison with those now demanded in mid-twentieth century nations. The great thrust of Soviet Russia, in a deliberate policy of maximizing its trained manpower, has become a worrisome challenge to the Western nations, and we in the United States have not been alone in trying to respond to it.

Western education stands out more clearly as an independent variable when we study its relations to political and social development where it has been exported to the non-Western world, and one may hope that intellectual excursions there will give fresh perspectives on the tangled web of interrelations in Western history. The fact that the great Western spread in the world took place at a time when Western societies still had much of their modern educational development ahead is an important historical fact. Nationalist political leaders throughout the world now reproach colonial masters for the insufficient and unsuitable education they brought to the non-Western world. The pace and quality might have been better than it was in many places. But it was largely set by ideas and traditions that Western nations brought with them and these were often quite different from those that now seem appropriate.

III. Western Education and Political Development in Africa

A. THE INTRODUCTION OF WESTERN EDUCATION

The contact of the Western world with the great array of peoples and cultures beyond it was, above all, a great demonstration of Western power. Whatever else the non-Western peoples may have thought of their invaders, they knew that they were formidable. The conquered had to submit to the introduction of Western practices and ideas as the colonial powers wished. Those, like Japan, who escaped conquest had to seek out the means of Western power and competence. A great spread of Western education resulted in both cases.

In Africa, as in many other places, the first agents of Western education were the missionaries. The presumption that Christianity was necessary to salvation provided recruits to teach even remote and primitive peoples. The effort in Africa dates from the Portuguese missions in the sixteenth century, and continued feebly until its great acceleration in the nineteenth and twentieth centuries with the partition of Africa among colonial powers. This missionary impulse made education in Western forms ancillary to religious purpose. Enough had to be taught to make Christian ideas comprehensible and to combat practices and beliefs that were regarded as barbarous or heathenish. An effort in elementary education with the rudiments of literacy and a strong emphasis on moral and religious training was implied. The broad spread of elementary education with relatively slight development at the higher levels which now characterizes African educational systems had its roots in the character and purposes of mission education. When the chief educational advisor to the Colonial Office sometime ago criticized Nyasaland education as a "bog of bush schools leading nowhere," he was commenting more on the results of mission efforts than on deliberate governmental policy. To note another example, from neighboring Southern Rhodesia, the much criticized fact that most African children in this territory acquire only two or three years of education in the vernacular and easily lose their scanty literacy, has again had much to do with the effort of missionaries to bring Christianity to as many people as possible.

The purposes of mission education meant that it could not be a merely neutral introduction of the techniques of reading, writing, and calculating to an African population. Even where teaching was done in the vernacular and the effort was to make the Christian doctrine available in African languages, an emphasis on standards of behavior and morality characteristic of the European world was to be found. One notes as critical an observer as Sir Harry Johnson, praising the order, cleanliness, and regularity which earnest Christian missionaries taught to Africans.[8] His reactions were shared by more pious colonial administrators who saw a "civilizing" influence in the mission schools. Their thinking was like that of nineteenth century conservatives who saw the spread of education for the poor as a means of making them loyal and reliable.

Some provision for education beyond the primary level grew from

[8] Roland Oliver, *Sir Harry Johnston and the Scramble for Africa*, New York, St. Martin's Press, 1958, pp. 127-129, 316.

the mission's concerns to have African catechists, ministers, and teachers for the multiplying schools. There was, consequently, in many places a growth of small teacher training and other institutions that reached up into secondary levels of education. In one notable case, Fourah Bay College in Sierra Leone, established in 1827, the demand for African ministers pushed the upper limits of education to what could be claimed as higher education. It is also worthy of note that the present relatively advanced state of Lovanium University in the former Belgian Congo had its beginnings in a concern to train Catholic priests at a time when any form of higher education for Congolese was regarded as doubtful policy by the government. The number of Africans who attained to more than elementary education was not large, but they were pioneers, and names like Boganda, Youlou, and Lumumba remind us of their importance in recent African political development.

Aside from encouraging mission education as a first step toward "civilizing" Africa, governmental efforts to bring Western education to Africans were at first weak and laggard. They appear occasionally in the plans and achievements of far-sighted colonial administrators who undertook to provide education which they thought would be necessary either to enable Africans to assist in the running of colonial societies or to prepare them for a more enlightened conduct of their own affairs. Faidherbe in Senegal marked one of the first steps in the 1850's with his school for educating the sons of chiefs. Kitchener's establishment of Gordon College in the year after the battle of Omdurman is another landmark. Both Faidherbe and Kitchener realized that if there was to be a progressive social and political development, the African peoples would have, in great part, to direct the management of their own affairs. Economy dictated this policy; and there were other reasons for it. Some degree of education was needed to supply African clerks, artisans, and minor functionaries. How high and widespread it became would depend on estimates of African potentials and the basic conceptions of colonial policy.

Looking broadly at the history of colonialism in Africa, one can distinguish two divergent tendencies of policy. The famous French policy of assimilation represents one pole; the other was the British policy of fostering indigenous institutions from whatever available beginnings might be found—a policy given its most clear-cut expression in Lugard's and Cameron's ideas of indirect rule. The kind of political development that has actually come about, with the emergence of independent African states from the matrix of colonial regimes themselves (and not from indigenous African institutions), was in large part an African achievement, overthrowing the designs of colonial powers. Colonial policy latterly accepted what was happening, and indeed was always forced into some position intermediate between assimilation and indirect rule. Educational policies varied with the general character of colonial policy and it is especially instructive to reflect on the educational principles of the polar tendencies.

The vision of an assimilation policy has seen the ultimate destiny of non-Western peoples as attaining the cultural characteristics that would make them acceptable as citizens on the same basis as their European fellows at home. Politically, the policy is careless of indigenous institutions and imposes a direct European rule. The educational policy that serves assimilation is clear; it must be education in the language and culture which is the goal of assimilation. Consistently, throughout French Africa, education has followed closely the syllabuses of the metropolitan school system.

It is a too-often repeated injustice to French educators that they made African children claim fair-haired Gallic ancestors; there has in fact been much adaptation of syllabuses, as inspection of any recent ones will show. But the conception that Africans needed and should have something radically different from what was given schoolchildren in France would have been out of keeping with the policy and the ideals of French colonialism. The farther an African went in an educational system of this type the more firmly he should be acculturated in the ways of the colonial power. Those who could rise the highest in the colonial society should thus be the most completely assimilated.

The traditional structure of European secondary education fits the assimilationist doctrine very well. It provides a screen through which aspirants to power and high positions must pass and which assures their possessing diffuse cultural attainments. There need not in principle be any educational ceiling under which colonial subjects must be kept, as long as their education is firmly within the culture, and up to the standards of the metropolitan powers. And they need not be confined by the occupational opportunities in their own colonies; when past the tests of assimilation, they were in principle welcome in the metropole as well.

The vision of evolution through indirect rule, on the other hand, was one in which the traditional leaders of African societies were to be gradually taught to assume more enlightened responsibilities and their institutions were to change slowly toward more advanced forms. Something necessarily had to be learned from Western schoolmasters. But the particularities of indigenous tradition needed to be recognized, and education had to be consistent with it for a long time. Education had also to be directed to the right people—especially to the chiefs and the traditional aristocracies where they existed. Thus in the Sudan in the heyday of indirect rule, a detailed hierarchy of educational attainments was envisaged—elementary school for the lowest order of chiefs, intermediate school for the next rank, and secondary school for the mighty ones.[9] The whole policy implied the carefully controlled development of an educational system in close timing with the evolution of the African political society—indeed a very complicated exercise in meeting the functional problems discussed above.

The assimilationist tendency is one that is attentive to the attachment of the educated to the colonizing Western power. It frankly assumes a break with the indigenous culture but provides, as it were, a port of destination. "Indirect rule" sought to avoid rootless or divided men by keeping them firmly in an evolving indigenous culture. The fact that neither of these policies controlled the course of events is evident in the spectacular demise of colonialism we have been watching in these last years. The reactions of Africans to the educational opportunities available were partly responsible, in addition to the failings of their colonial masters.

Throughout the greater part of Africa there was initially much resistance to putting children into Western type schools. In Muslim areas this had a religious basis, and was often treated respectfully, as in Lord Lugard's prohibition of Christian missionary activities in the muslim areas of Northern Nigeria. In the so-called pagan areas, there was less respect for African resistance, though it doubtless had similar bases. Former missionaries and district officers recall cajoling or ordering parents to send their children to school. But it did not take many years to see a distinct change in African attitudes toward schooling. The change occurred in part because Europeans were an elite in African societies and their characteristics and attainments came gradually to have the prestige and value which commonly is accorded an

[9] K. D. D. Henderson, *The Making of the Modern Sudan* (*The Life and Letters of Douglas Newbold*), London, 1953, p. 308.

elite. There was sober calculation, too. Even when European ways were mistrusted or hated, a yearning for the secret of their power directed Africans toward their schools, just as it did Chinese and Japanese on the other side of the world. The autobiographical account of a distinguished Senegalese tells how his responsible elders explained to him that he must go to the European school. One said, "Our grandfather and his elite were defeated. Why? How? Only the newcomers know. We must ask them. We must go among them to learn the art of winning without being right."[10] This sort of calculating and instrumental attitude toward the power of European education came quickly into prominence in Africa. It was not long before it became evident that literate men had opportunities for employment in the governments and other organizations brought by Europeans to Africa. Their positions as aides and agents of the Europeans gave them power. And until recent times there has been a scarcity value to literacy in Africa which assured men with a few years of elementary education a post of relative affluence among Africans.

In the early stages of educational development in Africa, there was a widespread effort, among the missionaries and in government schools as well, to adapt education to African conditions. There was in particular an emphasis on the manual arts, and on agriculture— the likely future occupations of many Africans. There were notable achievements like those of the Basle missionaries who set new standards for African artisans in the Gold Coast. But the evident fact that children who went to school long enough to acquire literacy in an European language were commonly brought into prestigious and lucrative government jobs brought an African demand for change in this emphasis. The English and French are now criticized by some Africans for the excessively "literary" character of the education they offered to Africans. In rebuttal they can and do point to African demands that the distinctions between metropolitan and African education be eliminated. This became a matter of principle, as in the last years of the Belgian Congo, but it was also in part a rational calculation based on where the most spectacular rewards for Africans lay. Thus leading mission schools like, e.g., Kings College in Uganda, dropped their early emphasis on the manual arts to become standard secondary schools as in England or France.

A widening of the gap between African backgrounds and the school

[10] Cheikh Hamidou Kane, *L'Aventure Ambiguë*, Paris, Julliard, p. 52 (my translation).

was inevitable, and has resulted in a strong alienation of schooled African children from traditional ways of life. The Ashanti Survey shortly after World War II gave striking evidence of the phenomenon in its finding that 95 per cent of the boys who had completed elementary school went to the towns and would not follow their elders' footsteps in traditional rural occupations, even in as rich an area as Ashanti.[11] This alienation has become very general in Africa. It was a source of the greatest concern to colonial administrators in their late days and it now troubles the rulers of new African states. But its first effect was a disruption of traditional African societies. The newly educated were not all the sons of chiefs. Indeed, the early resistance to education in places like Nigeria and Senegal, and doubtless elsewhere, gave a special opportunity to the humble, since they were most easily attracted to the European school. Moreover, the selection of boys for intermediate and secondary schools which European teachers and headmasters practiced was based upon scholarly achievement rather than distinction of family. The newly educated looked to Europeans, not to their traditional chiefs and elders, for advancement and for models of behavior. Their affluence and their links to European power made them a challenge to traditional prestige and authority.

This new social stratum in African society could hardly fail to become a political force, and with aid from reactions on the European side that inhibited easy assimilation, it became a spectacularly successful one.

It has been suggested above that colonial societies in Africa were ones in which the ruling European minority regarded itself as an elite and was so regarded by the African population. The effective management of these societies depended upon acceptance of Europeans as a powerful elite. During the first half of the twentieth century when colonialism in Africa was at its height, the superior position of Europeans was bolstered by feelings that they as civilized people were capable of doing things Africans could not do. The notion that Africans were not ready to govern themselves was put in terms of their cultural backwardness and their lack of capacity to administer a modern government. But the assumption of African inferiority went

[11] In her recent vivid account of Ghanaian conditions based upon long and intimate experience, M. J. Field includes numerous effective glimpses of the literate who is unable to find a place in paid employment in the towns: *Search for Security*, London, Faber, 1962.

much beyond the specific field of exercising responsible authority. There were types of work which were considered "European work" and types which were "African work." We find Africans still struggling to break away from these distinctions; in a recent debate in the Federal Parliament of Nigeria, one of the members held forth as follows: "At the moment it is one thing to say that we want carpenters, that we want bricklayers, but it is quite a different thing to have good workmanship from them. There are some of these carpenters who believe that carpentry is 'European work.' We should be able to tell these bricklayers and carpenters that the expression 'European work' is no more in existence. What we have now is 'Nigerian work,' and anybody who is to do any work should be able to do it with perfection. . . . Therefore the Government will be pursuing . . . the interests of the country by establishing more and more technical training schools."[12]

This setting did not make for ready acceptance and rapid advancement of the educated African. Although he had an impressive status among his fellow Africans, he received much less regard from the Europeans who controlled his best chances of occupational success. This was in part due to the nature of schooling in Africa. This schooling, it must constantly be remembered, was largely conducted in a language foreign to the Africans. After a few years of vernacular teaching in the English-speaking territories, or from the very beginning in the French-speaking territories, students tried to learn about the world in a language they had not spoken at home. The gap between the life of the school and life at home was a big one, and much of the matter of the school curriculum was unsupported by experience outside the school. A resulting verbalism was a common complaint of European schoolmasters and later employers. When words were foreign words and often about things otherwise unknown, it could hardly be otherwise. Coming themselves from societies in which there was a presumption that students in secondary and higher education had certain advantages of home background, Europeans were keenly aware of the poverty of African experience. Knowing as well that school successes need not assure positions of exceptional distinction in adult life, Europeans were much less impressed with the expectations of the new baccalaureate or graduate than Africans themselves.

[12] Remarks of Chief E. O. Okunowo, Member for Ijebu Central, Federal Parliament debates, Federal Government of Nigeria, April 2, 1962, column 688.

B. EDUCATED AFRICANS AND THE NATIONALIST REVOLUTION

In the recent political history of Africa the concrete datable events—the constitutions, demonstrations, and conferences—are solid, identifiable objects on top of a vast sweep of mass reactions. A profound social revolution has been going on in Africa, generating the forces which have made the rapid political evolution of recent years irresistible. Depending on which side one listens to, this social revolution gets much or little credit for African independence. The European tale of these last years stresses political and legal moves gradually extending the control of Africans over the governments of their countries, and ultimately culminating in the granting of independence. The aim of policy and hence the tone of description has been to make the whole shift an orderly and managed process. From the African side, the emphasis is on the force and persistence of African demands, on courage and sacrifice in a sometimes violent struggle for African rights. In this view of recent history, mass demonstrations, encounters with the police, and bold protests of African leaders win pride of place. Independence appears not as a grant but a prize wrested from laggard and unwilling colonial masters.

The African emphasis on struggle and achievement corresponds to the magnitude of the social transformation that was being achieved. For the movement to African independence was an overthrow of past subordination to a European elite in more than a political sense. In the era after World War II, when the notion became widely accepted that the colonial powers were only temporarily in Africa as trustees, the core issues of political development came to lie in the presumptions about African competence that could be established. Africans themselves had to come to the persuasion that they were capable of managing affairs that had previously been the business of the European elite. They had to make a thrust to self-confidence. When this thrust came, it was in a fashion quite different from that which European rulers had attempted to shape. It took the form of a general rejection of the assumptions of African inferiority on which the very structure of colonial regimes had depended. It was not a claim merely for special position for assimilated or "civilized" Africans, nor was it an argument that the old indigenous authorities had reached maturity. Rather it was a radically democratic or populist assertion of the rights and competences of all Africans that could be given one momentous and dramatic expression in winning control of their own countries.

Such assertion required plausible leadership that was found in educated Africans who were prepared to stress their Africanness and identify with all their people over against the Europeans. Some of the frustrations of educated Africans that made them ready for this identification, and the sources of their necessary prestige among Africans have already been noted. Once installed as representatives of Africans they could make a claim to authority based on popular sovereignty which Europeans found impossible to resist.

This, briefly, is the way Western education has wrought the revolution of African independence. If we look for suitable homage to this role of education, we may find it in a phase of the early history of independence in the Congo. University students have had a conspicuous part in African nationalist movements; in the annals of West African nationalism, student groups, often based in London or Paris have an honored pioneering place; in the Sudan there were the Gordon College graduates; farther east, the Somali Youth League. In the Congo, students seemed to miss an important public role, though they felt themselves to have great destinies. (One of the diversions of Lovanium University students in the days before independence was the distribution of future ministerial portfolios among themselves.) Then in September 1960 came General Mobutu's extraordinary experiment in statecraft; his entrustment of government to a squad of young university graduates as a college of commissioners should remain in history as a touching symbol of African faith in the educated.[13]

C. EDUCATION AND POLITICAL TENDENCIES IN THE NEW STATES

In a sense the great political decisions of African independence settled little, and indeed gave a new acuteness to many of the underlying tensions which provoked the great change. Our discussion suggests that Western education as introduced into Africa produced a new elite in African society that quite abruptly unseated the old European elite from political power. A new social integration would require either a sufficient establishment of the new African elite to give it a firm and unaided hold on the new African nations, or a good enough mutual adjustment of Africans and Europeans to permit effective cooperation. Political transition was so rapid that neither of these conditions could be well met. African political success rested on an African solidarity which tended to blur discriminating assessments

[13] For details see B. Verhaegen and J. Gerard-Libois, *Congo 1960*, Brussels, n.d., Vol. II, pp. 869-953.

of African competences, and it left unsettled disputes with Europeans about states of readiness for advancement and authority. The aftermath of independence thus is filled with problems of stabilizing and revising expectations within African societies, and great brittleness in relations with the passing European elite.

The hope of continued African-European cooperation played a central role in the liberal European position on the African independence movement. Methods were sought whereby European technicians, professional men, and administrators could continue to serve for and in African countries after their independence. Generous encouragement of this policy by providing people at the cost of the metropolitan government has been a French policy. British policy has been less generous but has increasingly included such measures as the payment of expatriates' differential in allowances, partial responsibility for compensation schemes, and most recently a straightforward commitment for the salaries of key personnel (as in the recent commitment of the Department of Technical Co-operation to bear half the recurrent costs of the East African research organizations).

This hope of cooperation has not proven easy to realize. The most dramatic example of its failure was, of course, in the former Belgian Congo. It was clear that the whole presumption of Congolese independence depended upon the continuation of Belgians in control of many activities, technical and otherwise, in Congolese society. The collapse of this control, in the Army and elsewhere, came with dramatic suddenness. The process of independence is a complex one but an outstanding difficulty for both Africans and Europeans is the control of demands for occupational promotion which independence brings. A general sense of having been held back under the colonial era is very widespread among Africans. Its justification in many places is unquestionably great, but it is also true that the revolt against European presumption dulled African self-criticism (Chief Awolowo once went so far as to call it "criminal").[14] The peculiarly brilliant success of the first African educated elite has made for great difficulty among Africans in realistically assessing the worth of secondary and higher education. Marshall Segall in his as yet unpublished research among the Banyankole of Uganda has noted a wild openness of expectations among secondary school students. Using a technique developed by Allport and Gillespie, which gave the students an opportunity to depict their future careers, he found an

[14] *Path to Nigerian Freedom*, London, 1947, pp. 33-34.

inflation of expectations among these Africans greater than has been reported anywhere else on the globe. The frustration of such great expectations is clearly beginning to show itself in the radicalism of university students in such places as Dakar and Ibadan. The situation is not made easier by the fact that the movement to African independence mounted as difficulties over the placement of Africans with modest levels of attainments grew. With expanded educational systems the scarcity value of literacy has gradually been reduced and it has become increasingly difficult to place those with only an elementary education in wage or salary jobs in African economies. The disappointments and frustrations of young Africans whose families and themselves had expected better rewards from their schooling provided one of the most clamorous forces behind the political agitation for independence. It would be difficult for any African politician to reconcile a vision of increased benefits for Africans in independence with the growing difficulty of providing jobs for school leavers. But this, in fact, has been the situation with which they are faced.

The seriousness of the pressures to hasty Africanization seems to vary inversely with the level of education attained in a country coming to independence. It is, for example, very serious in Tanganyika, where a late and scanty development of education before independence is notorious.[15] Places like Ghana and Senegal with more solid and longer educational development have been able to proceed more deliberately. Where a country has had some years of experience in the fact that a primary or even a secondary education does not provide assurance of a job, the pressures on African politicians are somewhat easier. It is also possible for them to hold to more realistic assessments of the qualifications required for the higher posts in government and business. Where such experience is scanty, it is extremely difficult to justify brakes on African promotion and the retention of expatriates in responsible and well-paid positions.

The revolutionary force of social change has led to a distinctly more rapid Africanization of governments and other institutions in Africa than had been anticipated. In Tanganyika, for example, where remarkable optimism about amicable cooperation was established by the moderation and good sense of Julius Nyerere's policies, almost a third of the European professionals and administrators in the civil

[15] In 1959, there were only 4,132 students in secondary schools, 428 pursuing higher education, and 70 university graduates (another 44 have post-secondary school diplomas). Figures from Dean A. B. Weston of University College, Dar es Salaam in *Yale Law Report*, 1961, Vol. 8, No. 2.

service had announced their intention to resign within four months after independence (550 out of a total of 1,700 by April, 1962).[16] Earlier, in West Africa, there had been similarly rapid departures though from rather better prepared civil services. Within this rapid movement, there have been differences in pace, which seem roughly correlated with political radicalism. There are, for example, a great many French civil servants still in conservative Ivory Coast and Senegal but almost none in Guinea and few in Mali.

The continuing pressures created by new expectations in African nations thus have had the general effect of loosening their ties with former colonial powers. They have also led to internal changes, in the educational system, and elsewhere, which have furthered the same process—one that appears, at least to Western eyes, as a drift to radicalism.

In the new African nations, one of the strongest demands is for universal primary education, and the motivations behind it have a great deal in common with those in Western history. African nationalism has been populist in the sense that it has insisted on the worth and rights of the humble many in African societies. A sense of solidarity of the people was the main source of strength in African nationalism and Africans are anxious to confirm this solidarity by a common education available to all. Individual opportunity for schooling is intimately linked with a sense of building nations. In a recent and engaging *Portrait of an African School*,[17] one reads: "Education in Africa is not just something your parents want you to have and which you go on getting until you can decently give it up. . . . Rather it is a means to an easy, easeful life, away from the toil and soiled hands and monotony of life in the village. It makes a person modern, up-to-date, enables a man to wear gloves, carry a brief case, and look like the young men in the advertisements. But ask any African teacher trainee why he is one, and the answer comes pat, 'Because I want to help my people.' "

Such responses are no mere hypocrisy. This sense of education being something essentially linked to the making of a nation and the proper service of its people has axiomatic force, and leaders who are well aware that they may be making grave trouble for themselves in strained budgets and disgruntled, unemployed school leavers exert themselves to expand education as far as possible. The tendency is

[16] Figures supplied by a Tanganyika government official.
[17] By W. G. McD. Partridge, London Missionary Society, 1961, pp. 9-10.

not uniquely African. F. C. Ward writes about Indian educators, "A system of education which, beyond its most elementary level has been charged with refining the few while excluding the many is now being scrutinized by its own graduates who, in the interests of the young democracy which they govern, appear to be quite prepared to rend their own nests."[18]

As Ward suggests for India, the populist impulse in African education is not only to broaden the base to take in all the people, but also to widen the hitherto restricted channels to higher levels of education. In doing so, there is inevitably a clash with the spirit and character of the traditional European education that colonizers brought. Secondary education in particular involves a difficult plunge into bookish cultivation that accords poorly with the populist, democratic spirit of the new nationalism. As in Western history, the tendency is to set technical and "practical" study over against this "literary" education, insisting that the nation is better served thereby. Some of this appeal for "practical" education is a challenge to the standards of the old elite. This tendency is strongly reinforced by the alienation of Africans from their traditional occupations. Reluctant to accept this alienation as inevitable, African leaders blame the nature of colonial education. Thus, a Nigerian leader, "Our people are lethargic about agriculture. To our schoolchildren, in our primary and secondary schools, when we talk of going back to the land it seems to them like a fairytale, because we have been so saturated with the colonial type of education, which is the education of pen-pushing. There is no technical touch in our educational system—it is all pen-pushing, all recitation—so that when we talk about going back to the land, even our own sons laugh at us."[19] New African educational schemes are thus full of provisions for manual work, especially agricultural, for all, and specialized technical education for as many as can be afforded.[20]

The effort to reshape educational systems to fit African societies has this "practical" bias as its most distinguishing feature. There is, of

[18] F. C. Ward, "Some Polarities in Indian Educational Thought," in J. M. Singer, *Introducing India in Liberal Education*, Chicago, University of Chicago Press, 1957, p. 91.

[19] Dr. K. O. Mbadiwe, Orlu North East, Federal Parliament Debates, Federal Government of Nigeria, April 2, 1962, c. 839.

[20] Thus, e.g. the 1961 plan of the Sudan Ministry says it proposes to introduce "practical subjects suited to the environment. . . . This practical side of education will insure that every citizen will leave school capable of doing manual work, instead of despising it and only looking for office jobs."

course, also a demand for Africanization of syllabuses, so that African culture and traditions are more justly represented. But despite manifestoes, this seems a weaker movement than that toward "practicality." Particularly in Africa south of the Sahara, the gap between African cultures and Western-style schools has been great enough to make a genuine integration barely conceivable. As new nations looking forward to being developed nations, the molding of a national cultural individuality must be a creative achievement, and it is more or less clearly seen as such. The goals of educational change and national development are linked in a vision of the future, more than in reconstruction of the past.

IV. Conclusion

Although the ideas set forth at the beginning of this chapter are quite general and may claim an essential place in any theory of the relations of education and politics, they hardly constitute a comprehensive theory in themselves. More is clearly needed on the role of education as an agency of political unity, and one might also wish for more symmetry in a well-developed theory through balanced attention to the effects of political development on the character and extent of educational systems. Some of these considerations were adumbrated in handling of the empirical facts of the African scene which indeed has ended with suggestions that political motivations may lie behind educational policies on the balance of primary and secondary education, or the content of curricula. But these efforts need to be handled more systematically and explicitly than they have been here.

There is also much to be done along the main lines of argument in this chapter. A certain concordance among educational systems, egalitarian tendencies, and the basing of modern states on popular sovereignty appears both in the review of Western education at home and in its African diffusion. This important theme deserves further clarification, and work on it may be a more promising approach toward a general theory than a start with apparently more general ideas.

CHAPTER 2

EDUCATION IN FORMER FRENCH AFRICA

MICHEL DEBEAUVAIS

IN THE developing countries, education is the sector that has the highest rate of expansion, both in enrollment in primary, secondary, and technical schools and universities, and in financial resources. As accelerated expansion gives rise to a variety of new problems, government scholars and international organizations try to elaborate a doctrine of planned educational development[1] and to study the economic and social factors of educational planning.

It is not yet possible to put forward a theory providing for the full integration of educational development with economic development, but studies in this area are making headway. The social factors relevant to education have been only partly explored, and with a rather negative emphasis. Sociologists have concentrated on the tensions and disharmonies that follow the introduction of Western educational systems into developing countries. Little has been done, however, to set standards, to lay down rules for educational systems fully adapted to the social structures of developing countries and the requirements of development. Nor has much attention been given to the relationship between education and political development. This paper will deal primarily with the main aspects that must be taken into account when analyzing the political factors in education in French-speaking, newly independent countries. For comparison with other developing countries, some of the conceptions implicit in the "models" described by Gabriel A. Almond and James S. Coleman in *The Politics of the Developing Areas* will be useful.

The Relationship between Education and Political Development

The role of education in the political life of new states may be examined from several points of view. On the one hand, education is one of the factors of political development; on the other, it is a matter for political decisions. As an institution, it may be analyzed from the standpoint of "input" political functions, that is, the func-

[1] *Educational Planning: A Bibliography*, Paris, International Institute for Educational Planning, 1964.

tions it performs in political socialization and in the recruitment of political cadres. In terms of "output," political decision making in the field of education establishes and modifies the system of education, determines the budgetary and other national resources turned over to it, and applies such decisions at the administrative level.

Education is construed, for the purpose of this chapter, in the narrow, institutional meaning of the term; the educational system is regarded as a specific institution whose aim is to train the young according to methods of universal applicability in primary and secondary schools and at the university level. We will therefore disregard the training provided by the family or the social group (units that exist in all societies and are given much importance by sociologists); in-service training, formal or informal; and adult education. The fact that systems of education are not the only available means of training should not, however, be overlooked; recognition of this fact leads to an awareness of their limits and to a clearer notion of their importance in terms of shaping and molding the individual.

In general, education has three main purposes:

1. It must train individuals and give each one a chance to develop his gifts and his personality, to "become that which he is." The human dimension of education knows no limits but those of human possibilities; it is the human aspect that educators most readily underline. It is also the most difficult to delineate because no country however well developed, has ever provided all its young people with the possibility of continuing their studies to the utmost limit of their gifts and aptitudes. Thus this aspect of education stands as an ideal as yet unattainable; its criteria are unclear, and the setting of priorities is impossible.

2. Education, by preparing children for active life, must train producers. This economic dimension is now systematically dealt with by assessing the manpower requirements of economic growth, so as to develop education as a function of over-all economic planning.[2]

3. Education must train citizens by making students aware that they belong to a nation; it must cross the boundaries of smaller groups—the family, in the narrowest or widest sense of the word, the tribe, the village, and so on. This political dimension of education consists in imparting to the young a notion of how they are situated in time

[2] Cf. in particular the Education Plan for Puerto Rico (Reimer), the long-term evaluation of manpower requirements in Nigeria (F. Harbison), Tunisia (M. Debeauvais), Italy (S.V.I.M.E.Z.), and France (Commissariat for Economic Planning).

and space. In new states the process is a dynamic one, creating the conditions for the birth and the development of a nation. To reach this goal, education must develop new attitudes to the state, the government, the administration, and the economy.

Through its political function education may play a decisive role in the modernization process by stimulating patterns of behavior which favor progress. It fulfills this aspect of its mission, however, only to the extent that it is systematically intended to do so. Educational systems are usually conceived of as passing down from generation to generation a pre-established body of knowledge and set of values and attitudes. Both the curricula and the teachers, as guardians of tradition, offer serious resistance to novelty. In Durkheim's terms, an educational system is both the product of a given society and the institution that determines that the society itself will endure. Inherent in this concept is the risk of perpetuating existing social structures instead of creating the conditions under which they may evolve. Here the specific task of education in emerging states is different from its role in industrialized nations: in the latter, progress in the economy and in society has preceded progress in education; whereas in new countries educational systems must be geared to a future objective, to a society and an economy as yet unknown. It is therefore necessary to place the problem of education in the broader context of the type of society that it is intended to create.

French Colonial Policy in the Field of Education

It is difficult to trace any general characteristics of France's policy in the field of education; indeed, one is almost tempted to say that there has been no over-all policy. Problems of education in overseas territories were never debated in Parliament; at the governmental level, the responsibility for educational measures was shared by the Ministry of Foreign Affairs (for Morocco and Tunisia), the Ministry of the Interior (for Algeria), and the Ministry of Overseas France (for colonies and territories under mandate). But in all instances the authority of colonial governors, in matters of education, was virtually exclusive, and decisions taken were based more on the personality of a governor than on guidance from metropolitan France. This autonomy was all the greater because colonial budgets were financed from local resources until 1945, and because the initiative in budget matters belonged to the governor, subject to approval in France.

Educational policies in overseas territories therefore varied widely, depending on circumstances and historical background. In some countries a school system existed before the colonial period; examples are the Koranic schools of Islam and the pagoda schools in Indochina. Broadly speaking, they were tolerated, but never assisted, financially or otherwise, by the French government, which never formulated a clear-cut doctrine concerning them. Such institutions were presumably looked upon as religious centers rather than as seats of learning, and were treated with untrusting neutrality.

No attempt was ever made to define the role that education was to play in the process of colonization. Reports of the colonial administration emphasized the need of training auxiliary cadres to fit either their own requirements or those of private business (clerks, primary school teachers, auxiliary medical staff, overseers, etc.), or stressed the political hazards of producing unemployed intellectuals. Moreover, no effort was made to define the type of education that should be given to a people subject to colonial rule. The few attempts to adapt education to local needs (the mutual teaching system in the Ouolof language in Senegal in 1816, the Franco-Moslem schools created by Governor Louis Faidherbe in Senegal in 1857, the bush schools in French Equatorial and French West Africa, etc.) were never followed up, with the exception of the Franco-Arabic secondary schools in Tunisia.

The stages in the evolution of educational policies in France had no exact counterpart in the colonies. When school laws in the 1880's provided for compulsory education for children from six to twelve years of age in France, the principle was not extended to overseas territories; in Algeria, where a part of French legislation was applicable, the obligation was valid only for French citizens, mainly French settlers and Jews of Algerian stock. From that time on, the network of schools in Algeria was developed so as to afford French citizens the same facilities as in metropolitan France. A similar evolution took place in Tunisia and later in Morocco, and also in the French West Indies and Réunion, territories where French settlers or people of French stock formed a substantial proportion of the population. This principle, however, was never embodied in a law or a governmental decision.

Similarly, the laws separating church and state, which put an end to religious schools in France after 1903, were not applied overseas. No concerted policy was devised for private schools. Schools created by Catholic missions were usually assisted and subsidized by the administration, but more in conformity with the personal preferences of colonial service staffs than with any over-all policy. (Protestant missions, often staffed by British or Americans, received no help.) Senegal offers an example of variations in the attitudes of the colonial administration. In 1841 the two public educational institutions which had existed since 1815 in Saint-Louis and Gorée were put under the guardianship of the Frères de Ploërmel, who retained a monopoly on teaching until Faidherbe's arrival in 1852. In 1864, however, the fourteen government schools were handed over to the Catholic missions (with the exception of the school at Saint-Louis). After 1884, when the school laws were adopted in France, public education was again developed, and French examinations were introduced (*brevet élémentaire et supérieur, certificat d'études primaires,* and *certificat d'aptitude professionnelle*).

While France had no clear educational policy for its overseas territories, aspects of its colonial policy nevertheless had repercussions on education. Most important was the so-called "direct administration," which resulted from the highly centralized French administrative system. Local government found no more favor overseas than it did in France. All powers were delegated to the governors, as to the prefects in France, and they, in turn, were assisted by *chefs de cercle* and *chefs de division,* all of whom were French. In Tunisia and Morocco the *contrôleurs civils* and the *adjoints de contrôle* played a similar role. These French civil servants, who wielded every form of authority—political, administrative, and even legal—worked side by side with traditional chieftains, whose jurisdiction was limited to the affairs of the native population. As the autonomy of traditional chieftains, however, was constantly encroached upon by the colonial administration, they often lost their powers, their positions, and thus their prestige. This traditional elite, which did not adjust well to modernization, was given little assistance by the colonial administration. Although Faidherbe did establish a school for chiefs' sons (dubbed the "school for hostages") in Senegal, it was an isolated and ephemeral example.

Centralized administration was not conducive to the development of education, for French citizens, trained in France, filled the vacancies at all levels of responsibility, and supplied the technical cadres as well. In settler territories such as North Africa and the French West Indies, most of the higher- and intermediate-level civil servants were recruited from among people of French extraction. Until the very eve of independence the number of French civil servants continued to increase, and by 1950 was more than 100,000: about 50,000 in Algeria, 35,000 in Morocco, 15,000 in Tunisia, and 15,000 in other territories. The substantial variations in the number of employees in different territories may be explained by two factors: (1) administrative staffing was heaviest in territories or areas where French citizens were most numerous, and (2) it depended on available budget resources. In general, the colonial administration employed natives only in the lowly positions of clerks and overseers in agriculture, husbandry, forestry, and so on. In private business firms, as well, the majority of cadres were of French origin.

Another feature of the French colonial system was the policy of assimilation, under which an indigenous elite was given a French-type education and thereby acquired rights equivalent to those enjoyed by Frenchmen. French officials have repeatedly stressed the fact that some colonials could obtain French nationality, and that the education offered in overseas territories was the same as it was in France. Closer investigation of the situation does not fully support all aspects of this claim. The few instances in which French citizenship was granted to individuals and families were exceptional and did not result from a systematic policy. Moreover, although the forms and the curricula of colonial education were patterned on the French model, the diplomas awarded were quite different. Before 1945 limited numbers of North African Moslems and West Indians had advanced to the *baccalauréat*, which gave them access to university education. In Indochina and sub-Saharan Africa such achievements were rare; although colonial degrees were on a par with those of France, they were not legally equivalent. The counterpart of the *certificat d'études primaire* was the *certificat d'études indigènes;* the two *brevets*, higher and lower, were matched by *brevets coloniaux;* and the *baccalauréat* was, in colonial terms, the *brevet de capacité colonial.* In the same way, administrative employees were classified as ordinary cadres, reserved in principle for Frenchmen, and native or local cadres.

It is fairly obvious that before 1945 French colonial policy did not envision education as a primary objective; certainly only a small proportion of budgetary resources were allocated to it. Not only was it limited in quantity, in terms of the number of institutions and openings for natives, but it was circumscribed legally, in terms of opportunities and the relative value of diplomas.

World War II marked a change in French colonial policy. The transformation was caused by well-known events, both domestic and external, in overseas territories (the Brazzaville Conference, the election of deputies to the French Parliament, the war in Indochina). The law of April 30, 1946, providing for the formulation, financing, and application of equipment and development plans for overseas territories, charted a new course which had implications for the field of education. Attempts to develop these territories through financial aid from France revealed the need for training new cadres.

A report by the French Ministry of Overseas Territories described the shortage of specialists: "Each large territory had but a few state engineers and private contractors, one or two surveyors, one or two geologists, and a few experts in forestry and agriculture, all of them overburdened by a daily round of tasks that would normally be assigned to three times as many officials. This skeleton staff is aided by a handful of Europeans and a few natives, trained either in vocational schools or simply in the field. Thus the stock of skilled personnel available in overseas territories was grossly inadequate." There was a similar shortage of skilled workers. The few bricklayers, mechanics, and carpenters were poorly qualified and insufficient in number to maintain roads, buildings, and equipment, and to carry out the public works normally provided for in territorial budgets.

The program of the Fonds d'Investissement pour le Développement économique et social des Territories d'Outre-Mer (FIDES) for 1947 defined its educational goals: "To double within five years and triple within ten years the number of pupils in elementary schools, and to double within ten years the number of students in secondary and technical schools and colleges." FIDES devoted a substantial part (roughly 10 per cent) of its equipment to technical and secondary schools. In the meantime, territorial budgets had, from year to year, increased their educational expenditures.

Only since that time has there been an educational policy that tended to increase school enrollments and to give Africans access to secondary, technical, and higher education. University colleges were founded in Dakar (1950) and Tananarive, and scholarships to be used in France were awarded to secondary school graduates. Degrees were made equivalent to those given in France, and entrance exami-

nations for service in the colonial administration were no longer reserved to French citizens. In the African territories, out of a total
population of some 30 million, school enrollment increased from
433,000 in 1938 to 503,000 in 1946 (272,000 of whom were in
public schools) to 654,000 in 1950 (370,000 of whom were in public
schools). A similar evolution took place in North Africa, but it is
more difficult to evaluate because the available statistics do not always
distinguish between Muslim and French students. Military operations
hindered progress in Indochina, and Hanoi University did not long
survive.

Broadly speaking, the forms and the curricula of French education
were applied overseas without substantial modification. The bush
schools and the attempt at basic education after 1945 were not pursued. At the elementary level French methods, textbooks, and curricula were used, except that an additional year was allowed for learning the language. Primary schools, rural and urban, comprised four
grades. Regional schools were the counterpart of the French elementary five-year cycle. The higher schools, initially intended to train
native auxiliary cadres, were gradually transformed *de facto* (and *de
jure* after 1945) into institutions patterned on those of metropolitan
France, such as teacher training colleges and schools of law and medicine, whose curricula approximated those of universities. Furthermore, educational reforms promulgated in France were faithfully
applied overseas; in 1945, after a merger was effected in France
between secondary and post-primary education, it became possible for
Africans to reach the *baccalauréat* level.

Because the French educational system is uniform and highly centralized, it was easily duplicated overseas. French school teachers, educated in teacher training colleges, have remarkably homogeneous views
on the essential values underlying the primary educational system,
evolved at the end of the nineteenth century. French instructors
sent overseas carried the same spirit with them, and trained native
pupils and future teachers as they themselves had been trained. Although the colonial administration had defined no educational policy,
and, before 1945, tended to place strictures on education rather than
to foster it, the teachers themselves discharged their responsibilities as they had done in metropolitan France. Thus it is necessary
to point out some characteristics of French education from the standpoint of political attitudes.

The French system of education is uniform, centralized, and hierarchical; curricula, methods, and even schedules are determined by the Ministry of National Education. The ministry also has the exclusive power to grant diplomas, a circumstance that tends to draw the public and private sectors of education closer together. The same is true overseas. In French West Africa, for instance, the best pupils of urban and rural schools (four-year course) had access to the regional schools (two-year course), which granted the primary school certificate; three years at the upper elementary school of the territory led to the appropriate diploma; later, an entrance examination gave access to the teacher training college in Sébikotane (Ecole William Ponty), which trained teachers, health officers, and civil servants and was the apex of the pyramid. After 1945 the system became identical with that of France.

French education is abstract in its programs as well as in its methods. Caring more for general ideas than for concrete facts, it gives a predominant position to abstract values. In admittedly oversimplified terms, its main objective is to inculcate in the child as much knowledge as possible, rather than to build his character or train him to adjust to society. The respect for knowledge thus engendered tends to become confused with a respect for degrees. For this reason the main motivation is competitiveness. From his first year at school, the pupil is given a weekly rating which is deemed more important than the actual marks obtained. The child is therefore taught to think in terms of his ranking among his fellows; he can become a "good pupil" only by turning in a better performance than theirs. The multiplicity of contests, which are always more important than examinations, makes the system even more markedly selective. The use of contests applies equally to the major schools, to employment in government agencies, and to the elementary schools and teacher training colleges in Africa. The spirit fostered by this system is at once democratic, as recruitment and promotion depend on merit rather than on wealth or family status, and individualistic, for success is necessarily obtained at the expense of others.

The same ambiguity is reflected in political attitudes. On the one hand, the French type of education leans toward the universal, and stresses values inspired by the French Revolution and the Declaration of Human Rights; it teaches the tolerance and equality of all men. On the other hand, it is nationalistic; it implicitly conveys the superiority of French civilization, and stresses the cultural heritage, the reason, the common sense, and the righteousness of France.

These various characteristics help to develop an abstract attitude toward the political sphere. The state is confused with the fatherland; national unanimity becomes all-pervasive. The distrust shown by the French Revolution toward intermediate bodies, local authorities, parochialism, and special interests still influences the citizenship courses taught in primary schools. It is taught that democratic principles are assured so long as citizens elect deputies to Parliament who supposedly have unlimited power to make political decisions; there is no mention of political parties, and local government agencies (town councils and *conseils généraux*) are merely wheels in the administrative machinery. There is no attempt to have special interests, economic or otherwise, represented; social inequalities or conflicts are disregarded; and the boundary between governmental decision making and the application of decisions is not clearly drawn. This abstract democratic ideal is linked with past history through the French Revolution and the Third Republic, and with the future through faith in human progress.

This type of education, when transplanted to colonial countries, pointed up obvious contradictions with actual conditions. It necessarily gave rise to demands for independence, in the name of the very values that it embodied. It is not surprising that teacher training colleges overseas were the main source for the recruitment of political elites at the time of independence. French educational features also accounted for some of the characteristics of political life in the new states.

The Present Situation

Some aspects of present-day life in the emerging states are clarified by the preceding considerations.

The educational system has played an essential role in the recruitment of political elites, especially in French West Africa but also, to a lesser extent, in French Equatorial Africa. After World War II the election of African deputies to the French Parliament and of African representatives to federal councils made it possible for the advocates of independence to express themselves politically. At that time the leaders of the Rassemblement Démocratique Africain (RDA) and other political parties were mainly recruited from among school teachers, who to this day constitute the majority of political leaders. The African bourgeoisie was much too weak to take the lead in independence movements. Trade was dominated by the great colonial firms, such as the Société commerciale de l'Ouest africain, the Compagnie française de l'Afrique occidentale, and Unilever, or by their Syrian and Lebanese go-betweens; property rights in land were virtually nonexistent, and in the Ivory Coast coffee planters were only beginning to realize profits. Traditional chieftains wielded some influence only in Sahara areas, where there was no economic progress. For precisely these reasons the Ecole William Ponty, a teacher training college, stood at the apex both of the educational pyramid and of social promotion. Through the screening process, based on examinations, the elites of all the territories in French West Africa were gathered at this hotbed of nationalism. Ouezzin Coulibaly, the RDA's most influential adviser, was for many years registrar at the William Ponty school, where most of the present-day African leaders were educated.

This kind of political recruitment was not based on ethnic or geographic origin, or on hereditary status. Although Modibo Keita and Sékou Touré may have benefited from the prestige of their illustrious ancestry, their commitment to political life is primarily owing to their activities as party or trade union militants. This democratization of political leadership encouraged the formation of interterritorial political parties, and even today, despite the Balkanization of Africa and the failure of the Mali Federation, it strengthens aspirations to African unity. The labor movement has also played an important role in training political elites, mainly through the unions of civil servants and teachers, who were recruited through the educational system.

Although the generalization that the educational system was the prime mover in the promotion of African political leaders may be justified, we must nevertheless note that it is difficult to delineate the political sphere; it would be quite arbitrary to establish strict boundaries separating political personnel, civil servants, and trade union cadres. In each French African state one party predominates, either legally or as the result of elections; decisions are made either by one person or by a very small number; the parliament and its members play a limited role. When political parties are very closely knit, as in Guinea and Mali, they tend to fuse with the civil service; in general, governmental administration is highly politicized. Even before independence, trade unions subordinated their particular demands to general objectives which coincided with those of political parties: the equality of rights, political independence, and labor codes. Neither the tradition of colonial administration, nor the French educational system, nor the exigencies of national unity have encouraged the creation of an autonomous political sphere or the separation of powers. The attempt by the political authorities of emerging states to control traditional chieftaincies, whose powers were abolished in Guinea as early as 1958 and more recently in Mali, is but another aspect of the tendency toward unification and centralization.

If we consider the machinery of state as a whole by including in it the political leaders, the senior ranks of the civil service, and trade union leaders, we might say that the rapid achievement of self-government and independence between 1956 and 1960 rested on the promotion of the leaders of independence movements, who had been recruited chiefly through the educational system and, in colonial times, served as teachers or civil servants. The needs were very great, for fifteen states with a population ranging from 300,000 to 5 million have each had to fill several hundred vacancies at a time when the intermediate ranks of the civil service were very thin. This general promotion has had several consequences:

1. The participation of the population in political life is a mass phenomenon; the electorate in French West Africa increased rapidly from 930,000 in 1945 to 10 million in 1957, out of a total population of 19 million. The vast majority of voters were illiterate, yet they supported the major interterritorial political parties and the educated elites who led them. Some leading groups drew their main support from certain ethnic groups, as in Dahomey, the Cameroun, the Congo, and Madagascar; nevertheless, political life developed on a national basis, and all leaders gave priority to the task of strengthening national unity within the boundaries drawn by the colonial powers at the end of the nineteenth century.

2. The widespread and rapid promotion of intermediate cadres to key posts created a vacuum in the machinery of government, for they could not be replaced by upgrading civil servants from the lower echelons whose educational level was too low. The functioning of central administrations, and even more so of provincial and local governments, was thus seriously handicapped; economic and social development and the execution of the central government's decisions were impeded.

3. Since secondary education developed only after 1946, African students did not begin to return to their native countries until 1956; by that time ruling groups had been constituted, and the integration

of new graduates into government service created serious problems. Even those given responsible assignments were reluctant to accept guidance from political leaders whose education was inferior to their own. Tension between leaders and students has appeared in countries like Guinea; it seeks a political outlet, but, as the political machine is controlled by the leading groups, the students have no political groups to join and no means of expression at their command.

The preceding remarks apply only to the countries of sub-Saharan Africa. Political developments followed a different course in Tunisia and Morocco, where a middle class of tradesmen, landowners, and professional people provided a source of political elites. In Indochina a distinction must be drawn between Vietnam on the one hand where the educational system was much more developed, and Cambodia and Laos on the other. Algeria, whose middle class has virtually disappeared, is in a class by itself. Indeed, each country calls for a specific study. In general, it may be said that the educational system was the salient factor in the recruitment and promotion of political elites. The existence of a bourgeoisie made the process slightly different. Although the French colonial system did not favor the economic development of a middle class, and debarred it from political power, its members had often obtained a French-type education, which, at the time of independence, added the prestige of education to that of wealth. This modern education has been a contributing factor in orienting the political life of new states toward modernization and centralization, away from local, linguistic, ethnic, or religious parochialism. Yet the rapid expansion of educational systems on the eve of independence raises new problems, as the present hierarchy in employment reflects less and less the hierarchy in degrees.

In the narrower field of educational policies, the attitudes of the leaders of new states have certain characteristics in common:

(a) African leaders view education as a political factor of overriding importance for national unity. It is essentially for this reason that French has been chosen as a national language wherever linguistic plurality might have favored one group over another. Moreover, leaders did not want to jeopardize the chances for African unity, and they hoped to facilitate technical cooperation with France.

(b) The French system of education has not been challenged. Owing to their own training and their desire to modernize, the leaders of all countries formerly under French colonial rule have been willing to maintain the French curricula. Fears of a downgrading of the academic level and misgivings that an adaptation of the educational process might reduce it to "cheap education" have prevailed over practical considerations that might have led to primary school teaching in the vernacular, as in former British territories. In countries where the national language has become official (Morocco, Tunisia, Mauritania, Cambodia, Laos, and Vietnam), educational reforms have been introduced. Except in Vietnam, French is taught from the fourth grade on, and in secondary education the French language is mainly used. These reforms have resulted in the addition of new fields (language, literature, history, and geography) without sacrificing any subject on the already crowded French curriculum. A rapid increase in enrollment is therefore very costly, and it is impossible to reduce the numbers of drop-outs and repeats, which were already very high. In sub-Saharan Africa, roughly 45 per cent of the pupils leave school without having completed the elementary grades. Under the Tunisian plan of education, 20 to 30 per cent of the pupils are expected to stay in the same grade for two years.

(c) New states consider the development of education as a high priority goal, and earmark from 15 to 25 per cent of their budgets for it. Limited financial resources, however, and the shortage of qualified teachers make it imperative to be selective in the allocation of funds; African ministers at the Addis Ababa Conference in May 1961 agreed that educational planning was necessary. Only Tunisia, however, has put such a plan into operation. Up to now African leaders seem to have given priority, for political and social reasons, to the development of elementary education. Although experts and international organizations recommend concentration on secondary education, which would train instructors as well as administrative and technical personnel, African leaders reply that they must first satisfy the needs for modernization and progress among the masses clamoring for schools. This attitude is a general one, although the situation varies from country to country; school enrollment is still very low in the Sahel area (less than 10 per cent in Mali, Niger, Upper Volta and Tchad) and is above the 50 per cent level only in Madagascar, the Cameroun, the Central African Republic, the Congo, and Gabon. The differences may be explained by the development of Catholic mission schools in these latter countries.

(d) The priority given to elementary education does not mean that secondary or technical education has been neglected. Enrollment at this level has been growing rapidly, but the rate of expansion depends on the number of additional teachers France will be able to place at the disposal of the new states. Almost all the teachers in secondary and technical schools are supplied through French technical assistance; administrative needs are too pressing, and the prospects of promotion in the civil service are too attractive, for African students to choose the teaching profession after graduation. At present, of the 20,000 teachers provided by the French government, 8,000 are in Morocco, 2,500 in Tunisia, 3,500 in sub-Saharan Africa, and 700 in Vietnam, Laos, and Cambodia.

(e) The leaders of new states are liberal in granting fellowships to students who have received their *baccalauréat*. The number of African students, nearly all of whom hold fellowships, who are pursuing higher education in France while the universities of Dakar and Tananarive are being developed is steadily rising (from 1,764 in 1959 to 3,122 in 1962). Tunis University already has 1,500 students, and 1,800 more Tunisians are studying in France.

The attitude of the population at large toward education is not very different from that of the leaders. The desire for schooling is widespread and intense, except in areas with a nomadic population; classes with a hundred or more pupils are not unusual, and in many villages the peasants themselves build schools to reinforce their demands for primary school teachers. The motivations of pupils and their families proceed not only from the desire to learn; education is regarded primarily as a means of social promotion which makes it possible to escape from the rural environment. It has often been claimed that young students are ambitious to become politicians or civil servants, but an inquiry conducted by the Institut d'Etude du Développement Economique et Social in Mali does not seem to support this claim. Of a sample of 788 pupils about to finish their elementary education (226 from rural schools, 562 from urban schools), 620 replied to a question as to the professions they intended to follow. The results were as follows: 241 chose teaching, 191 public health, 56 administration, 57 careers as technicians, 32 agriculture, 29 factory work, and 14 politics. Thus schooling does not seem to lead young people toward careers that offer little opportunity or are of only marginal interest to their country. Rather, it might accelerate migration from rural to urban areas, instead of stimulating modernization in a country where 80 to 90 per cent of the population is engaged in traditional agriculture. The breakdown of students from sub-Saharan Africa who are studying in Paris confirms this impression, for less than 10 per cent intend to take up agriculture. Contrary to a widespread opinion, however, only 15 per cent are studying law (See Table 1).[3]

Students are guided in their choice of a profession either by their own inclinations or by the government's fellowship policy; in several countries the student who is granted a fellowship must promise in writing to serve ten years in the civil service. The need for cadres, however, is ascertained on the basis of present shortages rather than of long-term forecasting. Some countries, such as Tunisia, Senegal, and Madagascar, have attempted to make such forecasts, but with little success.

Any satisfactory analysis of the relationship, past and present, between education and political development should make it possible to pinpoint the type of education likely to foster political development in the future. Such an effort presupposes a knowledge of the type of political development which is desirable. The application to developing countries of criteria elaborated from the political experiences of industrialized countries in the nineteenth century should be avoided.

Economists have substituted dynamic growth models for static ones. In the field of political science, dynamic typology must take into account the developmental requirements of the new countries; only then can political structures be analyzed with reference to the growth they may foster or hinder. The area of politics should be extended to include rule application, but the state's traditional task of maintaining a balance among interests, groups, and individuals must be distinguished from its dynamic task of furthering economic and social development. Then political structures may be assessed in terms of their aptitude to elaborate programs of actions, getting them under way, and reaching their objectives. For example, it would be helpful to know what kind of political structures would hasten economic and social modernization. Political stability, which depends on countervailing powers and parties governing in alternation, is an implicit criterion, but it may be less important than a concerted development policy. Similarly, in economics, price and currency stability, however important, is not enough to encourage economic development.

From the point of view of development requirements, education would not only be expected to convey political values and attitudes and provide for socio-professional mobility; it would also have to train the intermediate and upper-level cadres needed by the country.

[3] Cf. Remi Clignet, "Education et aspirations professionnelles," *Tiers Monde*, No. 17.

Thus conceived, the role of education would be to fit a manpower plan linked with the economic development plan. The technical problems of educational planning are beyond the scope of this study. But the main link between education and political development assumes dynamic significance when seen as a strategy for the development of human resources.

TABLE 1: STUDENTS FROM SUB-SAHARAN AFRICA AND THE MALAGASY REPUBLIC GRADUATING IN FRANCE

Sectors	1959	1960	1961	1962
Technical				
Non-specialized (Faculty of Sciences)	257	355	394	355
Specialized				
Agricultural				
Higher (including preparation)	96	126	142	128
Veterinary	73	74	87	77
Intermediate	115	170	138	110
Non-agricultural				
Higher (engineering schools, including preparation)	154	217	291	384
Intermediate	110	113	117	79
Total	805	1,055	1,169	1,133
Health				
Higher (medicine, 80%; pharmacy, 20%)	414	465	475	454
Intermediate	207	253	300	256
Total	621	718	775	710
Administration				
Non-specialized	458	538	528	499
Specialized				
Institut des Hautes Etudes d'Outre-Mer (IHEOM)	105	340	471	544
Schools of finance	100	190	235	213
Institut d'Etude du Développement Economique et Social (IEDES)	41	43	48	54
Others (including preparation)	66	62	279	414
Total	770	1,173	1,561	1,724
GRAND TOTAL	2,196	2,946	3,505	3,567

Source: Survey by Institut d'Etude du Développement Economique et Social.

CHAPTER 3

INDONESIA

JOSEPH FISCHER

～·～·～·～·～·～·～·～·～·～·～·～·～·～·～·～·～·～·～·

In INDONESIA, as in most countries, education is perhaps the most complex of all societal institutions. Disentangling the educational system from other systems in society and specifically identifying those organizations significantly involved in the educational process is at the outset the major task of research. It is both education as process and education as structure that must clearly be delimited before one can proceed very far with any analysis of the relationships between education and any other institutions. It must be recognized that education as a process can be found in a variety of organizations, many of which overlap and many of which are non-school in character. This is particularly noticeable in independent Indonesia, where the imported, formalized educational structure is of recent origin (75 years or so) and where the history of its most accelerated expansion has occupied less than a generation; where transfer of the process of teaching the young from traditional, often informalized situations to concrete organizations whose educational role is explicit is far from completed; and where there is very little hard data to validate the belief that even the most crucial aspects of the process of socialization and cultural transmission are being housed in a school system.

Truly, the most striking feature of Indonesian education today is its extremely fragmented structure. This is partly to be explained by the very small size of the Dutch-bequeathed educational system, the concomitantly high illiteracy rate (85 per cent) and the scarcity of skilled persons which compelled a host of diverse organizations to undertake instructional programs at the beginning of independence in 1948. In 1940 there were only 2,360,228 Indonesians in all schools and 637 in all faculties. Today there are over 1,000,000 students in high schools and approximately 50,000 in universities. In addition to family and village education by groups and in city schools, children and adults are confronted by a mélange of quasi-official and private agencies of instruction. Particularly in Java there exists what has been termed an *aliran* pattern which refers to the use by government and political parties of a number of voluntary social organizations directly or indirectly linked to them. Many government departments and most of the political parties (e.g., PNI, PKI, the Nahdatul Ulama, and, prior to its abolishment, the Masjumi) support vocational schools of many kinds, finance adult education programs, sponsor sundry youth groups, and through these and other means attempt to maintain official and party links with all levels of Indonesian society. In addition, Islamic schools of varying academic and religious quality are scattered about the country, particularly in Java and Sumatra. Instruction in factories, cooperatives, labor unions, and official in-service training programs further fragment the educational structure and make for an increasingly diffuse distribution of educational functions. While many of these agencies operate only intermittently and are of varying status, they have been understandably reluctant to divest themselves of an activity from which they acquire a certain prestige as well as government subsidies. And in fact it has been the central government in Djakarta which has in the past encouraged these "volunteer" programs and which has itself set up educational shop in organizations outside the control of its own Department of Education and beyond the pale of official authority.

The complex structure of Indonesian education requires, first, a definition of what constitutes the educational sector. We will consider education as here defined as the formalized process of teaching and learning which takes place within organizations called schools and which primarily involves three categories of persons: teachers, students, and administrators. Further, the formal educational structure will be emphasized and in particular the public section of it. We will treat three aspects of the educational process which relate to political development: the significance of school-state relationships, the content and effects of the instructional program, and the consequences of particular school environments. These aspects will be discussed mainly in terms of their relationships to specified functions of the educational system which bear upon the political process. Functions (as drawn from Merton) refer to those observable consequences or characteristics that relate to the adaptation of a system or relate to its maintenance and continuity. For characteristics that make for or aid in adaptation, the term "functional" will be used, while the term "dysfunctional" will refer to those which weaken or lessen the adaptation of a system. Functional and dysfunctional aspects of the educational system will be examined only as they are relevant to the political process and the structure in which it is housed. Primary emphasis will be placed upon those educational functions that are directly concerned with the process of building a unified and viable national state. In Indonesia this process concerns diminishing ethnic and religious diversity which manifests itself in political conflict, and concerns ameliorating regional particularisms which are enhanced by the geographic distribution of state resources. It is also relevant to utilizing the skills and knowledge of persons from a variety of social classes and backgrounds with widely differing levels of political maturity. To a very much lesser extent attention will be given to external aspects, that is, to Indonesia's international position and to the importation of ideologies and organizations.

This chapter is further limited by an almost exclusive concentration upon functions analyzed within certain educational organizations. The more concrete, less amorphous, less numerous organizations in the educational structure will receive the greatest attention, that is, high schools and universities. This emphasis can be defended on two grounds. First, it is the result of a search for an economy of method in countries like Indonesia characterized by enormous social flux, by national welfare planning in transition, and where, for the investigator, there exists little information about what is actually taking place.[1] Secondly, this orientation stems from an emphasis on the

---

[1] The major sources used in this chapter are the following: K. J. Brugmans, "Education and Economic Opportunity in the Netherlands East Indies" and "Education and Nationalism in the Netherlands East Indies," both in *Education in Pacific Countries*, Honolulu, Hawaii Seminar Conference, 1936; R. L. Djajadiningrat, *From Illiteracy to University, Educational Development in the Netherlands Indies*, New York, Institute of Pacific Relations, 1943; Joseph Fischer, "The Student Population of a Southeast Asian University: An Indonesian Example," *International Journal of Comparative Sociology*, Vol. II, September 1961, pp. 224-233; "The University Student in South and South-East Asia," *Minerva*, Vol. II, No. 1, autumn 1963, pp. 39-53, "Universities and the Political Process in Southeast Asia," *Pacific Affairs*, Vol. XXXVI, winter 1963, pp. 3-15, and *Universities in Southeast Asia*, Columbus, Ohio State University for Kappa Delta Pi, 1964; John S. Furnivall, "Education and Nationalism in Netherlands India," unpublished lecture, London, University of London, Education Department, 1946, *Educational Progress in Southeast Asia*, New York, Institute of Pacific Relations, 1943, and "The Training for Civil Administration in Netherlands India," *Journal of the Royal Central Asian Society*, Vol. XXVI, July 1939, pp. 415-439; Hla Myint, "The Universities of Southeast Asia and Economic Development," *Pacific Affairs*, Vol. XXXV, summer 1962, pp. 116-127; Marnixius Hutasoit, *Problems and Potentials of Indonesian Education*, Los Angeles, University of California Press, 1961; *Indonesia*, New Haven, Human Relations Area Files, 1956; Leslie H. Palmier, "Occupational Distribution of Parents of Pupils in Certain Indonesian Educational Institutions," *Indonesie*, Vol. X. Nos. 4 and 5, August 1957 and October 1957, pp. 320-348, 349-376; Soelaemon Soemardi, "Some Aspects of the Social Origin of Indonesian Political Decision Makers," *Transactions of the Third World Congress of Sociology*, Vol. III, No. 3, 1956, pp. 338-348; Justus Van der Kroef, "Educational Development and Social Change in Indonesia," *Harvard Educational Review*, Vol.

crucial role of elites during the first two to four generations of independence in countries that have short supplies of technical and technological skills and knowledge and limited or unexploited resources. The hunt for educational organizations that are concrete, relatively scarce, and that produce potential elites leads one invariably to high schools and universities.

In Indonesia, both types of organizations are in relatively short supply. Certain large cities (Djakarta, Bandung, Malang, Jogjakarta, Semarang, Medan, and Solo) contain most of the high-prestige public and private secondary schools of which there are, exclusive of vocational schools, only 600 with about 300,000 students compared with a primary school population of over 6,200,000. A survey taken of a sample population (1,000 students) enrolled in Gadjah Mada University in 1960 showed that 84 per cent came from metropolitan high schools and 60 per cent of these from only three cities. These figures are all the more remarkable when one considers that no more than 8 per cent of the total Indonesian population of 90,000,-000 reside in cities of over 100,000 and that some 75 per cent live in villages. Of the total university student population of nearly 50,000, approximately 26,000 are enrolled in only two universities out of twelve (Gadjah Mada and the University of Indonesia). Thus, the importance of certain urban high schools and a few universities has resulted in a monopoly of elite production. This will continue until the rapid expansion which is taking place at the primary school level compels broadening the high school and university base. This is, however, a decade or more away, and Indonesians as yet appear not to have taken political note of the fact that a half dozen cities and two universities virtually monopolize the only channels of highest social mobility.

Five functions have been selected with which to examine sets of relationships between education and political development in Indonesia: change, social mobility, socialization, acculturation, and the recruitment of potential elites. These functions are listed roughly in the order of their generality. The latter four functions are to be regarded in one sense as subordinate to the first function, that of change, as, when assessed together, they largely determine the quality and directtion of the educational system viewed as an agency of change or modernization. However, when evaluated separately these four func-

XXIV, Fall 1954, pp. 239-255; S. L. Van der Wal, *Some Information on Education in Indonesia up to 1942*, The Hague, Netherlands Universities Foundation for International Cooperation, 1961.

tions can be made to serve even a broader level of analysis. For the identification, description, and analysis of specific functions in specified organizations (i.e., school) of an institution in society (i.e., education) are a first step in the study of inter-institutional relationships, and also of comparative methodology in the social sciences.

In this chapter the starting points for analyzing function are always units of the educational structure. What follows is an attempt to relate the educational system (functions and structure) to those functions which have political consequences. No description or definition has been made of what is here called the political process. However, it is assumed that this process includes the distribution of power and the task of government to protect the whole society from external threat and internal dissolution. Educational functions have been selected which appear to have the most relevance to Indonesian political development and which are also regarded as basic to the maintenance of its social system. It must be pointed out that other functions could have been chosen and that the units of departure could have been within the political rather than the educational structure. A conventional professional basis has governed choice.

Assumptions of certain functions as being crucial to the operation and growth of society have been derived in part from Marion Levy. Also, while assenting to the usefulness of Talcott Parsons' division of society into a behavioral system and a social system, this investigation deals primarily with the latter.

After a general discussion of the dependent function of change, the educational system will be examined as an instrument of social mobility, particularly as it effects the possible entry of individuals into the political system. This refers mainly to the significance of completing various levels of schooling, of graduating from various types of schools (academic, vocational, etc.), and of attending certain schools in particular geographic locations. An evaluation will be presented of the educational backgrounds of elites and of the various groups, classes, and individuals for whom higher schooling and upward mobility in the political system are or are not synonymous.

Socialization as a function will be examined both in its content and in the environment in which it takes place. The content refers to those aspects of the formal transmission of culture, knowledge, and ideas that shape what may be called the political socialization of students, and the environment refers to the social milieu (system of human relationships, etc.) in which this process unfolds and from which it cannot be separated.

An analysis of the process of acculturation will be presented as it relates to decreasing or increasing cultural conflicts among youth and as it relates to creating national political loyalties.

The fourth and final function is that of the replacement of elites and refers to recruitment of individuals for the political system.

I. *The Educational System as an Instrument of Change*

This represents the most generalized level of function and has at least two aspects. The first involves a determination of the extent to which educational organizations are acting as agencies of change or modernization in relation to political development. Here we must consider: (1) the introduction into schools and universities by official authority of "new" or important ideas, practices, or knowledge which are considered necessary for "modern" political advance; and (2) the efforts of government to modify, abolish, or in any way alter certain ideas, customs, or practices already in existence which it deems are inimical to modern political development or which generally impede necessarily related social change. It therefore becomes necessary to assess the response of the units of the educational system to state-planned changes and political need, and the use and impact of particular organizations as instruments for introducing specific changes as well as their part in creating conditions or environments upon which general political change is dependent.

The selection of change as a primary function rests upon an assumption that the continuation and growth of a society and its social system depend in large part upon its general responsiveness and adjustment to changing ideological and material conditions. This would appear to be particularly applicable to traditional societies undergoing transitional periods marked by great conflict. It is suggested that the general adaptiveness of the social systems of such societies to varying and changing realities is perhaps the most essential feature of their ability to survive as they would wish. If this assumption is valid, one would expect such countries to utilize some of their national organizations for the purpose of rendering changes less haphazard. A further implication is that nations committed to national welfare schemes and balanced development should house programs of sponsored change in organizations that are subject to some type of decisive control. Schools are regarded by Indonesian politicians and administrators as public possessions administered, financed, and developed by government in the interests of the nation as a whole. If this is so, one might lay down the following hypothesis: the primary test of Indonesia's real commitment to socialism can be judged by the extent to which the government is actually in effective control of its educational system. The facts during the independence period indicate that so far the Indonesian government's direction of the educational system has been slight.

The formal structure of the Indonesian educational system is centered in Djakarta and in the Departments of Education and Higher Education, which have branches in all major cities and towns of the islands. These departments nominally control over 7,000,000 students enrolled in some 40,000 state schools. There are in addition some 5,000 private schools, all of which are subject to government inspection and more than half of which receive state subsidies. A widespread inspectorate system provides the departments with their major means of assessing schools, but the high ratio of schools to inspectors makes any productive inspection system virtually impossible. Private schools, because of their traditional isolation and autonomy, receive less attention from the departments despite the fact that many of the high-prestige middle and high schools are run by Dutch Jesuits and many Islamic schools are controlled by supporters of the now-illegal Masjumi Party. It is true enough that the extreme fragmentation and large size of the educational system in Indonesia handicaps control. It is also true that the government has acted upon the belief that any school is better than none, and that private schools lessen the state's educational burden. It is, nevertheless, surprising that the political elite has had only a half-hearted commitment to state control of education. But one must note that those responsible for expansionist educational policies are themselves the products of a severely restricted colonial system of education which was anathema to many of them. The Indonesian state and its political leaders are ideologically committed to free and equal educational opportunity for all its citizens. This belief has become a *sine qua non* not only for the elite but for the great majority of Indonesians, whatever their origin. The rapid expansion of the educational system that has taken place during the last decade is largely due to enormous social demand rather than to elite or government stimuli. State control over the vital parts of this system would require some effective type of braking instruments to regulate entry, but the extraordinary widespread and self-generating popular demand for education has made and would make such control politically hazardous. If attempted it would require police and military enforcement which as yet the elite of the dominant Indonesian Nationalist Party (PNI) has been unwilling or unable to use.

There is, furthermore, a notion of planning among many of the highly educated that amounts to a faith in, rather than a plan for, education. This faith is singularly naive and has dangerous political and economic implications for a loosely structured state in the process of harnessing partially exploited and unevenly distributed resources. There is a belief that the beneficial use of the educational system, particularly as it relates to accelerating economic development, is merely a problem of input—more and more students, teachers, facilities and *rupiah*, and that increases in these four areas are the major indicators of progress and success. The quality and utility of the products of the educational system—graduates, skills and research— are assumed somehow to correspond to national aims and needs. So long as a larger and larger number of people are taught to be literate and learn an increasing number of skills the elite believes the educational system to be functional. It is perhaps needless to point out that these assumptions have never been empirically validated in Indonesia, or for that matter in very many other countries in the world. Such criteria as are used for measuring Indonesian educational progress in relation to national development are predominantly quantitative—literacy rates, numbers of graduates, numbers of trained teachers, numbers of vocational schools, and so forth. In most cases data cited is applied to economic development, the political sector being ignored. However, even using these indicators, discrepancies between national aims and the performance of the educational system have been noticed by some Indonesian leaders.

In 1961 a separate Department of Higher Education was established partly as a response to the problem of an excess supply of graduates from non-technical faculties. For example, as of March 13, 1962 at Gadjah Mada University in Jogjakarta there were 2,472 students enrolled in the Faculty of Law out of a grand total enrollment of 15,747. Comparable figures from some other faculties were as follows: Medicine, 1,239; Engineering, 1,409; Agriculture, 770. From 1955 through 1960 the Faculty of Law at this university contained on the average 20 per cent of the student population. In other universities the popularity of law studies is much the same and is to be explained by the lingering high prestige of legal degrees as a legacy of pre-independence days. The disproportionate number of law graduates relative to national "needs" and available employment has only recently provoked official criticism and will probably result within the next five years in governmental regulation of faculty enrollment. Official concern is also shown in the dissatisfaction with the continuing domination of academic high schools and the low status and under-use of vocational high schools. The extreme faith of the government in vocational training has been at odds with the realities of the status system of traditional schooling. However, the Indonesian government's attempts at solution continue to demonstrate the *ad hoc* basis on which much of Indonesian educational planning has taken place.

In other spheres of national activity the Indonesian government has in great contrast to education exercised many of the assumed prerogatives of state control and influence. It has abolished political parties (the *Masjumi* and the *Partai Socialis Indonesia*), has established effective military censorship of the press, policed the political activities of labor unions and the Communist Party, and has virtually prohibited the Chinese from inland trading. Such forceful actions serve to underscore even more the contrasting apathy and indecisiveness of politicians and officials towards educational organizations. Once again this illustrates the fragmentary nature of Indonesia's commitment to centralization and to the instrumental use of schools for political or any other national purposes. This *de facto* abdication of state responsibility and power in the educational realm is not surprising considering present-day Indonesian political instability and the complex dilemmas of coping with a large, rapidly growing, conservative, and fragmented educational system which in part was a colonial heritage. But precisely because these conditions exist in a country where the rational allocation of resources is vital, the need for control and evaluation of the educational system is correspondingly greater. This is so if for no other reason than to justify the large proportion of national wealth diverted to the educational sector. In Indonesia some 15 per cent of the 1961 budget was allocated to formal education; and if one adds to this what is spent upon a variety of instructional programs and mass media outside of schools and universities this percentage would be almost doubled.

It follows from the foregoing that the formal role of Indonesian schools in planned change, particularly as it relates to the construction of a viable national state, is uncertain and may vary from school to school, from city to city, from province to province, and from island to island. It is clear that in the manifest use of schools for national political purposes implementation and planning cannot be separated and that desired results cannot be obtained without effective control. However, it is from another view that the Indonesian government's indirection and lax control has more serious consequences for national political development.

Purposefully or not, schools are involved in the process of change whether as instruments of transmission or innovation. It can be observed that certain functions basic to change are operating at certain levels of schooling or in certain types of schools. As will be demonstrated later, these connections can be specified and implications for the political process can be drawn. What is clear now in Indonesia is that the educational system is beginning to monopolize the time and instruction of youth from the ages of 7 to 14. The transfer of teaching the young from families and villages to schools is occurring rapidly though the quality and amount of this transference is not known. However, an examination and specification of various functions of units of the educational system with respect to political change can be made. Such a research effort would indicate whether or not, in what degree, and at what grade levels specified aspects of schooling are functional, dysfunctional, or not relevant to the development of a realistic and modern Indonesian polity. Formal education, despite its amorphous and complex nature, is after all not a secret process, and schools are far more open to scrutiny than, for example, most Indonesian political organizations. There is more misinformation and apathy in Indonesia regarding the school system than about almost any other organized sector of society. Discussion or appreciation of the educational system is generally phrased in terms of what education should or should not do, what is thought is being done or not being done, or what it can or cannot do. In a country that has not held a nationwide census since 1930, inconclusive statistics are publicly cited as refutation or validation. Rarely is the question asked: what are the realities of the educational system and what is it actually doing? Those with the competence or the power to change schools surely should know what it is they wish to alter.

One of the dilemmas confronting those Indonesian leaders who are realistic about their country's education is the inadequacy of current techniques of evaluation. Most methods lead inevitably either to descriptions of administration and the forms of structure or to the putative deficiencies of curriculum and teaching methods. These then are the points of examination and reform. The most superficial aspects of the educational system are the ones which appear to be constantly "changing." Countries like Indonesia in transitional periods of flux are bound to be caught in the ups and downs of political policies which do not ordinarily indicate the true nature of events. Schools are particularly sponge-like in their ability to absorb policies without undergoing basic changes in their composition. When one applies the usual professional criteria to the obvious and apparently concrete aspects of the Indonesian educational system, little of significance can be seen. Change bears little relationship to change as a function dependent upon other functions in a system. Thus except as noted previously the character of state-school relationships is not regarded as of primary importance and the formal content of the instructional program and its organization is not considered crucial. Thus the most meaningful designation of the educational system as an instrument of change depends upon the extent to which its organizations are involved in functions relevant to political processes of nation building and the way these functions produce or create conditions for political growth. Of the four functions to be discussed next it will be demonstrated that socialization and acculturation in the educational system are in many ways most significant to this process.

II. Educational Organizations as Instruments of Social Mobility

Mobility as a function rests upon the observation that modern societies must provide some concrete organizational means by which it is possible for individuals to enter a social system and find social and economic rewards which are commensurate with their abilities and desires. The units of a mobility system are also a primary means by which a society can identify and reward those individuals it needs to replace its aging or deceased members. Certain organizations have traditionally been crucial to the upward social movement of individuals; schools have been the foremost of these, particularly during previous generations when higher degrees were scarce and difficult to earn. In colonial Indonesia, high schools, higher institutes, and faculties capped the channels of mobility for Indonesians.

During the 350 years of Dutch occupation, the extremely small number of higher educational organizations and the very restricted nature of entry into them meant that for most Indonesians involvement in a mobility system dependent upon schooling lay outside their reach. Statistics dramatically attest to the magnitude of this denial of education to the Indonesian population. In 1942 with a population of 70,000,000, less than 1,000 Indonesians had completed a university education. It has been estimated that Indonesia began her independence with about 1,100 professional trained people: 400 technicians, 400 physicians, 250 lawyers, 4 philologists, 3 economists, and several veterinarians and agricultural experts. In 1940 there were 1,786 Indonesians enrolled in high schools compared to 5,688 Europeans. During the same year there were 2,360,238 Indonesians in *all* schools, but only 98,244 of this number were enrolled in schools providing a European-type education which was required for government employ except at menial levels.

Thus during the colonial period Indonesians who found themselves in an academic middle school had already begun their upward social progression. High school leavers and faculty graduates were always certain of desirable employment. There were, however, even for this group severe barriers against reaching the highest echelons of government service because of the great number of Dutchmen residing in Indonesia (mostly in Java) and the *de facto* preferences given to Eurasians. It must be noted that there were more Dutch citizens (some 50,000 families) residing in Indonesia between 1920 and 1939 than there were Europeans living in any other colony in the world. Out of 81,957 persons on active service in 1940 in the Netherlands Indies, 16,725 were Europeans who virtually monopolized the higher positions. Middle and high school leavers, of course, had no employment problems, but the few graduates felt the positions offered to them were not commensurate with the long and arduous period of study that they had completed. One out of two Indonesian faculty graduates, including those who earned degrees in Holland, became political dissenters, the hard core of which led the independence movement. The social and economic rewards were deemed by many Indonesians as not sufficient enough for their travail and many of them became revolutionaries. For Javanese, Sundanese, and South Sumatrans there were no alternatives to the lack of high government positions. Their own traditional social systems held commercial activities in low esteem and as private professionals (lawyers and doctors) they found themselves greatly disadvantaged by competition with Europeans and Chinese. The colonial educational system conferred high status upon Indonesians but did not guarantee high positions. It was not surprising that many refused government jobs or did not practice their professions and entered into oppositional politics during the colonial period.

Unfortunately there have hardly been any studies of the backgrounds of Indonesian elites. Such data as has been collected reveal that during the Dutch period about 95 per cent of high school leavers and graduates (exclusive of Europeans and foreign orientals) entered government service. The fact is evidence that diplomas and degrees were hallmarks of the highest possible social success to Indonesians. Over 85 per cent of these successful students came from families in which at least one parent had completed primary schooling and was a civil servant or a local official. Civil servants in Java have practically constituted a social class which is designated by the term *prijaji;* during the colonial period and since independence this group and their offspring have dominated Indonesian politics. During the colonial period completion of a high school or faculty education meant for an Indonesian a kind of automatic entry into the national political system either as a civil servant or as an agitator. The end of Dutch hegemony brought marked changes.

The first decade and a half of independence can be divided into two periods insofar as the importance of education for mobility and its political consequences are concerned. During the first ten years of independence about 75 per cent of all high school leavers gained admission to higher levels of education. These students were drawn chiefly from families whose fathers were civil servants or professionals, all of whom held academic degrees which were symbolic of the highest social prestige and status. Thus although students at the upper levels were coming from a wider social base than in pre-independence times, their fathers were overwhelmingly *prijaji.* These students were nurtured in a tradition in which social status was valued independent of economic reward or of actual academic performance but was determined by the educational level completed, or, in the case of a few, upon royal descent. University graduates from 1952 through 1958 were products of this older tradition and were largely willing to bear the burdens thrust up by an unwieldy and antiquated academic system. Though student frustration certainly must have been prevalent, rarely was it expressed through any organized dissent. Indonesian universities, in contrast with those in India and Burma, were not beset by problems of student discipline or political activity during this first decade. The demands of a vastly expanded government administrative system provided 85 per cent of all graduates during this period with state jobs. Those who remained outside government were mostly Chinese and some Sumatrans whose families had been traditionally involved in commerce. It was still obvious to most Indonesians that degrees and success were synonymous—the road to social eminence still began with schooling.

Indonesians have often stated that all levels of schooling have been free and open to all citizens regardless of ethnic origin, social class, or religion. Detailed data obtained from questionnaires, interviews, and student records at two universities tend to give considerable credence to this belief. This is a surprising feature of a country that has been constantly confronted with cultural conflict, and whose hopeful national motto is: "unity in diversity." However, the preponderance of university students came from *prijaji* backgrounds, an inheritance from the colonial system. The initial decade of independence in this respect was not dissimilar to the Dutch period. Java continued to dominate, and in effect still dominates, the high school and university prestige system. Great numbers of non-Javanese youth still sought entrance to schools in Java but found no insuperable barriers to their entrance and graduation. Many of them entered the government service and remained in Djakarta or Bandung; the great success of South Sumatrans in the area of elite politics attests to the usefulness of schools in achieving mobility. Thus the educational system maintained its position as the common denominator for personal advance among all Indonesians. Prestige and status continued to accrue not only to the individual but to his family as well. Education was and is the one area in which Indonesian parents are willing to make relatively large financial investments without the prior promise of quick, safe, and concrete returns.

During the colonial period the upper levels of schooling were the sole sources of status and prestige. All who were academically successful emerged from each higher school level with the same valued hallmark—the diploma or the degree. Distinctions among the rank of medical, legal, and technical degrees had social but no political significance. In such a system, ethnic, religious, and class differences among Indonesian graduates were of minor importance. Thus in a sense the social and academic qualifications for entry into the political system were the same for one and all. In this way colonial schooling provided a bridge and channel for diverse elements of the population and exposed the participants to common instruction and to generally similar environmental experiences. Those who took the reins of the revolutionary movement and who dominated the first decade of political independence were the members of a small, intimate circle in which until recently gross differences of ethnicity, religion, and personality were transcended. There were only eight high schools in the Indies of 1939 and seven of them and all the five faculties were located in Java. The potential elite thus not only attended the same schools but were required to live on one island and in the few cities that represented the center of Indonesian political life. Between the ages of eleven and twenty-four their realm was the national realm. The situation continued for the first decade of independence but has changed drastically since then.

The last five years have seen the beginning of a period of rapid expansion of education at all levels in numbers of students and kinds of schools. The system now is so fragmented and diversified that it confers differential status upon those completing various studies. The advent of vocational schools and the ease of entry into the formally forbidding and once highly academic middle schools means that the channels for mobility have multiplied and have become less clearly marked. After the primary school, the so-called *sekolah rakjat* (people's school), the channels for mobility lead in a number of directions. There are three types of academic high schools: SMA/A with a humanities bias, SMA/B for science, and SMA/C for economics and commercial subjects. There are in addition a host of vocational high schools from which it is possible to gain admission to a university. There is also an extraordinary proliferation of institutes, academies, and courses which stand between high school and university. Success in the high schools does not automatically confer high social status or satisfying economic rewards. Even the university degree has diminished in prestige, for it no longer guarantees the holder success in the occupational and social systems. The channels of political recruitment are muddled and the characters of potential elites are marked by differences rather than commonality. The great increase as well in schools and universities outside Java has begun to localize and regionalize what was a more unified national system of education. Mobility channels for non-Java students are local channels and entry into the highest levels of education means future entry into a local, not a national, political system. The lower status of non-Java schools draws those who are academically or financially unable to leave their home regions for more prestigious and better schooling. The use of schools as common instruments of social mobility now varies from island to island and from ethnic group to ethnic group, vastly complicating the political process.

III. Educational Organizations as Agencies of Socialization

The adaptiveness and advance of a society depends in part upon the existence of an effective communication network between individuals, groups, and institutions. The extent to which governments are in contact with descending levels of the social system and the extent to which there is a multiple flow and feed-back of information and response from individuals and organizations is one of the measures of the correspondence between social realities and the controlling political process. Communication is a product of socialization, that function by which the young are prepared for their roles as participants in the varied institutions of society. One of the possible uses of this function by a political elite is to transmit and preserve ideas, knowledge, and practices that influence and train youth for induction into the political sector of the national system. The impact of socialization upon youth can be both affective and instrumental. It is affective when its concern is to shape the feelings, attitudes, and values of youth towards, in this case, the political system in its homeland and other countries: for example, loyalty and feelings for particular levels of the political system (village, city, province, island, and national state); attachments to various political ideologies, principles, values, or symbols (democracy, colonialism, socialism, constitutions, etc.); and affinities for various organizations and personalities on the political scene. It is instrumental when it concerns the concrete aspects of politics: knowledge, facts, and practices concerning the workings of the government, the electoral process, political history, and foreign relations.

The connection between socialization and schools is of fairly recent origin, and in many of the newly independent countries the family has been and still is the most significant socializing agency. This is noticeably true in Indonesia, where the greatest part of the population resides in villages in rural areas. Within the context of the extended family the most fundamental objectives of the socialization process are being achieved. Nevertheless, today more and more of the basic elements of this process are in operation in the primary schools. It is generally believed that during the first four to six grades of schooling the most profound effects of socialization are to be seen. Most research tends to confirm that it is during the first school years that the young are in their most formative stage and are most easily impressed. Field work in Indonesia and other Southeast Asian countries tentatively indicates that as yet the greatest impact of the political socialization process is either in the family or in schools higher than the primary level. We will see that the political content is greater and the impact of the socialization process is more significant at high school and university levels. This effect is particularly noted in children reared and schooled in urban areas.

In transitional societies socialization appears to occur over a longer time span and thus its possible political influence through socialization is delayed until students reach school levels that are exposed to the political system. The lower one descends in the educational system in Indonesia, the further that system is from national political life. Primary schools are the least supervised of all educational organizations and in the rural regions they are the furthest removed from political influence. There are, of course, some exceptions to this. There is some evidence, for example, that the Partai Kommunist Indonesia is very interested in primary schools and that many primary school teachers have PKI affiliations or leanings. This is partly to be attributed to the widespread nature of PKI organizations and the lack of competition from other national parties in the rural areas. Observations and interviews at some thirty primary schools in supposed Communist strongholds in Central Java revealed that although some 30 per cent of the teachers were dissatisfied with Indonesian political leadership, schools had not yet been used as forums for their political feelings. Rather these teachers were apparently engaged in politicking among the non-school population. In Indonesia the majority of primary school teachers, particularly in small towns and village complexes, are the least qualified; many of them also hold additional jobs since school salaries at this level are very low. Political work is one of the only open channels for extra employment in the countryside and in many places in Central and East Java. This means involvement with the PKI.

The curriculum of the primary school in Indonesia has been traditionally dominated by the three "Rs" and the six-year primary school (*sekolah rakjat*) is common to all. In many areas, however, only four-year programs exist, due to limitations of finance and staff. The medium of instruction is optional, but in most cases the regional ethnic language is employed. Schools are required at the same time to provide instruction in the national language, *bahasa Indonesia*. In the largest cities *bahasa Indonesia* usually is the medium of instruction while the local language is offered as a subject for study. The existence and widespread use of a national *lingua franca* in Indonesia has had great political consequences. If the primary schools are not agencies of political socialization they are nonetheless propagators of a national tongue. In Indonesia this language has come to be regarded as synonymous with the very idea of an Indonesian state, and is symbolic of "unity in diversity." Practically all primary school children, from the tip of north Sumatra to the extremities of the Lesser Sundas some 2,000 miles eastward, speak *bahasa Indonesia*. One would think that in Central and East Java the Javanese, who represent 70 per cent of the total population, would have demanded more latitude in schools for their own highly developed language, but this they have never done. Even in Sumatra, where there was an anti-Djakarta insurrection in 1957, *bahasa Indonesia* is well entrenched in the primary schools—and it more than anything else signified to Bataks, Minangkabous, and Atjehnese the reality of a higher authority, the existence of an Indonesian state or nation of which, if by no other link, they were obviously a part.

Primary schools outside of Java have not yet been used for the purpose of creating anti-central government sentiment through local particularism. To be sure, there is a great deal of particularism in the schools, but it stems from quite natural factors rather than from external purpose. If the workings of primary schools in most areas of Indonesia (particularly Java and Sumatra) are any reflection, simultaneous loyalties to tribe, region, and state are being developed in a way which so far has diminished the cultural basis of political conflict in the nation. The most overriding factor has been a common language rather than the environment of socialization.

The students' entry into high schools begins a period of real exposure to political socialization. It is here that the content and environment become important. The curriculum reflects the efforts of the elites in power to construct a national ideology which is distinctive and which attempts to provide justification for a unified, central state. The five principles of *Pancha Sila* (one god, one state, religious tolerance, brotherhood, and peace) represent the first attempt to do just this—and in the sense that *Pancha Sila* is well known and constantly cited for a variety of public and private acts it is reasonably meaningful to both the semi-literate and the students. The name

Pancha Sila is distinctive and has long antecedents in Indonesian and imported Indian history. It is an ideology so general and so idealistic that it can be accepted by the majority and minorities alike. However, if the views of high school and university students are indicative, it is a kind of philosophy carried superficially "on the cuff" for the purposes of public discourse. Its very generality discourages individual commitment to any of its precepts. A good deal of Indonesian ideology is so amorphous and eclectic that it is difficult to transmit via teachers, schools, and texts. However, the major difficulty in the transmission of political beliefs and ideas in Indonesia is their great number and diversity. High school history and government courses are larded with a variety of conflicting ideologies emanating from Djakarta. Many are usually abbreviated for slogan purposes:

1. *Marhaenism*—Indonesian strength lies in the perseverance and morality of the common peasant and laborer.

2. *Manipol*—a return to the 1945 Constitution is necessary.

3. *Demokrasi Terpimpin*—a "guided" democracy is Indonesia's political salvation.

4. *USDEK*—socialism, democracy and economic development must be combined effectively.

5. *Gotong-rojong*—communal cooperation is the basis of political and economic advance.

6. Soekarno's *Konsepsi*—all major political forces and popular political parties must be reflected and represented in the central government (this applied particularly to the PKI, which received over 6,000,000 votes in the 1955 elections but had no representatives in the cabinet).

These slogans have been promulgated, modified, or withdrawn depending upon political circumstances, but most high school students refer to them in answering examination questions, in response to requests by foreigners for comments on Indonesia's strength and problems, and in private conversation among themselves. Their use of such terms reflects a kind of negativism towards politics which is especially characteristic of many young Javanese. Slogans for them become convenient substitutes for a personal involvement in politics which may endanger their position in any way. Such avoidance, and the concomitant withholding of personal views, is practically institutionalized and is considered a highly desirable virtue of the Javanese behavioral system. The widespread commitment to some form of socialism is quite apparent among the educated, but it has yet to be worked out either as a national ideology or a national plan.

The use of *bahasa Indonesia* in *all* high schools (public and private) has a politically socializing effect similar to that in the lower school levels, but here the basis of political socialization is deepened. The high school curriculum does not reflect much cultural bias or regional discrimination. The history courses are a case in point. Facts are stretched to give shape to the idea of the unity and inter-relatedness of the islands of the Indies. Much of the Indonesian claim to Irian Barat is based on the supposed affinity and historical connection of all the islands in the Dutch realm. Fortunately for the purposes of propaganda there is some truth in this, though certainly not in the case of Irian. The most dramatic aspects and the glories of Indonesian history have been inter-island; Sumatra, Java, and Bali all have figured prominently in the great Srivijaya, Şailendra, and Majapahit empires. National political policies have played up the historical unity of Indonesia while at the same time hoping to preserve the state from the disrupting effects of the cultural differences which in fact exist. High school students seem to emerge from this ideological training as loyal adherents to the Indonesian state while at the same time not losing their particular cultural identity. What seems to occur is a partial separation of cultural spheres from the political process. The political system as represented in the classroom appears to the young to be something new, modern, and Indonesian—something which is "natural," not at odds with individual desires, and which can be entered into without any substantial commitments or training. It must be noted also that the academic requirements of high school ordinarily take all the energies of students, leaving them little time for political interests or experiences. Entrance into the university brings them into a vastly different domain.

The urban locations of all major universities are important centers of national political life. Students entering the confines of university environments are surrounded by political realities which reflect the conditions of the prevailing political system into which they will later be drawn more directly. During the writer's residence in Indonesia (1956-1958, 1960) it was surprising, then, to find so little political activity on the campuses of the country. This has been explained previously as it relates to certainty of employment, and the traditional views of students towards Indonesian academic life. These things do not, however, account for the paucity of political party activities, the ineffectiveness of student movements, and student apathy to politics. Aside from traditional "avoidance" behavioral codes which are marked, much of this can be explained by the history of the nationalist movement which brought with it a young governing elite and a politics dominated by personalities rather than parties. The nationalist leaders were young, and it was they who had commandeered the revolution and the independent government that followed. University students considered that their interests were thus naturally being represented and that this youthful elite would reign for some time. Then, too, the power elite was small enough that many of its members were well known and in many cases had familial ties with students. In this case familiarity did not breed contempt, but rather heightened the predispositions of youth to harken to leaders rather than to their parties' ideas. In their turn, leaders did not concern themselves with students who were quiescent, politically unorganized, and whom many elite members knew personally. It was not considered necessary to politicize a passive and apparently already captured audience. The Partai Nationalis Indonesia which has dominated Indonesian politics since independence was until recently an agglomeration to which all and sundry could adhere and enter; propagandizing and recruiting activities on campuses were not necessary. The Masjumi and Nahdatul Ulama parties were considered conservative and represented by the banner of Islam, which had little appeal to most *prijaji*-class students. These parties did not regard university students as important elements to be politically won over and found in any case that the tenets of Islam did not provoke their support. The PKI based its programs on rural appeal and organization and apparently considered the children of educated civil servants as unlikely converts to a kind of agrarian Marxism. The only party that appeared interested in students and in their support was the Partai Socialis Indonesia. However, its organizational base was so narrow and its popular support so small that it could only woo students on an *ad hoc* basis, which proved largely ineffectual.[2]

It has been only within the last two years that university students have showed political initiative by becoming active in national youth parties. There is in evidence among the students at the three major universities, signs of a considerable anti-government feeling, but whether this dissatisfaction will be directed against the universities as

[2] The PSI was declared illegal and abolished in 1960.

in the case of India or against the government as in the case of Japan cannot as yet be determined. Nonetheless, the majority of university students are still apolitical and appear content to enter the *status quo* political system so long as there is rewarding employment available.[3]

The influence of the academic staff on the political views of students appears meagre. University teachers, professors, and deans are, first of all, only peripherally involved in politics themselves. There is a personal abstention from all formalized political activities, and at the same time a considerable involvement in national committees and quasi-political bodies. The national council established by President Soekarno to help guide the leaders of the Indonesian "guided democracy" includes many professors. Their role is nominally advisory, but in practice they do little else but attend meetings. During the past few years of political tension in Indonesia the premiums for silence have been all too obvious to academics. If students are to be influenced by a tradition which once cast the *guru* in an exemplary role, they are certainly not going to find any academic models for political behavior in Indonesian universities unless they are those for whom political abstinence is a cardinal principle.

The most obvious attempt to influence the political attitudes of university students may be seen in courses on *Pancha Sila* philosophy which are required of some 10,000 students at the major universities. The lectures are a hodge-podge of Koranic dictums, extracts from Marx and Dewey, the speeches of President Soekarno, all the various current ideological slogans, and a host of speculations which the majority of students find dull or irritating. The amorphousness of the political ideology of the Indonesian state makes it virtually useless for purposes of indoctrination, but so far few people seem to care about the efficacy of the attempt.

The social science and law curricula reflect many of the dilemmas and paradoxes of Indonesian political development. Let us take, for example, the content of economic courses at the largest Indonesian university. Most of the tests and lectures dwell almost entirely upon free enterprise and industry and devote little time to a discussion of state-controlled systems and the agricultural sector. Similarly, in other social sciences authoritarian systems of government receive scant mention, and in general much more time is spent upon European and American rather than local or relevant Asian experiences.

[3] The year 1964 has seen much more intense and widespread political dissent and indiscipline among Indonesian university students.

Success in the Faculty of Law is still predicated upon a knowledge of Dutch sources and of a colonial legal system rather than present realities and needs. University graduates are armed with knowledge, ideas, and techniques which do not correspond to the realities of the political system which most of them enter. Interviews of alumni from two universities who were employed during 1961 in the Departments of Home Affairs, Foreign Affairs, Economic Affairs and Justice indicate that most of them are faced with operational dilemmas and handicaps because of the discrepancies between their past university curricular experiences and the requirements of their jobs. The traditional Javanese behavioral system manages to contain much of the resulting frustration. Nevertheless, a great deal of inefficiency and apathy in the political system is the result of this gulf between educational training and current demands.

To summarize this section, the following should be noted:

1. At primary school levels the most significant element in socialization is the language of instruction.

2. The curriculum of schools does not have any manifest political content and does not appear to significantly affect students until secondary and university levels have been reached.

3. The most formal aspects of political socialization (curriculum, etc.) appear to have most significance at middle and high school levels.

4. The university environment (particularly student inter-personal relationships and associations) appears to have a greater impact upon the political socialization of students than many of the more formalized aspects of the instructional program.

5. Except for the existence of a national *lingua franca* and the widespread association of the name "Indonesia" with modernity, the instrumental role of the educational system in fostering loyalties to the Indonesian state has largely grown out of circumstantial factors rather than purposeful planning.

6. Non-school organizations (particularly the family) and locally based socializing systems appear most decisive in governing the political socialization of youths in schools.

7. The political system in Indonesia is so widespread, inclusive, and amorphous that it is difficult or perhaps incorrect to speak of *political* socialization as if the process were compartmentalized. Rather, socialization has its political content or its political referrents.

8. The role of the teacher in socialization appears to diminish as

one ascends the levels of schooling, while the importance of the school for the process appears to increase.

IV. Educational Organizations as Agencies of Acculturation

The term acculturation as employed here includes those changes produced in a culture by the influence of other cultures which result in an increased similarity or in an increased dissimilarity among any of them. It can be equated with cultural exchange and refers to a description of what is actually exchanged, the conditions under which the process unfolds and the net result among the exchangees. In the context of the Indonesian scene acculturation describes the cultural exchange and contact that takes place among diverse ethnic, religious and social groups within the educational system and how this relates to the nationalization or "homogenization" of youth in a country where political power is fragmented and political allegiances are divided.

At first view it would seem that Indonesia has never had the basic elements for a viable state. It is geographically fragmented—3,000 or more islands spread across an arc of 3,000 miles. It is ethnically diverse—30 major language groups and 300 local dialects. Its great resources and huge population are unevenly distributed—75 per cent of its people reside in Java and 75 per cent of its economic wealth lies outside Java in other islands. It abounds in religions and sects—varieties of Islam, Hinduism, Catholicism, Protestantism, and that catch-all of indigenous beliefs, animism. It has been dominated by Indian princes, Portuguese sea captains, an English lord, Dutch mercantilists, and Japanese militarists. With this background Indonesia has nevertheless managed to persist as a state since her independence despite two additional European military occupations and major insurrections in Sumatra and the Celebes. Certainly most of these historical facts have contributed to disunity, but there are harmonious elements as well.

The centers of "Indonesian" civilization have always been located in either Java and Sumatra, giving its history more continuity than would appear at first glance. These two islands contain 95 per cent of the total population and their lands harbor 85 per cent of the country's economic wealth; thus the problem of political viability is in many respects dependent on only two or possibly three rather than 3,000 islands. Religions are so many veneers on Indonesian civilization, and its constant eclectic borrowings has made religious toleration a feature of its life-style. All Indonesians shared to some extent foreign incursions, the long Dutch colonial rule, the Japanese oppression, and its revolutionary aftermath. Such experiences were shared by the small ethnically diverse elite that has held power since independence. Similar school experiences, kindred frustrations and successes had formed the basis of an elite camaraderie that transcended individual differences. In general, the forces of division have been contained, somewhat shakily it is true, but the state has not disintegrated and the educational system has so far played a functional role in this regard.

The basic political consideration related to schools and cultures within one country is the national language and the medium of instruction. The adoption of *bahasa Indonesia* as the first language of the new state met no resistance, largely because the language so established was not the language of the majority ethnic group—the Javanese. The imposition of an Indonesian language was not symbolic of the imposition of a majority—and this largely removed the whole question from the realm of politics. So long as provisions were made in schools for local languages, Indonesian could be accepted without concern. It is remarkable how quickly Indonesian has established itself as an effective *lingua franca* in many areas in which it was not used before 1945. To be sure, Indonesian was in use in commerce and in metropolitan government centers before independence, but its status was low and its literature practically nonexistent. Today the Indonesian language is the bridge of acculturation among diverse groups, thus diminishing cultural conflict and the problems of political communication. The educational system which uses Indonesian as the primary language of instruction for all first grades through all universities has been the most responsible agency in this process.

Indonesia may be divided for the purposes of this political analysis into three "culture" areas. The largest of these is the majority culture, and it includes the two major ethnic groups of Java—the Javanese and Sundanese. A second consists of the numerous minority cultures, those located outside of Java in what are often called the Outer Islands. A third area might be termed the "official" culture, that is, the amalgam of the majority and the minority cultures with the governmental structure and its politically "modern" ways. The "official" culture is half-formed, transitional, fragmented, and torn by conflict. It is nonetheless distinctive as its main task is to incorporate the local and traditional majority and minority cultures into an Indonesian culture which in turn represents the unity of an Indonesian state. The instrumental part played by schools in the process of acculturation is of vital importance here.

The higher the level of schooling in Indonesia, the more diverse is the school population, and the largest units at each level have the most diversity. This is largely a reflection of the scarcity of high schools and universities relative to demand and of the unequal distribution of educational units. It follows then that in each island the most diverse high school populations will be found in the largest cities and particularly in cities located near the confluence of various ethnic, religious, or social groups. Those schools which have the highest social and academic prestige will often draw students from most of the ethnic and religious groups, though not in proportion to the total size of each group in the country. Some groups have traditionally taken greater advantage of education in Indonesia than others (e.g., the Chinese, Catholics, and South Sumatrans) while others have been largely isolated from the educational system (e.g., Dayako, Buginese, and Lesser Sundra groups). The higher the level of schooling, the larger the size of higher schools, the greater their scarcity and the greater their prestige, the more likely one will find cross-sections within one group and representatives from a variety of groups. In Indonesia this progression leads directly to three universities (Airlangga, Gadjah Mada, and the University of Indonesia, with the latter two highest ranked). These universities are the only organizations in Indonesia where diverse, select youth live and study together for a period of five to seven years before they enter into the larger society. The fact that they are located in Java provides the logistic basis for the interaction of the three "cultures" previously described. Gadjah Mada University is particularly illustrative of this "cultural" setting.

At this university the conditions for acculturation have been ideal. Twenty per cent of its students have come from outside Java, with thirteen per cent of this total from Sumatra. Muslims represent 75 per cent and Christians 15 per cent. By occupation, students whose fathers are farmers count for 17 per cent, lower government officials for 23 per cent, teachers for 16 per cent, and private business and employ for 23 per cent. Cities of course send the most students (54 per cent), but villages and small towns still contribute a sizeable proportion of students (29 per cent). These figures represent almost a microcosm of the Indonesian population and a most representative sample of the children of elites. Data gathered from question-naires and interviews with alumni indicate great varieties of inter-ethnic association and suggest that the process of cultural exchange within the university environment tends to break down or at least modify cultural differences. Many graduates are therefore much more amenable to the impositions of the state and to the political realities which they face in such cities as Djakarta, Bandung, and Surabaya. The whole academic and social climate of Gadjah Mada has tended to promote conformity and a kind of homogeneity in the development of national loyalties. This process however operates quite incidentally, and the government has not as yet seen the possi-bility for effectively intruding its "official" culture into the university. Many of the alumni are thus disposed to work with all types of individuals, and they come with a much more "national" outlook, but they do not exhibit any real commitments, ideological or otherwise, to the central government and its programs. Politically speaking, they have been only partially acculturated.

The expansion of the university system will make the type of accul-turation that has been described much more difficult to achieve. Fur-thermore, the rapid expansion of secondary education in the Outer Islands will make it unnecessary for their youth to matriculate in Java, thereby decreasing early inter-cultural school contacts. Unless the central government can control the educational system more effectively and provide the conditions for a politically functional ac-culturation process, particularistic schools can increase cultural isola-tion and weaken the national political system.

V. Schools as Recruitment Centers for a Political Elite

High school leavers very rarely find their way into elite positions in the political process. If a student has managed to get through an academic high school, he ordinarily seeks education at higher levels. There have been no studies of secondary school leavers in Indonesia. However, from very limited data it can be suggested that about 20 per cent of high school leavers find employment in one or more of the political parties. The PKI, in particular, appears to be a haven for those leavers who either were unsuccessful in gaining admittance to a university or who dropped out before two years. No more than 10 per cent of the academic high school leavers attend a university, but this percentage is increasing rapidly as the opportunities at the top expand. Interviews with several PNI, PKI, and Nahdatul Ulama leaders indicated that they regard high school leavers as far better recruits for their parties than university graduates or university dropouts. In the main, it would appear that the aspirations of high school students more nearly coincide with party realities and party methods. However, a considerable number of various party officials have stated that they have great difficulties in recruiting workers for responsible positions. Politics is generally considered to be a part-time activity, not a vocation, and very few Indonesians are willing to commit themselves fully to it. The recruitment system under such circumstances is poorly organized and such system as exists is largely run by nepotism. Recruits are drawn into the political system through the attraction of personalities rather than parties or ideologies.

Universities hold a monopoly on the supply of potential elites in Indonesia. Two universities (Gadjah Mada University and the University of Indonesia) account for about 90 per cent of the graduates in government employ. Some 40 per cent of this number represent graduates who have been recruited into executive or administrative positions in the political system, which means into the Departments of Home Affairs, Defense, Justice, Foreign Affairs, or into the local levels of government. The largest number of recruits are employed in Djakarta with Bandung, Semarang, and Surabaja following. Graduates have invariably turned to these large urban centers, thereby increasing the already great urbanization of politics. These graduates rarely concern themselves with rural affairs and they usually support political parties like the PNI and the Nahdatul Ulama which do not adequately reflect rural interests. Once rural pressures begin to mount, the two major non-Communist parties will find themselves with an elite leadership so highly urbanized that it cannot effectively elicit rural support. In Indonesia, where "rural" population densities range from 400 to 700 per square mile, rural neglect may be politically disastrous.

During the period 1952 through 1960 more than half of non-Java university graduates did not return to their home islands, finding employment with the central government, primarily in Djakarta. Two-thirds of these non-Java graduates had completed legal studies; they generally obtained administrative positions in the government departments most concerned with the political process. The large number of minority persons in central government employ in many ways greatly facilitates the growth of nationhood since the national government is thus composed of a cross-section of various ethnic groups.

However, while having advantages for the nation, this loss of talent by the Outer Islands and by non-urban Java tends to have disadvantages for agricultural regions and ethnic minorities. Their most able potential elites are siphoned off by the central government, thus weakening their own position vis-à-vis the political center. Djakarta has furthermore established a rule-of-thumb policy that an elite minority person should not be sent to work with his own ethnic group or into his home region. Political talent has been scarce outside of Java. The present enormous expansion of government in the Outer Islands will, however, have the effect of reversing or weakening this placement policy.

Since two universities are the major centers for recruiting elites, and since to date practically all graduates have joined the government service, the composition of the past and present student population is indicative of who has been and who can be recruited into the political system. Tables 1-5 are based on samples of students from Gadjah Mada University.

TABLE 1: GEOGRAPHIC ORIGIN

	All Graduates 1952-1960	% of Total	New Students 1959-1960	% of Total	All Students 1962	% of Total
Java	711	82.86	1,969	80.69	12,640	79.63
Sumatra	108	12.58	333	13.64	2,329	14.69
Kalimantan	7	0.81	36	1.47	205	1.21
Bali	8	0.93	30	1.22	248	1.56
Celebes	17	1.98	39	1.59	200	1.20
Other eastern islands	7	0.81	33	1.35	251	1.58
Total	858	99.97	2,440	99.96	15,873	99.87

TABLE 2: RELIGIOUS BACKGROUND

	All Graduates 1952-1960	% of Total	New Students 1959/60	% of Total
Islam	673	78.43	1,844	75.57
Islam Java and Statistik[a]	10	1.17	6	0.24
Protestant	42	4.89	134	5.49
Catholic	42	4.89	244	10.00
Bali Hindu	8	0.93	30	1.22
Buddhist & Confucianist	3	0.34	14	0.57
No religion	5	0.58	3	0.12
No answer	75	8.74	165	6.76
Total	858	99.97	2,440	99.97

[a] Islam Statistik is a formal designation used by certain Indonesians to indicate that they are merely nominal followers of Islam.

TABLE 3: URBAN-RURAL ORIGINS

	All Graduates 1952-1960	% of Total	New Students 1959/60	% of Total
Metropolitan centers[a]	326	37.99	916	37.54
Large cities	227	26.45	433	17.74
Middle-sized cities	145	16.89	366	15.00
Small towns	123	14.33	429	17.58
Villages	37	4.31	296	12.13
Total	858	99.97	2,440	99.99

[a] Metropolitan centers include cities of 100,000 or more: large cities, 50,000 to 100,000; middle-sized cities, 5,000 to 50,000; small towns, 1,000 to 5,000; and villages, below 1,000.

TABLE 4: PARENTAL OCCUPATION

	Number of Fathers of All Graduates 1952/60	% of Total	Number of Fathers of New Students 1959/60	% of Total
Pension & lower government	280	32.63	567	23.23
Higher government	95	11.07	152	6.22
Village officials	35	4.07	112	4.59
Teachers	155	18.06	410	16.80
Police & military	20	2.33	69	2.82
Professional	35	4.07	61	2.50
Farmers	92	10.72	423	17.33
Self and privately employed	135	15.73	566	23.19
Artisans & unskilled labor	11	1.28	80	3.27
Total	858	99.96	2,440	99.95

TABLE 5: FACULTY ENROLLMENTS

	All Graduates 1952/60	% of Total	New Students 1959/60	% of Total	All Students 1960	% of Total	All Students 1962	% of Total
Law	132	15.38	474	19.42	2,179	19.38	2,472	15.70
Economics	18	2.09	199	8.15	1,509	13.42	2,472	15.70
Social & pol. sci.	267	31.11	523	21.43	2,021	17.98	2,421	15.38
Medicine & dentistry	65	7.57	258	10.57	1,380	12.27	1,497	9.57
Pharmacy	39	4.54	40	1.64	378	3.36	534	3.39
Biology	1	—	8	0.32	92	0.81	116	0.74
Engineering	220	25.64	302	12.37	678	6.03	1,409	8.22
Physics & mathematics	11	1.28	46	1.88	198	1.76	340	2.16
Education	18	2.09	347	14.22	1,330	11.83	2,528	16.05
Humanities	19	2.21	150	6.14	625	5.56	902	5.73
Veterinary	6	0.69	10	0.41	231	2.05	286	1.81
Agriculture	63	7.34	83	3.40	618	5.49	770	4.89
Total	858	99.94	2,440	99.95	11,239	99.94	15,747	99.34

These tables suggest some of the characteristics of those available for recruitment into the political system. Incomplete data, covering only the 858 graduates (those with terminal degrees) of Gadjah Mada University from 1952 through 1960, can be broken down in terms of present occupation as follows: 417 or 40 per cent are employed by the central government in the Departments of Defense, Justice, Home Affairs, Economic Affairs, and Foreign Affairs; 8 per cent are teachers; about 2 per cent are actively engaged in politics; 3 per cent are in private business; about 40 per cent are holding what might be termed elite positions, but most of these are administrative rather than policy making. From recent estimates during the last two years it appears that about 75 per cent of the graduates obtain government employ, but almost 30 per cent of this group become teachers. It must be remembered that the average time required to earn a degree with employment value is five years. Some attempts are being made to make the three-year baccalaureate degree terminal, but as yet such a degree would have very little prestige.

VI. Conclusions

In summary, some of the more significant aspects of the relationships of education and the political process can be stated as follows:

1. Schools are not inherently agents of political socialization and when instrumental they are not necessarily functional.

2. Functional acculturation and socialization can occur through circumstantial factors, but dysfunctionality is more likely in such situations, particularly if the educational system is loosely controlled.

3. Of all units in the organized sectors of national life schools are perhaps the most difficult to use and control for political purposes.

4. The rapid expansion and fragmentation of an educational system is likely to be at odds with many of the policies and requirements for developing and maintaining a viable unitary political system.

5. The educational environment and the mediums of political socialization and acculturation are perhaps more significant than the actual formal content of the process.

CHAPTER 4

NIGERIA

To ATTEMPT to analyze the different ways in which educational systems affect political systems amounts to treating educational systems as independent variables and political systems as dependent variables. Presumably this assumption comes from a political theory in which educational systems are regarded as major instruments of political socialization. Whatever may be the validity of such an assumption in theory, the facts of social life blunt it. In the case of Nigeria, for example, the political system, or more accurately, political change has affected the educational system as much if not more than the educational system has affected it over the same periods of time. Besides, other factors apart from education and political systems were at work at the same time. In such a situation it is not easy to disentangle what affects what.

Secondly, although there is a sense in which education during the colonial period in Nigeria is different from education since independence, it does not follow that the line of demarcation in temporal terms can be drawn at October 1, 1960, when Nigeria gained her independence. It makes better sense to draw the line at 1952, when the Regional Governments which came into existence set about modifying the character and tempo of educational change. Even this is open to some qualification. The earliest attempt to alter the structure of colonial education in Nigeria was inaugurated by the Ten Year Development Plan of 1946.

The third comment relates to the function of political socialization itself, which according to Almond means "that all political systems tend to perpetuate their cultures and structures through time."[1] Sutton has distinguished three tasks of socialization, namely, "(1) the definition of memberships and affiliations; (2) the inculcation of ideas, symbols, and disciplines that are part of the general culture and transcend particular relationships or affiliations, and (3) a differential instruction in the accomplishments and expectations that go

---

[1] Gabriel A. Almond and James S. Coleman, eds., *The Politics of the Developing Areas*, Princeton, Princeton University Press, 1960, p. 27.

with different statuses in the society."[2] By defining socialization and its tasks as they have done, Almond and Sutton appear to have defined by implication the tasks of the educational system as well. The legitimacy of this procedure is not in question. What has to be noted is that their educational system would be overly society-centered and underplay the responsibility of education for the individual, qua individual. By finding a rightful place for the individual, either conforming or deviant, in their behavioristic approach, we are likely to get a fuller picture which conceives of education as more than an instrument for producing "national" types; it will also make us mindful of the fact that the heart of all social change is the perpetual tension between society and some of its members who want themselves and the society to which they belong to be other than they are. The relevance of this to educational and political change in Nigeria during the colonial period will become clearer in the course of this chapter.

Almond has defined the political system as "that system of interactions to be found in all independent societies which performs the functions of integration and adaptation (both internally and vis-à-vis other societies) by means of the employment, or threat of employment, of more or less legitimate physical compulsion." The system includes not only parliaments, executives, bureaucracies, parties, and interest groups but also kinship lineage status and caste groups, and phenomena such as riots and demonstrations. We need a comparable operational definition of the educational system. In order to arrive at one, we must first ask ourselves what the hall-mark of educational activity is.

"Why does pedagogical activity exist at all? Why is it an occupation and a preoccupation of man?" asks Ortega y Gasset. "Man is occupied and preoccupied with education for a reason which is simple, bold, and devoid of glamour: in order to live with assurance and freedom and efficiency, it is necessary to know an enormous number of things, and the child or youth has an extremely limited capacity to learn. That is the reason."[3] Taking the cue from Ortega, we shall use the educational system to include all those individuals and agencies who contribute to this process of knowing: formal schools, schools run by government departments and commercial firms, apprenticeship systems and the activities of trade unions, political parties, the press

[2] See p. 51 above.
[3] José Ortega y Gasset, *Mission of the University*, Princeton, Princeton University Press, 1944.

and other mass media (as far as possible), professional organizations, as well as penal institutions. We shall also include the educational impact of non-indigenous groups resident in Nigeria. Just as the quantifiers of the income of nations allow for income from assets abroad in the value of the national product, we take account of Nigerians studying in educational institutions abroad.

If it is correct that the Ten Year Development Plan of 1946 was the first major effort to transform colonial education in Nigeria, the Second World War was the great divide. Before then government expenditure on education ranged from 1 per cent to 4.3 per cent of the budget; after it the figure went up to 10 per cent and above. There is a special reason for treating the Second World War as the watershed. It was in 1943 that the British Government sent out its Commission on Higher Education in West Africa. From the Commission's report[4] and other sources, it is possible to give a picture of colonial education in Nigeria as it was at the time of their visit. The features of the system which stand out are summarized in the following paragraphs.

The broad lines of educational policy were laid down in London and were contained in the various reports of the Colonial Office Advisory Committee on Education in the Colonies, especially its 1925 "Memorandum on Education Policy in British Tropical Africa" and another paper on "The Education of African Communities" issued in 1935. The broad principles which should form the basis of sound educational policy as set out in the 1925 Memorandum were as follows:

1. Governments should control educational policy, but they should cooperate with other educational agencies. Each territory should have an advisory board on which all educational interests should be represented.

2. Education should be adapted to the mentality, aptitudes, occupations, and traditions of the various peoples, conserving all sound and healthy elements in the fabric of their social life; adapting where necessary to changed circumstances and progressive ideas as an agent of natural growth and evolution.

3. Religious and character training is of the greatest importance.

4. The educational service must be made attractive to the best men from Britain.

---

[4] *Report of the Commission on Higher Education in West Africa, May 5, 1945,* Cmd. 6655, London, H.M.S.O., 1945.

5. Grants should be given to aid involuntary schools which satisfy the requirements.

6. African languages, as well as English, should be used in education.

7. African teaching staff must be adequate in numbers, in qualifications, and in character and should include women. The training of teachers is essential.

8. The system of specially trained visiting teachers is commended as a means of improving village schools.

9. A thorough system of inspection and supervision of schools is essential.

10. Technical training is best given in a system of apprenticeship in government workshops. "Instruction in village crafts must be clearly differentiated from the training of the skilled mechanic."

11. Vocational other than industrial training should be carried out through a system of learners in government departments.

12. The education of women is vitally important. There must be trained women teachers; education must be provided for adult women as well as girls.

13. A complete educational system should include primary (including infant) education, secondary education of different types, technical and vocational schools and institutes, some of which may hereafter reach "university rank" for such subjects as teacher education, medicine, agriculture, and adult education.

In Nigeria itself educational policy and execution was in the hands of the Director of Education and his predominantly British staff. There was an Advisory Board of Education on which the British Government in Nigeria, the voluntary agencies (both foreign missionary and indigenous), local authorities, and the Nigeria Union of Teachers were represented.

Apart from a few secondary schools and some primary schools in Northern Nigeria, the government left the running of schools to private initiative which it controlled through a system of grants-in-aid and inspection. Most of the assisted schools (i.e., schools which qualified for grants-in-aid) were run by the Missions. Non-assisted schools were by far the most important in terms of enrollment. According to the Elliot Commission, of the 276,000 pupils who were in infant and primary schools in Nigeria in 1942, 7,000 were in government schools, 8,000 in native authority schools, 82,000 in assisted schools, and 179,000 in non-assisted schools.

From the foregoing it emerges that the Nigerian contribution was considerable. What passed as mission schools were in fact mission schools in the sense that those responsible for organizing them belonged to Christian missions. The funds for running them (apart from grants-in-aid) came from the Nigerian members of the churches. When we add the secular schools run by Nigerians, the Nigerian contribution was truly substantial. Most of the secondary schools which the Commission found in Southern Nigeria were in fact community schools. Nigerian effort was also evident in the field of higher education. The Government of Nigeria awarded its first overseas scholarship for a degree course in 1937. By 1943 the number had managed to reach 11. For generations in Southern Nigeria, some families had sent sons and daughters for higher education abroad and just about the time of Commission visit the Ibibio State Union and Ibo tribal unions were sending young men abroad. Of the 178 Nigerian students in universities in the United Kingdom and Eire, only 40 were government scholars.

What did the Nigerian educational structure look like? The majority of schools were primary schools (including infant classes). There were a handful of secondary schools, all of the grammar school type. The only post-secondary institution which gave sub-professional training to future assistant medical officers, assistant forestry officers, assistant engineers, assistant surveyors, assistant veterinary officers, and secondary school teachers was the Yaba Higher College. The only technical and vocational training available was confined to government departments such as the Marine, the Public Works, and the Railway. The bulk of Nigerian boys got their training as carpenters, masons, bricklayers, goldsmiths, barbers, shoemakers, and so on from Nigerian master craftsmen under an indigenous apprenticeship system. Quite a few Nigerians also learned shoe-making and other trades in His Majesty's prisons!

What about the coverage of the Nigerian educational system in the early forties? According to the Elliot Commission, 17.7 per cent of school-age children attended school in Southern Nigeria and 1.7 per cent in Northern Nigeria. There were 34 secondary schools (30 for boys and 4 for girls) with an enrollment of 8,110. Of the 30 boys' secondary schools, only 1 was situated in Northern Nigeria. The above figures underline another feature of the Nigerian educational system, namely, its uneven development especially as between north and south. The poor quality of teachers was another. About 80 per cent of the teachers were without any training. Only ⅛ of secondary school teachers had university degrees. The ratio of girls to boys in the schools was 1 to 5.

In September 1960, a month before Nigeria attained independence, another historic report on Nigerian education was published. Entitled "Investment in Education"[5] it was the work of an international commission and was financed by the Carnegie Corporation. Although its specific term of reference was to report on post-school certificate and higher education in Nigeria, the commission brought the whole educational system within its purview. The report provides interesting parallels and contrasts with the situation that obtained in the early forties.

In less than a decade, the number of children in primary schools had risen from 970,806 to 2,840,000 in 1958. Universal primary education obtained in the south. There was also greater variety of educational provision. At the secondary level, there were technical institutes and modern secondary schools. Trade centers catered to the training of artisans and tradesmen. University College, Ibadan, with facilities for training graduates in arts, science, agriculture, medicine, and education, had been in existence ten years. Its extension activities covered the whole country. On the technological side, the Nigerian College of Arts, Science, and Technology ran professional courses for accountants, secretaries, engineers, and pharmacists.

Education was getting a bigger share of government expenditures. In the south close to 50 per cent of the budget was going into education. The education of girls as well as education in the north had both made impressive strides. There was improved science in many secondary schools. Sixth form work (two years advanced work after the secondary school course leading to the university) had become an important feature of the better secondary schools. Many more obtained the General Certificate of Examination at the advanced level or the Higher School Certificate (both qualifying tests at the end of the sixth form) by private study. Local and community effort, particularly in the field of secondary education in the south (virtually every town or district produced the required minimum deposit for one), had become almost an embarrassment to government; the problem was how to prevent secondary schools, which had little chance of securing qualified staffs, from being started.

[5] Nigeria, Commission on Post-School Certificate and Higher Education, *Investment in Education*, Lagos, Federal Ministry of Education, 1960.

The educational situation in 1958 nevertheless had a lot in common with the early forties. The shortage of qualified teachers was still a problem. Only 20 per cent of secondary school teachers and 17 per cent of the staff of teacher training colleges were university graduates. Almost three-quarters of primary school teachers were uncertificated or probationers. The teaching profession was still losing many of its valued members to other more attractive vocations.

The contrast between education in the south and in the north remained as glaring as ever. Only 9 per cent of the northern children were in primary schools as compared to well over 90 per cent in the south. Out of the 2 million children of secondary school age in the north, about 4,000 were enrolled in secondary schools. Students of northern origin at University College, Ibadan, numbered 57 out of a student body of a little over 1,000.

The Role of Education in Socialization

This was the Nigerian educational system on the eve of independence.

In his well-known book, *The Making of Citizens,* published in 1931, Charles E. Merriam attempted to draw together the threads of eight case studies of civic education which had been made of selected countries: France, Germany, Switzerland, the United States, Russia, Italy, Austria-Hungary, and Great Britain. He found eight mechanisms or techniques of civic education, namely, the schools, governmental services and officials, political parties, special patriotic organizations, political symbolism, language and literature, the press and other mass media, and love of locality. "In all the systems appraised in this study," he concluded, "the school emerges as the heart of the civic education of the political community. . . . In all cases the school system is the basic factor in the development of civic interest and loyalty, and the chief instrument for that purpose." The school was not utilized to the same extent everywhere. In five of the eight states studied—France, Germany, Switzerland, the United States, and Russia—Merriam found that the educational system occupied an important place of civic training and had been consciously employed for that purpose. In Italy, Austria-Hungary, and England, the school was used for less direct civic purposes.

Because Nigeria was until 1960 a British colony, special attention focuses on the English techniques of civic training. Merriam tells us that, like other systems, the English schools utilize history for the development of interest in national fortunes and national personalities, with inevitable emphasis on English traits and individuals. Although there was little direct teaching of governments in it, the English educational system was one of the most important of all factors in the growth of civic interest and allegiance. "This result is accomplished through the use of the schools as instruments for the development of self-government, through the utilization of certain schools and universities as training schools for governmental service, and by the use of the schools as agencies for the teaching of social distinctions and values. England has traditionally been governed by a type of English 'gentleman.' What constitutes his characteristics, and how they may be interpreted from time to time, is early taught in schools. The rules and the personnel for interpretation are both found there and the cult is fixed there. . . . What a gentleman should do or should not do was not set down, but was indirectly absorbed."[6]

To what extent was the educational system in Nigeria an instrument of socialization during the colonial period? We deal first with "political socialization into the general political culture of all those formally exposed to education." The most striking fact is that British put the foremost emphasis on character training. It was precisely because the Christian missions gave religious and moral training that the colonial government relied on them as the chief agencies for providing schools in Nigeria. Christianity was felt to be something good for the "natives."

Of formal civic training, apart from some instruction on "How Nigeria Is Governed," there was very little at the primary and secondary level. Greater reliance was placed on institutional devices, athletics, and other part-time activities. Every class in the primary school had its monitor and every teacher training college and every secondary school had its prefects. By giving monitors and prefects varying degrees of responsibility in the class or school, a crude attempt was made to inculcate the virtues of self-government. Some schools even had their fag systems, thereby moving closer to the tradition of the English public schools. No primary school was complete without its school uniform, not just caps and badges, but shorts and shirts, jumpers or girls' frocks made of the same material and cut in the same style. To complete the symbols of school solidarity, there was invariably a school band with possibly a flag.

[6] Charles E. Merriam, *The Making of Citizens*, Chicago, University of Chicago Press, 1931, pp. 96-97.

An important institution through which character training was fostered was the Boy Scout movement. The movement originated in England and has been described by Merriam as "a character-building organization," emphasizing cleanliness, truthfulness, readiness to help others, and hardiness. Another way in which character training was promoted was through games and athletics, especially in secondary schools and teacher training colleges. Through the schools what Nigerians call football and British soccer has virtually become the favorite sport in the country. Inter-school championship matches are a standing practice. The biggest event on Empire Day (May 24th) used to be an athletic competition. Two of the most popular athletic competitions were the Grier and Hussey Shield competitions named after two former British Directors of Education.

Although Nigeria had nothing to compare with the famous William Ponty school at Dakar which drew its students from all over what was formerly French West Africa, there were a few schools which drew their pupils and students from all over the country. Of these probably the most important were King's College for boys in Lagos, Queen's College for girls in Lagos, St. Andrew's College, Ojo, the oldest teacher training institution in the country, Hope Waddell Training Institution in Calabar, and the Higher College, Yaba. Through such schools and a few others many young boys and girls from different ethnic groups had an opportunity of living and mixing with one another. Many mission schools served a similar purpose, but there was one factor which worked in the other direction. The Christian missions were broken up into different sects, which to some extent made for mutual exclusiveness among their proselytes.

Since Nigeria was a British colony, it hardly was to be expected that the local British government would deliberately foster Nigerian solidarity or consciousness. In the early days, only English history was taught; later it was British Empire history. When the Nigerian child learned what passed for Nigerian history, it was an account of how British conquered Nigeria and governed her. He was told of no Nigerian heroes or national personalities. The many holidays were of two kinds: they were either official British holidays like Empire Day, the Queen's birthday and bank holidays, or Christian holidays. In spite of the official policy that African languages should be used for educational purposes, there was a penalty for speaking in one's mother tongue in some schools.

There was no teaching of Nigerian or African history in the real sense of the word until the early fifties when courses in the subject were introduced at University College, Ibadan, largely due to the initiative of Dr. K. O. Dike. The African history option quickly became one of of the most popular in the college. Through the work of Dr. Dike's former students who have gone out to teach in the schools, through the Nigerian Historical Society and its journal, interest in Nigerian history is growing apace among a wider public.

Before the Faculty of Economics and Social Studies came into existence at University College, Ibadan, about five years ago, the only course in politics was given in the history department. However, since the inception of the college in 1948, an increasing number of adults outside the walls of the college have been able to take advantage of the courses in government, economics, and other subjects offered by the Department of Extra-Mural Studies. The Elliot Commission strongly recommended the establishment of the department as a means of providing a link between the college in Ibadan and the Nigerian community at large. At a time when self-government was being envisaged, it was hoped that through the activities of the department many Nigerian adults who for some reason or other could not enter the university might be enabled to gain access to the facilities of the college. In this way it was hoped to build a body of well-informed citizens capable of exercising good judgment on public affairs. The second activity envisaged for the department were refresher courses for teachers, civil servants, and other responsible and key adults in the community.

The Extra-Mural Department has had a very good response throughout the country. In 1959-1960 with a full-time teaching staff of 10 situated at strategic centers in the country and about 80 part-time tutors it ran well over 170 evening classes attended by over 3,500 regular students. Its residential courses for teachers, agricultural extension officers, trade unionists, civil servants, and legislators drew almost another 500. The department played an important role in the years before independence. It ran development and comparative courses on selected problems of local government for local council members and chairmen. It pioneered special diploma courses at the college for the secretaries and treasurers who staffed the local councils in Southern Nigeria when they were modernized in the early fifties. Since its inception if has been largely responsible for promoting trade union education in the country. In cooperation with outside bodies it has run international seminars in and outside Nigeria on such topics as representative government in the new states, the press and progress in West Africa, and agricultural extension in Tropical Africa. For ten years it has taught courses in African literature, music, and art. It has successfully used the radio for the serious discussion of public affairs along the lines of the Canadian farm forum. Apart from the intellectual stimulus which it provided, the Extra-Mural Department of University College, Ibadan, furnished a neutral platform on which controversial issues of the day could be discussed as calmly and objectively as possible.

After the Second World War, the British government in Nigeria made an effort to push mass education and community development as a means of enabling the Nigerian adult to gain a better understanding of the modern world and to make a direct contribution to the uplift of the community. The mass education programs consisted mainly of literacy campaigns, and this may largely account for their limited appeal. Where they were combined with health, agricultural, and other programs they have fared better. Another problem was how to prevent the new literates from lapsing back into illiteracy. It was for this reason among others that the Gaskiya Corporation in Zaria was expanded to provide assimilable material for newly literate adults in the various languages of Northern Nigeria. For a long time, the *Gaskiya Ta fi Kwabo*, a Hausa newspaper run by the corporation, was the only outlet for the expression of opinion in print in that part of the country.

Community development in Nigeria is of course much older than the term. Most Nigerian schools, many a road and maternity center, and other public improvements are the result of one form of community development or another. The renewed interest by the British administration in the concept after the Second World War arose from the activities of a district officer whose work with the people of Udi attracted a good deal of publicity through the film "Daybreak in Udi." Community development became quite a vogue and a branch of government of which much was expected. The exaggerated enthusiasm has since cooled off and there is now a deeper appreciation of what community development can or cannot do. It seems clear, for example, that while community development may be a useful way of waking people up in rural areas it is not necessarily the most efficient way of getting things done. Besides, it has lent itself more to the creation of social services and less to economic improvements which make it possible to support social services. Two lessons seem to have emerged so far. First, community development has no chance of success unless community leaders get some training on how to set about organizing self-help. Second, instead of being a heroic program on its own, community development is best conceived as part of the general program of economic and social progress.

From 1952 until 1960 increasing political power came into the hands of Nigerians. How much difference has it made to the socialization of the young through the schools? The Nigerian governments, especially in the two southern regions, have thrown open the doors of education to many more young people. Indeed the phenomenal progress in quantitative terms reported by the Ashby Commission is due to their efforts. They have made some reforms of the school curricula through a greater provision for practical work and the study of Nigerian history. The government of Western Nigeria has launched a Yoruba Historical Scheme and finances journals on various aspects of Nigerian studies. The building up of Nigeria's historical archives has also gone forward. In spite of all this, the answer must be that Nigerians and their leaders do not as yet look up to the schools as instruments for the conscious fostering of a Nigerian consciousness or solidarity. One possible explanation may be in the federal structure of a country in which there is no single dominant political party and where education is a regional responsibility.

If the role of the educational system in the socialization of those formally exposed to schooling was as limited as we suggested above, the question may be asked whether there were other forces at work which helped to further the process, and if so what they were. At this point it should be pointed out that the indirect influence of the educational system counted more than its direct influence. One of the good things about education, especially if it goes beyond the primary stage, is that it furnishes a modicum of tools by which the possessor can extend his knowledge through reading and discussion with others; it provides at least a fair amount of the discipline of the mind which enables one to question and judge one's actions and that of others.

What, then, were the other agencies of socialization? One of the most important early in the history of Nigeria was contact with people of African descent from the New World as well as other parts of West Africa. It was while a pupil of Calabar's Hope Waddell Training Institution—a school which then numbered West Indians on its staff—that His Excellency Dr. Nnamdi Azikiwe first heard of Marcus Garvey and was inspired by what he heard. Many elderly Nigerians still remember vividly the impact of hearing Dr. Aggrey, who was visiting the country as a member of the Phelps Stokes Commission on education. Earlier still was the influence of Dr. Edward Blyden, as well as of Sierra Leoneans and West Indians who came to Nigeria as civil servants or professionals.

The Nigerian civil service itself was a great socializing factor in many ways. It gave many Nigerians an insight into the intricacies of modern administration. It brought many into direct contact with the British, thereby affording an opportunity to take a measure of their abilities and weaknesses. The civil service drew its membership from different ethnic groups, which proved important in developing a Nigerian outlook, especially since transfers up and down the country meant a firsthand experience of other localities. Children and wives profited most from such contacts. Through playmates and the market they picked up the local languages. It is interesting to record that a government commission—the Harragen Commission—recommended in 1946 that the civil service should be built up as the nucleus of a stable middle class in Nigeria.

Education abroad, especially in Europe and America, was another source of socialization. Nigerians at overseas institutions came into contact with new ideas, studied subjects like constitutional law, politics, and economics for which there were at that time no facilities in Nigeria. With the new ideas they had imbibed, the skills they had acquired, and the inferior status which awaited them if they chose to enter the Nigerian civil service, it was no surprise that they became critical of the *status quo* until the Second World War and played an active part in the nationalist movement from the earliest beginnings. The graduates of Fourah Bay College in Sierra Leone came back to occupy responsible positions in the church, secondary schools, and teacher-training institutions. For many years they were the only indigenous graduates in the teaching profession.

Before modern political parties with effective party machines arose in Nigeria, the press was probably the most influential agency for political socialization. In the hands of a skillful journalist and publicist like Azikiwe, for example, the press was a weapon for criticising and ridiculing the colonial administration, for instilling confidence into Nigerians on the basis of the achievements of men and women of African descent throughout the world, and for blue-printing plans on various aspects of Nigerian problems. It is no exaggeration to say that many Nigerians came to take their standards from the pages of the Azikiwe chain of papers. The Azikiwe is the best-known but the same is true to a lesser extent of other nationalist papers. Since then the number of newspapers, dailies, and weeklies in English and Nigerian languages has grown considerably. The vitality of the Nigerian press has been a contributory factor to Nigeria's comparative success in developing a parliamentary form of democratic government. In this respect she is unique in West Africa.

Without doubt, however, the major factor which made for socialization from 1945 to 1960 was the long process of public discussions and elections to local, regional, and federal assemblies which accompanied the transition of Nigeria from a country with a unitary government to an independent federation. During the period, political parties broadened the basis of their membership and participation: tribal unions, chiefs, and other members of the traditional elite, trade unions, university students, and women were drawn in directly or indirectly. A long debate took place on such topics as the following: how power should be divided between the federal and regional governments; what the bases of revenue allocation should be; how to ensure such things as an independent judiciary, a non-political civil service, and a police force which would not be dominated by any single political party. Through elections the issues were carried to the people in the remotest corners of Nigeria. It all amounted to a great and exciting exercise in political education in the best sense of the term.

When we turn to the way in which the Nigerian educational system has met the needs of the country for trained manpower, it would seem that the impetus came from political changes, or lack of them, in terms of ever-widening goals. Throughout the period of British rule one fact did not change: since there were no white settlers in the country or a considerable body of British officials, a modicum of Nigerians had to be trained to teach in schools, to man the various government services, and to serve the needs of trade and commerce. Up to the early thirties the more or less stagnant educational policy was partly due to the fuzzy and misguided policy of indirect rule which did not know what to do with the educated African, partly to the restricted goals of the maintenance of law and order which the British administration set themselves, and partly to the economic depression of the early thirties which kept down government revenues. But even by the early thirties doubts had begun to creep in as to whether the system of indirect rule was the wisest one. The decision to set up the Yaba Higher College for the training of Nigerians to fill middle-level posts was the first halting step in this direction. Throughout the period under discussion, admission to Yaba and to training courses run by government departments was strictly tailored to prospective vacancies.

The Second World War brought the first major break with the past in that for the first time the goal of ultimate self-government was explicitly made the cornerstone of policy. The Commission on Higher Education in British West Africa, which was sent out in 1943; the establishment of University College, Ibadan, in 1947-1948; the decision taken in 1948 to accelerate the training and promotion of Nigerians through an expanded program of some 400 higher education scholarships locally and abroad over a three-year period and through an intensified in-service training; the founding of the Nigerian College of Technology; and the setting up of a Public Service Board whose job, among others, was to accelerate the appointment and promotion of Nigerians to what were up to that time known as "European posts"—all these were manifestations of the attempt to suit education to the needs of constitutional advancement. The accession to power in 1952 of the first Nigerian ministers marked the beginning of a revolution in education which is still working itself out.

What did the Nigerian ministers and politicians find in 1952? First, they found that only nineteen per cent of senior posts were held by Nigerians. In the key posts of permanent secretaries, there was not a single Nigerian. It was obvious that for a country which was to be self-governing in the foreseeable future this was an intolerable position. It meant that higher education had to be expanded as fast as possible. Second, it was found that the base of the Nigerian educational system had to be considerably broadened at the primary and secondary levels if a bigger output of university trained graduates was to be obtained—hence the decision to push the expansion of primary and secondary schools. Third, it followed that more teacher training institutions had to be set up. Fourth, it was necessary to reform the school curricula. The Ten Year Development Plan of 1946 and the development programs of 1955 created additional demand for manpower, thereby adding to the urgency of turning out more trained men and women of all kinds.

The figures quoted earlier in this chapter give an indication of the colossal progress in quantitative terms made in Nigerian education between the early forties and the late fifties. Each of the two governments of the Eastern and Western Regions is currently spending about fifty per cent of its budget on education alone, that of the north almost twenty-five per cent. The figures exclude expenditures on the training of agricultural extension officers, cooperative officers, nurses, and medical auxiliaries; they also exclude what the various development corporations spend on staff training. On the eve of independence the proportion of Nigerians in senior posts had risen to almost two-thirds in the federal civil services, to a little under three-quarters in Eastern and Western Nigeria, and a bare tenth in the north. Nevertheless, supply, both from local and overseas sources, has not caught up with demand. In the federal service alone, a fifth of established posts were vacant in 1960.

The Ashby Commission on Post-School Certificate and Higher Education, which reported in 1960, was set up to study the problem of supplying educated manpower. Among the major recommendations of the Commission were the following:

1. There should be a massive effort to improve standards of primary education everywhere. The numbers of those completing primary education in 1970 should be stepped up to 25 per cent.

2. The intake of secondary schools should be increased from 12,000 per annum (1958) to more than 30,000 in 1970.

3. The bias of primary and secondary curricula towards academic subjects should be corrected by the introduction of an obligatory manual subject.

4. The imbalance in the system of post-secondary education should be corrected.

5. Of the 29,000 children who will complete secondary education in 1970, 21,000 should seek employment and some 8,000 should go for further training. Of these 8,000 some 3,500 should study the Higher School Certificate in existing secondary schools and in new national high schools to be financed by the Federal Government.

6. The goal should be to expand teacher training so that by 1970 the staff in secondary schools should be half graduate and half Grade I. At least one teacher in fifteen in the primary schools should be Grade I.

7. University development should be so planned as to ensure that by 1970 there will be an enrollment of at least 7,500, with a substantial growth beyond that figure in 1970-1980.

8. Every university in the country should have an Institute of African Studies.

9. Other recommendations include the modification of the content of university courses to suit Nigerian needs and the expansion of technical and vocational training.

10. An Inter-Regional Manpower Board should be established.

The recommendations, which were based partly on a survey of Nigeria's manpower needs by Frederick Harbison of Princeton University, have been accepted as minimum targets for the next years. Three new universities are to be built, bringing the number to five. They will all be national in character, attracting their students from all over the country. The implementation of this ambitious program will depend on substantial international aid.

Did the Nigerian educational system create a self-conscious elite? What is its composition? What role did it play in the nationalist movement? These and other questions were first studied by James S. Coleman in *Nigeria: Background to Nationalism* and more recently by Hugh and Mabel Smythe in *The New Nigerian Elite*.

Coleman and the Smythes agree that there is a Nigerian elite, but they differ in their definitions of the elite and their estimates of its size. Coleman's analysis runs in terms of the Western-educated elite, by which he means those who have completed or are in the process of completing primary education, post-primary education, and university education. He estimates that by the early fifties this group constituted no more than 1,166,600 or 6 per cent of the total population of Nigeria. The Smythes, for their part, define the Nigerian elite as a variable group of people consisting at least potentially of all those who have completed upper secondary school (eleven or twelve years of formal education). On the lower levels, such persons are the clerks and the teachers in the lower secondary school; on the upper levels, they are the professionals and top-ranking government figures or the most powerful traditional rulers. They estimate that "the elite of Nigeria" numbered at least 20,000 people in 1958 and not more than twice this many by even the most liberal estimate.

While the studies cited above are highly commendable as pioneer contributions to our knowledge of a difficult and important subject, it may be questioned whether they are not too dominated by Western categories of thought. In particular, it would be useful to know first who are regarded as the elite among as many of the ethnic groups in Nigeria as possible, and whether or not someone who is regarded as a member of the elite in one role is automatically regarded as a member of the elite in other roles. By adopting too narrow a definition of the business elite and placing undue reliance on the *Daily Times'* "Who's Who in Nigeria" and a sample of 156 Nigerians, the Smythes probably made too low an estimate.

What is not in doubt is that the educational system is the main source through which the Nigerian elite has been recruited. However, as in all generalizations, this statement has to be qualified. To the Muslim areas of the north, for example, the traditional elite is still relatively more important than the old elite farther south. This leads to the question whether the educational system in Nigeria has tended to preserve or to bring about fundamental changes in the class system. The answer is clearly affirmative as far as the south is concerned. Although a place has been found for the chiefs in governmental structure they play a subordinate role and political power has passed into the hands of the new educated elite. In addition, recruitment into the civil service is based on various levels of educational competence which are laid down and implemented by the Public Service Commissions. In the north as well, education is now enabling the newly educated to rise even at a more rapid rate in the regional and local government than in the south. What is not so clear is where power lies and whether education has altered the class system fundamentally. It is probably that education has modified the class system to some extent but not to the extent of changing the class basis of political power.

In passing, brief reference should be made to a number of institutions outside the educational system which are making a substantial even if intangible contribution to drawing the people of Nigeria closer together. Probably the most important are bodies such as the National Economic Council, the Joint (Economic) Planning Committee, the National Council on Establishments, the Consultative Committee on Education which bring representatives of the federal and regional governments together from time to time. They have helped in no small way to develop a greater sense of common purpose. Also working in the same direction are the national trade unions of which the Nigerian Union of Teachers if the most outstanding example. The N.U.T. is not only national in membership, but in the days before Nigerian politicians came to power it was the most effective and permanent pressure group which has been in many ways responsible for successful reforms in education. A patriotic organization about which more and more is being heard is the non-political and unofficial Nigerian Society. Its aim is to bring intellectuals together in order to make a more constructive contribution to natural development.

The major conclusion which emerges from this chapter is that the Nigerian educational system has made a decisive contribution to socialization in the country. It has shown remarkable adaptability in responding to the rapid constitutional and economic changes which culminated in independence in 1960. In quantitative terms alone the progress made in the fifteen years or so before independence is striking. Enrollment in primary schools went up from 276,000 to 2,911,619 and in secondary schools from 8,110 to 128,386. As against only one post-secondary institution with about 100 students (University College, Ibadan) at the beginning of the postwar period, two more universities were opened—the University of Nigeria, Nsukka, and the Nigerian College of Technology, which between them had 2,659 students. The number of government scholars in overseas institutions of higher education was over 2,000 as against 40 in the earlier period. Private students were estimated to be even more numerous.

Nigerian education has also become more diversified and at the same time more specialized at the post-primary levels. It was this combined with the increase in numbers, which enabled Nigeria to have at least the nucleus of a modern civil service with a fairly high proportion of Nigerians in senior posts. A quarter of the academic and administrative staff were Nigerians, a record without parallel elsewhere in West Africa.

It is true that the schools directly made little contribution to political socialization. Their indirect contribution was basic to the success of the other agencies responsible for the wider tasks of political education and integration.

This tremendous educational enterprise was the work of many hands, including the British, missionaries from overseas, and American foundations who gave invaluable assistance in ways too numerous to mention. Nigerians can justly feel proud, however, that through self-help and initiative they carried a major share of the burden. This in itself was an educational experience.

In higher education, Nigeria has managed to avoid some of the faults of universities in some developing countries. Her degrees are of good quality and half of the students in the five faculties of arts, science, economics and social studies, medicine, engineering and agriculture and veterinary science are in the scientific fields.

It has to be recognized, however, that the performance of the Nigerian educational system was due to one special circumstance. There was no ambiguity about what political development meant. It meant advance towards an independent and democratic Nigeria. That goal set the pace and direction of educational development. One problem which immediately arises when a country becomes independent is that some new goals have to be found and old ones redefined. A new goal which has been set since independence is a national six-year economic plan. Its successful implementation will set new targets for the educational system.

Since the former goal of independence has been achieved, the people of Nigeria will have to consider whether the schools should continue to give character training or whether their contribution should be broadened to include positive attempts to foster a Nigerian consciousness. With her federal structure, the present balance of political power and the powers of the Regions in the field of education, it is not going to be easy to reach agreement on this point. The important thing is that the question should at least be brought into the open. Through the kind of discussion and debate on public issues for which Nigeria is justly well-known, it should not be impossible to draw on the experience of other countries and arrive at a working Nigerian solution.

Up to now the main models for the Nigerian educational system have been drawn from Britain, with some recent accessions from the United States. The British models have served Nigeria reasonably well and the American models will probably do the same. However, since educational institutions are part of the cultures in which they originated, they can be imported only at some cost (sometimes at a high cost) and almost never without distortion. With the foundations already laid there is no longer any justification for copying educational institutions from abroad. The first thing is that Nigerians must recognize their educational needs and try to work out appropriate institutions. In doing so, there is a great deal to be gained by studying relevant experiences elsewhere—the fundamental ideals and principles that lie behind other institutions, what special problems they are designed to solve, how such institutions came to take the particular form they have, and how they work in practice. All this is obviously a challenge to creativity.

Unemployment of primary school leavers is not new in Nigeria. What is new is the dimension which the problem has assumed since 1960. It arises from erroneous educational thinking and lack of economic foresight. There is a tendency to think that primary education is something complete in itself, whereas it merely provides the most basic but elementary tools, mainly the three R's. It cannot and should not have a vocational content. That should be an extra, and a necessary extra. A possible way of avoiding unemployment among primary school leavers (that is, those who are not going on to higher schools) would be to make an extra year or two of some basic vocational training an integral part of the curriculum so that there is some needed labor the primary school leaver can perform. Also, the kind of economic planning which has gone on in Nigeria up to now has failed to take into account in specific terms the employment implications. It is equally true that educational planning has tended to underestimate the economic and financial implications. These two aspects will have to be brought right into the center of planning in Nigeria.

Education is conventionally thought to be the sole concern of educators. The various facets of educational development in Nigeria briefly touched upon in this chapter demonstrate this is not so. An activity which involves the making of Nigerians, the integration of the federation, the happiness of its citizens, the performance of its economy, and the use of scarce resources is one to which economics, political science, sociology, econometrics, and other disciplines must all contribute. This is the spirit in which Nigerian education should be conceived.

CHAPTER 5

TUNISIA

LEON CARL BROWN

When we were in the opposition and Tunisia belonged to others, not to us, we planned and resolved that when our country was independent and the state apparatus in our hands we must treat first the problem of education. . . .

Habib Bourguiba

IN 1881 at the beginning of the French Protectorate, Tunisia had a population of about 1,300,000,[1] and it has been estimated that only half of the people were completely settled. The ranks of true nomads were often swelled by those marginal farmers whom a bad year or an overzealous tax collector could drive off the land.

Consistent with the lingering medieval tradition, there was no concept of the positive state. The government was a group apart, collecting taxes for its own maintenance. A subject deemed himself fortunate if this ruling group kept taxes low while providing some public security against bedouin incursions. There was thus, *a fortiori*, no state system of education.

Schools did exist. The Islamic *kuttab* where a single master drilled his students aged five to sixteen in the memorization of the Quran could be found in all towns and villages—perhaps some 1,100 in all teaching about 17,000 students.[2]

From these schools a few students might go on to the Zitouna mosque-university which shared with the Qarawiyin mosque-university in Fes a prestige in North Africa comparable to that of Al-Azhar in Cairo for the Eastern Arab world.

However, these schools, financed entirely by religious foundations (*waqf* or *habous*) or by private subscription, constituted neither a state school system nor the possible nucleus for one. Several general

---

[1] The population today is approximately 4,000,000.

[2] Cf. d'Estournelles de Constant, *La Politique Française en Tunisie–Le Protectorat et ses Origines* (1854-1891), Paris, 1891, p. 449. The first Director of Education in the Protectorate gives an appreciably higher figure for Tunisia in the mid-1890's: 1,428 *kuttabs* with 1,432 teachers and 21,490 students. Louis Machuel, "l'Enseignement Musulman en Tunisie," *Revue Tunisienne*.

points about the religious education of *kuttab* and Zitouna should make this clear:

1. The *kuttab* and Zitouna training was in no way intended as general preparation for careers in government, business, crafts, or agriculture. It was designed solely to create a class of learned men who could carry out the ritual and the legal duties of the Islamic society and keep alive the inherited tradition.

2. Although teaching very young children by rote the Quran to the virtual exclusion of other subjects was not inconsistent with certain requisites of medieval theocentric Islam, such an education was a monstrosity by any post-Renaissance criterion.

3. Religious education was part of a closed system not meant to change. An evolution of such education into something else was ruled out *a priori*. Thus, knowledge was seen as self-contained. A learned man was one who had been able to commit to memory large segments of this unchanging whole. Analysis, criticism, and new interpretation were not valued.

4. Working also against change was respect for what had gone before which was instilled at all levels. Thus, one looked back with pride and regret to the "golden age" of Islam; one respected his parents, school master, the *ulama* who had studied the old traditions, the *shurafa* (descendants of the prophet, etc.).

Tentative moves away from this pattern of religious-based education had begun, however, before the Protectorate. Just as was the case with Egypt and the Ottoman Empire during the same period, the ruling elite in Tunisia had begun to feel the influence of a physically superior Western civilization and had, while still independent, begun the first cautious steps of integrating Western ideas and techniques into Islamic culture. The early modernist movement in Tunisia was sparked by the reforming zeal of Khayr al Din Pasha, a *mamluk* of Circassian origin who served as chief minister to the Bey from 1873 to 1877. His plans for adapting Western technology to the Islamic heritage were best symbolized and realized in Sadiqi College, founded in 1875 and still in existence.[3] Staffed by both foreign and native teachers, Sadiqi was designed to create the cadres of the hoped-for modern state. It was a cautious marriage of old and

[3] The school, named for the reigning bey, Muhammad Sadiq, was financed by the revenue from the confiscated properties of the former chief minister who was also Khayr al Din's father-in-law. This gives yet another indication of the extent to which "government" in that period was a tight-knit group, more or less divorced from the general society.

new—somewhere between the modern school and the educational system of the medieval *mamluk* regime of Egypt. Just as with the *mamluks* centuries earlier, each student received a thorough training in Arabic and Islamic studies before embarking on the secular curriculum. However, instead of attempting to wedge a few modern studies into the traditional system, Sadiqi adopted the Western pedagogical method almost in toto while adapting it to the special Tunisian need for Arabic and Islamic training as well.

Sadiqi College, with an average attendance of only about 150 students, began to decline soon after the departure of Khayr al Din. Also, just as the religious education was designed to produce a small religious elite, Sadiqi was never intended as more than an instrument of the equally small governing elite. Yet, Sadiqi, unlike the system of religious education, did serve as the nucleus of the eventual state educational system. Sadiqi College was the prototype of the Franco-Arab school which became the backbone of Tunisia's national education.

Little need be said about foreign mission schools which in other countries have been such an important influence. It is sufficient to observe that in 1853, for example, two schools run by the Frères de la Doctrine Chrétienne numbered 287 students, including 27 French, 81 Italians, 118 Maltese, 46 Jews, and only two Muslims. In 1880 three such European schools had only 4 "Arabs" of a total 465 students.[4]

This brief introduction may help set off in contrast the revolutionary change in education brought about under the Protectorate. Of course, education was merely one important part of the total impact produced by the French Protectorate, and it is often difficult to separate the part from the whole. The study of educational developments under the Protectorate is best understood within the framework of certain general categories of change. The following are suggested:

1. The slow development of the idea of a modern state, of public education as a state responsibility, and of mass education as an ideal.

2. The steady move away from a theocentric, static, and self-sufficient culture.

3. The intrusion of a new, technically superior culture challenging the old order and creating new problems such as bilingualism, the search for a new cultural identity, etc.

[4] Cf. F. Arnoulet, "La Pénétration intellectuelle en Tunisie avant le Protectorat," *Revue Africaine*, No. 98, 1954.

4. The rise of a new elite distinguished only by its Western training and its ability to manipulate the techniques of Western civilization, and the concomitant decline of an older elite deriving its position from family ties, traditional religious or governmental roles, leadership in pre-industrial crafts, or simply urban origins (especially the one great city, Tunis).

France began the Protectorate period predisposed to ideas of indirect rule and limited commitment. The idea of maintaining the basic structure of the beylical state was in favor, and a modest appreciation of the *mission civilisatrice* was in vogue. "Let us not seek to make pseudo-Europeans of them," a high official in the early administration insisted. "Let us recall that 50 years of living with us have glided over the Algerians without modifying them."[5] Out of this mentality came also the aim of scrupulously avoiding any interference with the existing system of *kuttabs* and Zitouna education—an aim which was generally respected during the entire Protectorate period.

The idea of limited commitment was rudely shattered by outside forces. The thrust of aggressive capitalism and the arrival of European settlers soon reversed the balance. A European population of about 12,000 in 1881[6] had climbed to 77,000 in 1895. By 1905 Europeans accounted for 129,000 or 6.4 per cent of the total Tunisian population—35,000 French and 81,000 Italians being the major groups.

Such a large concentration of French settlers in a French-administered state created a virtually irresistible pressure for French institutions, including justice, land tenure legislation, modern transportation, and communication facilities, and—certainly—French education.

Chiefly for this reason the Direction de l'Instruction Publique organized on a modest scale in 1885 was administering by the turn of the century a full-blown French primary and secondary education. On this point a contrast with Algeria is useful. It can be seen in retrospect that the intensive European settlement—the source of major difficulties in Algeria—probably served in Tunisia to accelerate the process of modernization and adjustment to the demands of a dynamic, technical society.[7] Tunisia was fortunate to be colonized

---

[5] d'Estournelles de Constant, *op.cit.*, p. 459.

[6] Almost all of whom were Italian at that date.

[7] And probably in Morocco as well. "The war in Algeria is a special case. The conquest of Tunisia was peaceful, and the colonization was not especially bloody. In Morocco this took place almost in an amiable fashion. There were chivalrous and

fifty years later, to be a Protectorate, and to have a small indigenous elite in existence.

The resulting school system was that of metropolitan France with a few minor changes to fit the situation in Tunisia, e.g., Arabic and Italian were offered as second languages, and history and geography of North Africa were added to the curriculum. All instruction was in French. In principle, classes were open to all, and although it was easy to deny access to Tunisian Muslims on the claim that they were not sufficiently prepared, did not know French well enough, or were too old, the principle was established. If in 1899 the one French *lycée* in Tunisia had only 10 Tunisian Muslims against 338 French and 160 Tunisian Jews, the situation in the primary grades was more encouraging. The total primary school population in the public schools for the same year was:

	French	Italian	Tunisian Muslim	Tunisian Jew	Other	Total
Boys	1,532	1,801	3,782	1,193	822	9,190
Girls	1,017	1,466	31	1,101	658	4,273

There was also considerable intermixture of Europeans and Tunisians in these classes. For the same year, 1899, all but 19 of the 78 boys or mixed boys-and-girls schools had European and Tunisian Muslim students studying side by side.[8]

Something approaching segregation was already beginning, however, with the inauguration of the Franco-Arab school designed especially for Tunisian Muslims. These schools, where theoretically one-third of the instruction was in Arabic, evolved both from the natural desire of the local population to maintain some instruction in their own language and from the growing prejudices of *colons* against having Tunisians studying with their children. However, the main battle was won. A Western lay system of education had been adopted by the Tunisian Protectorate government. The completely French schools were always open in principle to qualified Tunisians, and the Franco-Arab system was basically French education with some empha-

---

feudal wars after which the two sides embraced. In Algeria [colonial rule] was much bloodier from the beginning, and the later revolts were always drowned in blood. Doubtless because of this distinction the Tunisian and Moroccan revolts were based on hope while the Algerian insurrection was marked by despair." Habib Bourguiba in Roger Stephane, *La Tunisie de Bourguiba*, Paris, Plon, 1958, pp. 50-51.

[8] Louis Machuel, *L'Enseignement Public en Tunisie*, Tunis, Imprimerie Rapide, 1900. The negligible number of Muslim girls in school should be noted.

sis on Arabic and Islamic studies. As such they approached the standards of the completely French schools.

By the end of the Protectorate period some 15,000 or roughly one student in four of the completely French system was a Tunisian Muslim. The Franco-Arab system—the real foundation of Tunisian national education—provided in the same year, 1954, primary education to 125,000 Tunisian Muslims.

Sadiqi College, the prototype of the Franco-Arab system, became the training ground for the emerging elite. Reserved for Tunisian Muslims, all of whom after 1906 entered by competitive examination,[9] Sadiqi, with an attendance that never rose far above 700, has provided the native leadership from the 1880's to the present day. Its alumni include President Bourguiba and 8 of the 11 members of the present cabinet.

Several generalizations about the Protectorate school system can now be made:

1. It was of top quality. The French system blended completely into that of metropolitan France, and the Franco-Arab schools in many respects approached this standard.

2. If some Tunisians were thus beneficiaries of a first-rate education, they were hardly the intended beneficiaries. "Two tendencies seem to have presided over the erection of schools and the development of school enrollment: the concern of the authorities to assure the maximum instruction of French children, and the necessity to plan by priority the more important population centers for school building."[10]

3. Although a few Tunisians received a good education, the total number was disappointingly small. In 1904 there were 2,823 Tuni-

[9] According to the Delmas report to the Conseil de Perfectionnement de Sadiki in December 1906, as reported in *Le Tunisien*, February 14 and 21, 1907. Even so, it has been noted that the conscious Protectorate policy of recruiting sons of "old families" for Sadiqi gave way only after the First World War. De Montety has observed that after the First World War the best students from the primary schools began to sit for the competitive examinations at Sadiqi and "despite the consideration which the jury attempted to give to the sons of important families, the others captured most of the scholarships. The rigor of the competition was reinforced moreover when a Muslim co-director of humble origin, Si Attya, was placed at the head of this establishment in 1934. The majority of the professors as well were of modest condition." (Henri de Montety, *Enquête sur les Vieilles Familles et les Nouvelles Elites en Tunisie*, semi-official private publication, Tunis, 1939.)

[10] Jean Poncet, "La Scolarisation de la Tunisie et le Milieu Social," *Semaine Pédagogique*, proceedings of a conference organized by the Direction de l'Instruction Publique, Tunis, April 1949. This conference was itself symbolic of the new and more dynamic French educational policy during the last years of the Protectorate.

sian Muslims in the French or Franco-Arab schools (and almost 22,000 in the *kuttabs*). In 1930, when most of the present political leadership was in the primary school age group, only 35,000 Tunisian Muslims out of an eligible 476,000 (or 7.4 per cent) were in school. At the end of the Protectorate in 1955 only 26 per cent of the total primary school age children and 3 per cent of the total secondary school age children were actually in schools.

4. Even these modest figures of school attendance at the end of the Protectorate were essentially the result of the last decade. Only after the Second World War did France make a determined effort to increase the numbers of Tunisians in public schools. (In 1945, 66,000 or 9.5 per cent of the total eligible were in primary schools.)

5. This system produced graduates reasonably well prepared by French standards, but weak indeed in their native Arabic language and in their indigenous culture. Even the Franco-Arab system, which theoretically devoted ⅓ of its time to studies in Arabic, was actually more heavily weighted to the French part of the curriculum.

During most of the Protectorate period the public school system did not account for the majority of the few Tunisian Muslims who were in school. Yet so important was it as an influencing factor that any treatment of the continuing traditional education is meaningful only in terms of the intrusive new idea of education.

For example, as already noted the French wisely refrained from any great interference with Zitouna or the traditional *kuttab* education. Yet by the first decade of the Protectorate period an indigenous group was striving to reform and modernize education at Zitouna. This group, most of whom were later identified with the Young Tunisian movement, formed in 1896 the Khalduniya[11] designed to give modern studies (including foreign languages) to Zitouna students. Always viewed with suspicion by the official Zitouna leadership, the small Khalduniya played a role out of proportion to its numbers (99 students in 1901; 156 in 1905) as an entering wedge of modernism among the most traditionally inclined Tunisians.

Equally, Western techniques inspired the modern Quranic schools. Khairallah bin Mustafa, one of the original Young Tunisians who created the first such school in 1907, was interested in applying French pedagogy he had learned at the Direction de l'Instruction to form a modernized *kuttab*—a primary school which would maintain emphasis on Arabic and Islamic training while integrating modern

[11] Named for the famous Muslim philosopher and historian Ibn Khaldun (1332-1406), who was born in Tunis.

subjects and methods. By the end of the Protectorate period these modern Quranic schools—private except for limited state supervision and subsidy—had virtually replaced the old *kuttab,* accounting for 35,000 students or about one for every four in the public school system.[12]

At this point it might be useful to change the emphasis of our analysis and view these same Tunisians not as objects of new ideas and educational schemes but rather as subjects reacting to these ideas. As in many other countries, the educational institutions of the imperial power created a new elite, but more than most such new elites the Tunisian elite showed a greater awareness of how education was reshaping their society, accepted and even made an explicit goal the extension of such Westernizing education, and were less divided and concerned about the conflict between the traditional and the native as opposed to the new and foreign. In effect, the newly emerging Tunisian elite more nearly managed to demand the "rights of Frenchmen" without denying—or feeling that they were denying—their Tunisian identity. In another sense, there was created a self-conscious elite which was also a self-proclaimed elite, which did not shrink from openly announcing that their Western training was the essential basis of their claim to leadership.

This situation was especially true at the turn of the century with the early nationalist and reformist group, the Young Tunisians, and after the creation of the Neo-Destour in 1934. Between the two movements, during the era of the Old Destour, there was a certain tendency to fall away from the frank acceptance of modernization *à la française* while remaining nationalist.

The Young Tunisians were a small group of Western-trained intellectuals advancing ideas of modernization and Westernization at the turn of the century. By no means a mass political party, this small group, most of whom were by birth closely linked with the pre-Protectorate ruling class, saw its role as that of intermediary between their own "backward" society and the French protectors. Their social philosophy was best expressed in their weekly newspaper, *Le Tu-*

[12] These schools were later discouraged by the Protectorate authorities as potential centers of nationalist training, and the necessary licenses were often refused or long delayed. The nationalists not only used the schools for just this motive, they also used requests for schools as a goad to push the Protectorate government into greater educational activity. Cf. Bou Hasna (Henri de Montety), *Etudes Tunisiennes—Structure Administrative et institutions du Protectorat français en Tunisie (1938),* Paris, 1939, pp. 83ff. That the modernizing Tunisians of the Neo-Destour had no great regard for the modern Quranic schools except as a means to pressure the Protectorate government is clearly revealed by their acts after independence.

nisien, which appeared from 1907 to 1912.[13] Perhaps as much as 25 per cent of the coverage in this newspaper dealt with education. To the Young Tunisians it was the sole weapon capable of bringing Tunisians to the point where they could form a modern state and gain acceptance of their claims from the French.

The Young Tunisians wanted an education for native Tunisians in no way inferior to that of the French themselves, and having willed the ends they did not shrink from the means. They insisted on education in French and openly avowed that Arabic was not yet adapted to the needs of modern technology.

Most of the Young Tunisians led by their informal leader, Ali Bach Hamba, even had reservations about the modern Quranic schools initiated, as had been seen, by another Young Tunisian. To them simple piece-meal improvement was not enough. One must either attain the educational standard of the French ruler or remain forever in a secondary position. For the same reason they attacked any Protectorate scheme for trade schools, seeing in this a design to educate Tunisians only up to the level where they might become more effective "hired hands."

The period after the First World War saw Tunisian nationalism blossom quickly into a full-grown mass movement. The sudden move to mass politics meant an appeal going well beyond that of a clique of "Young Tunisians" all of whom had been exposed to French education. Consequently the views expressed on this subject become more tradition oriented. The Young Tunisians had insisted, "Our new mentality is the product of the French mind. We have taken over its vast domain and made it our own."[14] *La Tunisie Martyre*, on the other hand, insisted that Tunisia wanted "national, scientific education" and all she got was French, "as foreign to us as Chinese education is to France."[15] Yet it is interesting to note that even this period

---

[13] Significantly, in French although an Arabic edition was added in 1908.

[14] First issue of *Le Tunisien*, February 7, 1907.

[15] Anonymous (Abd al Aziz al Tha'albi and Ahmad Saqqa), *La Tunisie Martyre: Ses Revendications*, Paris, Jouve, 1920, p. 49. This book, which belongs to the period of the Old Destour origin, is the best single source both of Old Destour demands and its mentality. In many ways a well-written political polemic, *La Tunisie Martyre* depicted a pre-Protectorate "golden age." This, we would suggest, was more than just polemics. It indicated a real psychological need to reject the intrusive French culture and return to the traditional. It is in this tendency, in part, to look backward that the Old Destour stands in contrast to both the Young Tunisians and the later Neo-Destour. Of course, there were many French-trained and quite Westernized people in the Old Destour, and the party was by no means an all-out reactionary group. Still, by contrast with the earlier Young Tunisians and the later Neo-Destour the generalization is valid.

was more nearly a pause in order to contact the emerging masses rather than a reversal. Demands for reform and modernization of Zitouna increased in intensity, as the students felt more strongly the competition for positions from graduates of French or Franco-Arab schools.

More important, in this period after the First World War the cumulative effect of many French innovations (not necessarily planned for such a purpose) in land tenure, economic policy, transportation and communication, capitalistic exploitation of resources, all served to give Tunisians greater mobility, greater access to openings that had once been the closed preserve of the Tunis elite, and (certainly for many finding their traditional pattern of life threatened) the stimulus of a greater need to exert some initiative. Given this setting, even the elementary idea of competitive examinations for scholarships and government posts could be revolutionary. By the 1920's the sons of modest, frugal provincial Tunisians were climbing into the role of the new elite—through the sole device of Western education. In the 1920's such Tunisians as Habib Bourguiba from Monastir, Tahir Sfar from Mahdia, and Bahri Guiga from Testour were pursuing higher studies in France. They would be heard from later.

It was only a few years later, as it happened. Following this era of the Old Destour, with its reserve toward French culture and education, came the period of the Neo-Destour. This party, now the ruling political group in independent Tunisia, was organized in 1934 by a group of French-trained Tunisians, mostly of modest, provincial origin, who had the dedication and good sense to go right back to their own people in organizing a mass party rather than using their education simply as an entree into the rapidly declining Tunis elite. For the first time the Old Destour idea of a mass party was combined with that of outright Westernization advocated by the Young Tunisians. Here was a group insisting that the Western tools provided a means of national liberation. Habib Bourguiba in the inaugural congress of the Neo-Destour described himself and the political executive of the party as young men who "entered the political battle after having spent many years in Europe pursuing their studies, regarding Europe's peoples and their method of opposition. They learned these beneficial methods and then came back to apply them in their home country."[16]

[16] Speech to the 1934 Neo-Destour congress, *Congresses of the Neo-Destour Party* (in Arabic), Ministry of Information, Tunis, n.d., 1956?.

In essence two fundamental changes were taking place during this period. The medieval Islamic tendency to avoid government and leave it in the hands of a small, and often foreign, group was crumbling before an active competition for positions in the administration. At the same time the provinces which for centuries had been alternatively ruled and ignored by the forces in the capital were becoming politically active. Education was playing a leading role in this development.

A few statistics taken from a 1939 study will indicate the social change being spearheaded by education. In 1935 the competitive examinations for admission to Sadiqi College revealed the following results for the two major areas of Tunisia:

	District of Tunis	District of Sousse-Sahel
Number of candidates	148	106
Number accepted	32	49
Percentage accepted	21%	46%

In 1938 it was estimated that only 15 per cent of the students of Sadiqi were sons of "old families."

The later careers of these Sadiqi graduates is also significant. An estimated 80 per cent were absorbed into government. By contrast only 20 per cent of the Tunisians in the fully French lycées went into government.[17] Since the absence of Arabic training in the lycées put these graduates at a disadvantage in the examinations for government employment, they gravitated toward the liberal professions.

Yet Arabic language competence was not alone sufficient to obtain government employment. The almost complete rout of the Zitouna graduate by those having been trained in the Franco-Arab system was manifest by the late 1930's. In 1938 results of the examinations for posts of probationary *khalifa* (the beginning grade in the local administration) were as follows:

Educational Background	Number of Candidates	Number Accepted
Zitouna	135	5
Sadiqi	23	10
Primary Superior	12	3[18]

[17] In 1939 there were 400 enrolled in Sadiqi, and 750 Tunisian Muslims in the lycées.

[18] All of the above statistics are from de Montety's previously cited *Enquête sur les Vieilles Familles et les Nouvelles Elites en Tunisie*. Primary Superior was a modified form of Franco-Arab education giving a post-primary training forming a well prepared bilingual graduate. It was designed in large measure to provide native teachers.

A system of public lay education was not only playing a vital role in producing such changes; it was itself providing a new career for Tunisians. The number of Tunisian Muslims serving as teachers in the French and Franco-Arab schools increased very slowly but steadily, and it is probable that no profession (not even law—as in Egypt under the Wafd) can rival that of teaching as the seedbed of a nationalist elite. Aside from the obvious mechanics of teaching which permit, even require, the instructor to serve as leader and guide for the youth, there was in Tunisia another factor of incalculable importance. The French teaching staff in Tunisia reflected in large degree certain well-known characteristics of their colleagues in metropolitan France. They were usually anti-clerical, leftists of the radical or socialist variety, and active trade unionists. Many, of course, joined the *prépondérants* in the colonial situation, but many indeed tutored their Tunisian colleagues in the principles of Socialist anti-imperialism, mass organization, trade unionism, and, more generally, the rights of the "people."

It is thus not surprising that 4 of the 12 Tunisian cabinet members in 1961 had been teachers. Of these, 2, Mahmud Messadi and Ahmad bin Salah, had at one time been the head of the teachers' trade union.

In addition to these changes in the Neo-Destour phase of the Protectorate several earlier problems remained unsolved. There were continued attempts to reform Zitouna, and that school did greatly increase its attendance and expand the number of secondary school annexes. However, the problem of introducing modern studies without impinging upon the requisites of an essentially theological training was never resolved. In terms of social status this fostered a vicious circle—fewer opportunities for Zitouna graduates leading to fewer competent applicants for Zitouna education.

At the same time the Tunisians again rejected a proposal for rudimentary education, the Gau plan of 1936, designed to eliminate illiteracy and give the rural population a simple education geared to their agricultural needs. Just as previously, the Tunisian elite saw this plan only as a divice to perpetuate the subordinate role of Tunisians vis-à-vis the French by making impossible the creation of Tunisian "cadres."

In sum, by the end of the Protectorate period a cohesive national movement led by a French-trained elite had gained acceptance in pledging Tunisia to the dual aim of independence and the creation of a modern social state. It would be an exaggeration to say that the French-inspired public education had created the national movement, but it is certainly true that the national movement had been fostered in the classrooms.

Why did this happen? Why, for example, was there no movement tending to reject everything French in the process of struggle against French political control? Why was there no equivalent in Tunisia to the Muslim Brotherhood or the Algerian Association of Ulama? Only a few tentative suggestions can be offered here:

First, the new Tunisian elite made a virtue of their French training as a mark of leadership. Rather than saying (and who has not heard variants of this in colonial situations?) "I am French-trained, but I am still a good nationalist" they insisted "We are better trained and thus have a larger responsibility in the Tunisian national movement."

Then, too, the old religious elite made a poor showing. Not only was Zitouna unable to achieve practical reform, but many of the ulama were marked by their complaisance before the French authorities. The bitter campaign against French naturalization in 1932—spear-headed by the group later to form the Neo-Destour—made this clear. A significant article appeared in *L'Action Tunisienne* at the height of the campaign. Entitled "Our Revenge" and signed by "a student" the article observed that many Westerners had thought Western education would sap the Muslim faith of the students, and the ulama with their continual cries of alarm had supported such an idea. Now had come the naturalization campaign and who were the true Muslims—those "pontiffs" or the youth who contributed to save Islam?[19]

Lastly, the contact of the emerging Tunisian elite with French leftists (especially in academic circles) in Tunisia and in France facilitated the acceptance of things French while rejecting French political control. If certain French citizens could vaunt the tradition of the French Revolution, condemn capitalist imperialism, reject the "superstitions" advocated by clerics, and advocate modern lay education—then the Tunisians need feel no qualms about using certain "French" ideas in their national struggle.

The Independence Period

Bourguiba and the Neo-Destour had always considered their struggle as twofold: against external control and against internal "back-

[19] *Action Tunisienne*, 27 April 1933.

wardness."[20] The *idée force* of creating a modern Tunisia politically, culturally, and economically sparked a host of reforms in the immediate post-independence period: granting women the vote, an intensive campaign against the veil, the abolition of *shari'a* courts and the institution of a single national legal system, the abolition of polygamy, the abolition of public and private *habous*, the enactment of a nationality code giving citizenship a territorial rather than a religious base, earmarking over 12 per cent of the budget to improvements in public health, and the institution of a system of work projects designed to reduce unemployment and underemployment and to advance the principle that any unemployed person presenting himself to the provincial governor must be given work. Yet perhaps the most important single project was the impressive educational program.

In a very real sense the Tunisian leadership saw the entire post-independence program as one of mass education. "When we were in the opposition," Bourguiba affirmed in 1958, "and Tunisia belonged to others, not to us, we planned and resolved that when our country was independent and the state apparatus in our hands we must treat first the problem of education."[21] There were two reasons for this priority—one made explicit, the second, and perhaps most important, was implied.

First, Tunisia needed the cadres to run a modern state, not to mention the more ambitious plans of economic development. A government report insisted: "A policy of reduced or only slowly increasing school attendance implies a choice of underdeveloped or at least a resigned attitude toward a permanent protraction of economic and social underdevelopment . . . (but the opposite policy) can help carry out successfully any plan of transforming the economic and social structure of the nation."[22]

Second, there was the implicit idea that each graduate of the "modern" education became a convert to the ruling elite's plan of

[20] "The Neo-Destour party in its first decade fought on two fronts. It struggled against the French who opposed it at times with special laws and suppressive courts and at times with fire and steel. It also fought a more difficult and trying battle against passiveness, submission, outdated mentalities, disunity and illusions which overwhelmed a large proportion of the population in order to arouse the hearts, ignite the minds, abolish superstition, destroy outdated customs, tribal particularism and odious fanaticism, and to create a revolution in the depths of the souls. As a result the people today are not what they were in the past." (Ali Belhouane, *Revolutionary Tunisia*, in Arabic, Cairo, 1954, p. 72.)

[21] Speech at Sadiqi College, June 25, 1958.

[22] Ministry of Education, *Perspectives décennales de l'enseignement*, Tunis, n.d., 1958?

social revolution. In a program which was essentially Ataturkism without its constraint it was vital that the base of those intellectually and emotionally committed to the ideals of the ruling elite be rapidly expanded. It is no exaggeration to argue that the government of newly independent Tunisia sought with classroom to forestall any possible traditionalist reaction that might be able to exploit either religion or the idea of a return to Arabism in order to challenge Western-inspired principles of social organization.

In another sense expanding modern education was to be the most dynamic factor in the process of social revolution. The Neo-Destour and its ancillary organizations—of agricultural workers, labor, business, women, youth, and students—could, of course, provide considerable indoctrination, and certainly they were essential to providing the necessary discipline for the transitional period. However, education offered the best chance of creating the "new Tunisians," completely emancipated from a theocentric culture and at home in a this-worldly humanism devoted to the national solving of problems in a technical world.

Only viewed in this light can the emphasis given education in independent Tunisia as well as some of the decisions taken in implementing the educational program be properly understood.

In 1947 a Tunisian professor at the newly created (November 1945) Institut des Hautes Etudes wrote in an Arabic language review: "It is a sacred principle of general pedagogy—the necessity of safeguarding the cultural unity of a country. This is a corollary of the idea which we have developed earlier: education is social integration. If the society is a living reality, one and indivisible, the culture will be so as well, and the pedagogical system must be a harmonious whole given the task of not letting the unity of the whole be placed in peril. To ignore the principle of cultural unity is . . . to sow the seeds of discord and—another unavoidable consequence—to place it in peril of death."[23] Some eleven years later the author of this article received the chance and the challenge to put his ideas to the test, for in May 1958 Mahmud Messadi became Minister of Education.

Equally important as this "sacred principle" of cultural unity, and perhaps of greater political urgency, was the task of rapidly increasing total school attendance. There had been great strides in the last ten years of the Protectorate, but even so in 1955 only 27 per cent of

[23] Mahmud Messadi in *Al Mabahith*, October 1947.

the primary school age children and 3 per cent of the secondary were actually in attendance.

The first two years of independence saw considerable advancement. Total primary school attendance was raised from 227,000 to 322,000 and both the Zitouna secondary school annexes and the modern Quranic schools were integrated into a single national school system.

By 1958, however, it was apparent that little more progress could be made without facing several difficult problems of choice: Which took priority—the quick return to education in Arabic, the national language, or the maintenance of the existing high standards even if instruction was in a foreign language—French? Was it consistent with Tunisian independence to have such a large number of French citizens in the teaching establishment? Zitouna graduates, although lacking in modern technical education, at least had a good command of Arabic and the Islamic tradition. Should not this resource be exploited to the full? Was it of greater importance to increase school attendance even at the risk of letting standards decline, or should the maintenance of previous standards override even the pressing problem of moving toward universal education?

Never was the peculiar Tunisian trait of sober realism in greater evidence than in the choices made. The principle—at least in the short run—of bilingual education was confirmed. At no point was the introduction of a greater degree of instruction in Arabic permitted at the risk of lowering standards. In spite of all the outstanding disputes with France and the deteriorating Algerian situation, Tunisia moved eagerly into a cultural convention with France assuring French teachers for the Tunisian school system. And in the face of an acute shortage of teachers over 800 Zitouna-trained teachers were released as sub-standard. Finally, refusing to accept the dichotomy of either quality or quantity the Tunisians are striving for universal education while maintaining the former high standard.

The decisions taken were embodied in a ten-year educational plan. With his usual flair for the effective gesture, President Bourguiba announced the plan at the June 1958 commencement exercises of Sadiqi College, the best symbol of modern Tunisia and the school which he himself had entered just fifty years earlier.

The major points of the plan are as follows:[24]

[24] It is only just to point out that this plan owes a great amount of its inspiration and detail to the French 20-year plan for Tunisia, 1949-1969. Equal credit, however, is due the Tunisian authorities for being willing to accept what they realized was valid from the Protectorate heritage.

1. Universal primary education is to be achieved in 10 years, after which time it will become compulsory. This will require an average annual increase in school attendance of about 50,000.

2. In order to compensate for the existing shortage of teachers two important changes have been made in the primary education: (a) For the first two years of primary school there will be two shifts of students, each attending for one-half day or 15 hours of instruction per week. (b) The seventh year of primary education will be eliminated. These changes alone increased the potential primary schools enrollment by almost 30 per cent.

3. Since French will continue for an indefinite time to be the vehicle of instruction for various technical subjects,[25] French is introduced in the third grade. For the total primary school period, almost 50 per cent of the instruction is in French as the following table shows:

| Primary School | Language of Instruction in Hours Per Week | |
	Arabic	French
1st year	15	0
2nd year	15	0
3rd year	10	15
4th year	10	15
5th year	10	15
6th year	10	15
Total	70	60

4. In secondary school education the language of instruction remains almost exactly as it was under the Protectorate—about two-thirds in French, one-third in Arabic. Although the ultimate aim is 100 per cent instruction in Arabic, officials are not yet even speculating what the ratio might be at the end of the ten-year period. It seems fair to conclude that the next generation will be bilingual.

5. Two types of secondary school education have been established: (a) a six-year program modelled on the traditional Franco-Arab school (itself patterned on the lycée) though with greater emphasis on the natural sciences and (b) a three-year terminal intermediate program designed to give a more practical training to those who will not be going on to higher studies. Both types of secondary school will recruit by competitive examination, and it will be possible for an

[25] Cf. M. Messadi in *Le Figaro*, 3 November 1959, "We have committed our country to a *de facto* bilingualism. We would like to conserve the importance of your French culture. It depends on France whether this plan will succeed or fail" (i.e., by providing needed teachers).

especially bright student to transfer later from the intermediate to the six-year secondary school. Still, even at the end of the ten-year program only one primary school graduate in three will be able to go on to either type of secondary school.

6. Tunisian authorities deliberately moved slowly in higher education. The University of Tunis was officially established in March 1960, but impressive numerical gains in higher education are expected to begin only after 1964, when the products of the present secondary school program begin to enter college. For the present the Tunisians are concerned that the national university be more than a premature manifestation of young national pride. Their ideal is again found in France, and the gratuitous manner of culturally turning their back on the Arab East is indicated in the following statement from an official report: "The example of certain young universities created in the last forty years in various countries formerly dependent or underdeveloped, notably in the countries of the Arab Near East, demonstrates that a university which is not sufficiently concerned with research rapidly becomes a teaching institution, the level of which approaches some sort of complementary secondary education."[26]

For such an ambitious plan even partial success will be remarkable. A brief examination of the quantitative results after the first two years shows that the Tunisians are almost keeping up to the proposed pace:[27]

TABLE 1: EXPANSION OF TUNISIAN EDUCATION

	1958-59 Actual	1960-61 Planned	1960-61 Actual	1968-69 Planned
Primary school	320,362	428,071	408,758	836,913
Terminal intermediate	7,864	10,119	12,012	36,293
Secondary	15,568	24,840	23,147	93,790
Ecoles Normales	874		1,193	

[26] Ministry of Education, *Study of the Creation of the Tunisian University*, Tunis, n.d.

[27] (a) Terminal intermediate training is replacing the former Centers for Professional Training which were thought to be too elementary. The totals include both the new terminal intermediate and the remaining classes of the old system. (b) The totals exclude 3,965 students who started their secondary education under the old Zitouna system before 1958 and who will be permitted to finish under the same system. Thus the old Zitouna secondary system will disappear completely in four more years. (c) Projections for the Ecoles Normales were not included in the ten-year reform program.

The magnitude of the educational program is also indicated by the national budget. Between 17 per cent and 19 per cent of the annual budget is earmarked for education.

Success in the rapid acceleration of Tunisian education depends in large measure on foreign assistance. Without U.S. economic aid, which for education alone has averaged $2,000,000 to $3,000,000 per year since 1958, the school building program and especially the equipment of intermediate schools would be far behind schedule.

More pressing in the short run is the need for teachers who—in view of Tunisia's educational past and goals—can come only from France until sufficient Tunisians are trained. By Franco-Tunisian agreement the French government provides Tunisia needed teaching personnel and pays approximately 40 per cent of the total salary and allowances. In the past few years there has been a yearly average of about 1,300 French teachers in the Tunisian national school system. This meant that for the 1959-1960 school year there were (in addition to the 44 French teachers in higher education): 212 French teachers in secondary schools or about 1 for every 5 native Tunisians; 94 French teachers in technical schools or about 1 for every 8 native Tunisians; 928 French teachers in primary schools or about 1 for every 7 native Tunisians.

In addition to the 1,300 French teachers in the Tunisian national school system there were in 1959-1960 over 1,400 teaching in the remaining French schools in Tunisia. Even these totally French-staffed and French-financed schools designed to service the needs of French nationals remaining in Tunisia provide assistance to Tunisia—giving primary and secondary education to some 8,000 Tunisian Muslims and 6,500 Tunisian Jews as well as 19,600 children with French citizenship.[28]

This imperative need to rely on foreign assistance until the Tunisians are able to create their own cadres has strongly influenced the new state's foreign policy, a fact helping to explain how in spite of many difficulties and at times outright provocations Tunisia has managed to maintain working relations with France. Nor was the timing of Bourguiba's *démarche* easing tension over the 1961 Bizerte crisis with France unconnected with the desire to have a renewed cultural convention with France by the beginning of the school year.

---

[28] These are the figures for 1959-1960. There was little change in the following year. Figures for 1961-1962 (after the Bizerte crisis) are not available, but there was probably a considerable drop in attendance.

Tunisia reveals an equal willingness to look to the former protecting power for the higher education requirements which cannot be filled in Tunisia. Table 2 for 1960-1961 shows the almost exclusive reliance on France:

TABLE 2: TUNISIAN STUDENTS ON SCHOLARSHIPS ABROAD, 1960-1961

Country	Total Students	Number Receiving Scholarships from Host Country	Number Receiving Scholarships from Tunisian Government
France	1,064	600	464
Lebanon	80		80
Iraq	61	61	
United States	55	55	
Italy	25	25	
Switzerland	24		24
West Germany	17	15	2
Belgium	15	10	5
United Arab Republic	13		13
United Kingdom	6	1	5
Netherlands	1		1
Total	1,361	767	594

It has been observed earlier how the forces brought into play by the French Protectorate created a new elite and gave the provincials the opportunity to break the previous monopoly on power and wealth held by Tunis. The educational program of independent Tunisia remains committed to extending this goal until all great regional disparities are removed. Studies by the Ministry of Education of school attendance for 1959-1960 revealed rates of primary school attendance varying all the way from 17 per cent of the total school age children in Kasserine province to 65 per cent for the province of Tunis. (The national average was 43 per cent.) These studies by province were also projected for the ten-year period of the plan in order to know the annual rate of increase required by province in order to achieve universal primary education by 1969. To date there has been considerably more school construction in these deprived areas.

It is most likely that the final phases of the ten-year-plan will break down in the sparsely settled and economically underdeveloped provinces. (By contrast, the French 20-year plan for Tunisian education, 1949-1969, aimed at universal primary education only in the urban and semi-urban areas, and for attendance of roughly two-thirds of the total primary school age children in other parts of the country.) One might even go farther and insist that by any purely economic criterion the investment in the socially and economically more backward areas will never reap an economic growth commensurate with what might be possible in the coastal provinces from Bizerte to Sfax. However, such a criterion will not be decisive in the thinking of the Tunisian leaders. The concept of cultural and political unity plus the militantly "populist" general orientation of the new elite dictates this plan of unifying and equalizing Tunisia in every respect.[29]

Equally, the disparity of school attendance between boys and girls remains a matter of continuing concern for the Tunisian authorities. Minister of Education Messadi in his September 1960 press conference at the beginning of the school year took pride in the gains achieved but went on to deplore the situation in which only 27 per cent of the primary school age girls (as opposed to 57 per cent of the boys) were in school. He pledged increased efforts to close this gap. The Bourguiba government is dedicated to the idea of bringing Tunisian Muslim women into full participation in society; and the President himself, according to the top leader of the Union Nationale des Femmes Tunisiennes, "is the first feminist."[30]

Noteworthy also in the present scheme of Tunisian education is the planned move away from classical and liberal arts studies, early specialization and a heavy increase in graduates with technical skills. "A Zitouna *shaykh* who has passed his day teaching theology wants, as soon as he gets home, to take a bath or listen to the radio. To maintain and better this modernism, to assure the comfort and well-being, we need to create specialists and technicians, to push our youth forward toward familiarizing themselves with this field essential for the future of our country." With this homely example, Bourguiba advanced the point in one of his weekly speeches[31] concluding that "henceforth the man in the blue jacket must be esteemed as he deserves."

There seems to be a healthy response to this challenge. Of 200

---

[29] The classification suggested by Morroe Berger distinguishing "pre-populist" from "populist" states is especially apt for Tunisia. Cf. his *The Arab World Today*, New York, Doubleday, 1962, pp. 419-421.

[30] Bourguiba's recent divorce of his wife (originally French) in order to marry a younger Tunisian may have somewhat tarnished this reputation. It is difficult to judge the impact of this move by the very muted criticism heard in Tunis.

[31] Speech, June 27, 1957.

students recently applying for government scholarships, 63 per cent expressed a preference for higher studies in the natural sciences. Only 20 per cent opted for law, and 17 per cent for letters.

Of great importance is the elusive question: what sort of "new Tunisian" is being created by this education? What are the ingredients making up this greatly prized "cultural unity" which independence has presumably made possible?

Certain indications come from the curriculum itself. As has been seen, there is an almost equal division between Arabic and French as the language of instruction in primary school, and in secondary school there has been virtually no change since Protectorate days. This is in large measure dictated by necessity. Tunisia must rely on French-speaking teachers for years to come. Even so the division of time among the various studies in primary education reflects more than this problem of bilingualism, as may be seen in Table 3. Most sig-

TABLE 3: SUBJECTS TAUGHT IN PRIMARY EDUCATION
AVERAGE HOURS PER WEEK

Subject	Hours
Arabic	7½
French	5
Arithmetic	3½
Practical studies (drawing, singing, physical education, etc.)	3
Nature and geography	½
History and civic instruction	⅓
Quran and moral studies	1

nificant, perhaps, is the extremely modest share given to Quran and moral studies. Nothing more concisely sums up the change that has taken place since 1881 than this prosaic point—physical education now commands as much time in primary schools as the Quran and moral studies.

In secondary education almost as much time is devoted to the teaching of French language and literature as Arabic. Harsh reality or conscious choice? The necessity of continuing to teach many subjects *in French* is not disputed, but does not the continued emphasis on teaching French language *and literature* (an average of 5 hours out of 30 per week for the first four years as against an average of 6 for Arabic) involve a more deliberate choice?

Official publications have often noted the need to reintegrate Islamic philosophy into independent Tunisia's educational system. The official program for secondary education lists in a single fascicule the subject "Philosophy and the Study of Islamic Thought." This sounds intriguing—a synthesis of Western philosophy and traditional Islamic studies? Actually the title is confusing. They are two completely different subjects taught in the last year of general secondary education according to Table 4.

TABLE 4: HOURS PER WEEK (TOTAL PROGRAM 30)

Subject	Modern Letters	Degree Program Classical Letters	Science	Math	Normale
Philosophy	7	7	4	4	5
Study of Islamic Thought	2	3	1	1	2

Further, the extent to which even the modest degree of Islamic education is to be given in a modern rather than traditional Zitouna framework is indicated by the following explanation of the general aims of the course taken from the official program: "In a word, the methods to be relied upon in teaching Islamic thought should be those employed in what is today called the study of religious thought from the sociological point of view. This is the method with attempts to go beyond the investigation of any given ideology in order to discover the substantive factors which determined its various viewpoints just as they determined the solutions and the problems arising out of that very ideology in any given age. This method in short calls not for simply receiving and believing but for thought, investigation and criticism."[32]

The genuine effort being made to give equal educational opportunities to both sexes has already been noted. This new mentality seems to be striking roots. In a recent lecture on modern Tunisian literature there was only one poem cited by the speaker which drew guffaws and catcalls from the audience (about three-fourths students)—a poem written in the early 1930's by a conservative exhorting women to remain true to their religion by keeping their veils and habits of seclusion.

It would appear that the existing education does serve to inculcate in the young ideas generally shared by the ruling elite. Both the

---

[32] Translated from the Arabic. The program for Islamic thought covers 10 pages in Arabic; that for philosophy 22 pages in French.

present political leadership and the younger graduates of independent Tunisia's schools seem committed to a modern, secular, Western-inspired cultural outlook in a way which exceeds in boldness the various modernist movements found in other parts of the Arab world. This is not necessarily political Francophilia or pro-Westernism. It is rather the modernism of Sartre and Sputnik—of the rights of man and of successful five-year plans. The views of Tunisia's leaders and the youth they are seeking to train are more ambivalent toward their older traditions and the Eastern Arab world. This elite realizes that the Eastern Arab world has not made a very impressive showing in adjusting to the mid-twentieth century. They also resent what often appears as a rather patronizing approach of the Arab East in dealing with the Maghrib. Still, there remains a certain inner uneasiness about the sharp break with Tunisia's past, the relatively debased state of the native Arabic language, and the lack of more substantial ties with the rest of the Arab and Islamic world.

In short, the search for a new cultural identity continues. The choice of many Western techniques and ideas was made for pragmatic and tactical reasons. Many such techniques and ideas have now become so firmly rooted that they might be considered national and Tunisian. Others are still judged simply by a utilitarian standard. At the same time the traditional impulses of Tunisian society, though now eclipsed, are far from dead.

This only returns the question to the implied purpose of independent Tunisia's educational program—broadening the base of the elite which fully accept the leadership's idea of social revolution.

There seems good reason to believe that the leadership's purpose will be achieved. The continual concern of Tunisia's government and ruling political party for the students suggests that a new generation will grow up feeling a sense of identity with its leaders. For example, a young pro-Communist Tunisian professor gave a lecture on the social implications of modern Tunisian literature. To his surprise he was personally praised and awarded by President Bourguiba for his important work and concern in this field. It is significant also that a top Tunisian leader usually travels to Paris whenever there is an especially important change in Tunisian policy in order to explain the move to the Tunisian students in France.

Finally, just as in the Protectorate period, the overwhelming majority of Tunisia's graduates enter government service. To date there has been no problem of absorbing these graduates. In short, the educational institution, the party and its branch organizations, and the government are interlocked. This closed system brings obvious danger of a stultifying bureaucracy, political despotism, or both. Thus far, however, the dynamism generated by independence, expansion in education, projects for economic development, and *élan* which comes from the feeling of belonging to a going concern has managed to avoid such dangers while recording some tangible results.

Several brief conclusions about education and the process of political change in Tunisia might now be suggested:

1. As in most, if indeed not all, formerly colonized countries, the educational institution of essentially Western inspiration served as a major element in creating a new elite.

2. Equally, modern education was perhaps the most important single factor in broadening the social and the geographical base of political participation in Tunisia.

3. A distinguishing point about Tunisia has been the existence of a native elite aware of the creative impulse given by modern, Western education. This awareness goes back to the turn of the century, and after a short, backward step in the 1920's it came into equally sharp focus from the period of the Neo-Destour to the present.

4. Education in independent Tunisia maintains a high degree of continuity with Protectorate experience, which suggests the extent to which Tunisia wants to build on this legacy rather than reject it.

5. There has been a conscious and deliberate effort in independent Tunisia to use education as the vanguard of the proposed social revolution.

CHAPTER 6

EGYPT

MALCOLM H. KERR

IN EGYPT the impact of education on political development revolves chiefly around the prospective economic and social role of the large numbers of university graduates being produced in the country. Egypt is beset with the problem of a crowded and rapidly growing population living on very limited resources. The demand for economic development is urgent, particularly in the industrial field, and unless substantial progress can be made toward this objective, most educated Egyptians will find themselves without a satisfying role to perform; indeed, such a role is lacking today.

Industrialization requires a greatly increased force of skilled workers and foremen. So far the educational system has produced very limited numbers of such persons and instead has created a surplus of university graduates in such unproductive fields as law, commercial accounting, and liberal arts. There are two main reasons for this. The first, which will not be examined in any detail here, is a general problem of entrepreneurship having to do with the traditional inhibitions of employers regarding labor paractices, with inadequate industrial planning, and with a low level of appreciation of the economic value of personnel trained specifically for the technical tasks at hand. In short, the educational system responds not to theoretical national needs but to the job market, and, until recently at least, the one has not been effectively translated into the terms of the other. The second reason, with which we are more directly concerned, is that social traditions and attitudes have for a long time placed a high premium on membership in the genteel professions, even if economically unrewarding. The university graduates accordingly constitute a growing force of unusable manpower, whose social and economic expectations have been raised to unrealistic levels by their education and whose rapport with the military elite ruling the country is tenuous. The result of mass higher education has thus been to redistribute poverty in the name of social equality, in a manner that threatens simply to replace an illiterate class of unemployed proletarians with a literate and more sharply alienated one. This discontent has been subdued over the past decade, yet its potential explosive force has been increased by the educational policies of the regime. Also it is likely that the spread of literacy through mass elementary education may also generate social and economic problems for an even larger class, which will ultimately pose a dangerous political situation. This, however, lies in the more distant future.

Historical Summary of the Educational System

Modern secular education in Egypt dates from the first half of the nineteenth century with the efforts of Muhammad Ali, the illiterate Albanian soldier who seized power in 1805 and founded a new dynasty, to lay the foundations for a modern army and an efficient administration. During his rule (1805-1849) Muhammad Ali sent some 339 students to Europe, chiefly to France, for scientific and technical training, brought European doctors, engineers, and military officers to Egypt as instructors, and opened a medical college, a printing press, a translation office, a number of technical and agricultural schools, and primary schools in the towns and largest villages. He also established for the first time a government Department of Education. These efforts were continued sporadically under his successors up to the British occupation of Egypt in 1882, at which time there were in the country 270 government primary schools as well as 200 European and many more privately run Egyptian schools.

Alongside this new system there continued to exist the traditional Islamic educational system that had survived in Egypt over many centuries. This included the *kuttab*, or elementary Koran-memorization school, which was the only road to literacy for the bulk of Egypt's children, but was in fact attended by a small minority; the *madrasa* or mosque-school, run in the larger towns by local religious scholars in traditional Islamic fields of learning such as Arabic grammar, theology, Islamic law, and including perhaps a smattering of history; and at the apex of the system the ancient university of Al-Azhar in Cairo, itself the leading *madrasa* of the country, in which boys and young men of widely differing ages would sit at the feet of a teacher by a pillar in the courtyard and memorize the contents of traditional grammatical or religious texts. Students who attended long enough to pass an oral examination would graduate with the title of *Alim* (plural, *Ulama*), i.e., "savant," and subsequently also lecture under a pillar in the Azhar or else become judges in the religious courts, mosque preachers, leaders in local mystic brotherhoods, or possibly functionaries in the bureaucracy.

Muhammad Ali's educational measures thus did not supplant traditional learning but created a dichotomy of culture that has persisted to the present. A considerable number of students from the traditional system, however, found their way into the modern one by being sent to Europe or enrolling in one of the higher professional or technical schools in Egypt. A number of such persons, hybrid products of two contrasting cultural traditions, have made interesting contributions to the intellectual and political life of Egypt over the last century, reflecting the tensions and conflicts of the two traditions in a manner that reveals something of the complexity of present-day political and social attitudes that are sometimes encountered among educated Egyptians. Muhammad Abduh and Saad Zaghlul are perhaps the best-known past figures to represent this cultural ambivalence to the outside world; within Egypt such types are commonplace.

The period from 1882 to the present may conveniently be divided as follows: (1) The period of British military occupation from 1882 to 1922, when Egypt became nominally independent. During this period an autonomous Egyptian government functioned, theoretically under the suzerainty of the Ottoman Porte but in practice subject to the decisive influence of a British Resident acting through the medium of British advisers in the various government departments. (2) Egypt's period as an independent constitutional monarchy, from 1923 to 1952. (3) From the military coup of 1952 to the present. These three periods are more or less distinctive as regards the general educational endeavors of the regime. However, the structure of the educational system, and some features of the political culture to which it contributed, underwent a steady evolution independent of the nature of the regime in power.

It is important to bear in mind that it would be somewhat oversimplified to speak of a period of colonial rule in Egypt, since Egypt was never a colony. British authority, though very real, was ill-defined, even after a Protectorate was unilaterally declared in 1914. After declaring Egypt independent in 1922, Britain continued to enjoy considerable internal influence until the treaty of 1936. Furthermore, until 1936 not only British but other European communities in Egypt enjoyed a privileged commercial and legal, as well as social, position under the Ottoman Capitulations (extraterritorial conces-sions), so that culturally and economically Egypt was, so to speak, everyone's colony, with French the primary foreign language rather than English. Until some years after the 1952 revolution large num-bers of Egyptian as well as European children attended French, Ital-ian, American, Greek, and English private schools, and thus were educated in a foreign curriculum and in a foreign language. The most precise distinction one can make between a "colonial" and an "inde-pendent" period is, however, in reference to government-run schools. Until 1922 not only was British control of general state finance complete, but the internal finances of the Ministry of Education were closely supervised by a tight-fisted Scottish adviser named Douglas Dunlop, so that whatever the structure of the government school system, the resources devoted to its development at various levels was a matter of British rather than Egyptian policy.

The habitual complaint by Egyptians that Britain did shamefully little to promote education before 1922 is amply justified by budget-ary statistics. After 24 years of British control, in 1905-1906, the proportion of the state budget devoted to education was still less than 1 per cent, and in 1919-1920, on the eve of independence, it was less than 2 per cent. In the latter year the total education budget amounted to only about five shillings per child of elementary school age, and only about 15 per cent of the total sum was allotted to mass elementary education. By contrast, with the advent of Egyptian inde-pendence, the proportion of the total budget allotted to education jumped to 6.8 per cent in 1925-1926 and to over 12 per cent in 1945-1946; it is now over 15 per cent. When Lord Cromer left Egypt in 1907, after 23 years of effective control, an estimated 94.6 per cent of the total population was still illiterate; ten years later the figure had decreased only slightly to 92.1 per cent.

It is true that until virtually the end of Cromer's period the neg-lect of education was partly justified by the pressing need to restore order to Egypt's debt-ridden finances. It is also true that in England itself in the late nineteenth century the resources devoted to state education were small by today's standards. But Cromer's claim that "it may well be a matter for surprise, not that so little, but that so much progress . . . has been made in so short a time" toward edu-cating Egyptians for self-government[1] strikes one as humbug, as does also his startling observation that "the best test of whether the Egyp-

[1] Cromer, *Modern Egypt*, London, Macmillan, 1908, Vol. II, p. 526.

tians really desire to be educated is to ascertain whether they are prepared to pay for education. On this point, the evidence is conclusive. In the early days of the British occupation, nearly all the pupils who attended the government schools were taught gratuitously. Before many years had passed, by far the greater proportion paid for their education."[2] It is more instructive to note that a specially constituted Anglo-Egyptian commission on elementary education in 1918 pronounced the government's record in this field a failure. In 1920 a subcommittee of the Milner Commission, sent by Whitehall to investigate the political unrest in Egypt, castigated "the failure of the administration to establish any system of education which extends to the mass of the people" and asserted that "no true social, economic, or political progress can be looked for without a complete revision of the educational system in Egypt." The subcommittee found that the privately run elementary schools in Egypt were "carried on with complete incompetence and under quite unsanitary conditions," which encouraged the schools to "become a centre of insubordination and even of political propaganda," that the expansion of technical, agricultural, and commercial training schools was "urgently necessary," and that the Egyptian University, established under private auspices in 1909, was a virtually useless institution for lack of government encouragement.[3] Government secondary schools, meanwhile, were so neglected that by 1925 their total enrollment was only 8,100, as compared to 222,761 in primary and elementary schools.

The first effort of the newly independent Egyptian regime after 1922 was to expand facilities and enrollment at all levels, particularly in elementary and primary schools. By 1950-1951 enrollment in this category reached 1,030,486 in government schools and approximately 250,000 in private and foreign schools. The chief impetus to this expansion was the promulgation in 1925 of a law providing for free and compulsory elementary education. For various social as well as economic reasons, however, practical implementation of this program was slow. The 1950 enrollment represented only about 30 per cent of the elementary-age children, and as late as 1960-1961, after considerable further expansion, this percentage had risen only to perhaps 65 per cent. Public secondary school enrollment continued to lag

[2] *Ibid.*, pp. 531-532.

[3] "Recommendations of Subcommittee 'A' on EDUCATION," manuscript, Private Papers of Lord Milner, New College Library, Oxford, England. Extracts here are quoted by permission of the Historical Section of the Cabinet Office, London.

badly until the end of World War II; since then there has been a sustained growth.

An Egyptian state university was opened in 1925 at Cairo. The floundering, hitherto private university of 1909 was transformed into the College of Arts; the existing professional "higher schools" of law, medicine, commerce, engineering, and agriculture became its other colleges. Similarly diversified universities were opened in Alexandria (1942) and Ain Shams, a district of Cairo (1950); the University of Assiut (1957) concentrates on scientific and technical fields. Total university enrollment, which has quadrupled since the war, reached 87,000 in 1960-1961, in addition to about 20,000 in university level teacher training and technical institutes, and about 4,000 university level students out of the 41,000 enrolled at Al-Azhar and its affiliates.[4]

Since the 1952 revolution the government's most notable attentions have been devoted to continuing the spread of elementary education, which it is hoped will be universal by 1965, and to expanding the facilities for university instruction in science, medicine, and engineering. There has also been a moderate increase in the enrollment in technical secondary schools and an improvement of their facilities. Academic secondary education has shown only a modest increase, but the proportion of those going on to university has risen sharply, and is now well over half of all secondary graduates. Efforts were also made by the military regime to improve and standardize the primary and secondary curriculum, about which more will be said below. Private Egyptian schools, which largely came under effective government control in 1943, have since been taken even more firmly in hand, and foreign schools have almost all passed into Egyptian hands.

Until 1951 one of the most notable, and notorious, features of the school system was the distinction between primary and elementary education. Primary schools (which were few in number) led on to an academic secondary education and thence to the university, a professional "higher college," or a white-collar job in the bureaucracy. The elementary school, on the other hand, led nowhere, except into the medieval curriculum of Al-Azhar, a handful of ill-managed trade schools, or back to the cotton fields and often a relapse into illiteracy.

<hr>

[4] Figures are from United Arab Republic Central Ministry of Education, *Summary Report on Development of Education in the United Arab Republic during the Year 1960-1961* (in English), pp. 24-25.

This dual system was not without its rationale, for the purpose of the elementary school was to combat illiteracy in the villages among a class who otherwise would not attend school at all and who were in need of a simple and practical curriculum which could be taught tolerably by the only prospective teachers available in sufficient numbers: men who themselves had little or no education beyond elementary school. But, as Lord Milner's subcommittee had complained as early as 1920, the primary school ladder "provides for a privileged class and in view of the relative absence of general elementary education, serves rather to widen the breach between that class and the bulk of the people." While fees were abolished in elementary schools in 1925, they continued in primary schools until 1943, and until the latter date the government made little effort to expand primary facilities, instead leaving the field open principally to foreign and private schools. The elementary schools, although expanded greatly in numbers between 1925 and 1945, were of such poor quality and so overcrowded that it was widely felt that the impressive statistics of rising enrollment were almost meaningless, and that in any case until the elementary-school graduate was entitled and qualified to continue his education, the social purposes of mass education would not have been served. Accordingly, after a decade of preparation, a 1951 law unified all early education in a single six-year primary course ending with an examination and a certificate. However, this remained largely a paper reform, for the bulk of the former "elementary" schools were simply not equipped to offer the full prescribed program. The chief stumbling block was the teaching of a foreign language (usually English). It had once been the practice to introduce this subject early in the primary curriculum; eventually it had been put back to the fifth year, but after 1951 it was still required for entrance into secondary school. Since the former elementary schools were for the most part unable to provide foreign language teaching, the result was that their graduates were barred as before from admission to the secondary schools.

Accordingly a law of 1953 reorganized the entire system by ending primary school two years earlier than before, following which it substituted a "preparatory" school of four years (later reduced to three) and finally a revised secondary course of three years. This enabled all qualified primary students to move on to preparatory schools, in which foreign language instruction was begun.

From 1949 to 1953 the secondary system was plagued by almost yearly radical changes instituted by successive governments, at a time when the number of primary graduates was increasing very rapidly and existing facilities were under heavy pressure. A 1949 law had provided free tuition for the first two years of academic secondary school to students scoring above a certain grade in their primary examinations; then the Wafd Government of 1950, in a demagogic bid, decreed free secondary tuition to all, regardless of grades, although in fact the existing secondary schools were not remotely equipped to handle the resultant influx. With their eyes set on eventual admission to universities and therefore a job in the already overstaffed bureaucracy, a flood of primary graduates in 1951 jammed the secondary schools, while the secondary technical and trade schools, which had achieved some expansion over the previous decade, incurred an actual drop in enrollment. With this unnatural increase in high career expectations of students and the pressure on the budget to expand secondary education at the inevitable expense of improved primary facilities (at a time when Egypt was still 75 per cent illiterate), the result of this new policy, if continued, could only have been what one Egyptian authority referred to as a "social catastrophe."[5]

The situation was partially retrieved by the military regime in 1953 with the announcement that although tuition would continue to be free, admission to academic secondary schools would be limited to those best qualified.

Despite a number of changes since 1953 the secondary curriculum has continued to be burdened by overcrowding and low standards, by heavy emphasis on languages, overcentralization of teaching materials and examinations, and a shortage of qualified teachers. The heavy schedule of state examinations at the end of secondary school has traditionally haunted students throughout their final year and turned much of their schooling into a cram course; indeed, before 1953 a number of governments sought political popularity by issuing blanket permission to failing students to repeat the examination.

Secondary technical and commercial schools, though greatly improved since the war, continue to be scorned by students anxious to pursue the status symbol and imagined open-sesame of a literary or scientific university degree. From 1943 to 1953 technical school en-

---

[5] Ismail Qabbani, "Tatawwur al-tarbiya fi al-jumhuriyya al-misriyya khilal al-sanawat al-'ashr al-akhira" ("Developments in Education in the Egyptian Republic during the Last Ten Years"), in Habib Kurani, ed., *Muhadarat fi nuzum al-tarbiya* (Lectures on Educational Systems), Beirut, 1956, pp. 130-131.

rollment increased only from 16,000 to 27,000. Under the post-1952 regime it rose to 75,549 in 1960-1961, but even the latter figure is modest when compared, for instance, with the total university enrollment of 87,000 in the same year.

Not only has the university population skyrocketed, but it has done so out of all proportion to the rise in secondary school graduates. In addition, the Egyptian government continues the practice originated by Muhammad Ali a century and a half ago, of sending students abroad. In 1960-1961 some 967 undergraduate and graduate students and 686 government officials attended foreign institutions at government expense, in addition to 3,456 other students paying their own way. In the Egyptian universities budgetary priority has been given in recent years to improved facilities in the medical, scientific, and poly-technical faculties, and the need to staff these faculties with qualified personnel partly accounts for the size of the body of students sent abroad. Nevertheless an even greater proportion of the increased university enrollment has fallen upon other departments, all of which consequently suffer from the problems of poorly paid, overworked teachers (much of whose time is often devoted to other jobs on the side), poorly prepared students lacking in initiative and in intellectual horizons, and crowded classrooms. A further handicap to standards has been that of language: English is the language of the engineering and medical schools, while at the law colleges some subjects are taught in French; yet not many students are really proficient in these languages.

At all levels of public education in Egypt the most obvious and pressing problems come down to the matter of money: funds are continually short for new buildings, better trained and better paid teachers, equipment, etc. Equally serious if less obvious, however, is the problem of the social background of the students, who generally come from homes where encouragements to cultivation are lacking and where formal education is regarded as primarily a ticket to social and economic promotion. Job expectations exert a powerful and usually harmful influence on the operation of the school system, just as schooling for its part stimulates the social ambitions of Egyptians. Hence the government's educational policies have long been the subject of political controversy, since education is the cornerstone of the whole notion of equality of opportunity that has dominated the political consciousness of the Egyptian masses since the war.

Political Importance of the Intelligentsia

There is often a tendency to overestimate the scope of political socialization among the Egyptian rural and urban masses and to imagine that basic literacy is all that is needed to create a more or less permanently active force out of the resentments of these deprived people. In reality only a small—though growing—educated urban minority figures more than marginally in any calculation of the politically important forces of the country for the foreseeable future.

On the one hand it is misleading to speak of the 1952 Land Reform as having broken the political strength of the rich land-owning class by depriving them of their economic influence over their peasant tenants. The landlords' political power had been derived less from their ability to intimidate the peasant than from the wealth and social prestige that their ownership of land enabled them to wield within the privileged circles of Cairo and Alexandria. It is true that after 1952 the landlord could no longer deliver the rural vote in elections, but this was not because of land reform, and in any case pre-1952 elections had had little more influence on the conduct of state than those under the Nasser regime. The peasant continues to be an obedient voter; but, literate or not, it is chiefly his physical isolation that limits his relevance to politics.

On the other hand the peasant's migration to the city, which is sometimes stimulated by his own or his sons' literacy, draws him only one step closer to political participation, from which as an urban proletarian he is still somewhat removed. As urban migration tends to concentrate the unemployment problem under unfavorable social and psychological conditions, and as literacy is apt to sharpen the pangs of unemployment and the sense of disillusionment with the promises of the regime (which cannot hope to employ everyone in its industrialization plans),[6] it seems a reasonable assumption that the spread of basic literacy contributes to the build-up of a potentially serious discontent, although this stage probably lies well in the future. Nor is it as true as is often supposed that pre-Nasser politics were dominated by the constant threat of urban mob violence. The

[6] See the discussion by Frederick Harbison and Ibrahim Abdelkader Ibrahim, *Human Resources for Egyptian Enterprise*, New York, McGraw-Hill, 1958, pp. 137-139, where the likelihood is mentioned that Egyptian industrial production could probably double in volume without a net rise in employment, by the use of more modern equipment, and by more intensive training of a limited work force.

only occasion in this century when a genuine mob spontaneously took control in Cairo—in the famous "Black Saturday" riot of January 1952—was an exception which arose under the unique circumstances of the heedlessness and paralysis of an unusually degenerate government. The riot did not crystallize any definable political forces: it was aimless and did not serve anyone's particular advantage.

On other occasions mass riots and demonstrations have been made not by real mobs but by more limited and well-defined groups: most often students, occasionally trade unionists, with a fringe of rag-tag stragglers passively filling the ranks, as for example in the pro-Naguib demonstrations organized by the Moslem Brotherhood (principally students) and the pro-Nasser counter-demonstrations (trade unionists) in early 1954. The huge crowds swarming around such national leaders as Zaghlul, Nahhas, or Nasser on the occasions of their open-air speeches in Cairo and Alexandria are not mobs, any more than the peasants who used to clutch pathetically at General Naguib's sleeve during his village tours in 1953. They are not political forces of any kind, but simply noisy, helpless spectators. Nasser addresses them, but his words are most often aimed at the limited group of at most 1,500,000 Egyptians (out of 29 million) who have enough education to form political opinions, enough status to aspire to middle-class security, and enough skills to make their loyalty and enthusiasm a matter of economic consequence.

This group primarily consists of those possessing at least a partial technical or academic secondary education, plus a small number of less educated but highly skilled trade union members. Most important, at the core of this group, are the 250,000-350,000 university graduates, of whom half are under thirty years of age. In terms of social origins this group as a whole is the product of the great upsurge of social mobility that has swept Egypt for the past generation. The vast majority of its members have received more education than their parents and, in aspirations if not in real income, have risen higher on the social ladder. Only those few who attended the better European secondary schools in Egypt, such as the Ecole St.-Marc or Victoria College in Alexandria, or who attended European universities as undergraduates, are likely to have come from privileged families. The bulk of secondary and university graduates come from families in which few books if any are found, in which no foreign language is spoken, in which little knowledge of the modern world has been imparted, in which the mother, if not the father, is illiterate, and in which education is regarded first and last as the path to economic betterment.

Educational and Cultural Content

Against this background primary, intermediate, and secondary education tend to be highly abstract and theoretical. A very high proportion of time throughout is devoted to Arabic and foreign languages. Written Arabic is as different from the spoken dialect as Latin is from Italian, and its immense vocabulary, its grammatical structure, and its alphabet make it a difficult language to read rapidly. Hence literary skills beyond the most elementary do not come easily. Knowledge of foreign languages is important for many types of office employment in Egypt, for all science and some arts courses at university level, and for a wider range of reading than modern Arabic publications currently provide. Until 1938 primary school students began studying English or French at the age of eight, and a second foreign language at fourteen, while continuing a heavy program of Arabic. This load has been somewhat lightened, so that at present the first foreign language begins at the age of ten and the second is restricted to secondary arts students in their final two years. University students in most fields are obliged to continue foreign language study for either three or four years, and in the Colleges of Medicine and Engineering the examinations, as well as some lectures, are conducted in English. Nevertheless the foreign language is seldom learned well, even by those who major in it at the university; yet the time devoted to it naturally detracts from the attention given to other subjects.

Curricula in secondary school and above involve a heavy class schedule in an inordinately long list of subjects. A survey published in 1949 gave the following breakdown of the first four years of the secondary curriculum: of a total of 144 hour units (thus an average of 36 hours of classes a week), Arabic absorbed 28, the first foreign language 30, the second foreign language 12, mathematics 18, sciences 17, history, civics, and geography 16, and other subjects 23.[7] A fifth year was devoted to concentration in mathematics, science, or letters. This schedule has now been partially eased by the postponement by one year of the second foreign language and the devotion of the last two years rather than one to specialization. But upon entering

[7] Roderic D. Matthews and Matta Akrawi, *Education in Arab Countries of the Near East*, Washington, American Council on Education, 1949, p. 58.

the university the student continues to be subjected to a long and rigidly prescribed series of classes and subjects. Most arts majors, for example, require twenty-four weekly class hours in six to eight subjects a semester, with virtually no room for choice. Concentration in the departmental major begins in the first year. Thus, for example, the candidate for the B.A. at the University of Cairo majoring in economics takes, over a four-year period, 138 hours in economics courses alone, out of a total schedule of 191 semester hours. His non-economics courses included 28 hours of English, French, or German, various required cognate courses, and only a total of 4 hours of electives. This very heavy schedule, as well as such other factors as the ancient Moslem tradition of transmitting inherited knowledge in memorized packages, contributes to the stifling of the imagination and curiosity of the student and tends to leave him at the time of graduation like a horse in blinkers, with limited breadth of knowledge or perception. He is likely to have developed little taste for independent reading, and being unable to afford expensive foreign books (which he finds difficult to read anyway), his knowledge of the outside world comes either through the limited and unreliable medium of Arabic translations or through the propaganda-drugged Cairo press. Fortunately the range and quality of Arabic translations has greatly improved in recent years, particularly as a result of the efforts of the Franklin Institute and the Egyptian Higher Council for Letters and Arts.

One result of the above situation is that in forming his political views the Egyptian secondary or university graduate is often as exclusively dependent on local propaganda as the man with only a few years of primary education. An abundance of such material is served up to them by a half-dozen mass-circulation daily newspapers, two or three leading news-and-gossip weeklies, and the ever-present radio. The technical standards and facilities of these media are excellent; *Al-Ahram*, the most prestigious daily, also has a fairly wide range of world news coverage and a generally constructive and interesting page of editorial features. But throughout the press the news is heavily slanted in tone and content to serve the government's purposes. This was the case as much before as after the nationalization of the press in 1960. Educated Egyptians are well aware that their press is a vehicle of propaganda, and on domestic matters, about which more informal means of information are often at hand, they are often skeptical of what they read. But for foreign affairs few of them are exposed to any other source of news.

Prior to the 1952 coup the Egyptian secondary and university student learned surprisingly little in school about the political, social, and economic problems of his own country. Even the B.A. candidate in political economy at the University of Cairo found his schedule crammed with such subjects as an Arabic adaptation of French constitutional law. The major in Arabic literature, concentrating on the ancient and medieval classics of the language, was no closer to reality. Efforts have been made at both the secondary and university levels over the past decade to rectify this situation. University economics and sociology programs, for example, both include a number of courses on Arab and Egyptian problems. A compulsory course entitled "Egyptian Society" (later renamed "Arab Society") was introduced in the final year of secondary school, and subsequently required for freshmen throughout the universities, higher technical schools, and the military academy. However, examination of the contents of various of the textbooks that have been used for this course reveals little serious discussion of social or political problems, but a great deal of propaganda and historical mythology. When asked why the historical chapters almost entirely ignored four centuries of Ottoman rule in the Arab East, the co-author of one of the texts disarmingly explained that the Ottoman age was a dark period in Arab history and that he and his colleagues had decided to treat only the brighter periods.

Nasser himself has publicly complained about the failure of university teachers in the social sciences to bring more relevance into their tests and courses: "At the Law College you teach political economy—Adam Smith's theory of supply and demand—and you say that . . . such theories are ideal. People would then look at us in surprise and say: What we have learned at the Law Faculty differs from what is being applied here. I say: No, the process [in Egypt] is not one of supply and demand. We are forging a new system. . . . Some authors have written books on economics that were simply copied from other countries. Who has written a book on the economy we are now dealing with? . . . When I realize that these economics books are merely a repetition of what we were taught at the Law Faculty in 1936, then I am filled with endless disappointment."[8]

Mass education since the war, and more especially since the 1952 coup, has contributed significantly to the unification of cultural life in the country (and cheapened its quality) by proportionally reducing

[8] Speech of November 25, 1961.

the graduates of foreign schools to a much smaller minority than before. The Egyptianization of British and French schools after Suez (Victoria College was renamed "Victory College"), and eventually, as announced in January 1962, the Egyptianization of all other foreign schools as well, with foreign teachers in all but 20 per cent of total positions to be replaced by Egyptians, put the seal to this development. It is true that over the past century the foreign schools have maintained much the best standards and enjoyed great prestige among those Egyptian parents who could afford to send their children to them, but they have been a mixed blessing, for while contributing to the once-celebrated cosmopolitanism of Cairo and Alexandria they have also perpetuated the problem of a mixed linguistic culture, with many of their Egyptian graduates being virtually illiterate in their native Arabic. Furthermore, it was to a disproportionate extent the minority communities—Copts, Jews, Syrians and Lebanese, as well as Greeks and Italians—whose children attended these schools, and who as a result were best qualified upon graduation to fill commercial jobs in the cities requiring fluency in foreign languages. Such positions will now increasingly be filled—not always as capably—by Moslems, and a long-standing social grievance against the minorities will be at least partly removed.

A more persistent problem has been that of the cultural gap between the graduates of modern secular schools and those of Al-Azhar. Over the past two generations a series of reforms have introduced such subjects as foreign languages, science, and sociology into the Azhar, but these remained marginal to the core of its ageless curriculum, and the Azhar continued to produce graduates who were out of touch with many of the problems of modern life and ill-equipped to fill useful positions except as teachers of the Arabic language. A major change in this situation was heralded by the enactment of a law in June 1961 providing for the conversion of the Azhar into a modern-style university offering degrees in the full range of scientific and humanistic secular disciplines alongside those of Islamic law and theology. A presidentially appointed committee was charged with supervising these innovations. In principle this reform constitutes a revolutionary step. How rapidly and to what extent it will substantively affect the number, training, and outlook of students in the traditional field of learning remains to be seen.

Islamic culture in Egypt, unlike the indigenous traditional culture of some African and Asian countries, is neither primitive nor conceded by all educated persons to have been made obsolete by Western culture. The result is that the contact between the two cultures has been one of more bitter and protracted conflict, and has caused much pain, uncertainty, equivocation, and proneness to illusion and emotionalism. The conflict exists not only between the clearly recognizable partisans of the two distinct cultures, but also at various intermediate stages, and often within the mind and conscience of the individual.

The attempt to bridge the gap through apologetics which insist that there is no conflict between modern science and the Islamic cultural heritage, that Islamic law is as flexible and utilitarian as modern statutory law, that early Islam was the first democratic and socialist society, and so forth, does not always ease the tensions and doubts in the minds of young Egyptians. For such arguments make it all the more difficult for the regime to project Egypt's need to learn, to look forward and outward rather than backward and inward. The cultural attainments of Islamic society in its golden age were remarkable and in some ways the legacy is a source of pride and confidence, but in another sense it constitutes a psychological and social burden.

Economic and Social Prospects of the University Graduate

The overriding concern of the new graduate of the secondary school or university in Egypt continues to be what it has been since the turn of the century: to find a job. It used to be remarked of law students that in their first year they aspired to become prime ministers, in their second year cabinet members, in their third year judges, and by the time of their graduation simply to find whatever work they could. The number-one employer, not only for law graduates but for graduates of all kinds at all levels, has traditionally been the state, whose massive and immobile bureaucracy has operated as a national employment and relief agency since the days of Muhammad Ali.

There are various reasons for this. Muhammad Ali, in tailoring his educational program to his bureaucratic requirements, set a precedent which eventually encourage precisely the reverse principle: that the requirements of the bureaucracy should be expanded to meet the demand for jobs. In one sense this was not new, for not only in Egypt but in Ottoman Turkey and in other Moslem regimes the bureaucracy had traditionally been a prime employer of literate skills. But the educational system begun in the nineteenth century was an altogether new one, being modern and secular; and therefore it was of fateful significance that its products, instead of being steered toward private commercial enterprise and membership in a new-born bourgeoisie, simply became modern versions of an age-old class of clerks and secretaries. The state, which from time immemorial in Egypt had been the only sizeable organized institution, thus failed to gain a rival but instead became stronger still, while the development of modern commerce and industry was left to a collection of foreigners, Levantine minorities, and traditionally wealthy families who were incapable of providing the foundations for a large, independent, mobile, indigenous Egyptian Moslem middle class in which new generations of educated youth would find their place.

Furthermore, from the late nineteenth century onward the rapid growth of population made the bureaucracy an outlet of shrinking promise for graduates of the schools. As the number of applicants for jobs increased, the proportionate number of vacancies declined, as did the economic and social attractions inherent in them.

It would seem to have been sensible, as early as the 1882-1922 British period, for the educational system to lay increasing stress on vocational and technical training as a means of diverting talents into productive enterprise and encouraging the development of a technological mentality. The failure to do this was noted in particular by Lord Lloyd, who complained that Cromer, Dunlop, and others had half-heartedly fostered a second-rate literary education, wholly outclassed by private French schools in the country, at a time when Egypt's true needs lay in elementary and technical education.[9] The Milner Commission's education subcommittee commented that:

"The course of education given in the Primary and Secondary Schools was originally designed to produce a lower grade of Egyptian civil servant to fill the posts which previously to the occupation had been occupied almost exclusively by Copts or by Jews and Syrians. The supply of such candidates has long exceeded the demand, both of the Government service and the professional colleges, but the course followed in the Primary and Secondary Schools remains unmodified and vitiated by its original design. It prepares with moderate success for professional occupations, but fails conspicuously to educate for life. . . . We therefore consider it very important that education should be dissociated from examinations qualifying for the public service and that there should be no justification for a presumption that any certificate attained in the schools carries with it a title to

[9] Lloyd, *Egypt since Cromer*, London, Macmillan, 1933, Vol. I, pp. 56-68.

government employment. This presumption, indeed, no longer corresponds with facts, for the number of certificate holders largely exceeds the number that can actually be employed by the State. But it is still cherished by large numbers of Egyptians, and their inevitable disappointment is among the prevailing causes of unrest. . . . We have heard many complaints from young Egyptians and their parents that the Government is breaking faith with them by not giving them employment on the strength of their certificates."

In succeeding decades after 1920 this problem was to increase in severity, and remains unsolved in 1964; for the solution is not, as the above report implies, simply to be firm in turning away graduates who knock on the door of the government, but to create satisfactory alternatives, which is primarily an economic matter.

Even in recent years civil service recruitment, job classification, salary, and promotion have been tightly and systematically geared to academic degree qualifications. Indeed, with the growing tide of university graduates in the country, the bureaucracy in its higher reaches has become more fully staffed with degree holders than its counterpart in many more advanced countries, despite the fact that it pays them as little as $30 a month. Applicants continue to besiege government officers for the obvious reason that many have nowhere else to go. Until recently a large proportion of major business and commercial enterprises in Egypt were owned by foreigners or cosmopolitan-minded minorities who tended to give preference in white-collar employment to their own people, partly because they had the requisite language skills. The rapid construction since 1957 of a state-owned industrial and commercial empire, and the nationalization of all of the larger private enterprises since 1961, will presumably broaden opportunities over the years, but the growth of the university-attending population, which has doubled in less than a decade, has outstripped the rise in opportunities. With about 3.6 university students per thousand of population, Egypt's ratio in 1960-1961 was almost twice that of Great Britain.[10]

---

[10] Admittedly these figures signify less than may appear to be the case, given the number of British students enrolled in technical and professional colleges outside the confines of the universities. In 1960-1961, 111,451 full-time students were enrolled in British universities, or almost 2.1 per thousand of total population. Only about 15,000 of these were students of technology. Outside the universities some 82,350 full-time students were enrolled in higher institutions of technology, commerce, art, etc. (See *Commonwealth Universities Yearbook*, 1963, pp. 894, 901.) It is, however, the enrollment in the non-technological fields of higher education, which in both Britain and Egypt means primarily the universities, that is particularly relevant to the point we wish to make here.

It might appear fortunate for a developing country to possess such a large supply of educated manpower, but such an impression would overlook two essential considerations. One is that the cultural level of most graduates is very low, as many Egyptian university teachers are the first to admit.[11] The other is the fact that about 70 per cent of the university enrollment is in the Faculties of Arts, Law, and Commerce, and for the vast majority of these graduates there is no demand; there is meanwhile a pressing need for scientists, doctors, and engineers, and the 20 per cent enrollment in these fields absorbs the best student talent. The arts, law, and commerce graduates, therefore, constitute a large and rapidly growing group whose skills are largely substandard and unwanted, and whose native talents are mediocre, but whose sights have been trained since childhood on the attainment of a dignified job carrying economic rewards and social prestige. The disappointments are naturally sharp as these thousands of not-so-bright young men in their soiled collars and cheap suits eke out a shabby and insecure but desperately respectable existence on ten pounds a month as minor clerks, bookkeepers, school teachers, and journalists. They are assured from time to time in the press and in the president's speeches that as educated men they are the "vanguard" of the nation's progress, but they are impotent to fashion even their own progress, and they can only listen anxiously to the officially propagated theme of equal and widening opportunities under the new socialist economic development plan which ambitiously pledges to double the national income in ten years.

It is this explosive compound of the high aspirations and self-conscious dignity instilled by university education and the unpromising conditions of the job market that has made university students and graduates a continuing revolutionary force throughout the past half-century in Egypt—as, for that matter, in a half-dozen other Near Eastern countries. At the time of the revolutionary nationalist agitation in Egypt in 1919 led by Saad Zaghlul (appropriately, a former Minister of Education) and his Wafd Party, British residents and officials in Cairo were quick to remark the strength of Zaghlul's appeal to students and young graduates, and the prominence of young lawyers in particular among the nationalist organizers and agitators. The school system and especially Dunlop's record were much criticized as being the ultimate cause of much of the agitation. "The result," wrote one British resident, "has been to produce a large number of

[11] This was the consensus of a panel of university teachers whose discussions were published in *Al-Ahram*, December 25, 1961 to January 2, 1962.

semi-educated youths, imbued with a false sense of their own capacity, and a dangerous veneer of civilization, whose ambition is to enter the already overcrowded professions of the Government service, law, and medicine. These openings are limited to a small proportion, and the remainder, mostly unsuitably trained for agricultural, industrial, or commercial pursuits, swell the ranks of the déclassés."[12]

Throughout the inter-war period and even more in the violent and anarchic years from 1946 to the revolution in 1952, the anomic irruptions of students into the political arena became increasingly familiar, until the new military government imposed their discipline by stationing troops at the gates of the University of Cairo and (more subtly) introducing in 1954 a mid-winter period of examinations to keep student attentions occupied. A number of student demonstrations and strikes were over apparently scholastic questions. In 1938, for instance, students at the rival institutions of Al-Azhar and Dar al-Ulum struck and counterstruck over the question of government appointment of their respective graduates as teachers of Arabic in the public schools. But for the students this was above all a matter of economic security, particularly as the Azharites, being more often than others from poor rural families, had little other prospective source of livelihood on the strength of their traditionalist education.

Politics in Egypt have often tended to intrude into peripheral issues. When in March 1937 a delegation of students appealed to the Rector of Cairo University to introduce religious instruction in the curriculum, the most immediate consequence was a series of bloody clashes among adherents of the rival Wafd, Young Egypt, and "Blue Shirt" parties, in shifting combinations, at Al-Azhar and Cairo Universities.[13] In the years after the war the Moslem Brotherhood attracted a good number of students into its conspiratorial activities; as late as February 1954, at the height of the Nasser-Naguib contest for power, student supporters and members of the Brotherhood demonstrating against Nasser clashed violently with the police. The suppression of the Brotherhood later that year coincided with the end in Egypt of student agitation against established authority. Student political activity is now a tame affair organized in support of the regime through various officially inspired channels such as the Arab Socialist Union, which is the sole and official party. Indeed, students and the

[12] "Report of the Council of Cairo Non-Official British Community to the British Mission of Inquiry," Milner Papers.

[13] See Sylvia Haim, "State and University in Egypt," in Chauncy D. Harris and Max Horkheimer, *Universität und moderne Gesellschaft*, Frankfurt am Main, 1959, pp. 105-107.

younger intelligentsia as a whole are now perhaps among the most reliable enthusiasts of the regime, to which they look to provide them with opportunities for successful careers. But they continue as always to be a revolutionary force, for their enthusiasm rests on their faith in the social and economic revolution that now at last—twelve years after the military coup—appears to be genuinely in progress, and for the present it is they, rather than Egypt's unemployed and illiterate masses of urban laborers and rural fellahin, who constitute the proletariat that Nasser's dictatorship represents.

Whether the regime can justify their faith in the long run depends on the pace and distribution of economic growth; and in a country facing such deep-seated ills as Egypt it is difficult to be optimistic. The future of the legal profession is a characteristic example of the problem. This profession, already said to be overcrowded in 1920, tripled its membership from 1949 to 1958, and since the latter date it has continued to grow.[14] In addition there are still larger numbers of law graduates who do not practice law. The Lawyers' Association has studied a variety of plans for improving the economic welfare of its members. In 1961 it decreed an increase in its pension payments and proposed a plan for sharing out the opportunities as court-appointed counsel in criminal cases, a limitation on the number of companies a single lawyer may represent, and the creation of a fund from which to pay apprentices a wage.[15] Other proposals have been widely circulated for the creation of a lawyers' cooperative which, by charging low rates, could open up a wider clientele, and there are hopes that the newly nationalized economic empire of the state will provide additional jobs for lawyers. But all these measures either are designed simply to redistribute opportunity within the profession or are temporary palliatives. The scheme for apprentice wages drew fire from one leading lawyer on the ground that many present apprentices did not seriously expect to practice law but were simply "waiting for the government bus"—i.e., a job in the bureaucracy—and that the payment of wages to such persons would not only be a waste of money but would attract still more hangers-on to the profession.[16]

The general problems of lawyers are those also of certain other

[14] In 1949 the Lawyers' Association registered 4,433 practicing members; in 1958 it listed 8,098 (of whom 3,831 were still serving apprenticeships) plus approximately 5,000 other enrolled members who were not actively engaged in practice. Meanwhile 13,017 were enrolled at the three law schools in 1955-1956.

[15] Mustafa Baradi'i, President of the Lawyers' Association, in *Al-Ahram*, November 11, 1961.

[16] Hasan al-Basyuni in *Al-Ahram*, November 13, 1961.

professions. Most conspicuous are the accountants, who graduate in comparably large numbers from the Faculties of Commerce of the three universities only to find the profession overcrowded, financially unrewarding, and dominated by a tight circle of inordinately successful persons. To a lesser degree the same was once true of doctors, as it was only in the larger cities and among a limited clientele that a doctor could earn a living, but it now appears that the development of government programs of medical care and public health services is turning the profession into a highly promising one. If the disappointed lawyers, accountants, and arts graduates constitute (on the strength of their anxieties) a revolutionary body of support for the regime, the doctors, engineers, industrial managers, and scientists whose skills are in such high demand have by contrast a vested interest in what the regime is already accomplishing and are hence its conservative supporters.

In a sense the very existence of the problem of underemployed arts and law graduates seems absurdly unnecessary. With jobs scarce, the universities jammed, and the standard of secondary education unsatisfactory, how simple and rational it should have been ten or even twenty years ago to restrict university admission to only a select minority of those who actually were admitted. As early as 1944 the then Dean of the Law Faculty of the University of Cairo, Dr. Ali Badawi, proposed such a limitation, but was overruled. In 1957 President Nasser's Minister of Education, Kamal al-Din Husain, modestly attempted to restrict the acceptance of extension candidates for university degrees, only to have the National Assembly respond by voting to recommend the admission of *all* secondary school graduates to university status. The government managed to resist this proposal successfully; but in 1963 it announced that all secondary graduates were henceforth assured placement in one institution of higher learning or another (though not necessarily a university). A placement office has for some years served as a clearing-house for university admission applications and determines in which faculty, at which university, each applicant may enroll, in accordance with his qualifications, residence, and order of precedence. This process serves to restrict the enrollment in medicine, engineering, and science to superior students in the limited numbers that facilities allow, but it has not been used to curtail enrollment of the overflow in the colleges of arts, law, and commerce. The passively accepted assumption is that in these fields, where tuition fees are very low and nothing tangible is

sacrificed by increasing the attendance at lectures, freedom of opportunity should be the rule. In reality, of course, a great deal is sacrificed, for not only does the quality of education drop, but a serious
social problem is made worse, and thousands of students beginning
their secondary schooling continue to be encouraged to aim for the
universities rather than for the secondary technical education which
would be more useful to themselves and to the economic progress of
the country. Indeed the complaint is made that even many of those
who are turned away from academic secondary schools because of
poor grades and are therefore compelled to attend an industrial trade
school, subsequently go in search of a government office job, and,
failing this, end up as elementary school teachers; from this vantage
point they then demand the right to enter the university as extension
students in order to raise their teaching qualifications and draw a
better salary.[17] Thus all roads lead to Rome.

Military Leadership and the Intellectuals: The Problem of Self-Expression

The army officers who took power in 1952 and have consolidated
their position since that time represent a new class of leadership in
more respects than is indicated by their wearing of uniforms. In fact
the uniform suggests a false continuity: it links them with the count-
less generations of military governors who have usurped civilian
power in Islamic society since the time of the Abbasid Empire,
whereas in truth the present officers are distinctive in the progressive-
ness and rationality of their ideas and the special brand of esprit de
corps furnished them by a common modern military academy education.

They are also to be distinguished from their more immediate civilian predecessors. Their education, unlike that of such civilian nationalists as Mustafa Kamil, Saad Zaghlul, Mustafa Nahhas, and Muhammad Husain Haikal, was technical rather than literary and
legal, and English in model rather than French. Pre-1952 Egyptian politicians were predominantly lawyers who spoke French;
Nasser and his colleagues speak English. Many of the politicians,
especially those of better family, had studied or travelled in Europe;
hardly any of the officers had been anywhere. They lacked social
contact with political leaders before 1952, having had neither the
necessary seniority nor the necessary social antecedents to move in the

[17] Qabbani, op.cit., p. 124.

same circles. Nor did they have much contact with other civilians, as their own military profession naturally tended to isolate them. (The work of doctors, lawyers, engineers, and journalists brings them into contact with all sorts of people; the work of the soldier brings him together only with other soldiers.) These considerations may perhaps help to explain why it was that after the officers seized power they found it difficult to share it with civilians, except as trusted technical experts in diplomacy, economics, and engineering.

The advent of the military junta has posed the rather odd problem that, despite all the publicity directed toward building the self-esteem of college graduates (the "elite," the "future leaders" of the country, etc.), in practice the intelligentsia have no avenue to political power nor even a forum from which to speak frankly. A generation ago the educated class tended to be a distinctive social class, by virtue not only of its culture, but also of its wealth and family connections. Today the great majority of the educated come from humbler origins; they are also relatively younger. Under the constitutional civilian regime before 1952 the educated youth had a certain natural claim to political influence as an elite group, but, being disorganized and inexperienced, they split their energies among a variety of radical groups and movements. Under present conditions the situation is quite different, for those in control of the government represent a distinct group of their own, and implicitly possess a justification of their own right to govern, more clear and convincing than any that a disarrayed group of university graduates could conceivably put forward.

Since it is the officers who are in and the "intellectuals" who are out, it is the latter who face the problem of coping with a loss of self-esteem. Whatever resentments some of them may feel inwardly, they are publicly encouraged to blame themselves: this is the substance of a number of articles that have appeared intermittently in the press on the topic of "The Crisis of the Intellectuals,"[18] and on the reasons for the selection of "trustworthy men" (i.e., officers) rather than "experts" (i.e., civilians) for responsible positions in the government. Journalists and university teachers may debate at great length in the press about the failing of their own class, provided the conclusion is drawn not that the army has monopolized power and deprived intel-

---

[18] See in particular the series by Lutfi al-Khawli and others in *Al-Ahram*, March 12-21, 1961, and that by Muhammad Hasanain Haikal, also in *Al-Ahram*, weekly beginning June 2, 1961.

lectuals of the right to free self-expression, but that the intellectuals had ignominiously abdicated responsibility before and after 1952 and that the army was obliged (reluctantly) to step forward.

Breast-beating has thus become a fixed posture of the intellectual in the public press as he self-consciously discusses the "crisis" of the university, the "crisis" of the free professions, and even the "crisis of the journalistic conscience" under the new socialism, and searches for reasons why it is not his class that has lately stood in the forefront of change. But perhaps it would be more logical to turn the question around and ask, not why the revolution was not led by intellectuals, but rather why anyone should suppose that it should have been. For while true intellectuals—men with a depth of knowledge, insight, and independence of mind—are as few in Egypt as elsewhere, there is no lack of what one would call intelligentsia—people who have been far enough through school and are well up enough on the news to have conventional opinions. But there is no reason to expect the latter group to display unity, foresight, or courage, given their origins and circumstances. They are characterized, as one caustic observer remarks, by an absence of culture.[19] Their education has furnished them with a certain mode of expectations and has steered some of them into positions from which they are accustomed to express themselves such as journalism and teaching, but it has not furnished them with ideas or principles. They are not a cohesive and self-conscious elite. Those among them trained as technical specialists (doctors, engineers, scientists) do form an elite in Egypt today, but not a political one; their ambitions, which are professional, are generally satisfied. The mass of other university graduates, on the other hand, constitute not an elite but an amorphous, unhappy, helpless class. They are relatively more literate but scarcely more cultivated and independent in their thinking than a million other Egyptians who have not been through the university.

The real problem of self-expression is that of the small minority among the non-technical literati who do possess ideas of their own and a desire to engage in honest criticism—the intellectuals. What they suffer from is not exclusion from power, but censorship and the heavy-handed tendency of the regime to regard all intellectual activity as simply another resource to mobilize. It is scarcely encouraging to serious intellectuals for President Nasser, surrounded by white

---

[19] Georges Ketman, "The Egyptian Intelligentsia," in W. Z. Laqueur, *The Middle East in Transition*, London, Routledge and Kegan Paul, 1959, p. 481.

peace doves, little girls scattering roses, and his hard-faced military friends, to tell an assembled "Knowledge Day" gathering at Cairo University that "the new culture which we want is a reflection of the new order. . . . The culture we want is the culture of the people, hostile to imperialism, to political, economic, and social exploitation. . . . The cultural revolution places itself at the service of the political and social revolutions."[20]

What the regime is in fact carrying out is not a "cultural revolution" but what has been called a "communication revolution."[21] By a frontal attack on illiteracy plus the concerted use of mass media for political indoctrination, it has attempted to raise the productive potential of the masses while simultaneously staving off any uncontrollable political consequences of mass social consciousness. There seems no reason for the time being to doubt the practicality of this policy. But the majority of those favored with a higher level of education are still being bought off with promises that are hard to fulfill and with appeals to their emotions, and here lies the foremost potential of disaffection. Never before have so many different classes of Egyptians been drawn into so common a level of political discussion and orientation. But this may prove deceptive. The masses have been drawn in only marginally and passively, as half-comprehending listeners; the integration of those who are better educated into the prevailing modes of nationalist and socialist ideology is tentative, for it has not been anchored by any assured economic role for them to fill. Thus the prospect of creating a stable and well-integrated political culture comes down to the same difficult problem of economic productivity that underlies every major social question in Egypt.

[20] Speech of December 18, 1961. Text and news account in *Al-Ahram*, December 19, 1961.
[21] Daniel Lerner, *The Passing of Traditional Society*, Glencoe, The Free Press, 1958, p. 251.

CHAPTER 7

BRAZIL [1]

FRANK BONILLA

∿∿∿∿∿∿∿∿∿∿∿∿∿∿∿∿∿∿∿∿∿∿∿∿∿∿∿∿∿

THE FAITH of Latin Americans in education as an instrument for the rapid achievement of desired fundamental changes in the social and political order has been no less exaggerated than in other parts of the world. From the beginnings of independence, democracy and education have been linked in political rhetoric, educational doctrine, and the popular symbolism of a free society. In the southern nations of the New World the intellectual preoccupation with problems of national political development predates and in a vital sense runs deeper than the more recent fascination with the processes of industrial growth and economic expansion. Efforts to analyze and explicate chronic political failures have, moreover, always been more distressing emotionally, more menacing and disturbing than similar examinations of economic backwardness. Though the more direct links between political and economic institutional forms have not been overlooked, the roots of economic underdevelopment have been more easily traced to external forces and conditions or to deficiencies of a material or technological variety for which an abundance of plausible remedies were readily conceivable. A nation can live with itself with some dignity despite the knowledge that it is poor, that its industry and agriculture are primitive technologically, or even with the awareness that it is caught in a network of economic relationships that makes the hope of a genuine economic emancipation problematical. But the continued failure to achieve a stable, honest, equitable, and efficient political machinery strikes deeply at the moral sensibilities of Latin Americans. The area's chronic political insolvency questions in a profound way the human capabilities of its people and the social and cultural foundations of regional life.

Much of the discussion of political development problems is thus

[1] The author has for two years worked closely with Kalman H. Silvert of the American Universities Field Staff on a four-country study of the relationships between education and economic and social development. While little direct reference is made in this paper to that research and Professor Silvert is not accountable for the ideas expressed here, this collaboration has sensitized the writer to materials and lines of exploration that might otherwise have been overlooked. This intellectual debt is gratefully acknowledged.

[195]

clouded by the deep insecurities and defensiveness it both elicits and sometimes seeks to anticipate. Nevertheless, there exists a massive literature on these themes—the larger and better part of it of native origin—that attempts to penetrate beyond the surface day-to-day polemics, the scramble for political advantage and power, and to chart in some meaningful way the see-sawing struggle for political and social democracy in Latin America. For it is worth noting that in debating the problems of political development the most broadly accepted canons have been specifically democratic and republican and that the implicit model of democratic government, though aggressively eschewed and attacked on occasion, imperfectly understood, and sometimes idealized out of all proportion, has been the United States.

Thus, though quick to sense disparagement in the writings of outsiders, Latin Americans have not hesitated to undertake conscientious and unsparing self-scrutinies that at times become almost morbid self-indictments. The more visible symptoms of the area's political malaise have been extensively catalogued, tirelessly iterated, and intrude sufficiently into the public consciousness so that a list like the following could be produced by any moderately well-informed individual. One can begin as is most common by noting the excessive personalism of political life without halting for the moment to inquire whether this is indeed another among other external symptoms or a more basic, pattern-setting characteristic. Whatever the case, once that key element is established, much of the rest seems to follow implacably—the extreme concentration of power in the executive arm, the weakness of legislatures and political parties, the corruption and inefficiency of government bureaucracies, the lust for power and tenacity in office of politicians, the consequent leaning toward strong governments provoking violent protest and subversion, the repeated violation of constitutional procedures and the irregular changes in national charters, the denial and abuse of individual rights, particularly of persons in political opposition, the persisting patterns of fraud in elections, the discontinuities in national policy from one government to the next, repeated military interventions in political life, widespread disregard and evasion of the law especially among privileged groups, the pillaging of national treasures and the misuse of government funds and facilities.

These are heavy burdens indeed for a people to bear, and social theorists have advanced many explanations for the capacity of such political behavior to endure and flourish in the presence of a passionate commitment to its eradication. These explanations cover the full gamut of developments in social theory over the last century. Racial arguments of a refined variety—taking into account not only the global Iberian contribution but regional variations within the Iberian peninsula as well as variants in both the African and Indian stocks that constitute the main elements in the Latin American racial mix—have been periodically forwarded. Climate, terrain, topographical barriers to communication and transport, the existence of refractory indigenous communities, the inheritance of semi-feudal forms of social organization that quickly took root in areas readily adapted for profitable exploitation through mono-culturative or mono-extractive enterprises, a gradual but firmly cemented dependence on foreign markets and foreign financial interests, the absence of a middle class, the irresponsibility and rapacity of traditional elites, the incapacity or lack of "civic culture" of the masses—all have been seen as contributing to, when not reflecting, the chronic shortcomings of political institutions.

Brazil has had greater success than her neighbors in evading the more dramatically destructive manifestations of these political ills, though certainly within the republican period since 1889 the grim bill of particulars outlined above is as fully applicable there as elsewhere in the hemisphere. But perhaps because the struggle there has been less bloody, less open, and less organized—more institutional in the sense of not pitting rigidly defined groups of people against each other—theorizing in Brazil about the process of political development and national growth has reached unusual levels of sophistication and has for many years been sensitive to the fundamental importance of social structure and competing institutional loyalties and institutionalized values in this process.

Brazil entered the Republican period after nearly three hundred years of Portuguese domination followed by almost a century of government by monarchs who were moderate but jealous of their prerogatives. Eighty per cent of her people were illiterate and bound in economic relationships that had been only mildly ameliorated by the gradual legal emancipation of the nation's slave population. Still ingenuous prognostications about the quick democratization of the nation through universal public education were proclaimed by the handful of liberal and republican thinkers who gave an intellectual and ideological patina to what was basically a military insurrection.

Now, after some seventy years of Republican government Brazilian education, both public and private, can be said to have made only limited advances. It continues to be attacked as a reactionary, regressive, and stratifying force. As attention has shifted from the quantitative insufficiencies of the system, in themselves staggering, efforts have been turned increasingly toward the study not only of the limiting effects of certain features of the social structure on the capacity of the educational system to stimulate broad changes, but also of complex notions such as that of "school climates" and their effects on the social selectivity, pedagogical efficiency, and value orientations of various types of schools in the country.

Primary Education

In 1920, thirty years after Brazil embarked on the construction of a modern educational system, 75 per cent of the nation was still illiterate. By 1960 the national illiteracy rate was just over 50 per cent but in many rural areas it still hovered around the 80 per cent figure that was the national average in the last days of the empire.[2] The total in-school population was then estimated at about ten per cent of the nation in contrast to the three per cent thought to be in school attendance around 1890. These modest relative gains are small comfort in view of the massive growth of population; the actual number of illiterates and persons with only marginal schooling in Brazil is now a good many millions larger than half a century ago. The number of illiterates in the population over 15 years of age alone increasing from 6,348,869 to 15,272,632 between 1900 and 1950.[3]

The Brazilian primary school has been assailed as anti-democratic, as a system whose intent and function is to select and prepare a small group for advancement to the secondary school. Other critics point to the marked lack of continuity between the primary and secondary

[2] Statistics and other descriptive data on education for Brazil are taken from three chief sources: J. Roberto Moreira, Brasil, Inventário das Necessidades de Educacão Para o Desenvolvimento Socio-Econômico, Rio de Janeiro, Centro Latino Americano de Pesquisas em Ciencias Sociais, 1961; UNESCO, Proyecto Principal de Educación, Boletín Trimestral, Enero-Marzo, 1962; and UNESCO, La Situación Educativa en America Latina, Paris, 1960. For more detailed historical accounts see J. Roberto Moreira, Educacão e Desenvolvimento no Brasil, Rio de Janeiro (Centro Latino Americano de Pesquisas em Ciencias Sociais, 1960, and Manoel Bergstroem Lourenco Filho, "Education" in Lawrence F. Hill, editor, Brazil, Berkeley, University of California Press, 1947.

[3] Anuário Estatístico do Brasil: 1959, Rio de Janeiro, IBGE, Conselho Nacional de Estatística, 1959, p. 24.

school; the primary school, they affirm, neither leads logically into higher levels of schooling nor imparts anything in itself of real value to the students it manages to hold. Current estimates are that half of the youngsters of primary school age (7 to 11 years) never see the inside of a school. Those who enroll average between two and three years of schooling, thus failing to complete even the basic four-year elementary course. Less than ten per cent of those initially entering the school system get beyond the first four years.[4]

The failure of the schools to reach and to hold students reflects not only inadequacies of the system itself, though it is not very realistic to expect high levels of motivation to attend schools that offer so little. The school selects and rejects; it encourages dropouts. The social situation of most students is such as to promote high absenteeism, early school desertion, early frustration and discouragement through incapacity to meet the rigid demands of examinations. The absence of material, moral, and intellectual support from the home is not offset by the provision of such help for those who need it most in the schools. On the contrary, it is where these problems are most grave that the school's deficiencies are most pronounced. It is in the rural areas that there are fewest schools, the greatest proportion of incomplete schools, the most poorly paid and least trained teachers, the greatest shortage of teaching materials, the least adequate provision for helping the student with books and materials, food, clothes, health problems. In addition, the rapid pace of the growth of the cities has overcrowded urban schools almost to the point of eliminating the advantages they may have had over their rural counterparts in the past. Greatly expanded enrollments have been accommodated by increasing the size of classes and shortening the school day to permit two and three daily shifts in the same school plant, thus further weakening an already tenuous school experience.

Though the main guidelines for all education are set in federal law, the states in Brazil have chief responsibility for primary education.[5] About three-fifths of the total primary school enrollment is in state-operated schools, about one-fifth in municipal schools, and another fifth in privately maintained schools, largely Catholic. In 1957 the median annual salary for primary teachers in state schools was

[4] J. Roberto Moreira, *Brasil, Inventário das Necessidades de Educacão Para o Desenvolvimento Socio-Econômico*, p. 8ff.

[5] Law No. 4024, laying down the basic orientation of national education, was passed on Dec. 20, 1961. Some controversial features of that law will be commented on later in this chapter.

$733 (U.S.), in municipal schools $200, and in private schools $452. The salary range in the state schools was from $200 to $1,100 and in some municipalities teacher salaries were as low as $40 and $60 a year.[6] In these isolated and chiefly rural municipalities that remain political fiefdoms, education like all else depends on the whim of the local chieftain. Teacher appointments frequently are made on the basis of the political reliability of the candidate or his family. A recent study of two Amazon municipalities reports that politicians created and closed schools and appointed and dismissed teachers at will. Most of the teachers employed had no training; many were working in schools to which they were not assigned or had been replaced informally by relatives with even less training than themselves.[7] Though directly linked to the pitiable salary scales prevailing, this lack of professional training is also commonplace outside the municipal systems. Of some 200,000 primary school teachers in service in 1960, about 95,000 had no formal teacher training. The normal school for the primary level is widely regarded as an appropriate finishing school for women so that of the nearly 91,000 enrolled in such schools in 1960 only a fraction can be expected to enter the profession. A majority of the normal schools in operation were in fact private and church sponsored, with only 476 out of 1,234 normal schools being run by the states, which have by law major responsibility in this sphere.[8]

The goals of economic expansion and industrialization are currently uppermost in the minds of Brazilian policymakers, though Brazil has been more attentive to the political demands of development than other hemisphere nations. Thus the newly proposed concentrated effort to eliminate illiteracy and to bring all school-age children within the school system for a minimum of four to six years looks chiefly toward the rapid incorporation of the mass of Brazilians into the production and consumption opportunities already enjoyed by those within the developed sectors of the society. Proposed reforms over the next decade, which will concentrate on expanding facilities in cities and the urban periphery and in extending the use of educational radio in rural areas, are expected and intended to have some political consequences as well, though these remain less well

[6] J. Roberto Moreira, *Brasil, Inventário*, pp. 15 ff.

[7] Oracy Nogueira, Klaas Axel Woortmann, Roberto Decio de las Casas, and Sarah de las Casas, *Relatório Preliminar Sobre a Situacão do Ensino em Santarém e Itaituba, Estado do Para*, Santarém, Campanha Nacional de Erradicacão do Analfabetismo, 1959.

[8] J. Roberto Moreira, *Brasil, Inventário*, p. 16.

defined. Brazil is in the paradoxical position of having achieved very substantial economic gains and some more precarious and less easily documented political advances despite the abysmal situation of the machinery for basic education. As a result, the expansion of education is seen in certain quarters not so much as a way of furthering continued economic gain or social or political reforms but as a means of salvaging the national honor, of erasing an unseemly blot on the record of a nation that on most other current indices of national progress scores fairly high.[9] Understandably, in the face of the glaring insufficiencies reflected in the figures that have been quoted, the main remedies continue to appear to lie in the eradication of illiteracy and the imparting of a basic mastery over letters and numbers to as many Brazilians as possible. But, as will be seen, at least some political analysts in Brazil have for a long time taken a much more complex view of political development and the place of education in the process of nation building.

The Secondary Schools

After the four-year primary school, which in some cities includes a fifth year preparatory for secondary school (this may be skipped by passing an entrance examination to the secondary level), Brazilian education branches out into a complex system of specialized institutions covering ordinarily seven years. Here again the final year may be bypassed by surviving another "vestibular" examination to the university school in question. A basic common core of four years with a number of variants within the *ginasio* leads on to the more specialized two, three, and four year courses. Since 1953 all of these courses that cover at least seven years legally qualify the student to compete for entry into a university. Despite the fact that the academic, normal, commercial, and technical courses are by law considered equivalent, secondary school enrollment continues to be heavily concentrated in the academic courses. Of 1,177,427 secondary students in 1960, nearly three-fourths were enrolled in the academic *ginasio* or the classical or scientific courses in the *colegio*, 16 per cent were in commercial courses, eight per cent in teacher training, and two per cent in vocational or technical schools.[10] The secondary school has thus been almost totally unresponsive to the changing manpower

---

[9] Pompeu Accioly Borges, "Graus de Desenvolvimento na América Latina," in *Desenvolvimento & Conjuntura*, Ano V, No. 2, February 1961.
[10] J. Roberto Moreira, *Brasil, Inventário*, p. 43.

needs of the nation; the two per cent of students preparing for occupations in industry are absorbing nearly 30 per cent of the secondary school budget largely because of the low enrollment. The increased enrollment in commercial schools has been attributed more to the fact that these courses are cheaper and less taxing intellectually than to a genuine expansion of professional interest in the field.

The ruthless selective process that begins on the threshold of the primary school proceeds relentlessly to its culmination in the secondary school. Private schools, which constitute only about 12 per cent of the establishments offering primary instruction, account for nearly seven out of ten secondary school units.[11] Thus despite a constitutional provision that all who can demonstrate need will be afforded free secondary and university training, the capacity to pay enters decisively at this juncture. Inevitably the tremendous regional, urban-rural, class, and ethnic inequalities in economic capacity are directly mirrored in the school system. The great proliferation of secondary schools has concentrated in the larger cities and in the more prosperous states. About nine per cent of the young people between 12 and 18 years of age are in the secondary schools; even in the free public schools these are overwhelmingly of upper and middle class origins, only about a fourth coming from working class families. This economic and class selectivity serves to eliminate black Brazilians from the educational process at an early stage. As in the primary schools, enrollment is concentrated in the lower years of the seven-year secondary cycle; only 15 per cent of those who begin secondary schooling complete seven years. By the termination of secondary school the winnowing is almost complete. A majority of the small elite who complete high school manage to go on to a university though not necessarily to the school or in the field of their preference.

The shortage of qualified teachers has disastrous proportions at this level. Only about one in five secondary school teachers meet the legal requirement demanding four years of university training as the basic teaching qualification. The great majority have little more than high school preparation themselves, training of the same shallow quality that they go on to impart to others. Having in view this lack of preparation among staff not only in teaching method but in the subject matters that they subsequently teach with heavy schedules and for extremely low pay, one is less impressed at finding the equivalent of fifth- and sixth-grade children in the United States taking

[11] *Ibid.*, p. 71.

Latin, French, and seven other subjects in addition to their own language. Outside of the few institutions where high standards of excellence are pursued and maintained, such instruction neither expresses nor inspires the broad humanism that its defenders hail as its moving justification. Curricula and teaching plans become more encyclopedic lists of topics, which the instructor covers as best he can, reverting often to some familiar text or timeworn notes of earlier courses. Schooling at the secondary level becomes narrowly utilitarian, compartmentalized, mechanical, dogmatic, and pretentious.

The University

The weakness and disorganization of Brazilian education are most apparent in the universities. Unlike some of the Hispanic countries that have a university tradition extending back to the seventeenth and eighteenth centuries, the first grouping of institutions of higher learning into something that could be called a university did not take place in Brazil until 1937. With the expulsion of the Jesuits in the eighteenth century the gradual evolution of some secondary schools toward a classical university was cut off. Isolated professional schools of law, medicine, engineering, pharmacy, and dentistry were established after independence, but these served only a tiny fraction of the nation. It will be remembered that at the turn of the century, some seventy-five years later, only three per cent of the nation was in schools of any kind. This lack of formalized tradition has some advantages in that it opens an avenue for creative innovation in university organization, which can be observed, for example, in the Universities of São Paulo and Minas Gerais, and most dramatically in the plans for the new University of Brasilia. It has also lent itself to the proliferation of isolated schools or faculties, especially Faculties of Philosophy that train secondary school teachers and that are in many cases only poor extensions of the secondary school with the legal status of universities.

In 1960 there were 418 establishments offering university instruction with an enrollment of 93,202 students and a teaching staff of 21,064 in Brazil. Two hundred and twenty-eight of these were single faculties leaving 190 that are associated in groupings that encompass more than one field of training. Forty-four per cent of the university enrollment is in private institutions, 38 per cent in federally operated universities, and 17 per cent in state universities. The remaining one per cent is in a handful of municipal university centers. A quarter of the total enrollment is in schools of law and another 22 per cent in faculties of philosophy, arts, and sciences. Engineering (12 per cent), medicine (11 per cent), business, dentistry, and other professional schools make up the remainder.

All the defects of the secondary schools are carried over into the university with the additional aggravation that the failure to maintain or attain reasonable standards of scholarship here puts the seal of finality on a terrible hoax. The apparent excess of professors to pupils —there is a teaching staff member for every 4.4 students in Brazil —masks with few exceptions a system of irregular, haphazard, routinized instruction with few contacts between students and the teaching staff outside of those situations in which the fulfillment of some bureaucratic transaction requires such an encounter.

The decades-old movement for reform in the Latin American university has always focused on the government of the university, on the selection and tenure rights of professors as the key to any real improvement.[12] But the drive for genuine student participation in university government has not been as extensive or as successful in Brazil as in some other countries. In June 1962 the National Student Union called a strike of all university students and presented demands for student participation in university councils to a meeting of all the rectors of Brazilian universities. Whatever concessions students are able to pry from university authorities through such actions take time to consolidate and do not guarantee lasting improvements. Student intervention in university affairs does occasionally make for excesses and for a hyper-politicization of academic issues, but professors and university administrators are in a weak position as long as they frequently show even less competence and sense of responsibility than students. Student pressure, it is to be hoped, will continue as long as the university remains a place of privilege and entrenched mediocrity, where a passing acquaintance with a large number of topics is passively absorbed—as long as the feeling persists that education that is more than ornamental must be sought outside the country.

Political Integration and National Development

The fact that an indictment of the educational system as complete as the above can be built exclusively from official Brazilian sources suggests that the situation is not without hope, that there exists a

[12] Gabriel Del Mazo, *La Reforma Universitaria y la Universidad Latinoamericana*, Buenos Aires, Cia. Editora y Distribuidora del Plata, 1957.

FRANK BONILLA

disposition to examine national problems in objective fashion, to face squarely the fundamental value conflicts that divide the society. Clearly the educational system is on the whole not sweeping the country along into momentous changes. It is cementing old forms of stratification, closing opportunities for self-advancement to the growing mass of young people, falling behind in supplying the new manpower needs of the nation, failing to relieve the intellectual and social isolation of the rural and urban masses who are still excluded from any real participation in national life. But all of these statements imply that Brazilian society is moving in new directions, albeit without the support of the educational apparatus. What are the directions of this national development, particularly within the political sphere?

Jacques Lambert made popular the phrase "the two Brasils," contrasting the "archaic," agricultural, familistic, technologically primitive, and hunger-plagued Brazil that exists side by side with the highly industrialized, technologically advanced, and consumption-oriented Brazil of the major cities.[13] This social dualism, affirms Lambert, means not only inevitable conflicts and institutional disharmonies born of internal imbalances in the pace of development. It means that even shared forms of organization—as, for example, representative democracy—will take quite different shapes in the "developed" and the "underdeveloped" sectors of the same society. These polarities of the "traditional" versus the "modern" have been explored in a variety of useful ways in the development literature and a number of paradigms have been advanced of what those societies that are now "emergent" or "in transition" are moving away from and where they are headed. A pressing task now is to move from the contemplation of these polar idealizations and begin to deal with the reality of countries like Brazil that are already complex amalgams of old and new elements, to begin to examine the focal points of contact and tension, change and accommodation, the gradual shifts in value base and institutionalized loyalties, the changing nature and distribution of power.

Brazil has one of the fastest expanding economies in the world. Industrial production in 1961 increased by ten per cent despite an inflation rate of four times that magnitude and despite a year of prolonged political crisis and stalemate. In 1961 Brazil inaugurated a

[13] Jacques Lambert, "Les Obstacles Au Développement Provenant de la Formation d'une Societé Dualiste," in *Resistencias a Mudança*, Rio de Janeiro, Centro Latino Americano de Pesquisas em Ciencias Sociais, 1960.

[205]

new president, Jânio Quadros, who promised and undertook a substantial shift in policy from the previous government. Seven months later President Quadros resigned, claiming that unbearable pressures had been placed on him from abroad and by political extremists of right and left at home. An attempted coup by conservative elements in the armed forces designed to thwart the legal succession of the elected vice-president followed the Quadros resignation. A combination of civil resistance centered in the legislature, the political parties, the state governments, the press, and labor unions, and a political split within the armed forces frustrated the military leaders behind the coup. Armed conflict was avoided and surface legality honored by a compromise parliamentary regime that ostensibly sharply curbed presidential power. The new government falteringly but with increasing confidence undertook to push forward along much the same new lines of policy established in the short-lived preceding regime.

Recurrent crises such as this throw into focus the fundamental political nature of the development process. They reveal the underlying struggle that has to do with political decisions about how the gains and costs of economic development are to be shared within the nation, and with the outside interests allowed to participate. Involved here are questions concerning desired rates and priorities for expansion and norms for the distribution of income. These crises have to do as well with the changing scope, nature, and base of political power centered in the state.

Political development in Brazil can be charted within the framework of a secular struggle between privately and publicly organized power. Brazilian political analysts have carefully examined this process, not only as a surface organized contention between the centralized power and recalcitrant localized and family-based interests, but as a competition between institutionalized systems of social organization.[14] This insight is essential to an assessment of the role of education in political development in Brazil.

[14] Only a handful of the major writers who have most intensively developed this theme can be mentioned here. Alberto Torres, *O Problema Nacional Brasileiro*, São Paulo, Cia. Editora Nacional, 1938, third edition. The first edition of this book appeared in 1914. Oliveira Vianna, *Populações Meridionais do Brasil*, São Paulo, Monteiro K. Lobato & Cia., 1922, second edition; *Instituições Políticas Brasileiras*, Rio de Janeiro, Livraria Jose Olympio Editora, 1949, two volumes. Victor Nunes Leal, *Coronelismo, Enxada, e Voto*, Rio de Janeiro, Revista Forense, S.A., 1948. The account most useful for the argument as developed here is in Nestor Duarte, *A Ordem Privada e a Organização Política Nacional*, São Paulo, Cia. Editora Nacional, 1939.

A permanent symptom of the failure to develop a stable and genuinely effective central political power in Brazil has been "the disparity between the area of social expansion and the area of political effectiveness."[15] The vast territory, larger than the continental United States and at present still peopled by only some sixty millions, swallowed the trickle of colonial population even along the more heavily settled coastal areas. The enormous initial land grants, accompanied by almost unrestricted powers and immunities, transferred to the new nation a system of social organization in which the fusion of family and property in the *latifundio* and the close bonds of family and church created a capacity for local control that the newly forming central administrations could not rival. In Portugal itself the municipal charters of the Middle Ages were in effect concessions to the rights of local *families*, individually bargained for, and within which only heads of families won political rights. Within the process of national consolidation and the rapid expansion of empire, the Portuguese remained more a private individual than a political person or citizen: ". . . the Portuguese remains impenetrable to the State because he is above all organized in groups that are anterior to or run counter to the meaning of the state, such as the familial or religious, in order perhaps to better protect and conceal his anarchic individualism. . . . Christianity distinguished private virtues from public virtues, demeaning the latter and elevating the former, and placed God, the family, the human person above the nation, above the citizen."[16] In Brazil as in Portugal the political power early assumed by the family and the church, together or separately, was absorbed into the private sphere.

The slow penetration of the Brazilian hinterland was not a process of conquest for the crown or a consolidation of state power, but a new form of private and church activity. The *bandeiras*, at first raiding parties in the quest for slaves and later in the search for mineral wealth, were private armed bands in the service of individuals and often refused military service to the crown. This tradition of armed violence continues to pose a problem in rural areas. "The *bandeira*," says Oliveira Vianna, "was a fragment of the *latifundio*."[17] In the interior there are few cities and little of note architecturally except the

[15] Nestor Duarte, *op.cit.*, p. 96.

[16] *Ibid.*, p. 16. Duarte notes that the trend toward totalitarianism or fascism in these situations reflects an effort to build national power on the same basis that the family and church build power.

[17] Oliveira Vianna, *Populacões Meridionais do Brasil*.

churches in the mining towns of the colonial era. The presence of the central government is barely evident. "The Church was capable of penetrating more deeply into the colonial territory and into the hearts of the people than the Portuguese state."[18] The family and the church were the basic associative elements absorbing all loyalties and impeding the formation of any broader political notions of community.

Conditions in Brazil were thus propitious for a throwback to a familistic society that, given the enormous territory, the political weakness of the central government, and the rapid establishment of a slave-based plantation economy, could flourish even more successfully in the new setting than in Portugal. Brazil knew no real revolutions because local power and control was never really contested. The crown yielded or accommodated itself to the power rooted in the "big house" of the plantations; the republic and the political parties have done the same with the rural "colonels," who in many areas continue to resist the slow process by which political loyalties are gradually being pried loose from the narrow local identifications and controls. This is not a simple battle between centralists and defenders of state or municipal rights. The municipality in Brazil has never been a democratic force standing between an overweening central power and the impotent citizen. The *latifundio* and the family-based plantation economy absorbed and controlled not only the mass of slaves and servants but whatever fragments of a free society grew up around it and in the small towns.

The modern survivals of *coronelismo* are not identical with traditional forms of patriarchalism. They are a compromise between the weakened private power of the landowners and the weakly consolidated power of national governments and political parties. The colonel guarantees the vote of his local clientele in exchange for local freedom of action. Municipal autonomy has not been a big issue because the local group in power has always had free rein as long as it has been in accord with the state governments. The policy of weakening the *municipios* to circumvent local oligarchs merely put in the hands of the state governments and the political parties the choice of which oligarchs would run which municipalities. Political development in Brazil, both in the rural areas and even in the cities, has fundamentally to do with the breaking up of the varied adaptations of patriarchalism to representative democracy—with a process of political differentiation in which political values and loyalties are slowly

[18] Nestor Duarte, *op.cit.*, p. 101.

lifted from patterns rooted in familial relationships and expanded to a broader communal and national identification, and to the rational and instrumental treatment of political decisions that a major power like Brazil requires of its citizens.

"In a history in which everything went against the state, favoring on the contrary the victory and revival of other groups and principles of command and organization, the political institution, in addition to having only a precarious objective projection since it did not extend into the centers of force and discipline in the community, nor to its habits and customs, lost likewise its power of reaching into the spirit of that community, and was unable to imprint upon it a clear, unequivocal, differentiated public sense.

"It is under this criterion, in the light of its own history, that Brazil is a new nation in that it has yet to complete its process of political differentiation. It is an old people living under an old order insofar as it persists in preserving and remembering the spirit and form of preexisting structures which history itself guards and transmits to contemporary reality."[19]

Political Behavior and Political Culture

Contemporary analyses of the process of national growth in Brazil depart from the assumption that there have been very substantial changes in the extent to which the mass of Brazilians have internalized a new sense of national identification, thus expanding the capacity of the nation to mobilize along new political lines in behalf of freshly defined economic goals and political objectives in the international sphere. Current nationalist theorizing, much of it from a fairly unique Brazilian institution, the Instituto Superior de Estudos Brasileiros (ISEB), postulates a continuing *tomada de consciencia*, or mass awakening to nationhood, which allegedly received its first major impulse from the 1930 Vargas revolution and has accelerated sharply in the years since World War II.[20] In this view it is this *tomada de*

---

[19] *Ibid.*, pp. 230-231. Summarizing his own studies of the political psychology and behavior of south central Brazilians, whom he regarded as the most advanced group in the country, Oliveira Vianna, writing around the time of World War I, reported: "I studied their consciousness of the nation-state, their feelings about the interests of the national collectivity—and I recognized that as a social group, as a people in the mass, they lacked a democratic sense of the nation. Psychologically considered this sense was moreover extremely tenuous in the spirits of these south central Brazilians. It was only an idea, with a low emotional coefficient, and therefore, with little determining or coercive force." (*Instituicões Políticas Brasileiras*, p. 322.)

[20] An extended analysis of the work of ISEB is given in Frank Bonilla, "A National Ideology for Development: Brazil," in Kalman H. Silvert, ed., *Expectant Peoples*, New York, Random House, 1963.

consciencia that makes national development the logical and necessary cornerstone and objective of present policy. The qualitative change in individual political awareness and commitment revitalizes the nation, making it now an active agent rather than a mere object of history, and helping to break the bonds of economic and political dependence on other nations. The man in the street not only acquires the idea of the nation and the possibilities of national development; he is himself *possessed* by these ideas.[21]

The fact is that very little can be said and supported with solid knowledge about the basic political orientations of Brazilians in the mass. The large numbers disfranchised through illiteracy, the persisting and profound social and regional inequalities in income and living standards, the continuing isolation from national life of the rural masses and the marginal slum populations in major cities—all throw into question the extent and effective impact of this alleged collective *tomada de consciencia*.

Some recent research seeking to test a particular theoretical formulation of the nature of national identification studied three groups in Brazil: managers of industrial enterprises, skilled workers, and urban slum dwellers or *favelados*. The desire was to contrast in Brazil two groups intimately involved in the nation's rapid industrial advance and a third group similar in social origins to the skilled workers but still marginal to industrial development.[22] Different groups were studied in Argentina, Chile, and Mexico. For preliminary analysis a rough four-item index of "national identification" or "loyalty and confidence in the system" was constructed. The items included one indicator of support for the state as arbiter of conflict in an area where a strong competing authority, the church, claims primacy; indicators of the disposition to accept the right of the state to impose certain social obligations or controls on occupation roles and the economy; and a final item testing whether acceptance of state power is rational or pragmatic rather than "patriotic."

The managers scored significantly higher than both *favelados* and skilled workers on this index, the pattern of response among workers being close to that of *favelados*. This was true despite the fact that the skilled workers were in terms of subjective class identifications, values related to the sphere of work, and personal development val-

[21] Alvaro Vieira Pinto, *Ideologia e Desenvolvimento Nacional*, Rio de Janeiro, Instituto Superior de Estudos Brasileiros, 1960.

[22] K. H. Silvert and Frank Bonilla, *Education and the Social Meaning of Development: A Preliminary Statement*, New York, American Universities Field Staff, 1961.

ues much closer to the managers than to the *favelados* to whom skilled workers were closer in origins and objective social situation. The broad differences in a variety of attitudes and values observed among skilled workers and *favelados* was not matched by a significant shift of orientations toward the central political mechanism. Moreover, political activity among all groups sampled in Brazil was very low. Managers differed from others primarily in how much they talked about politics rather than in their participation in party life as such. In fact, *favelados* were somewhat more likely to have worked recently for a party or a candidate than were skilled workers or managers. The political activity of the two latter groups was apparently almost entirely confined to interest groups (unions and trade and professional associations) rather than parties. There is little substance offered here for the hope that political reform, stability, and responsible participation will grow naturally through the simple expansion of the industrial occupational sector.

Some additional evidence suggests that it is the expansive capacity of the economy and the presumed openness of the social system rather than a sense of political efficacy or confidence in the machinery of state that give many Brazilians a sense of commitment.[23] Favela dwellers were asked whether they believed in the sincerity of the desire of various outsiders (including the president of the nation, the state governor, the military, journalists, labor unions, etc.) to help solve the problems of *favelados*. The response was on the whole overwhelmingly negative. Large numbers of *favelados* and skilled workers, moreover, have little faith in the potential benefits of political action. Nearly half of the *favelados* affirmed that there is nothing to be gained from political activity; about the same proportion of skilled workers said they attach little or no importance to their political opinions and activities. Still the workers, who have moved into the nation's new industrial elite, almost unanimously believe that high status occupations in almost every field are open to any capable person in Brazil.[24] A majority of *favelado* men similarly believe that the way up is not barred to their children, especially in business and

[23] Frank Bonilla, *Rio's Favelas: The Rural Slum within the City*, American Universities Field Staff Report, Vol. VIII, No. 3, East Coast South America Series, 1961.

[24] The major conclusions of the most intensive study of social mobility in Brazil are the following. "First, industrial development did not produce a dissolution of class barriers as had been anticipated. Second, the greater access to the educational system did not produce an increase in social mobility." (Bertram Hutchinson, *Mobilidade e Trabalho*, Rio de Janeiro, Centro Brasileiro de Pesquisas Educacionais, 1960, p. 229.)

government service. Though few of the *favelados* questioned felt that their own situation had improved in the last five years, most said that the growth of industry in the country is benefitting people like themselves. Among these deprived and newly mobile social groups political apathy, inaction, and cynicism seems balanced by the belief that the society offers hope of advance for them and their children.

A survey of congressional and public opinion conducted independently at about the same time as the above research offers some confirmatory data. Summarizing his findings on "popular discontent" based on national cross-sections of opinion, the author, Lloyd A. Free states: "In a basic way, however, the general picture in terms of popular protest or revolt is encouraging from the point of view of the political stability of the Brazilian nation. The people, both urban and rural, appear not to be overly frustrated at this stage, despite their very real problems in connection with standard of living. They have some sense of progress over the past five years, both personal and national. They are highly optimistic both about their own personal future and the nation's future. They appear to have confidence in the existing system and way of life." On the prospects for development, Free remarks: "Our data show a strong desire for economic and social development among Brazilians generally and a fairly extensive awareness of the potentialities for an improved living standard presented by the technological age. Brazilians are psychologically ready for basic economic progress. Our survey also provides evidence of willingness in Congressional and normally conservative circles to adopt 'liberal' approaches, such as land reform, to accomplish such development."[25]

These remarks point to two important components in the political picture in Brazil. The first is hope, the continuing faith that the nation's expanding wealth will be shared to some degree by most Brazilians, that economic progress will push forward even if these gains can be won only in the dead of night "while the politicians sleep." The second is the generalized feeling that there is still room for the transaction of existing conflicts and inequalities. A great deal has been written about the Brazilian "genius for compromise," the national capacity for conciliation and accommodation that is reflected in the relatively peaceful evolution of the nation and that was pre-

[25] Lloyd A. Free, *Some International Implications of the Political Psychology of Brazilians*, Princeton, N.J., The Institute for International Social Research, 1961, pp. 74-75.

sumably in part inherited from the Portuguese. While the true foundations, consequences, and the very reality of such broad attributes of national character are extremely difficult to document, few visitors to Brazil who are familiar with other countries in Latin America fail to remark this basic difference in the political climate.

". . . few persons who know Brazil will deny that the forms of domination elaborated by the groups who have traditionally held power here and in large part continue to do so have been singularly effective in mitigating violent social conflict. . . . In no other country in Latin America do such staggering inequalities (material, social, political, racial, and regional) seem so little productive of individual tensions and resentments or of intransigent, regimented collective strife. This cannot be explained simply as mass apathy or fatalism, or as the incapacity of the exploited to mobilize themselves for the defense of group interests. All of these are factors in the avoidance up to the present of more violent internal conflict, but the nation is not inert politically. The country is now in fact in the grips of a great political struggle in which popular groups (*o povo*) are more than passive or docile spectators. There is nevertheless an almost exasperating blandness underlying the public façade of combativity affected by politicians and a bewildering lack of rational connections among apparent interests, organized political groups, and points of view espoused. The disposition to yield among groups at the top, though not extravagant, seems often more than apparent pressures from below would reasonably demand just as the disposition to accept small concessions among lower groups seems often out of line with the urgency of their need or their apparent power at given moments. In short, there is an element of civility, a capacity and a disposition to work out dispute peaceably in Brazilian political life that one would hardly expect to find in conjunction with such harsh inequities, the generally low cultural level, the sad record of corrupt and irresponsible government, and the vulnerability and rudimentary organization of political institutions."[26]

Danger signs that this kind of social entente may be crumbling, particularly in the rural areas, can be seen in all regions of the country though they are concentrated in the famine-ridden northeast. Rural leagues and workers associations led by both priests and poli-

[26] Frank Bonilla, *Rural Reform in Brazil: Diminishing Prospects for a Democratic Solution,* American Universities Field Staff Report, Vol. VIII, No. 4, 1961, East Coast South America Series, pp. 2-3.

ticians have begun to make stronger demands and to meet violence with violence. Control of the rural areas by the two major parties, the Partido Social Democrático (PSD) and the União Democrática Nacional (UDN) is being challenged by the Partido Trabalhista Brasileiro (PTB), which has a stronger representation of town-based shopkeepers and workers in rural *municipios*.[27] The multiplication of candidacies and tickets as the town vote in rural areas becomes more independent is a further sign of the beginning breakdown of the unitary control until recently exercised by local chieftains.[28]

But the multiplication of parties, the elimination of the grosser forms of electoral fraud, and the emergence in the towns and cities of a mass vote that is not easily manipulable does not mean that older forms of political allegiance and action have disappeared. The PSD and the UDN, which are much alike in social composition, represented initially a split in the traditional ruling elite into pro-Vargas and anti-Vargas forces. The PTB is an urban-based, popular voting force also organized under Getulio Vargas, who as a moderate dictator ruled Brazil from 1930 to 1945 and who continues to cast a shadow over Brazilian politics since his death by suicide in 1954. No clear ideological distinctions can be made among these parties, the men who lead them, or the policies they incorporate into platforms or attempt to follow when in office. In the absence of more than momentarily crystallized connections among parties, personalities, and principles, the vote in Brazil remains an intensely personal exercise. It has been affirmed that for many electors the vote is not a political act, but a personal gift, bestowed on the candidate in much the same way that the rural worker gives a basket of oranges or a stalk of bananas to the local landlord. This pervading personalism can also be seen in the proliferation of parties, the instability of the party vote from one election to the next, the impunity with which major figures cross party lines. Around the time of the 1960 presidential election a newspaper poll asked a sample of Rio voters what they would do in a situation in which the best candidate was being backed by the worst party and the

[27] In elections since 1945, when national parties made their appearance in Brazil, these three parties have accounted for about 75 per cent of the national vote. Fifty-eight of the 62 senators and 251 of the 326 deputies in the legislature elected in 1958 came from these three parties. The nine other parties with representation in the legislature are chiefly of local importance and are concentrated in the larger cities (São Paulo, Rio de Janeiro, Recife) where there is a large enough vote to sustain a multiplicity of parties.

[28] Orlando M. Carvalho, *Ensaios de Sociologia Eleitoral,* Belo Horizonte, Universidade de Minas Gerais, 1958.

best party was supporting the poorest candidate. Seventy-seven per cent said they would take their chances with the best candidate rather than with the best party.[29]

Of the fifteen and a half million Brazilians who were eligible to vote in 1960 about ninety per cent went to the polls (the vote is obligatory for all Brazilians 18 years of age and over who are able to write their name). The campaign was long and arduously contested, the vote free, the tally fair, and the result remarkably decisive in view of the baffling barrage of contradictory stimuli to which the electorate had been subjected. But the clarity of the vote was not indicative of sure knowledge as to the candidate's intention. There was real suspense among the best-informed Brazilians as to any concrete measure the new president might take until he went into action. In Brazil, the candidate reveals himself in office; the electorate is asked to express faith in the man and not in a set of policies to which the candidate binds himself.[30]

The security of the candidate depends not only on the successful courting of the popular vote, but also in more complex and less visible ways on support from the church and the armed forces. No full-scale study exists of the ramifications and extensions of church power into secular affairs in Brazil nor of the exact ways in which religious and civil powers mesh, balance, and conflict. Without doubt the church holds a firmly consolidated position within the present framework of power. In a country with such an overwhelming majority sharing a particular faith, it is perhaps inevitable that there be many informal links between religious and governmental authorities. Substantial amounts of federal, state, and muncipal funds destined for education, health, and other social welfare services are administered through the church and religious organizations. No important legislative or executive policy decision is made without consultation with the prelacy, and these soundings of opinion are often made publicly. Though when opinion is sharply divided it is almost always possible for every major faction to find some religious authority to endorse its viewpoint, the fact remains that the church's sanction is seen

[29] *Côrreio da Manhã*, Rio de Janeiro, September 23, 1960.
[30] These difficulties are compounded in legislative elections by the system of proportional representation and the fact that there is no legislative districting within states. In the 1962 election there were 1,274 candidates to the Senate, Chamber of Deputies, and the State Assembly in Guanabara state alone. Guanabara is the former federal district. *Boletim Informativo*, Washington, D.C., Embaixada do Brasil, No. 90, May 25, 1962.

as highly useful if not indispensable in enlisting the support of an important sector of the public for governmental policy. Though the church generally refrains from openly supporting specific candidates or parties in electoral contests, few candidates fail to make a well-publicized appearance at some religious ceremony during the campaign, and "independent" but religiously identified organizations for "screening" candidates seldom fail to appear. In the political crisis of August 1961, the forthright appeal of prelates for respect of the constitution and the legal succession was generally acknowledged as one of the keys to the peaceful compromise that allowed João Goulart to take the presidency over military opposition.[31]

Similarly, one of the questions routinely raised about a candidate to national office is whether he has *cobertura militar*, or adequate backing among the military. However, only when military intervention becomes as flagrant as in the move to impede the succession of João Goulart in 1961 does one get any concrete notion of what the military *do* in a political way. Except in moments of crisis, all such activity is shrouded in a circumspect rhetoric that seeks to justify the discreet tuition over the nation's affairs that military men regard as their prerogative since they forced the abdication of the emperor and gave republican government to Brazil. The military, we are told, act only to protect the national interest and security, the inviolability of the constitution, and the preservation of democratic institutions.

The military and the church lay claim, in part justifiably, to being the only genuinely national institutions. The military feel they are the only major power factor that is not bound by narrow regional or personal interests and ambitions, that they alone see problems on a national scale and have an overriding commitment to the nation. Only the soldier, they contend, knows every corner of Brazil well enough to have any real idea of what the nation means. The church similarly feels itself the receptacle and instrument of a moral and spiritual unity that binds Brazilians together in ways that political loyalties have never matched. To the extent that this kind of rationalization has some foundation, the church and the military are seeking in different ways to fill existing weaknesses in the central politi-

---

[31] Frank Bonilla, *A Franciscan Bishopric in the Amazon: Some Contemporary Problems of Brazilian Catholicism*, American Universities Field Staff Report, Vol. VIII, No. 5, 1961, East Coast South America Series. In early June 1962, Cardinal Jaime de Barros Camara announced in Rio de Janeiro the formation of a "family electoral alliance" to protect the voter in Guanabara State from political deception. *Boletim Informativo*, Washington, D.C., Embaixada do Brasil, No. 95, June 1, 1962.

cal institution: the simple absence of the central government as a physical presence in large areas of the nation, the absence of an effective civil and secular mechanism for aggregating and articulating interests on a national scale, the absence of a firmly internalized commitment to and confidence in the central political machinery as an instrument for rational and equitable government.

Part of the importance of the work of the Instituto Superior de Estudos Brasileiros mentioned earlier in these pages has been its concern about the non-ideological, unplanned aspects of national growth and their connections with nationalistic policies of development. These thinkers have thus been much less concerned about the building of a specifically nationalist political party or organization than with the "rehabilitation" of the state. This means not only the elimination of corruption and inefficiency from government but a genuine democratization of the political system, the creation of a new confidence in public power, the generation at all social levels of a new kind of political loyalty centered on the state and capable of transcending class and sector interests.

Education and Political Socialization

Up to the present, then, the educational system in Brazil has been only tangentially an active agent, reflecting in only a limited fashion, among a small number of educators and model institutions, the dynamism that characterizes other sectors of Brazilian society. The school system is neither national nor democratic nor genuinely educational. The overwhelming backlog of the totally unschooled and functionally illiterate and the educational demand accumulating in a rapidly growing and youthful population tax resources to a degree that restricts efforts within a compass that thoughtful educators and even many political leaders clearly see as inadequate. The primary education system, especially in rural areas, increasingly functions as little more than a massive and superficial literacy campaign. And though literacy is basic to the exercise of the vote in Brazil, it does not lead directly to the kinds of political sentiments, skills, and behaviors envisioned in national educational legislation and programs. No one really knows the kind of training required for democratic citizenship within the sharply contrasting contexts of Brazilian society, nor can the nation wait for the research to be carried out that might give some guidance in this area. But clearly education by itself cannot break the stranglehold of political traditionalism and its contemporary variants on the Brazilian countryside. This would be a formidable task even if the rural schools were capable of undertaking on an effective scale some systematic training for citizenship. But as late as 1961 the Ministry of Education was campaigning for private support to equip for the first time thousands of primary schools with a national flag and pamphlets containing the words to the national anthem. The school is least accessible, most transitory as a life experience, and most out of touch with national reality where the social milieu is most refractory. "For the political education of the people," wrote Oliveira Vianna nearly half a century ago, "there is only one efficient school—the school of custom, tradition, use and social institutions . . . now that school of custom and tradition was always lacking for our rural population."[32] Many of those presently resisting proposed agrarian reforms insist that education is a prior need to any changes in land tenure patterns or attempts to raise technological levels and productivity in farm areas. But few situations make clearer how ineffectual is any piecemeal approach to social reform. Literacy training and the minimum job of social promotion into national life that the primary school can undertake in rural areas will remain politically ineffective until they become part of a generalized restructuring of social relationships.

The equally class-bound and class-binding nature of secondary and higher education in Brazil is fixed by its extreme selectivity and the large proportion of private institutions at this level. Recent estimates of class distribution in Brazil place some 26 per cent in the middle class and about 4 per cent in the upper class. The 26 per cent middle class is divided into 2 per cent upper middle, 6 per cent middle-middle, and 18 per cent lower middle. Calculations based on the assumption that all children of upper and upper middle class families are enrolled in secondary schools lead to the surmisal that all but 33 per cent of those in secondary schools come from the uppermost social levels and that practically all the enrollment from lower levels is in agricultural, commercial, and industrial or vocational schools.[33] It is useful to know as some recent psychological research suggests that the story completions of some seventh-grade Brazilians are more like those of children in less dominating or democratic cultures than like those of children in authoritarian cultures.[34] But it becomes almost a

[32] Oliveira Vianna, *Instituições Políticas Brasileiras*, p. 327.

[33] J. Roberto Moreira, *Brasil, Inventário*, p. 46.

[34] Harold H. Anderson and Gladys L. Anderson, *Social Values of Teachers in Rio de Janeiro, Mexico City, and Los Angeles County, California; A Comparative Study*

matter of indifference whether the social relationships *within* the school at this level, where a high degree of social homogeneity is achieved not only in the student body but in the school as a whole, are democratic or conducive to freedom and creativity. In terms of national or social integration the secondary school is anti-national and a promoter of class division by its very exclusivism. Other research documents the class-centered rigidities, the paternalism, and bureaucratic nature of relationships between teachers, school administrators, and pupils and their parents in metropolitan primary schools.[35]

The widely shared sense of national expansion and the belief in a partly spurious "openness" in Brazilian society stem from a genuine growth in the actual numbers of those in middle class sectors, which makes without question for a qualitative change in the society. But the school continues to function primarily as a certifier of status rather than as a real channel of mobility and provides little opportunity for experiences that support increased understanding and solidarity across class lines.

The bleak situation of Brazilian education is not just a historical accident, the simple outcome of the indifference or incapacity of national and local governments. It is the object of a hard-fought struggle to which the mass of Brazilians has only partially awakened but is increasingly alerted. The bitter public and legislative controversy over a basic educational law (A Lei de Diretrizes e Bases), which dragged on over more than a decade until late 1961 and has yet to find a definitive resolution, threw into the open the complex class, religious, material, and political interests pitted against each other. The present law established that private schools receiving government funds are obliged to provide scholarships to needy students in amounts corresponding to those received as subsidies. It further stipulates that no government financial assistance shall be given to any institution that refuses enrollment to a student because of race, color, or social condition. These legal safeguards, like other legalistic solutions to grave social problems, serve to mask more fundamental cleavages. The basic issue remains—who is to define national educational policy, who is to supervise and administer national education? To an important extent this has become a raw political struggle be-

---

of Teachers and Children, paper presented before the American Educational Research Association, Atlantic City, New Jersey, February 1962.

[35] Luiz Pereira, *A Escola Numa Area Metropolitana*, São Paulo, University of São Paulo, Faculty of Philosophy, Science and Letters, 1960.

tween the small but powerful number who do not need state education, who are impatient with its shortcomings, who do not trust secular control of educational institutions, or who can profit from the continued expansion of private education against the mass who have little hope of breaking into national life without good, free schools.[36]

The extent to which education has itself become a prime value for people of all social levels in Brazil and in all Latin America is not to be underestimated. The four-country study mentioned earlier touched a dozen distinct groups ranging from the highest to the lowest status levels. The right to a free education was uniformly ranked as first or second in importance along with equality before the law among citizen rights including a minimum wage, access to social services, and an effective voice in politics. Equal unanimity appears to exist about the obligation of the state to provide free university education to all capable persons.[37]

The political dangers of a "proletarization of the intellectuals" or an "intellectualization of the proletariat" are increasingly pointed to in developing countries as a possible outcome of an expansion of education that outpaces economic growth and opportunities for remunerative work and social betterment. Despite serious imbalances in the training offered by the universities and lower level schools as against the present and anticipated manpower needs in Brazil, the nation is not in the immediate future threatened by an educational surplus of this kind. But even if it were, the implication that future political unrest can be avoided in Brazil or elsewhere by withholding or "rationing" education is not only inhumane but unrealistic. It would be the greatest folly to imagine that the tensions of persisting inequities and newly awakened aspirations can be avoided under present conditions by this kind of intellectual blindfolding. Insofar as the nation is committed to pursuing democratic solutions to existing problems, only a new kind of organic political unity can see Brazil through the successive crises of growth it will continue to face. Education cannot create that unity by itself and is clearly making a weak contribution at present toward its achievement. But the cause of political development will not be advanced by setting out to disarm a generation politically. National integration and political stability cannot be won within a democratic framework by sealing off potentially

[36] Roque Spencer Maciel de Barros, editor, *Diretrizes e Bases da Educacão Nacional*, São Paulo, Libraria Pioneira Editora, 1960.
[37] K. H. Silvert and Frank Bonilla, *op.cit.*, p. 158.

disturbing elements from the political arena but only by forging new and meaningful loyalties and identifications among all in the nation. The effort must be made to unravel within the complexity of over-lapping and competing sources of desired normative change those that have their natural place and chief strength within the educational system.

Part II:

Patterns of

Polity-Directed Educational Development

INTRODUCTION TO PART I

JAMES S. COLEMAN

~·~·~·~·~·~·~·~·~·~·~·~·~·~·~·~·~·~·~

THE relationship between the political and the educ
in the modernization of the Soviet Union, Japan, and ᴛʜᴇ Philippines
presents a striking contrast to the variant patterns discussed in Part I.
First, these countries are educationally far more "developed," according to the statistical indices usually employed to measure such development, than the countries discussed in Part I. The difference is
clearly brought out by the figures in Table 1. Second, in the Soviet

TABLE 1: RELATIVE WORLD RANK[a] OF SELECTED COUNTRIES
IN INDICES OF EDUCATIONAL DEVELOPMENT

Country	Literacy	Primary School Enrollment	Post-Primary School Enrollment
Japan	17	34	5
USSR	25	20	11
Philippines	49	37.5	16
Brazil	59	68.5	56
Egypt	79	81	33
Tunisia	97	91.5	59
Indonesia	90	66.5	79
Nigeria	104	100	114

[a] Total countries ranked was 136.
Source: Norton Ginsburg, *Atlas of Economic Development,* Chicago, University of
Chicago Press, 1962, pp. 38, 42, 44.

Union, Japan, and the Philippines, the educational system has been
consciously used for a generation or more as an agency for political
socialization, to build a national political culture congruent with and
supportive of existing political institutions. Finally, these countries,
despite their extensive educational development, have been able to
contain or avoid the politically destabilizing consequences of an unemployed educated class. These similarities are the rationale for
grouping these three countries together, although their patterns of
historical development have otherwise been markedly different.

These three countries have a high degree of educational development principally because, from the very beginning of the process of
deliberate modernization launched by their respective elites (the Communist Party elite in the Soviet Union in the early 1920's, the Samurai

..ng class in Japan in the early 1870's, and American colonial
..ialdom in the Philippines at the turn of the century), mass education, with an explicitly political or civic content, has been regarded as an
indispensable precondition for modern nationhood. This strong instrumental commitment to education by a Russian Communist, a Japanese feudal, and an American colonial oligarchy, operating under
very different political assumptions and values, is brought out vividly
in the chapters by Azrael, Passin, and Landé. The comparatively
high-ranking position each country holds on the world's educational
ladder is the end product of this very early and continuous emphasis
upon educational development, considered both as a proper function
of government and as a requisite of a modern nation.

National unification, civic loyalty, and a technically competent,
"enlightened," and allegiant population were common educational
objectives in the Soviet Union, Japan, and the Philippines. In the pursuit of these objectives, however, the educational system has been
used by the polity in quite different ways. The Soviet Union has built
up a single monolithic educational system under omnipresent party
control with heavy inputs of political indoctrination at all levels. In
Japan the pattern has been dualistic, embracing political indoctrination of the mass of the population at the lower elementary levels, and
academic freedom, without polity-directed indoctrination, in the institutions of higher learning. This ingenious dual system, described by
Passin, was a product of the famous Mori reform of 1885. In the
Philippines, although the educational system has from the beginning
been under strong central control, a markedly different concept of
political education has prevailed.[1] Following the American pattern,
it has been aimed, Landé notes, at fostering "a faith in and a desire
for democracy . . . [and] habits of citizenship appropriate to such a
form of government." Citizenship training at the lower levels was a
significant component in the curriculum. At higher levels political
institutions and practices were studied objectively and comparatively,
in the tradition of free universities in the Western world.

These three case studies not only illuminate the variant patterns of

---

[1] As used here, "political education" is a generic concept subsuming at least two
very different processes: (a) "political indoctrination" in a specific political ideology
intended to rationalize and legitimate a particular regime, and (b) "civic training"
in the nature and functioning of one's own polity and in how a good citizen participates
in it. Political education in the schools of most societies characteristically includes both
components. The difference among societies is in the emphasis given to each component. In Soviet schools, for example, it is preponderantly indoctrination; in American
schools, the emphasis is primarily, but not exclusively, upon civic training.

political education; they also bring out some of the key issues we confront in evaluating the effectiveness or the significance of manifest socialization in the schools. The Soviet experience described by Azrael, for example, suggests that formalistic and authoritarian instruction in the classroom is not necessarily the most effective means of political indoctrination. In the Philippines, one feels, actual popular participation in formal democratic institutions has been a far more decisive factor than teaching about democracy. Regarding Japan, one wonders whether the effectiveness of thoroughgoing indoctrination in the elementary schools has been owing to curriculum content, to the authoritarian teacher-student relationship in the classroom, or to the strong hierarchical element in the Japanese family pattern. Or has it been owing to the reinforcing congruence among all the socializing agencies—curriculum, school environment, and family, as well as other institutions, such as the army? If the latter factor is responsible, then the drastic changes since the end of World War II in all these spheres will no doubt alter the cumulative character of these influences.

The experiences of these three countries demonstrate convincingly that educational systems can be powerful instruments in forging national unity, in developing a common language of political communication, and in providing exposure to, if not inculcating a positive affect for, national symbols and goals. Both Azrael and Passin, however, query the effectiveness of an educational system for the inculcation of total conformity and of uncritical loyalty to a regime. Boredom, political passivity, and positive disaffection are just as likely to be the result of explicit politicization as is unquestioning loyalty. The experience of the Soviet Union and Japan is suggestive but inconclusive, and it is this very fact that makes the 1958 Khrushchev reforms described by Azrael particularly in point for the further study of this problem.

The third major respect in which the experiences of these three countries have been similar is their success in containing or avoiding the politically destabilizing consequences of educational development. All three have been affected in one way or another by the disequilibriums of uneven growth and by the frustrated groups produced by educational expansion. In each country there have been disaffected and unemployed intellectuals, aggrieved and disadvantaged minority groups, new inequalities, and other similar consequences which could have been—as in the developing areas they threaten to be—dysfunctional to the political system. The point here is not that these three countries completely escaped the characteristic tensions of rapid educational expansion, but that for various reasons they either controlled or successfully resolved them.

What are the reasons for their success? The Soviet experience shows some of the ways in which a totalitarian state can handle the disequilibriums of rapid educational expansion. It can impose rigid and comprehensive control over both input and output of the educational system, limit the number of persons allowed to proceed to higher levels, reduce both old and new inequalities, and otherwise manipulate the educational system so as to ensure a close fit between its products and the needs of the economy and of society. The continuing dissatisfaction of the Soviet elite with the educational system suggests that the system must be constantly monitored and adapted to correct new disequilibriums and inequalities. This same issue is raised by Lewis in Part III, in his discussion of the Communist Chinese experience.

The path of totalitarian manipulation has not been followed by Japan and the Philippines. As pluralistic societies, both have faced potentially serious political problems in the emergence of large numbers of unemployed educated persons. Both countries, however, have thus far been able to contain these situations. Passin describes how Japan has successfully dealt with two separate waves of educated unemployed. The first, which reached ominous proportions during the interwar period, was dissipated by military conscription and industrial mobilization after 1937, and then by World War II; the second wave, coming after World War II, has been kept within manageable bounds by Japan's postwar economic boom. World War II, in its own cruel way, also temporarily extinguished the problem of the educated unemployed in the Philippines.

But totalitarian direction and international wars have not been the only, or even the most important, solutions to the problem of the educated unemployed in these three societies. At least two additional factors are pertinent: the relationship between education and mobility, and the character of academic traditions. On the education-mobility issue, these countries have shown a striking resemblance in that in none of them has education ever been thought of as conferring a special right to political elite status in particular, or as being the only channel for upward mobility in general. This fact goes far to explain the unrestrained commitment to mass education by the modernizing elites in all three countries. Mass education in the Soviet Union and in post-Restoration Japan was aimed at unification of the nation and at the creation of loyal and dutiful subjects; in the Philippines its object was the creation of participant citizens in an American-type democratic society. In no instance was education linked to political elite status, either in the minds of the early elites who introduced mass education or in the expectations of the recipient peoples. It was equally true of the Soviet Union and the Philippines that, as Passin notes for Japan, when a modern national school system was established, the distribution of political power and the processes of political recruitment were not significantly affected. As development proceeded, education increasingly became a criterion for recruitment to bureaucratic, technical, and professional positions, but the channels of political recruitment to top political elite status either became pluralistic, as in Japan and the Philippines, or remained under firm party control, as in the Soviet Union. Moreover, the very fact that education became the prerogative of nearly every citizen meant that it could hardly be the decisive determinant of entry into the political elite.

This lack of correlation among education, upward mobility, and political power stands in sharp contrast to the elitist and aristocratic assumptions regarding the role of education which prevailed among ruling groups in most modern European countries, and which in turn influenced, or even determined, the perspectives of governing elites in the former European colonies which are now the new states. Particularly in Britain and France, members of the higher bureaucracy, indeed, all members of the Establishment, were characteristically recruited through the elite institutions of a narrowly based educational system.[2] The British public schools and the Napoleonic *lycées* in France were virtually the only channels for recruitment into the elite stratum. In both countries high bureaucratic status carried prestige and visible power; in the public mind there was a clear link

---

[2] Joseph Ben-David has noted that "European societies used to have—and perhaps still have—relatively closed and permanent central elites. Universities have been closely linked to these elites, and tended to adopt conservative policies concerning academic innovations." (Joseph Ben-David, "Professions in the Class System of Present-Day Societies," *Current Sociology*, Vol. XII, 1963-1964, p. 272. Also see Joseph Ben-David and Awraham Zloczower, "Universities and Academic Systems in Modern Societies," *European Journal of Sociology*, Vol. III, 1962, pp. 45-84. For an analysis of the elitist character of the French *lycée* see Michalina Clifford-Vaughan, "Enlightenment and Education," *British Journal of Sociology*, June 1963, pp. 135-153; for the British public schools see Rupert Wilkinson, "Political Leadership and the Late Victorian Public School," *British Journal of Sociology*, Dec. 1962, pp. 320-333.)

between education and elite status. The consequences of such a system, particularly when transferred to a milieu lacking other channels of mobility, has been described by Joseph Ben-David: ". . . an elite-oriented education, placing the upper class way of life as an ideal before the students, as well as restricting their range of occupational choice, produced intellectuals unable or unwilling to perform the concrete tasks necessary for the gradual transformation of their societies into modern states. Such education gave the educated no other means than political action for achieving their aims."[3]

The second common feature helping to explain why the Soviet Union, Japan, and the Philippines have circumvented the problem of the unemployability of intellectuals is the character of their systems of higher education. Although these systems differ from one another, they are, in contrast with the conservative academic tradition of Western Europe, strikingly similar in their flexibility, practicality, and adaptability to the changing needs of a developing society. These traits are common to the academic traditions of both the Soviet Union, at least in the fields of science and technology, and the United States, which has had so marked an influence upon higher education in Japan and the Philippines.[4] The political consequences of this type of academic system in a changing society have been succinctly summarized by Joseph Ben-David: "Once . . . institutions of higher education are divested of their upper class associations and transformed into pragmatic institutions of teaching and research in a growing variety of basic and practical fields, the relationship between them and the class system changes. Instead of serving as agents for the selection of the few middle or working class people destined for upper elite careers, they become auxiliary channels of mobility for a growing range of occupations, decreasing, incidentally, the social distance between elite and other callings. . . . The much wider scope of studies creates a more flexible standard of achievement and, as a result, a greater variety of attitudes and motivations can be satisfied within the educational system. . . . Educational mobility and the rapid expan-

---

[3] *Op.cit.*, p. 276.

[4] The common element in the Soviet and the American traditions of higher education has been the process of constant differentiation and innovation, the incorporation into the academic framework of fields of intellectual and occupational interest which elsewhere remained outside, and, as Ben-David observes, "the readiness to satisfy every industrial or agricultural demand . . . [and] the virtually unlimited opportunities for the realization of new ideas about the possible uses of higher education for training specialists, without paying much attention to existing academic traditions." (*Ibid.*, pp. 270-271.)

sion of higher education were made possible by this flexibility."[5] As a result, a rather tight fit has developed between the pragmatic and diversified educational systems of these countries and their occupational structures. This development has helped to prevent the emergence of a class of alienated intellectuals, not only in the totalitarian Soviet system, but also in the more pluralistic Japanese and Philippine systems, which have been oriented toward the American pattern.[6]

Comparisons of the historical development of educational systems in modern societies strongly support the proposition that where alternative channels of mobility exist, a politically dysfunctional intellectual proletariat is less likely to appear. Ben-David concludes that, in European development, "the existence of alternative channels of mobility depends, in its turn, on the size, strength and cultural development of the middle classes prior to the rise of modern universities."[7] Although the Japanese and Philippine course of evolution, as described by Passin and Landé, did not follow the sequence marked out by Ben-David, it nevertheless strongly suggests the crucial importance of a vigorous and expanding private sector in coping with the dysfunctional consequences of educational expansion. Alternative careers outside government employment can provide status, as well as political influence. Moreover, in highly competitive, achievement-oriented societies, the blame for educational and career failure can be projected against one's self rather than against the system or

---

[5] *Ibid.*, pp. 276-277, 294.

[6] Seymour Martin Lipset has noted that "the two nations which have invested more in education in terms of both money and manpower than any other in the 'third world' are the Philippines and Puerto Rico. Yet one does not have the impression that their university students or graduates constitute a major danger to the polity. Rather, both have relatively stable political institutions." ("Research Problems in the Comparative Analysis of Mobility and Development," *International Social Science Journal*, Vol. XVI, No. 1, 1964, p. 42.)

[7] *Op.cit.*, p. 275. Ben-David's argument is that in the more developed countries of Western and Northern Europe, Switzerland, and presumably the United States, where a strong and articulate middle class was in existence when universities developed in the nineteenth century, its tradition of education and culture was capable of competing with the "academic-professional culture. . . . The flocking of all the potential elite to the universities was thereby prevented, while the existence of a middle class widely dispersed over the country created at the same time conditions for a greater decentralization and wider absorption of professional services among the population. Thus professional people did not become a separate class, and were far from alienated. Rather they became an integral part of a prosperous and educated middle class." (*Ibid.*, p. 274.) Cf. Walter M. Kotschnig, *Unemployment in the Learned Professions*, London, Oxford University Press, 1937, pp. 168-178 and 283-286, where "overcrowding" in the professions in several European countries in the 1930's and its consequences, particularly in Germany, are discussed.

the government. These and other factors help to create a societal capacity to manage politically destabilizing tensions, a capacity demonstrated by both Japan and the Philippines, but lacked by most new states because of the weakness of the private sector of their economies, and the consequent absence of alternative channels for upward mobility. Moreover, in most new states the private sector is likely to remain weak, not only because of the strong statist orientation of governing elites, but also because of the habituation of the mass of the population to a bureaucratic and statist polity. The real dilemma confronted by the leaders in such societies is that they possess neither the disposition to emulate the Japanese or Philippine pluralistic example, nor the organizational and administrative capacity to pursue effectively the totalitarian alternative.

CHAPTER 8

SOVIET UNION

JEREMY R. AZRAEL

I

WITH A FEW notable exceptions, students of Soviet politics have largely neglected, or at best treated only indirectly, the process whereby Soviet citizens, and more particularly Soviet youth, acquire their political values, attitudes, perceptions, and sentiments.[1] The task of this chapter is to help fill this gap by discussing one major agency involved in the process of political socialization in the USSR —the educational system.[2]

There are good reasons for making a study of the educational system the first step toward a broader study of the process of political socialization in the Soviet Union. In the first place, a good deal of relevant data, though by no means enough, is available. In the second place, the Soviet rulers aspire to transform the educational system into *the* primary agency of political socialization for Soviet youth. However, the present effort is limited in scope. There is, for example, no discussion of pre-school institutions or "schools of special purpose" such as military and party schools.[3] Similarly, the focus is almost ex-

---

[1] See Samuel W. Harper, *Civic Training in Soviet Russia*, Chicago, University of Chicago Press, 1929, for the first systematic study of this process by a political scientist. See Allen H. Kassof, "The Soviet Youth Program: Socialization in a Totalitarian Society," unpublished dissertation, Harvard University, 1960; Kent Geiger, "Winning Over Youth," in Alex Inkeles and Kent Geiger, eds., *Soviet Society*, Boston, Houghton Mifflin, 1961; Ralph T. Fisher, Jr., *Pattern for Soviet Youth*, New York, Columbia University Press, 1959, and Alex Inkeles and Raymond A. Bauer, *The Soviet Citizen*, Cambridge, Harvard University Press, 1959, for other studies dealing with various aspects of the general socialization process in the USSR.

[2] See Herbert Hyman, *Political Socialization*, Glencoe, Free Press, 1959; Gabriel Almond and James Coleman, eds., *The Politics of the Developing Areas*, Princeton, Princeton University Press, 1960, pp. 26-35; and David Easton and Robert D. Hess, "Problems in the Study of Political Socialization," in S. M. Lipset and L. L. Lowenthal, eds., *Culture and Social Character*, New York, Free Press, 1961, for discussions of the process of political socialization.

[3] In addition, there is no discussion of the extensive system of adult education. Nor is there any treatment of "extracurricular education," though it should be noted that in Soviet life almost all social institutions are assigned pedagogic functions. The trade unions are labelled "schools of management," the collective farms, "schools of communism," etc. Even penal institutions are supposed actively to "re-educate" their inmates. In sum, this essay deals only with the central core of the formal educational system whose clientele is the bulk of Soviet youth.

clusively on the past two or three decades of Soviet educational history. No attempt is made to discuss the first period of Soviet education during which a combination of revolutionary zeal for "progressive" pedagogical experimentation and concern to undercut the authority of the temporarily irreplaceable "bourgeois" teachers led to a thoroughgoing transformation of the traditional educational system.[4]

In addition, another, more fundamental, word of caution is in order. Those suggestions which follow and attempt to correlate the influence of the educational system as an agency of political socialization with the political behavior of those who have passed through it (or for that matter are still in it) are at best very general and tentative; they are offered with extreme trepidation. In the first place, the educational system is but one agency of political socialization, and its influence cannot be appraised with confidence unless the roles of other critical agencies such as the family, the peer-group, the communication media, non-school institutions and organizations, etc., are analyzed in some detail. In the second place, political behavior cannot be viewed simply as a product of political socialization unless political socialization is treated in a purely reductionist fashion—i.e., unless all other variables are reduced to the single variable "political socialization." Political socialization often determines the tenor of political behavior, sets limits to it, etc., but behavior is determined by situational and other variables as well. What is true of the political behavior of individuals is even more true of the processes of political change in society at large. Thus, if the suggestions which are offered on the interrelationship between the functioning of the educational system and political behavior are very general and tentative, those which are offered on the interrelationship between the functioning of the educational system and basic processes of political change are doubly so.

Given this orientation and these limits, the central question which is posed in this essay might be put as follows: what degree of success has the Soviet educational system achieved in meeting its assigned task of creating a "new man"? To put the question in this way suggests the existence of a number of potentially instructive comparisons, since in other countries as well, and notably in some of the newly independent nations, the political rulers have assigned the educa-

---

[4] See George Z. F. Bereday et al., eds., *The Changing Soviet School*, Boston, Houghton Mifflin, 1960, pp. 50-74 for a brief treatment of Soviet education in the first decade or so after the Revolution.

tional system a key role in the transformation of traditional values, beliefs, attitudes, and sentiments. However, if the Soviet educational system is considered in its own terms, comparisons of this sort can be valid only up to a point. The "new *Soviet* man" whom the Soviet educational system is supposed to produce is not merely "civic man" and "industrial man" but also "totalitarian man." There is persuasive evidence that *ultimately* political cohesiveness and rapid economic development are merely instrumental values for the Soviet rulers, and that the latter's end goal is the construction and consolidation of a political system in which total power is concentrated in their own hands. As leaders of the Communist Party, the Soviet rulers have claimed that status of exclusive custodians of an all-embracing, action-oriented ideology—Marxism-Leninism. Since at least 1928, they have interpreted this ideology as postulating and legitimizing the creation of a polity in which the entire populace is kept in a state of perpetual mobilization, all primary groups and secondary associations are transformed into malleable "transmission belts" controlled from the center, and all traditional loyalties are subverted or uprooted. They have attempted to establish a totalitarian political culture—an all-inclusive, monolithic, and homogeneous political culture character- ized by values, beliefs, attitudes, and sentiments which foster absolute devotion to the Communist Party, undeviating adherence to the principles set forth in the party line, and enthusiastic obedience to the directives of the party leadership.[5] Few, if any, of the rulers of the "new nations," even where they have borrowed Soviet organizational techniques, aspire to such total power. Nor is a nationalistic ideology conducive to the creation of such a polity or the establishment of such a political culture, since, no matter how revolutionary its spirit, na- tionalism usually implies and entails some legitimation of and respect for traditional social arrangements and cultural principles. In the Soviet system, as will be shown, the attempt to achieve political cohe- siveness and rapid economic development has forced modification in, and in some important respects placed obstacles in the course of, the quest for total power. However, that quest has been persistent, and its pursuit has had a decisive influence on the nature and functioning of the Soviet educational system. In the next section of this chapter the nature of this influence will be described; in the third section the obstacles which the educational system has encountered in its effort to

---

[5] See Gabriel Almond, "A Theory of Political Culture," unpublished manuscript, for a discussion of the concept, "political culture."

induct Soviet youth into the totalitarian political culture will be analyzed, and in the fourth and fifth sections an attempt will be made to
discuss and appraise recent changes in the educational system.

II

In this and the following section the discussion will be focused on
the educational system during the decade or so immediately prior to
the "Khrushchev educational reform" of 1958.

STRUCTURE AND SCOPE

In the period prior to 1958 (and still today) the educational system
was part of the monopolistic, centrally controlled communications
network of Soviet society. The Department of Schools of the Party
Central Committee supervised the functioning of the entire system
and each link of the latter was subject to tight control by local party
organs.[6] Policy-making authority in the sphere of higher education
was officially centralized and in the remaining spheres, which were
formally under the jurisdiction of the several republics, the Russian
Republic Ministry of Education set the basic policy line on all important educational issues. What operative decentralization there was derived from the need to take special local conditions into account in order
better to realize centrally determined objectives and tended to be
almost exclusively administrative in character.[7] A single basic pattern
of school organization prevailed throughout the entire country. The
law provided for universal, compulsory, seven-year, or *incomplete*
secondary education beginning at age seven, although, in fact, in the
years immediately preceding the 1958 reform, only 80 per cent of
Soviet children who entered the first grade finished the seventh.[8]
Upon completing their compulsory education, the overwhelming majority of students followed one of three paths. One group went more
or less directly into the work force. A second group enrolled in *technicums*, where they received a *complete specialized* secondary education which qualified them, after three or four years' study, as low- or
middle-level technicians. A third group, consisting of those whose
parents could meet the moderate, but by no means inconsequen-

---

[6] See George Z. F. Bereday and Jaan Rennar, *The Politics of Soviet Education*,
New York, Praeger, 1960, Chap. 3, for a discussion of party control over schools.
[7] See Bereday, *The Changing*, Chap. 5, for a discussion of school administration.
[8] Prior to 1943, the starting age for school children was eight (Bereday, *The
Changing*, p. 82). See N. S. Khrushchev, "On Strengthening the Connection of the
School and Life," *School and Society*, February 14, 1959, for the 80 per cent figure.

tial, tuition payments which applied from 1941 on and who received the highest scores on the rigorous qualifying exams which were instituted in 1944, was allowed to enter the so-called "complete secondary" or ten-year school, where, for three years, they received a *complete general* secondary education.[9] During most of the period under discussion, the first group constituted approximately 60-65 per cent of the total; the second, 15 per cent; and the third, some 20-25 per cent; although, as we shall see, in the years immediately preceding the 1958 reform the relative size of the first group decreased and that of the third grew rapidly.[10] Of those students who entered the work force, the preponderant majority pursued their education no further, although there did exist a skeletal network of so-called "schools of working and rural youth" in which they could continue their studies in their free time.[11] Similarly, graduation from the *technicum* was ordinarily the final step in the education of students in the second group, although the top 5 per cent of *technicum* graduates were permitted to apply for immediate admission to higher education, and the remainder could do so after having worked at state-assigned jobs for at least three years.[12] The normal route to higher education was graduation from the ten-year school, and, in fact, prior to 1954, a complete general secondary education was not only a virtual prerequisite for but also a virtual guarantee of admission to higher education.[13] Higher education, which normally lasted five years, was provided in universities or technical institutes and was culminated by enrollment in the lower ranks of the Soviet elite.

CURRICULUM

Just as a single pattern of school organization prevailed throughout the entire USSR, so a uniform core curriculum was found in all

[9] See Bereday, *The Changing*, pp. 74, 83.

[10] See E. Koutaisoff, "Soviet Education and the New Man," *Soviet Studies*, Vol. II, October 1953, p. 123, for these estimates, which refer to 1952-1953. It is possible that the introduction of fees led to a decrease in the percentage of students going on to the ten-year school, since, according to one source, in 1940-1941, 43.3 per cent of all seventh graders continued their education (K. Hulicka, "Political Education in Soviet Schools," *Soviet Studies*, Vol. II, October 1953, p. 147). In the post-1954 period, there was a rapid increase in this percentage, and, by 1958, 70 per cent of those who completed the seventh grade entered the eighth (Nicholas DeWitt, "Upheaval in Education," *Problems of Communism*, Vol. VIII, No. 1, January, February, 1959, p. 29. See below, pp. 252-253, for the consequences of this rapid increase.

[11] See Nicholas DeWitt, *Education and Professional Employment in the U.S.S.R.*, Washington, National Science Foundation, 1961, p. 92.

[12] Bereday and Rennar, *The Politics*, p. 12.

[13] See below, p. 252.

schools of the same basic type. The only significant variations had to do with the language of instruction and, at the upper levels of the educational system, with the particular technical specialty that was stressed.[14] Ideological consideration militated against the development of special programs for "gifted" or "backward" pupils, since the desire for political homogeneity led to an insistence that, within fairly narrow limits, all students were equal or could become equal if they so chose.[15] The same factors led to the politicization of the entire curriculum, although the major indoctrinational burden was carried, as one would anticipate, by the social sciences and humanities.[16] In these fields politicization was particularly intensive and proceeded according to a carefully organized plan designed to synchronize substance and method with the maturation process as understood by Soviet educational psychologists.[17] Broadly speaking, the indoctrinational techniques used corresponded to those which were characteristic of the rest of the Soviet communications network. At the lower levels of the system primary reliance was placed upon *agitation*, with the main effort devoted to inculcating the "spirit" of Bolshevism, conditioning responses to a few relatively simple symbols, acquainting the students with the party's slogans and principal platform planks, and "explaining" in gross outline the policies of the regime. At the upper levels, and above all in the universities and institutes, increasing reliance was placed upon *propaganda*, with the main effort devoted to "the intensive elucidation of the teachings of Marx, Engels, Lenin, and [prior to 1956] Stalin, and of the history of the Bolshevik Party and its tasks."[18] At all levels, however, the general outlines of the "message" were the same.

In the primary and middle grades an intensive effort was made to establish in the minds of students a full identity among political community (nation), regime (party), and government (state system and ruling authorities) and to channel commitment from one to another "level" of the political system without discrimination or differ-

---

[14] See below, p. 249.

[15] See Bereday and Rennar, *The Politics*, pp. 64-65.

[16] See Fred M. Hechinger, *The Big Red Schoolhouse*, New York; Doubleday, 1959, p. 167; and G. S. Counts, *The Challenge of Soviet Education*, New York, McGraw-Hill, 1957, p. 93, for examples of the politicization of the natural science curriculum.

[17] See *Soviet Education*, Vol. I, No. 2, December, 1958, pp. 53-91, for an example of such a plan.

[18] Alex Inkeles, *Public Opinion in Soviet Russia*, Cambridge; Harvard University Press, 1958, p. 41 and also pp. 40-43.

entiation.[19] Early initiation into the cult of Lenin and—prior to 1956—into the cult of Stalin was considered an especially useful means of cementing this identification. According to Soviet educators, experience had shown that "children progress most easily to the feeling of love for their motherland, their fatherland, and their state through a feeling of love for the leaders of the Soviet people—Lenin and Stalin," that "they [the children] associate with the concrete images of Lenin and Stalin the Party of Communists, the Party of Bolsheviks created by [the] great leaders," and that "they quickly begin to perceive that under the leadership of the Party of Lenin and Stalin we both build and defend our Soviet state, our fatherland."[20] The desired orientation toward the monolithic political system was summed up in the concept "Soviet patriotism," and the supreme task of the curriculum was to inculcate "Soviet patriotism."[21]

At the lower levels of the education system, "Soviet patriotism" was interpreted primarily in terms of the political community. Thus, history texts—and the primary school song book and readers as well —were designed to convince students that "everywhere, in all spheres of science and art, industry and agriculture, in the works of peace and on the battlefields, the Soviet people march in the forefront of other nations and have created values which are unequaled anywhere in the world."[22] As this suggests, a dichotomous image of the world was an integral part of the inculcation of "Soviet patriotism." While elaborating the glories of the Soviet Union, teachers were instructed to regale their students with vivid "human interest" stories of life in the West—stories of a sort which would insure that

[19] See Easton and Hess, *op.cit.*, for "levels" of the political system. The effort to establish an identity among the various "levels" is reflected clearly in the introduction to the official fourth grade history text where "land of socialism," "Motherland," "Party," and "Soviet state" are used almost interchangeably. (See Counts, *op.cit.*, p. 120, for a translation.) It is noteworthy that the Soviets are pursuing a technique which they recognize as having been characteristic of tsarist education: "In inculcating devotion to the tsar, the Ministry of Public Enlightenment constantly joined the concept 'fatherland' to the concept 'tsar,' striving to consolidate the two concepts." In the case of tsarist education, of course, the consolidation was sought for "reactionary" ends. (M. A. Zinoviev, *Soviet Methods of Teaching History*, Ann Arbor, University of Michigan Press, 1952, p. 43.)

[20] G. S. Counts, *I Want to Be Like Stalin* (New York, J. Day, 1947), p. 54. (This is a translation of a Soviet pedagogical text.)

[21] See Frederick C. Barghoorn, *Soviet Russian Nationalism*, New York, Oxford University Press, 1956, esp. Chapter One, for a discussion of "Soviet patriotism." See Counts, *The Challenge*, p. 118, for the primary place assigned the cultivation of "Soviet patriotism" in the curriculum.

[22] Zinoviev, *op.cit.*, p. 90. See also Merle Fainsod, "The Komsomol: Youth Under Dictatorship," in Inkeles and Geiger, *op.cit.*, p. 115; and Counts, *I Want*, pp. 53-54.

students knew "not only with their minds, but with their hearts that capitalism is hunger, unemployment, and eternal fear of tomorrow."[23] It was expected that an emotionally charged juxtaposition of the glories of Soviet life and the horrors of life in the West would "foster a hatred for the exploiters," "teach the students to struggle," and reinforce the students' love of the Soviet system.[24] Out of this syndrome of emotions, in turn, the students would develop a feeling that they stood in debt before their own society and were obliged to repay its beneficence with endless and unstinting service.[25]

The type of service which was expected was made clear to school children by appropriate models. Primary school readers were replete with tales of the careers of political leaders (above all Lenin and Stalin), valiant soldiers, famous scientists, and production heroes.[26] The style of these "biographies" was at once hagiographic and intimate, and they were designed not merely to exemplify right conduct and inspire reverence, but also to facilitate the internalization of desirable "ego-ideals." Full identification was encouraged by including many "heroic" children, ranging from the notorious Pavlik Morozov to young partisans killed in the "Great Fatherland War" (World War II). In addition, almost all the "biographies" of adults began with glimpses of the childhood years of their heroes. The fact that the Great Lenin was once *Volodya* Ulyanov and the Great Stalin was once *So-So* Djugashvilli was stressed, and the idea was constantly driven home that the character traits of the heroic adult were consciously cultivated by the child.[27] As for the character traits themselves, those which were most exalted were love of labor, and, in general, the "protestant" economic virtues so central to industrial development; "personal self-sacrifice with the aim of bringing victory to the fatherland"; and "devotion to revolutionary and scientific

[23] V. A. Sukhomlinsky, *Vospitaniye Sovietskovo Patriotisma u Shkolnikov*, Moscow, 1959, pp. 25-26. This pedagogical manual was published after the 1958 reform but is in most respects a reliable guide to pre-reform methods where "Soviet patriotism" is concerned.

[24] Zinoviev, *op.cit.*, p. 83.

[25] *Ibid.*, p. 90. See also Sukhomlinsky, *op.cit.*, pp. 25-26.

[26] See Fainsod, *op.cit.*, p. 155; Counts, *I Want*, p. 39; Zinoviev, *op.cit.*, p. 91.

[27] See Vasileva, "Study of Episodic Stories from the History of U.S.S.R. in the Fourth Grade," *Soviet Education*, Vol. III, No. 5, 1960; M. I. Kalinin, *On Communist Education*, Moscow, 1959, pp. 108-109. It is this effort to achieve full identification with appropriate "heroes" which justifies Counts entitling his translation of sections from a Soviet text *I Want to Be Like Stalin*, although the text itself is entitled simply Pedagogy. (See, however, Bertram D. Wolfe, *Communist Totalitarianism*, Boston, Beacon Press, 1956, p. 114.)

ideas."[28] And, once again, as in the case of the picture of the world at large, graphic examples of "negative heroes" were juxtaposed to the portraits of "positive heroes" in order to reinforce commitment to the character traits of the latter. The dichotomous image of the world was complemented by a dichotomous image of human nature, and every effort was made to inculcate a radical intolerance of ambiguity.[29]

At the upper levels of the educational system, the indoctrinational themes were essentially the same. However, the approach became increasingly sophisticated. One change of note was the devotion of progressively more time and energy to the development of proper orientations toward the regime and governmental "levels" of the political system. All complete secondary school students were required (usually in the tenth grade) to take a course on "The Constitution of the U.S.S.R." Here the status of the Soviet state as "the most democratic in the world" was elaborated, the institutional setting of Soviet politics was clarified, and students were instructed in the nature and norms of "socialist legality." History was increasingly party history, and more and more time was devoted to the contemporary period.[30] While the inculcation of absolute devotion to the nation as such was by no means abandoned, and history texts continued to cultivate not merely chauvinism but xenophobia, the concept of "Soviet patriotism" was more and more infused with manifest political content.[31] Increasing attention was devoted to cultivating a "class point of view" and to training students to "unmask" and "expose" the "class essence" of ideas.[32] Prior to 1953, all students from the senior grades on were required to be intimately familiar with the *History of the Communist Party of the Soviet Union: Short Course* with its exaltation of Stalin, its cries for vigilance against any political deviation, and its vigorous assertion of the vanguard role of the

[28] Zinoviev, *op.cit.*, p. 91. See also Counts, *I Want*, pp. 125-126.

[29] The stress on model "heroes"—positive and negative—was not confined to historic personages, nor was it limited to primary education. It was a major theme in the teaching of literature in the secondary schools as well. (See Frederic Ligle, "The Study of Literature in the Soviet School," *Studies in Comparative Education*, December 1959, p. 34.)

[30] It must be noted, however, that no formal course in party history was offered below the university-institute level.

[31] See Martin Levit, "Content Analysis of a Soviet History Text for University-Level Courses," *Studies in Comparative Education*, December 1959, for a content analysis of the official university text on Soviet history.

[32] Zinoviev, *op.cit.*, pp. 63, 79, 85-90.

party. After Stalin's death, texts and guides of generally similar character, though minus the somewhat hysterical tone and the "cult of personality," were gradually substituted.[33]

In the middle and senior grades there was no separate study of Marxism-Leninism or, as the sequence ran prior to 1953, Marxism-Leninism-Stalinism. The role of the party as exclusive custodian of the ideology was stressed constantly, but no effort was made to cultivate real ideological sophistication. The fact that the party had a "scientific" theory at its disposal was emphasized in order to generate "convictional certainty." This "convictional certainty" was to rise out of but transcend the emotional predispositions built up in the earlier grades. To the students' emotional revulsion against the West was added a "conviction in the inevitable victory of socialism."[34] However, emphasis was *not* placed upon the niceties of historical and dialectical materialism. What was sought was total loyalty to the party, and there was an implicit recognition that until such loyalty was secured, familiarity with the ideology *per se* could lead to "confusion" and provide a standard by which to judge the party and resist changes in the party line.[35] It was only in the institutions of higher education—after the students had been exposed to an all-out attempt to socialize them into party loyalty—that the formal study of Marxism-Leninism was introduced. At this level, however, it was a required subject and occupied an important place in the curriculum.[36] Instruction in ideological theory was designed to consolidate the world view of that segment of Soviet youth which was destined to enter the ranks of the Soviet elite. It was designed to insure that they would not approach their future assignments from a "narrowly professional" point of view and would make the proper choice—i.e., the choice in conformity with the regime's current schedule of priorities—among the conflicting goals which would confront them as they moved up the lad-

[33] See Bereday, *The Changing*, pp. 88-89, for a discussion of some of the consequences of "de-Stalinization" for the formal school program. See below, pp. 254-257, for some of the more politically relevant consequences.

[34] Zinoviev, *op.cit.*, pp. 3, 84.

[35] See Hyman, *op.cit.*, p. 19, for the important role of party loyalty as opposed (at least partially) to programmatic loyalty in preparing the ground for acceptance of social change.

[36] See *Report of IIE Seminar on Education in the Soviet Union*, New York, 1960, p. 34. "Marxism-Leninism," together with "The History of the Communist Party of the Soviet Union" and "Political Economy," which were also required subjects, occupied over 600 curricular hours over the course of five years' study in institutions of higher education. In addition, all applicants for graduate degrees were required to pass an examination in "Marxism-Leninism," irrespective of their proposed field of concentration.

der of success and were accorded more and more operational autonomy.[37] It was designed to insure that they would become worthy members of an *aktiv* on one or another of the "fronts" of Soviet life. And, finally, it was designed to guarantee that they would be sensitized to the special semantics of Soviet political life and hence able properly to "interpret" the measures of the regime to the masses. It was designed, in other words, to prepare them to serve as agitators in their own right, thus perpetuating the cycle of indoctrination through which they themselves had passed.[38]

ATMOSPHERE AND SPIRIT

Within the educational system, manipulation of the atmosphere and spirit of school life was considered at least as important as manipulation of the formal curriculum in guaranteeing the proper "political upbringing" of youth. Throughout the system, the atmosphere was pervaded by a spirit of discipline and hierarchy.[39] At the lower levels, lessons were marked by the formal recitation of material drawn from the assigned textbooks and by catechetical drill, while at the higher levels standardized lectures propagating the official version of the Truth predominated. Among the very first requirements imposed on entering pupils was that of memorizing and obeying the highly authoritarian "Rules for Schoolchildren" which constituted "a program for the cultivation . . . of habits of disciplined and cultured behavior" both inside and outside the school.[40] It was hoped that behavior, become reflexive, would produce corresponding thought-patterns and that habituation would be the first step in the development of self-discipline. Self-discipline was desired, in turn, because with it *conformity and obedience [would] become more perfect.*[41] The ultimate goal, in other words, was the internalization of the attitudes toward authority that the "Rules" reflected. Teachers were reminded that they were the principal authority figures with whom school children had contact and that they had to

[37] Cf. Jeremy Azrael, "Political Profiles of the Soviet Technical Intelligentsia and Managerial Elite," unpublished dissertation, Harvard University, 1961, Chap. v; David Granick, *Management of the Industrial Firm in the U.S.S.R.*, New York, Columbia University Press, 1954, p. 284.

[38] See Inkeles, *op.cit.*, pp. 42-43.

[39] See above, p. 234, for the brief mention of the quite different atmosphere which characterized the education system in the decade or so following the Revolution.

[40] Counts, *I Want*, p. 97. See *ibid.*, pp. 149-150, for a translation of the "Rules for School Children."

[41] *Ibid.*, p. 108 (italics mine). See also *ibid.*, p. 96.

conduct themselves accordingly, never forgetting, as the late Soviet president Kalinin put it, that "a pedagogue is an engineer of human souls."[42] An authoritative text, after pointing out that "submission to the will of a leader is a necessary and essential mark of discipline," directed teachers to "assume from the outset a firm and impressive tone" and warned them not to coax students but rather to demand obedience, for only in this way would students develop the desired moral qualities.[43]

"Conformity and obedience" were secured not only by casting the teacher in an authoritarian role and imposing rigid rules upon the individual pupils, but also by carefully structuring relationships among the pupils. Here the role of the *kollektiv* was crucial. Indeed, *Pravda* proclaimed a strong *kollektiv* to be "the foundation of foundations of the Soviet educational system" and stressed that it was essential that "the organization of a *kollektiv* and the cultivation in each child of a feeling of collectiveness . . . [begin] from the first grade."[44] Teachers were instructed in the ways and means of shaming recalcitrant students into obedience by mobilizing the *kollektivs* against them, thereby at once buttressing their own authority and training students from a very early age to use and respond to such fundamental institutions of Soviet political life as criticism, self-criticism, denunciation, confession, and recantation.[45] However, the *kollektiv's* area of "legitimate" concern was considered to extend well beyond the walls of the classroom, and it was manipulated to break down all attempts on the part of students to develop or maintain a "private" sphere of existence.[46] An attempt was made through the *kollektiv* to

[42] Kalinin, *op.cit.*, p. 93.

[43] *Ibid.*; Counts, *I Want*, pp. 122, 140.

[44] Counts, *I Want*, pp. 84, 85.

[45] *Ibid.*, pp. 110, 102, 89, 93. At the lowest levels of the educational system the operative *kollektiv* was the class *kollektiv*. From the third grade to the seventh the class *kollektiv* was in effect a local unit of the All-Union Pioneer organization which strove to embrace all children between the ages of nine and thirteen (ten to fourteen after 1958). In the 1930's there had been an all-union organization for younger children, the Octobrist organization, embracing children from seven to nine, but this was abolished before World War II and not reestablished until 1957. At the upper levels of the system, the school-wide or faculty-wide (in institutions of higher education) *kollektiv* became increasingly important. It in effect constituted a local unit of the All-Union Komsomol, which strove to include all or nearly all *students* in the eligible age range (fourteen to twenty-six prior to 1958, fifteen to twenty-seven thereafter). In 1949, over 50 per cent of students from grades seven through ten were members of the Komsomol and in recent years 80 or 90 per cent of all students in institutions of higher education have been members. (Kassof, *op.cit.*, p. 204; Bereday and Rennar, *The Politics*, p. 52.)

[46] Counts, *I Want*, pp. 84-85.

exploit the natural vulnerability of youth to peer-group pressure. This was a particularly strategic control technique because, as Kassof has pointed out, the *kollektivs* operated on such a highly personal level and, where they were successful, turned "the abstract question of obeying official norms into issues of friendship and personal emotional security."[47] The first step was to create "citizens . . . able to put social above personal interests," but the long-run goal was "to educate a person . . . who [had] no interests opposed to the collective interests."[48] The hope was that the student would ultimately come to make his standing in the *kollektiv* the basis for self-appraisal and would develop such a "passion for unanimity" that coercion would be superfluous.[49]

The *kollektiv* functioned as an agency of mobilization as well as an agency of control. Here the involvement of the *kollektiv* in "socially useful labor" was considered to be of particular importance.[50] At the lower levels of the educational system, class and school *kollektivs* competed with each other in the collection of scrap metal, the planting of trees, the tending of public parks, etc., while at the upper levels Komsomol organizations mustered their members for "Saturdays" and "Sundays" of labor on nearby construction projects and for summer stints on collective or state farms. The objectives which were sought through student participation in "socially useful labor" were chiefly political and ideological, and in only a few instances was student labor of major economic significance. In the first place, participation was designed to inspire respect for physical labor, thereby, at one and the same time, strengthening the appeal of the regime's image as a bulwark of the proletariat and inhibiting the growth of "class-consciousness" within Soviet society.[51] In the second place, it was designed to bring home the reality of socialism. There appeared to be

[47] Kassof, *op.cit.*

[48] Counts, *I Want*, pp. 88, 37.

[49] See Margaret Mead, *Soviet Attitudes Toward Authority*, New York, W. Morrow, 1955, p. 108. There is obvious tension between the regime's effort to induce students to internalize strong, "ego-ideals" on the one hand and its effort to rely on group-pressure as a critical technique of social control on the other. Ideally, of course, the two efforts are designed to reinforce each other, but practically considerable tension probably results and the two efforts may tend to contradict each other and lead to tremendous ambivalence on the part of the individual. Further research along these lines might be fruitful, though data would be very difficult to acquire.

[50] "Socially useful labor" can also be viewed as a control technique in so far as it was designed to fill and insure supervision over the use of their leisure time by students. (See Jeremy R. Azrael, "Soviet Urban Attitudes Toward Leisure," *Social Problems*, Vol. IX, No. 1, summer 1961, pp. 75-76; Kassof, *op.cit.*, pp. 140-141.)

[51] See below, pp. 251-252.

faith in an inverted Lockean logic, whereby, by dint of mixing their labor with the construction projects of the regime, students would develop a sense of the reality of *their* ownership—socialist ownership through membership in the *kollektiv*—of all of the resources of Soviet society.

Finally, the *kollektiv* functioned as an important channel of political recruitment. This function was most marked, of course, at the upper levels of the educational system, but even in the primary grades the operations of the *kollektiv* were considered particularly useful in permitting teachers to identify "children of initiative." Once the latter were identified, the task was to discipline them without reducing them to apathy. On the one hand every effort was made to insure that "initiative not be exhibited impulsively."[52] On the other hand something more than "just blind obedience" was desired. The objective was to restrict the exercise of initiative to a purely instrumental level where it would find expression as "an independent search for the best way to fulfill a command."[53] To accomplish this delicate task, initiative had to be "directed into organized channels." Here again the *kollektiv* occupied a key position, serving as a forum and a framework for the development of initiative of the desired sort and guaranteeing that "out of children of initiative good organizers . . . [would] come."[54] In the earliest years the position of "class monitors," which entailed assisting the teacher with such things as distributing supplies and maintaining classroom discipline and "cultured" standards of student behavior, served as a training ground for "children of initiative."[55] In addition, from the primary grades on, such children were encouraged to assume special "social obligations" above and beyond their participation in "socially useful labor." "Social obligations" in the lower grades ranged from aiding more backward classmates with their school work to writing articles for local children's newspapers.[56] Later "social obligations" entailed such things

---

[52] Counts, *I Want*, p. 128.

[53] Hadley Cantril, *Soviet Leaders and Mastery Over Man*, New Brunswick, Rutgers University Press, 1960, p. 45, quotes the following definition of initiative by two of the leading educational theorists of the late Stalin era: "Not just blind obedience but an independent search for the best way to fulfill a command." The point, of course, is that there must be a command.

[54] Counts, *I Want*, p. 128.

[55] *Ibid.*, p. 89. In the primary grades "monitors" were directly appointed by the teacher; later they were "elected" by the *kollektiv*, but the influence of the teacher on the outcome was usually decisive.

[56] See Jeremy R. and Gabriella Azrael, "Sasha, Vovo, and Natasha," *The Reporter*, April 27, 1961.

as the assumption of leadership (under the guidance of the teacher concerned) of a lower-level class *kollektiv* or Pioneer detachment, participation in the regime's various agitational campaigns, etc.[57] Those students who undertook major "social obligations" and fulfilled them with enthusiasm and skill were singled out, in turn, for further and more intensive initiation into the rites of responsibility. They were apt to be moved into the Komsomol apparatus itself, to be accorded early party membership, to be enrolled in the special "cadres reserve" maintained by leading party committees, and thus to be placed on a course which could lead not merely to elite status, but to membership in the "power elite" itself.[58]

III

The educational system prior to 1958 accomplished many of the tasks set it by the Soviet rulers and, in the process, won admiration and prestige for the regime abroad and support for the regime at home.[59] It transformed an overwhelmingly illiterate population into an almost universally literate one. It fought a largely successful battle against the influence on youth of such traditional institutions as the church. It helped socialize a predominantly tradition-oriented population into the cultural patterns of an industrial society. It trained the technical and managerial cadres without whom rapid industrialization and the maintenance of a high tempo of industrial growth would have been impossible. It educated scientists whose researches enabled the regime to pioneer new developments in a wide variety of fields. It played an important role in persuading the bulk of Soviet youth of the merits of socialist principles of production and distribution.[60] It helped generate enough consensus to enable the political system to survive severe shock from within and without. And, finally, it was instrumental in producing enough highly motivated, ideologically committed, and politically active young people that the regime was able to institutionalize tremendously rapid social and economic change and to establish a "permanent purge" of key officials without losing its essential political continuity.

These were no small accomplishments, and the foregoing catalogue

[57] See F. Vigdorova, *Diary of a Russian Schoolteacher,* New York, Grove Press, 1960, for the role of leader of a class-collective.

[58] See Tim Callaghan, "Studying the Students," *Soviet Survey,* No. 33, July-September, 1960, pp. 131, 240.

[59] Inkeles and Bauer, *op.cit.,* pp. 131, 240.

[60] *Ibid.,* p. 254.

is by no means exhaustive. However, despite its many "successes," the educational system had not managed to create the sort of all-inclusive, monolithic, and homogeneous political culture that the rulers desired. Its efforts to create such a political culture had been beset by a number of problems which it had been unable to resolve. To be sure, in many cases, the fault lay not with the educational system proper but rather with forces in the broader economic, social, and political environment within which it functioned, but the problems at issue were often rendered more acute by the consequences of its functioning. The most critical of the problems which beset the educational system were those which derived from (1) the multi-national character of Soviet society, (2) the tendency of the rigid status hierarchy which the regime had established to turn into a general system of social stratification and take on "class content," and (3) the capacity of the human mind to resist, remain immune to, "misinterpret," or become apathetic in the face of intensive indoctrination.

THE PROBLEM OF NATIONALITIES

The educational system was still far from having eradicated all of the sources of tension and discord inherent in a multi-national polity. It had accomplished a great deal in this direction and had in large measure succeeded in creating a sense of shared destiny among the polyglot nationalities of the USSR.[61] Even in this respect, however, there were significant exceptions, and, although reliable data are scarce, there is persuasive evidence that educational successes in the area of political socialization were consistently greater among Russian than among non-Russian youth.[62] In part this was a consequence of the fact that the launching of the five-year plans had produced a more far-reaching social and cultural upheaval in many of the non-Russian regions than in Russia proper and, quite apart from any strictly political considerations, had engendered widespread hostility against the Bolsheviks as agents of "modernization." Moreover, there was a not altogether unjustifiable tendency to identify the Bolsheviks as Great Russians.[63] This introduction of a nationalistic dimension into an already complex situation made the task of the educational

[61] See *ibid.*, Chap. 15; and Barghoorn, *op.cit.*

[62] The fact that the regime felt it necessary to admit that collaboration with the Germans was widespread in several national republics is indicative of the existence of exceptions to the above generalization.

[63] Barghoorn, *op.cit.*, pp. 68-69.

system more difficult. The difficulty was further compounded because the regime had assimilated many—though by no means all or the most important—of the traditional values and attitudes of the Russian people in an effort to win support among the dominant nationality during the "transitional period" to full-fledged totalitarianism.[64] For example, throughout most of the period under discussion, the concept of "Soviet patriotism" was heavily infused with the spirit of Russian nationalism.[65] This unquestionably heightened its appeal to Russian youth, but this was scarcely the case where Ukrainians, Uzbeks, or Tadzhiks were concerned.

One step which the regime had taken to make its indoctrinational "message" more palatable (as well as to insure its wider diffusion) was to propagate "socialist content" in "national form," and most non-Russians were given an opportunity to receive their education, including their higher education, in their native languages.[66] This unquestionably tended to appease nationalist sentiment in some respects, but it also had dysfunctional consequences. For one thing, the perpetuation (or in some cases creation, at least in written form) of native languages served almost automatically to preserve and in many cases to strengthen consciousness of a separate identity. In addition, it reduced the incentive to learn or teach Russian well and contributed to the rise of a situation in which, although the intensive study of Russian was required in all native-language schools, even graduates of native-language secondary schools and institutions of higher education were not really fluent in Russian.[67] This was dangerous for the Soviet system because Russian was the primary language of science, technology, and administration, and was hence a prerequisite for "progress" as the regime conceived it. The existing situation made it difficult for the regime to utilize native cadres and, at the same time, meant that non-Russians educated in native-language schools faced more limited career prospects than Russians with equivalent education.[68] They could normally make their way at the local

---

[64] See *ibid.*, on the assimilation of traditional Russian values. See Dinko Tomasic, *The Impact of Russian Culture on Soviet Communism*, Glencoe, Free Press, 1953, for an extreme statement of the degree to which traditional Russian values were easily assimilable to Bolshevik values.

[65] See Barghoorn, *op.cit.*

[66] However, see *ibid.*, pp. 44-45, for a reference to the absence of such an opportunity in the former Polish Ukraine.

[67] See Bereday, *The Changing*, pp. 196-197; Bereday, *The Politics*, pp. 76-77; and below, p. 269.

[68] Some non-Russians had the option of attending Russian schools in the non-Russian republics, and this option was often exercised by the ambitious. (See Makhma-

level, but the odds were disproportionately against them at the national level.[69] The aspirations of the most ambitious were thus apt to be frustrated, while many other educated non-Russians had their tendencies toward "local nationalism" reinforced precisely because their occupational and professional frames of reference were "sensibly" local in character. Opportunities for advancement and access to positions of responsibility were extensive enough that there did not appear on the scene a wholly alienated native intelligentsia similar to that produced by the functioning of so many other "imperial" educational systems. Concessions to national pride were extensive enough that little real separatist spirit developed. However, "localist" tendencies were prevalent, and forthright nationalist sentiment was by no means eradicated among highly educated non-Russian youth. That this should have been so graphically demonstrated by the violent reaction of Georgian university students to the destruction of the "personality cult" of their co-national Stalin was ironic but, at the same time, both symptomatic and symbolic.

THE PROBLEMS OF STATUS, MOBILITY, AND STRATIFICATION

The Soviet rulers accompanied their turn to a policy of rapid industrialization and total planning with the establishment of a rigid status hierarchy in all walks of life. Extreme wage differentials, clearcut symbols of rank and office, etc., were introduced in an effort to buttress managerial authority and to create a system of incentives which would draw maximum effort from the labor force and attract the ambitious, but ideologically hostile or indifferent, to the service of the regime.[70] At the same time, however, the rulers were committed to the maintenance of a rapid rate of vertical social mobility. The establishment of a rigid status hierarchy constituted a clear betrayal of those key tenets of Marxist-Leninist ideology which posited social egalitarianism, and the rulers hoped to mask this betrayal by pointing to universal *equality of opportunity* and the complete dependence of status on achievement. More important, the rulers counted upon a rapid rate of vertical social mobility to play a significant part in pre-

---

tov, "The Outlook for Tartar Schools," *Soviet Education*, Vol. II, No. 5, 1959-1960.) However, this option existed only in urban areas, and even in urban areas the number of places in Russian schools was limited.

[69] Distrust of the minorities and Great Russian chauvinism also limited the career opportunities of non-Russians, but here only factors related more or less directly to the functioning of the educational system are at issue.

[70] See Nicholas S. Timasheff, *The Great Retreat*, New York, E. P. Dutton, 1946.

venting the transformation of the status hierarchy into a general system of social stratification. Fearing a system in which status would cease to be wholly impersonal, a mere reflection of the regime's evaluation of the benefits which accrued to it through the exercise of various social and economic functions, the rulers hoped that rapid mobility would inhibit tendencies toward the consolidation of privilege and automatic transmission of privilege independently of the direct sanction of the regime. Rapid mobility was viewed as a desire to help insure against the status gulf's growing into a class gulf and unleashing pressures for social "routinization" and a reduction in the "tempo" of Soviet life. In sum, the commitment of the rulers to the maintenance of a rapid rate of vertical social mobility within the established status hierarchy was part and parcel of their commitment to the consolidation of total power in their own hands and to the creation of a totalitarian political culture.

The rulers always expected the educational system to serve as a major channel of rapid social mobility. In fact, as industrial maturation made problems of management and administration both increasingly critical and increasingly complex, the educational system almost perforce became the primary channel of social mobility. However, although it trained hundreds of thousands of "proletarian specialists," the educational system never managed to create a situation of equal opportunity for all, and in the period after World War II it began to show signs of functioning more and more as an instrument of social stratification.[71] Note has already been taken of the fact that in recent years, despite the seven-year compulsory education law, only 80 per cent of Soviet children who entered the first grade actually completed the seventh.[72] The great bulk of the "delinquents" were concentrated in rural areas. The "delinquency" of rural children was attributable in large measure to the low quality of rural education, the necessity most of them faced of having to transfer to schools in towns and cities in order to continue their education beyond the fourth grade, the inadequacy of transportation and near absence of boarding facilities for transferees, etc.[73] The "under-representation"

[71] See Azrael, "Political Profiles," pp. 252-255; Feldmesser, "Aspects of Social Mobility in the Soviet Union," unpublished dissertation, Harvard University, 1955.
[72] See above, p. 237.
[73] See DeWitt, *Education and Professional Employment*, pp. 142-143. Dropping-out was encouraged also by the relative cultural impoverishment of the home and social environment of the bulk of rural children and by the fact that even young children were an economic asset in the countryside, particularly for work on the family's private garden plot. The factors noted in the text were, however, much more

of the peasantry increased as one ascended the educational ladder.[74] This was due to the operative effects of low social status which were not confined to the peasantry although it hit them with particular force.

Among the urban population also differential rates of access to the upper levels of the educational system had become characteristic. Universal seven-year education was a reality in the cities, but the children of the workers were increasingly underrepresented as one moved into the upper reaches of the educational system, access to which had become a virtual prerequisite for entrance into the elite. The necessity of paying tuition fees in the ten-year schools and institutions of higher education, which applied between 1941 and 1956, militated against the children of workers continuing their education.[75] An additional factor was the inability of working-class parents to bring pressure or influence to bear in order to secure places in institutions of higher education for their children. This factor acquired great importance in the years following Stalin's death, for in these years, due partly to widespread knowledge that the abolition of tuition fees was imminent and partly to a rise in income which made the payment of fees less burdensome, more and more working-class children did enter and finish the ten-year schools.[76] Since the institutions of higher education did not increase their enrollments, an intensive competition for openings began, and parental status determined the outcome in many instances.[77] The combined effect of the fee system and

---

critical, and, as their character suggests, they were ultimately rooted in the failure of the regime to provide adequate resources to the educational system.

[74] See Inkeles and Bauer, *op.cit.*, pp. 136-137.

[75] See above, p. 7. Tuition fees were also demanded in technicums, but scholarships were rather widely available for the latter. The question of why tuition fees were introduced in 1941 has never been satisfactorily resolved. Some have suggested that they were designed to cover the costs of school construction, but the revenue brought in was never very substantial. Others have suggested that their purpose was to provide more manpower for the labor force by limiting educational opportunities. This is plausible, but the method chosen was bound to bring a derogation of ideological legitimacy, to cause widespread resentment among the masses, and to increase the danger that a system of stratification independent of achievement as appraised by the regime would arise.

[76] The abolition of fees had been foreshadowed in 1952 at the Nineteenth Party Congress which decreed a transition to ten-year compulsory education to be completed in the cities by 1955 and in the countryside by 1960.

[77] Khrushchev, "Educate Active and Conscious Builders of a Communist Society," *School and Society* (February 14, 1959), p. 66; and Khrushchev, "On Strengthening," p. 73. The number of openings in institutions of higher education was not expanded due to the fact that the regime faced an acute adult manpower shortage as a result of

parental influence is suggested by the fact that in 1958 60 to 70 per cent of the students in institutions of higher education were children of "officials" and "members of the intelligentsia."[78] This represents a marked change from the situation which prevailed in the early 1930's, when the drive to "proletarianize" education was at its height and a significant change from the situation which prevailed in 1938 (after the "proletarianization" drive had been relaxed) when only 42 per cent of university students were children of professional, administrative, or white-collar parents.[79] This change could not but be highly disturbing to rulers whose ideology posited a movement toward "classlessness," whose political system numbered a widespread opportunity for education among those of its attributes which attracted major support from the population at large, and who were desirous of preventing the transformation of a "service elite" into a "social elite." It was the more disturbing because it was accompanied by a growth of "class consciousness" which the schools seemed powerless to prevent and often subtly encouraged, e.g., by stressing that the fate of academic failures was to become common workers.[80] The growth of "class consciousness," in turn, threatened to generate patterns of solidarity and antagonism in society which the regime could not wholly control, and which could undercut its drive to eliminate all dimensions of autonomous social interaction. It also was largely responsible, in the eyes of the regime, for a disturbing tendency on the part of many students to take their privileged

---

the "generational gap" brought about by World War II. (See below, p. 259.) Between 1954 and 1958 the "surplus" of ten-year school graduates over higher education openings reached 3,000,000.

[78] Khrushchev, "On Strengthening," p. 74. These figures referred to institutions of higher education in Moscow, and elsewhere the situation was probably more satisfactory. However, Moscow represented a general trend, and a trend that may actually have been more extreme than Khrushchev's figures revealed, since he suggested that many of the children of workers and peasants in institutions of higher education were extension and correspondence students. The quality of correspondence and extension education was lower than that of resident education, and the former probably brought fewer opportunities for rapid advancement.

[79] See Inkeles and Bauer, *op.cit.*, p. 137; Nicholas DeWitt, *Soviet Professional Manpower*, Washington, National Science Foundation, 1955, p. 100; Azrael, "Political Profiles," p. 223; especially note 63; Feldmesser, *op.cit.*

[80] According to a major article in *Pravda*, the educational system had contributed to the growth of a situation such that "the editors of youth newspapers frequently had to answer such questions from readers as, for example: 'Can a schoolgirl have a boyfriend who is a worker?' or 'I have a job and study at night, while a friend of mine is a full-time student. He is condemned for his friendship with me. Is this right?' Etc." (*Pravda*, January 10, 1962, p. 4. See also *Izvestia*, November 24, 1961, p. 6; and Bereday and Rennar, *The Politics*, pp. 80-87.)

status for granted and respond with indifference or hostility to the educational system's attempts to mobilize them.

THE PROBLEMS OF DISAFFECTION AND APATHY

Had the Soviet educational system fulfilled the entirety of the political socialization plan that was assigned it during the period under discussion, the official "de-Stalinization" campaign that began in 1956 would, in one way or another, have resulted in the disintegration of the entire fabric of Soviet life. At a minimum it would have resulted in moral anarchy among the younger generation of Soviet citizens.[81] According to Soviet sources, "de-Stalinization" did cause "a trauma in [some] impressionable young souls" and led a certain number of students to become "skeptics" and "nihilists," believing in nothing and no one.[82] However, despite its disorienting consequences, it would appear that "de-Stalinization" did not profoundly disturb the bulk of Soviet youth, and it is the author's distinct impression that it left the majority of students remarkably untouched.[83] In launching the "de-Stalinization" campaign, Stalin's successors gambled that the educational system had failed in its ultimate task of inculcating an undifferentiated image of community, regime, and government, with faith in Stalin as the unifying cement. They won their gamble, but their very victory could not but disturb them, for it was clear that in part it was due to pervasive political indifference among a sizeable segment of Soviet youth, and they were no more willing to tolerate indifference than Stalin had been before them. Moreover, the relaxation of control which accompanied "de-Stalinization" quickly revealed that there was a group of students at the upper levels of the educational system who were politically disaffected and whose disaffection could not be eradicated by the kind of political changes which they, Stalin's heirs, proposed to institute.

[81] Some further sense of the place of the Stalin cult in the school curriculum is provided by the following report which appeared in the official Soviet teachers' newspaper: "From the first day at school our children were brought up in the spirit of genuflection to the personality of I. V. Stalin. The idea was daily inculcated into the schoolchildren that their happy childhood had been created only by him and precisely he had given them the right to education. All the victories gained by the Soviet people both in the struggle against enemies and in creative work were explained only by the genius and wisdom of one man." (*Uchitelskaya Gazeta,* August 22, 1956.)

[82] See Speech of A. N. Shelepin to the Thirteenth Congress of the Komsomol translated in *Current Digest of the Soviet Press,* Vol. x, No. 16, pp. 2-9; also, *Current Digest of the Soviet Press, Vol.* IX, No. 27, p. 12; *The Soviet Review,* Vol. II, No. 11, p. 14; S. Dmitriev in *Molodaya Gvardiya,* April 1962, pp. 278, 283.

[83] This impression derives from an academic year (1958-1959) spent at Moscow State University.

Disaffection, derived from a wide variety of sources, took diverse forms and appeared with varying degrees of intensity. Here only a few major variants can be noted.[84] Among some students disaffection took the form of "pandering to Western tastes." Often this amounted to little more than *stilyagism* or "style chasing," indulged in more or less for its own sake as a protest against the drab, puritanical atmosphere of Soviet life and the depressing uniformity of official Soviet style. Sometimes, however, "pandering to Western tastes" involved genuine cultural "cosmopolitanism" and represented an effort on the part of some of the most cultured members of the younger generation to break free of the stultifying esthetic canons of the regime and to reestablish contact with the main streams of Western art, literature, and music. In a few cases, there was concern with Western political concepts and institutions as well, but most of those who cultivated an interest in the West were not interested in political liberty so much as in liberty from politics. They tended to be apolitical, although in the Soviet context to be apolitical was to be politically defiant.

The major substantive sources of articulate and directly political disaffection were not to be found in the contemporary West, but rather in Marxist-Leninist theory and in the Russian cultural heritage. The students concerned tended to elaborate an "immanent critique" of the political system, contrasting Soviet reality with the theories which were used to legitimize it. The imagery they developed was that of "Russia betrayed" or "the Revolution betrayed," and their goal was to recover the pure nucleus which they believed had been present at the inception of the political system, but had been stifled and contaminated by the bureaucratic rigidities and institutionalized brutalities of Stalinism. They were, in a word, idealists—but idealists whose zeal the educational system had failed to harness to party loyalty and whose enthusiasm it had failed to discipline and direct into "constructive" channels.[85] Although the source of their disaffection was Stalinism, their conception of Stalinism embraced almost the whole of

---

[84] See Callaghan, *op.cit.*, and Burg, "Observations on Soviet University Students," *Daedalus,* summer 1960, for further discussion

[85] Often it was only when these young people left the educational system that they discovered the full extent of the contrast between theory and reality. Only then did they learn the extent to which evasion, suspicion, deception, and dissimulation were built into the prevailing political system. As one young Soviet recently put it: "When we graduated . . . we had no idea what a complex joke life could sometimes be. We walked into it with eyes shut. Many of us got our heads bloodied, and that first painful collision turned into something of a moral crash." (*The Soviet Review,* Vol. II, No. 12, p. 51.)

the contemporary Soviet system, and the selective "de-Stalinization" and wary return to Marxism-Leninism that Khrushchev was attempting seemed merely hypocritical.

The disaffected students, while disturbing, were nonetheless a small minority among the student body. A much larger group was politically indifferent and apathetic. As was the case with disaffection, the sources, forms, and degrees of political apathy were highly varied. A sizeable group of students, including many of the best students in the pure and applied natural sciences, had developed a deep sense of professionalism and a somewhat technocratic orientation which made them shun political involvement and become restive at political interference in their own spheres of primary interest, be it interference in the form of demands that they perform political functions or that they pursue their professional callings from a "Marxist-Leninist perspective." Another group was apathetic from sheer overwhelming boredom aroused by the dogmatism and repetitiveness of all political communication sponsored by the regime, whether in the classroom, the Komsomol, or the mass media. And yet a third group—perhaps the largest of all—developed an attitude toward politics that was purely instrumental. Political involvement was for them but a part of the process of acquiring prestige and status. The students in the group were adept at expressing zeal and enthusiasm at appropriate moments and were politically active when occasion demanded, but they were basically self-satisfied and complacent.[86] The artificial quality of the activism of this group was demonstrated with particular force in the years after 1954 when the number of ten-year school graduates began greatly to exceed the number of openings in institutions of higher education.[87] A great many of those ten-year school graduates who were denied admission to the university or institute of their choice refused to enter the labor force and engaged in endless attempts extending over a period of years to gain admittance to *any* department of *any* institution of higher education. They were unwilling to serve the regime in any but a "suitable" station despite the fact that the regime was facing a manpower shortage and could offer such challenging perspectives as labor in the Virgin Lands. As Khrushchev put it, they disdained and had a contemptuous attitude toward labor, and this was not only ideologically disturbing but also boded ill for

[86] See Callaghan, *op.cit.*, and Burg, *op.cit.*, for further discussion of the apathetic and "careerist" students.

[87] See above, pp. 252-253.

the quality of their work when and if they achieved "suitable" positions.[88] Soviet executives no less than Soviet laborers were supposed to be "shock workers," and "disdain for labor" was unlikely to be translated into the desired entrepreneurial behavior.

IV

The inability of the educational system to cope with the major problems discussed in the preceding section was one of the critical motive forces behind the "Khrushchev school reform" of 1958.[89] It was also the critical motive force behind Khrushchev's campaign, which began in 1956, to establish an extensive network of boarding schools. While this campaign preceded Khrushchev's major intervention in the field of educational policy, the two are intimately related, and the former may have even greater long-run significance than the latter.

The *immediate* function of the boarding schools, which presently number more than 2,000 with some 700,000 students enrolled, is to spur social mobility by increasing the educational opportunities of lower-class children, and it is from among such children that the students of the boarding schools are being primarily drawn.[90] *Ultimately*, however, as the President of the Russian Republic Academy of Pedagogy and many other authoritative spokesmen have made clear, "the boarding schools will become the new school of communist society," and will dominate or even monopolize the Soviet educational scene.[91] As this goal is realized, the function of the boarding schools increasingly will be to withdraw all children from parental

---

[88] Khrushchev, "On Strengthening," p. 73; Khrushchev, "Educating Active and Conscious Builders," pp. 65-66. Khrushchev tended to attribute this complacency to "upper class" origins but its prevalence among students who did not gain admittance to institutions of higher education suggests that it was marked among students of worker and peasant origin as well. The educational system tended to inculcate status-consciousness and a variety of "anticipatory" class-consciousness in its own right irrespective of the social origins of those involved.

[89] See below, p. 259, for a recognition that the precise timing of the reform was heavily influenced by the existence of a serious manpower shortage. It should also be noted that Khrushchev's original proposals for reform were more radical even than those adopted. Khrushchev was persuaded or compelled to compromise on some issues, due primarily, it appears, to opposition from educators and members of the "new class." However, the compromises did not affect fundamentals and have already been abrogated in some respects (e.g., with respect to "schools for the gifted").

[90] See *Current Digest of the Soviet Press*, Vol. XIV, No. 3, p. 24, speech of Kairov to the Twenty-Second Party Congress. Cf. also *Current Digest of the Soviet Press*, Vol. XIV, No. 2, p. 17, speech of Mukhitdinov to the Twenty-Second Congress.

[91] *Current Digest of the Soviet Press*, Vol. XIV, No. 3, p. 28, speech of Kairov to the Twenty-Second Party Congress.

influence and place their "upbringing" under the complete control of the regime. Through the boarding schools, it is hoped, it will be possible to shield children from traditional values and attitudes reflecting status- or class-consciousness. Ideally, all children will be exposed to identical influences and will be treated with complete equality, thus laying the basis for a wholly impersonal, wholly objective process of social and political recruitment. The boarding schools, in other words, represent the beginning of an attempt to eliminate the family as a significant agency of political socialization and as a final, natural (as opposed to institutional or societal), limit to the consolidation of totalitarian power.[92] They represent a decisive attempt to lay the basis for the establishment of a "consensual" or "popular" totalitarianism.

At least for the immediate future, due to a combination of serious construction difficulties and parental resistance to the boarding school concept, the ordinary schools will remain in existence and will embrace the great majority of students.[93] These schools have, however, been fundamentally reorganized, this reorganization constituting the "Khrushchev school reform" proper, as proposed by Khrushchev in a speech before the Thirteenth Congress of the Komsomol in April 1958, and subsequently elaborated, modified, and authorized by the Central Committee and the Supreme Soviet.[94]

STRUCTURE AND SCOPE AFTER THE REFORM

The 1958 reform did not envision major changes in the grade structure of the educational system. The most notable change was the conversion of the seven-year schools into eight-year schools and the (temporary) conversion of ten-year schools into eleven-year schools, but this was a derivative of the "polytechnicization" of the curriculum and has no independent significance.[95] In terms of scope, however, a

[92] See *New York Times*, May 3, 1961, for a report on one of the nursery boarding schools already in existence. See *Novy Mir*, July 1960, for an article in which the dean of Soviet economists, S. G. Strumilin, depicts the Communist future as follows: "Any Soviet citizen who enters the world will automatically be placed in a nursery, moving on to a children's home and then, at the appropriate age, to a boarding school. . . . We are completely opposed to the tradition which regards children as the 'property' of parents."

[93] Within the ordinary school system, however, it is noteworthy that the "extended day school" is being more and more widely introduced. In addition increased stress has been placed on the need to expand and improve public crèche and nursery facilities. Both of these measures can be seen as steps toward the ultimate boarding school ideal.

[94] See above, footnote 89.

[95] See below, pp. 261-262. More accurately, the conversion was a derivative of "polytechnicalization" combined with a desire to preserve the bulk of the old curricu-

number of important changes have taken place. The compulsory education requirement has been extended from seven to eight years.[96] Steps have been taken to overcome at least some of the obstacles that led earlier to rural "deviations" from the legal educational norms. The network of schools for "working and rural youth" has been expanded and the quality of education offered in the latter has been improved. The most fundamental change has been that the great majority of complete secondary school graduates have been compelled to enter the work force for at least two years in consequence of a provision that 80 per cent of all places in institutions of higher education are reserved for young people with at least two years' work experience.[97] One effect of this measure has been a considerable increase in the size of the work force during the current period when the Soviet Union faces a serious manpower shortage resulting from the decline in the birth rate in the years 1941-1947. A desire to fill the manpower gap was no doubt responsible for the timing of this measure.[98] However, the measure

---

lum. In the winter of 1963-1964 suggestions that the eleven-year schools be reconverted back into ten-year schools began to appear in the Soviet press. (See, for example, *Current Digest of the Soviet Press*, Vol. xv, No. 41, p. 15), and in the fall of 1964 this reconversion was officially decreed. In addition, in the summer of 1964 the term of higher education for certain specialties was reduced by periods of 6 to 12 months.

[96] See Utechin, *op.cit.*, p. 127. Eight-year compulsory education is already established in the Ukraine and in the Russian Republic. Eight-year compulsory education represents, of course, a retreat from the goal of immediately realizing universal compulsory ten-year education—a goal slated for realization in 1960 by the Nineteenth Party Congress and reaffirmed by the Twentieth Party Congress. There has been considerable discussion of the possibility of accommodating the additional year of compulsory education provided by the reform by enrolling children in school at age six instead of age seven. For the time there has been no action in this regard, but such a change seems a likely possibility, since it would mean that there would be no delay in youth's entering the work force and would bring youth under the direct supervision of the regime earlier, thus curtailing the role of the family and of unorganized peer-groups as agencies of political socialization.

[97] In 1960, only 67,500 of over 1,000,000 secondary school graduates were admitted to higher educational establishments (*Pravda*, January 26, 1961). Already well over 50 per cent of matriculating university students are meeting the requirement of two years' prior work in production (*Current Digest of the Soviet Press*, Vol. xii, No. 20, p. 9; *Pravda*, October 22, 1963, p. 1). Probably the bulk of the students who are exempted from this requirement are those especially gifted in physics, chemistry, mathematics, and the performing arts (Bereday and Rennar, *The Politics*, p. 38). It should also be noted that the reform provides that the bulk of the university students acquire the first two years of their higher education by correspondence or through evening study while remaining on the job. Again exceptions are ultimately to be made only for aspiring scientists whose education depends on access to laboratories. At present 56.5 per cent of all matriculating students are evening or correspondence students (*Current Digest of the Soviet Press*, Vol. xiii, No. 20, p. 11).

[98] A desire to fill the manpower gap may also be responsible for some temporary reversal of the hitherto prevailing tendency to permit more and more children to continue full-time study beyond the level required by law. However, the author knows of no evidence to support the implicit suggestion of members of the Comparative Education Society that there will be a dramatic reversal of this tendency in conjunc-

has much broader significance. It appears to be designed, among other things, to improve the position of young workers who complete their secondary education in their free time relative to graduates of regular complete secondary schools (*and technicums*) in the competition for admission to higher education. It has the effect of confronting those in the latter group with the necessity of using their spare time to maintain their knowledge or else of losing the benefit of the scholastic advantages which they initially enjoy over the students of the "schools for working and rural youth." What seems to be involved is a conscious policy of academic "leveling down" in order to increase equality of opportunity and, since most children of elite families will continue to attend complete secondary schools, in order to increase social mobility.[99]

Still, the bulk of university students will probably continue to be complete secondary school graduates. Where this group is concerned, the rulers believe that two years in production will make it possible to identify the most highly motivated students and insure that only they are admitted to higher education, and what is even more important, will help eradicate the class- and status-consciousness which characterized so many graduates of the old ten-year schools. Forcing students into production will, it is hoped, reveal to watchful eyes those students who are adversely affected by the discovery that the reality of Soviet life does not square completely with the theories professed in the schools. It will instill a healthy discipline into those students who are inclined to nonconformity or who entertain dissident notions.[100] And it will induce the complacent students to overcome

---

tion with the school reform. (See Bereday, *The Changing*, p. 268, where it is stated without any reference that under the reform it is planned that 60 to 75 per cent of eight-year school graduates will be inducted directly into . . . the work force, while only 10 per cent will be allowed to go to complete middle schools.)

[99] Cf. E. L. Manevich, "Obliterating Distinctions Between Mental and Physical Labor," *Voprosy Filosofii*, Vol. 9 (1961), translated in *The Soviet Review*, Vol. II, No. 2, February 1962: "Henceforth all students without exception will be required to work in production for a certain period before being admitted to college. Of course, children of brain workers will *still* (italics mine) for a time enjoy certain advantages in that they have more favorable conditions of study at home.(?) However, the entire system of training, the obligatory nature of work in production . . . will . . . become instrumental for youth" (p. 23).

[100] See Cantril, *op.cit.*, pp. 43-44. Cantril and some others suggest that the measure under discussion was adopted in order to reduce the pressure on institutions of higher education, the theory being that after two years in production, many ex-students will have ceased to aspire to higher education. It may have this effect, but this was probably not its purpose, since the regime recognizes that in the long run, more and more engineers and technicians will be needed for the maturing economy. The measure is designed not to discourage applicants for higher education, but to eliminate the

their "disdain for labor." In sum, it is expected to insure a "health-ier" university population and hence, ultimately, a "healthier" elite. And, in order to make certain that only those who respond "posi-tively" to their experience in production are permitted to go on with their education and that no "extraneous factors" such as family pres-sure interfere with the selection process, the reform law provides that admissions be contingent not only upon school records and the results of entrance examinations, but also upon the recommendations of "public organizations" (trade-union, Komsomol, and party organiza-tions) at the applicant's place of work, and that representatives of "public organizations" sit on all admissions boards.

CURRICULUM AFTER THE REFORM

The most dramatic changes in the educational system have taken place in the curriculum. Above all, increased attention has been de-voted to "polytechnical training," and, as already noted, it is the in-troduction of a wide range of polytechnical subjects into the curricu-lum that is responsible for the conversion of the seven-year into eight-year schools.[101] At the lower and middle levels of the educational system, "polytechnicalization" means that a much greater amount of time is now devoted to "shop" courses, whereas in the complete secondary schools (which have been rechristened "labor-polytechnic schools with production training") the students now spend one-third of their time actually working in industry or agriculture.[102] In addi-tion, at both levels, there is a de-emphasis of theoretical in favor of applied science. One of the purposes behind "polytechnicalization" is to provide students with vocational skills so that when they enter the work force—even if for only two years—they will not need ex-tensive on-the-job training.[103] Indeed, the production training which

---

belief of complete secondary school graduates that they are entitled to education. Under the new system it is hoped that only the highly motivated will apply. The long-term effort, however, is to produce young citizens who are highly motivated and hence will apply.

[101] Cf. *Pravda*, November 10, 1956, for a curious threat by Khrushchev to have dissident students relegated to work in factories where the workers would teach them discipline.

[102] Cf. Bereday and Rennar, *The Politics*, Chap. 2, for a fairly thorough discussion of "polytechnical education," including its historical background. It should be noted that "polytechnical education" is sanctified in Marxist theory, that it was a major component of the Soviet curriculum prior to the "traditionalization" of the educa-tional system in the 1930's, and that it was reintroduced into the curriculum by the Nineteenth Party Congress, although it was not until the 1958 reform that a campaign to realize this decision was launched.

[103] See *Soviet Education*, Vol. I, No. 11, September 1959, p. 22.

complete secondary school students receive is supposed in many cases to be equivalent to a full-fledged apprenticeship in one or another production skill.[104] However, vocational training is not the sole purpose behind "polytechnicalization," and perhaps it is not the most important one.[105] According to leading Soviet educational officials, polytechnical and production training have "become the most effective factor in the ideological education of students. While learning a trade, the student becomes imbued with working class spirit, with the spirit of collectivism, discipline, and organization."[106] In other words, polytechnical and production training are designed to inculcate a respect for labor, to generate enthusiastic commitment to the economic objectives of the regime, to bring home the reality of socialist ownership, to inhibit the growth of class and status consciousness, etc. They are intended to play the same rôle in the political socialization process as the compulsory two-year assignment upon graduation. What one has, in effect, is the traditional technique of "socially useful labor" elevated to a formal place in the curriculum and given a much wider and more intensive application.[107]

The tremendous emphasis placed upon polytechnical training and the great store set by its power as an ideological-indoctrinational weapon have not led to a diminution in the scope of the traditional program of political education. If anything, the latter has been expanded and intensified. Thus, courses in "The Fundamentals of Political Knowledge" and "Social Science" have been introduced in the complete secondary schools (usually in the eleventh grade), while at the higher education level, new courses in "The Foundations of Scientific Communism," "Marxist-Leninist Esthetics," "Marxist-Leninist Ethics," and "The Foundations of Scientific Atheism" have been established.[108] What is involved here is an effort to buttress official political, esthetic, and moral theory in the face of deviant tendencies

---

[104] See Utechin, *op.cit.*, p. 128. Currently, about 25 per cent of those students entering the work force after completing their compulsory education receive preliminary job training for brief periods in special vocational schools.

[105] *Soviet Education*, Vol. I, No. 11, September 1959, p. 22.

[106] *Ibid.* The fact that plant managers often show considerable hostility to students engaged in "production training" indicates that the economic benefits of the latter should not be exaggerated. The presence of students in plants on only a part-time basis (two days a week usually) has a disruptive effect on production. Economically, short-run losses may outweigh long-run gains.

[107] *Soviet Education*, Vol. III, No. 3, January 1961, p. 29. See also *Soviet Education*, Vol. II, No. 7, May 1960, p. 28.

[108] See *Soviet Education*, Vol. II, No. 6, pp. 39-43; *Kommunist*, Vol. 3, February 1962, p. 29; *Soviet Education*, Vol. II, No. 5, p. 11; *Soviet Education*, Vol. I, No. 9, p. 27; *Pravda*, January 22, 1964, p. 4; *Pravda*, February 8, 1963, p. 4.

unleashed or called forth by the post-Stalin "thaw." More broadly, however, the aim is to arouse active ideological commitment. This effort was characteristic of the Stalin period as well, but on a much diminished scale. Now it is felt that exposure to relatively "pure" ideology is not as potentially dangerous as it was because reality contrasts less starkly with theory. In addition, the rulers feel that theory is more necessary now because terror is not so readily available or so effective as a technique of social mobilization, and ideological commitment alone can fill the gap and prevent routinization.[109]

As a natural concomitant of the increased stress on inculcating Marxism-Leninism considerably more attention is being devoted to developing appropriate orientations toward the regime and governmental "levels" of the political system. The history program in the schools has been revised by order of the Central Committee (October 8, 1959) to accord more time to the history of the Soviet periods in general, and current history in particular.[110] Simultaneously, the content of Soviet history as taught in the schools is being altered in an effort to weed out all traces of the Stalin "personality cult."[111] The Lenin cult is still very much present and history teachers are still instructed to present their subject in such a way that the students are acquainted with appropriate model "heroes" to imitate. However, once one moves beyond the period of the Revolution—which is now treated at even greater length than earlier in order to inspire youth with "revolutionary romanticism"—individuals recede and "the People" and, above all, "the Party" become the chief characters on the historical stage.[112] Among other things, this increased stress on the Soviet period and on the regime and government is probably part of an effort to reduce nationality tensions in Soviet life

[109] See below, pp. 266-267.

[110] See *Soviet Education*, Vol. II, No. 1, p. 35; *Soviet Education*, Vol. II, No. 6, pp. 38-40; *Soviet Education*, Vol. III, No. 3, p. 14; *Soviet Education*, Vol. II, No. 9, p. 37.

[111] How long and slow a process this is is suggested by the continuing appearance of complaints from the highest officials that even current texts and study guides contain reflections of the "cult of personality." (See, for example, the remarks of Suslov in *Kommunist*, Vol. 6, February 1962.)

[112] See *Soviet Education*, Vol. II, No. 10, p. 8; *Soviet Education*, Vol. II, No. 11, p. 47; *Soviet Education*, Vol. II, No. 6, pp. 39-40; *Soviet Education*, Vol. III, No. 5. There was certainly no "Khrushchev cult" resembling the Lenin cult or the old Stalin cult, but there were signs that a modified "Khrushchev cult" was in the process of formation as the Soviet press began to charge following Khrushchev's deposition. One sign of "recidivism" was an immensely adulatory biography of Khrushchev. (See P. Bogdanov et al., *Rasskaz o Pochyotnom Shakhtyorye*, Stalino, 1961.)

by diverting attention away from historical traditions which are often divisive and from the question of community identification which is so intimately related to historical traditions. This is particularly important, because, where the community is concerned, the regime has felt compelled to make concessions to the minority nationalities by reducing the peculiarly Russian component in the concept of "Soviet patriotism" and by granting permission to devote more class time to the history of the local nationality. The schools are warned that local history must be taught as an integral part of the history of the USSR and that great care must be exercised to combat any manifestations of "bourgeois nationalism," but the concessionary policy still has inherent dangers that make it all the more imperative to inculcate values and attitudes which lead to support for the regime and government.[113]

ATMOSPHERE AND SPIRIT AFTER THE REFORM

In conjunction with the school reform it was recognized that the authoritarianism and rigidity that characterized the atmosphere and spirit of school life were partly responsible for the widespread apathy and indifference among students. In consequence an attempt has been made to introduce some modifications. While the "Rules for Students" remain in force and the formal recitation and the lecture remain the standard pedagogical techniques, teachers have been urged to permit more individual student initiative, to venture outside the confines of the prescribed texts, and to honor the questions of students and make an effort to discover those issues that concern them.[114] What is involved, however, is not a quest for intellectual independence. Education is still defined, as it once was by the late Soviet President Kalinin, as "the definite, purposeful, and systematic influencing of the mind of the person being educated in order to imbue him with the qualities desired by the educator."[115] It has simply been recognized that such

---

[113] See *Soviet Education*, Vol. II, No. 7, pp. 33-36; *Current Digest of the Soviet Press*, Vol. XI, No. 40, p. 24; *Current Digest*, Vol. XI, No. 37, pp. 14-15; *Current Digest*, Vol. XI, No. 46, pp. 33-34. Another aspect of the concessionary policy is that the study of Russian in native-language schools has now been put on a voluntary basis. However, it is unclear how meaningful this provision has been in actuality. (See Bereday, *The Politics*, p. 119; *Current Digest*, Vol. X, No. 5, p. 3; *Current Digest*, Vol. X, No. 48, p. 16; *Current Digest*, Vol. XI, No. 39, pp. 3-7; *Kommunist*, Vol. I, *January* 1962, p. 68.)

[114] See "Improve in Every Way the Methods and Organizational Forms of Instruction," *Soviet Education*, Vol. I, No. 10; *Pravda*, January 10, 1962, p. 4; *Current Digest*, Vol. IX, No. 1, pp. 11-12; "Elimination of Formalism in the Make-Up of Lessons," *Soviet Education*, Vol. I, No. 3; *Izvestia*, May 9, 1963, p. 3.

[115] Kalinin, *op. cit.*, p. 126.

"influencing" requires a more sophisticated approach on the part of teachers. The following words of the party's leading journal indicate the concern which animates the regime: "If the student is given no answers to his inquiries on matters that interest him, he will nonetheless continue to search for one. To avoid answering questions on subjects of concern to students is to open the way for all kinds of false rumors, to weaken the struggle against the bourgeois and petty-bourgeois ideology which reaches our country by way of the radio, the press, etc. That is why it is necessary to take up the questions raised by our youth and where necessary . . . to unmask the inner contradictions of erroneous views."[116]

Essentially this same concern lies behind the effort which has been launched in conjunction with the school reform to revitalize the functioning of the student *kollektivs*. It is hoped that by making the *kollektivs* more independent of direct control by teachers and school administrators, by giving them a wider role in the school and society at large, and by observing the forms of internal democracy, the *kollektivs* will be better able to fulfill their assigned tasks—tasks which are unchanged—in the political socialization program.[117] Under the old system, it is now recognized, manipulation was too direct and too obvious, and, in consequence, large numbers of students viewed their membership in the *kollektivs* with indifference and approached their involvement in the activities of the *kollektiv* with resignation rather than with enthusiasm. As a result, group pressure on the individual tended to have a highly artificial quality which reduced its effectiveness as a technique of social control. At the same time, by freeing the *kollektivs* from their excessive subordination to the educational authorities, the regime hopes to guard against the contamination of the former by the "special interest" orientation of the latter. Academic success will no longer be able to serve so easily as a shield against punishment for nonconformist behavior and intellectual brilliance will no longer be accepted, as it sometimes was earlier, as an excuse for political passivity.[118] Activism will be a *sine qua non* of success.

V

The "Khrushchev school reform" should be viewed as an effort to overcome many of the "failures" of the old educational system in its

[116] *Partinaya Zhizn*, Vol. 22 (1956).

[117] See *Current Digest*, Vol. XII, No. 30, p. 16.

[118] See *Current Digest*, Vol. XIV, No. 1, p. 29, for what is, in effect, a protest against this new situation from a prominent scholar, Academician I. Tamm.

endeavor to socialize all Soviet youth into the official, totalitarian political culture. As has already been noted, these "failures" are far from telling the entire story of how the Soviet educational system functioned prior to 1958. Its "successes" were manifold and impressive, and, in a number of important instances, the "failures" were at least partially direct or indirect consequences of these "successes," although this made them no less intolerable from the point of view of the regime.[119] The "failures" of the educational system became particularly intolerable after the death of Stalin in view of the succession leadership's decision greatly to curtail the application of terror. To a degree this decision itself was no doubt a consequence of the "successes" achieved by the system. In the first place, Stalin-style terror had become increasingly costly with the economic development of Soviet society, and the educational system played a significant role in the process of economic development. In the second place, the educational system had created enough consensus and support that Stalin-style terror was no longer absolutely essential to the retention of governmental power in the hands of the Party leadership.[120]

The decision to curtail the application of terror also was prompted by a desire on the part of the leadership to rally further support, and there was no doubt that the decision would make it easier for the educational system to contribute to this process. Terror had made the tasks of the educational system more difficult by discouraging initiative, by heightening the tension between family and school, by enlarging the gap between professed theory and reality, etc.[121] At the

[119] See above, pp. 247-248.

[120] Other factors in the decision to relegate terror to the background were the desire to preserve "collective leadership," the desire on the part of the party leadership to reduce the possibility of using the police apparatus as a power base in the succession struggle, the desire not to revolt world opinion, and, possibly, the desire to shed forever the horrors of Stalinism. It makes little sense, in the eyes of the author, to say that industrial maturation or a vastly increased level of education had made terror impossible. Stalin was evidently planning an extensive violent purge in 1952 and there seems no valid reason to assume that he would have abandoned his plan or that its execution would have brought about his downfall. The cost would have been unprecedentedly high, but it could have been met. It is possible that now, after terror has been relegated to the background for nearly a decade, its re-establishment would be impossible in the sense that it would bring about the downfall of those who launched it. Soviet society has become somewhat more resilient, thanks to the prolonged absence of widespread and violent terror, and it might show greater powers of resistance. Even this is far from certain, however, and in the immediately post-Stalin period society was still so atomized that a united succession leadership could have proceeded to atomize it further through the application of terror without undue risk to its own domestic power.

[121] See Callaghan, *op. cit.*, p. 15, for some brief comments on terror and student disaffection.

same time, however, terror had tended to compensate for (as well as to conceal) the "failures" of the educational system. It had functioned to uproot traditional loyalties, to inhibit the growth of group solidarity (among co-nationals, co-professionals, etc.), to frustrate attempts to consolidate and transmit status, to prevent the growth of class-consciousness (partly by making the possession of privilege less enviable since it meant a vastly increased likelihood of arrest), to maintain rapid social mobility, to enforce conformity, and to produce activist and entrepreneurial behavior. These were crucial functions in the totalitarian scheme, and a mere increase in generalized support and consensus did not render their exercise superfluous.

Generalized support and consensus, while desirable in many respects, did not guarantee the sort of behavior that the leadership considered essential to the maintenance and consolidation of its total power, and they were positively dangerous if they were rooted in a spirit of demobilization and were oriented toward the *status quo*. Terror and education had been harnessed to the same goal in Stalinist Russia; their joint task had been to facilitate the accumulation of total power in the hands of the party elite. The succession leadership's decision to relegate terror to the background meant that the educational system was called upon to assume a double burden. The ultimate goal of the educational system had been to render terror superfluous by establishing a *totalitarian* consensus in society and creating a "new man" characterized by the sort of self-control and self-mobilization that would permit the establishment of a wholly "consensual" or "popular" totalitarianism. Now, with terror held in abeyance and with the possibilities of its extensive use perhaps increasingly atrophying, this ultimate goal has taken on much more immediate and pressing operational significance.[122]

Whether the "Khrushchev school reform" has or will actually further the realization of this ultimate goal is doubtful. The first thing to be noted in this connection is that, because of its association with the current manpower shortage, the reform has probably meant decreased exposure to the educational system for many Soviet children.[123] To the extent that this continues to be the case, the reform will produce an increased cultural gap between the average Soviet youth and

---

[122] See above, footnote 120; see Zbigniew K. Brzezinski, *Ideology and Power in Soviet Politics*, New York, Praeger, 1962, Chapter 3, for a somewhat similar appraisal, though without specific reference to the educational system.
[123] See above, p. 259, and footnote 98.

his comrade who achieves the upper reaches of the educational sys-tem.[124] Secondly, the regime has been unwilling (or, as some evi-dence would indicate, unable) to allocate to education the funds that alone could permit the new system to have a major impact on the rate of social mobility in society, particularly upward social mobility. In-adequate funds are primarily responsible for the countryside's contin-uing to lag behind the cities in meeting the compulsory education requirement,[125] and to a considerable extent for the continued infe-riority of the "schools for working and rural youth" to the regular complete secondary schools.[126] This latter fact, combined with the fact that the need for manpower has made it difficult to reduce work-ing hours to the point where after-hours study does not represent an immense and often intolerable drain on energy, means that the bulk of those matriculating in institutions of higher education still are graduates of the regular complete secondary schools and are disproportionately likely to be children of the elite.[127] The threat of an increased cultural gap is serious enough in a political system committed to cultural homogeneity; it becomes doubly serious in the absence of a high rate of social mobility to insure that the lines of cultural division do not parallel prevailing class and status lines and reinforce class-consciousness. There is even a possibility that the "Khrushchev school reform" by increasing the cultural gap without greatly increasing mobility will further rather than overcome the propensities toward the development of class-consciousness which are widespread among children of the elite.

Nor is the hope that the necessity of working two years in pro-duction will overcome these propensities likely to be fulfilled. The work experience tends to be viewed by many complete secondary school graduates as simply a normal interlude in their progression toward relatively certain inclusion in the Soviet elite. In cases where

---

[124] See Nicholas P. Vakar, *The Taproot of Soviet Society*, New York, Harper, 1961, p. 147.

[125] See *Soviet Education*, Vol. III, No. 7, p. 59; *Soviet Education*, Vol. III, No. 9, p. 5; *Soviet Education*, Vol. III, No. 1, p. 48.

[126] See *Soviet Education*, Vol. II, No. 9, p. 29; *Soviet Education*, Vol. III, No. 1, p. 56. This drain on energy was one of the factors leading to a 30 per cent drop-out rate among senior grade students in "schools for working and rural youth."

[127] Apart from their much better academic background, elite children probably have a much easier time getting included in the quota of students admitted to institutions of higher education without work experience. Parental influence plays a part still, nor is there any reason to doubt that parental pressure continues to influence ordinary admissions procedures, despite the involvement of public organizations in the latter. (See *Current Digest*, Vol. XIV, No. 16, p. 9.)

it does not prove to be merely an interlude, extreme disaffection may result and cause problems more serious than those which widespread apathy now causes. Disaffection generated by frustrated ambition may, moreover, prove less amenable to coercion or persuasion than purely intellectual disaffection. As for the latter, it is doubtful that experience in production will dissolve it. The regime is relying on the workers to exert a "healthy" influence on the disaffected students, but, at the same time, it is increasing the possibility that the workers themselves will be "contaminated." While the potential explosiveness of the situation should not be exaggerated, the reform does have the effect of providing the small band of dissident intelligentsia an outlet to the masses which it lacked earlier, and what evidence is available indicates that discontent is already more pervasive among the masses than among the bureaucratic elements who earlier provided the main social contacts of the student-dissenters.[128]

The same sorts of considerations apply in estimating the probable effectiveness of the "polytechnicalization" of the curriculum. However, there are several additional factors which must be considered in discussing "polytechnicalization."

The "polytechnicalization" of the curriculum has created particular problems with respect to the minority nationalities. Throughout the USSR, despite the addition of a year to the normal education cycle, "polytechnicalization" has meant a reduction in the time allotted to the humanities in the educational program. In the national republics the Russian language is among those subjects whose time allotment has been reduced, thus compounding an already bad situation.[129] And finally, by devaluing "pure" science, "polytechnicalization" threatens to slow the pace of technical innovation in society in the long run, thus reducing the regime's relative power in the world arena and calling into question the regime's claim to represent the forces of "progress" in all walks of life.[130]

As for the other non-structural aspects of the reform, the attempt to

[128] See G. L. Kline, "Russia Five Years After Stalin: Education," *New Leader*, Vol. 41, No. 24, June 16, 1958, p. 9. By creating a "single culture," "one nation" instead of two, the educational system has in large measure eliminated the problem of communication between the intelligentsia and the masses, which was so important an element in the frustration of revolutionary movements in the nineteenth century.

[129] See *Soviet Education*, Vol. II, No. 9, p. 35; *Current Digest*, Vol. XIV, No. 2, p. 17; *Izvestia*, April 14, 1962, p. 1.

[130] This is also likely to be the consequence of the work requirement. Students entering the institutions of higher education from production are less well prepared than those who enter direct from school. (*Current Digest*, Vol. XIII, No. 20, p. 9.) Higher motivation, even where present, may not compensate.

overcome boredom and political indifference among the students by enlivening and liberalizing the school atmosphere has probably yielded some positive results, but of limited scope. The force of training and habit combined with deeply ingrained timidity make it extremely difficult for most Soviet teachers to modify their rigid and authoritarian pedagogical style. In addition, the regime itself has made it unmistakably clear that liberalization must not mean tolerance for "demagogic excesses" and "unprincipled criticism," thus setting definite but undefined boundaries to student independence, free discussion, etc., and reinforcing the temptation of teachers (as well as Komsomol leaders at another level) to maintain the status quo. Finally, the regime continues to insist that rather crude and overt indoctrination play a prominent part in the educational process. In consequence, boredom remains rife among students, political passivity is induced, and the educational environment remains too rigid and formalistic to prevent or deal with the disaffected student.[131]

Even this brief discussion of the "Khrushchev school reform" should suffice to make clear that the reform has been and can be no "cure-all" for the problems that beset the old educational system and that it has and will create new problems of its own. The Soviet educational system is still not a perfect instrument of totalitarian consolidation. However, the Soviet rulers have not abandoned their attempt to make it so. Whether this attempt is inevitably doomed to frustration is a moot point. As has been shown above, many of the "failures" of the old system and of the new are rooted in inadequate resources. Despite their faith in the almost unlimited possibilities of social and psychological engineering through education, the Soviet rulers have never put education at the apex of their priority schedule. Other goals have been considered more pressing. Moreover, these other goals, in addition to diverting resources from the educational system, have led the rulers to divert the attention of the educational system from its ultimate goal and, in some cases, to establish programs which conflicted with that goal. In the 1930's, for example, the educational system was required to train hundreds of thousands of engineers and technicians at so rapid a rate that thorough political training had to be by-passed; and, even today, the attempt to use polytechnical training in lieu of industrial

[131] See *Soviet Education*, Vol. ii, No. 5, pp. 16-17; "Improve in Every Way the Methods and Organizational Forms of Instruction," *Soviet Education*, Vol. i, No. 10; *Kommunist*, Vol. 3, February 1962, p. 25; *Current Digest*, Vol. xiii, No. 49, p. 29; *Current Digest*, Vol. xi, No. 27, p. 12; *Komsomolskaya Pravda*, xxx October 6, 1961.

apprenticeships in order to bridge the manpower gap reduces the possibility of using such training to full indoctrinational effect. However, the ultimate goal of creating a "new Soviet man" has never been abandoned and, in fact, has recently been reaffirmed with renewed vigor. The author's belief is that in the future the educational system will receive more and more resources. In particular, the boarding school program, which entails immense expenditures, will be pressed. While short-run considerations may prevent any rapid movement in this regard and may even lead to some retrenchment from announced goals,[132] the boarding schools are a "natural" outgrowth of the quest for total power, given the current "stage" of development in the USSR, and Khrushchev's successors are likely to be as committed to this quest as was Khrushchev himself. Resources alone, of course, are not enough to ensure the successful functioning of the boarding schools. The "new Soviet man" cannot be his own teacher, and the necessity of using "old" teachers in the new boarding schools will give "survivals of the past" a renewed lease on life. However, if Khrushchev and his successors press the boarding school program and tolerate no long-term opposition to it, the possibility of the educational system's actually accomplishing its ultimate task of socializing Soviet youth into totalitarian political culture cannot be rejected *prima facie*, except by those who believe that there are anti-totalitarian traits inherent in man. Even the "successful" functioning of the boarding schools would not, to be sure, guarantee the establishment of a "popular totalitarianism." As was pointed out in the first pages of this essay, political socialization continues beyond the period of youth. The broader "postgraduate" milieu of Soviet life will, for a long time to come, be such as to challenge the values, beliefs, attitudes, and sentiments inculcated by the education system with alternative, and often conflicting, values, beliefs, attitudes, and sentiments. Though there is comfort in this for lovers of freedom, the danger that a "consensual" or "popular" totalitarianism is in the offing is unprecedentedly real.

[132] It has, for example, been reliably reported that the secondary classes in most boarding schools have recently been suspended and the students assigned to regular schools.

CHAPTER 9

JAPAN [1]

HERBERT PASSIN

≈≈≈≈≈≈≈≈≈≈≈≈≈≈≈≈≈≈≈

I. The Japanese Educational System

THE BEGINNINGS

Many people speculate on the mystery of Japan's extraordinary growth, writes Seiichi Tōhata, the distinguished agricultural economist. The answer is—in effect—that Japan developed a comprehensive educational system rapidly. Her social investment in education is now paying off.[2]

TABLE 1: ELEMENTARY SCHOOL ATTENDANCE RATIO
FOR SELECTED YEARS[a]

Year	Ratio	Boys	Girls
1873	28%	40%	15%
1883	51	67	34
1893	59	75	41
1903	94	97	93
1913	98	99	98
1923	99	99	99
1933	99.58	99.58	99.58
1943	99.76	99.75	99.77

[a] Figures taken from Mombusho (Ministry of Education): *Gakusei 80-nen-shi* (80 Years' History of the School System), Tokyo, 1954, Table I, pp. 1037-1038.

Within four years of the Meiji Restoration, in 1872, a Fundamental Code of Education was promulgated, envisioning the creation of a fully modern and comprehensive system of education, to be in principle universal and compulsory. (England achieved this in 1870, and France only in 1882.) Education, the preamble declares, is the key to personal development and to success in life. It is not the exclusive privilege of the samurai, as used to be thought in the past, but rather

[1] The themes of this paper are elaborated more fully in Herbert Passin, *Society and Education in Japan*, Comparative Education Series, New York, Bureau of Publications, Teachers College, Columbia University, 1964, Chs. 6-8.

[2] *Nihon Keizai* Newspaper, May 14, 1962. Also see the recent studies on financial return from "educational investment," Mombusho, *Nihon no Seichō to Kyōiku* (Japan's Economic Growth and Education), 1962, substantially translated into English as Ministry of Education, *Japan's Growth and Education*, Tokyo, 1963.

the duty of all the people. "There shall, in the future, be no community with an illiterate family, or a family with an illiterate person." Even though the bold plan for the immediate establishment of 8 universities, 256 middle schools, and 53,760 elementary schools could not be put into effect as quickly as optimists had hoped, progress was rapid enough. In 1873, 28 per cent of school-age children (40 per cent of the boys, 15 per cent of the girls) were in school; and by the first years of the twentieth century attendance was virtually complete.

Compulsory attendance was first set at four years, and by 1907, once it had taken hold firmly, raised to six years.[3] In 1941, it was proposed to increase compulsory schooling to eight years; although wartime conditions prevented the system from going fully into effect, 67 per cent were already taking some form of secondary education.[4] In 1947, under the American Occupation's reforms, the period of compulsory schooling was raised to nine years, that is, through the lower secondary grades (corresponding to the American junior high school). By 1955-1957, 98 per cent of all children in the appropriate age groups were enrolled in lower secondary schools.

In upper secondary school education (senior high school level) the latest figures (62 per cent enrollment)[5] now place Japan among the leading countries of the world. By 1970, the enrollment ratio is expected to reach 72 per cent. And in university attendance (700,000 students), Japan (along with the Soviet Union) ranks second only to the United States in ratio of university students to population—sub-

---

[3] The legally required years of schooling changed several times in the intervening years because of the difficulties in establishing schools and maintaining children's attendance, particularly in rural areas and in poor urban districts. (For an account of these problems, see Tamaki Hajime, *Nihon Kyōiku Hattatsu-shi* [History of the Development of Japanese Education], 1954, Chapter 1.) The changes may be seen in the following table:

Compulsory Attendance

Year	Relevant Legislation	Term
1872	Fundamental Code of Education	4 years
1879	Education Ordinance	16 months
1880	Revised Education Ordinance	3 years
1886	Elementary School Ordinance	4 years (3 years also possible)
1900	Elementary School Ordinance	4 years
1907	Elementary School Ordinance	6 years

[4] And by the end of 1946, just before the educational reforms, about 75 per cent.
[5] 63.6 per cent boys; 60.3 per cent girls (Mombusho, *Nihon no Seichō to Kyōiku*, Table 5, p. 39). However, an additional 24.7 per cent are enrolled in continuation schooling of a secondary type (*ibid.*, Table 6, p. 40).

stantially higher, for example, than Great Britain, France, and Germany.

TABLE 2: PROPORTION OF STUDENTS IN HIGHER EDUCATION
IN SELECTED COUNTRIES
(per 1,000 population) [a,6]

	University Students Only	University Students Plus Students in Higher Teacher Training Institutions
England (and Wales)	1.77	2.35
East Germany	3.45	3.84
West Germany	3.61	4.00
France[b]	4.76	4.87
Japan	6.37	7.00
USSR	6.46	10.00
United States[c]	15.31	17.06

[a] Calculated from data for the year 1957-58 in UNESCO, *World Survey of Education, III*, New York, International Documents Service, 1961.
[b] Excluding overseas territories and foreign students.
[c] Excluding overseas territories and Alaska, Hawaii, and Puerto Rico.

It should not be supposed, however, that the Japanese suddenly acquired the idea of a school system from the West and then set out to copy it. Schools had been an important part of Japanese life for several hundred years.[7] The end of the Tokugawa period (1603-1867) found something on the order of 17,000 different schools in Japan, among them reaching a considerable portion of the population. Most of these had come into existence after the middle of the eighteenth century. Official schools, largely for the education of the children of the samurai classes, had been established first by the Shogunate and then by the lords of the various feudal domains.[8] Shogun Ieyasu himself, the first of the Tokugawa, had laid down as Article 1 of his laws for the military families (*Buke Shohatto*) the injunction in 1615 that the samurai must "pay heed" not only to "tactics, archery, and horsemanship," but also to "learning," which he placed first

[6] Since 1957-1958, the period on which these figures are based, university attendance has gone up in all of these countries by from two to fifteen per cent (as of 1962).

[7] See Passin, *op.cit.*, Ch. 2.

[8] There were 21 Shogunate schools, including the highest-ranking ones in the land. (See Mombusho: *Nihon Kyōikushi* [History of Japanese Education], 1910, pp. 241-243.) The figures for the domain schools are not entirely certain, but may possibly reach a total of 300. An early estimate by the Ministry of Education placed the number at 212; but later calculation by Kasai Sukeji yielded 276. (See his: *Kinsei Hankō no Kenkyū* [Studies of the Domain Schools of the Late Pre-Modern Period], 1960.)

on his list. This injunction was piously repeated by later Shoguns, such as Ienobu in 1710 and Yoshimune, who came into office in 1716, and by the great feudal lords in their own domains. In addition to the official schools, private schools (*shijuku*) grew rapidly in numbers following their first appearance early in the seventeenth century.[9] They provided instruction in a wide variety of fields, including the classics, practical sciences and arts, and medicine. By the end of the Tokugawa period, they were increasingly opened to commoners.

For the common people in both towns and villages, the *terakoya*, or "parishioners' schools,"[10] of which there were about 15,000 by the end of the Tokugawa era, provided the elements of literacy and moral instruction; they were usually conducted by civic-minded commoners, *samurai*—both in and out of service, priests—both Buddhist and Shintoist, and doctors.[11] There were also a small number of schools for commoners that emphasized moral training, which were called *gogaku*, or "village schools."

To be sure, these did not add up to a modern, comprehensive, integrated educational system reaching all classes of the population. But they did give Japan what was probably a more extensive, more widely based system of formal education than could be found in any other pre-modern nation in recent history. If, as Ronald Dore points out, "In Ieyasu's time a samurai who could express himself cogently on paper was a rarity, and total illiteracy was common . . . by the end of the 19th century, [Saikaku] already speaks of an illiterate samurai as sadly behind the times, and by the middle of the 19th century the situation was vastly different."[12] Not only was the samu-

---

[9] The Ministry of Education (*Nihon Kyōiku Shiryō* [Materials on the History of Japanese Education], 1890-1892) estimated 1,500 of them. However, later materials suggest that there were very likely many more. Itō Tasaburō (in *Kokumin Seikatsushi* [History of the People's Livelihood], Part III: *Seikatsu to Gakumon Kyōiku* [Life and Academic Education], 1958, p. 367) found 118 in the single province of Echigo alone, more than earlier studies showed.

[10] Although they were called "parishioners' schools," by the end of the Tokugawa period they rarely had anything to do with the temples. The name was carried over from the fifteenth and sixteenth centuries, when the temples had in fact carried on this kind of common elementary school.

[11] Ishikawa Ken (*Terakoya* [Temple Schools], 1960, p. 122) found the following distribution of *terakoya* teachers:

Commoners	4,174
Samurai	2,697
Buddhist Priests	1,884
Shinto Priests	790
Doctors	927
	10,472

[12] Ronald Dore, "The Legacy of Tokugawa Education" (unpublished).

rai class largely literate, but large numbers of them could show substantial achievements in learning, the practical arts, administration, and the arts of political and philosophical dispute. Nor did official neglect necessarily mean complete illiteracy among the lower orders. The curve of popular education rises rapidly throughout the Tokugawa period to the point that an estimate of about 40-50 per cent male, and about 15 per cent female, literacy as of its end would not be far wrong.[13]

The first debates on the modernization of education, which began after Commodore Perry's arrival in 1853, were not therefore entirely unencumbered by deeply rooted vested interests. These were, essentially, three: the Confucianists, the national scholars (*kokugakusha*), and the Western scholars. Competition among them led to many hybrid plans as, for example, the proposal that national education should be the center, with Chinese and Western learning as the wings.[14] But the Meiji leaders, urgently aware of the need for a modern, unified educational system to catch up with the West, plumped down firmly on the side of Western learning. The Education Code of 1872 argues, in strongly utilitarian terms, that "learning is the key to success, and no man can afford to neglect it. . . . Learning being viewed as the exclusive privilege of the samurai and his superiors, farmers, artisans, merchants, and women have neglected it. . . . Even those few among the samurai . . . who did pursue learning . . . indulged in poetry, empty reasoning, and idle discussions, and their dissertations, while not lacking in elegance, were seldom applicable to life. . . ."[15]

Since education was self-evidently in the interests of the people themselves, the Educational Code provided that the costs of elementary education were to be borne by the people and the local districts.

[13] This rough figure is arrived at from many different directions. One of the most interesting attempts to estimate the extent of literacy at the end of the Tokugawa period is that of Ototake Iwazō on the basis of detailed interviews with 3,000 oldsters, whose schooling age would have come in the pre-Meiji period. (The interviews were carried out between 1915 and 1917.) His estimate, which is based largely on recalled school attendance rates, is between 40 and 50 per cent male literacy. This figure, it should be noted, corresponds closely to the figure for male school attendance in the first "modern" schools in 1873—40 per cent—as may be seen in Table 1 of the text. (See Ototake Iwazō: *Nihon Shomin Kyōiku-shi* [A History of the Education of the Common People in Japan], Vol. 3, 1928, pp. 926-946.)

[14] See Okubo Toshiaki: "*Meiji Jidai no Kyōiku*" (Education in the Meiji Period), *Rekishigaku Kenkyū* (Historical Research), 1935. This was stipulated in the regulations of the Kyōtō Kōgakusho (Kyoto Imperial School) and of the Kangakusho (School of Chinese Studies) in September 1868.

[15] Quoted from Baron Dairoku Kikuchi, *Japanese Education*, London, John Murray, 1909, pp. 68-69.

Tuition charges varied between 25 and 50 *sen* per month (in some districts this could be paid in installments of as little as 3 *sen* each). Although these sums seem small, in many areas they were burdensome enough on poor families to hold down school attendance. It was not until 1900 that education became entirely free.

The utilitarianism that is implicit in the 1872 Code was not, of course, the only operative principle in the development of Japanese education. In fact, its language may not have been entirely representative of Japanese thinking of the period. Once the early wave of Westernization had died down, the language of the "native scholars" begins to creep back into the educational documents. This time, however, it was held firmly within the framework of the views of modern statists, such as Itō Hirobumi and his Education Minister, Mori Arinori, who emphasized the primacy of the needs of the state and the development of a proper civic morality. The purpose of education, as it is clarified in the course of national debates and experience, is not only to educate the people but to make them loyal subjects as well. The well-known Imperial Rescript on Education of 1890 reflects both the spirit of the national scholars[16] and the views of the "state-first" modernists.

PREWAR

After two decades of debates and experiments, an educational structure finally took shape which remained, in all essentials, unchanged until the postwar American reforms. Foreign influences and ideas were undoubtedly present, but they combined with distinctively Japanese notions and methods, and both together were adjusted, through practical experience and ideological competition, to the dominant political ideas and needs of the new state. American ideas, for example, had been very strong in the early Meiji years. But based as they were on the distinctive American experience of decentralized schools and extreme individualism, they could not be easily accommodated to Japanese conditions. What remained of them in the end was the co-educational common school, the system of normal schools, and scattered influences in certain fields. The model for the centralized educational system, under the control of a Ministry of Education, was provided by France. For the universities, Germany provided the main model.

[16] See Donald Shively, "Motoda Eifu: Confucian Lecturer to the Meiji Emperor," in David Nivison and A. F. Wright, *Confucianism in Action*, Stanford, Stanford University Press, 1959, for a fascinating account of the behind-the-scenes activities of the Confucianists during the education controversies.

The resulting system may be visualized graphically in Chart I. At the base lay the comprehensive elementary schools, compulsory and co-educational.[17]

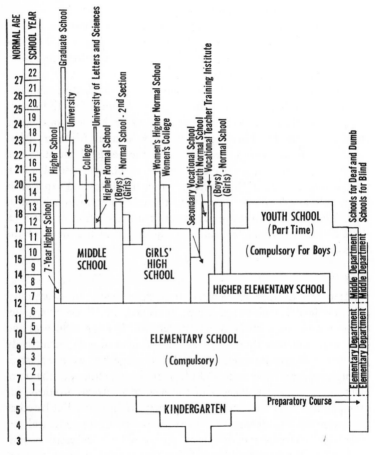

CHART I. JAPANESE SCHOOL SYSTEM, 1937

Source: Herbert Passin, *Society and Education in Japan,* New York, 1964, p. 308.

After the six years of elementary schooling, pupils faced their first, and perhaps most important, streaming out. This separation once accomplished, it became extraordinarily difficult, if not impossible, to transfer from one stream to another. The first major separation was

---

[17] The majority of these were public schools.

between boys and girls. The middle schools were not coeducational: girls took their middle-school training in special girls' schools (called "girls' high schools") and the boys went on to exclusively male institutions. Among boys, the major separation was between those going on towards higher education (about 10 per cent) and those either terminating with elementary school or aiming for terminal training at the middle-school level. For the former, there were the middle schools; for the latter, a wide variety of institutions, including advanced primary, continuation, vocational, technical, and normal schools. The main-channel middle schools, that is, those leading on to higher education, were for five years.

It was at the next step—the transition from middle school to the university-preparatory school, called the "higher school" (*kōtō-gakkō*)—that the student encountered the most radical streaming. Because facilities for higher education were far below demand, competition was ferocious and ruthless. Only one out of 13 middle-school graduates could expect to enter higher school, and only one out of 25 the prestige higher schools that opened the way into the Imperial Universities. Normally the number of applicants ran about seven times more than the number of places. How narrow this gateway was may be seen in the following figures: in 1929 there were almost 70,000 middle-school graduates; of these, about 5,000 were accepted into the 33 university-preparatory higher schools. This stage was decisive for the child's future. Without university, he could not expect to enter the higher channels of business or government; his life chances were demonstrably poorer.

The anxiety of parents for their children's future, the anxiety of the pupils for themselves and their feeling of obligation to their parents created an unbearable pressure which has come to be known as the *shiken jigoku*, the "examination hell." Students and parents both awaited the results with frantic anxiety, and suicides for failure were not uncommon.[18]

Successful candidates proceeded to the three-year higher school, which was preparatory to the university. Others had the choice of terminating their education, entering an inferior channel (such as the normal school or military school, which were important outlets for poor, but bright boys who could not attend the higher schools or

[18] "Second-chance" channels were not entirely absent, as for example the *kentei-shiken* (licensing examination), through which non-secondary school graduates could go on to higher school or college; or the normal school course leading to the "higher normal school" and from there (after their establishment in 1929) to the two Universities of Arts and Sciences. But these channels were limited.

could not leave their home area for one reason or another), or going into the special and higher technical colleges, the *semmongakkō*. These institutions were junior to the university, even though they provided a wide range of professional and even literary curricula. Through them one could become a doctor, dentist, engineer, architect, or pharmacist, but at a lower level than professionals trained in the universities. Once one entered the *semmongakkō* channel, it was extremely difficult (although not completely impossible) to transfer to a university. The highest education for girls (who had already been streamed into their own channels after primary school) was in the "women's universities," which ranked at the level of the *semmongakkō*.[19] Therefore, many ambitious young men and women, finding themselves unable to enter the university channel in Japan, went abroad, and often to the United States, for their higher education. Unfortunately, their expectations were frustrated by the fact that overseas education was considered inferior to Japanese, and American university graduates were often treated in business and government at the same level as *semmongakkō*, rather than as university graduates.[20]

What intensified the competition was the hierarchical ranking of schools. Ambitious elementary school graduates aimed not only for middle school, but for the best ones. The competition for the famous higher schools, where hierarchical ranking was explicit in its consequences for the future, was most intense of all. In order to enter a high-ranking university, with all this meant for one's career, it was necessary to come through a high-ranking higher school. The best way, for example, to reach Japan's elite university, Tokyo Imperial,[21] was through the First Higher School. The elite course came to be defined as Tokyo First Middle School–First Higher School–Tokyo Imperial.[22] Among higher schools, the state and public ones ranked above the private, and among the state schools, the First, Third, and Fourth outranked all the others. The middle-school grad-

[19] A few universities opened their doors to a small number of women, usually at the graduate level or as auditors.

[20] It should be noted, however, that the Japanese student entered university after 14 years of schooling, compared to only 12 years for the American, so that the Japanese university started at the equivalent of the 3rd year of the American university. See J. Bennett, H. Passin, and R. McKnight, *In Search of Identity*, Minneapolis, University of Minnesota Press, 1958, for a full discussion of this subject.

[21] First called "Tokyo University" in 1877; then "Imperial University" in 1886; and finally "Tokyo Imperial University" in 1897, when another imperial university was established in Kyoto. Since the war, it has reverted to the title "Tokyo University."

[22] The full range would include the Seishi Primary School in Hongo Ward, Tokyo.

uate had therefore not only to try for higher school, but preferably for one of the elite state schools. Otherwise he would find himself qualified only for second- and third-ranking institutions, usually private, which meant calculable limitations on his career chances. "(It) is estimated," wrote Keenleyside and Thomas in 1937, "that an Imperial University graduate has at least twice the chance of finding a satisfactory post as has a graduate of equal ability from a less prominent institution."[23] Among the 45 prewar universities, the "Imperial" universities ranked highest, and among the Imperial universities Tokyo stood unchallengeably first; in the next rank came the remaining government universities plus a small number of private schools; well below these came the 23 remaining private universities. The result of this elitism was not only the crushing competition for the good schools but a concentration of the best students in the small number of prestige schools. First Higher School students were, in fact, better than students of other schools, at least in their academic preparation; and Tokyo University concentrated in its halls the flower of the Japanese university world.

If one passed through higher school, however, entrance into university was almost automatic. For the graduates of the government higher schools, entrance into a leading national university was virtually assured. Others had to scramble and content themselves with a lesser institution.

Once in the university, the pressure relaxed. The successful entrant was virtually guaranteed a diploma, the all-important passport into the high-ranking main channels of Japanese society. No matter how the student might slack off in his university years, it was extremely unusual for him to be dropped from school. Thus the rhythm of the Japanese educational system was almost the inverse of the American —and rather like the European, particularly the French. American schools are relatively easy and non-competitive at the lower levels, gradually becoming more demanding as the school level rises. The Japanese schools, like those of France, were extremely competitive in the early stages, and then eased off at the university level.

The rate of attrition from elementary school through university completion was extremely high. Of every 1,000 elementary school

---

See Masuda Takaharu: *Gakubatsu—Nihon o Shihai-suru Akamon* (School Clique— The "Red Gate" That Controls Japan), Tokyo, Yūki Shobo, 1957, p. 20.

[23] Hugh Keenleyside and A. F. Thomas, *History of Japanese Education and Present Educational System*, Tokyo, Hokuseido, 1937, p. 274.

entrants, about five[24] would finish university. The reason was not, of course, only the ruthless competitiveness of the system, but the economic difficulty for many of carrying their education beyond the elementary or secondary level.

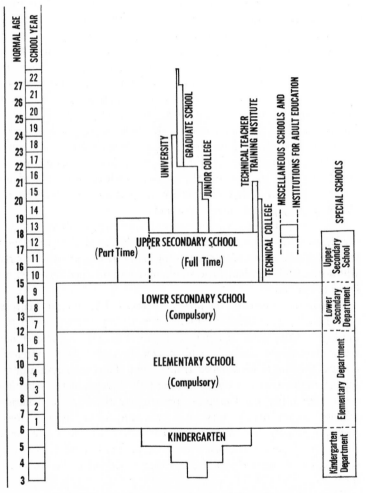

CHART II. JAPANESE SCHOOL SYSTEM, 1963

Source: Herbert Passin, *Society and Education in Japan,* New York, 1964, p. 309.

What effects the differential ranking of universities had on career chances in prewar Japan we shall see in a later section of this chapter.

[24] This figure varied somewhat from year to year, ranging between three and eight.

POSTWAR

In 1947, under the influence of the American Occupation, this entire system was reorganized, both in structure and curriculum. Without going into the entire story of the American reforms, we might profitably note the most consequential of the changes.

In the first place, Japan shifted from a multi-channel to a single-channel structure (see Chart II) each level qualifying students for the next higher level. The separate tracks were consolidated at each level, the *semmongakkō* absorbed into the university, and the university level lowered. A separate although rather limited junior college system on the American model was later added.

Compulsory education was increased to nine years of schooling, and a 6-3-3-4 structure was adopted (six years of elementary school; three years of lower secondary, corresponding to the American junior high school; three years of upper secondary, corresponding to the senior high school; and four years of university).

Coeducation, which was formerly limited to the elementary school, was now "recognized" by law, and a common curriculum for boys and girls became the pattern for all schools. In spite of the opposition of many parents, fearful of its consequences for morality and the traditional family system, coeducation has been widely accepted and now dominates the school system. Women's education has been placed on the same footing as that for men; they can attend the same schools and go on to the same universities.[25]

[25] Women number about thirteen per cent of the total university population (excluding the "junior colleges," where they number over sixty per cent). In the leading universities they usually constitute less than five per cent of the student body. However, there is a marked tendency for them to cluster in certain departments and fields as, for example, literature or English literature, in particular. In these fields they often outnumbered men by a substantial margin. A few examples for 1962-1963:[a]

University	Proportion of Women Students in Literature Department
Gakushūin (formerly Peers' College)	89%
Aoyama Gakuin	87
Rikkyō	64
Jōchi	44
Keiō	44
Waseda	33
Tokyo	11

These figures, if anything, underestimate the proportions of women in pure literature, because in the division of Japanese faculties, the "Literature Department," or "Faculty," also includes such fields as philosophy, sociology, history, etc.; in other words, the "humanities" in general. In the English literature course at Gakushuin University, for example, only 9 out of 294 students are men, so that here women represent a full 96 per cent of the total.

[a] *Japan Times*, November 29, 1962.

Today all boys and girls attend lower secondary school, and over sixty per cent go on to senior high school. The percentage is expected to rise to 72 by the year 1970.

In order to meet the increased demand, the number of universities jumped from 49 in 1942 to over 245[26] (565, if we include the new junior colleges with 2 or 3 years of schooling), and the student population from about 85,000 to its present high of more than 700,000.

So radical a change in the educational system has profound implications for Japanese life and society. One obvious effect is to keep young people out of the labor force for a prolonged period, which means that they must be supported for that time by their parents and that they very likely entertain higher expectations than early labor-force entrants before the war. The level of qualification requirements constantly rises, so that jobs that formerly required only an elementary school certificate now require lower secondary, or even upper secondary, education; white collar positions, formerly available to middle-school graduates, now increasingly require a university degree.

The growth of the university population may be seen in Table 3.

TABLE 3: UNIVERSITY ATTENDANCE (UNIVERSITY AND GRADUATE SCHOOL)[a]

	Students[b]	Teachers[c]	Schools
1877	235	91	1
1882	563	123	1
1897	1,974	191	2
1907	6,272	503	3
1917	7,291	924	4
1927	34,633	4,643	37
1937	49,546	6,334	45
1947	87,898	8,259	49
1952[d]	399,513	36,978	220
1957[e]	564,454	55,345	231
1960[e]	626,421	61,021	245

[a] The figures through 1947 are from Mombusho, *Gakusei 80-nen-shi, op.cit.*, Table II, pp. 1,062-1,063.

[b] Includes university students and graduate students: excludes preparatory students, students in *semmongakkō* attached to universities, etc.

[c] This figure is for teachers of all classes of students "connected with" the universities, not necessarily only the true university-level students listed in the column "students."

[d] *Ibid.*, Table 20, p. 1,083.

[e] Bureau of Statistics, Office of Prime Minister, *Japan Statistical Yearook 1961*, Tokyo, Mainichi Shimbun, 1962, p. 463.

[26] England has 18, France 17, and West Germany 18 (plus 14 technical schools of university level). By 1948, in anticipation of the reform of the school system, the number of universities in Japan had gone up to 64.

With an almost nine-fold increase in the number of university students, competition has intensified for the limited number of prestige jobs. Before the reforms, the university student was a rare bird; today he is one of a vast throng jostling for attention and prestige. In the same way, the scarcity value of the professor has also declined with the enormous increase in university faculty members.

Although we cannot disentangle the specific effects of coeducation from all the other postwar changes affecting women, certainly they are considerable. Not only have women entered the labor force in much larger numbers and at much higher levels of skill and pay than ever before, but they are moving rapidly from an automatic acceptance of the traditional role of Japanese women. A woman who has gone through higher education in competition with boys and who has come to associate with them daily has a different outlook on such matters as dating, absolute obedience to husbands, companionship in marriage, and the inherent inferiority of women from that of her mother—whose schooling and school life were entirely different.

Since upper secondary education is now guaranteed by the state, the point of competitive stress in the system has shifted from the middle school–higher school to the high school–university transition.[27] In 1955, there were 658,343 applicants for 136,467 announced openings in the universities (4.8:1).[28] Since then the ratio has become somewhat more favorable, although there are still on the average more than five times as many high-school graduates as there are university vacancies. Not all of them apply, however, but the

[27] The newspapers constantly carry reports such as the following: "A youth despondent over his failure to pass a college entrance examination committed suicide by electrocuting himself on a high tension wire. . . . The youth carried a note in his pocket which said he felt he could no longer live in this world because he was too weak-minded." (*Japan Times*, July 10, 1962.)

Although Finland and Austria have suicide rates that are comparable to Japan's, in the 15-24 age group, Japan outstrips them by far.

	Selected Suicide Rates[a]			
	All Ages[b]		15-24 Age Group[c]	
	Male	Female	Male	Female
Japan (1955)	31.6	19.0	60.8	36.7
Finland (1956)	37.0	9.0	18.1	—
Austria (1956)	32.4	14.5	17.4	8.1

[a] From United Nations, *Demographic Yearbook*, 1957, Table 17.

[b] Per 100,000 population.

[c] Per 100,000 population of the 15-24 age group.

[28] *Kyoiku Nenkan 1957* (Education Annual 1957). Data current as of May 1, 1955. The figures are probably a slight overestimate because many high-school graduates apply to more than one school. In 1960 of 809,275 applicants, 172,444 were admitted (4.7:1).

rates today are running at about 25 per cent. Of the applicants, more than one-third will not be able to get into any university at all. For the great metropolitan areas of Tokyo, Kyoto, and Osaka, the applications outrun vacancies by more than three times, and for the prestige universities in some years only one out of ten or twenty applicants will be accepted.

The forced-draft creation of new universities, hastily knocked together from prewar higher schools, *semmongakkō*, technical schools, and normal schools, has, if anything, intensified the quality gap, and with it, the competition for entry into the better schools. If university education has much less scarcity value than before, the individual student must make up for this by the quality of the school he goes to. The result is that in spite of all efforts to equalize quality throughout the country, the former Imperial Universities (now called national universities) still outrank the private universities, and the gap between the older universities, whether public or private, and the newly formed institutions is even greater.[29] Tokyo, with one-third of the universities and one-half the student population of the country, still remains the target of the ambitious.

This pressure has created a new social phenomenon, the *rōnin* (named for the masterless samurai of the Tokugawa period)—students who, failing to pass the entrance examinations for the first-rank schools, spend years cramming for a retake rather than enter an inferior institution. By now they form a significant proportion of the new entrants to such schools as Tokyo University, thereby cutting down the number of openings available for applicants fresh from senior high school. What we have, a leading Japanese scholar once wrote, is not a 6-3-3-4 system but a 6-3-x-3-x-4 system, "x" representing the years spent trying to get through the entrance examinations for the better senior high schools and universities.[30] (Some would add an-

[29] With the single exception of the newly formed International Christian University, whose students rank among the highest. In the 1953 National Scholastic Aptitudes Test, for example, ICU ranked among the top four.

School	Test Score
Tokyo University	60.63
International Christian University	55.57
Hitotsubashi University	55.37
Osaka University	55.00
Average for all Japan	35.50

[30] In a recent year, for example, 271,000 of Japan's 1,000,000 high school graduates applied for the 72 national universites. But in addition there were 100,000

other "x" after the 4 years of university—for the "university hospital.")

The competition at the senior high school level is not quite so pressing, but it is there nevertheless. Efforts to equalize their quality and distribution by means of controlled school districting have not been successful. Many parents find ways to send their children to good schools outside their home districts. The problem has become so serious that good school districts in Tokyo openly levy a special "voluntary contribution" on non-resident pupils. Falsified residential documents are arranged, and in some cases a mother may move into a particular district with her child so that he can go to the good school. According to a survey in 1957, in a class of 62 pupils in a well-known school in Tokyo, only 27 actually had their residence properly within that school district.[31] The result is that it is widely known that certain schools are better than others and offer a greater probability of entrance into the better schools on the next higher level.

In some ways the channels have even narrowed. Before the war, although it is true that the probability of entering Tokyo Imperial University was much higher for First Higher School graduates, graduates of the other national higher schools were also taken in significant numbers. Today, now that the First Higher School has disappeared (it has been absorbed into Tokyo University as its School of Liberal Education—*Kyōyōgaku-bu*), there are now four high schools in Tokyo that provide a disproportionate number of successful applicants for entry, and between 50 and 60 per cent of Tokyo University students come from the Tokyo area. Therefore, the proportion of good students from the good provincial high schools who get into Tokyo University is even smaller than before. However, this may reflect a greater equalization of the level of good schools, so that good students in the provinces are able to go to a first-class university somewhat closer home.

These quality differences are explicitly recognized by society. A Tokyo University degree is obviously much more highly regarded than a degree from a new provincial university. The better compa-

---

rōnin applicants from previous years. According to Shimizu Yoshiro, *Shiken* (Examination), 1957, in 1947, of 13,485 applicants to Tokyo University, 66 per cent had spent from one to three years as *rōnin*, only 34 per cent applying fresh from high school. Of the 2,004 successful applicants, 72 per cent were *rōnin*, and only 28 per cent were straight from high school. (The corresponding percentages for all national universities are 50 fresh from high school and 50 *rōnin*.)

[31] Masuda, *op.cit.*, pp. 21-22.

nies, which are the main target of the university graduate, maintain either implicit or explicit quotas on the number of entrants to be taken from various schools. The graduate of a good school has a demonstrably better chance to secure a job, and a good job, than the graduate of a lower-ranking school.

II. Education and Society

JOB AND CLASS

It was a remarkable achievement of the young Meiji leaders that although they knew very little of the outside world they were able to see so quickly the need for a comprehensive modern educational system. Along with the abolition of feudalism in 1871 and the establishment of national military service in place of the feudal service of the hereditary warrior class, educational reform ranks as one of the key measures for the transformation of Japan from a feudal to a modern, unified national state.

Education not only supplied the skills needed for military and economic development but also furthered the creation of a national state out of the 280 or so feudal domains into which the country had been divided. Through the use of uniform textbooks and teaching materials and the diffusion of a national language (a modified version of the Tokyo dialect), the schools helped promote a common sense of nationhood and the displacement of regional by national loyalties. All these went very far towards unifying the country, shifting loyalties from feudal to national symbols, and involving wider strata of the population in the modernization process. Moreover, in the explicit view of the Meiji reformers, it opened the way to the full utilization of the intellectual resources of the country; men of talent, even if of commoner origin, were more valuable to the new state than unqualified samurai. "Self-cultivation" and "merit" became the watchwords of the day.

In feudal Japan family, class, and personal connections had formed the main pathways to recognized achievement, even though within these limitations personal merit carried some weight.[32] But once the turmoil of the transition period had subsided and the new school system, as well as the other reforms, were well on their way—say,

[32] See, for example, Thomas Smith, "Merit in Tokugawa Bureaucracy" (unpublished); Ronald Dore, "Talent and the Social Order in Tokugawa, Japan," *Past and Present*, No. 21, April 1962.

within 20 years—new channels of achievement and mobility began to take on institutional shape. To get ahead in the world it was no longer sufficient simply to come of a good family; one had to go to a good school and do well in it. Education became the new escalator for talent and achievement, and the demand for qualified men far exceeded the capacity of the schools to provide them.

In spite of the tremendous national effort, university development was a slow growth. In 1885, for example, 17 years after the Meiji Restoration, Tokyo Imperial University (established in 1877) was still the only university in the country. Many ambitious youths had to go abroad for higher education. As late as 1904, Tokyo Imperial had only produced about 5,000 graduates (the newer Kyoto Imperial, established in 1897, about 100), and between 1912 and 1925, Japan produced a total of only 42,000 graduates.[33] As against these small numbers, the needs in various fields were overwhelming. According to a survey conducted by Tokyo Imperial University in 1904, of 1,700 judicial officers (including judges and procurators), only 300 were university graduates, of 4,300 secondary school teachers only 300, and of 40,000 physicians and surgeons only 60 had university training.[34]

This slow development of university education fixed at an early point several endemic features of Japanese education: the extreme competitiveness, the rigorous examination system, and the elitism.

Once universal education came into full operation, the educational ladder became the skeletal core of the social-achievement ladder. Those with elementary education went into agricultural or manual-labor jobs; middle-school graduates into white-collar positions; and university graduates into the higher administrative and executive positions. Although it was not entirely impossible for a person with elementary-school education to go up in the ranks, it was not likely that he would go very far. Enterprises were usually divided into two entirely separate channels, a labor, or production, channel, and an administrative channel. Once a worker entered a firm in the production channel, he was able to move up the ranks through seniority and personal merit, but he could not move over into the administrative channel.

In the larger enterprises, a further distinction was usually made between a lower administrative and a higher executive channel.

[33] See Ministry of Education, *Demand and Supply for University Graduates—Japan*, August 1958, pp. 64-65, Appendix 1.

[34] Alfred Stead (ed.), *Japan by the Japanese, A Survey by Its Highest Authorities*, London, William Heinemann, 1904, p. 238.

These two were somewhat less impermeable, but it was unlikely that someone who had started in the lower channel would go very high in the executive line. At the lower levels of the administrative channel differences in school background might not stand out. But as one goes up the ladder, the differences begin to appear. The example of X-pharmaceutical company may serve to illustrate this. At the lower executive level, the section chief (*kachō*), 11 per cent were Tokyo University graduates. This means that 89 per cent came from schools ranked below Tokyo. But as the executive level rises, so does the proportion of Tokyo graduates. Thirty-three per cent of the bureau chiefs (*buchō*) and fully 50 per cent of the directors (*jūyaku*) are from Tokyo.[35] The separation worked the other way as well. Companies would not accept persons with higher education in production or other low-grade jobs.[36] No greater tragedy could be imagined than for educated people to be forced by economic conditions to take inferior jobs, as in the 1920's and 1930's, when "*Tōdai* (Tokyo University) policemen" and lower-grade civil servants came to public notice. This may have had something to do with the alienation of intellectuals from the regime that developed so rapidly in the 1920's and 1930's.

Similarly, in government, a distinction was made between the higher administrative posts and the ordinary civil service. For the higher ranks one had to come from a proper university. In some cases the university qualification was specified; in other cases, the choice was assured by the examination and personal-interview system, which virtually guaranteed that only graduates of the proper schools would be appointed.

The hierarchical distinctions that grew up among the universities and the *semmongakkō* had immediate consequences for one's career chances. Many companies, for example, took college-level entrants only from a particular school or schools; in other cases, they might have a quota for entrants from different schools. The Japan Broadcasting Corporation, for example, before the war used to give Imperial university graduates a starting salary of 80 yen per month, private-university graduates 75, and *semmongakkō* graduates 70. In 1927, to take another example, the Mitsubishi enterprises paid new

[35] Calculated from materials in *Kaisha Shokuin-roku* (Company Membership Lists), edited by the Dayamondo Publishing Co., Tokyo, 1957.

[36] The best discussion in English of company-recruitment policies is to be found in James Abegglen, *The Japanese Factory*, Glencoe, Free Press, 1958.

company entrants starting salaries on the following scales: Imperial engineering graduates, 90 yen per month; Imperial law graduates, 80; Commercial University graduates, 80; Waseda and Keio, 75; other private universities, 65-70; *semmongakkō*, 65-70.[37] For the higher and most desirable posts in Japanese life, it was almost essential to have gone to the elite schools. The lesser universities provided entrée into the lower levels of government and lesser businesses.

The universities not only provided training and connections, but they were perhaps even more important as the source of one's lifetime identification with a clique. These cliques, or *batsu*, as they are called, are intimate, informal groups based upon personal loyalties that span many fields from the university into business, the professional world, government, and politics. A person without a *batsu* faces Japanese society unsupported, with no one to sponsor him or to help him out in times of crisis. It is one's *batsu* that opens the closed doors. Characteristically each *batsu* has its own sphere of influence, which it guards jealously against outsiders and opens only to its intimates. Universities form their own *batsu*, and even particular departments within the university may have their own spheres of influence.

The elite positions in Japanese society have been largely dominated by the graduates of the elite universities—Tokyo Imperial, Kyoto Imperial, and Tokyo Commercial University (and to a lesser extent the other former Imperial universities). How overwhelming this can be we may see from a few figures. Before the war Tokyo University had about 12 per cent of the total university population: the "big three" (Tokyo, Kyoto, and Tokyo Commercial), about 23 per cent; the six Imperial universities, about 30 per cent; the government universities as a whole, about 34 per cent.[38] Expressed as a percentage of the total population of "higher schools," that is, including *semmongakkō* and the higher technical schools, to whom top management positions were also theoretically open, these become:

[37] See Matsunari Yoshie, Tanuma Hajime, Izumiya Hajime, Noda Masaho, *Nihon no Sarariiman* (The Japanese Salaryman), Tokyo, Aoki Shoten, 1957, Table 3, p. 66. Similar data are compiled there for 14 companies.

[38] Based upon data for the year 1933-1934, in *Jiji Nenkan* (Jiji Yearbook), 1935. There are some discrepancies among the various compilations of educational statistics. The figures cited here are notably lower than those reported in the *Jiji Nenkan*, but the difference may be accounted for by the fact that the Ministry of Education compilation excludes students in preparatory schools and in *semmongakkō* that are attached to universities, while the *Jiji Nenkan* undoubtedly includes them. Keenleyside and Thomas (*op.cit.*), reporting on the same year, again give rather different figures. But in no case are the dimensions calculated here significantly altered.

Tokyo Imperial University 4%
The Big Three 6
The Six Imperial Universities 10
The Government Universities 12

For the postwar period, to take the sample year 1958,[39] the proportions become:

Tokyo University 1.7%
Big Three 3.2
Six Former Imperial Universities 4.8
Government Universities 34.4

As against these small numbers, these schools have contributed remarkably disproportionate numbers of leaders of the high-ranking, prestigeful layers of Japanese society.

Let us start first with the higher civil service. In 1935, for example, of 99 successful applicants for higher civil service positions, 81 were from Tokyo University. In 1937, of 1,264 higher civil servants, 74 per cent were Tokyo University graduates (and 46 per cent from Tokyo University's Law Faculty alone).[40] In a sampling for the year 1957, of 10 bureau chiefs of the Foreign Office, 9 graduated from Tokyo and 1 from Tokyo Commercial University; all 12 bureau chiefs in the Ministry of Finance were Tokyo graduates. A survey completed in 1958 shows the following distribution among the highest-ranking government officials (Classes I, II, and III):

TABLE 4[a]

Educational Background	Class I	Class II	Class III
National University graduate	97.6%	81.6%	57.1%
Private University graduate	0.	5.6	8.9
Semmongakkō graduate	2.4	11.6	23.6
Middle-school graduate	0.	0.9	7.0
Other	0.	0.4	3.4
Tokyo University graduate	80.5	67.2	39.9
Number:	(41)	(558)	(2,317)

[a] Calculated from *Kakushochō Kachō-kyū Ijō no Gakureki, Shikaku, oyobi Keireki* (The Education, Qualifications, and Records of Branch Chiefs and Above in All Departments and Bureaus), mimeographed report of survey by the Japanese Government, June 1959.

[39] From Kyōdō Tsūshinsha, *Nihon Gensei 1958* (The Present Situation in Japan, 1958). These figures are based upon attendance at four-year universities and exclude two- and three-year junior colleges.

[40] *Jinji Kōshinroku* (Who's Who), March 1937, reported in Inoki Masamichi, "The Civil Bureaucracy," in Robert E. Ward and Dankwart A. Rustow, eds.,

This connection of Tokyo University and the higher civil service has a long history. During the Meiji period the ambitious and patriotic young man was likely to aim for the Law Faculty of Tokyo University (and later of Kyoto Imperial), which was virtually an open channel into government. In fact, during this period, the majority of Tokyo University students were in the Faculty of Law, and even as late as 1959 the Law Faculty registration, with 38 per cent, outnumbered all other faculties.

Until 1915 the majority of graduates entered government service rather than private industry.[41] The preferment in government for Tokyo law graduates was so great that for a while they were assigned posts without examination simply on the basis of their school grades.[42] An agreement between the Prime Minister and the President of Tokyo Imperial in August 1887 specified that graduates were to receive entering salaries on a sliding scale between 450 and 600 yen per month, depending upon their school records.[43] "Don't despise the student"—a popular song of the period runs—"the *sangi* [the highest rank in the civil service] was once a student too." If he were not interested in a government career, the prestige of his Tokyo law degree would open many other high-ranking administrative and executive positions to him. *Hōka bannō*[44]—the almighty law graduate—it was said. With this background, we can understand better the complaint of a recent graduate of a private university, one that must have been repeated many times in the last 75 years: "As everyone knows, Chuo University students passing the judicial officer examination exceed those from Tokyo University by a wide margin,

---

Political Modernization in Japan and Turkey, Princeton, Princeton University Press, 1964.

[41] The turning point came about 1918, when for the first time graduates entering the business world outnumbered those entering government.

[42] Imperial Decree No. 37, July 23, 1887.

[43] At present prices, this is the equivalent of between 1.0 and 1.5 million yen per month (about $2,800 to $4,000 U.S.). A starting government worker at the same level would today receive about 23,000 yen (about $64); he might reach 100,000 yen (about $280) if he were promoted to a high post after 20 or 30 years of service. Some figures for the period may place this in perspective. One *koku* (5 bushels) of rice (which today sells for about 10,000 yen) cost about 6 yen. The Director of the National Bank received a salary of about 300 yen *per year*. According to the *Kōgyō Iken* (Memorandum on the Promotion of Industry), published by the Ministry of Agriculture and Commerce in 1884, the average *annual* income of the upper-income group in Japan in 1883 was ¥110.82 per capita (13 per cent of the population); for the middle-income group (29 per cent of the population), ¥60.45; for the lower-income group (57 per cent), ¥20.15. A cabinet minister received ¥800 per month (¥9,600 per year), and a cabinet councillor ¥500 per month (¥6,000 per year).

[44] "*Bannō*" means omniscient, omni-capable.

but when they become judicial officers, they find very few seniors from their alma mater. . . . Soon after the war, a senior graduate of our college managed to become under-secretary in the Construction Ministry, but even then he was about six or seven years behind the graduates of Tokyo University."[45]

Surveys in the business world show much the same story. A listing of 108 top business and political leaders in 1952 shows 60 Tokyo graduates, and 71 in all from national (former Imperial) universities.[46] A survey of 2,592 executives in 283 companies conducted in 1954 shows 38 per cent of them Tokyo graduates, and a total of 63 per cent graduates of the "big three"—Tokyo, Kyoto, and Hitotsubashi (formerly Tokyo Commercial University).[47] A more recent survey of the background of executives of firms with a capitalization of one billion yen or more, that is, of the largest firms in Japan, gives similar results: 35 per cent from Tokyo, and a total of 52 per cent from the big three.[48]

Lower ranking universities have had to carve out their own spheres of influence, and in this many of them have been successful, even if they were excluded from the top positions in government and the leading companies. Particular areas or institutions fell within the sphere of influence of particular universities. In a recent sampling, for example, it was found that Keio, one of the two leading private universities of Japan, has its dominant influence in insurance companies and department stores; Waseda, the other leading private university, in certain newspapers and the construction industry.[49] Therefore, a student bent upon a particular career has to be sure to get into the proper channels. Keio would open the way to a satisfactory business career, and Waseda one in journalism; for government, the Foreign Service, leading banks, and corporations, he would have to go to Tokyo. "But woe betide the graduates of a college having no company faction," warns the *Nippon Times*,[50] for these unfortunates usually have to be satisfied with jobs in small and medium

[45] *Nippon Times*, December 9, 1955.

[46] Natori Giichi: *Seizaikai-jin no Meiun* (The Fate of Political and Business Leaders), Tokyo, Hokushindo, 1952.

[47] Iwai Hiromichi: "*Kyōsō, Seikō, Shusse*" (Competition, Success, and Getting Ahead) in *Dayamondo Shushoku Annai* (Dayamondo Job Guide), 1954.

[48] Productivity Institute Survey, 1959. Reported in Noda Kazuo, *Nihon no Jūyaku* (The Japanese Executive), Tokyo, Dayamondo-sha, 1960, pp. 160-161.

[49] Fukumoto Kunio, "*Gakubatsu, Ningenbatsu, Shihonbatsu*" (School, Personal, and Capital Cliques) in Sakamoto Fujinaga, ed., *Genzai no Keieisha* (The Manager Today), Tokyo, Chisei-sha, 1959.

[50] December 9, 1955.

enterprises—unless they are lucky enough to find their way into the movie world, which is the only enterprise in Japan where talent counts above everything else and the 'old school tie' holds no domain."

SUPPLY AND DEMAND IN HIGHER EDUCATION

In an ideal world, there would be an exact correspondence between the demand for higher education and the facilities available for it and between the number of trained graduates and the number of socially useful and satisfying places for them in society. When there are substantial discordances, serious personal and political problems arise. On the first score, applications for university entrance in Japan have always run well ahead of vacancies, and this has meant a rigorously competitive system and much personal unhappiness. But on the second score at least, the Meiji period was one of those euphoric moments in history when every graduate could find a useful, productive, and remunerative outlet for his training and talents. The demand for trained people far outran their production by the universities. But with the growth both of the industrial sector of the economy and of the university population, two problems began to appear. In the first place, graduates seeking "good" jobs found themselves in an increasingly competitive situation. In the second place, the universities were turning out too many in the humanities and too few in the sciences and technology. With their high expectations and the substantial investment in their long years of training (a minimum of 17 years of schooling, as compared to 16 required in the United States for a B.A.), the university-educated were particularly vulnerable to economic insecurity.

By the middle of the second decade of the twentieth century, government was no longer able to absorb as high a proportion of graduates, even from Tokyo and Kyoto universities, as it had before, so that students had to direct themselves towards private employment. In 1900, for example, of 2,247 graduates of Tokyo and Kyoto Imperial universities to date, 68 per cent went into government positions and 32 per cent into private industry. As late as 1915, 59 per cent of them were still going into government. But by 1918, the proportions had reversed: only 48 per cent went into government and 52 per cent into private industry.[51] Since then the trend has accelerated to the point that of 2,083 students in the 1959 graduating class of Tokyo

[51] Compiled from various annuals of the Ministry of Education.

University, only ten per cent went into government service (plus one per cent into local government service);[52] and even among graduates of the Law Faculty, the traditional breeding ground of top bureaucrats, fully 75 per cent went into private enterprise.

The *"sarariiman,"* the educated white-collar worker, made his appearance in Japan for the first time. No longer the bold, self-confident builder of the nation, a contemporary song describes him "crossing the Kanda Bridge at five in the morning, wearing his frayed Western-style clothes and carrying his lunch-box, briskly clip-clopping towards his miserable pittance."[53]

Thus, in spite of the extremely selective, carefully limited, elite character of the system, within a few decades of its establishment it was already producing too many graduates for the economy to absorb satisfactorily. By the 1920's and the 1930's intellectual employment became a serious political problem. In the year 1936, for example, 44 per cent of the university graduates were unable to get jobs.[54] The employment rate for law, economics, and literature graduates dropped below fifty per cent in 1923 and 1930.[55] Discontent and bitterness among the highly educated, combining as it did with the new influences coming from the Russian Revolution, a new wave of enthusiasm for Western democracy as against German authoritarianism, and the penetration of Marxism among students and intellectuals, made the organized protest movement a significant element in Japanese politics. As against the absolute over-production of educated persons, there was a shortage of technically qualified personnel. In the same year of 1936, in spite of the unemployment among university graduates, according to R. K. Hall, "the technical schools were able to supply only 16.4 per cent of the 17,630 technicians needed in industry."[56] In 1937 the shortage in electrical and mechanical engineering and applied chemistry was even worse.[57] A longer-term survey of employment rates for the years 1913-1956 concludes that

[52] See Noda, *op.cit.*, p. 154.

[53] The "Scholar Song" (Sukaara Songu) by Kaminaga Ryōgetsu, quoted in Matsunari et al., *op.cit.*, p. 37. The quotation is full of puns and Japanese references that cannot be literally translated.

[54] Robert K. Hall, *Education for the New Japan*, New Haven, Yale University Press, 1949, p. 228. The survey of employment rates (*Demand and Supply* . . . , *op.cit.*, Figure 10, p. 17) shows a lower estimate of unemployment, but the discrepancy may be attributed to the base of the calculation—in Hall's case *"university* graduates," in the other "university and college (that is *semmongakkō*) graduates."

[55] *Demand and Supply* . . . , *op.cit.*, Figure 11(a), p. 19.

[56] Hall, *op.cit.*, p. 228.

[57] Keenleyside and Thomas, *op.cit.*, pp. 327-328.

"The curve for engineering graduates is seen to have been a relatively stable seventy to ninety percent . . . ,"[58] and the range for technical school (*semmongakkō*) graduates is approximately the same.[59]

From 1937 until the end of the Second World War, military conscription and industrial mobilization solved the problem of unemployment. More than half of the young students of the country, it has been estimated, were taken into service.[60] But the end of the war brought it back with even greater severity, and it was further exacerbated by the enormous increase in the university population resulting from the American educational reforms. The threat of unemployment and the difficulty of finding satisfactory work, in spite of years of sacrifice and effort, provided an enormous reservoir of support for socialist and anti-conservative movements.

Until the past three or four years, it was by no means certain that all university graduates could find a job, and even less certain that it would be a job for which they felt themselves properly qualified. Although the situation has been improving, there are great differences among the various classes of universities in the job success of their graduates. While in 1959, for example, 79 per cent of university graduates found jobs within three months of graduation, only 55 per cent of the junior-college graduates were able to do so.[61] Moreover, if we were to distinguish between the prestige universities and the low-ranking ones, we would find a further gap: the chances of securing any job at all were about twice as high for the graduates of the former than of the latter. If we introduced a further distinction in the desirability of jobs, the difference would be even more extreme. The over-supply, however, is selective not only in university ranking, but also in the field of study. In scientific, technical, and social science fields there has been, if anything, a shortage; the surplus has been primarily in the humanities (literature, history, philosophy, and fine arts), such women's fields as "homemaking" and nursing, and to a lesser extent in education.[62]

---

[58] *Demand and Supply* . . . , *op.cit.*, p. 18.

[59] *Ibid.*, Figure 11(b), p. 19.

[60] At the start of the war, university students were exempted, but by 1943 special student exemptions in the fields of social sciences and humanities were ended.

[61] Ministry of Education, *Education in 1959*, Annual Report of the Ministry of Education, March 1961, p. 62.

[62] Based upon data reported in Ronald Anderson, *Japan—Three Epochs of Modern Education*, Washington, U.S. Dept. of Health, Education and Welfare, Bulletin 1959, No. 11, pp. 144-145.

Even if, as appears to be the case from the most recent statistics, Japan's economic boom is absorbing almost all of the university graduates, the competition remains severe, particularly for the desirable companies. The overwhelming majority of the 160,000 or so university graduates every year must go into private business, and they all aim for the first-class companies. Of Japan's approximately 440,000 companies,[63] only 2,000 can be considered "large," and it is to these that university graduates try to go; if they fail, they then move down to medium- and small-scale enterprises. In a survey among 1,000 of these 2,000 leading companies, it was found that there are on the average about ten applicants per job opening.[64] In 1961, one of Japan's elite newspapers found itself with 3,000 applicants for only twenty openings. The competition for desirable government positions is, if anything, even more extreme. The average number of applicants for the senior diplomatic channel of the Foreign Office is about 600; 16 to 18 are chosen, of whom 10 to 14 are from Tokyo University. (In one recent year, there were 1,100 applicants for six openings.) Since this narrow entrance way is already so rigged in favor of the better schools, competition and frustration are extreme.

From late fall through early spring, the fourth-year university student must scramble for a job, applying to many places and taking innumerable entrance examinations, some of them more difficult than anything he has taken during his academic career. Every failure is a heartbreak for the student and his family; the level of ambition clicks downward one step. The result is a typically Japanese phenomenon, that books with such unpromising titles as *Compulsory Subjects for Company-Entrance Examinations*, or *Job-Getting Policy Encyclopedia*, become best-sellers, with sales running into the millions every year.

POLITICS

The men of Meiji, who began the modernization of the country, were not themselves the product of modernity. They were men of the *ancien régime*, and even of its privileged orders—most of them lower-ranking samurai—who had been educated in the orthodox fief

[63] Noda, *op.cit.*, p. 156. However, *Japan Statistical Yearbook 1961* (p. 61) lists 746,000 under its definition of "corporations." This undoubtedly uses a different definition of corporations.

[64] Surveys of the Japan Federation of Economic Organizations. The ratio of acceptance among technical applicants was somewhat higher than for administrative applicants.

schools or the *shijuku*. Disaffected, or at the very least discontent with the *status quo* and their position within it, they were quickened into political activity by their awareness of the great power of the West, both as a military, colonial threat and as a system of ideas that traditional Japan would have to come to terms with. The dominant slogans of the day, *fūkoku kyōhei* (prosperous country, strong military) and *bunmei kaika* (civilization and enlightenment), expressed the consensus that held them together in a tight oligarchy for a good thirty years: a unified modern state; national strength—both economic and military; the selective import of Western technology. In the light of retrospect, it might be argued that this apparent consensus papered over an inherent fault-line, one that was later to show itself in the conflict between the conservative nationalists and the liberals; but in the event, it was powerful enough to hold the elite together.

The establishment of a modern school system did not, therefore, in the first instance affect the distribution of political power. This was already solidly held by an elite formed in the pre-Meiji period. The early products of the school system fit into their designs, manning the newly opened bureaucratic posts and institutions, and moving cautiously into the slowly developing modern economic sector. Most of the graduates of the higher schools were immediately drawn in.

But the very existence of a school system and its entrenchment as the main channel for access to government position, business, and power brought about important changes in the composition of the elite. The samurai, as a legally privileged class, had been on the downgrade rapidly and, particularly after the abortive revolt of Saigo Takamori in 1877 (the very year Tokyo Imperial University was established), had to face increasingly vigorous competition from the other classes. Although persons of samurai origin remained disproportionately high among the elite and among those with higher education[65] (as they do even today),[66] their absolute dominance

---

[65] According to Shimizu, *op.cit.*, p. 109, in 1878, one year after commoners were permitted to enter the Tokyo University Preparatory School, 8 out of 10 students were still of samurai origin, but 10 years later, the proportion had gone down to 6 out of 10. In the regular university departments, according to Mombusho (*Nihon no Seichō to Kyōiku, op.cit.*, Table 3, p. 35), the proportion of students of samurai origin declined from 73.9 per cent in 1878 to 51.7 per cent in 1885. (The 1878 figure includes students from the law, science, and literature faculties; the 1885 figures add students from the medical faculty.)

[66] See the revealing study of the social composition of business, political, and intellectual elites by James Abegglen and Hiroshi Mannari, "Leaders of Modern Japan," *Economic Development and Cultural Change*, 1960.

continued to diminish in tandem with the rise of the former under-privileged classes. The emergence into the national political commu-nity of the former lower orders is a process that has been going on slowly throughout the ninety years of modern Japanese history, and in a sense it can still be said to be going on. The first enfranchised electorate in Japan numbered about 400,000 people (Japan's popula-tion at that time was about 40,000,000). By means of tax and prop-erty qualifications it was held down to the well-educated, the people of means, the wealthier farmers, the growing class of industrialists and entrepreneurs. Only in 1925 did universal manhood suffrage bring the working class and the peasantry into the national political community. (Full universal suffrage, including women as well, down to the age of twenty years, came only with the American Occupa-tion.)

But in spite of this restriction of the electorate, the growth and differentiation of society, governmental institutions, and the economy went on rapidly. New classes—a modern working class and a modern industrialist class, for example—came into existence, and these ex-panded in numbers and influence at the expense of the older classes. The rise of military power and the political party system transformed politics from a monopoly of the oligarchy into a three-way struggle, in the course of which there were many compromises and coalitions. The bureaucracy-business-political party coalition of the 1920's was displaced by a military-bureaucracy coalition which finally led Japan into the China and Pacific Wars.

The intellectuals and university graduates of the Meiji period had been essentially a political elite, taking part in the governance of the country. Whether in government itself as members of the bureauc-racy, in one of the important national institutions (such as the army or the school system), in politics, or in a private capacity, the edu-cated classes felt themselves committed members of a common na-tional effort. But as the Meiji period began to draw to its close and the great Restoration leaders to leave the scene, the products of the new universities and the school system began to enter the market-place. Where in an earlier day any educated person could feel that he was making his personal contribution to national affairs, whether or not he held official position, now a gap began to appear between the bureaucratic and civil elites. For the first time there were modern intellectuals who felt themselves outside the national political com-munity, or even hostile to it. The early Meiji leaders had all been "generalists," cultivated men with a strong sense of national dedication, rather than technical specialists in particular fields. The new university products included increasing numbers of technicians, engineers, and even writers and artists who looked upon politics as a condition of life rather than as an arena for their own activity. A Mori Ōgai could still feel that the intellectual must serve the nation (he was an MD and novelist) but Shimasaki Tōson and others were already arguing the priority of personal vision and morality as against the state. The educated classes began to divide into two broad streams: a bureaucratic elite taking part in public affairs in one form or another; and a civil element, which again consisted of two parts— the holders of stable, respectable, mainline positions who identified themselves with the "Establishment," and a new intelligentsia, disaffected and inclined towards all the great heresies of individualism, radicalism, liberalism, and Westernism.

Entrance into the Establishment was therefore through the educational channels, but the educational system could not completely channel all of its products. Some of them went into opposition and found arenas of activity in non-mainline channels that were growing up: the trade union and radical movements; Christian institutions (churches, schools, colleges, social work, etc.); foreign-connected institutions; the growing communications and entertainment industries; and free-lance creative work. In the more organized political and social movements, they joined with the leaders arising from within these movements to form a new leadership which in itself became a counter-elite to the elite of the Establishment.

To reach high political, as distinct from bureaucratic, position, therefore, there were channels other than those of the school system. Local bosses with their own areas of control could be elected to the Diet, even if they had very little schooling. Leaders of mass movements or wealthy businessmen could also do so. Thus the grass-roots politicians often had their own independent bastions of support from which to negotiate with the official cliques. But within the framework of the party, the various *batsu* had to compete among themselves and make effective coalitions to carry on the practical work of politics, and here the bureaucratic element, with its school-based *batsu*, played a very important part. Internal party life was essentially a question of struggle, compromise, and coalition among factions. The higher the formal level of political power, the more clearly do we find clique lines. While the party back-benchers in the Diet might come from many different backgrounds, there is increasing homogeneity as we go up the scale to, say, party executives and cabinets.

In the February 1962 Diet, for example, 35 per cent of the members of the House of Representatives had less than university education. But even among the university graduates, there was considerable scatter, as may be seen in the following table:

TABLE 5[a]

Members of the House of Representatives	100 %	N^{b} 461
With some university education	64.6	298
Completed university education	61.8	285
Government universities	37.3	172
Private universities	22.5	104
Other	1.9	9
(Tokyo University)	(26.4)	(122)

[a] Calculated from Nihon Seikei Shimbunsha: *Kokkai Binran 37* (Register of the National Diet, 1962). Tokyo, February 1962, pp. 99-130. Data for the years 1947, 1949, 1953, and 1958 can be found in Appendix, Chart 8, pp. 164-167, Robert Scalapino and Junnosuke Masumi, *Parties and Politics in Contemporary Japan,* Berkeley and Los Angeles, University of California Press, 1962.

[b] The Diet membership is actually slightly larger, usually about 467, but with deaths, resignations, and incomplete information, this was the best number on which I was able to make calculations.

However, when we reach cabinet level, the prestige university graduates are clearly dominant. In the first Ikeda Cabinet, for example, formed in 1960, 13 of the 20 members were from the "Big Three," and 14 in all from the national universities.

TABLE 6: FIRST IKEDA CABINET (JULY 19, 1960)[a]

School Background	Number of Cabinet Ministers
Tokyo Imperial University	7
Kyoto Imperial University	3
Tokyo Commercial University	3
Tōhoku Imperial University	1
Waseda University	3
Nihon University	1
Wesleyan University (U.S.)[b]	1
Department of Agriculture Fisheries Training School[c]	1

[a] Source: *Asahi,* July 19, 1960.
[b] This was the one woman member of the Cabinet.
[c] Middle-school level.

In the second, formed on July 18, 1962, 11 of the 20 were from the "Big Three," and 12 from the national universities.

TABLE 7: SECOND IKEDA CABINET (JULY 18, 1962)[a]

School Background	Number of Cabinet Ministers
Tokyo Imperial University	7
Kyoto Imperial University	3
Tokyo Commercial University	1
Tōhoku Imperial University	1
Waseda University	3
Senshū University	1
Tōyō University (incomplete)	1
Japan Women's University[b]	1
Industrial School[c]	1
Business Training School[c]	1

[a] Source: *Asahi*, July 18, 1962.
[b] Equivalent to the *semmongakkō* level.
[c] Middle-school level.

Opposition politics is less dominated by university-based cliques, as may be seen in the following table:

TABLE 8[a]

	Liberal-Democratic Party	Japan Socialist Party
Diet members with university education	74%	52%
Government universities	46	21
Tokyo University	33	13

[a] Calculated from Nihon Seikei Shimbunsha, *op.cit.*

The sources of leadership are more diverse—from trade unions, farmers' organizations, or popular movements—but, as against this, the intellectuals among the leadership stand out more conspicuously as a distinct group.

On the surface, Japanese politics today appears about as polarized as it can be. And yet the old school tie still makes it possible for politicians of the left and the right to maintain some kind of communication across the political gap. It has not been unknown for a socialist to leave the podium after blood-and-thunder denunciation and declaration of war unto the death, only to join a conservative friend in a pleasant social gathering. Every close observer has his own favorite examples of these cross-party friendships and of how unexpectedly far they can go. It may be that this is an element that makes the polarization of Japanese politics somewhat less bitter and irreconcilable than it often appears to be.

III. Education and Ideology

Except for the totalitarian states, no modern nation has used the schools so systematically for purposes of political indoctrination as Japan. Although the early builders of the modern school system spoke a utilitarian language, they did not for a moment forget problems of morality and patriotism. They simply took them for granted. The purpose of education was, as it had been during the Tokugawa period, to create loyal as well as trained citizens, and there were always people ready to see to it that over-enthusiastic utilitarians and Westernizers did not go too far. Although the "national scholars" had failed to maintain their early control of the school system, by the late 1880's and 1890's, together with the Confucianists, they made a strong re-entry into the field. Under the influence of Motoda Eifu and Nishimura Shigeki, the Imperial Rescript on Education, which was drafted by the then Minister of Education, Inoue Kowashi, was promulgated on October 30, 1890, as the basic document governing the operation of the school system:

"Our Imperial Ancestors have founded our Empire on a basis broad and everlasting. . . . Our subjects ever united in loyalty and filial piety have from generation to generation illustrated the beauty thereof. This is the glory of the fundamental character of Our Empire, and herein also lies the source of Our Education. Ye, Our Subjects, be filial to your parents, affectionate to your brothers and sisters; as husbands and wives be harmonious, as friends, true . . . pursue learning and cultivate arts, and thereby develop intellectual faculties and perfect moral powers; furthermore, advance public good and promote common interests; always respect the Constitution and observe the laws; should emergency arise, offer yourselves courageously to the State; and thus guard and maintain the prosperity of Our Imperial Throne coeval with heaven and earth. . . ."

The reaction against the pro-Western "excesses" of the early Meiji period, which began to set in in the late 1880's, involved not only the national scholars, who looked to antiquity for the model of what a modern Japanese state should be, and the Confucianists who were fearful of the effects of Western utilitarianism and "materialism" on morality and public virtue, but the hard-headed pragmatic Meiji leaders themselves, who were out to establish firmly the concept of the supremacy of the state. Already this concept was central in the draft of the new constitution, for which purpose Itō Hirobumi, who was responsible for its drafting, had drawn upon German ideas and advisors.[67] "In the administration of all schools," wrote Mori Arinori, the first Itō Cabinet's Minister of Education in 1885, and himself considered pro-Western and even pro-American, "it must be kept in mind, what is to be done is not for the sake of the pupils, but for the sake of the country."

But for the "sake of the country," it will be recalled, implied not only obedience but "training" as well. Obedience might be a necessary, even the basic, civic virtue, but quite clearly it was not likely to bring Japan the new knowledge and techniques necessary for becoming a major world power. On the other hand, the critical, skeptical temper of the West, important though it might be for the development of Japanese science and technology, was a threat to the constitutional absolutism envisioned by the Meiji oligarchs. The resolution of this dilemma was the work of Mori Arinori,[68] and so ingenious was

---

[67] Itō visited Europe in 1882-1883. He attended lectures in Berlin specially prepared for him by Rudolf von Gneist, a distinguished German constitutional authority, and then spent time with Lorenz von Stein in Vienna. On his way back to Japan, he stopped off in England for one lecture by Herbert Spencer on representative government.

[68] My own views on Mori have been deeply influenced by Prof. Hayashi Takeji of Tohoku University, Sendai, Japan. See in particular his "Kindai Kyōiku Kōsō to Mori Arinori" (The Structure of Modern Education and Mori Arinori), *Chūō Kōron*, September 1962; and "Mori Arinori to Arai Osui ni kansuru Oboegaki" (Memorandum on Mori Arinori and Arai Osui), unpublished. Prof. Nagai Michio has written several influential articles on Mori, rather more harsh in judgment than Prof. Hayashi. See his "Chishikijin no Seisan Rūto (Intellectual Production Route), in *Kindai Nihon Shisōshi Kōza* (Lectures on the History of Modern Japanese Thought), Vol. 4, *Chishikijin no Seisei to Yakuwari* (Production and Role of the Intellectuals), Tokyo, Chikuma Shobo, 1959, and also his "Mori Arinori: Meiji Kyōiku no Kensetsusha" (Mori Arinori: Builder of Meiji Education), *Asahi Journal*, May 20, 1962.

Mori (1847-1889) was a remarkable and controversial figure. At the age of 18 he was sent to study in England and returned to Japan in 1868 after a trip through Russia and the United States. At the age of 23, in 1870, he was appointed Japan's first minister to the United States, where he came Christian influence and became an advocate of religious and academic freedom and male-female equality. "Progress can only be achieved," he wrote, in a manner reminiscent of Thomas Paine, "through revolutions and trials. . . ." Yet later in his life he was considered a leading advocate of ultra-nationalism and militarism. As Nagai explains in his brilliant articles, this was not as much of a contradiction as it appears. Mori's primary moti-

it that it remained essentially unchanged until the end of the Second World War.

What he did was to establish a dual system: on the one hand a compulsory sector heavily indoctrinated in the spirit of the traditional morality and nationalism, on the other, a university sector for the elite in an atmosphere of the greatest possible academic freedom and critical rationalism. Although the relative freedom for the university involved a certain degree of risk, Mori felt that it was minimized by the fact that all students would come to it only after a thorough nationalistic indoctrination in the lower schools. The gap between higher and lower education was bridged by the normal school, and to this Mori devoted a great deal of attention. Normal school students, who were state-supported, lived in dormitories under strict military-style discipline. Mori's solution has resulted in that curious dichotomy between the relative academic freedom of the Japanese university and the severely controlled and indoctrinated system of lower education.

With these ideas, the Japanese quite naturally found Prussian pedagogical theory much more congenial than the Anglo-Saxon, which had until then been dominant. In the Japanese reading, what Herbart was saying was that "moral training," rather than individual development, was the center of education, and for this national history and literature were the best curricular instruments. This was an eminently agreeable notion and concorded well with the ideas of the national scholars, the Confucianists, and the oligarchy itself.

---

vation was the strengthening and modernization of Japan. In this sense, he was always nationalistic and even militaristic. But he saw academic freedom, religious freedom, and his other "progressive" ideas as instruments of national development, rather than as absolute values.

When he returned to Japan in 1873, at the age of 26, he joined Fukuzawa Yukichi and other leaders of the "enlightenment" in Japan in the formation of the Meirokusha (Meiji 6—that is, 1873—Society) for the promotion of Western thought and soon became its chairman. In 1875 he went abroad again as Japan's consul in China, and then in 1879 he went as consul to England. In the early 1880's, he came into personal contact with Itō, then studying European constitutional developments in preparation for the writing of a Constitution for Japan. Their ideas coincided so closely that when Itō became Prime Minister in 1885, he made Mori his Minister of Education in spite of the considerable opposition of the Confucianists around the Emperor Meiji.

Within three months of his appointment he put into effect the Imperial University decree and one month later the Primary School, Middle School, and Normal School decrees, which set the basis for the modern educational system of Japan. In February 1889, on the day of the promulgation of the new Constitution, he was assassinated by a fanatic nationalist youth, the son of a shrine priest.

From 1890 on until the American Occupation, the inculcation of loyalty and an official version of national morality became central to the mission and methods of the school system. The official doctrine taught in the schools was essentially that of the "Japanists" (*Nihonshugisha*): Japan is a unique family-state, descended from a common ancestor. The Emperor, as the direct descendant of the Imperial ancestor, has qualities of divinity and embodies in his person the unity of the state and the people. The unique Japanese family system is based upon reverence for ancestors, the power and responsibility of the family head, obedience, and filial piety. Filial piety is the model for the relation of the citizen both to the state and to superiors.

Although both the family and the state ideology preached in the schools were drawn from the Japanese tradition, they represented only a selective adaptation of traditional principles. The divinity of the Emperor and the obligation of absolute obedience to him, for example, were essentially revivals of the pre-feudal period. During feudal times, the Emperors had been eclipsed, and primary loyalty was owed to one's personal overlord. What the Meiji leaders did was retain the principle of unquestioning loyalty but transfer it from feudal lord to the Emperor. And since the Emperor system was the kingpin of the unified national state, it was all the more important to fix this loyalty firmly. In the same way, the family ethic preached in the schools was essentially the Confucian ethic of the upper classes; it was not that of the lower classes. But the Meiji leaders set out to inculcate the samurai ethic as the national ethic, and the school system played the key role in this transformation.

Family and state ethics were considered, both by supporters and opponents of the doctrine, to reinforce each other. Filial piety was the prototype for loyalty to superiors, the state, and the Emperor. The subordination of the self to the needs of the collective family group was concordant with the more generalized notion of subordination of self to the national collectivity. *On*—unending obligation to parents —was the basis of loyalty to the father-Emperor.

> Precious are my parents that gave me birth,
> So that I might serve his Majesty.

might serve as a statement of the doctrine in a nutshell. The notion that one owed unlimited obligation and obedience to all one's superiors, just as one did to one's parents and the Emperor, was promoted in many ways, leading to the doctrines of "*on* to the teacher," "*on* to one's benefactor," etc.[69]

The principal instrument for the inculcation of these ideas was the morals course (*shūshin*). A minimum of one hour per week of morals was mandatory in all schools, from elementary through the secondary school. But apart from the formal morals course, the ideas were worked into the curriculum and into school life in any way the ingenuity of the educators could devise. Wherever subject matter permitted, they were to be worked into the textual material. "The essential aim of teaching Japanese history is to make children comprehend the fundamental character of the Empire and to foster in them the national spirit," read the regulations for the teaching of history. "Children should be taught the outlines of the establishment of the Empire, the continuity of the Imperial dynasty. . . . It is above all important to keep in touch with the teaching of morals:"[70] In geography, "The essential object . . . is to give children a general knowledge of the condition of the earth's surface . . . to make them understand in a general way how our country stands in the world, and to instil into their minds the love of their country."[71] Morals indoctrination even turned up in such unlikely subjects as arithmetic, language, and music.

Outside of class, the official doctrine was promoted in a variety of ways. There were frequent ceremonial assemblies requiring the reading of the Imperial Rescript on Education, the showing of the Imperial Portraits, the raising of the national flag, etc., and these were carried through with the utmost protocol and graveness to make a proper impression on the children. The reading of the Imperial Rescript was more a religious incantation than the recitation of a secular document. The reader had to carry the sacred scroll reverently, hold it in white-gloved hands, and read it impressively and perfectly. So sacred were these symbols that in case of fire they were to be saved before everything else, even at the risk of life. The slightest impropriety led to disgrace and humiliation. Dramatic cases have been reported of teachers or principals of schools, accidentally responsible for some impropriety—as, for example, dropping the Imperial Rescript, or making a mistake in its reading—committing suicide. The cult of the state, which has come to be known as State Shinto, was brought into close relation with

---

[69] See Ruth Benedict, *Chrysanthemum and the Sword*.
[70] Quoted in Keenleyside and Thomas, *op.cit.*, pp. 179-180.
[71] *Ibid.*, p. 183.

the school system. Its doctrines were taught, and pupils were required to participate in its rituals and visit its shrines on ceremonial and national occasions. Schools organized pilgrimages and outings designed to strengthen the pupils' loyalty and devotion to the national cult.

With the arrival of the militarists to power, the deliberate indoctrination was intensified, and became even more specifically directed towards the goals of the militarists and the ultra-nationalists. The demand for orthodoxy and conformity turned into an official system of thought control, more than ever strictly policed by Special Thought Police, Special Higher Thought Police, etc. . . . In 1941, General Araki Sadao was appointed Minister of Education, and the military was in virtual control of the indoctrination program. The aim of moral education was not only the exaltation of the Japanese state, but more specifically "to make students realize the moral mission of the Empire, and by training them in practical morality, to cultivate virtues based on the principles of the Imperial Rescript on Education."[72] Delmer Brown has estimated that about one-third of the curriculum had a strongly nationalistic content in this period.[73] In the official morals textbooks which, of course, dealt not only with the state but with the family, the school, etiquette, and the individual, a content analysis has shown that materials on the state went up from about 20 per cent in 1933 to about 38 per cent in 1941.[74] In the same way, stories about famous men, which used to include international figures like Benjamin Franklin, George Washington, Einstein, etc., became increasingly nationalistic. By the beginning of the war, the only foreigners mentioned were Beethoven, Galileo, and Edward Jenner—Beethoven and Galileo from allied countries and Jenner from a neutral country; but all Englishmen and Americans had been dropped. By the middle of the war, even Beethoven and Galileo were dropped. An inspection of the first pages of first-year language texts shows a similar story.[75] In the liberal 1920's, the first pages read: "Flower (page 1); Dove, bean, scale (page 2); Here is a crow, and here also is a sparrow (page 4)." In the 1930's, the opening lines read as follows: "It has blossomed, it has blossomed, the cherry has

[72] Ministry of Education Order No. 4, March 14, 1941. Quoted in Anderson, op.cit., p. 17.

[73] Delmer Brown, Nationalism in Japan, Berkeley and Los Angeles, University of California Press, 1955.

[74] Karasawa Tomitarō, "Changes in Japanese Education as Revealed in Textbooks," Japan Quarterly, July-September, 1955.

[75] These items are from Karasawa Tomitarō, Kyōkasho no Rekishi (History of Textbooks), Tokyo, Sōbun-sha, 1956.

blossomed."[76] Then: "Advance, advance, soldier, advance." The war-time text opened with: "The rising sun (Japan's national flag), red, red." The contents for the first pages of reading training include references to military matters such as "Navy task force," etc. According to Karasawa, about 76.4 per cent of the content of the language textbooks was nationalistic during the war period.[77]

The indoctrination was supported both within and without the school. Teachers were often formal and stiff with their pupils, and strict respect relations between them were considered proper. Self-expression was discouraged and disagreement with teachers and elders severely frowned upon.

Outside of school, the teaching was reinforced by family life itself. The Japanese family was, as someone has observed, a "training ground in hierarchy." Relations within the family had a strong hierarchical element: the head of the family had superordinate authority legally enjoined by the Civil Code, over the family members; females were subordinate to males; juniors were subordinate to seniors; younger brothers were subordinate to the elder brother, the heir-apparent to the headship of the family. Where extended family relations were maintained, these too were characteristically hierarchical in character, with the "main house" holding authority over the "branch houses," who in turn owed obedience and often service to the former. It is not without significance that Japan's leading sociologist of law, Kawashima Takeyoshi, has entitled one of his main books *The Family System as Ideology*.[78] In all public institutions the same ethics of hierarchy was insisted upon, and in the army, to which most Japanese men were obligated for a period of service, the indoctrination and its exemplification in military life reached their high point.

How effective this system was is a different matter, and no easy answer can be given. Japanese sociologists, anthropologists, psychologists, and historians are still trying laboriously to piece the whole story together. It is clear, however, that there were strong elements of resistance to the penetration of the official doctrine. In spite of the indoctrination of an official orthodoxy, the suppression of academic freedom, and ultimately the imposition · of a system of thought control, there were many products of the school system who

---

[76] The cherry blossom, which blooms for only a brief moment of glory and then dies, is the symbol of the warrior's spirit.

[77] Karasawa, *op.cit.*, p. 381.

[78] *Ideorogii to Shite No Kazoku Seido*, Tokyo, Iwanami, 1957.

opposed the official views. This was particularly the case at the higher levels of education where, as Mori had seen, the necessity for comparison, critical thought, and the study of outside ideas makes the imposition of an official doctrine more difficult. Students in higher institutions were evidently more affected by their general reading and studies than by the official morals courses. The schools were so open to outside ideas—through foreign books, libraries, and the inherent conclusions of reading and reflective thought—that no official attempts could completely close them off. Nor was this seriously attempted until the militarists came to power. Until the rise of politically organized mass movements, the universities provided the main centers of resistance to official ideology, and even extreme suppression could not wipe them out.

Similarly there were other deviant channels of Japanese life and thought, sustained by the outside world or by particular life experiences, that resisted orthodoxy: Christian institutions, foreign-linked activities, liberal and radical political movements—even to some extent the private universities—in general, all those for whom the *bunmei kaika* (civilization and enlightenment) part of the Meiji consensus was more important than the *fukoku kyōhei* (prosperous country, strong military) part.

Nor is there any evidence that the officially promoted morality penetrated as deeply among the masses as the leaders might have hoped. For many people, the official dogmas were mere formalities, external to themselves and their way of life. Even among the less educated sections of the population, as in isolated rural areas, Kawashima[79] has shown us that the ethical precepts of *on*, *giri*, and *chū* were by no means so widely accepted nor were they accepted in precisely the manner intended. The popular norms of morality and family relations were far less austere than, for example, observers like Ruth Benedict had been led to believe.

It may be that the rulers of Japan were half-hearted, or that their indoctrinating impulses were too spasmodic. But the Japanese experience suggests the equally plausible—and comforting—conclusion that perhaps the life of thought has its own momentum and logic. Once you start to educate people, it is very likely that some of them are going to reach their own conclusions about the nature of life and

[79] For example, his "On no Ishiki no Jittai" (A Field Study of the Consciousness of *On*), *Chūō Kōron*, Vol. 66, No. 3 (Whole No. 745), March 1951.

society. And when, as in the higher reaches of thought, this involves comparison, reflection on personal and social life, debate, critical judgment, and the development of independent canons of truth, unorthodox thought may perhaps be suppressed, but it is unlikely to be wiped out.

CHAPTER 10

The Philippines

CARL H. LANDÉ

~·~

*Introduction: The School System during the Spanish
and American Colonial Periods*

FROM THE beginning of the Spanish occupation of the Philippines in 1565 until 1863, when a public school system was created, responsibility for education in the Islands was left entirely in the hands of the church. It continued to remain largely under the actual direction of the church until the end of the Spanish regime in 1898, though during its last years a number of private schools were established by some distinguished Filipinos.

Among the aims of the church-controlled educational system during the Spanish period were the Christianization of the Philippines as a whole, and the Hispanization of the Filipino upper class. These were fundamental cultural changes. As for political socialization, the schools in the Spanish Philippines sought to make the natives obedient subjects of the Spanish king. Preparation for more active political roles was an unintended by-product of Spanish education. The system produced a small but influential Filipino educated class which was steeped in European tradition, was familiar with European political ideas and institutions, including those of countries enjoying more liberal government than Spain, and aspired to a more active role in the government of the Islands while remaining loyal subjects of Spain. When such a role was denied them, they took arms to win a brief period of independence before losing it again to the United States. The Filipino leaders produced by the Spanish colonial educational system were men of outstanding ability who wrote a democratic constitution for their short-lived Republic, and gave the country outstanding leadership during the early years of American rule.

Educational policy beginning early during the American colonial period, which lasted from 1898 until the Japanese occupation of World War II, was heavily influenced by the knowledge of American officials that the colonial regime was to be a temporary one, and that the Islands were to be granted independence when their people had demonstrated their ability to govern themselves by means of the largely democratic institutions of government which were established soon after the end of armed resistance to American forces.

Political socialization—in this case the deliberate inculcation of values appropriate for the citizens of a democracy—became a manifest aim of the educational system, and was pursued both by American colonial officials and by Filipino political and educational leaders.

Several other features came to characterize educational policy during the American regime, and largely continue to characterize it since the achievement of independence. These were: that large expenditures be incurred to establish a system of free public primary education which as many children as possible should attend; that publicly financed education be secular; that the language of instruction be English; that the curriculum follow that customary in the United States but that special emphasis be placed upon the extension of literacy, upon citizenship education, and upon vocational and physical training; that the entire educational system, both public and private, be subject to a high degree of centralized governmental control.

The effect of the mass education program upon the rate of literacy is of interest. The census of 1903 showed that of the population over ten years of age, 20.2 per cent could both read and write. At that time only 1.6 per cent had received the equivalent of a common school education.[1] In 1938, literacy was estimated at 48.8 per cent of the population ten years of age or over, the basis being the ability to read and write in any language or dialect.[2] The 1960 census showed the rate of literacy among those ten years and over to be 72.0 per cent.[3]

The importance accorded to education was reflected in the fields of administration and of budgeting. During the period of American control, the Secretaryship of Public Instruction was held by the American Vice Governor. In 1937, shortly after the establishment of the Commonwealth, and for some time before that year, the Philippines appropriated a sum for education which constituted about 20 per cent of all national and local governmental expenditures.[4]

From the beginning, stress was placed upon the training of teachers and upon the construction of schools. The resulting increase in the number of teachers in the public schools was as follows:[5]

[1] Joseph Ralston Hayden, *The Philippines: A Study in National Development*, New York, Macmillan, 1950, p. 937, n. 1.
[2] *Ibid.*, p. 604.
[3] *Handbook of Philippine Statistics*, Manila, Bureau of Printing, 1960, p. 13.
[4] Hayden, *op.cit.*, p. 480.
[5] *Handbook of Philippine Statistics*, 1960, pp. 25-26, and unprinted records of the Department of Education.

School year	Teachers
1903-1904	149,298
1934-1935	4,195
1962-1963	27,855

Attendance at public schools increased as follows:[6]

School year	Public elementary schools	Public secondary schools	Public universities and colleges
1902-1903	227,000	none	none
1934-1935	1,150,000	52,000	between 1,000 and 2,000
1962-1963	4,598,097	226,890	27,604

The population during this period increased as follows:[7]

Year	Population
1903	7,635,426
1935	14,731,300
1963	30,241,000

As these data indicate attendance at what until World War II were tuition-free elementary schools (since the war, outside Manila, only the four primary grades have been tuition-free) far exceeds attendance at secondary schools and colleges. In fact, a great many students leave school before the completion of the primary grades. The heavy and early drop-out rate, which is especially severe in the rural areas, has been a source of continual concern to Filipino and American educators, many of whom feel that less than four years of education is largely a waste of time and money. Efforts to lessen the drop-out rate have met with little success.

While a large number of students quit school after a few years of primary education, many continue on and graduate from high school. This in turn has created great pressure for admission to colleges and universities, with the result that the old church-controlled institutions, and a few new ones which were established during the American period, have been unable to accommodate the throng of applicants. The pressure has been absorbed in part by state institutions established during the American period, the most important of which is the University of the Philippines. But state institutions of higher learning are distinguished for quality rather than quantity. The pri-

[6] *Ibid.*, pp. 23-24, and unprinted records of the Department of Education. Figures for 1962-1963 do not include attendance at Zamboanga State College, for which no information could be obtained.
[7] *Ibid.*, p. 5, and unprinted records of the Bureau of the Census and Statistics. The figure for 1963 is an estimate.

mary commitment of the state to the provision of free elementary education for the masses has prevented it from offering facilities for college training to more than a small proportion of those who desire it.

The gap was filled by private venture colleges. Starting from small beginnings before the war, and organized initially largely as family undertakings, the number of such institutions and their enrollment have grown rapidly since the war and many of them have converted themselves into highly profitable joint stock companies. These private venture college-level institutions vary greatly in size and quality. The largest private venture university, and one of good reputation, is Far Eastern University, which in 1962-1963 had an enrollment of 47,777, and operated night and day. Another outstanding institution is Philippine Women's University. At the other extreme are innumerable large and small diploma mills which are engaged in a continual battle to maintain their accreditation with the Bureau of Private Schools.

For the year 1962-1963 the ratio of enrollment in private as compared with public collegiate institutions was roughly 15 to 1. (Private institutions include both private venture and church-affiliated ones. Figures published by the government fail to distinguish between the two.) Thus while the state has assumed the bulk of the burden of providing elementary education, higher education is left almost entirely to the private profit-making and religious sectors. Secondary education, which is offered both in public and in religious and private-venture high schools, falls roughly in between.

It should be pointed out, however, that collegiate education in the Philippines is not, and under present circumstances cannot be, the equivalent of collegiate education in the United States. Quite aside from the fact that instruction through the medium of a foreign language lessens the amount of substantive information which can be absorbed by a student, there is the added fact that since 1940 students have been admitted to college after but six years of elementary school and four years of high school (before 1940, there were seven years of elementary school). Thus two years less of pre-college education is required than in the United States. Finally, the data on Philippine college attendance signifies a broader and more shallow distribution of college education than would the same percentage figures in the United States, for a large proportion of those who enter college never graduate.

Nonetheless, the large number of Filipinos who "have been to college" has political and economic consequences of considerable importance. The situation has produced a large number of individuals who think of themselves as persons of education and who attempt to take an educated approach to politics. It also has produced a large number of individuals whose education does not really prepare them for white-collar positions demanding a high degree of training, but who are unwilling to settle for non-white-collar employment and in particular for agricultural employment. While in the Philippines such people do not riot or join radical political parties, they do place a heavy economic burden upon hard-working parents and relatives who, as good Filipinos, feel it their duty to support them. Insofar as this reduces the working Filipino's ability to save, it impedes economic development.

The lowering of the quality of a public elementary school education as a result of the cutbacks discussed above has brought increased pressure for admission to private elementary schools. The Ateneo de Manila currently has some 1,000 applicants yearly for entry into its first grade—of which only 200 can be accepted. This competition for placement in the best schools at all levels has enabled such institutions to make greater demands of their students in terms of scholastic performance and graduation requirements. While one cannot object to the efforts of schools favored by the wealthy to raise their standards, the simultaneous decline of standards in schools attended by the less privileged students, particularly the public elementary schools, places their graduates at a serious disadvantage in the job market and must tend to maintain the very gap between common people and gentry which the public school system was designed to lessen. Because of the difference in standards between public and private schools at the elementary and secondary levels, public school students find it increasingly hard to gain admission to the better colleges, both public and private. This in turn strengthens the hold of the diploma mills, which will accept almost any student who desires a college degree and can pay tuition.

On the whole, educational policy since the achievement of full Filipino control over that policy in 1935 has held fast to the principles established earlier, although certain changes of emphasis have resulted from the postwar self-examination which goes under the designation of nationalism. Thoughtful Filipinos have come to the conclusion that their intensive exposure to the admittedly impressive culture imposed upon them, largely with their consent, by the Americans has prevented the nation from concentrating upon the development of a distinct culture of its own. They realize that as a consequence of both Spanish and American rule, and of the failure of any of the great Asian civilizations to sink firm roots outside of the southern island of Mindanao, they are irrevocably a part of Christendom, and in large measure a part of the West. Their inability to be thoroughly "Asian," though tied to Asia by race and geography, makes them especially determined to preserve the distinctness of their syncretic culture and not to permit themselves to become another Hawaii, a little Malayan America outside the Union. Specifically, they wish a respite from the continual bombardment of American culture sufficient in duration to enable them to absorb what has been accepted, and to take control of their own cultural development.

The current mood has resulted in the hostility of much of the educated class to their government's decision to accept American Peace Corps volunteers. At the same time it has resulted in such positive measures as the establishment of an Institute of Philippine Culture at the Ateneo de Manila and an Institute of Asian Studies at the University of the Philippines. Finally, it has resulted in a tendency to look to countries other than the United States for some of the foreign contacts which no one denies are desirable. Significantly, until the early 1960's when admiration of Indonesia's anti-Western neutralism became pronounced among left-wing "ultra-nationalists" the countries looked to have been European and not Asian. Among them are not only England but also the earlier colonizing power, Spain. A result has been the institution, at the insistence of the "nationalists," and to the despair of most Filipino educators, of compulsory courses in Spanish in high schools and colleges.

Yet, as individuals, Filipinos remain determined to obtain American training. While on grounds of principle they may argue that Philippine education should be better adapted to the needs of a predominantly agricultural society and that Filipino merchants should study the methods of Chinese shopkeepers, Filipino industrialists, publishers, scholars, and politicians who really count among the country's leaders continue to send their sons to Harvard. And young Filipino nationalists of the elite, who object to the Peace Corps efforts to improve the English language skills of village children, know full well that their own professional success depends upon their mastery of that tongue, and they display that mastery by impressive contributions to their country's English language literature.

The growing interest in American social science and the execution of numerous empirical village studies by teams of Filipino social scientists will help educated Filipinos to obtain a better understanding of their own society. By achieving a greater understanding of what they are, and by keeping the myth-building and self-deception which seem to accompany surges of nationalism to a minimum, Filipinos will be better equipped to transform their society into what they want it to be.

Education and Nation Building

One of the most important changes which have taken place in the centuries since Spain first seized the islands has been the creation of a sense of Philippine nationhood. Education played a crucial role in this development.

The importance of the Spanish contribution is suggested by the state of affairs which existed in the mid-sixteenth century when Spain established itself in the Philippines. At the time the Islands constituted the least civilized fringe of the Malayan world. The population was probably under half a million as compared with the estimated 27.5 million of 1962. With few exceptions, communities were small and scattered. Archaeological evidence and anthropological inference from the institutions of surviving indigenous peoples of the region suggest that the political system of most of these communities were quite simple and did not extend beyond the confines of the community. There were no states of the sort found in Indonesia and mainland Southeast Asia. A few larger coastal settlements, which depended upon trade with Arab and Chinese merchants, contained sufficiently large clusters of population and wealth to support substantial local chieftainships. But these trading settlements and their political structures were of recent origin, only briefly antedating the Spanish conquest. Isolation permitted the development of large numbers of related but often mutually unintelligible languages throughout the Islands. Nothing that could remotely be called a Filipino nation existed when Spain began its rule in the archipelago. By the end of the Spanish period, a nation had come into being.

Among the major purposes of Spanish rule were the religious conversion of the natives and, in the framework of mercantilism, the economic exploitation of the country. Both ends were served by a policy of regrouping small scattered communities, some of them made up of wet rice agriculturists, many of them consisting of shifting cultivators, into larger and more permanent towns and villages. As a result of this measure, the natives were made more susceptible to conversion and religious supervision by the clergy, whose numbers otherwise would have been insufficient for this purpose. Resettlement also facilitated the extraction of the surplus of the agricultural produce of the cultivators. It is probably no accident that the area under wet-rice cultivation, which yields a far greater surplus than does shifting dry-rice cultivation but which involves permanent settlement, greatly expanded during this period.

By these policies of settlement and indoctrination, Spain not only converted scattered agriculturists into a peasantry and facilitated the entry of that peasantry into Christendom—a process which profoundly affected though it did not basically alter the native folk culture of the common people throughout the archipelago—but also provided the economic preconditions for the gradual emergence of a Filipino and mestizo landed gentry. This landed gentry was subjected to a much heavier degree of Hispanization. While the peasantry received religious instruction in their own diverse languages, the children of the gentry throughout the Islands were taught to speak and read Spanish, the first *lingua franca* of the Islands. Those who sought higher education came to Manila and a few other centers of population where colleges established by the religious orders were to be found. A few who could afford it studied in Spain or in other European countries. Thus diverse local elites intermingled and intermarried, and over the course of time developed a sense of common nationhood which trickled down to the common people as well and which became sufficiently strong to culminate, at the close of the nineteenth century, first in a full-scale revolution against Spain and then in a war of resistance against the American effort to replace Spain as the ruling colonial power.

The educated class, particularly its literary members, played a major role in giving direction to the revolution against Spain. Propagandist activity for administrative reform had its center among Filipino students in Spain. Newspapers and novels critical of colonial policy and advocating reform were published by them in Madrid, and found their way back to the Philippines, where they aroused intense interest among members of the literate class who could not speak out openly in the Islands.

After the turn of the century, the process of nation building, an unwitting by-product of Spanish rule, continued now wittingly under the American colonial regime. It took three forms: the dissemination of a new lingua franca, the systematic inculcation of patriotism and civic responsibility in the public schools, and regular practice in the actual operation of democratic institutions of government on a national scale. The first two of these processes involved formal instruction. The last was clearly intended by the colonial power to be a nation-wide educational experience.

Religious instruction aside, formal education, including the learning of written and spoken Spanish, had been confined largely to the upper classes during the Spanish period. The introduction, with the approval of Filipino leaders, of mass primary education employing English as the medium of instruction from the first grade onwards, gave—as it was intended to give—a common language to a substantial proportion of the common people.

The availability of English as the language employed in virtually all public documents and as the language actually spoken among officials at the higher levels of government if not in local administration has helped to reduce the importance of regionalism in national politics. It permits candidates for national office to campaign and to win votes throughout the country despite their ignorance of local languages other than their own. It enables legislators from all parts of the archipelago to communicate with each other in a tongue which is understood not only by themselves but by petty politicians and other opinion leaders in their home provinces and by a large proportion of the interested electorate as well. It permits the Manila English language press to be the nation-wide press, entertaining a truly national point of view. It makes possible the assignment of civil servants to posts throughout the country, far from their home provinces.

After the establishment of self-government under the Commonwealth in 1935, Tagalog, the local tongue of central and southern Luzon, was made the national language. Though not the language used in government, which continued to be English, it was taught as a separate subject in the schools throughout the country. Tagalog and English are now the most widely known languages in the Philippines, being spoken by 44.4 per cent and 39.5 per cent of the population respectively, according to the census of 1960, and the knowledge of the former is increasing at a more rapid rate than the latter. Tagalog is the lingua franca of the Manila marketplace, and the growing number of non-Tagalogs who live in Manila soon learn to speak it. It seems probable that in time it will join or replace English as the language of debate in the Congress. But that time would still seem to be far off.

While since 1957 the schools have employed the local vernacular of each region rather than English as the language of instruction in the first two grades, a proposal emanating from nationalist quarters that English be replaced as the language of instruction in elementary schools has met with little support. The reaction of the Secretary of Education was blunt and practical: "Take away English and we will be a nation of ignoramuses."[8] No responsible leaders have suggested the replacement of English at the high school and college levels, nor has there been any move to replace it as the language employed in civil service examinations.

It may well be that the acceptance of English as a second language, if not as the language of ordinary conversation, has passed the point of no return. The almost exclusive reliance of newspaper readers upon the English language press assures that English skills acquired in school receive constant practice. Manila is dominated by six large English language dailies. Two Tagalog papers, subsidiaries of larger English language dailies, obtain their readers mainly among the urban proletariat. Neither is doing well, and one has changed recently from a daily to a weekly schedule of publication. Surviving Spanish language newspapers fare no better.

What is more, the same state of affairs prevails in the provinces, where one might expect a vernacular press to thrive. Much of the readership of the Manila English language press is in the provinces. Even the many small local papers published in various provinces favor English over the language of the locality. Of 38 such papers surveyed by a national digest of the provincial press, 24 are printed in English, 2 in the local vernacular, and 1 in Spanish. Eight print news both in English and the vernacular, and 2 employ English and Spanish. While several weekly family magazines published in the vernacular and English have a large readership, it is quite evident that English publications are the main medium of printed news.

This will affect the political socialization of Filipinos in the sphere of foreign relations. For some time to come, newspaper readers will continue to obtain most of their foreign news from American or Commonwealth press services. And college students will continue to be exposed to the ideas of American authors.

[8] Statement attributed to Alejandro R. Roces, Secretary of Education, in the *Philippines Herald Magazine,* June 2, 1962.

The widespread demand for higher education in recent years has encouraged geographic mobility, thereby also furthering the growth of national feeling. The concentration of institutions of higher learning in Manila has filled that city with a flood of young men and women from all parts of the archipelago. Intermarriage among students in Manila and the acquisition of language and professional skills which can be employed anywhere have led to the settlement of graduates in provinces other than those of their birth. In the process narrow regional feelings have declined as sons and daughters have brought home spouses from other parts of the country.

Filipino school children not only acquired a common language during the American period. They were subjected as well to a common indoctrination in loyalty to the Philippine nation through textbooks and courses which stressed citizenship training and which imparted a knowledge of Philippine history and culture. The willingness of colonial authorities not merely to permit but to encourage the inculcation of Filipino patriotism helps to explain the weakness, until recently, of the anti-American ingredient in Filipino nationalism. While hostility to the continuance of American influence has become widespread among sectors of the Filipino intelligentsia in the course of the past decade, the mass of the electorate, especially in the rural areas, appear to be little affected, as was demonstrated at several elections in recent years when candidates who made anti-American appeals made rather poor showings at the polls.

Other aspects of American colonial policy contributed to nation building as well. Spain during her three and a half centuries in the Islands had failed to bring a number of important regional minorities under effective rule. In the southern island of Mindanao several Muslim groups, collectively known as "Moros," had been fairly successful in resisting Spanish attempts to subjugate them. Since the periodic Spanish expeditions against the Moros were composed largely of Christian Filipino troops, and since Moro pirates and slave hunters made a practice of raiding the Christian Filipino coastal settlements of the Visayas for slaves and booty, the feelings between Christian Filipinos and Moros were, and to some extent still are, feelings of mutual fear and antipathy. Moro independence crumbled early during the American period when American troops, with superior armament, subjugated the area and imposed American colonial government. They also imposed an American educational system with the same rigor as elsewhere. Half a century later, most Moros under their Manila- and United States-educated English-speaking leaders had reconciled themselves to and now in large part welcome participation in the Filipino nation. Tradition-bound Moros still send their children to Muslim religious schools. But more progressive Moros consider these to be vastly inferior to the government's public school system, and have used their political influence to secure the establishment of a branch of the state university in Mindanao. Participation in the mainstream of Philippine education has been the key to Muslim political effectiveness. When traditional leaders, lacking such education and the use of English which accompanies it, have been sent to Congress, they have not been taken seriously and as a result their constituents have suffered neglect. But when literate and articulate Muslims have been elected, they have been as effective as congressmen from other regions.

Much the same can be said for the Igorotes, a number of tribal groups who form much of the population of Mountain Province in Northern Luzon. Left to themselves in their impenetrable mountains by the Spaniards, the Igorotes were head-hunting pagans until the American colonial government began to build roads into the area. Provided with schools and taught to play baseball and politics in lieu of taking heads, these mountain people, like the Moros, have been brought into the Philippine body politic.

The cultural homogeneity and national feeling which developed during the Spanish and American periods, both as a result of and as a reaction against colonial rule, is reflected in the sphere of informal political organization. The country has two major political parties, the strength of both of which is evenly distributed throughout the Islands. Minor parties of a manifestly regional sort have been rare. Even the leaders of such distinctive regionally based minorities as the Moros and Igorotes have made no effort to create parties of their own but have divided themselves between the major parties in the same fashion as the Christian Filipinos. Politicians from diverse regions work together with a minimum of inter-regional misunderstanding.

Thus an area which at the beginning of the Western impact was among the most fragmented parts of Southeast Asia, a chain of islands inhabited mainly by a thin scattering of agriculturists and fishermen, with but a slight exposure to a common higher civilization and with no history of common subjection to any native empire, is now politically the most united country of Southeast Asia, Thailand not excluded. It seems evident that this development was due in large part to the uniform system of education, both religious and secular, which came into being during the colonial period.

Education, Culture Change, and Political Socialization

A former American Vice Governor of the Philippines has noted that from the beginning of the American period, the Philippine school system was given a task different from that of the schools in the United States, where "the traditional function of the schools has been to supplement the home in imparting the more formal part of the established national culture to the coming generation . . . to preserve the traditional national institutions rather than to destroy or rapidly modify them." Instead, "the Philippines under American guidance," having "set out to modify profoundly its political, social and economic institutions . . . deliberately planned its educational system to hasten such changes in the national character as might seem necessary for the accomplishment of these purposes."[9]

This effort met with some success. The indigenous peoples of lowland Southeast Asia, with a few highly localized exceptions, share a common social structure, and their traditional patterns of culture and behavior, which underlie the diverse foreign cultures that have been superimposed upon them, are remarkably similar. Yet visitors from other countries of the region are struck by the "Americanized" ways of the present-day Filipinos, ways which go beyond fashion and manner and involve deep-going changes in their orientation towards action.

These changes affect various aspects of life. We shall confine ourselves here to those which bear upon economic activity and politics. The former is included because of the effect upon the Philippine political system of the recent emergence of a successful and aggressive Filipino business community.

While United States economic policy towards the Philippines, namely, the involuntary inclusion of the colony within the American tariff wall, discouraged the industrialization of the islands prior to independence, more farsighted educational policies adopted by American officialdom in the Islands prepared the way for rapid industrial growth at a later time by helping to create a labor force equipped by training and outlook to man modern industrial establishments.

[9] Hayden, *op.cit.*, pp. 512-513.

Next to the spread of literacy, the principal instrument for this development was a large-scale program of vocational education. The aim of this program was not merely to teach skills, but also to inculcate attitudes towards manual work of a sort likely to lead to the exercise of such skills. Spanish colonial society had looked upon manual labor as degrading, and Filipinos had shared, or come to share, this prejudice. American colonial officials and Filipino educators thought it desirable to inculcate a belief in the "dignity of labor," and to that end all school children were required to take at least some vocational courses which forced them to work with their hands.[10]

While during prewar years the official stress upon vocational education encountered some criticism on the grounds that a predominantly agricultural economy was not yet ready to absorb a large number of persons trained in this fashion, such criticism is not heard today. The accumulation of a pool of skilled laborers and technicians has paid off in the rapid growth of Philippine industry which began shortly after the war as a result of the erection of obstacles to the duty-free and unlimited entry of American manufactured goods. The need for even more skilled workers and technicians is attested to by the numerous technical schools and colleges that have sprung up in the Philippines since the war, and now attract large numbers of fees-paying students.

In a broader sense, the schools and the government in and since American times sought to inculcate achievement values in a country where open-handed spending was more admired than frugality and saving, and where dependence, not to say sponging, was common and accepted. Under the new colonial regime the themes of self-reliance and industriousness were stressed in school textbooks. Thus a book written by the foremost Filipino educational official and writer of textbooks was "designed to aid in the tremendous undertaking of character education—nothing less than the reconstruction of the character of the citizens of a new nation—to lay the foundation for the formulation of a philosophy which centers on the serious business of life."[11] With the same objective in mind, the *Commerce and Industry Journal*, a publication of the Bureau of Commerce and Industry, quoted such aphorisms as "The man who never gets over difficulties

[10] Hayden, *op.cit.*, p. 519.
[11] Quoted by Samuel N. Seidman in "Enterprise and Entrepreneurship in the Philippine Republic," unpublished Ph.D. dissertation, Dept. of Economics, New York University, 1963, from Camilo Osias, *The Filipino Way of Life: The Pluralized Philosophy*, New York, Ginn and Co., 1940, p. xi.

never gets very far," and "High aims form great characters, and great objects bring out great minds."[12]

The effort to inculcate an achievement orientation probably contributed to the emergence of a Filipino entrepreneurial class. In the past, commerce in the Philippines had been dominated by the Chinese and other foreigners, in large part because the qualities which make for success in business—hard work, frugality, reliability, and a habit of thinking in long-run terms—were not highly esteemed in Philippine society, which values leisure, conspicuous consumption, and the right to change one's mind.

During the American period, the values of much of the elite underwent a transformation, drawing its members not only to the professions but to non-agricultural enterprise as well. A current study of Philippine entrepreneurship finds that: "While most of the creative, daring and imaginative leaders were engaged in politics, the foundations for entrepreneurial activities were being established. Marked changes were made in the 'latent' factors influencing entrepreneurs: . . . Reward for individual effort was exemplified; business pursuits and the profit motive were no longer ignominious; action was given the same importance as ideas; and, access was provided to accumulated scientific and technical knowledge. The prestigeful position of entrepreneurship in American society was obviously impressive to Filipinos. Also much was done to inculcate an understanding of the behavioral pattern associated with entrepreneurial status. Familiarity with entrepreneurial behavior was being developed through theory and folklore in the American-inspired school system."[13]

At the University of the Philippines, which attracts the children of the respectable middle class and especially of civil servants, only 2.5 per cent of the students were enrolled in the school of business administration in 1959-1960. But in the private colleges and universities, 29 per cent of the student body in 1957-1958 were enrolled in the commerce course. It would appear that many of the commerce students enrolled in private institutions, especially in the "diploma mills," appear to be men and women who aspire to minor jobs as accountants, clerks, and secretaries, a fact which nonetheless gives an indication of the growing importance of business in the life of the Philippines.

[12] Quoted by Seidman, *op.cit.*, from *Commerce and Industry Journal*, Vol. IV, April 1928, p. 11.
[13] Seidman, *op.cit.*

However, at the Ateneo de Manila, which more than any other college educates the sons of the social and economic elite, more than half of the undergraduates now major in economics. The Ateneo's role in training future captains of industry is of special interest because of that school's American connections. Originally a Spanish Jesuit institution, the college was taken over by the American branch of the order in 1921. While American educators have ceased to exert influence at the strongly nationalistic University of the Philippines or upon the public school system in general, American Jesuits at the several branches of the Ateneo now play a crucial role in inculcating in the sons of the Filipino elite the spirit of capitalism which Max Weber associated with the Protestant ethic.

Among those most strongly affected by their exposure to American values have been those members of the middle and upper classes who have spent some time in the United States. There they have discovered that the behavioral injunctions found in Philippine school books are not empty aphorisms but constitute the ground rules of a real society which many Filipinos—though by no means all of them—admire. Those who find it exhilarating to live in a society where the fruits of ambition are not siphoned off by sponging relatives, where people help total strangers as a matter of course, and where efficiency appears to prevail, often make major adjustments in their own behavior, remain under the influence of their stateside experience throughout their lives, and transmit that influence to their children. Some simply remain in the United States.

It is the returning Filipinos, a growing number of whom are graduates of American business schools, who have formed and who give aggressive leadership to civic organizations such as the Manila Jaycees. This group in particular has undertaken an impressive program of privately organized public service not only within the Philippines but—as in the case of "Operation Brotherhood's" medical teams in Vietnam—in other parts of Southeast Asia as well. Civic organizations of this sort are relatively new to the Philippines, where traditionally a wide range of obligations to one's kinsmen has left little time or money for philanthropy outside of one's kindred. The new civic organizations have played an aggressive role in organizing upper-class pressure upon Congress and various administrations in favor of good government and other public-interest objectives.

Let us turn to the role of education in political socialization. The schools since the beginning of the American period have sought to foster a faith in and a desire for democracy, and to teach habits of citizenship appropriate to such a form of government. Classes in citizenship were introduced at the third grade level as early as 1904. Since then, more emphasis has been placed on instruction in citizenship than is customary in the United States.[14] And as in the United States, such instruction has had an immediate practical purpose. For from 1907 onwards, young Filipinos found themselves called upon to exercise their citizenship skills in national elections at which substantial powers of government were placed in the hands of native leaders of their choice.

It would be erroneous, however, to assume that the considerable success of democracy and the high degree of public interest in elections and governmental affairs in general is to be attributed mainly to foreign-sponsored indoctrination. Much of the resemblance of the Philippine democratic process to that of the United States is due, rather, to certain traditional features of Philippine society and behavior.

For social structural reasons which are discussed elsewhere,[15] social life in the Philippines may be described as a never-ending popularity contest in which victories depend to a large extent upon the ability to distribute material rewards. It is hardly surprising that a society of this sort should have adopted with enthusiasm a political system which embodies the principle of the popularity contest, particularly when the government's coffers were so early put at the disposal of Filipino politicians by a cooperative colonial administration.

Again, Philippine society is somewhat anarchic. Clashes of interest or opinion are likely to have violent results. For this reason great care is usually taken to forestall open displays of aggressiveness, and to avoid pushing one's opponents to the wall, and much effort is made to achieve compromises capable of saving the faces of everyone concerned, even at the risk of sacrificing matters of "principle." This too facilitates the avoidance of the sort of open clashes of irreconcilable groups which in some countries make majoritarian democracy difficult to maintain.

On the other hand, when attitudes and behavior traditional to the Philippines are inconsistent with those suitable to the smooth working of a democratic system, serious problems arise. Thus American teach-

[14] Hayden, *op.cit.*, p. 485.
[15] Carl H. Landé, "Leaders, Factions, and Parties: The Structure of Philippine Politics," New Haven, Yale University Southeast Asia Studies, Monograph Series, 1965.

ers and officials tried to teach Filipinos to accept political defeat with grace and for this reason placed much emphasis upon the introduction of American sports in the schools. But in a society in which popularity is so important and in which substantive issues are of so little real significance, electoral defeat is far more hard to bear than in the United States, where a defeat can be shrugged off as the result of the public's unwisdom in matters of public policy. In a Philippine election, a candidate's prestige and self-esteem, and those of his relatives and friends as well, are at stake to an extraordinary degree —hence the unwillingness so often displayed by losing candidates, among them the losing candidate in the most recent presidential election, to admit that they were defeated by honest means.

Similarly, the effort of the schools to teach future civil servants to make decisions on an impersonal basis and to refuse to yield to pleas from friends and relatives for favored treatment has been but partially effective, to say the least. Yet the stress placed, in the citizenship classes of the American-sponsored school system, upon the necessity of accepting the outcome of elections and upon the undesirability of "anomalies" in government does seem to have left an impression upon those not directly affected, the educated public, as we shall see, and helps to account for the strength of democratic institutions in the Philippines today.

The general public's refusal to tolerate a high incidence of anomalies in government and their readiness to vote against politicians whose anomalies are thought to be excessive appears to have been the main reason for the three postwar expulsions from power of a ruling party. The frequency and amplitude of the reversals in the electoral cycle are explained in part by a clash between traditional and foreign values. The urge to favor friends and relatives is exceedingly strong among Filipinos because of a deep-seated feeling that favoritism of this sort is "right." Yet Filipinos also have come to believe that favoritism by public officials is bad for the country. As a result, politicians who upbraid the governing party for its anomalies when they are in opposition find it very hard to resist the pleas of their relatives when they themselves are in power. Yet the public will not tolerate such weakness and the politician soon finds himself ejected from office. This seems to be the principal reason for the rapid turnover of the membership of the Congress.

Education, Social Mobility, and Political Recruitment

Social stratification and the means of social mobility have also undergone major changes during the periods of Spanish and American colonial rule. Education has helped to bring about these changes.

Social stratification was shallow in pre-Spanish times. A thinly scattered, frequently shifting population in an area of abundant land impeded the establishment of power over people. During Spanish times, the most important basis of status was that of race. Spaniards were on top. Pure Filipinos were at the bottom. Eurasian "mestizos" were in between. Chinese immigrants, as pariah capitalists, were in a special category of relatively low status.

Yet during Spanish times a Filipino gentry, largely mestizo in composition, began to take shape. The probable connection between the resettlement of the natives, the spread of wet rice agriculture, and the growing importance of land ownership has been suggested above. The emergence of a class of wealthy landed Filipinos was probably stimulated by the growth of an export trade for Philippine agricultural commodities during the last century and a half of Spanish rule.[16]

In Spanish times the Filipino gentry were set off from the purely vernacular speaking common people not only by their wealth but by their Spanish speech, culture, and education. During the American period mass education lessened the cultural if not the economic gap between landowners and the "common tao." It also helped to greatly expand the professional middle class and in general opened new channels for the upward social mobility of individuals.

This does not mean that education per se became the major criterion of high social status, though certainly education did contribute to high status. Rather, education became a widely available means for the acquisition of those attributes which traditionally have been the main source of high status in Philippine society: wealth and popularity. Both of these attributes are of a sort that can be acquired rather quickly, as compared with descent, an ascriptive criterion, which has been less essential to status in the Philippines than in many other traditional societies.

[16] For a discussion of the growth of Philippine exports in the eighteenth century see Thomas R. McHale and Mary C. McHale, *Early American-Philippine Trade: The Journal of Nathanial Bowditch in Manila, 1796*, New Haven, Yale University Southeast Asia Studies, Monograph Series No. 2, 1962.

Wealth and popularity are closely interconnected in the Philippines. Each helps to produce the other. Wealth enables a Filipino to gather about him a cluster of dependents who become his loyal followers, which in the Philippine sense of the word makes him a popular man. Conversely, the power obtained from the ability to mobilize followers facilitates the appropriation of wealth.[17]

In late Spanish times the opportunities for the acquisition of land, the main basis of wealth, and thus of popularity and power were sharply restricted in the more densely settled portions of the Philippines. Share-cropping peasants, often perennially in debt, found it difficult enough to subsist, and few were able to accumulate a sufficient surplus to permit the purchase of land. The Filipino land-owning elite, once it had come into being, tended to be a closed group.

In American times, the establishment of electoral politics introduced a new and easier way to acquire popularity and wealth. By organizing a following among his fellow villagers or townsmen, an ordinary Filipino might win local public office or help someone else to win office. Having done so, he obtained access to spoils and patronage with which to reward his supporters and to increase his following. Then he might run for a higher office and obtain more spoils which he might use to finance his campaign for an even more exalted office and to enrich himself in the bargain. Thus by employing his skill as a manipulator of people, and public money as capital, the son of a peasant might—and not a few did—escape the poverty of his early surroundings and raise himself to a position of fame and fortune. In the course of his career he might marry into a wealthy family and consolidate his position within the social elite. Because of the relatively slight importance given to descent in the Philippines, this consolidation has usually been fairly complete.

The relative ease with which successful politicians of humble origin are absorbed into the upper class has had the effect of depriving the common people of leaders dedicated exclusively to the interests of the common man. It is notable how often Filipino politicians of humble origin adopt the conservative point of view of the gentry once they have made their political fortunes. Yet they retain their rapport with, and their ability to manipulate, the common people from whom they stem. This is one reason why Philippine political parties succeed

[17] For survey data attesting to the close relationship between wealth and status, see Frank Lynch, S.J., *Social Class in a Bikol Town*, Chicago, University of Chicago Philippine Studies Program, 1959.

in winning support from all social and economic strata simultaneously.

While the number of men who have climbed from nipa huts to the halls of Congress has been small in terms of absolute numbers, the belief that such ascent is possible has made a strong impression on young Filipinos of recent generations, and helps to account for their fascination with politics. This political Horatio Alger myth has also had the effect of diverting attention from the rigidity of the economic class system.

Education helps open the way to a political career and thus to higher social status. Filipino politicians agree that formal schooling, preferably in the fields of law or medicine, is a pre-condition to success at the polls. An uneducated man of wealth may deliver many votes to others. But he will win few votes for himself if the public knows him to be a man of little schooling.

Education also opens an indirect route into politics by way of a prior career in the civil service. In view of the availability of free public primary education, of the existence of a large number of inexpensive secondary schools and colleges which a working student can attend, many poor boys have been able to prepare themselves for the civil service examinations. Since English early became the language of administration and because candidates who took the civil service examinations in English had far better career opportunities than those who took them in Spanish, the linguistic inheritance of the sons of the old Spanish-speaking elite gave them no advantage, and the cards were not stacked heavily against linguistically talented village boys. In a sense this very fact lessened the prestige value of civil service positions, for the entry into such positions of large numbers of poor boys has made the public service in the Philippines a middle class rather than an elite profession. Nonetheless the fact that the civil servant is in a position to exert power over people and, sometimes, to extort tangible rewards for himself, lends great attraction to a civil service career, for as we have noted, power—which in the Philippines means popularity—and wealth are the main sources of prestige in Philippine society.

At the same time, in view of the even greater power and opportunities for income associated with elective office and of the great satisfaction which Filipinos seem to find in the public display of oratorical and combative skill and in the conspicuous distribution of largesse, it is a rare Philippine civil servant who would not exchange his bureaucratic post for an elective office. A great many poor but ambitious boys appear to have this in mind when they enter the public service. Their bureaucratic apprenticeship permits them to acquire inside knowledge of politics and to accumulate political capital: civil servants stationed in Manila generally make a point of doing favors for their townsmen and province-mates in preparation for the day when they plan to return to their respective home towns and throw their hats into the political ring.

An examination of the biographies of members of the House of Representatives confirms the contribution of mass education to a broadly based pattern of recruitment to positions of political leadership. Many congressmen appear to be of relatively humble origin. Most of them are the products of public primary, intermediate, and secondary schools and make a point of mentioning this fact in their published biographies. While a few attended the high-prestige colleges of the religious orders, two-fifths have studied at the University of the Philippines. The rest—with the exception of the handful who had no higher education—are products of the less distinguished commercially run colleges which cater to the working part-time students of lower or lower-middle-class parentage whose preparation of funds are insufficient to gain them admittance to the more prestige-worthy schools. The biographies of these congressmen reveal a passion for education. Many have attended several colleges and professional schools, perhaps because of the need to interrupt their studies to earn their tuition. Some have studied in the United States. As might be expected, a large proportion have law degrees, though this does not necessarily mean that they have practiced law. Many began their government careers at the bottom, holding minor clerical jobs and then rising in the civil service until an opportunity to enter politics presented itself.

Of those members of Congress who did not enter politics by way of the public service, all but a handful are professionals: lawyers, doctors, dentists, and civil engineers. That is to say, they are men who prior to entering politics obtained their living by the exercise of skills acquired through higher education, and only partly if at all from an independent income obtained through the ownership of land. Such men are part of the growing professional middle class whose contribution to Philippine politics will be touched upon below.

We have suggested that the present pattern of education in the

Philippines promotes a good deal of social mobility. But it also has less felicitous social implications, which stem from its imbalance. We have dwelt on the high rate of college attendance. Yet we have noted that the drop-out rate in the elementary grades is also very high. The contrast between the two phenomena becomes evident when one compares the Philippines with other countries. A recent cross-national report on rates of enrollment in higher education showed the Philippines to rank second from the top in a list of 121 countries or territories. Its rate, per 100,000 population in 1957, was 909. Only the United States, with a rate of 1,816 in 1955, surpassed it. But in its rate of literacy among persons aged fifteen or over, the Philippines ranked 76 from the top of a list of 153 countries and territories, with a modest 60 per cent literacy among this age group.[18]

The rapid expansion of higher education among those who can afford to attend private colleges while a large proportion of the population remains virtually uneducated may produce serious frustration among those in the latter category as they find their social status and economic opportunities declining in relation to those of a mushrooming educated class. This suggests the need for a renewed stress upon public elementary education.

Education and Democracy in the Philippines

A. LITERACY, ELECTIONS AND DEMOCRACY

The high rate of Philippine literacy has made possible the employment of procedures for the conduct of elections which have the effect of maximizing the voter's freedom of choice among candidates and parties. Such procedures help to account for the highly competitive character of Philippine democracy.

Elections in the Philippines are conducted by means of write-in ballots. Printed ballots contain nothing but a list of the offices to be filled. The voters must write in the names of the candidates for whom they wish to vote. Furthermore, no official list of candidates is posted in the polling booths. To find out the names of the candidates and their party affiliation, the voters are left to their own devices. To help them, parties, candidates, and individual political leaders arrange for the printing of "sample ballots" containing the names of

[18] "Basic Data for Cross-National Comparisons: Provisional Profiles," Research Monograph No. 1. Yale University Political Data Program, 1963.

their favorite candidates which they distribute among the voters on or before election day. Each hopes that the voters will copy the names from his sample ballot when they cast their votes.

The write-in ballot system of conducting elections, together with the weakness of party cohesion which is a feature of Philippine politics, prevents party leaders, especially national party leaders, from restricting candidacy for a local and provincial office to that member of each party who is favored by its leadership. The national headquarters of each party can and does submit a list of "official party candidates" to the Commission on Elections. But anyone else who wishes to run may also submit his name to the Commission and may advertise himself as being a member of whichever party he wishes. As a result it is not unusual for a party's "official candidate" to be beaten at the polls by a self-proclaimed member of the same party who has a larger personal following in the constituency. This makes the local party conventions, which nominate "official candidates," and the national party leaders, who "proclaim" them, extremely wary of imposing unpopular choices as candidates for municipal and provincial officers and for the House of Representatives. The "sample ballot" system for making known the names of candidates brings the center of gravity of political power near the grass roots level. While national party headquarters, as well as individual candidates running for high national offices, arrange for the printing of large numbers of sample ballots containing the names of their party's national candidates, and while they send batches of such ballots to political leaders in various provinces, the spaces for the listing of candidates for provincial and municipal offices are usually left blank, in the belief that local leaders will be more willing to distribute the ballots to their followers and to the voters at large if they are left free to insert the names of the local candidates whom they prefer. Even so, it often happens that the name of a national candidate— perhaps even the name of the senatorial candidate who paid for the printing—is scratched out and replaced by the name of another candidate who happens to have made an impression upon a local leader. Thus the petty leader at the grass roots level has the final say as to the names which will appear on the sample ballots which he distributes. Yet even he has but limited control over the outcome of the voting. For the voter receives many sample ballots from rival leaders in his locality. In the secrecy of the polling place he can copy down names from several of them or disregard all of them and fill in the blanks of the official ballot with whatever names he prefers. As a result, disciplined straight-ticket voting is far harder to enforce than is the case in countries where an illiterate electorate permit the nation's political elite to restrict the voters to a choice between symbols or colors representing the pre-selected slates of the political parties.

B. THE EDUCATED MIDDLE CLASS AND THE DEFENSE OF DEMOCRACY

It has often been argued that the success of democracy depends upon the presence of a fairly large middle class. It is often assumed, further, that this must be an entrepreneurial middle class similar to that which came into being in recent centuries in the towns and cities of Western Europe.

In the Philippines, until a few years ago, the entrepreneurial skill of Chinese immigrants and of other foreign businessmen, as well as the absence of strong incentives for the development of domestic manufacturing, inhibited the growth of a large Filipino business community. This state of affairs is now undergoing change, due in part to the enactment of legislation designed to exclude the Chinese from retail trade, in part to the adoption of protectionist measures which have been administered in such a way as to favor native Filipino industrialists. As a result, the Filipino business community has grown markedly in recent years both in its numbers and in the wealth and aggressiveness of its leading members. Filipino businessmen have been among the most vocal critics of corruption in government, for such corruption has added to the cost of doing business. But they have not held democratic institutions of government to blame for corruption. Instead they have placed the blame upon an excess of governmental controls over the economy. The writer knows of no Filipino businessman who advocates the abandonment of the present system of government in favor of a more authoritarian one. Rather, Filipino businessmen and their organizations have thrown their support behind efforts to perfect Philippine democracy. At the same time, they have sought to play a greater political role themselves, both as members of organized pressure groups and, with increasing frequency, as candidates for elective and appointive public offices. There is good reason to believe that if Philippine democracy were to be threatened in the future, the business community would be among its staunchest defenders.

But during the crucial early years of Philippine independence, before the Filipino business community attained its present power and élan, the defence of democracy rested mainly in the hands of two other and somewhat older sectors of the middle class: the landed gentry and the professional and semi-professional people whose achievement of middle-class status is the result of their education.

The rural gentry appear to be quite satisfied with the present system. They have gained both pleasure and material satisfaction from the game of democratic politics as they have played it at the local level during the past half century. By and large, they have been hostile to, and refused to cooperate with what sometimes appeared to be centrally directed attempts to restrict or terminate the game.

Of the professional middle-class defenders of democracy, the public school teachers are of particular interest from the point of view of this study. Teachers seem to be especially influential as leaders of opinion in the more remote and backward villages where few other persons of education are to be found. On the other hand, in villages where the spread of education has led to the appearance of other educated persons—doctors, pharmacists, lawyers, educated farmers, and the like—the relative prestige and influence of the school teachers has, to some extent, declined.

The civic role played by school teachers has been affected by their status as public employees. Like other civil servants, public school teachers are supposed to eschew partisan politics. In practice they often find themselves under pressure from local and provincial politicians to use their influence with the parents of their pupils in favor of one or another candidate. But in view of the fact that most school teachers are not natives of the villages to which they are assigned, and as the factional and partisan divisions which largely determine voting in most communities have their roots in long-standing familial alignments and rivalries in these communities, it is doubtful whether many teachers exert much influence over the outcome of elections even when they wish to do so. Thus school teachers must leave the task of expelling unworthy politicians from office, and of replacing them with good ones, to local leaders—many of them self-employed or privately employed professionals—who were born in the villages where they reside and who are not barred from partisan activity by civil service rules.

In non-partisan matters, however, the school teachers' position as public servants invest them with special responsibilities with respect to the promotion of civic action and the guardianship of the democratic process. Thus various agencies of the central government charged with the task of teaching villagers to organize projects for community self-help—projects stimulated in part by the hope that they will inculcate democratic habits at the village level—draw heavily upon the off-duty labor of village school teachers for their local direction. And at election time school teachers, as ex-officio chairmen of the bipartisan boards of election inspectors, bear a major responsibility for the maintenance of honest elections at the precinct level.

From the point of view of their attitudes towards democracy, there appears to be far less difference between the entrepreneurial, landowning, and professional sectors of the middle class in the Philippines than is the case in some other developing nations. The great majority of the members of all three sectors are graduates of the American colonial educational system and have been subjected to heavy schooltime doses of indoctrination by teachers who had few doubts about the superiority of democracy and about the applicability of that form of government to the Philippines. When the prospects for democracy seemed gloomy after the "dirty" elections of 1949, members of all three sectors joined or supported the National Movement for Free Elections. This organization and others like it, formed at a later time, established a most impressive network for the discovery and reporting of election anomalies. Together with a free and outspoken national press, such organizations have created an atmosphere of public vigilance sufficient to forestall any large-scale attempt to repeat the anomalies of 1949.

It is of some importance that most of the educated middle class and its leaders are not and do not regard themselves as being an "intelligentsia" in the Continental sense of that term, but rather as practical men: skilled professionals, technicians, and entrepreneurs. They display little interest in theory, but take much interest in practical politics as a means of achieving practical results. There is a small group of academicians and newspapermen, neither of whom constitute more than a minority in their professions—though a vocal minority—who lean in the direction of a Marxian point of view. But this group, and "intellectuals" in general, lack the influence among the educated class and the students which intellectuals enjoy in most other developing nations. As compared with practical men, Filipino intellectuals—the term is rarely used in the Philippines—occupy roughly the same role in the public life of their country as do intellectuals in that of the United States. One must conclude that it is the American direction of the Philippine educational system, and the American training of most of those who studied abroad, which is in large part responsible for this state of affairs.

C. EDUCATION, COMMUNICATION, AND GRASS-ROOTS PARTICIPATION
IN GOVERNMENT

Filipino politicians report that the readiness of rural voters to take advantage of the freedom of choice given them by the write-in ballot system has greatly increased in recent years. Before World War II, great national leaders such as Quezon and Osmeña rarely came to the villages at election time. Instead, they confined their campaigning to the important towns and relied upon provincial leaders to deliver the small town and village votes.

But since the end of the war, and especially since the time of President Magsaysay, who in 1953 set a new pattern of village-to-village campaigning, candidates for high offices have found it necessary to go from one village to another and to appeal directly to petty village leaders and to the village electorate at large. In doing so, they often by-pass the middle-level politicians who in the past delivered the villagers' votes.

Conversely, petty village leaders who in earlier years appealed to town and provincial leaders for help in securing nationally financed benefits for their villages, have learned to direct their requests straight to persons high in the national government, often traveling to the national capital to do so. This development has served to strengthen the village leaders at the expense of the leaders of municipalities and provinces.

In part this trend can be attributed to the increased competitiveness of politics at the higher levels which resulted from the re-establishment of a two-party system after a long pre-war period of one-party dominance. But in part the change may be seen to be a long-term consequence of mass education. For mass education has given villages access to reliable political news dispensed by the Manila press and by national periodicals, and has lessened their dependence upon verbal news and rumor, relayed and rationed by the middle-level leaders in the towns.

The improvement in the flow and accuracy of communication between Manila and the villages helps to account for the high degree of rapport that obtains between voters and politicians, a rapport which serves to distinguish Philippine politics from that of a good many other developing nations and makes it more nearly resemble that of the United States. Travelers through the provinces in the Philippines during a pre-election period are struck by the intimate and accurate knowledge of political developments in Manila and elsewhere which is displayed not only by local politicians but by ordinary educated citizens. In forming judgments about the administration and the opposition, people in the outlying areas take their cues from the Manila press and from such colorful leaders of the city as the late Mayor of Manila. As a result, once an administration loses the confidence of such independent leaders of opinion in the capital, its support is likely to decline rather quickly throughout the country. This accounts for the frequency with which parties have been turned out of power since the end of the war.

In turn, national leaders in Manila have detailed and accurate information concerning political moods and trends in the provinces. The government, the political parties, and the newspapers have created diverse and elaborate networks to sound opinion among local leaders and the general public. This means that electoral tides usually are predicted with sufficient accuracy to permit well-directed last-minute efforts to influence the results, or to adjust to them. More generally, it accounts for the high degree of governmental responsiveness to the desires of diverse sectors of the public. This in turn may account for the rarity of explosions of "anomic" behavior in the Philippines. Politicians take great care to inform themselves of public opinion. With a number of notable exceptions, they have been able to discover surges of popular indignation and to appease or deflect them before they have reached the point of explosion.

D. MASS EDUCATION, A PLURAL ELITE, AND THE FAITH IN POPULAR GOVERNMENT

The relatively slight political influence exerted by the "intelligentsia" has been noted. Furthermore the Philippines lacks a clearly recognizable "Establishment." While there certainly is an upper class, there is no small cohesive, self-conscious elite group which sets itself off from the rest of the populace and regards itself, and is accepted as being, especially qualified to govern the nation. Some of the reasons for the absence of such an "establishment" are traceable to the educational system.

The first reason stems from the sheer number of people who have received a substantial amount of education. In a country where the rate of college enrollment is almost as high as in the United States and where not to have had a few years of schooling is to be under-privileged, higher education does not give those who receive it a sense of being members of an elite.

Second, the Philippine educational system is not divided into two programs, one designed for the laboring class, one for those destined to work with their minds. While it is true that the parochial elementary and secondary schools are generally thought to be of higher quality than the corresponding public schools, and while a few special trade schools exist, the public school system on the whole is a uniform one, and it is common for students to pass entirely through that system and to graduate from the very prestige-worthy University of the Philippines. Furthermore, the large number of persons who have received one or two or three years of full- or part-time schooling at one of the numerous second-rate colleges obscure the boundary between the college-trained and the high-school-trained sectors of the population.

Third, the diversity of good universities—public, Catholic, Protestant, and private venture—has prevented the emergence of a corps of graduates from a single institution, united by the knowledge that they are destined to run the country.

As there is diversity among colleges, so there is diversity among the occupational groups which exert influence upon government. Power is shared by bureaucrats, lawyer-politicians, businessmen, planters, absentee landowners, the press, and various other occupational groups. There is no self-conscious elite administrative corps comparable to the Indian Civil Service. It was not the American intent to foster the development of such a corps. Politicians, who give orders to bureaucrats, must bow to pressures from interest groups. No single interest group is dominant, and all interests need the good will of powerful bureaucrats. All power holders are subject to harassment by the press. All are liable to have their power augmented or diminished as a result of what have been, in the case of the great majority of presidential elections, thoroughly intelligent and generally well-received popular judgments at the polls.

Education and Political Integration

One of the striking characteristics of Philippine political life is the great measure of agreement which exists among diverse sectors of the population as to the type of society and state in which they wish to live, and as to the means of achieving these goals—in short, the high degree of integration of political culture.

We have noted the effects of education in creating a nation out of diverse and widely dispersed linguistic groups. We have also noted its effects in lessening the danger of class conflict by facilitating social climbing on the part of those who might otherwise become radical political leaders of the poor. Education has furthered political integration in two additional ways.

First, the gap between the culture of the most tradition-bound sectors of Christian Filipino society and of the most modern ones is relatively slight as compared with similar gaps in other former colonial societies. This accomplishment is largely the work of Spain, which, during her three and a half centuries of colonial rule, introduced not only the Filipino elite but also the Filipino peasantry into Christendom. As a result all sectors of society, with the exception of the small non-Christian minority, are sufficiently "Westernized," if not in their way of life, then certainly in their ideological commitments, to ensure that the country is not troubled by serious political conflict between "Westernized" leaders and a "traditional" counter-elite and peasantry deeply committed to "Asian" ways, who balk at being "Westernized."

Second, the gap between the political cultures of the rural and urban Philippines, though substantial, appears to be far less great than is the case in many other developing societies. Here, too, education deserves much of the credit. We have noted that a large number of Filipinos who were born in the provinces come to Manila for their studies. While many of them remain in Manila after graduation, a good many others return to their home towns to practice their professions or manage their families' farms. Many of those who remain in Manila maintain close ties with their country cousins and make a point of visiting their home towns from time to time.

As a result, the educated and professional urban middle class in the Philippines does not consist merely of burghers of long standing, separated from the rural folk, but to a large extent is made up of citified countrymen. Because of their education, members of this group play an important role in transmitting an urban and national point of view to their rustic kinsmen and in bringing an awareness of rural needs to the cities. This was reflected in the surprisingly close similarity of rural and urban opinion on a variety of political matters revealed in a survey conducted by the writer.[19] It is also to be seen in the lack of much difference between rural and urban election-time preferences as to candidates and parties.

The high degree of consensus which is found among Filipinos in regard to the type of government which they desire for their country is largely responsible for the successful functioning of democracy in the Philippines. As constitutional democracy is the type of government desired by the overwhelming majority of Filipinos, there are grounds for concluding that *politically* the young Philippine nation has come reasonably close to achieving its major objective. Henceforth, the task will be to perfect the system: to reduce the scale of "anomalies," to develop more severe criteria for the selection of officials, to produce party leaders who will devise more consistent and effective policies and rely less on muddling through. But, despite the current imperfections, the relative success of the nation in setting its political house in order leaves it free to concentrate upon its economic tasks. Here, too, the presence of a largely literate public, an educated middle class, and a highly trained elite should contribute to a steady rate of progress.

Conclusions

Philippine society has undergone great changes since the middle of the sixteenth century when Spain established her rule. Had not certain of these changes occurred, it seems doubtful whether the country would be capable of maintaining democratic institutions of government on a national scale today. From a political point of view, the most important changes were those which helped to make the Philippines a nation and those which prepared the mass of its people to play the role of intelligent voters in a democratic state. The first change came about mainly during the Spanish period. The second took place largely during the much shorter period of American rule and of Philippine independence which followed it.

The changes, especially the more recent ones, involved the acquisition of new skills: literacy and a common language in the case of a large proportion of the common people; higher education in the Western tradition in the case of a smaller sector of society which comprises the propertied class and of a substantial number of up-

[19] Carl H. Landé, "Political Attitudes and Behavior in the Philippines," *Philippine Journal of Public Administration*, Vol. 3, No. 3, July 1959.

wardly mobile children of more humble origin; administrative skills in the case of the large numbers of civil servants needed to staff a modern government; managerial, technical, and mechanical skills in the case of the entrepreneurs, technicians, and workers which were needed if rapid economic progress were to be made during the early decades of independence.

The changes involved an acceptance of new loyalties and beliefs: a common loyalty to a Filipino nation, and a strong belief in the desirability and feasibility of constitutional democracy in the Philippines.

Most important, the changes involved the learning through continual practice of new techniques for the achievement of political ends. Over the years these techniques became habits and finally the conventions of a relatively stable political system, which few would care to change. Among them are the habit of choosing and controlling public officials through free and competitive elections in the case of the people at large, and the habit of appealing for the votes of one's social inferiors and of accepting the outcome of the voting in the case of the political elite.

Finally, the changes involved major alterations in the structure and character of society: the growth of a substantial Filipino propertied class which, while to a large extent residing in the countryside and maintaining lines of communication with the peasantry, yet was sufficiently modern and Western in its experience and aspirations to educate its sons and daughters in the Western, and lately in the American, tradition and to accept modernization and Westernization as an appropriate goal for all classes. The development of a lower class which no less aspired towards modernity, and which now leavens the country's governing elite by contributing to it the most capable of its educated and upwardly mobile youth.

These changes are the result of a combination of forces at work in the Philippines over several centuries. To what extent particular changes may be attributed specifically to education is impossible to say. But it is quite clear that both during the Spanish and American colonial periods, educational policies designed to bring about some of these changes were implemented with both enthusiasm and persistence. Some of these policies involved formal instruction: religious and secular instruction by the Spanish clergy, secular instruction alone by American-trained school teachers. Others involved training through practice: practice in the operation of democratic institutions of government. Some changes were intended by the colonial power:

the implantation of Christianity in Spanish times, the spread of linguistic skills and of literacy and the acquisition of new political habits during the American period. Other changes which laid the foundations for the modern Philippine state were not intended or desired by the colonial power, but were side effects of other changes which were intended: the growth of Philippine national consciousness which was stimulated by the reception of a common foreign culture and by the improvement of inter-island travel and communication during the late Spanish period.

The fact that two colonial regimes, each in its own way, were able to bring about fundamental changes in Philippine society and culture may be explained by a number of factors. First, many of the most fundamental changes were planned changes, not accidental ones. Unlike some other ventures in colonization which were launched with little more in mind than commercial or strategic advantage for the colonizing power, both Spanish and American colonial authorities sought not merely to exploit the Filipinos but also, for better or worse, to change them. For this purpose elaborate programs of religious and secular instruction were introduced. These programs had the benefit of being based upon prior experience: the Church's experience in the religious instruction of Europeans and American Indians, and United States experience in the mass education and citizenship training of American youth.

Second, these programs of planned change were carried out over extended periods of time. Spain began its effort to Christianize and Hispanize the Filipinos three and a half centuries before its rule came to an end. American colonial authorities began their program of formal and practical training of Filipinos for self-government nearly half a century before the country won final independence.

Third, both colonial regimes sought to change not only the Filipino elite but the great mass of people as well. Spanish priests wished to save the souls of all Filipinos, not merely those of the upper class. American education and political training were aimed at all sectors of the population.

Finally, Spanish and American efforts to transform Philippine culture met with the approval and, in many respects, with the enthusiastic collaboration of those whose culture was to be changed. As a result, even after former colonial rulers have lost their ability to force changes upon their colony, the latter, now an independent nation, continues to strive to make itself more Christian and more modern and democratic in a specifically Western sense.

The reasons for Filipino collaboration with their colonial rulers' efforts to change them deserve some comment, for they stem from a combination of circumstances not found in many other Asian colonies of Western powers.

First, Spanish culture and to a slightly less extent American culture appeared to colonial Filipinos to offer something superior to the culture which they knew. Except for some small groups of Filipinos who had been converted to Islam—and these the Spaniards found harder to convert—the bulk of the Filipinos in the mid-sixteenth century were pagans with but a primitive technology and few if any supra-local social or political institutions. Having no great Asian civilization to look back upon and no great native states to command their loyalty, they sought—or at any rate put up but little resistance to—conversion and Hispanization. Later, when Americans replaced Spaniards in the Philippines, the culture which they brought with them was not a totally alien one, but merely a more progressive version of the European culture which Filipinos had imbibed in Spanish times. Filipinos appear to have been convinced that Western education, offered to them by the American-instituted public school system, was essential to the individual social and economic success of their sons and daughters. Furthermore, while Filipino ways of thought may appear to differ somewhat from those of Western Europeans, they differ from them considerably less than do, say, the ways of thought of various other peoples of what to many Westerners remains the inscrutable East. For this, too, the influence of Spain and of generations of Spanish priests in the Islands would seem to be responsible. Thus Filipinos were both eager for and capable of mass education in the Western tradition when this was offered to them in American times. As for the political institutions which Americans sought to impose on the Islands, these differed little from the liberal institutions of government which Filipino nationalists, educated in the West or in Spanish schools in the Islands, had sought to obtain from Spain for many years. Thus, in contrast to some other former colonies, there was not much foot-dragging by native traditionalists bent on protecting their culture against that of the West.

Second, both American colonial policy and the international climate of opinion of the early decades of the twentieth century, when the aims and tactics of Filipino nationalists became fixed in a form which still persists, were such as to encourage Filipino nationalists to choose democratic practices and aspirations. The American regime, almost from the beginning, made it clear that independence would be granted when Filipino voters and leaders had demonstrated their ability to run their country in a democratic fashion. Further, the American regime, from 1907 onward, made it possible for Filipino leaders to achieve positions of great power and prestige by playing the game of Politics according to the American rules. Thus to learn the political lessons Americans wished to teach was both patriotic and profitable. To reject the lessons was unpatriotic and self-defeating, for there was at that time no anti-colonial bloc of nations to snap at the heels of the colonial powers, demanding that independence be given to subject peoples whether or not they were prepared for it.

Furthermore, Philippine democracy became a national goal and in large part a reality at a time when it was widely thought to be axiomatic that constitutional democracy was not only the best form of government but a form applicable to all peoples. European total-itarianism, of either the Marxist or nationalist variety, had not yet established claim to be the wave of the future, and its non-Western imitators were not to assert similar claims until after the dissolution of other European empires following the Second World War. By that time Philippine democracy was a successful going concern.

Third, Philippine democracy, as it evolved before World War II, served the needs and in general operated to the satisfaction of those sectors of the society that might have been in a position to sabotage it. During that period democratic politics in the Philippines took the form of an amiable, profitable, and socially undisruptive competition for office among the gentry. As the lower strata became more asser-tive, they too found it possible to obtain benefits for their class through the shrewd employment of the ballot and the exercise of pressure upon gentry or lower middle-class politicians. In short, the effective electorate was broadened gradually, somewhat as in Eng-land during the preceding century, with the difference that the pres-ence of a benevolent colonial power reduced the effectiveness of rear-guard resistance on the part of the upper class. Today as in earlier years, most Filipinos feel that the maintenance of constitutional de-mocracy serves their interests.

We have seen that, by and large, Filipinos welcomed the American effort to prepare the country for democratic self-government, and sought to make that preparation a success. It remains to be asked whether the preparation was sufficient to ensure the survival of democratic institutions of government in the face of serious efforts to subvert them, once the restraining hand of the colonial power had been removed. Pessimism in this regard was widespread after the "dirty" elections of 1949, and many feared that the elections of 1951 or 1953 would be even dirtier, and might signal the end of Philippine democracy. Instead, these elections served as a challenge to which the champions of Philippine democracy responded with verve, organizational skill, and most important, with the general support of the educated public. Partly because of the anticipated effectiveness of measures designed to expose "anomalies," partly because those in high places who may have considered committing anomalies had pangs of conscience about taking steps which they no less than their critics knew to be bad for the country, the elections of 1951 and 1953 turned out to be cleanly conducted. The same can be said for the elections held since that time. There has been a great deal of vote buying, much of it ineffective, it is true. But there has been little centrally directed violence, intimidation, or fraud at the polls. When such anomalies have occurred, they have usually been of local inspiration, uncoordinated, and designed mainly to assure the election of one or another candidate for local office.

This suggests some final observations concerning the relationship between education and Philippine democracy. One of these is that the indoctrination and practical training of the previous half-century helped to create a climate of opinion which would have subjected whoever might have tried to destroy democracy to the intense and sustained condemnation of their peers and of the public at large.

The other is that the most important political lesson which Filipinos have learned is one which they have taught themselves: that they can take effective steps to guard their democracy. Until the system was threatened and defended successfully, this question remained in doubt. Now, few thoughtful Filipinos have much fear that their system cannot be defended in the future, at least against internal threats. Nations as a whole learn in times of crisis. It seems unlikely that the Philippines, after the self-taught lessons of 1951 and 1953, will be quite the same again.

Part III:

The Education of Modern Elites

in Developing Countries

INTRODUCTION TO PART III

JAMES S. COLEMAN

A REMARKABLE amount of attention has been given to the education and training of elites in developing countries. Several factors explain this concern. The academic traditions inherited from England and the countries of Western Europe, as we have seen, were markedly elitist in their concept of the social function of education.[1] Colonial policies and practices fostered an elitist mentality by sharply differentiating the "educated elements" from the illiterate masses.[2] The emphasis placed upon "strategic human capital" or "high-level manpower" as prime requisites for development has strengthened the tendency to attach high priority to elite education.[3] This assumption has significantly affected the aid strategies of the more highly developed donor countries, as well as of international agencies. Indeed, a concern with cadres and leadership groups, existent or presumptive, almost saturates the literature on development.

The concern for elite groups is reflected particularly in the treatment of university students in or from developing countries. Such students are regarded as though they were, by definition, members of

---

[1] The character of this imported elitism, and the consequences of importing it, are perceptively analyzed by Eric Ashby, *African Universities & Western Tradition*, Cambridge, Harvard University Press, 1964, pp. 4-12, 21-42.

[2] This differentiation was particularly true of Africa. As I have noted elsewhere, "In the eyes of missionaries, an educated African was *ipso facto* superior because he was, in most instances, a Christian African. Moreover, throughout Africa the Western-educated class was referred to officially as 'the progressive or civilized elements' (British Africa), the 'elite,' *'notables évolues,' or 'élite noire'* (French and Belgian Africa), the *'evoluido'* or *'assimilado'* (Portuguese Africa), and the *'emancipado'* (Spanish Africa). This uncritical equating of education with special rights and legitimacy has endowed the educated African with an exaggerated sense of superiority and special legitimacy. Politics have been permeated with the presumably uncontestable assumption that the educated have a divine right to rule." (Gabriel A. Almond and James S. Coleman, eds., *The Politics of the Developing Areas*, Princeton, Princeton University Press, 1960, p. 283.)

[3] The occupational categories covered by Harbison and Myers' definition of "strategic human capital" include entrepreneurial, managerial, and administrative personnel, professional personnel; teachers, technical personnel; and "top-ranking political leaders, labor leaders, judges, and officers of police and the armed forces." (Frederick Harbison and Charles A. Myers, *Education, Manpower, and Economic Growth: Strategies of Human Resource Development*, New York, McGraw-Hill Book Co., 1964, pp. 15-16.

[353]

an elite in gestation.[4] The conferment of presumptive elite status, irrespective of demonstrated qualifications or leadership, has been particularly marked in reference to students at universities abroad.[5] Whether in countries of the Eastern bloc or the Western world, they have uncritically been regarded as strategic target groups by those seeking to influence the course of political evolution in the developing countries concerned. These influences have produced an unreal and inflated climate of elitism, reflected not only in the students' own exaggerated expectations, but also in the perspectives and assumptions of external observers and analysts.

A climate of elitism can be produced by various types of situations, of which three are particularly in point here: (1) The aristocratic type exists in a society characterized by a very narrow-based educational pyramid, a rigid hierarchical stratification system, limited upward mobility (or none at all), and the restriction of the higher educational levels to the upper classes. (2) In the elite-school type there may be substantial equality of educational opportunity for persons from all strata, and substantial upward mobility, but the apex of the educational pyramid is dominated by a limited number of elite or prestige institutions which impose a distinctive elite culture upon there graduates (such as Ivy League prep schools, British public schools, French *lycées,* and German gymnasiums at the secondary

---

[4] Douglas E. Ashford has observed that "Moroccan and Tunisian college students are quite conscious of their influential position. The radio and the newspapers are filled almost daily with pleas for trained people. . . . A privileged young person in North Africa, and undoubtedly in much of Africa and Asia, cannot grow up without being told how important he is long before he is asked to demonstrate his skill or talent. This is very different from the student's position in an advanced society." (*Second and Third Generation Elites in the Maghreb,* Policy Research Study, U.S. Department of State, Washington, Government Printing Office, 1964, p. 24.)

"The university," Seymour Martin Lipset states, "has the primary responsibility to train the future elites. This is particularly true for professional and governmental roles. In the developing nations, the role of the university is particularly significant, since almost all elite roles in the modernizing sectors of the society are filled from the ranks of the university-educated." ("The Political Behavior of University Students in Developing Nations," paper prepared for presentation at the UNESCO Conference on Students and University Education in Latin America, Bogotá, Colombia, July 13-19, 1964, p. 2.)

[5] Students at universities in the developing countries themselves are also actively courted. As Seymour Martin Lipset has observed, "In many of the underdeveloped nations in which it is clear that university students will form a considerable portion of the future elite, all parties have devoted a considerable portion of their energies to winning student support." (*Op.cit.,* p. 16.) See also William John Hanna, "Students," in James S. Coleman and Carl G. Rosberg, Jr., eds., *Political Parties and National Integration in Tropical Africa,* Berkeley and Los Angeles, University of California Press, 1964, pp. 413-447.

level, and Harvard-MIT, Oxbridge, French *grandes écoles*, and the Tokyo Imperial University at the university level). Graduates of these schools usually regard themselves, and in turn are regarded by others, as presumptive members of a national elite reservoir. (3) The "limited-output" type may provide equality of educational opportunity and upward mobility for all strata, but may lack recognized elite schools; yet the narrowness of the educational pyramid, juxtaposed against the continuously adequate number of elite career openings, endows university graduates, and even entering students, with a recognized claim to elite status.[6]

The climate of elitism in developing countries often reflects a mixture of all these types; the aristocratic and the elite-school standards of the inherited European academic tradition may be coupled with the scarcity resulting from the disparity between the output of the institutions of higher education and the demands for high-level manpower. Such a development is particularly characterized of post-colonial Africa. The elitist climate there, however, is probably transitory, not only because the trend toward educational eclecticism, multiple dependency, and indigenous innovation will dilute and transform it, but also because the expansion of indigenous secondary and higher education will deflate it insofar as it is produced by educational scarcity.

Elites have attracted special attention in developing countries because elites generally have heightened visibility and greater discretionary power in societies undergoing rapid change. In older and more stable societies, national political institutions and the national political culture exert a constraining influence upon leadership groups. In such societies, "elites are merged with the objects, habits, and manners of their age. . . . The timeless, functional aspects of their roles . . . [are] apparent primarily during periods of social transition or crisis."[7] The comparative fragility of national institutions and the absence of national cultural traditions in many developing

[6] Lipset has argued that elitist systems tend to be less productive of student political unrest because they "tend to assure those who succeed in reaching the university a guaranteed place in the upper levels of society. To enter, remain in, and graduate from systems of higher education is all-important. . . . Students may realistically expect to enter the elite, and thus they tend to identify with the existing one. The consequences of alienating oneself from the power elite will be very great." (*Ibid.*, p. 31.)

[7] Suzanne Keller, *Beyond the Ruling Class: Strategic Elites in Modern Society*, New York, Random House, 1963, p. 5.

countries allow political elites to function with few institutional and cultural restraints.[8] Their main problem is to establish and maintain their supremacy over other elites, a struggle characteristically marked by the subordination of sub-national—usually traditional—elites, and the assimilation or the neutralization of actual or potential modern counter-elites at the national level. This pre-eminence of elites in transitional societies explains the strong interest of development planners and social scientists in elite education, orientation, and succession, and in inter-elite relationships.

In discussing such broad concepts as "developing areas," "education," and "elitism," it is deceptively easy to impute to them a homogeneity that does not in fact exist. This pitfall, of course, is the inevitable consequence of the effort to simplify complex phenomena and reduce them to broad generalizations. Certain features are generic to the developing areas; yet, as the country studies in this book show, the countries concerned reveal enormous differences. Similarly, although education can be, and unfortunately tends to be, regarded as a homogeneous substance differentiable only in quantitative terms, there is a wide variation among different types of education, not only qualitatively as to content, but consequentially in terms of the impact of the variant types and mixes on the perspectives and behavior of their respective recipients. Again, it is useful to speak of a single "elite political culture," or of an "elite-mass gap," when discussing the gross features of the social structure and culture of the developing countries; yet in all societies, except perhaps in primitive tribes or in autocratic dictatorships, there are plural elites. And when they are examined in detail it is their heterogeneity, their diverse orientations, their conflicting political sub-cultures which are their most arresting features.

Elites are differentiated not only by their functional position in and their relative significance for the total society, but sometimes, even more importantly, by their educational experiences. A shared experience may have a homogenizing influence on the political perspectives of the elites of a particular generation, or indeed of successive generations. For example, during the pre-independence period, as we have already noted, a common outlook was created among indigenous nationalist elites who have attended the same secondary school or uni-

<hr>

[8] See James S. Coleman and Carl G. Rosberg, Jr., eds., *Political Parties and National Integration in Tropical Africa*, Berkeley and Los Angeles, University of California Press, 1964, p. 2.

JAMES S. COLEMAN

versity; usually only one leading institution functioned as a national center for elite homogenization. The extent to which a shared educational experience can produce a uniform political orientation is, of course, limited, as Dwaine Marvick brings out in his study of African university students in Chapter 14. On balance, however, such an experience does at least enhance understanding, communication, and predictability among those who have shared it. Also, in all likelihood, their political values and orientation will be more congruent than if they had not shared the experience.

Educational development means not only expansion and proliferation of schools to enlarge educational opportunities, but also increased specialization to accommodate the intensified professionalization and occupational differentiation characteristic of a modern society. In a developing country, separate educational institutions inevitably emerge to provide specialized training for the different groups that make up the "strategic elites."[9] The functional differentiation of elites obviously necessitates expansion of the educational system: military academies, police training colleges, schools of public administration, institutes of education—these and other institutions are set up to provide the cadres of a developing society. Unless deliberate measures are taken to counteract the drift toward an ever-greater compartmentalization of socializing experience, the educational system may become an instrument for parochializing and isolating, rather than homogenizing and integrating, a society's strategic elites. In most Western societies the drift toward elite heterogeneity is not politically dysfunctional, partly because of a fairly general consensus on the "rules of the game," and partly because of the overlapping affiliations of the members of specialized elites.[10] Heterogeneity may be dysfunctional in many developing countries, however, because political elites are still trying simultaneously to create a basic societal consensus, to establish their own legitimacy, and to consolidate and preserve their supremacy over other elites.

Malintegration and tension between incumbent political elites and other elites (actual or potential) in a developing country may be very pronounced where divergent socializing experiences have produced

[9] Keller (*op.cit.*, p. 20) defines "strategic elites" as the leadership groups that are "important for society as a whole . . . [and] have a general and sustained social impact, . . . [in short, as] those whose judgments, decisions and actions have important and determinable consequences for many members of society."

[10] Lester G. Seligman, *Leadership in a New Nation*, New York, Atherton Press, 1964, p. 20.

incompatible political orientations. As the several chapters in Part III show, one of the most pervasive problems of interelite relations in developing countries is generational discontinuity.[11] Rapid and fundamental transformation in social structure and power relationships is bound to make the problem of elite succession acute, unpredictable, and highly visible. When an essentially static society marked by widespread illiteracy and a predominance of ascriptive criteria moves toward a dynamic and modernizing society where education is the principal criterion of upward mobility and stratificational position, each successive wave of better-educated persons presents a challenge to its predecessor. This phenomenon largely explains the prevalence of generational discontinuity in many developing countries at two points of tension: (1) the gap between traditional elites and the first wave of modern educated elites, and (2) the division between the latter and the succeeding generation of better educated and professionally more qualified persons. It also accounts for the schizoid character (simultaneous anti-traditionalism and anti-intellectualism) of the outlook of many of the incumbent political and bureaucratic groups in new states. It is an important ingredient in the tension between political elites and university students; between the politically dominant leaders who carried out the revolution (nationalism or Communist) and the second post-revolutionary generation of technicians and managers; between a less educated "older generation" (many still only in their thirties) of nationalists entrenched in the upper reaches of the bureaucracy or army, who were the beneficiaries of the meteoric upward mobility prevalent at the time of the transfer of power to indigenous leadership, and the second and third generations of more highly trained persons who, finding promotion almost impossible, must mark time interminably at lower pay, status, and perquisite levels.[12] It is not simply education per se which accounts for

[11] On the concept of generational discontinuity in broader perspective see Keller, *op.cit.*, pp. 246-251. Lipset has observed that "The conflict of generations is greatest in periods of rapid social change, when the older generation still adhere to values which are increasingly challenged. Opinion surveys in a number of rapidly developing societies indicate extremely wide discrepancies among the attitudes of different generations." (*Op.cit.*, p. 23.) On the serious consequences of generational discontinuity in societies disturbed by a major event which breaks the normal succession of generations see Sigmund Neumann, *Permanent Revolution: The Total State in a World at War*, New York, Harper & Brothers, 1942, pp. 234-256.

[12] William J. Foltz, "Building the Newest Nations: Short-Run Strategies and Long-Run Problems," in Karl W. Deutsch and William J. Foltz, eds., *Nation Building*, New York, Atherton Press, 1963, p. 125. Foltz notes that in Senegal it was necessary for the party leaders "to remove the prime minister and dismantle the planning and administrative apparatus under his control when they seemed to threaten party primacy."

inter-generational tension; rather it is the whole complex of change in perspectives and assumptions associated with the higher valuation education acquires at certain stages in a developing society.

The elite relationship between the incumbent older generation of politicians in control of state power and the newer generation of technicians and specialists who staff the bureaucracy and other structures deeply involved in the modernization of the society is particularly marked by tension. If economic development is really given serious priority by political elites in new nations, "one may expect to find a new center of power created in the planning ministry, allied or not allied with the civil service against the party and regime."[13] In the Soviet Union the tension between the two groups constitutes one of the two most significant threats to the system: ". . . the continuing tension between the political leadership in the Party apparat and the social, economic, intellectual, military, and other specialized elites which share in the direction of Soviet society . . . runs like a thread through the more specific issues of Soviet politics. . . . To what extent . . . [for example] are the key positions of political leadership to be pre-empted by apparatchiki and to what extent are they to be shared with industrial managers, military chiefs, scientists, and professional bureaucrats?"[14] Statements like these underscore the belief that the relationship between the two elite groups is critically determinative of future political development in a wide range of societies.

The relationship is often one of mutual contempt and distrust. On the one hand, the political elite fears displacement by or loss of power to a new class of technicians and managers who are not only "inexperienced and lacking [in] real roots among the people,"[15] but also ideologically unreliable. On the other hand, the new class tends to view with contempt the frailties and the incompetence of the politicians; it is impatient with their willingness to sacrifice efficiency to ideological purity or political expediency; and it is disinclined to endorse continued legitimation of the dominant elite on the basis of long-past epochal events, such as the "struggle for liberation" or "the revolution." These and other elements are found in varying combinations in many of the developing countries where there is a confrontation of the two groups.

What is the likely influence of this relationship on the future course

[13] *Ibid.*, p. 125.

[14] Zbigniew Brzezinski and Samuel P. Huntington, *Political Power: USA/USSR*, New York, Viking Press, 1964, pp. 415-416.

[15] David Abernethy and Trevor Coombe, "Education and Politics in Developing Countries," unpublished ms., p. 13.

of political development in such countries? In his chapter on Communist China, Lewis concludes that the answer can be only conjectural: "It is probable that the elite will not be able to divert individuals with high achievement aspiration into subordinate technical posts supervised by technically unqualified political cadres without causing increasing dissatisfaction." Yet in his analysis of what he calls the "second New Class" in the Communist mobilization systems of Eastern Europe—a not dissimilar situation—Carl Beck suggests that it is unlikely that this new class, although its existence and importance can be demonstrated, will ever achieve a dominant position.[16] In the Soviet Union the "threat to Party supremacy from the demands of other elite groups is one of slow erosion. It is also limited. . . . Conceivably, the apparatchiki could be displaced by a military coup d'état or a managerial revolt. The probability of this, however, is very low."[17] We have been cautioned by Merle Fainsod not to "be unduly beguiled by that special variety of technological determinism which assumes that those who possess important technical skills in a society inevitably transmute these skills into political power. There is no iron law which prevents dictators from presiding over the destinies of highly industrialized societies."[18]

How relevant are the experiences and the future development probabilities of Communist mobilization systems for developing countries having a superficially similar confrontation of an older political elite and a younger better-educated class of technocrats and specialists? Several contrasting circumstances suggest that their relevance is doubtful. The ruling elites in the Communist systems have had and will continue to have at their disposal the enormous power of a systematic and pervasive ideology, a monolithic party-state structure, and an educational system that for nearly a generation has been deliberately manipulated to inculcate loyalty and conformity to the regime. Because the old Communist countries are far more advanced industrially than most developing countries are likely to be for some

[16] Carl Beck, "Bureaucracy and Political Development in Eastern Europe," in Joseph LaPalombara, ed., *Bureaucracy and Political Development*, Princeton, Princeton University Press, 1963, p. 296.

[17] Brzezinski and Huntington, *op.cit.*, p. 416. They continue: "Ideology cannot replace engineering, physics, military science, or even economics. Nor can engineers, scientists, generals, or economists manage a modern state without becoming politicians. . . . [The Party apparat could be displaced only if it] . . . were first weakened by an assault not from below but from above, not from the pluralistic tendencies in Soviet society but from the autocratic ones."

[18] Merle Fainsod, "Bureaucracy and Modernization: The Russian and Soviet Case," in LaPalombara, *op.cit.*, pp. 262-263.

time, they have a markedly greater capacity to absorb new groups. Although industrialization theoretically increases the threat of counter-elite activity because of the proliferation of professional and technical groups, historically it has tended to strengthen the political system that brings it about.[19] By contrast, most developing countries lack an integrating ideology; political elites seldom possess the institutional and organizational strength to contain or absorb dissident counter-elites; remarkably few attempts are made to use the educational systems in a coherent way to support the regime; and the pace of economic development is usually not rapid enough to provide meaningful careers for the new groups that emerge from the increased functional specialization of the educational system and other dimensions of the modernization process. In short, incumbent political elites in most developing countries are presumptively far more vulnerable to a military or bureaucratic take-over or to revolutionary movements by alienated intellectuals, as well as to sheer stagnation.

The presumptive vulnerability of a political elite does not necessarily mean that counter-elite coups will actually occur, or even be attempted. Indeed, political elites in many developing countries have demonstrated a remarkable staying power in spite of cultural malintegration, institutional fragility, weak and intermittent penetration of central authority into the rural areas, a large number of unemployed intellectuals, and a sluggish economy kept going only by foreign assistance. This capacity for elite survival in seemingly hopeless circumstances, where all objective indicators point to imminent collapse, may sometimes be explained simply by the lack of any visible alternative. Another explanation is that potential counter-elites (army officers, technical, managerial, and bureaucratic cadres, and so forth) do not in fact seek political power. One reason for their failure to do so is that their ranks are small, and they recognize the futility of an attempt to acquire political power. Another reason may be that they are recruited from the same social strata, or the same ethnic or cultural groups, as members of the dominant political elite, so that there is a mutual dependence and integration among elites in the different institutional spheres. A third reason may be the pervasive spirit of professionalism among members of a managerial or technical elite. For example, as William Gutteridge suggests in Chapter 13, army officers possessing a strong sense of military professionalism may be

[19] Henry A. Kissinger, *The Necessity for Choice*, New York, Harper & Brothers, 1961, p. 318.

disposed to relinquish authority to civilians because they realize that officers cannot effectively be both expert soldiers and efficient civil administrators.

Another reason for political indifference or inactivity by potential counter-elites is that their members may be ideologically incompatible and hostile and not, therefore, disposed to engage in collective political action. On the contrary, if their orientations are highly fragmented and if dissension is strong, the different factions could neutralize one another in terms of common action by the elite concerned. The lack of political consensus among members of an elite group may come from many factors, but differential socialization, particularly as reflected in divergent educational experiences, is frequently the decisive one. Just as inter-elite heterogeneity in educational backgrounds may cause malintegration and tension among the strategic elites of a society, so intra-elite differences in educational experiences may affect the capacity and the disposition of the members of a strategic elite to engage in common political action in the competition for power.

One of the more arresting features of strategic elites in most developing countries is the increasing heterogeneity of their educational experiences, particularly of their post-secondary professional training. A substantial proportion—in some instances the overwhelming majority—of their "strategic human capital" has been or is being (and, for the next decade or so, probably will continue to be) trained in the universities and professional schools of the more developed countries of the world. This phenomenon is not, of course, peculiar to the developing areas of the present generation; throughout modern history relationships between host training countries and less developed countries have been marked by educational dependency.[20] That dependency, however, has never occurred on so large a scale and with such multiple and crosscutting involvement as in the present period.

Educational ties between a developing country and an educationally advanced country have usually been predominantly, or sometimes exclusively, bilateral, particularly during and immediately after the colonial period. Since the end of World War II, however, there has been an enormous diversification and multilateralization of dependency relationships. Except for former French colonial areas, where the metropolis still serves as the main pole of gravitation, "it is rare for a single host country to enjoy a virtual monopoly of foreign

[20] Japan leaned heavily upon Prussia first, and then upon America. Germany served as the host country for numerous countries.

students from one particular developing nation."[21] The degree to which such diversification has occurred is illuminated by the figures in Table 1.

TABLE 1: DISTRIBUTION OF STUDENTS FROM THE DEVELOPING COUNTRIES STUDYING ABROAD, 1959-1961

HOST COUNTRY	Brazil	Burma	Ceylon	Congo (Leopoldville)	Ghana	Guinea	India	Indonesia	Iraq	Peru	Sudan	Syria	UAR
Australia	—	35	21	—	1	—	68	225	—	—	—	1	—
Austria	13	4	...	...	4	...	40	5	112	8	5	187	599
Belgium	11	...	1	221	...	1	3	16	2	2	1	42	49
Canada	14	7	8	...	31	...	155	49	1	16	1	3	16
Czechoslovakia	...	...	...	...	...	...	4	60	16	...	18	...	119
France	95	1	6	14	5	147	89	6	121	37	3	22	24
Germany, West	...	...	...	...	...	...	843	...	278	...	...	...	1,476
India	...	102	937	...	...	...	.	16	1	...	11	...	...
Italy	5	...	...	...	5	...	76	6	1	8	12	57	26
Japan	8	12	12	—	—	—	9	33	2	4	—	—	2
Netherlands	1	...	...	...	...	...	15	365	...	...	...	...	...
Spain	19	—	—	—	—	—	1	1	4	265	—	4	6
Switzerland	27	1	...	...	17	10	67	22	44	15	3	60	195
UAR	...	...	...	...	...	...	19	54	90	...	406	...	.
UK	14	72	251	2	371	—	1,660	47	490	9	153	43	344
USA	521	220	83	39	201	58	5,621	653	700	464	135	298	923

[a] Table does not include the number of foreign students in the Soviet Union, Communist China, and other Eastern bloc countries, as figures are not available. It is estimated that about 11,000 foreign students were in the Soviet Union during this period. (See M. Brewster Smith, "Foreign vs. Indigenous Education," in D. C. Piper and Taylor Cole, eds., *Post-Primary Education and Political and Economic Development,* Durham, Duke University Press, 1964, p. 51.)

Source: UNESCO, *Study Abroad,* Vol. XIII, 1962, Paris, 1961, pp. 678-683; Vol. XIV, 1963, Paris, 1962, pp. 702-709.

The reasons for this global proliferation of educational links are also diverse: the enormous demand for high-level manpower in the developing countries juxtaposed against the inadequacy of local educational institutions and the inability of the universities and professional schools of any single foreign country to meet the demand; the widespread commitment of the more developed nations to the princi-

.[21] M. Brewster Smith, "Foreign vs. Indigenous Education," in D. C. Piper and Taylor Cole, eds., *Post-Primary Education and Political and Economic Development,* Durham, Duke University Press, 1964, p. 51.

ple of international technical assistance; and the Cold War competition, as Eastern and Western nations seek to establish and extend their influence in the developing countries through the ideological and professional socialization of the presumptive decision-makers of the future.

The political motivation of host nations is reciprocated by the developing countries. In their determination to achieve full decolonization, they consciously seek to diversify their educational dependence in order to reduce the post-colonial influence of the former imperial power. Their policies of positive neutralism lead them toward a pattern of balanced dependence upon both East and West, as well as toward new relationships with historically neutral nations or with other nonaligned countries of the Afro-Asian world. There are, as Brewster Smith has observed, a variety of considerations which govern the direction of the flow of foreign students from developing countries. These include factors of educational, linguistic, religious, and cultural tradition, proximity, financial support, political ideology, and intangible prestige.[22] During the past decade, however, the political motives of both host and sending countries have greatly accelerated the trend toward increased diversity.

It is difficult to assess the political consequences of this increasing heterogeneity in the higher education and professional training of a particular elite. It obviously raises the question of what criteria are to predominate both in recruitment into, and in the determination of relative status within, the elite concerned. As already noted heterogeneity could weaken an elite's cohesion and propensity for common political action, and precipitate and intensify factionalism within it. At least two lines of cleavage are particularly significant. One is the division between the segment that is defending a prior homogeneous (single foreign model), initially dominant educational tradition, whose members are a product of that tradition, and newer elements aggressively seeking to establish the validity of their foreign scholastic credentials. Characteristically the former seek to stay on top by controlling the rate and the criteria of recruitment; the latter agitate for eclecticism in educational background, or assert the primacy of the educational pattern they represent by extolling its virtues and denigrating the older tradition. This type of cleavage is particularly prevalent when American- or Soviet-educated graduates return home to countries where French or British educational patterns are en-

22 *Ibid.*

trenched.[23] The second type of intra-elite division, probably more determinative of political development among the next generation, separates elements that received their training in the West and those that received it in countries of the Eastern bloc. If these two lines of cleavage converge and are mutually reinforcing, the resulting intra-elite tension may have significant political implications in a developing country.

Heterogeneity in educational experiences may not only create or aggravate intra-elite divisions and tensions, but it may also have a positive impact upon development. Where conservative educational patterns are entrenched, the intrusion of a more dynamic pattern may stimulate the adaptation and evolution of the established educational system toward a pattern that is more congruent with the development process and more genuinely "national": ". . . the growth on the African scene of an appreciable segment of intellectuals trained in the more pragmatic and instrumental tradition of American higher education might serve as a catalyst to induce change in the status-oriented features of indigenous higher education, which has . . . disadvantages for political and economic development. . . . Moreover, providing developing countries . . . with alternative educational models may widen their range of effective choice and increase the likelihood that indigenous educational institutions may develop along lines more closely adapted to national needs than is possible for any postcolonial echo of overvalued metropolitan practice."[24] Diversity may also foster a climate of tolerance, flexibility, and responsiveness to innovation, supportive of a new synthesis, as well as elite integration. Among peoples in quest of their own identity and sense of distinctive nationhood, eclecticism and pragmatism have a particularly strong attraction.[25]

[23] Returnees who are products of an educational tradition different from that which predominates in their home country suffer marked disadvantages in the competition for jobs and status; presumably they are, therefore, more vulnerable to political disaffection and opposition. Brewster Smith has analyzed some of the difficulties returnees encounter when they have found themselves in competition with the products of an established indigenous system. Among Mexican student returnees, for example, "American training was seen as a source of handicap, failing to produce degrees or credentials that corresponded to those locally honored, and involving, as it did for many, the loss or restriction of potentially influential contacts. Given the anti-*Yanqui* climate of opinion, they had in any case to avoid the appearance of Americanization." (*Ibid.*, p. 70.)

[24] *Ibid.*, pp. 67-68.

[25] Indiscriminate and aimless eclecticism, inspired and nourished mainly by the impulse to reject one particular external model on zenophobic grounds, may be both costly and ineffective. Sir Eric Ashby's comments on one zealous effort at applied

Thus, there are several likely consequences—constructive as well as dysfunctional—of heterogeneity in the higher education and professional training of strategic elites. Systematic comparative survey data are lacking, however, on the relationship between exposure to a particular type of foreign educational experience and subsequent political orientation and behavior.[26] What evidence we do have is inconclusive. The divergent political orientation of similarly trained military leaders in Pakistan and India suggests, as William Gutteridge points out, that the character of professional military training is not a decisive factor in subsequent political behavior. Indeed, this and other evidence (for example, the accommodational behavior of ideologically radical overseas students returning to conservative milieus) indicate that positional and situational determinants can be far more decisive.

Also bearing on any assessment of the political implications of the multi-lateralization and diversification of elite education is the extent to which really significant differences exist among the various patterns of education in the host countries concerned. Here again we lack systematic comparative data as well as agreed standards of measurement and analysis. Authorities are sharply divided, for example, even over the character and the magnitude of differences in the political content of education in the Soviet Union and the United States.[27] It is probable that, apart from explicit efforts in political indoctrination, educational curricula—indeed, educational systems in general—are becoming increasingly more alike throughout the world. This trend is particularly true of professional, scientific, and technical subjects, and is even discernible in some of the social sciences, although

---

eclecticism (the draft constitution offered to the University of Lagos, Nigeria, by a UNESCO commission—a "sort of anthology of fragments from British and Continental university procedure") are in point: "To attempt to run a university on these lines would have been like asking a mechanic to construct a car from a mixture of components, some from Ford and some from Volkswagen." (Ashby, *op.cit.*, p. 77.)

[26] A sizable body of literature on the impact of an American educational experience upon the attitudes and prospects of foreign students has developed from the researches of a group of social scientists during the past decade. The studies that emerged are listed by Smith, *op.cit.*, p. 49. These studies are suggestive, yet as Smith notes (p. 49), "We know virtually nothing about the effect of an American. study sojourn, for example, on arousing in foreign students higher levels of achievement motivation that David McClelland holds to be the central ingredient of the entrepreneurial spirit and an important precondition of economic growth." Lipset has stressed the need for "comparative studies of university-educated elites, to investigate the influence of socialization within different types of university milieux." (*Op.cit.*, p. 66.)

[27] Cf. G. Z. F. Bereday and B. B. Stretch, "Political Education in the USA and the USSR," *Comparative Education Review*, June 1963, pp. 9-16, and Brzezinski and Huntington, *op.cit.*, pp. 80 ff.

admittedly great differences still exist. Educational systems are particularly resistant to change. Nevertheless, to the extent that a world educational culture is emerging, even if only partially, diversity in the foreign education of members of an elite will not necessarily have a politically significant differentiating impact. Once again, however, we must enter the caveat that formal education is only one, and not necessarily the most important one, among a variety of socializing influences at work. American, Soviet, British, and even Communist Chinese schools may increasingly tend to follow a similar pattern, but the extra-university social and political environments in these countries will probably continue to be very different.

In many developing countries teachers and former teachers, as a categoric group, are among the more politically prominent and influential of the strategic elites. Their special political importance is not a peculiarity of the present era; rather, it is characteristic of certain phases in the evolution of many societies undergoing basic structural transformation. The principal reasons for their prominent role in such circumstances have been succinctly summarized by Joseph Ben-David:

"The crucial place of teaching as a stepping-stone for both intra- and inter-generational mobility . . . [has been] . . . of particularly great importance in countries emerging from dependent status into independence, as well as in countries at the first stages of the disintegration of rigid traditional class distinctions. . . . The reason for this is that teaching is the only profession at those stages of development which is practically open to the subject, or low class population, and into which their entrance is even encouraged by the government. As a result it attracts many people of high ability and energy who otherwise would enter more highly placed professions. As teachers they are placed in a marginal position between two reference groups. Their work places them in an elite position among . . . the lower classes from which they originate . . . [but it also places them] . . . on the lower levels of the professional class which creates among them a personal dissatisfaction with their position. Therefore they do not regard teaching as a terminal but rather as a transitory position. . . . Political activity is one of the most legitimate channels for . . . [upward mobility available to them]."[28]

[28] "Professions in the Class System of Present-Day Societies," *Current Sociology*, Vol. XII, No. 3, 1963-1964, pp. 281-282. The same point is made by Harbison and Meyers (*op.cit.*, pp. 56-57): "In the educationally least developed countries of Level I

The validity of this summation is given fresh support by Dwaine Marvick's findings, analyzed in Chapter 14. These reveal that in one African university nearly two-thirds of all students expected to become teachers, and at least half among the largest contingent aspired to roles in their national legislature or to ministerial office.

In colonial countries teachers played an extraordinarily active part in the agitation for independence, both as ideologists and as key organizational leaders. After independence they have in many instances constituted the single largest categoric group in national legislatures, as the figures in Table 2 show. The proximate reason for their

TABLE 2: REPRESENTATION OF FORMER TEACHERS IN
LEGISLATURES IN SELECTED AFRICAN COUNTRIES[a]

Country	Total Number of Members in Legislature	Former Teachers as Per Cent of Total
Nigeria		
Federal	301	32.5
East	86	37.2
West	121	35.5
North	132[b]	19.7
Ghana	109	34.9
Kenya	41	46.3
Tanganyika	48	22.9
Uganda	52[c]	40.4
Senegal	79	26.6
Mali	67	32.8
Congo (Braz.)	58	31.0

[a] Presumably these legislatures were elected in the late 1950's or early 1960's.

[b] Sample out of total of 170.

[c] Sample out of total of 77.

Source: Guy Hunter, The New Societies of Tropical Africa, New York, Oxford University Press, 1962, p. 285.

strikingly predominant political role in the immediate post-colonial period is their leadership in nationalist movements; as the legitimate legatees of imperial power they inherited the higher statuses their political disaffection and marginality had impelled them to seek.

there is) . . . an acute shortage of indigenous secondary school teachers, and it is likely to exist for a long time. A major reason is that the qualified local teachers, by virtue of the scarcity of people with equivalent education, are already members of the intellectually elite group, and they tend to move rapidly into high positions in the government. In Nyasaland [Malawi], for example, the great majority of the new African ministers are former secondary school teachers. In the Level I countries, teaching at the secondary level is a major avenue of access to the upper ranks of government service, as well as to industry and commerce. . . . The competent local teacher . . . is not likely to remain in the service of education."

Also, as the most geographically dispersed of the modern strategic elites—other elites are concentrated in urban centers, mainly the national capital—they had an inherent numerical advantage in the national legislature of a polity based upon the representative principle. As an important group among the "educated elements" they were endowed with the enormous, if transitory, prestige flowing from the inflated valuation education acquires in a period of maximum scarcity. As the most "modern" and prestigious persons in rural communities, as well as the most qualified, because of their superior education, to deal with central authorities, or to articulate and represent local interests at the national level, teachers were frequently able to build a fairly strong local power base.[29] Thus, in most developing countries that have progressed or are progressing from pure colonialism to independent statehood, teachers have tended to be among the most predisposed, available, and qualified elite categories to participate in political life.

The unusual political prominence of teachers is transitory, a fact implicit in Ben-David's analysis quoted above. At later stages of development teaching ceases to be the rapid escalator to higher status through politics: "With the introduction of mass education, the teacher's status tends to suffer a relative decline, because he is imparting to others the very skills which used to raise him above them."[30] This progressive devaluation of the relative status of teachers, coupled with their diminished prestige, both locally and nationally, and the loss of their own sense of self-esteem, is an element in a deflationary syndrome leading to political apathy and alienation. The situation holds special significance because teachers are a professional category inherently vulnerable to political disaffection and characteristically inclined toward a critical stance regarding the society in which they live.[31]

[29] Abernethy and Coombe, op.cit., p. 15. The authors point out, however (on p. 17), that teachers do not invariably have rapport with or command the esteem of the local people: "[The teacher] is often acutely uncomfortable in his rural environment (which might not be the one in which he was raised), a stranger by birth or preference to local customs, and painfully aware of his isolation from other educated people. As the tutor of the young in admittedly necessary but unwelcome ways and ideas, he might encounter resentment and opposition from the elders of the society. If his own political persuasion is different from that of his community, his alienation from that community is likely to be nearly complete."

[30] Ibid., p. 17.

[31] "In the underdeveloped or emerging nations, the critical stance of the educated strata has been enhanced by the very fact that the system goals are in a state of flux. . . . [They are] especially prone to feelings of national inferiority." (Lipset, op.cit., pp. 13-15.)

Political alienation among teachers has potentially serious dysfunctional consequences for the nation- and polity-building processes in new states. Teachers are important both as socializers and as communicators. Schools are not self-socializing institutions; schoolteachers are the active agents. Indeed, they occupy one of the most strategic positions in the whole socialization process. They are also key agents in political communication in view of the wide elite-mass gap in developing countries, as well as the fragmentation and underdevelopment of communications media.[32] Their personal political attitudes and orientation, their teaching style and effectiveness, significantly affect the quality of their performance in these two roles. If they are cooperative and supportive, as the *instituteur* has been in modern France,[33] they can maximize the impact of manifest political socialization in the schools, help to contain the volatility and radicalism characteristic of school milieus, and serve as an important link between the elite and the mass. If they are apathetic and indifferent, they will aggravate the atmosphere of flux and the aimlessness prevalent in most societies undergoing rapid change, and will fail to bridge the discontinuities in communication. If they are politically hostile and embittered, they can use their strategic position in many subtle ways to denigrate the regime and to inculcate an oppositional or cynical mentality. Thus, even though teaching may eventually cease to be the assured stepping-stone to higher status and political power, the teacher as socializer and communicator continues to be a crucial agent in political development.

The chapters in Part III of this book are concerned with the relationship between education and various types of elites. Five elite categories, which are admittedly overlapping, command our special

[32] Cf. Lucian Pye, ed., *Communications and Political Development*, Princeton, Princeton University Press, 1963. As David Abernethy and Trevor Coombe (*op.cit.*, p. 16) have put it, "The teacher straddles two ways of life. . . . Through him ideas of nationalism are transmitted from the political leaders and the press. He is often—whether or not this is legally permissible—a party activist involved in proselytizing, political organizing, and political education. And it may be that through him some of the less articulated needs of the rural people are made known to the leadership."

[33] Cf. Georges Duveau, *Les Instituteurs*, Paris, Editions du Seuil, 1954, pp. 48-51, and Michalina Clifford-Vaughan, "Enlightenment and Education," *British Journal of Sociology*, Vol. XIV, June 1963, pp. 135-143. Clifford-Vaughan (at p. 139) states that the *instituteur* was "a civil servant from the administrative point of view. . . . In the local community his participation in the political and administrative life enhanced his intellectual prestige. [He was] . . . the central figure in the republican conception more or less consciously advocated by the Radical Party and rationalized by Alain, of substituting an intellectual elite to aristocracies of birth and money. The teaching profession at all levels had the task of selecting it."

interest: (1) traditional political elites possessing residual authority in surviving (usually subnational) structures; (2) modern bureaucratic, managerial, and technical elites emerging from the expanding and increasingly specialized educational system, and constituting the key cadres for carrying out modernization; (3) modern professionalized military elites having a distinctive and characteristically isolated socialization experience,[34] who are frequently impatient with or distrustful of political elites; (4) university students (usually the core of political opposition in new states), some of whom may be recruited into the bureaucratic, technical, and military elites, while others will swell the ranks of the educated unemployed; and (5) intellectuals —usually disesteemed by the political elites—who constitute the latent leadership of incipient or potential revolutionary movements, and whose ranks include not only university faculty, but also, at certain stages of development, schoolteachers and university students.[35] Other elite groups, such as business, labor, or religious leaders, sometimes play a decisive role in political development. For our purposes, however, the five groups noted above are particularly relevant. They are critically examined within the context of variant cultural and political milieus in Chapters 11 through 15 by Kirk-Greene, Lewis, Gutteridge, Marvick, and Shils, respectively. These chapters provide added insight into the character and the role of these elites in political development; they illuminate some of the problems of inter-elite relations; and they help to explain how these relationships are affected by different educational experiences.

[34] Cf. Stanford M. Dornbusch, "The Military Academy as an Assimilating Institution," *Social Forces*, May 1955, pp. 316-321, and Morris Janowitz, *The Military in the Political Development of New Nations*, Chicago, University of Chicago Press, 1964, pp. 49-62.

[35] Edward Shils has pointed out that in developing countries the concept "intellectuals" is far more elastic and all-embracing than in developed countries. It includes not only those categories of persons normally thought of as intellectuals in the conventional sense (that is, those persons who belong to the modern intellectual community he discusses in Chapter 15), but also university students. "In advanced countries, students are not regarded as *ex-officio* intellectuals; in underdeveloped countries, they are." ("The Intellectuals in the Political Development of New States," in John H. Kautsky, ed., *Political Change in Underdeveloped Countries*, New York, John Wiley, 1962, p. 203.) By this elastic definition, schoolteachers, as a categoric group, could also, it would seem, be recognized as part of a nation's intellectual community.

CHAPTER 11

BUREAUCRATIC CADRES IN A TRADITIONAL MILIEU

ANTHONY H. M. KIRK-GREENE, M.B.E., M. A. (CANTAB.)[1]

Introduction

THERE can be few, if any, African or Asian countries where a new set of Western-style governmental institutions has not found itself in a state of uneasy co-existence with the old indigenous authority system institutions. What I propose to do in this chapter is to examine within the Northern Nigerian framework some of the problems and pressures originating from the impact of new leadership cadres on a society characterized by a highly structured and traditionalist administration; that is, to analyze the tension-areas that appear when an alien but indigenous bureaucracy, predominantly selected by merit and trained along contemporary civil service lines, comes into contact with an established and largely heredity-conscious native administrative hierarchy.

As my model I am taking Northern Nigeria, primarily because it reflects a political system which, marked as it was by a high degree of economic specialization, administrative sophistication, and political homogeneity, has been universally recognized as a classic among highly structured authoritarian societies of the pre-European contact period. Northern Nigeria represents what no less an experienced authority than Lord Hailey has ranked as "the scene of one of the most effectively organized systems of indigenous rule to be found south of the Sahara."[2] Under the cementing influence of Islam, the original Hausa kingdoms had here developed an enviable fiscal system, an accepted code of land tenure, a trained judiciary, and a regular method of local administration through agents appointed from the center.

In developing nations possessing centralized political systems, authority may be so concentrated and restricted in its exercise that it tends to hinder the introduction of modern bureaucracy, with its em-

---

[1] This is a condensed version of the original paper read at the Lake Arrowhead conference. The ideas expressed are personal to the author and are in no way to be understood as expressing an official viewpoint.

[2] Lord Hailey, *An African Survey: Revised 1956*, London, Oxford University Press, 1957, p. 453.

phasis on diffused, uncommitted, and impersonal decision making. Where the centralized authority is presumptive and is enforced by hereditary titled offices or has gerontocratic leanings, the new leadership cadres encounter opposition, often of a sociological origin, that reflects on the efficacy of their function as bureaucrats.

I

THE ADMINISTRATIVE STRUCTURE OF HAUSA SOCIETY

Let us now turn to our model. The first thing is to acquire a clear understanding of the pre-European contact structure of local administration in the emirates of Northern Nigeria. In this task we are fortunate in having at our disposal a first-class account of the old Habe (sing: *Kado*; the original Hausa inhabitants) political system, backed up by a brilliant piece of research from a leading contemporary sociologist, M. G. Smith.[3] The systems of government so analyzed are peculiarly valuable because together they enable us to study what has been the commonest pattern of indigenous government in the Northern Nigerian emirates, namely, the Fulani adoption and adaptation of the pre-jihad systems of government.[4]

[3] The Hausa versions by M. Hassan and M. Shu'aibu, *Makau, Sarkin Zazzau na Habe* and *Tarihi da Al'adun Habe na Abuja*, Zaria, 1952, are available in English translation by F. Heath, *A Chronicle of Abuja*, Ibadan, Ibadan University Press, 1952. Dr. M. G. Smith's study has been published under the title of *Government in Zazzau: 1800-1950*, London, Oxford University Press, 1960. Much of the next three pages of this paper owes an intellectual debt of gratitude to these valuable sources.

[4] The kind of political system we find complies with the model defined by M. Fortes and E. E. Evans-Pritchard (*African Political Systems*, London, Oxford University Press, 1941), as "those systems which have centralized authority, administrative machinery and judicial institutions—in short, a government—and in which cleavages of wealth, privilege and status correspond to the distribution of power and authority" (p. 5). The executive structure in such societies conforms to the general idea of a state as a political system distinguished by the conduct of its government through a series of offices. It need not be supposed that these were operated with the neat, rational, and antiseptic impersonality that seems to be the hallmark of today's efficient bureaucracies. The essential difference between the traditional authority and the new bureaucracy is to be found in Weber's distinction between the motivations of their respective administrative personnel: on the one hand, personal loyalty to the chief, blurred definition of responsibility, and advancement depended on caprice or whim; on the other, loyalty to an anonymous tradition of service, legalized jurisdiction, and stabilized and publicized career-terms. In the pure type of traditional authority, the following features of a bureaucracy are absent: (a) a clearly defined sphere of competence subject to impersonal rules; (b) a rational ordering of relations of the basis of free contract; (c) a regular system of appointment and promotion on the basis of free contract; (d) technical training as a regular requirement; (e) fixed salaries, in the type case paid in money. In place of a well-defined impersonal sphere of competence, there is (in traditional systems of authority) a shifting series of tasks and powers commissioned and granted by the chief through his arbitrary decision of the

In the original Habe kingdom of Zaria, then known as Zazzau, there were seven classes of chiefs and title holders. Each *sarauta* (ranked and titled office) was permanent and self-contained. These groups were: (1) the chief councillors; (2) the turbanned councillors; (3) the body servants; (4) the emir's eunuchs; (5) the household servants; (6) the children of the ruling houses; (7) the imams or *malamai*. These were the key organs of government.

Among the four chief councillors, the most important was the holder of the title *Madawaki,* who ranked next to the emir and was commander of the army. It was his prerogative to advise the emir on the appointment and dismissal of all title holders. Interestingly enough, the remaining chief councillors were all eunuchs. This may well have been because, consideration of harem charge apart, since their condition disqualified them from passing on to a notional family any personal power, they could be trusted in senior administrative positions as being without ambition and were consequently no threat to a government based on hereditary chieftainship. The second group, the turbanned councillors, were chosen from among the most important men in the capital. These were titles to which slaves could aspire. A number of turbanned councillors followed each of the superordinate chief councillors and were "his" men. The functions of the body servants and household servants are self-evident. The children of the ruling houses included the heir presumptive. The imams were the religious officials, among them being the emir's chief scribe, *magatakarda,* who also officiated as the royal chaplain. Such titles have been described by Smith as providing the enduring structure of political relations, "a framework of established offices and statuses which act as relatively fixed points about which political relations of authority and competition are articulated at an individual level as well as between groups."[5] Outside the capital, six principal chiefs were responsible for the administration of the main towns. Each of these had his own representative at court (some of the chief councillors also played this role), and the chief would report any incident in his district to this representative, who would in turn inform the emir. Supervision of the smaller towns was divided fief-wise among the councillors and children of the ruling houses. The chiefs of all these

---

moment." (Max Weber, *The Theory of Social and Economic Organization,* ed. Talcott Parsons, New York, Oxford University Press, 1947, p. 315.)

[5] M. G. Smith's introduction to M. F. Smith, *Baba of Karo,* London, Faber and Faber, 1954, p. 31.

towns and the headmen of the lesser villages paid tribute, collected from their people, to the emir, one-tenth of what eventually reached the capital being the share of the district representative at the royal court.

The officers directly responsible for administration were the two groups of the chief councillors and the turbanned councillors, known as the *rukuni* (senior) and *rawuna* (junior) orders.[6] These officials were charged with responsibility for tax collecting, execution of justice, and district administration. This last-named territorial allocation of responsibility took the form of fiefs. The *rukuni*, under the *Madawaki* (a freeman), had special military functions and numbered freemen in their group. The *rawuna*, under the *Galadima* (a eunuch) assisted by two other eunuchs and a number of junior public officials who were freemen, were specifically responsible for civil administration such as police, prisons, markets, meat supplies, roads, ferries, and provisions in general for the capital and for the army. During times of war, the *Galadima* did not accompany the army, but remained behind in Zaria to oversee the civil administration.

THE SOCIAL STRUCTURE OF HAUSA SOCIETY

Hausa society distinguished four major status divisions, "each of which found expression in the official hierarchy as a condition of eligibility for particular offices."[7] These status conditions were: royalty, slavery, freedom, and eunuchhood. Perhaps we should reckon the *malam*[8] class as a fifth status condition, for though freemen they constituted a closed, self-promotional series by means of their religious calling. Habe society therefore recognized differentiation by rank and function.

The first differentiation is that between Fulani and Habe, though this has been modified by the shared culture of Islam. Another is that between freeman and slave, a social classification that has extended well beyond the legal abolition of slavery in Northern Nigeria. The former serfs (*dimajai*), born in slavery but not themselves enslaved and consequently never alienable by sale, even today constitute a

[6] The Hausa term *rukuni* (pl. *rukunai*) derives from the Arabic and denotes a group of persons, sometimes with the specialized sense of "those who matter." *Rawuna* is the plural form of *rawani*, a turban or, by extension, an office: e.g., *ya ajiye rawani*, he resigned his appointment.

[7] M. G. Smith, *op.cit.*, p. 43.

[8] From the Arabic *mu'allim*, a teacher. At this period the Hausa term was restricted to Koranic scholars.

sizeable element in the population of Zaria. A third, of recent introduction but acute proportions, is that between Muslim and Christian.
The most frequently quoted status distinction is that of the *sarakuna*
(chiefs) and *masu-sarauta* (title-holders) contrasted with the *tala-
kawa* (men-in-the-street, commoners). Within Hausa society there
are also to be found several occupationally distinguished strata. This
system, Smith maintains, "is at once a description of their society, a
guide to behavior, and a normative frame."[9]

But there is a further subdivision within these classifications, often
overlooked in the generalized lineup of patricians and plebeians. This
is the status distinction drawn, within a bureaucratic or an occupational group, between those who inherit office (ascriptive) and those
who are appointed to office (achieved). The Hausa have terms for
these modern sociological concepts, *karda* and *shigege*.[10] *Karda,* an
hereditary occupation, enjoys greater *daraja* (prestige) than *shigege,* a
freely and individual-chosen métier. The distinction between *karda*
and *shigege* extends to offices of authority as well as to economic
pursuits. The concept of *karda* versus *shigege* will, along with the
concept of *sarauta* (titled office and all the prestigious respect that
attaches), reappear from time to time in my argument. For I am of
the opinion that, despite the changes wrought by the modern bureaucratization of authority, these two typical Hausa attitudes are
inrooted enough not only to persist but to regain—perhaps modified,
but in direction only and not in degree—their eminence and lustre as
an ambition even in the minds of the new civil service.

OFFICES UNDER THE FULANI

When the Fulani captured Zaria in 1804, they instituted a monoc-
racy, in which the king exercised absolute authority through his control of appointments to offices of state. They based their territorial
organization, outside the personal *rumada* or slave-villages, on the
local chieftainship of community units. The typical community was
focussed on a walled town, where the local chief would maintain a
relatively impressive compound. Such towns would be conspicuous by
their mosque, their ceremonial praying ground, and their regular

[9] M. G. Smith, "The Hausa System of Social Status," *Africa,* Vol. XXIX, 1959, p.
250.
[10] Although the modern Hausa generation recognizes *shigege* in its secondary
meaning of an interloper, very few know its primary meaning of a person who adopts
a calling different from that of his ancestors. I have yet to meet a Hausa undergraduate who has ever heard of *karda,* although older men know it.

market, all of which peripheral satellite villages would attend. Within each community the village chief administered its population through a hierarchy of ward-heads, whom he was free to appoint to office, to promote or dismiss. These local communities were administered as fiefs by the state officials, who now resided in the capital and owed their office to the emir. Known as *hakimai* (overlords) and generally related to the ruling dynasties, they supervised their distant fiefs through a staff of titled subordinates, some of whom were appointed as *jekadu* (intermediaries) to one or more of the overlord's fiefs. These agents were appointed, promoted, dismissed, and titled at will by the *hakimai*.

Certain titles were allocated among persons of royal status. As the Fulani rule continued, the number of offices appropriated by the ruling dynasties continued to increase. The general effect of this progressive transfer of titles to the royal rank order was to increase the instability of promotional arrangements: "not only were office-holders liable to peremptory dismissal on the death of their royal patron, their offices also were liable to be transferred to another rank and given to persons of different status, since the allocation of office was governed by the king's political situation and needs."[11] Inherent in this short-term autocracy—the term is Smith's—was the assumption that the king should personally direct policy in the light of his own interpretation of the political situation and should have person-to-person contact with his fief-holders and officers without any intermediary stages. Office had now become, under the Fulani regime, an administrative organ, and the emir exercised administrative authority, supreme though never absolute because of his suzerainty to his liege lord, the Sultan of Sokoto, and the threat of rival machinations for succession to the throne.

II

THE ROLE OF THE GOVERNMENT ADMINISTRATOR

Hailey has summarized the political organization of Hausa society as "a central control by the Emir and his Councillors, local rule being exercised through appointed District Heads and Village Heads. . . . The District Heads were appointed by the Ruler, sometimes from his own or other important families, sometimes from the traditional chiefs of the subject peoples comprised in the unit of which they were

[11] M. G. Smith, *Government in Zazzau*, p. 46.

in charge."[12] When the British colonial government set up its administration in Northern Nigeria, it believed it was essential to its doctrine of indirect rule that as many of these indigenous forms of authority as possible should be preserved. "We must utilize the existing machinery and endeavor only to improve it," wrote Lugard in his *Political Memoranda*, declaring his aim to be "the regeneration of Nigeria . . . through *its own governing class* and its own indigenous institutions."[13] The italics are mine, for this concept is at the root of the problem discussed in this chapter. It remains for us to understand what the role of the new bureaucracy, in the shape of the Political and later Administrative Service, staffed by British District Officers for the first sixty years and since 1957 by Northern Nigerians, has been in its relations and responsibilities towards the traditional emirate administrative structure.

There is no succinct yet comprehensive description of the role of the District Officers. If they had been a French service, doubtless all would have been codified and catalogued, and they would have been duly catechised before confirmation; but they are a British service, with a fine disregard for written constitutions despite the skill of the British at writing them for emergent nations. Pragmatic empiricism has been the guide, a state much rued by the new Nigerian bureaucrats, who would have preferred a comprehensive handbook. In one of the few "open" directives ever issued to District Officers in Nigeria, and about the only one since Sir Donald Cameron's *Principles of Native Administration*, a 1952 circular made some attempt to define the work of the Administration vis-à-vis the new, "political" government. "The District Officer now has two principal tasks: firstly, as the local representative and agent of the Government, he is required to coordinate all its activities, to see that the ideas of technical experts are adapted to local conditions and, as Dr. Marshall puts it in his report on local government in the Sudan, 'to deal in a common-sense way with the needs of the "people" and ensure that a comprehensive view is taken of human problems.' Secondly, he is the medium through which local government is to be made a living force, and it is he who must develop representative local institutions, train the members of those institutions in their work, and educate the people in their public responsibilities. . . . He must always keep in mind that

[12] Lord Hailey, *Native Administration in the British African Territories*, London, H.M.S.O., 1951, Vol. III, p. 46.
[13] Lugard, *Political Memoranda*, London, 1918, Memo. IX.

the ideal of the highest efficiency and rapidity of execution must be subordinate to the main policy of encouraging and training the Native Authorities to undertake the functions of administration with ever-increasing quality of attainment." Much emphasis was still, as late as 1952, put on the Administrative Officer's proverbial role of jack-of-all-trades. The directive concluded with the following triple definition of his functions: "To assist the African to govern himself; to train the people to build up efficient institutions of local government which satisfy their wishes and are at the same time adequate for modern needs; and finally to foster the emergence of an intelligent and responsible public opinion so that Nigeria may ultimately take her place as a useful member of the Commonwealth of Nations."[14]

Even this 1952 directive is not so far removed from the tenets of indirect rule. To date in Northern Nigeria, the new indigenous, leadership cadres have done little more—have indeed been expected to do little more—than take over from expatriate colleagues the same responsibilities of Government adviser to the Native Authorities.[15] But today the advisers are the same people as the advised, counselling, with the splendid temerity of youth, the very authorities who have been administering their emirates since the British burnt Washington. *A holi Falijo habre ka'e?* asks a Fulani proverb: Are you trying to teach a Fali warrior how to fight with stones? Whether this virtual *status quo* of the administrator's functions can continue "under new management," as it were, is an aspect of the problems of new leadership cadres to which we shall return.

III

THE BACKGROUND AND RECRUITMENT
OF THE NEW LEADERSHIP CADRES

Who are the new leadership cadres in Northern Nigeria? Where have they come from, and how have they got there? What has been the extent of their political socialization? This is the next set of questions to pose in our analysis of the potential conflict-field between the old and new bureaucracies.

[14] All the quotations are taken from *Duties of the Administrative Officer in Northern Nigeria*, Kaduna, Government Printer, 1952.

[15] Since this paper was written, Northern Nigeria has rationalized its policy by passing the Provincial Administration Law of 1962. For a detailed historical analysis of its evolution see A. H. M. Kirk-Greene, "A Redefinition of Provincial Administration," *Journal of Local Administration Overseas*, Vol. IV, January 1965.

It may be safely assumed that no one has entered the new public service who has not had some exposure to Western education. This is by no means the case in the local services, the Native Administrations, where tradition and family can still outpoint literacy. In Zaria Native Authority, for instance, the number of Native Authority officials who in 1945 had ever attended a school where writing was taught in Roman (*boko*) instead of Arabic (*ajami*) script was only 79 out of a total establishment (excluding the education department) of 506 office-holders. In the same Native Authority, 343 posts were held by those related to the leading Fulani lineages (and over 200 of them from only five families) against 186 held by non-Fulani officials.[16] Chart 1 is a representative, though hypothetical, picture in this context of Native Authority employment patterns in the top leadership echelons during the early 1950's. In the public service it may also be accepted that over the past five years there has been a marked rise in the minimum standards required for entrance to the civil service, in direct ratio to the increasing output from secondary schools. The last six years have also seen a big-scale series of deliberately designed Africanization programs for the new leadership cadres at all levels, including one for the Administrative Service.

Who has been offered the golden key of Western education as the inevitable road to the no less ineluctable goal of a job in the new bureaucracy? Can any change in the ranks from whom leadership cadres have been drawn be distinguished between the non-European power-elite of the period 1930-1950, and that of the 1960's?

Among the very earliest experiments with Western education in a doubting, Islam-dominated, Northern Nigeria was, as one might expect from a British-sprung regime, the establishment of a school for the sons of chiefs. Lugard had very soon after his arrival affirmed his faith in the Fulani as the right people to rule the emirates. Gradually the normal British-colonial type of education pattern spread into the emirates. Senior primary schools and secondary schools were recruited by open competition from the junior primary schools. This acceptance of anonymous and objective ability as a basis of selection is important because here is the seed of a new elite growing up which does not necessarily derive from or is reinforced by the established authority-group.

Exactly the same process of recruitment through ability rather than

[16] Based on M. G. Smith, *The Economy of Hausa Communities of Zaria*, London, H.M.S.O., 1955, p. 84.

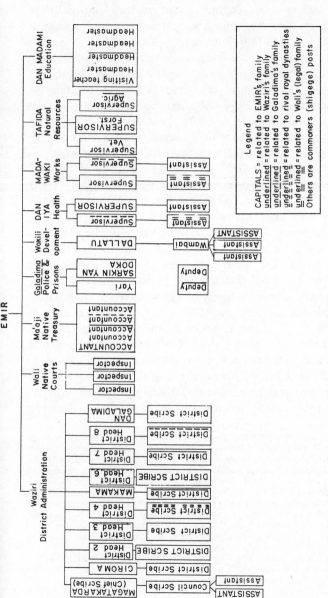

CHART I

SYNTHESIZED STRUCTURE OF A TYPE-EMIRATE ADMINISTRATIVE HIERARCHY: c. 1950

1. The most "open" departments are Education and Native Treasury, where Western education is essential. The most "closed" appointments are those of District Heads, where some posts may continue to be hereditary (karda).

2. Alkali families tend to be hereditary and to specialize in legal work.

Source: A.H.M. K-G., Zaria, 31/5/62.

Legend

CAPITALS = related to EMIR's family
underlined = related to Waziri's family
underlined = related to Galadima's family
underlined = related to rival royal dynasties
underlined = related to Wali's (legal) family

Others are commoners (shigege) posts

lineage has marked the northernization of the civil service. The Public Service Commission has sought to accept candidates, especially for senior grades, on their experience and qualifications. By and large it has paid scant attention to their parentage. The fact that there have been delicate problems of ethnic balance to face up to is an inescapable condition of present-day Nigeria, and this in no way invalidates the substance of our argument here that the primary criterion for appointment to the new leadership cadres has been ability, without regard to social origin or occupational background.

In a study of the recruitment of the administrative and executive grades through the government's specialist training programs, representing about 90 per cent and 75 per cent respectively of the total direct intake into these senior bureaucratic posts since the training schemes started in 1957 and 1960, the picture that at once emerges is one of intensive social or occupational mobility, with little suggestion of any persistent presence of royal families.[17] (See Table 1.) This is borne out for Nigeria as a whole by the Smythes' study of the new elite: two-thirds of their informants were of common stock. Elsewhere, Smythe has noted that the new leader is unlikely to have come from a very prominent family background but has pushed himself up by education, talent, opportunism and "the consequences of changing times."[18] By contrast, in Great Britain, nearly 40 per cent of a recent survey of higher civil servants[19] had fathers engaged in professional and technical occupations and about 25 per cent were salesmen and clerks. Some 17 per cent owned their own businesses or farms, while an equal proportion of fathers were classified in the domestic servant-manual worker category. A study of American

[17] "Indiscriminate recruitment into the Christian fold (entrance into which meant opportunity for Western education and eventually high status in the emergent territorial society) brought about a status reversal in many societies. Africans drawn from the lowest social stratum of traditional society have been elevated, through the activities of missionaries, to the highest strata of the social structure of the larger territorial societies. Thus, one finds in some instances central government officials, frequently of humble origin, placed over chiefs for whom their fathers were slaves. It is doubtful whether in the modern world such rapid vertical mobility has ever been equalled." (James S. Coleman, "The Politics of Sub-Saharan Africa" in Gabriel A. Almond and James S. Coleman, eds., *The Politics of the Developing Areas*, Princeton, Princeton University Press, 1960, p. 279.)

[18] Hugh and Mabel Smythe, *The New Nigerian Elite*, Stanford, Stanford University Press, 1960; Hugh H. Smythe, "The African Elite in Nigeria," in *Africa Seen by American Negroes*, Paris, Présence Africaine, 1949, p. 78.

[19] R. K. Kelsall, *Higher Civil Servants in Britain*, London, Routledge and Kegan Paul, 1955, pp. 188, 200.

higher public servants undertaken by the University of Colorado[20] revealed 28 per cent as the sons of professional men, 29 per cent of farm owners, and 10 per cent of laborers. An examination of candidates accepted by the Ecole Nationale d'Administration has shown that 65 per cent of the successful candidates for the French public service came from families in the professional, manager, technician, and employer category.[21]

It is evident from Table 1 that there is a challenging shift in the familial provenance and occupational history of Northern Nigeria's new bureaucrats, and that the traditionalists are by no means extending their direct presence into the new leadership cadres. Whether they are, however, indirectly continuing their social influence on the new leadership cadres is another question.

IV

SOME ATTITUDES OF THE TRADITIONALISTS:
THE CRITERIA FOR RESPECT

It is clear that one of the basic difficulties which the traditional authority sees in the advent of the new bureaucracy is that of "class." In traditional Hausa society, the gradations of social status can often be no less rigid, sensitive, or accepted than they are in English society.

We have already seen how the criteria of selection and appointment in the new leadership cadres have, by and large, ignored familial status and concentrated on ability. The result has been first the creation and then the reinforcing of a genuine middle class. The existence of such a professional middle class has often been acclaimed as the political strength of Western democratic countries, just as its startling absence until recently has been described as a regrettable political weakness in many emergent countries on the African continent.[22] The middle class is as yet not so much a class as a number of individuals, but its beginnings are encouragingly perceptible.

So it is that the traditional authority, in the form of the dynastic

---

[20] Reinhard Bendix, *Higher Civil Servants in American Society*, Boulder, University of Colorado Press, 1949, p. 23.

[21] Quoted in Morroe Berger, *Bureaucracy and Society in Modern Egypt*, Princeton, Princeton University Press, 1957, p. 45.

[22] See, for example, the proceedings of the 29th I.N.C.I.D.I. Congress on *The Development of a Middle Class in Tropical and Sub-Tropical Countries*, 1955.

TABLE 1: SELECTED ATTRIBUTES OF ADMINISTRATIVE LEADERSHIP CADRES IN NORTHERN NIGERIA AND OF SOME PARALLEL ADMINISTRATIVE TRAINEE RESOURCES IN EAST AFRICA

Attribute	ASTC[1] 1.	ASTC 2.	ASTC 3.	ASTC 4.	ASTC 5.	EGTC[2] 1.	EGTC 2.	EGTC 3.	DPA[3]	GOVT. COLL.[4]	TANG 1.	TANG 2.	UGAN-DA 1.	UGAN-DA 2.	KENYA
					NORTHERN NIGERIA								EAST AFRICA[5]		
Age group															
20-25	13	32	31	39	35	80	83	96	81	—	4	8	15	18	5
26-30	44	48	31	46	61	20	17	4	19	—	52	20	46	56	14
31-34	37	10	28	11	0	0	0	0	0	—	28	68	31	27	27
35 plus	6	10	10	4	4	0	0	0	0	—	16	4	8	0	54
Father's occupation[6]															
KARDA															
Chief	0	0	4	4	0	0	0	8	0	0	—	0	—	—	—
Traditional title holder	6	22	18	32	36	15	17	12	15	13	—	4	—	—	—
Alkali/Koranic *Malam*	19	18	11	4	4	5	5	0	2	3	—	4	—	—	—
SHIGEGE															
Govt. employee	6	0	0	0	0	0	0	16	9	6	—	8	—	—	—
N.A. employee	19	15	8	15	8	15	5	16	19	14	—	9	—	—	—
Commercial or corporation employee	6	0	0	0	0	5	0	4	2	1	—	0	—	—	—

TALAKA															
Farmer	37	37	41	31	36	55	46	36	45	47	—	48	—	—	—
Trader	0	4	11	7	8	5	5	8	3	7	—	8	—	—	—
Evangelist	0	0	0	4	4	0	5	0	2	5	—	16	—	—	—
Tailor/carpenter/messenger/laborer	6	4	7	7	4	0	17	0	3	4	—	12	—	—	—
Previous job															
Govt. (executive)	44	30	46	35	35	10	0	0	18	—	36	40	46	36	100
Govt. (junior)	0	12	0	4	0	35	10	28	13	—	32	4	38	55	0
N.A.	44	27	11	32	27	25	5	4	11	—	0	8	8	0	0
Teacher	6	24	33	18	27	0	10	8	10	—	20	28	8	0	0
Commercial/corporation	0	0	5	7	7	25	17	24	17	—	4	0	0	9	0
College student	6	4	5	4	4	5	58	36	31	—	4	0	0	0	0
Politics	0	0	0	4	0	0	0	0	0	—	4	0	0	0	0
Religion															
Muslim	81	82	79	69	77	60	56	64	28	—	—	16	—	—	13
Christian	19	18	21	31	23	40	44	36	72	—	—	84	—	—	87

Figures are expressed as percentages.

[1] ASTC refers to the special Administrative Service Training Courses held at the Institute of Administration, Zaria.

[2] EGTC refers to the Executive Grade Training Courses at Zaria.

[3] DPA refers to the Diploma in Public Administration Course held at Ahmadu Bello University.

[4] Government College relates to a sample 1962 intake.

[5] The East African figures all refer to Administrative Service Training Courses.

[6] Under "Father's occupation," the groups are ranged in descending order of traditional social status.

Source: A.H.M. K-G. Zaria, 31/5/62.

emir or the *sarauta*-succession councillors, may, meeting a representative of the new bureaucracy in the Nigerian District Officer, have found themselves in a class-conflicting social situation, one which can be as novel as it is embarrassing. Such a conflict of standards has already been the lot of senior Native Authority officials in their relationship with the younger, schooled staff. "Traditionally," writes Cohen in a paper on an emirate political organization, "a fief holder controlled his fief completely; and everyone in the area was ipso facto his political subordinate. The Native Administration personnel, however, are less easily turned into subordinates. They have departmental responsibilities as well as traditional links of loyalty and respect for the position of the District Head."[23] Relative and accepted social ranking is a determinant of person-to-person behavior. Must a senior, title-holding councillor really accept administrative "advice" from the teenage-plus son of a commoner, when in the normal social intercourse of the emirate slave-born families are still recognized as inferior? Must a Moslem emir defer in council to the advice of a Northern Christian District Officer—not only a Christian but almost certainly one whose grandfather was a *kafir* or *arna* (unbeliever) and whose great-grandfather may well have belonged to a traditional slave-raiding area? Can it be borne that the son of a client (*bara*) is now able to say good morning to a member of a royal family on an equal, if not superior, footing? Insofar as Hausa society is birth-conscious and status-differentiated, it is understandably discomforting for such a society to accept as *their* D.O. (and the sense of proud possessiveness over District Officers has been very noticeable) the son of a *talaka* (commoner), a farmer—or worse. If office holding on hereditary grounds (*karda*) is held to be socially preferable to that of a *shigege* appointment, it is hard for an hereditary title-holder to respect the authority of a man who has chosen the civil service as a career or who, like a eunuch or slave in the last century, has earned his position by ability alone, the very hallmark of bourgeoisie and middle-class professionalism.

Another vulnerable spot in the equipment of the new bureaucrat is his relative youth. This I believe to be an active cause of tension. Inevitably, given the recent development of secondary education (up to 1950 there was only one government secondary school in Northern Nigeria; the West African School Certificate was first taken by gov-

---

[23] Ronald Cohen, "The Analysis of Conflict in Hierarchical Systems," in *Anthropologica*, Vol. IV, 1962, p. 102.

ernment colleges in 1949, and the Higher School Certificate not until 1960), over 85 per cent of those with a full secondary education and beyond are under 30. This education pattern is indicated in the age group of the 90 candidates short-listed for the first of the Ahmadu Bello University courses to be announced (see the heading "DPA" in Table 1). In any African society respect has traditionally been given in direct proportion to age. Not for nothing have we come to refer to the traditional leaders as "elders." But today along comes the new African civil servant, with an average age of 25, to tell or show his elders what to do—"elders" in the fullest meaning of the word. *Magana ba iko maganar banza*, the Hausa say: "talk without authority is a waste of breath." Also can the traditional authorities accept being "ruled," however indirectly, by a young man whose father they know as nothing "better" than a farmer, and who himself they often laughed at as a naked child playing in the sand outside the emir's palace? *Mutatis mutandis*, many a young graduate in the United Kingdom has preferred to wait a decade before returning to teach at his alma mater, for fear the staff would be too liable to retain the image of him as a recent schoolboy rather than to regard him as a new colleague.

Another by-product of higher education has been that Hausa youths marry later.[24] This trend has been most noticeable among undergraduates, where it is now unusual for 18-20 year olds to be married whereas in traditional society this was the accepted age. The result is that the new leadership cadres are often unmarried when they graduate at 23-25. But Hausa society rejects the unmarried as a threat to the community (*tuzuru ya fi gwauro barna*, they say: "a bachelor is more dangerous than a widower") and classifies any unmarried adult as *karuwa* (prostitute), irrespective of sex. This is yet another difficulty confronting the civil servant in his new position.

Admittedly, the European administrator was no less exposed to the disadvantage of youth when working in African society. But he was able to offset this liability by a number of qualities peculiar to him, which set him apart and lifted him out of the context of local society: his aloofness, his unfamiliarity, his undoubted superior academic or technical skills, and, in the last instance, his support from a foreign governmental machine.

[24] A parallel phenomenon in Ghana has been discussed by T. Peter Omari, "Changing Attitudes of Students in West African Society Toward Marriage and Family Relationships," *The British Journal of Sociology*, Vol. XI, 1960, pp. 197-210. It also features in Gustav Jahoda, *White Man*, London, Oxford University Press, 1961.

I have just referred to the expatriate administrators' "undoubted superior academic or technical skills." The traditional authorities do not always take such a quality for granted in the new administrator. While due deference is still paid to technical and professional officers, whose period of training and standards of achievement have perforce been the same as those set for expatriate officials, the same cannot always be said of the administrative officers. As a service they have, in nearly all the *térritoires d'expression anglaise,* been characterized in their formative years by crash-training programs and emergency commissions. Curiously enough, we now have the possibility of a status *volte-face* reflected in a society which has, generally speaking, been wont to consider the administrative service as the heaven-born and the technical officers as second-class citizens, now respecting the technical officer for his training and qualifications but feeling that the new administrative officer is not always any better trained than some of the new Native Authority officials; and whose youth in any case cannot compete with the administrative experience gained by the older Native Authority staff nor the *savoir-faire* acquired by those councillors from their experience as sophisticated politicians at the national level.

What other grievances, proved or potential, is the traditional authority apt to bear against the indigenous civil servant of the level we are discussing? The following observations are the result of my discussions with students—with the next generation of the new leadership cadres, the senior school-leavers and undergraduates whom I have known in Nigeria and at universities overseas.

The young bureaucrat's adjustment to a new social milieu, his finding of a new social level, must also be seen from the standpoint of the traditional authority. The emir (or at least his courtiers) is often suspicious, anxiously wondering whether those of his people who visit the District Officer are carrying unwelcome tales from the town: often the local authority personnel are firmly warned against mixing socially with their *African* District Officer lest he learn and betray the local secrets. Conversely, there has here and there existed the fear on the part of the new District Officer's expatriate senior officer that too much intimacy with the Native Administration officials will lead to involvement, which will in turn lead to the exertion of improper influence on the District Officer. A plausible thesis could be maintained that one of the strengths of the old Indian Civil and

Colonial Services has been in its social aloofness. The ability of its servants to withdraw to their bungalows and their clubs to render themselves socially self-sufficient, has been a favorite target of nationalists, and not without some justifications. But, to take a wider view, such social isolation has provided an impregnable defence against "involvement," in all its pejorative connotations and in all its consequential permutations, with local affairs. Such a social (and hence political) asylum is not granted to the new Nigerian bureaucrat.

Here is another instance of sociability gone suspect in the eyes of the local authority. A young administrator, keen on extramural activities in the manner of the British *beau idéal* of a ball-hitting, extrovert, public-school administrator, gathered round him a thriving local boys' club to play football and go on picnics, activities that in Hausa society are popular yet require outside stimulus. But to the *sarauta*-centered Native Administration councillors there could be only one kind of *jamiyya* or association: any other must per se be a potential focus of anti-N.A. feeling. So the District Officer's enthusiasm met with the local cold shoulder and, in what was considered to be the best interests of all, he was not reposted to that emirate.

Accusations of disregard for the accepted forms of *gaisuwa* or *fadanci* (greetings with or without gifts, a highly institutionalized custom of Hausa society) to traditional leaders is another stumbling block. It is a phenomenon of every generation to accuse the new one of having fallen away from the standard of manners and behavioral codes observed by the previous generation: a Hausa proverb runs *yaran zamani tun ba su tafasa ba su kan kone* ("modern boys are burnt before they come to the boil," i.e., the younger generation tries to run before it can walk). Such an attitude is poignantly current in a society like the one we are examining in our model, where the normal generation-shift in patterns of behavior has been accelerated by the eagerly welcomed carriers of a novel culture. If a UK or USA graduate in the new leadership cadres of the north is reluctant to kick off his shoes and squat on the ground when calling on the emir, the emir finds it no less repugnant to see one whom he and his traditional councillors are bound to consider, at the best, a mere youth, enter his palace with his shoes on as if he owned the place. This may seem a minor alarum, but such an instance can assume a critical and significant magnitude in the minds of both the new bureaucracy and the less enlightened of the traditionalist courtiers and councillors.

V

THE NEW LEADERSHIP CADRES: THEIR SEARCH FOR LEGITIMACY

Now let us look at the reverse of the coin and consider how fearful and frustrated the new leadership cadres are at some of the sociological problems that their new positions of executive responsibility bring in their wake. The first problem is that we have just been discussing from the point of view of the traditionalists, namely, the relationship of the indigenous civil servant with other people.

We can calculate, from what we have heard and already know about the emir's position, exactly how the average new bureaucrat will regard the emir—in a word, awesomely. If you have, since birth, been brought up in an atmosphere where everyone salutes the emir with great and quite sincere respect, removing his shoes and prostrating himself in genuine reverence, and if you have equally practiced great courtesy in the presence of your father and uncles and grandfather, you do not lightly cast aside these forms. Etiquette, like table manners, is stubbornly conservative. One of the problems that, along with the question of "how are we to be identified as the new District Officer?" has agitated the minds of the new administrative officers has been "how shall we greet the emir?" If, they reason, we follow our indigenous tradition, we have lost the battle in the first round, for how can the Native Authority believe in the firmness of government's agent when we have just been seen to prostrate ourselves, in the accepted token of allegiance, before the emir? If we follow the administration's tradition and expect, gently but unquestioningly in that effective way of the Englishman's natural leadership,[25] a chair in the council chamber and to keep our shoes on, we have at once offended, if not the emir, at least his less tolerant courtiers. Again, once this hurdle is cleared, do we offer our hand to the emir or should he offer his first? In the answer may lie the public evidence of who is on top.

In this matter of personal relationships, one of the most marked characteristics of the new bureaucrat's rejection is his vehement dislike for the bush life and touring. Nor is this to be wondered at. He is actively shunning the resurgence of what he has spent his whole life

---

[25] Cf. Lugard, *The Dual Mandate in British Tropical Africa*, London, W. Blackwood and Sons, 1926, pp. 212-213: "The British gentleman needs no prompting in such a matter—his instinct is never wrong."

running away from: the bush existence. To some extent this is simply a manifestation of boredom inherent in the familiar. Yet I suggest there is something more to it than this. The mental malaise and dissatisfaction are deeper. If I may generalize, the new Northern Nigerian bureaucrat, because he is so often the first generation that is "educated" in the world sense, totally lacks any cultural resources on which to fall back. He does not read for the pleasure of reading; he has no hobby such as bird-watching or botany; amateur anthropology or linguistic research have no attraction for him among his own people; and he finds no romance in safari, an experience ruined for him by its tedious *faute de mieux* in his childhood. But, more importantly, the African is too gregarious ever to enjoy periods of living quietly alone. Without the town amenities of electricity and the cinema, without friends and without the ability to create his own recreation, the Nigerian bureaucrat in out-stations can become utterly lost and miserable. "The District Commissioner was a lonely figure," Professor Macmillan perceptively wrote some years before the evidence we today have was available, "but his African successor may well be lonelier still: the new men, predominantly urban, certainly feel the masses as a drag on their progress and are not readily attracted to work in the 'bush,' in technical services or even agriculture; the aristocratic tradition may be temporarily in eclipse, and with it the tradition of service."[26]

Does the new bureaucrat fare much better in the city? The well-educated has his problems wherever he is, and those educated overseas too often find themselves suffering from cultural ambivalence: marginal men and women with double standards.[27] It is doubtful whether the Northern Nigerian bureaucrat plays a full part in the prevailing social life of the outstations, still largely European-styled. He may find his own level once his own people are in the majority, but there remain awkward moments while there exists a sizeable group of new civil servants who are nevertheless in the minority.

[26] W. M. Macmillan, *Road to Self Rule*, London, Faber and Faber, 1959, p. 27.

[27] In addition to the valuable series on the attitudes of foreign students in the United States published by the University of Minnesota Press, the dilemma of Westernized Indians has been closely analyzed by J. Useem and R. Useem, *Western-educated Man in India*, New York; Dryden Press, 1955, and Professor Edward Shils, "Intellectuals between Tradition and Modernity: The Indian Situation," *Comparative Studies in Society and History*, The Hague, Mouton, 1961. Curiously enough, no such study has yet been undertaken on the African student, though the Institute of International Education has just published a preliminary report, *IIE Survey of the African Student*, New York, 1961.

Yet another related problem which must shortly affect the new bureaucracy is the alarming quantitative gap between the men and the women of comparable educational standards: a "been-to" sooner or later begins to expect a wife in whom he can find the same kind of compatible companionship that he has been used to enjoying in his undergraduate years abroad. Here we have no more space to comment on this tangential problem other than to emphasize that the question of where the new leaders find the kind of wife they want is especially critical in two "bureaucrat" situations: one, in careers such as the Foreign Service, the Armed Forces, the central Civil Service and academia, where public social performance is at a premium; the other, in assignments where society is in-looking and is often called upon to be self-contained, such as the camp life of the District Officer, the period on detachment by the military officer, or the early months of the young diplomat in a foreign capital.

Then there are the behavioral mores of the new leadership cadres towards society as a whole. From a purely personal and bureaucratic standpoint, I am inclined to doubt whether it is possible absolutely to reconcile the accepted civil service code of behavior with the traditional African way of life. Aside from any question of criteria or attitudes, one other reason will suffice: family obligations. How can—to quote from my case study notes—a member of the new cadres live up to the standards his superiors (for the time being expatriate) demand of him and which he indeed sets for himself, when on returning home from the office and bringing his Resident with him as a guest, he finds the house has been suddenly and without notice taken over by a dozen cousins, who have emptied the ice box and are sprawled asleep all over the living room? The bureaucrat in this case resigned and joined the Foreign Service in order, as he told me, to put a safe distance between him and his social environment. Again, how can a police superintendent live within his means when because he earns an adequate wage, his friends ceaselessly drop in and drink him out of house and home? I have known potential leaders to refuse promotion to the $1,000 scale because they know that once this financial upgrading was noised abroad they would be besieged by relatives and left with a lesser net salary than if they had remained on their former $500 level.[28] These comments must not be construed as an

[28] "An African salary earner in government service in the town usually has many relatives living at his expense in or near the house. These have been attracted from his village, not by employment but by the fact that their relative has a cash income. As

attack on the African family system wholesale, for it has much to commend it. But in its present form it can be seriously injurious to the growth of a healthy, independent civil service. It is a problem that the new leadership cadres have yet to face squarely, although those who have had a university education are becoming more and more vocal in their awareness that the time is approaching when in their own interests they will want to redefine the dimension and direction of kinship obligations.[29]

In the analysis of the problems consequent on the political socialization of the new leadership cadres, the supreme problem is what may be termed their quest for recognition, their search for the legitimization of their new power-position. Dr. Michael Banton has reminded us that every relationship is structured by the rights and obligations of its participants: "social change occurs when . . . new norms develop as to these rights and obligations, for until new ideas gain general acceptance and become norms any infraction of the existing code will call forth sanctions and result in a reinforcement of the traditional pattern."[30] The new bureaucrats are introducing new norms in their relationships with traditional society and have thus taken on the composite role of being both the carriers and the outcome of social change. But in their performance, especially where it is related to public office, their behavior is conditioned by one dominant *Angst:* their search for security in their positions of new authority. This is the essence of the tension, the nub of the inner conflict. "They have no Golden Stool," Professor St. Clair Drake said in a recent address at Ibadan,[31] "and unless they are Moslems they have no *baraka* to reinforce their claims. Whenever their authority is challenged by either the formal colonial rulers or local traditional authorities they can be expected, as one West African political leader has phrased it, 'to show them where power lies.' "

Before a person can legitimize his authority, he must let others literally see that he claims it as his right. This very question of how

---

the African says 'come and eat' to the man who passes his house while he is eating, so the salaried clerk finds it normal to keep five relatives in idleness." (N. Heseltine, *Remaking Africa*, London, Museum Press, 1961, p. 101.)

[29] The Hausa have a proverb *dan uwa rigar kaya ne*, "a brother is a coat of thorns," i.e., you cannot rid yourself of it.

[30] Michael Banton, "The Restructuring of Social Relationships," *Social Change in Modern Africa*, Aidan Southall, ed., London, Oxford University Press, 1961, p. 115.

[31] Given at the International Conference on Representative Government and National Progress, sponsored by the Congress for Cultural Freedom in March 1959.

people will recognize that they are the new leaders has constituted a deep and perennial source of anxiety to the new cadres in training. The question "how will people *know* that I am a District Officer?" unconsciously expresses the profound anxiety that motivates the new leaders' attitude towards their new office, their search for legitimacy and recognition.

Certain outward status symbols are, of course, a *sine qua non* of bureaucratic office, old or new. The modern ones have become the aspiration of every Nigerian schoolboy and junior civil servant because it is by their display that others will know that the owner has arrived. The most important of these is an automobile, for without an automobile no new bureaucrat has the slightest hope of convincing anyone that he has made the grade. The car in Nigeria is the status symbol *par excellence*, and within that category there are gradations of status according to the size and make of the car.

Next in the value of status symbols comes a house. The occupation of a "senior service" quarter, by virtue of its immediate advertisement that the new tenant is "a Somebody," as the West African languages have it, is a pre-condition of legitimizing new authority. These twin motivations are well expressed in Wole Soyinka's lines describing how the "Other Immigrant" steels himself to endure the tribulations of his exigent existence in London as an African student only.

> By thinking of his government house,
> Senior Service car,
> And hordes of admiring women awaiting me.[32]

But if the car and the house, and probably the orderly or government messenger in the case of the Administrative Officer, offer some unmistakable form of identity in certain circumstances, the new bureaucrat has still no confidence in his instant recognition. He fears, as an illustration, that a European—especially those on contract, in the majority and less knowledgeable about local society—may mistake him for a junior clerk, or the local peasantry may take him for a Native Authority scribe. This explains the demand for an official uniform for daily wear, so insistently heard in the early years of training the new administrators.

Here it is pertinent to ask how the European District Officer sur-

[32] Wole Soyinka, "Two in London," in *An African Treasury*, Langston Hughes, ed., New York, Pyramid Books, 1960, p. 183.

mounted such an obstacle. The answer is, that his white skin *was* in a sense his uniform. Europeans were *ipso facto* people in authority. Similarly, it is no less pertinent to ask how the senior Native Authority official is recognized, or even the Member of Parliament. The answer is manifold: by the way he dresses (only title-holders or royalty wear turbans, multiple gowns indicate *daraja*); by the unpurposeful and unhurried way he walks; by having an expensive automobile and a personal driver (no new bureaucrat can afford a driver, either financially, or socially as long as he has expatriate colleagues) or praise-singer; by having a host of menials to follow behind him or carry his portfolio; or by his ostentatious wealth and conspicuous consumption.

What are the difficulties the new bureaucrat is likely to face in legitimizing his authority vis-à-vis the traditional authority? One is an unconscious response to the *karda/shigege*-differentiated attitudes of traditional Hausa life. If the old bureaucracy consider a freely chosen title and occupation inferior to and less respectable than an inherited one, the new civil servant may take precisely the opposite view. Trained from his earliest schooldays to consider appointment and promotion (to prefect and college, for instance) as dependent on ability and merit and in no way connected with blood or patronage, he carries this attitude with him into his new post. He finds that the same principles hold good in the civil service. But when he starts to work in close contact with the local authority, he is likely to find that in the Native Authority promotion still goes predominantly to those in the *karda*-status category. An analysis of family connections of District Heads in any emirate lends weight to this. As Smith has shown in his study of the political system in Zaria emirate, the Fulani, numbering in the political society there only 54,000 against the 252,000 Habe, receive preference over the non-Fulani as regards employment by the Native Authority in the ratio of two to one; the dynastic Fulani receive preference over the other Fulani, holding as much as 40 per cent of all the salaried posts; and members of the ruling dynasty receive preference over their rivals, enjoying 22 per cent of the posts. Small wonder, then, that only a minimal percentage of secondary school boys and a nil return from college graduates seriously consider taking up Native Authority employment.

In many respects the unconcealed social stratification can go much deeper among contemporaries than it does in English society. At an English school, the sons of a duke and dustman are, if they find themselves in the same form, equals at least as far as school life extends. But this is far from being so in Northern Nigeria. In our training courses we have remarked how an emir's nephew or even an older student is rarely called by his name among his co-students but is given the honorific salutation of *ranka ya dade*. A student of mine who received a letter from a boy only a year younger than he could not understand why I teased him about the deferential opening of "Dear Sir."

Patronage and clientship of the nature that we have earlier noted in traditional Hausa society can continue, sometimes modified and sometimes almost unadulterated, in the bureaucratic society and are quite untrammelled in the political society. The new bureaucracy—especially those who have been trained abroad but including also many of those who have been to higher educational institutions within Nigeria—openly admit how much they resent the cramping insistence on the tradition of *fadanci* (paying personal court) which is often expected from them. The new bureaucracy enviously admire other colleagues who hold degrees and are therefore, in the present limitless seller's market, able to show a much greater spirit of indepence than those whose services would on the open market command a lesser price than they have won in government service. My impression is that this group of bureaucrats, irked by the social limitations imposed on them by the hang-over structure of their own society, will eventually effect a social (and hopefully quite bloodless) revolution in the amount of control hitherto exercised on their private life by the transference of a traditional Hausa town social code to a non-traditional cosmopolitan city way of life.

VI

FOUR CONCLUDING PROPOSITIONS

In concluding this discussion on some of the strains and stresses that the new bureaucracy are exposed to when they begin to operate in an atmosphere still redolent with a traditional system of social and authority ranking—described by Smythe as "the situation of the indigenous elite so encrusted with the weight of ancient Islamic tradition and continued feudal patterns and attitudes that the 'old families' have continued to resist successfully the stress upon individual accomplishment which obtains in Southern Nigeria"[33]—I wish to

[33] Smythe, "The African Elite in Nigeria," p. 81.

put forward four propositions. None of these is to be construed as a call to sweep away the present social ethics. Northern Nigerian society has a tremendous amount to commend it, but it must, as its shrewdest leaders recognize, move with the times if it is to survive. "We of this Region," said the Premier of Northern Nigeria in his address at the independence celebrations in October 1960, "put a high value on our traditions which have given us a stable society and an orderly administration. We intend to do all in our power to preserve what is good in our way of life. But we have no illusions about the sanctity of traditions and are fully conscious of the need to keep pace with the march of time. We shall not allow ourselves to become a static society; for we shall be unworthy of our legacy if we ourselves do not pass it on to future generations with the impress of our times."

The first proposition is this. Whatever the strength of the traditional authority (and in the Northern Nigerian context we have remarked how strong it is) and however much revivalism there is in West African society (cultural, social, and religious), in the final analysis we are going to witness an increase in the authority of the new leadership cadres at the expense of the traditional power-structured system. This is by no means saying that the chiefs and their traditional hierarchies will be swept away; they still have a role to fill in Hausa society. What it does say is that there will ensue a marked shift in the balance of the power in favor of the new political and bureaucratic societies.[34]

This prediction is based on several observations. What is the attitude of the average schooled Northern Nigerian to the traditional authority system? He sees it as a mixed blessing. He genuinely likes and needs the security and orderliness it affords, but his education has taught him that this is no longer the best of all possible worlds. The traditionalists have lost the confidence of the new generation; few

[34] I am aware that the Jones report in Eastern Nigeria (1957) declared that "a lot of people in the East feel that democratic forces have steamrollered the old social system out of their life, and that there should be a place for the traditional authorities in the life of the country," but this apparent demand for the regalia and office of chieftainship in an area where such an institution was little recognized before has to be read against the political situation—a caveat confirmed by the manner in which appointments to the House of Chiefs have been made. More realistic, I suggest, is the representative nature of the report of the Cambridge Summer School on the place of chiefs in African society, with its conclusion that "prerogative powers are unlikely to increase and where they exist at present are likely to diminish in time as the result of being called in question." (Colonial Office, African No. 1190, 1957, p. 85, para. 24.)

educated men aspire to their office. The new generation is represented in Native Authority service only by the educational failures; the civil service is the magnet.[35] The significance of the refusal of the first son of the Emir of Kano in 1961 to resign his senior career appointment in the Foreign Service and to take up the traditional, prestigeful, and powerful office of Ciroman Kano was not lost on the Nigerian Press. The new Northerner therefore seeks to retain as much of his sincere respect for traditional authority as possible, especially where it is sanctioned and strengthened by its Islamic content; but at the same time he insists that merit rather than blood, ability rather than kinship, objectively attained qualifications rather than hereditary ties, should be the passport to high office. This strong emphasis on "opportunity" is, I think, the key. It is, in short, the opportunity of being given an equal opportunity to become unequal.

The second proposition is that in spite of the authority dichotomy between the old and the new bureaucracy, the situation will not erupt into violence. Why has there been no overt clash between the traditionalists and the young Northern Nigerian civil servants? Why has there been no repetition of the Aba riots, which shook Eastern Nigeria in 1929 after an alien form of bureaucracy had been imposed on the traditional system of tribal authority? There are several explanations for this, the full answer doubtless being an amalgam.

First, we must remember that the localization of the civil service in Northern Nigeria has been a deliberate and regulated process, not a wholesale changeover. It has, in fact, followed the classic Northern Nigerian approach to most of its problems: the doctrine of gradualism. In brief, the expatriate has been retained to hold the hand of the new indigenous bureaucrat, to ease him into his position of fresh authority. Very few African countries have maintained their administrative service at over 50 per cent expatriate for two and a half years after self-government or have delayed the full indigenization of their Permanent Secretary and Resident cadre for nearly four years.[36] But Northern Nigeria has, and is proud of it, and is pleased at not only

[35] See, for instance, the high percentages quoted by P. Mercier in his analysis of career ambitions of school children in Dakar, "Evolution of Senegalese Elites," *International Social Science Bulletin*, Vol. VIII, 1956, p. 441. These figures are supported by sample surveys in other African territories.

[36] Speaking in the House of Assembly in March 1962, the Premier of Northern Nigeria announced that he hoped to "Northernize" all these posts by the end of the year. The region achieved self-government in March 1959.

the resultant governmental stability but also the way in which such a situation was welcomed by its electorate.

Secondly, the way for a shift in the balance of power has, gently but perceptibly, been paved over the past decade. The emir and all that he symbolizes is not the absolute authority that he was in 1950, although Native Administrations have sought to compensate for their reduction in authority by an increase in their sphere of influence. Gradually the Native Authorities have been brought into a position where they must respond to the beginnings of democratic feeling in the north engendered by the spread of education, both scholastic and political. For instance, the title of "sole chief" was abolished in 1952; in 1954 the Native Authority Law imposed, *inter alia,* elected majorities on all subordinate councils; in 1956 and again in 1960 the judicial powers of the emirs' courts were drastically readjusted; in 1961 and 1962 three major commissions of inquiry into the working of senior Native Authorities were ordered by the Premier himself, who sternly warned that "any Native Authority, large or small, which is obstructive or takes the line that it can please itself must be prepared to face investigation. . . . My colleagues and I cannot sit idly by and allow maladministration and corruption to go unchecked";[37] and now one of the last powers of the emirs, that over land, has been modified by the proposed Land Tenure Law, 1962. All the time, too, there has continued a steady pressure by the Administration for the cancellation of the royal prerogative to make personal levies of produce or service, for broadening the Native Authority council by the inclusion of educated, non-traditional elements, and for setting up impartial committees to scrutinize Native Authority appointments and promotions. Perhaps the war-time air force phase of a "softening-up process" best describes this phased relaxation of control.

Thirdly, with the introduction of politics in 1951, there has been a continuous and quite proper transfer of power away from the Administration to the elected representatives. Here a vicious circle can now be discerned. The Ministers derive their position from the power of the Native Authorities. It seems beyond doubt that no Northern Peoples' Congress (the ruling party) candidate is nominated for election to the House of Assembly or the House of Representatives without the approval, implicit or explicit, of his nomination by the

[37] *Speech by the Premier of Northern Nigeria . . . to Zaria Native Authority Council, 3 August 1961,* Kaduna, Government Printer, p. 6.

emir. "In Nigeria," comments one internal observer, "political parties seek the support of the chiefs in order to secure the votes of their followers."[38] In two historic cases where the emir preferred his own candidate to the party nominee, the latter lost the election; in three others, the emir's influence is held by external observers to have decided the balance between two candidates. As Dr. Lucy Mair commented in a recent article on the position of chiefs in the African political society, "it is a feature of contemporary West Africa that hereditary chiefs, though they have lost their political functions, have by no means lost their influence."[39] A dramatic instance of this persistent power was illustrated in 1958 by the Moro Naba, chief of the Mossi in Upper Volta, when he laid siege to the Territorial Assembly with an armed force in protest against the usurpation of his power.[40] At the same time as the Ministers rely on the Native Authorities for their support, they must, as elected representatives, gradually bring the Native Authorities to a stricter conformity than had been the case under the policy of colonial indirect rule. Such a tightening up and centralization of discipline has been a feature of nearly every African country on its attainment of independence. In the middle of this tug-of-war for authority, there has arrived the new bureaucrat. The new bureaucracy has drawn some hope from the proposed Provincial Commissioners' legislation, whereby the civil service Resident gives way to a political appointee who becomes a kind of Resident Minister. If the latter can look after the delicate political problems and leave the civil servant to handle the executive functions of a government agent, a Western-style bureaucracy has a chance to survive and to continue to attract the best brains.

Lastly in this list of reasons why no head-on clash has taken place between the old and new authorities is the remarkable phlegm and flexibility of the Hausa temperament. This resilience in the face of adversity and in times of difficulty has been characteristic of the whole history of Hausaland and its people: "Situated between the two powerful empires of Songhay and Bornu, the Hausa states had already felt the tide of conquest sweep across them more than once in

[38] H. O. Davies, *Nigeria: The Prospects for Democracy*, London; Weidenfeld and Nicolson, 1961, p. 69. See also R. Sklar, *Nigerian Political Parties*, Princeton, Princeton University Press, 1963.

[39] Lucy P. Mair, "Representative Local Government as a Problem in Social Change," *Journal of African Administration*, Vol. X, 1958, p. 20.

[40] See report "Upper Volta Vortex," Michael Crowder, *West African Review*, January 1959, pp. 14-16.

their long existence, but as the waters of war subsided they had always emerged with independence and by means of stubborn courage and diplomatic payments of tribute they had retained the individuality of their political life. Like a bed of rushes they had ever allowed the storms of encircling forces to beat over their heads. At times they appeared to be laid low, but when the hurricane had passed they raised themselves, none the worse for the buffeting of fate."[41]

My third proposition does not concern the relationships between the new bureaucracy and the old bureaucracy, but carries the potential conflict a few years ahead, when one of the most meaningful crises in other emergent countries, as well as Nigeria, threatens to erupt within the new bureaucracy itself. Let me present the problem in a series of succinct and related propositions:

1. The new bureaucracy, especially the key administrative service, has because of the near-total absence of degree-holding candidates been filled up by officers of, whatever their merits of character and experience, a sub-university academic standard.

2. These civil servants have done well in the field, but they have been unable to cope with the secretariat schedules of a Ministry desk or to lead a district development team which includes fully trained professional officers.

3. Their entry at a time of critical shortage, exacerbated by the rapid retirement of senior expatriate administrators, has favored their accelerated promotion to high rank.

4. Their age means that under normal circumstances they can expect at least 25 years more (hitherto the span of a total career!) in the high posts they have already attained, a situation which can lead to a demoralizing promotional freeze.

5. This promotional velocity has meant a shortfall of experience, so that one finds Residents who have never run a division and Permanent Secretaries who have had marginal or no experience of field administration. This in turn means a dearth of accumulated experience to pass on to the fresh entrants.

6. The consequence of this lack of a normal age-spread within the bureaucratic hierarchy has been pinpointed by Coleman as "the absence of those gradations in experience and wisdom that are vital for the preservation and the passing on of service traditions, and for the

[41] A. H. M. Kirk-Greene, *This Is Northern Nigeria*, Kaduna, Government Printer, 1956, p. 30.

inculation of loyalty to and respect for the legal norms and processes of the public services among the new recruits."[42]

7. Will the graduate be attracted to a career so structured? Will the best students still opt for the administrative service, or will it become a repository of third-rate minds? When the young African is so alarmingly concious of his academic standing, will the B.A. be content to serve under the equivalent of a twelfth grader for the next twenty-five years? Already the latter-day emergency intake of administrators, with their Higher (freshman year) or School (11th-12th grade) Certificates, are looking askance at those above them in the staff list with their Secondary IV (10th grade) or even Secondary II certificates.

8. If not, what is to happen? Is the first generation of new bureaucrats to be diverted out of the main promotional stream? Or sacrificed? Or do we breed a generation of dissatisfied civil servants and unemployed graduates, a nightmare for any political leader in an emergent nation?

This leads me to the final proposition. By its very nature, it comes nearer to offering a solution to these aspects of socio-authority conflict than do the others. I believe that, aside from questions of recruitment calibre, not until there is a radical reorientation of the role and responsibilities of the new bureaucracy, especially in the vital administrative and executive grades, can the new civil servant stand a fair chance to fulfill his designated function in the kind of authority-structured society represented by the emirates of Northern Nigeria.

As we have seen, the primary role of the administrative officer in colonial Northern Nigeria has been that of adviser rather than of government executive. Yet it is unambiguously clear to all who have had the opportunity to reflect on the situation that even if the structure and ideals of the provincial administration at the actual time of independence are superficially no different, save in the nationality of the administrator, from those of five or fifteen years ago, the whole philosophy of an independent government is in fact utterly different. Sooner rather than later the functions and forms of the provincial administration must change.[43] I would go further. Indirect rule may

---

[42] James S. Coleman, in a paper presented to the 32nd conference of the International Institute of Differing Civilizations, 1959.

[43] That they had not immediately done so with the coming of independence struck visiting South African Ezekiel Mphahlele at once: "The educated African in a colonial context has thus merely stepped into the colonial administrator's shoes." *The African Image*, London, Faber and Faber, 1962, p. 63.

be the very essence of a colonial administration; certainly independence demands direct administration. Self-rule needs executive agents, not advisers, it requires something more than a reproduction of the European District Officer. Superb as I know him to have been, he was but a creation of his age; and the age of the archetypal District Officer has passed.[44]

To put it another way: while the administration that most of us have known and worked in has been primarily a government of law and order, the dynamics of modern administration in these communities must be geared to a government of social and economic development. "The new independent Tanganyika," Adu has urged, "requires that civil servants should not merely apply and interpret the necessary routine regulations; but they should also share with the government the vital role of leadership in the community."[45] Kenyatta was voicing the thoughts of many African leaders when he said that the indigenous administrative officer must not only work *for* the people, as his expatriate predecessor had done, but also *with* the people. Julius Nyerere has gone even further, declaring that his party's conception of the President's office in their new republican constitution rules out the theory that public services ought to be politically impartial: "Civil servants are human beings; they do have political views and this must affect their work. Policies they like are executed with enthusiasm, those of which they disapprove are implemented reluctantly or may even be slowed down. . . . *We cannot afford the luxury of administrators who are neutral.*"[46] In what used to be French West Africa the same conviction prevails: "All civil servants must at all times be at the service of the Nation, that is to say, at the disposition of the Party and of the Government which are the expressions of the Nation's strength. . . . The Administration must mobilise all its own staff as well as the traditional village and town authorities to reinforce the Party."[47] Example rather than orders, leadership rather than supervision, are the requirements. The

[44] This is an abridgement of a theme developed in my unpublished memorandum *New Dimensions in Administrative Training Programmes for African Governments*, submitted to the Bridges Commission on Public Administration set up in Great Britain in 1962.

[45] A. L. Adu, *Report of the Tanganyika Salaries Commission*, Dar-es-Salaam, Government Printer, 1961, para. 102.

[46] Julius Nyerere, "How Much Power for a Leader?" *Observer* (London), June 3, 1962. Italics added. Ghana followed suit in 1964.

[47] Quoted in *Le Niger*, Niamey, from Débats de l'Assemblée Nationale, May 1961. I am grateful to Mr. T. G. Brierly of the British Embassy, Dakar, for drawing my attention to this parallel.

administrative officer is still urgently needed in developing territories, often in greater numbers than ever before; but he must, like Nicodemus, undergo a rebirth.

CONCLUDING OBSERVATIONS

Can the new bureaucracy exercise its role of dynamic leadership in the community when the community already has its own established leadership? If in such societies governments continue to look on the task of the new bureaucracy as the same kind of work as was being done by the District Officer for the past sixty years—primarily the responsibility for law and order crystallized in an advisory capacity to the local administration in the form of the Native Authority—then the answer in traditional, authority-structured societies must be "no." I am aware that such a conclusion runs contrary to Lloyd Fallers' hypothesis that "Societies with hierarchical, centralized political systems incorporate the Western type of civil service structure with less strain and instability than do societies having other types of political systems—e.g., the segmentary ones."[48] But there is room for a reinterpretation of this authoritative claim in the light of the level and, more important, the ethnic composition, of the bureaucracy under question. If, on the other hand, governments perceive that a reorientation is required in the functions of the bureaucracy, proceeding from a motivation more closely allied to economic and social development, and if they transfer the political cares to their own party representatives in the field while reinforcing and legitimizing the executive authority of the new bureaucracy as the recognized agents of government, the answer can be "yes."

In the meantime, it is impossible to expect the indigenous District Officer to continue the laissez-faire, personality-gauged, "advisory" policy of indirect rule. Cranford Pratt has remarked in his study of British administrative policy in Uganda[49] that although stress has always been put on the role of the District Officer as a sympathetic counsellor to the chief, the very nature of his responsibility has meant that his authority greatly exceeded that of advice *pur sang*. This role

[48] Lloyd A. Fallers, *Bantu Bureaucracy: A Study of Processes and Types of Domination*, East African Institute of Social Research, n.d., p. 242. This premise led to lengthy discussion at the 13th Conference of the Rhodes-Livingstone Institute for Social Research: see *From Tribal Rule to Modern Government*, Conference proceedings, Raymond Apthorpe, ed., Lusaka, 1960.

[49] D. A. Low and R. C. Pratt, *Buganda and British Overrule, 1900-1955*, London, Oxford University Press, 1960, p. 172.

of the modern administrators, neatly described as "advisers, prompt-
ers and brakesmen—a position somewhat vague from the juridical
point of view, but one of high esteem from the human, and also one
for which a sanguine temperament appears an inappropriate, but
phlegm (provided it is shot through with cordiality) a most enviable,
attribute,"[50] is demanding too much from the young bureaucrat
launched into the kind of society we have discussed here. At the
bottom level of bureaucracy, administration is largely a question of
efficient control and competent execution. But at the higher levels of
decision making, the administrator requires some of the qualities of
the diplomat. "The logic of efficiency loses force as we approach the
top of the pyramid," Selznick has expressed it; ". . . the executive
becomes a statesman as he makes the transition from administrative
management to institutional leadership."[51] In such a face-to-face
game, the dice are loaded against the new bureaucrat in Northern
Nigeria.

My thesis has also suggested that, although the new bureaucracy
rejects the curb on individualism imposed by the authority and rank
patterns of traditional Hausa society, it is nevertheless in danger of
finding the Hausa power and prestige-system reproduced at the political and older civil servant level, with identical demands for personal
loyalty, traditional respect, and positive relationships that are outside
the accepted civil service code of behavior. Berger has noted how in
the Egyptian civil service the persistent influence of the local community way of life has tended to politicize interpersonal relations so that
individuals assess one another in terms of social position and power.
A similar social legacy may be the lot of the Nigerian civil service.

Furthermore, I have suggested that if the civil service succeeds in
overcoming this phenomenon of the Native Authority pattern of behavior being projected and repeated at the central government
spheres of influence, there remains a grave likelihood of the new
bureaucracy establishing itself as a closed power-elite—an outcome
that would bring the wheel back to the full turn of *karda*.

Here the Hausa concept of *sarauta* is showing itself exceptionally
tenacious. The new bureaucracy has so far displayed no less enthusiasm in the search for *sarauta* than their ancestors and elders exercised

[50] Baron Van Asbeeh, *Leaps and Approaches Towards Self Government in British
Africa*, Leyden, 1953.
[51] Philip Selznick, *Leadership in Administration*, Evanston, Ill., Row, Peterson,
1957, pp. 3-4.

in traditional Hausa society.[52] On a narrower plane, an identical manifestation has already been spotted by Smith in the reaction of the Zaria aristocracy to the British introduction of departmental heads. "They recall the old occupational orders in the specificity of their technical interests. . . . They have therefore been easily accommodated to the prevailing concepts of *sarauta* which involved title, rank political clientage, administrative responsibility, compounds, remuneration, promotional careers."[53] Inevitably, the display and exercise of power are major concerns of a new elite. *Sarauta* at once advertises the fact that its possessor is in a position to render favors and wield authority. This is no less true in the post-British Nigerian society than it was in the pre-Fulani Habe society. A catalyst is required if the traditional lure of *sarauta* is to be resisted. "To train Africans," writes David Apter, "in the complex jobs of modern administration and government, both in standards of work and in standards of political judgement, demands first a shattering of traditional standards and judgments. The tribal criteria for activity can no longer apply."[54] Unlike the West, where, as Berger points out, "political responsibility, democratic institutions, and private economic power have diminished the awe in which the trappings of the state are viewed by the ordinary citizen,"[55] in areas like the Middle East civil servants see their own power as the main determinant of public respect for the service.

It is in the sociological embarrassments deriving from the efforts of the new leadership cadres to legitimize their position in the eyes of a society which already recognizes its own authority system that one of the most fertile fields of political research lies. Western-type civil services have "evolved a form of loyalty to a given task irrespective of one's economic relationship to it,"[56] but this type of moral commitment to a job is as yet largely unknown among the values current in traditional, highly structured political systems. In its place is preferred a personal evaluation. We can perhaps do little more than

[52] Davies, *op.cit.*, p. 73 concludes a perceptive analysis of the intensive nature of the power struggle in Nigeria by declaring that "Economically, ministerial government is a restratification of society into a new form of plutocracy." C. S. Whitaker, in a brilliant unpublished dissertation (Princeton, 1962), has assembled a wealth of examples illustrating the theme of traditional authority and society reproducing itself in the guise of novel democracy as I have sought to develop it here; to this phenomenon Whitaker gives the neat label of "institutional convergence."

[53] M. G. Smith, *Government in Zazzau*, p. 233.

[54] David Apter, "Africa and the Social Scientist," *World Politics*, Vol. VI, 1954.

[55] Berger, *op.cit.*, p. 111.

[56] *Ibid.*, p. 114.

observe, record, and formulate models, for I doubt whether anyone who has not actually lived in this kind of society can ever hope to understand fully the stresses and influences and demands to which the new leadership is exposed during this period of transition from a traditional to a more rationalized system of administration.

That the new leadership cadres will triumph there is little doubt—even though a fully Westernized civil service is unlikely to develop—for society itself is becoming more and more impatient in its demands for a change of heart in leadership. James Coleman foresees an inexorable advance in the process of state formation "not only because the modern state remains the unchallenged symbol of personal and group freedom, but also because of the belief that it provides the only respectable and legitimate arena for the exercise of power, the realization of democracy, and the attainment of economic prosperity."[57] "Traditionalist" can be a term of abuse, its synonym "reactionary," its antonym "progressive."

Time is on the side of the new bureaucracy. Meanwhile, it is the young bureaucrat himself, in danger of being a marginal man as he stands at the crossroads between tradition and modernity,[58] who needs our understanding and sympathetic encouragement;[59] for in the final analysis bureaucracy, despite its tight-lipped and impersonal efficiency, is still made up of human beings.

[57] Coleman, *op.cit.*, p. 56.

[58] "Ours is the difficulty of this transition stage" is the way a young medical graduate from the other side of the African continent put it. (Noni Jabavu, *Drawn in Colour: African Contrasts*, London, Murray, 1960, p. 129.)

[59] Last week one of Northern Nigeria's new bureaucrats wrote to me: "I have been a pioneer throughout my career: the first class in a new secondary school, the first class to do pre-college studies, the first set to join the administrative cadre. Now you advise me to enroll in a brand new university. Can I never expect to move into a defined, established position? Must I always be a pioneer?" Perhaps in the Africa of the 1960's there is only one answer to this common kind of question: "You are the pioneer generation."

CHAPTER 12

PARTY CADRES IN COMMUNIST CHINA

JOHN WILSON LEWIS

Functions of Traditional Chinese Education

RECENT monographic studies of the Ch'ing period (1644-1912) draw attention to the balance of conflicting Chinese socio-political interests and make clear that the traditional educational patterns were vital in the preservation of that balance.[1] This introductory analysis of the operation of the nineteenth-century Chinese educational system highlights the political function of Ch'ing education and sets the current problem of education and political development in a meaningful context.

A description of Ch'ing society begins with the extended family, organized on patrilineal lines, and the rigidly structured, mutually exclusive lineage (or clan) and village groups.[2] The family and localized groups monopolized the most important life functions, including the maintenance of order and social discipline under the authority of the patriarchs and group elders.[3] The so-called family system was relatively immobile geographically and socially, although physical and social positions were far from fixed.[4] Permanence and continuity prevailed, however, and the classical sanctions preserved the established order against the complicating intrusions from outside China and social decay from within. Ancestors and heirs were consid-

[1] In this discussion I have used Knight Biggerstaff, *The Earliest Modern Government Schools in China*, Ithaca, Cornell University Press, 1961, esp. Chap. 1; Chung-li Chang, *The Chinese Gentry: Studies on Their Role in Nineteenth-Century Chinese Society*, Seattle, University of Washington Press, 1955, introduction and pt. 1; Kung-ch'uan Hsiao, *Rural China: Imperial Control in the Nineteenth Century*, Seattle, University of Washington Press, 1960, pp. 3-10, *passim*; Franz Michael, "State and Society in Nineteenth-Century China," *World Politics*, Vol. VII, No. 3, April 1955, pp. 419-433; and Teng Ssu-yü and John K. Fairbank, *China's Response to the West; A Documentary Survey, 1839-1923*, Cambridge, Harvard University Press, 1954.

[2] See Hsiao, *op.cit.*, Chap. VIII; T'ung-tsu Ch'ü, *Law and Society in Traditional China*, Paris and The Hague, Mouton, 1961, pp. 15-20; Fei Hsiao-t'ung, *Peasant Life in China*, New York, E. P. Dutton, 1939, esp. pp. 90-95; Maurice Freedman, *Lineage Organization in Southeastern China*, London, Athlone Press, 1958, Chap. 1; and Sybille van der Sprenkel, *Legal Institutions in Manchu China*, London, Athlone Press, 1962, Chap. VII.

[3] Ch'ü, *op.cit.*, pp. 20-41.

[4] Robert M. Marsh, *The Mandarins; The Circulation of Elites in China, 1600-1900*, Glencoe, Free Press, 1961, pp. 186-194.

ered evidence of continuity, the timeless Chinese witnesses to a stable system sanctified by the Confucian classics and the loosely defined folk religions. Social prescriptions acclaimed the existing "holistic" order, and these prescriptions underlay the education of children.

The philosophy of the Chinese state assumed the disciplined regulation of the decentralized social base, and the training of children, however unconscious, was crucial to the stability and cohesion of that base. Although generally speaking the education of Chinese children lacked overt political content, Chinese social discipline and cohesion provided the indispensable foundation for elite action and for the demands by the elite on the Chinese population. Under the mounting challenges from the West in the nineteenth century[5] and the extreme internal crises,[6] the elite's claims on the Chinese people multiplied as the cohesive social base disintegrated.

The Ch'ing officials[7] in the late nineteenth century numbered about 40,000[8] in a population of probably less than 400,000,000 and were drawn from a reservoir of local elites or "gentry" who varied in number between 1.1 and 1.4 million. The non-official gentry had important political and social functions, and those who had passed the civil service examinations provided the ready pool of recruits for officialdom. This pool monopolized China's scholar leaders. Among the political functions exercised by the scholar-gentry who did not hold official posts were political indoctrination (in the so-called *hsiang-yüeh* or lecture system),[9] liaison between officials and the general populace, and transmission of the ethical lore which purported to bind all in the Middle Kingdom.

In addition to these political functions, the gentry also assumed responsibility for indoctrinating prospective candidates for official positions and transmitting orthodox thinking and behavior to the potential heirs of the policy apparatus. By a tradition that had roots in the Former Han dynasty (201 B.C.-A.D. 8) and that was formalized in the Sui (589-618) and T'ang (618-907) periods, the Chinese re-

[5] Teng and Fairbank, *op.cit.*; Joseph Levenson, *Confucian China and Its Modern Fate; The Problem of Intellectual Continuity*, London, Routledge and Kegan Paul, 1958, esp. pp. 146-155; and Mary C. Wright, *The Last Stand of Chinese Conservatism: The T'ung-chih Restoration, 1862-1874*, Stanford, Stanford University Press, 1957.

[6] An idea of the dimension of these crises may be gained from S. Y. Teng, *The Nien Army and Their Guerrilla Warfare*, Paris and The Hague, Mouton, 1961.

[7] John K. Fairbank, "The Manchu-Chinese Dyarchy in the 1840's and '50's," *Far Eastern Quarterly*, Vol. XII, No. 3, May 1953, pp. 265-278.

[8] Chang, *op.cit.*, pt. II.

[9] Hsiao, *op.cit.*, Chap. VI.

stricted elite membership to humanistically trained literati who had demonstrated mastery of the ancient classics and literary forms. The training regimen required to absorb the basic literature was compensated by rewards of coveted degrees granted to the successful competitors in the examination sequence. Social prestige, official position, and numerous material perquisites awaited the most competent winners in the examinations, which were theoretically open to all except the "mean" people[10] but actually closed to those who could not afford the lengthy study program.

The examination system[11] infused officialdom with values which proved disastrous to the political order in the late nineteenth century. Educated to compete in bureaucratically administered examinations which tested the mastery of authoritative texts, the candidates eventually acquired a political style or manner of official operation which was also competitive, authoritarian, and bureaucratic.[12] The examinations were rituals designed to stamp aspiring students with the acceptable political style, and prestige and position came to those whose examinations indicated the highest potential for adopting that style. Moreover, political style derived from the ancient literature undermined innovation and impeded the emergence of specialization. Lacking the distinctive identity and job security of the specialist, the Ch'ing official tended to exhibit a suspicious, mechanical, and often artificial style of operation, although there were notable exceptions in the Ch'ing hierarchy.

The imperial court applauded these tendencies in the bureaucratic environment. The "ideal" official in many societies is impersonal and impartial, a faithful servant bound by the "rules," but the Emperor in Peking also welcomed the Chinese model of a competitive, even faction-ridden, bureaucratic apparatus. The principal values of this model, however, ran counter to habit patterns learned by the elite (and the general population) as children, and Ch'ing officials were under constant pressure from below to abide by family and kinship

[10] Ch'ü, op.cit., p. 129, defines "mean" people as slaves, prostitutes, entertainers, government runners, and some regionally defined groups.

[11] For a recent analysis of the Ch'ing examination system, see Wolfgang Franke, Reform and Abolition of the Traditional Chinese Examination System, Cambridge, Harvard University Press, 1960. An excellent Chinese study is Shang Yen-liu, Ch'ing-tai k'o-chü k'ao-shih shu-lu (An Account of the Ch'ing Civil Service Examinations), Peking, San-lien shu-tien, 1958.

[12] See C. K. Yang, "Some Characteristics of Chinese Bureaucratic Behavior," in David S. Nivison and Arthur F. Wright, eds., Confucianism in Action, Stanford, Stanford University Press, 1959, pp. 134-164.

obligations and to accord special privileges based on loyalty and other personal ties.[13] In the broadest terms, therefore, the leaders of the Chinese polity attempted to inculcate and sustain a pattern of official behavior strikingly dissimilar to habits and attitudes formed in childhood. The education of children emphasized the values of the family and kin groups and compatible personal relationships, in contrast to the political education of the gentry, which stressed individuated, impersonal, and competitive behavior. To prevent the emergence of family values in the bureaucracy, the elite established disciplinary constraints managed through a moderately effective Censorate[14] which provided a channel for imperial control and frustrated nepotism.[15] Moreover, the underlying division in the behavioral patterns of the elite and the general populace encouraged divergent political strategies of the commoners and officials. The first desired protection, some local improvements, and passive rule, whereas the latter sought strong centralized government and control. The political tactics of the ordinary Chinese were based on manipulation of relationships, the jockeying for favors, and the nurturing of personal obligations; the comparable tactics of officials as dictated by their style of training and official strictures were impersonal and authoritarian, frequently utilizing modified strategies of force (armies and police) but often manipulating the relational structure for control purposes.

Given the fundamental differences between the bureaucratically organized elite and the general society in the Ch'ing dynasty, the Chinese thus demonstrated an impressive genius in binding the political and social systems into an operative whole. It was here that the role of the educational system *qua* system was vital. For, despite the pernicious influence of the values it fostered, the educational system bound the two socio-political elements together by utilizing common ethical standards and by its promotion of a widespread belief in the possibility of access to the elite and consequent mobility for all who "qualified." Comparing the political elite and the general society, the inculcation of the Confucian dogma followed markedly dissimilar paths, but by the use of the semi-open examination system, the Chinese were able to maximize the fact that there was only one dogma in the final analysis.

[13] Yang, *ibid.*, esp. pp. 156-163, makes this point in another context.

[14] Charles O. Hucker, "Confucianism and the Chinese Censorial System," in Nivison and Wright, *op.cit.*, pp. 182-208.

[15] Robert M. Marsh, "Bureaucratic Constraints on Nepotism in the Ch'ing Period," *Journal of Asian Studies*, Vol. XIX, No. 2, February 1960, pp. 117-133.

Thus, as form and ritual in the education of children, the Confucian values created the appearance of a national consensus, but these same values when incorporated in scholarly literature and elite education distinguished leaders from commoners in the total society and thereby deprived that consensus of real content. Basing elite selection on Confucian values, the examination system appeared to establish social continuity from the village to the central government, but simultaneously it prevented the proliferation of potential leaders and the loss of the leadership's distinctive identity. In general, the basic education of Chinese children emphasized values without literacy and formal repetition without critical thought. The prestige of the literati, on the other hand, stemmed from the fact that they alone were literate, knew the content of the classical literature, and could exercise (though few did, of course, for other reasons) interpretative judgment. The Chinese reserved the classical education for the cultivation of succeeding generations of elites and thereby preserved the clear boundary lines of the political system and created a self-conscious, identifiable leadership. The extent to which the elite reproduced itself may be seen from the fact that more than 80 per cent of the official elite was drawn from existing gentry families in the nineteenth century.[16] What the socio-political order could not have withstood was a large literate base outside the elite, and one of the probable reasons for the failure to reestablish central authority after the downfall of the Ch'ing was the rapid expansion of the number of scholars (particularly in missionary schools) who could not be effectively employed at the same time that secret societies and other local institutions attained a competitive position to recruit leadership. Uncontrolled learning proliferated potential leaders outside official regulation. These "leaders" found positions in regional and local organizations and dramatically contributed to the power of local rulers.

The demand for Western learning that accompanied the Western thrust into China was a threat, then, of many dimensions. Western scientific standards challenged the internalized standards of achievement in the family and the ancient learning at the same time that it and Christianity undermined the validity of the common ethical pattern.[17] One catastrophic result of this Western challenge was the

[16] Marsh, *The Mandarins*, p. 82.

[17] For a discussion of the encounter of Chinese and Western systems of thought, see Levenson, *op.cit.*

elimination of the examination system in 1905. When coupled with the progressive disintegration of the family and lineage, the elimination of the institution of examinations destroyed the official foundation of the bureaucratic ethic and the delicate balance of "qualified" officials and those "preparing for qualification" within the polity. Without the examinations, who was to say which educated man was qualified? Western education was politically destructive in that it failed to maintain the sense of unity which helped bind the society and polity or develop the standards for national leadership. From 1905 until the establishment of the Chinese People's Republic in 1949, the Chinese sought to create indigenous educational institutions which might cultivate a competent modern elite and reunite the society and polity.

The Search for a New Educational System, 1911-1949

The establishment of the first modern government school, the T'ung-wen Kuan, in 1862, initiated a period of intensive reappraisal of Chinese education.[18] This reappraisal, which has usually been attributed to China's reaction to Western penetration, culminated in the creation of a comprehensive school system in 1902-1903, and a Ministry of Learning in 1906.[19] The 1903 system envisaged a multi-stage training program which was to last twenty-one years. Although political factions obstructed the implementation of this program, official concern for a new educational pattern survived the chaotic transitional years leading up to and immediately following the 1911 Revolution. The pre-1911 emphasis of education to "save China" remained central in Chinese thought, moreover, and the intensity of the search for model educational programs and reforms after 1911 reflected the mounting political disintegration.

This search ended temporarily in 1922. The so-called *jen-hsü* reorganization of that year provided for six years of elementary school, three years of junior middle school, three years of senior middle school, and four years of college or university. The political tone of the new system is suggested by these official criteria: "(1) satisfaction of the needs of community progress; (2) promotion of the spirit of civilian education; (3) promotion of individualism; (4) attention to the potentiality of the national economy; (5) empha-

[18] Biggerstaff, *op.cit.*, pp. 94-153.
[19] J. Chester Cheng, *Basic Principles Underlying the Chinese Communist Approach to Education*, Washington, Office of Education, 1961, pp. 16-17.

sis on 'education for living'; (6) popularization of education; and (7) adaptability to local conditions."[20] Thus conceived, the *jen-hsü* system, which laid the basis for achievement-oriented education discussed below, persisted for the next quarter century and in 1949 became the foundation of the Chinese Communist educational structure.

Despite the flamboyant inaugural, however, the new educational institutions floundered in the years of near anarchy and failed to bind the new intellectuals to a common political platform. After the death of Sun Yat-sen in 1925, the Kuomintang (Nationalist Party) under Chiang Kai-shek injected additional political content into the curriculum within the general framework of Sun's Three People's Principles (nationalism, democracy, and people's livelihood). Social order, national pride, and guided training on behalf of China became the dominant political themes in education, while the courses in the curriculum stressed science, economics, and engineering. The Nationalists also increasingly paid lip service to traditional Confucian values and, in 1934, launched a rather ineffective movement (New Life Movement) to instill the ancient virtues of loyalty and filial piety. In the politically competitive atmosphere, the Nationalists failed to attract the support of large numbers of youths and intellectuals, and, after the collapse of the abortive united front of 1937, "education" became a race between the Nationalists and Communists for the minds of the young intellectuals.[21]

The Basic Principles of Chinese Communist Education

The Chinese Communist Party seized power in 1949, armed with a comprehensive program for "a new society and a new state."[22] The "people"[23] of the new state could "educate and remould themselves by democratic methods on a national and all-round scale" in order to eliminate reactionary influences and evil vestiges and to "continue to

[20] Chiao-yü pu (Ministry of Education), ed., *Ti-i tz'u Chung-kuo chiao-yü nien-k'an* (First Yearbook of Chinese Education), Shanghai, 1934, Vol. I, p. 3.

[21] See Mao Tse-tung, *The Orientation of the Youth Movement* [May 4, 1939], Peking, Foreign Languages Press, 1960.

[22] The Common Program of the Chinese People's Political Consultative Conference, September 29, 1949, preamble. Text in *The Important Documents of the First Plenary Session of the Chinese People's Political Consultative Conference*, Peking, Foreign Languages Press, 1949, pp. 1-20.

[23] By "people," the Chinese Communists mean "the working class, the peasantry, the petty bourgeoisie and the national bourgeoisie. . . ." See Mao Tse-tung, *On People's Democratic Dictatorship* [June 30, 1949], Peking, Foreign Languages Press, 1959, pp. 11-12.

advance and make progress towards a socialist and communist society."[24] Mao Tse-tung, chairman of the party and state apparatus, simultaneously called on the Chinese to learn from all who "know the ropes" and to "overcome difficulties and learn the things we do not know." Under Mao's direction, Communist leaders placed education in a central role for the formation of the transitional society and state.

The essence of the 1949 educational proposals was summarized in the Common Program of the Chinese People's Political Consultative Conference, which called for cultural and educational work to "train personnel for national construction work, liquidate feudal, compradore and fascist ideology, and develop the ideology of serving the people" (Art. 41). Articles 46 and 47 of the Common Program added the important stipulation that the proposed educational system would unify "theory and practice" and systematically form the educational process into a planned, comprehensive instrument. The universal education promised in the Common Program was reaffirmed as a right of all citizens in the 1954 Constitution of the Chinese People's Republic (Art. 94).[25]

Although the Communists have thus far failed to replace the 1922 school system, they have made impressive strides in developing a new educational doctrine. "Our educational policy," Mao said in 1957, "must enable everyone who gets an education to develop morally, intellectually and physically and become a cultured, socialist-minded worker."[26] In this key passage, Mao also directed "all departments and organizations concerned . . . especially heads of educational institutions and teachers" to "spread the idea of building our country through hard work and thrift."

The Communist reasoning here is elementary: the leadership must consciously create the new state; political and economic "construction" require hard work; the central task of education therefore is to teach people to work hard for socialist construction. Following this "logic," the Chinese Communists have consistently given priority to labor as an integral aspect of learning. In the Communist view, the traditional scorn for manual work presents one fundamental barrier

---

[24] *Ibid.*, p. 13.

[25] Text in *Documents of the First Session of the First National People's Congress of the People's Republic of China*, Peking, Foreign Languages Press, 1955, pp. 131-163.

[26] Mao Tse-tung, *On the Correct Handling of Contradictions Among the People* [February 27, 1957], Peking, Foreign Languages Press, 1958, p. 44.

to a "strong and prosperous [China] within a period of several decades."[27] The Marxist-Leninist rationale behind this view relates work to the adoption of the new, prescribed political habits and values. "Work is struggle";[28] education is a form of struggle;[29] therefore work and education are part of the same process to remake China. Participating in hard work will cause a "cultural revolution," and, according to China's leading spokesman on education, Lu Ting-yi, "cultural revolution means that the masses of workers and peasants become well educated and the intellectuals become identical with the working people."[30] The work ethic thus replaces the Confucian ethic as the great unifier. Progressively "higher" knowledge occurs within the new unity, however, and, as will be seen below, presumably thrusts advanced "activist" and cadre elements into contention for membership in the leadership elite.

Marxist-Leninist epistemological theory also binds education to the leadership of the Chinese Communist Party.[31] In brief, the Communists define "knowing" as a process which integrates both theory and practice and the objective and the subjective. The accumulative acquisition of knowledge proceeds according to pre-set standards of correctness and actively involves the person who aspires to "know" in guided practice. The first stage of this process trains the adherent to follow interrelated steps of "perception,"[32] "conception," and "verification," which lead him to new dimensions of moral[33] choices and increasing commitment. The second general stage presages a "higher" form of understanding based on the "proper" recognition of the integrating function of "contradictions" in "objective reality." This recognition is possible only in the performance of revolutionary tasks which are determined and judged by the party elite. Although one may wish to ask how the Communist "vanguard" was chosen in the first place, such questions are now deemed irrelevant. What is rele-

[27] *Ibid.*
[28] Mao Tse-tung, *Selected Works*, Peking, Foreign Languages Press, 1961, Vol. IV, p. 58.
[29] Liu Shao-ch'i, *On Inner-Party Struggle* [July 2, 1941], Peking, Foreign Languages Press, n.d., p. 29.
[30] Lu Ting-yi, "Message of Greetings," in *The National Conference of Outstanding Groups and Individuals in Socialist Construction in Education, Culture, Health, Physical Culture and Journalism (Important Documents)*, Peking, Foreign Languages Press, 1960, p. 6.
[31] For a typical article, see *Jen-min jih-pao* (People's Daily), June 2, 1961. See also, John W. Lewis, *Leadership in Communist China*, Ithaca, Cornell University Press, 1963, Chap. II.
[32] See *Jen-min jih-pao*, November 1, 1961.
[33] See *Kuang-ming jih-pao* (Bright Daily), December 6, 1961.

vant flows from the second-stage guidance of the trainee along a path of perpetual tension[34] and struggle. This struggle theoretically re-creates the personality of the individual and prepares him for elite membership. Generally speaking, the first stage knowledge is correct knowledge and applies to all Chinese. When learned in the process of guided work, this knowledge produces a unifying consensus in China. The second stage knowledge, on the other hand, is "socialist" knowledge, which guides the lower stage of knowing. The acquisition of "socialist" knowledge equates struggle to education and teaching to party direction. Those who have socialist knowledge qualify for the political elite.

As sloganized by Lu Ting-yi in 1958, "the educational policy of the Chinese Communist Party has always been that education should serve the politics of the working class and be combined with productive labour."[35] In the Communist interpretation, this policy integrates epistemology, political development, and party-directed education. "Socialist education is inconceivable without Communist Party leadership," Lu said. "Socialist education is one of the powerful weapons for transforming the old and building the new society."[36] Education assists those "who promote . . . the development of the productive forces" against those who impede it; education combining theory with productive labor fosters "fully developed" individuals. At the stage of "socialist" knowledge, these individuals become generalists, versatile in production, experienced in administration, skilled in a specialization, and distinguished by political study. According to Liu Shao-ch'i's famous 1957 injunction, "all must strive to make themselves 'red and expert' specialists."[37] When the momentum of revolutionary struggle waned in the years after 1959, a readjustment in the scope of "socialist" knowledge thus became inevitable because of the fundamental role of that struggle in the educational process. As discussed below, in 1961, the Communists modified their program designed to cultivate "red and expert" generalists in favor of separate training programs for political cadres and technical specialists.

[34] Liu Shao-ch'i, "Report on the Work of the Central Committee," *Second Session of the Eighth National Congress of the Communist Party of China*, Peking, Foreign Languages Press, 1958, p. 44.

[35] Lu Ting-yi, *Education Must Be Combined with Productive Labour*, Peking, Foreign Languages Press, 1958, pp. 3-4.

[36] *Ibid.*, p. 3.

[37] *Lun yu hung yu chuan* (On Red and Expert), Peking, Chung-kuo ch'ing-nien ch'u-pan she, 1958, p. 3.

The Communist Chinese Educational System

A joint Communist Party and State Council directive of September 19, 1958 dictated the policies to implement these foregoing principles.[38] Coming during the "high tide" of socialist construction, this directive modeled education on the pattern of the Great Leap Forward: mass movements, emulation, total planning, unparalleled experimentation, and extraordinary claims of achievement. Thus conceived, education reached out beyond the formal school system to embrace virtually every Chinese in some form of organized study. In June 1960, the Minister of Education stated that in China "over 300,000,000 persons are studying in schools at all levels or in kindergartens."[39] Other millions, he said, "are making strenuous efforts at their study and are on their way to becoming masters of science and culture in our country."

Literacy drives were stepped up, and greater emphasis fell on mass techniques than on the former intensive methods, particularly the method of the "small group" meeting.[40] The fundamental educational principle combined "unity with diversity," a single doctrine taught in a variety of ways. Full-time,[41] part-work part-study,[42] and spare-time schools[43] proliferated. School administration became decentralized with particular stress placed on schools formed by factories, mines, communes, and military units. An earlier (1957) "curriculum in socialist education" for party cadres and university students[44] blended with technical, scientific, and Chinese and foreign language training.[45] Workers were directed to become teachers, and teachers,

[38] Text in *Jen-min jih-pao*, September 20, 1958.

[39] *Jen-min jih-pao*, June 15, 1960.

[40] Information derived from refugee interviews conducted by the author in Hong Kong, 1960-1961.

[41] See Leo A. Orleans, *Professional Manpower and Education in Communist China*, Washington, National Science Foundation, 1961; and Theodore Hsi-en Chen, *Teacher Training in Communist China*, Washington, Office of Education, 1960. On the 1960 educational reforms, see *Current Background*, No. 623, 1960, pp. 1-24; *Current Background*, No. 630, 1960, pp. 1-10; and Robert D. Barendsen, "The 1960 Educational Reforms," *China Quarterly*, No. 4, October-December 1960, pp. 55-65.

[42] See Robert D. Barendsen, "The Agricultural Middle School in Communist China," *China Quarterly*, No. 8, October-December 1961, pp. 106-134.

[43] See Munemitsu Abe, "Spare-time Education in Communist China," *China Quarterly*, No. 8, October-December 1961, pp. 149-159.

[44] *She-hui-chu-i chiao-yü k'o-ch'eng ti yüeh-tu wen-chien hui-pien* (Collected Readings and Documents for the Curriculum in Socialist Education), Peking, Jen-min ch'u-pan she, 1957-1958. For a discussion, see H. Arthur Steiner, "The Curriculum in Chinese Socialist Education: An Official Bibliography of 'Maoism,'" *Pacific Affairs*, Vol. XXXI, No. 3, September 1958, pp. 286-299.

[45] Orleans, *op.cit.*, app. B and C.

cadres, and other leading personnel were ordered to become students and workers.[46] From our perspective of "seeing" China through limited documents and scattered refugee reports, the Chinese society of 1958-1961 resembled a mammoth schoolroom under the tutelage of the Chinese Communist Party. Guided by the "mass line" in education, party committees encouraged maximum local initiative, and local bodies adopted the previously inner-party techniques of thought reform: "open and free airing of views," during which participants "inspect themselves, criticize themselves with self-awareness, affirm their own correct points, denounce their own incorrect points, analyze the sources of incorrectness, and develop ways to reform, criticize, and help each other."[47] The walls of Chinese towns and villages became classroom blackboards pasted with large-character posters (ta-tzu pao). The general population participated in unending meetings, self-study movements,[48] demonstrations, and work-plus-discussion sessions.

The 1958 changes emphasized certain basic themes long extant in the Chinese Communist approach to education.[49] Education had long been viewed as a political tool with "education for education's sake" belittled as a "bourgeois slogan." In 1934, Mao stated that education "aims to educate the broad working masses with the spirit of communism, to cause culture and education to serve the revolutionary war and the class struggle, to combine education and labor, and to turn the broad masses of Chinese into a people who enjoy civilization and happiness."[50] Mao's objectives have consistently been to create the general popular environment in which leadership not only would enjoy active, dedicated support but in which "advanced" personnel would also be continuously promoted.[51] For more than a generation, the creation of a vital, uniform, and national political "culture" has been a primary educational task,[52] the fulfillment of which would separate enemies from friends, backward from ad-

[46] Hsinhua News Agency Release, May 1957, item 051421, pp. 120-121.
[47] Jen-min jih-pao, August 17, 1961.
[48] For a typical article, see T'ien-feng (Heavenly Wind), No. 9, 1960, pp. 20-21.
[49] A collection of earlier essays and documents on Chinese Communist education is found in Michael Lindsay et al., Notes on Educational Problems in Communist China, New York, Institute of Pacific Relations, 1950.
[50] Quoted in Mao Tse-tung t'ung-chih lun chiao-yü kung-tso (Comrade Mao Tse-tung on Educational Work), Peking, Jen-min chiao-yü ch'u-pan she, 1958, p. 15.
[51] Mao, "On Methods of Leadership," Selected Works, London, Lawrence & Wishart, 1954-1956, Vol. IV, pp. 111-117.
[52] Mao, On New Democracy [January 1940], Peking, Foreign Languages Press, 1954, esp. pp. 18-27.

vanced, followers from leaders. Within the framework of Marxism-Leninism, the Chinese Communists have devised a "mass line" technique of leadership which simultaneously supplies the means to indoctrinate the Chinese people, isolate opponents, and recruit and train prospective elite members. Leading, educating, and becoming educated fuse into one process.

When speaking of education, the Chinese Communists divide the period from 1949 to 1958 into two stages. The first stage, 1949-1952, was dominated by internal rehabilitation, the Korean War, and the wide ranging reform movements against bureaucratic corruption and malpractice.[53] The second stage, 1952-1958, emphasized economic growth under the "general line of transition to socialism." In the first period, the Chinese made minimal changes, built schools, and investigated foreign (particularly Soviet) educational institutions as possible models for future reforms. At the first National Conference on Educational Work in December 1949, the then Vice Minister of Education, Ch'ien Chün-jui, singled out economic reconstruction as the central goal in educational work.[54] Attuned to this goal, the party gave priority to education for workers, soldiers, and peasants and to the reform of intellectuals, choosing to transform adult education and the composition of adult structures (including the elite itself) before tackling the formation of a new socio-political environment. The training of children received secondary emphasis.

The stress on reforming and restructuring (in class composition) cadres, teachers, university students, and officials intensified during the second phase. Although the basic directive for the new curriculum in 1951[55] contained some guarantees for general education, the institutional innovations were minimal. The basic structures continued to be those inherited from the Nationalists. Fundamental institutional changes did not occur until the second phase, and these changes stemmed directly from the movements to remold intellectuals. Utilizing the reform weapons fashioned in the party rectification movements, Communist cadres after 1952 rigorously instructed intellectuals in the acceptable patterns of thinking and acting under Communism. The cadres were urged to avoid stereotypes in reforming the intellectuals, and the inventory of ingenious and varied techniques was bolstered by the personalization of targets, by a new lan-

---

[53] See H. Arthur Steiner, *Chinese Communism in Action*, Los Angeles, mimeographed materials for U.C.L.A. Political Science 159, 1953, Pt. III, Chap. X.

[54] *Jen-min jih-pao*, January 6 and April 19, 1950.

[55] Text in *Jen-min jih-pao*, October 3, 1951.

guage, and by the disguising of inner-party rituals under such labels as "blooming and contending."[56] The coverage of intellectuals after 1952 gradually expanded to keep pace with the programs of agricultural collectivization and the socialization of industry and commerce.

Arguing in 1956 that the basic character of society had undergone a revolutionary transformation by the completion of the initial collectivization and socialization program, Mao Tse-tung then turned to the question of the relationship of this change in the "economic base" to the "political and cultural superstructure." The new preoccupation with superstructure directly shaped plans for China's intellectuals. At the January 1956 party Central Committee meeting on intellectuals, Chou En-lai stated that continued socialist construction demanded "the energetic labour not only of the working class and the broad masses of the peasants, but also of the intellectuals."[57] At every point in the superstructure, the intellectuals of China played a key role, Chou added, and their mobilization and use undergirded "the fundamental tasks of the transition period."

As the intellectuals of China moved through the "hundred flowers" and rectification periods over the next four years, one of their prescribed tasks became the reform of the educational structure and the basic curriculum from kindergarten through university. The consequent innovation and experimentation produced a series of conclusions which in 1960 formed the core of "a plan to carry out a reform program . . . step by step and phase by phase in our full-time middle and elementary schools in the next ten to twenty years."[58] This plan envisages scrapping the 1922 twelve-year system in favor of a nine- or ten-year program of study. Students would begin primary grades earlier, concentrate heavily throughout the ten years on language and mathematics, and complete first-year college courses by the end of the tenth year. Those not continuing in full-time university work[59] would study in spare-time higher schools. According to the proposal, academic standards would be raised and increased

[56] For a general discussion of the reform of intellectuals, see Theodore H. E. Chen, *Thought Reform of the Chinese Intellectuals*, Hong Kong, Hong Kong University Press, 1960.

[57] Chou En-lai, *Report on the Question of Intellectuals*, Peking, Foreign Languages Press, 1956, p. 5.

[58] Lu Ting-yi, "Our Schooling System Must Be Reformed," in *Current Background*, No. 623, 1960, p. 2.

[59] On higher education, see Joseph C. Kun, "Higher Education: Some Problems of Selection and Enrollment," *China Quarterly*, No. 8, October-December 1961, pp. 135-148.

attention would be paid to manual labor. The 1960 program restored the classroom focus to Chinese education.

The Communist goals for the gradual extension of universal primary education to universal education in the higher grades involve the party in a staggering undertaking. By reaching 300,000,000 in schools and anti-illiteracy classes, the party directly or indirectly guides and influences virtually every person in China. To handle this training enterprise the party works through 3,000,000 full-time and 10,000,000 amateur teachers.[60] Radio, television (including television schools), newspapers, and even telephones are employed in a systematic program of education and propaganda. Moreover, the schools constitute merely one arm of the institutional apparatus. Education embraces all organizational life in China, whether in the army, the family, the commune work teams, the state organs, or the factories. The model educational institution is the party branch, which operates to remold and educate the more than 17,000,000 party members.[61] In addition, the Communist leaders stress the unique role of the Young Communist League (YCL) in the education of Chinese youth. "Our Young Communist League has become an efficient subsidiary of the party," YCL leader Hu Yao-pang said in 1959, "and a core for drawing in and uniting all youth of China in the heroic struggle for socialism."[62] At age nine, children become eligible for membership in the YCL-supervised Young Pioneers, and at fourteen youngsters may apply for membership in the league. With 50,000,000 in the Young Pioneers and 25,000,000 in the league, a preliminary political screening occurs for the more than 193,000,000 (1958) young people within the ages of ten through twenty-four.[63] Thus slightly more than one out of three children merit and choose membership in party organizations by the age of twenty-five, and all who apply for party membership before the age of twenty-five must be league members.[64] "Political consciousness" and successfully

[60] *Jen-min jih-pao*, June 15, 1960. A general review of Chinese Communist propaganda techniques is found in Franklin W. Houn, *To Change a Nation; Propaganda and Indoctrination in Communist China*, New York, Free Press, 1961.

[61] *Peking Review*, No. 26-27, July 7, 1961, p. 10.

[62] *Jen-min jih-pao*, October 1, 1959

[63] Figures from *Current Background*, No. 600, 1959, pp. 8-13; *Survey of China Mainland Press*, No. 2511, 1961, p. 11; and John S. Aird, *The Size, Composition, and Growth of the Population of Mainland China*, Washington, Bureau of the Census, 1961, p. 82.

[64] Chu Yü-chin et al., *Ho ch'ing-nien t'an ju tang wen-t'i* (Talk with Youth concerning Problems of Entering the Party), Hankow, Chung-nan ch'ing-nien ch'u-pan she, 1952, pp. 32-33.

proved leadership abilities are central to this selection process which becomes determinant in later admission to the cadre hierarchy of the party elite.

Education and Political Development: A Study of Pre-School Training Programs

The central question of how the process of political development in China actually inter-operates with the forming social environment may take as its starting point the Chinese Communist concept of economic development which remains the principal goal of the political system. The "new battle" is against nature, Mao Tse-tung said in 1957. "Our basic task is no longer to set free the productive forces but to protect and expand them in the context of the new relations of production."[65] The current over-all framework for party policies is now the "general line of socialist construction," and the "basic significance of this general line," Liu Shao-ch'i said in 1961, "is to utilize to the maximum the enormous potentiality of the socialist system for developing the productive forces of society, to mobilize all the positive factors, to unite with all the forces that can be united with, to put into effect the series of policies of 'walking on two legs,' to develop our national economy in a planned and proportionate way and at high speed so that our country can change at a comparatively fast rate from a backward into an advanced country."[66] The vaunted "three red banners"—the general line, the big leap forward, and the people's communes—apply directly to economic development.

The conscious emphasis on economic change in China permits us to use two propositions concerning development which have been suggested by David McClelland's important study, *The Achieving Society*.[67] These two propositions concern change and achievement orientation and may be used to clarify the probable patterns of behavior of successful Chinese students. They are: first, in a society undergoing conscious, directed economic development, individual achievement will tend to be the predominant behavioral objective between the ages of five and eight; and, second, in a society which is likely to

[65] Mao, *On the Correct Handling*, pp. 27, 30.

[66] *Peking Review*, No. 26-27, July 7, 1961, p. 8.

[67] David C. McClelland, *The Achieving Society*, Princeton, D. Van Nostrand, 1961. See also David C. McClelland et al., *The Achievement Motive*, New York, Appleton-Century-Crofts, 1953; and John W. Atkinson, ed., *Motives in Fantasy, Action, and Society*, Princeton, D. Van Nostrand, 1958. I am indebted to Professor Arthur P. Wolf for his suggestions and criticism in the preparation of this section and to Mr. Kau Yin-maw for his research assistance.

succeed over the long run in attaining developmental goals, the educational programs will emphasize public opinion or "other directedness" rather than institutional norms.

On the basis of an examination of these propositions, we shall attempt to relate the results of pre-school behavior to current Communist problems in cadre leadership. Chinese Communist education in Kiangsu kindergartens was used as a model. This education, it will be seen, heavily accentuates individual, competitive achievement as defined by McClelland and, when combined with family and later school education, probably creates a set of attitudes and motivations which basically run counter to prescribed leadership techniques. Child education, in contrast to the education of political cadres, takes its cue primarily from the priorities of economic development rather than from the revolutionary political priorities. The question will be raised concerning the relevance of the revolutionary model for the coming generation of the elite.

The selection of data from teachers' manuals for Kiangsu kindergartens requires preliminary comment.[68] According to McClelland and others, child training data such as contained in the Kiangsu teaching materials hold a significant key to understanding economic development. Stories, songs, and games provide an important insight into achievement and other motivational variables critical to rapid development. "It may come as something of a shock," McClelland adds, "to realize that more could have been learned about the rate of future economic growth . . . by reading elementary school books than by studying such presumably more relevant matters as power politics, wars and depressions, economic statistics, or governmental policies."[69] In an earlier study, McClelland had also concluded that certain propensities concerning achievement motivation are developed before the eighth birthday and are scarcely affected by later adult education.[70]

Supporting evidence for the two propositions above is provided

[68] Chiang-su sheng chiao-yü t'ing (Kiangsu Provincial Education Office), ed., *Yu-erh-yüan yu-hsi chiao-ts'ai* (Teaching Materials for Kindergarten Games), Nanking, Kiangsu jen-min ch'u-pan she, 1956; and Chiang-su sheng chiao-yü ting, ed., *Yu-erh-yüan yü-yin chiao-ts'ai* (Oral Teaching Materials for Kindergartens), Nanking, Kiangsu jen-min ch'u-pan she, 1956. Kiangsu, a province on China's coast, straddles the Yangtze River and crowds over 45 million Chinese onto its fertile plain. Twenty-five per cent of Kiangsu Chinese live in towns and cities, exemplified by the great cities of Nanking (1.3 million) and Soochow (500,000). Kiangsu typifies the variety of China but possibly with a higher flavor of pre-1949 Western contacts.

[69] McClelland, *op.cit.*, 1961, p. 202.

[70] In Atkinson, *op.cit.*, pp. 319-320.

through an analysis of the following aspects of kindergarten training in Kiangsu: In each of the three kindergarten levels (age levels 3-4, 5-6, 6-7), 22 physical games are prescribed. Each of the total of 66 games was rated according to McClelland's scale of competitiveness and individuality, which in general measures the level of achievement-motivated behavior desired from the educational experience. Then, the stated objectives for these 66 physical games and for 91 educational play situations were enumerated and classified. The results of the ratings and classifications of games and play situations were also compared to 63 kindergarten story themes rated for achievement imagery, affiliation imagery, and power imagery and for their stress on public opinion ("other-directedness") and political emphasis.

ACHIEVEMENT[71]

The Kiangsu manuals reveal a highly sophisticated program of training conducive to individual achievement motivation. This program, which has apparently been in operation since the late Republican period,[72] can best be understood in the scope of this brief discussion by looking at a "typical" Kiangsu child. The traditional Chinese family provided a non-competitive, group-oriented environment based on compatible relationships.[73] Raised for his first three years in tradition-bound households, the Kiangsu child enters a kindergarten in which the teachers have the tasks of weaning him from dependence on his family and of cultivating the exercise of rudimentary "achievement" practices. Gradually, teachers stress games which are more competitive and individualist.[74] The trend away from non-

[71] McClelland defines "achievement motivation" as "competition with some standard of excellence" (in Atkinson, *op.cit.*, p. 181). In his 1961 book, McClelland enumerates some of the attributes of persons with high levels of achievement motivation. These include self-reliance, better memory, increased activism, eagerness to volunteer, more apt to "choose experts over friends as working partners," more likely to take moderate risks, and more likely to initiate action.

[72] Fourteen Chinese educated in the Republican period were interviewed to ascertain the extent to which achievement-based education prevailed in Nationalist China. The picture remains somewhat confused because of the variety of educational systems, but a clear emphasis on achievement was present. This would explain the otherwise early entrance of achievement-motivated Chinese into the Communist elite after 1949.

[73] See Atkinson, *op.cit.*, pp. 205-207.

[74] The Chinese emphasis on individualist, competitive sports such as track, swimming, gymnastics, and table tennis continues this pre-school training. See *Sport Flourishes in New China*, Peking, Foreign Languages Press, 1955. Group sports (soccer, ice hockey, and volley ball) are also popular in China, and some observers have noted an intensive group atmosphere in play. See Bernard Ullmann, "China's

competitive, group games reinforces the proliferation of individual skills learned in physical games and educational play.[75] The formation of the self-reliant child receives additional support in the last two years through high "achievement imagery" in stories, songs, and poems.

Kiangsu kindergarten training, moreover, constitutes a far more ambitious undertaking than the normal independence training often encountered in pre-school education. The inculcation of high levels of achievement motivation may be conceptualized from the Kiangsu materials as the teaching of self-reliant, competitive behavior.[76] The successful kindergarten pupil utilizes elementary standards of judgment which have become his "own" (even though they may have been induced by political cadres, as will be seen) rather than the impersonal prerogative of family, lineage, or traditional village institutions. An examination of the themes of the stories indicates that the most prevalent themes include socialism, conquest of nature, hard work, and science. These themes help to form a model for the child's "standards of excellence," and such standards, according to a parents' manual for Liaoning Province, also require dedicated cultivation by the family in order to provide a high level of character and knowledge required for the socialist and Communist enterprise.[77] Thus eventually the break with the family for the child entering pre-school should become progressively less severe. Parents are cautioned to be adept at developing their children's "independence, motivations, and activeness" as central elements of the new "character" which *must not be* "blindly following, nor submissive."[78] Later, as a primary and middle school student, the former kindergarten pupil

---

Grim Winter: A Reporter's Notebook," *New York Times Magazine*, February 19, 1961, p. 50. Also, the training books which the author has been able to locate all predate the communes. For McClelland on group play, see *op.cit.*, 1961, pp. 197-201, 400-401. The author is indebted to Professor John M. Roberts for his suggestions on the role of games in type cultures. See John M. Roberts and Brian Sutton-Smith, "Child Training and Game Involvement," *Ethnology*, Vol. I, No. 2, April 1962, pp. 166-185. An important Communist analysis of a sample of 81 games is in *Chung-kuo ch'ing-nien pao* (China Youth News), May 29, 1962, in *Survey of China Mainland Press* (hereafter cited as SCMP), No. 2765, 1962, pp. 12-14.

[75] Children in kindergarten learn to read and write and to solve simple arithmetic problems. See *Jen-min jih-pao*, June 7, 1960.

[76] McClelland, *op.cit.*, 1961, pp. 413-417.

[77] *Tsen-yang chiao-yü hai-tzu* (How to Teach Children), Shenyang, Liaoning jen-min ch'u-pan she, 1956, p. 1. More recent discussions which reemphasize the points in this manual are in *Kuang-ming jih-pao*, May 31, 1962, and *Jen-min jih-pao*, June 1, 1962.

[78] *Tsen-yang chiao-yü hai-tzu*, p. 4. See also *Jen-min jih-pao*, January 2, 1962.

will be cautioned not to be "satisfied with learning ready-made conclusions by rote in study."[79] As an intellectual, he will be told to "criticize and discuss" in "blooming and contending";[80] as a cadre, he will be swamped with demands in the party press that he "investigate and study" (*tiao-ch'a yen-chiu*) each question;[81] and as a Chinese, he will encounter daily the slogan of "toppling superstitions, emancipating the mind, promoting the communist style of thinking, speaking and acting boldly."[82]

Although McClelland's first proposition has not yet been proved in the Chinese Communist case, the evidence strongly suggests a preschool educational policy designed to foster skilled, self-motivated individuals. These individuals may have a strong commitment to Communist programs and goals but with an equally strong incentive to interpret and modify, to demand recognition and to create.[83] The new course of study aims to "educate children in accordance with their special characteristics."[84] Throughout the school system, the curriculum is overwhelmingly geared to the cultivation of advanced "intellectuals" in all fields but particularly in applied and technical science and mathematics. Although the Chinese Communists believe that children develop according to general laws ("children will only accept those measures which conform to the laws of the development of children"),[85] each child, teachers are now repeatedly reminded, presents a unique challenge. The approach to the Chinese people as "the masses" has been both a Chinese and a Communist failing in the past. Great pressures—which probably developed first in the Nationalist period—may be at work to replace that approach with a new, achievement-oriented, competitive, and individualist one.

PUBLIC OPINION

Although McClelland found in his 1961 study that in general nursery school experience only slightly affected achievement motivation in many cases, the limitation clearly did not apply to China: "On

[79] See, for example, *Chung-kuo ch'ing-nien* (China Youth), No. 10, 1961, in *Selections from China Mainland Magazines*, No. 273, 1961, pp. 36-38. *Jen-min jih-pao*, May 19, 1962, emphasizes the reading of novels, short stories, and biographies on heroes, science, and achievement for pre-adolescents.

[80] See *Peking Review*, No. 12, March 24, 1961, pp. 6-9.

[81] See Lewis, *op.cit.*, Chap. v.

[82] See *Ten Glorious Years*, Peking, Foreign Languages Press, 1960, p. 16.

[83] See Sidney H. Gould, ed., *Sciences in Communist China*, Washington, American Association for the Advancement of Science, 1961.

[84] *Jen-min jih-pao*, June 1, 1961.

[85] *Ibid.*

balance, exposure to partial educational influences which might increase . . . achievement [motivation] do not appear very effective when they are unsupported by 'ideological conversion' of the total group in which the experience occurs. . . . Attempts to introduce changes gradually or indirectly without strong ideological conviction and fervor may do more harm than good."[86] High intensity reform movements which create "a high level of aspiration set by people at the top" may provide the most effective arena in which to encourage "very high standards of achievement."[87] The previous sections have highlighted the Chinese Communist cultivation of such standards within the context of total ideological conversion.

According to McClelland's evidence, the creation of an arena conducive to high levels of achievement motivation partially corresponds to a shift in the social direction of the individual. In brief, a society which promotes high levels of achievement motivation must simultaneously foster public opinion or "other-directedness," a concept which McClelland borrows in modified form from David Riesman to describe a society which is "less 'fixed' and more open."[88] In most high achievement societies, individuals become more conscious of public opinion as a controlling factor in their lives than of impersonal, traditional institutions. McClelland views this emphasis on "other-directedness" in an achieving society as a probable prerequisite for social cohesion to offset higher levels of individuality and self-reliance. "Other-directedness" differs from the need for affiliation, then, because it represents a regulating social norm, not a basic, internalized motivation. Generally speaking, a society with a high level of affiliation motivation does not require a social norm to check and discipline autonomous individuals; a society with a high level of achievement motivation does need such a norm. The problem in research is to distinguish social norm from individual motivation, to assess—in this case indirectly through documents—the balance between the collective and the individual.

The evidence of "other-directedness" in Kiangsu kindergartens is inconclusive. Part of the problem involves the lack of a base-line to separate current levels of public opinion from village public opinion in the traditional society. Themes which unambiguously emphasize public opinion appear with a constant but low frequency in the

[86] McClelland, op.cit., 1961, pp. 416-417.
[87] Ibid., pp. 412-413.
[88] Ibid., pp. 192ff.

Kiangsu kindergarten stories, songs, and poems. A problem related to judging these themes, moreover, involves the Communist use of "collectivism." Collective opinion in Communist China usually means party opinion, and the party cadre has frequently attempted to mimic family patriarchs or village elders as the voice of "impersonal, institutional authority."

The current trend in education appears to be toward generalized norms and the personalized approval of one's group. In this respect, McClelland has found that group collectivity need not stifle individual achievement for "a man may get achievement satisfaction from having contributed to the success of a group enterprise, so long as it is he who made some of the decisions contributing to a successful outcome and he therefore has some way of telling how well he has done."[89] The Chinese Communist "mass line" of leadership, as I have attempted to demonstrate elsewhere, theoretically encourages individual initiative and responsibility within the confines of rigid general policy.[90] The individualist, competitive training in the Kiangsu kindergartens and throughout the lower school grades also emphasizes "love of Chairman Mao" as the representative of the Chinese people and seeks to harmonize the bold young individualist and the "collective spirit." Stories for Young Pioneers laud the child who puts his problems "before my schoolmates for discussion and asks them to give their opinions."[91] From the author's interviews in Hong Kong, however, as of early 1961 there still appeared to be a progressive loss of "group collectivity" in the course of the socialization experience and a substitution of the specific party cadre for the "general other." Although genuine public opinion may operate in the lower grades, all Chinese interviewed stated that the so-called "public" increasingly fronts for Communist orthodoxy in the higher school grades and pre-adult organizations. This apparent discrepancy, however, tends to support a major finding in the next section with respect to cadre leadership and elite socialization.

Elite Socialization and the Fate of Politics

Elite socialization in China essentially refers to the training of cadres. "Cadres" (*kan-pu*) are the leading officials at all levels within

---

[89] McClelland, *op.cit.*, 1961, pp. 230, 399-401.

[90] Lewis, *op.cit.*, Chap. III.

[91] Chang Tien-yi, *Stories of Chinese Young Pioneers*, Peking, Foreign Languages Press, 1954, p. 7. See also *Young Builders of China*, Peking, Foreign Languages Press, 1953; and *Kuang-ming jih-pao*, December 14-15, 1961.

party and non-party organizations, and the Chinese Communist Party has long given first priority to their training for leadership posts. In fact, the education of cadres appears to be intimately related to their initial selection, assignment, promotion, and dismissal, although we are only beginning to determine specific details.[92] In general, the Communists believe that cadres must be rigorously trained politically and ideologically and that training must keep pace with ever-widening cadre responsibilities. To free higher-level cadres for leadership tasks, greater emphasis has fallen on the education of the novice cadre in the hope that later "struggle" would nurture and test the techniques and skills implanted during the periods of intensive indoctrination. Cadres simultaneously study, participate in various movements, and maintain a rigid schedule of supervision, policy administration, and physical work. Newspapers, training manuals, and group sessions provide the substantive core of study and thought remolding, and the study results are incorporated in the cadre's permanent record. A tiny percentage of the cadres are regularly sent to specialized schools.

The proper cadre "style of work" acquired in this educational process is non-competitive, collectivist, and selfless. According to party Secretary-General Teng Hsiao-p'ing, "arrogance, arbitrariness, rashness and habits of pretending to be clever, of not consulting the masses, of forcing one's opinions on others, of persisting in errors to keep up one's prestige" oppose the correct style.[93] Rectification of cadre working style has dominated inner-party reform movements. Particularly in the 1942-1944 and 1957-1958 reform movements, the evils of "bureaucracy, sectarianism, and subjectivism" led the inventory of cadre sins, the central themes of which are independence and "individualism." In the party literature, "individualism" means the erroneous tendency to give priority to personal ambitions and relationships. According to Mao's description of the "mass line" method of leadership, cadre behavior must be "correctly" responsive to group pressures and to the cultivation of generalized relationships with the common people.[94] "All Communists and revolutionary cadres," *Red Flag* stated in 1961, "must treat others on an equal basis, consider themselves ordinary workers, share the joys and suffering with the

---

[92] This discussion on cadres is based on Lewis, *op.cit.*, Chap. v.

[93] Teng Hsiao-p'ing, "Report on the Revision of the Constitution," *Eighth National Congress of the Communist Party of China*, Peking, Foreign Languages Press, 1956, Vol. I, p. 179.

[94] Mao Tse-tung, "On Methods of Leadership," *passim.*

masses, be closely concerned with the interests of the masses, and mingle with the masses."[95]

Style theoretically reflects the political consciousness of the cadre, and political consciousness takes priority in the evaluation of cadres. Party manuals make the point that cadres generally are "recruited from within the masses" while higher or party cadres come from the rank and file of the Chinese Communist Party. Only the thin thread of political consciousness theoretically separates the cadre from ordinary Chinese: "A cadre is not a permanent profession; nor is he a special class."[96] Cadres must continually develop and advance their consciousness in order to merit retention or promotion.

Mao's revolutionary model of elite socialization neatly fuses political study and actual production experience in order to prepare party recruits for advanced leadership posts. A brief glance at the recent history of this socialization process, however, reveals a striking difference between this process and the general education of children and youth. In contrast to general education, which has been conceived as a continuous, accumulative process reaching back to kindergarten, political socialization for the elite has comprised a program of *re*-education. Increasingly since 1958, the Chinese Communist Party leaders reveal that they do not trust the political indoctrination and evaluation performed by schools and by the youth organizations set up for those purposes. Rectification since 1957 has emphasized the serious deficiencies of the newer cadres and party members entering the ranks of the elite—those members, that is, who have had the longest period of formal Communist-directed education. Eight out of the last twelve 1961 issues of the Central Committee journal, *Red Flag*, carried at least one major article on the Communist style of work, with frequent references to "some cadres" who "lack experience and . . . have not yet had systematic Marxist-Leninist education."[97] An increasing proportion of the more than 17,000,000 party members (more than 80 per cent joined after 1949) have known only Communist education, but with each wave of new young members has come an even greater stress on reform and re-education.

More is at stake here than simply discontinuity in political sociali-

[95] *Hung-ch'i*, No. 13, July 1, 1961, p. 17.

[96] Chinese Communist Party, Central Committee, Research Office of the Organization Department, ed., *Tang ti tsu-chih kung-tso wen-ta* (Questions and Answers on Party Organization Work), Peking, Jen-min ch'u-pan she, 1959, translated in *U.S. Joint Publications Research Service*, No. 7273, 1961, p. 29.

[97] *Hung-ch'i*, No. 13, July 1, 1961, p. 9.

zation. Thoroughly trained in the Communist-run schools, the youth of China most qualified for advanced positions may be the least attracted to Communist ideology. Youth with high levels of achievement motivation more naturally adopt a pattern of behavior which is self-confident and self-reliant. A generation of these youth trained in the late Kuomintang period and throughout the Communist years probably began to enter the vast complex of organizations soon after the Communist take-over in 1949. Although political activity and party membership led to the ladder of success, Chinese youth on the rungs of that ladder did not adopt the mass line style of behavior. "Political excellence" could, of course, be adopted by youth with high achievement motivation as their standard of excellence, but the Communist formulation of political style apparently discouraged such a development in China. Self-confident, competitive, achievement-motivated youth could not be expected to adopt—except as a masquerade—a self-abnegating, non-competitive, affiliative style, but the official endorsement of that style undermined the emergence of an operative "public opinion" as postulated by McClelland for an "achieving society."

For these and other reasons the revolutionary heritage has become a mere schoolbook legend for China's new youth whose motivational preferences now sharply vary from the mass line techniques and style. In February 1957, Mao Tse-tung reported "a falling off recently in ideological and political work among students and intellectuals."[98] Referring to this speech three months later, Hu Yao-pang stated that "a trend has begun to gain ground among some of our youths where emphasis is laid on professional pursuits at the expense of political studies."[99] One reason for this trend, Hu stated, was that "youths now around twenty . . . have not had much of the dark life of the old society and have never participated in the gruelling class struggle." As a result, youths had shown an increased concern with "name, position, and material compensation." At the Eighth Party Congress a year earlier, Teng Hsiao-p'ing noted this concern in the party when he said: "(I)t is easy to find people who have joined the Party for the sake of prestige and position."[100]

In 1957-1958, Communist leaders reacted to these developments by launching mass rectification and educational movements under the

[98] Mao, *On the Correct Handling,* p. 43.
[99] *Jen-min jih-pao*, May 16, 1957.
[100] Teng, *op.cit.*, p. 209.

slogan "politics in command." The party required all political and technical personnel to become "red and expert" and apparently expected achievement-motivated youth to adopt a mass line style and politically oriented personnel to become achievement motivated by an act of will and by dedicated struggle in mass movements. These expectations partially explain the 1958 emphases in education. The new emphases dramatized the emotional response of the party elite to the fact that the Maoist style of operation developed in the life-and-death struggle of civil war had lost its immediate relevancy and appeal in the upsurge of economic development. Party directives gave political education a decisive role, therefore, to hold the revolutionary line. Cadres without political "talents" were repudiated as "rightists" and reactionaries with the reasoning that "the greater their 'talent' is, the more detrimental they will be to the revolutionary enterprise."[101] The entire cadre structure was reorganized by the technique of *hsia-fang* under which many cadres were demoted and all cadres regularly worked in factories or communes. Universities were also periodically emptied by sending students to work in production in order to steel them in the "great furnace of labor." Throughout the following years, the party leadership held divergent tendencies in check by an increased emphasis on discipline and organizational constraints.

Political education, mass mobilization, and imposed discipline failed, however, to solve the deepening crises of the "period of the great leap forward," and in 1961 a marked shift occurred in the "red and expert" focus of education. An increased stress on the basic technical subjects and on the vital role of subject-matter instruction in the schools first signalled the changes ahead.[102] The fundamental modification of the original 1957 conception of "red and expert"—the training of each cadre to be an advanced technician and political specialist—officially came on August 10, 1961, in a speech delivered by Vice-Premier Ch'en Yi to the graduates of higher institutes of learning in Peking.[103] In the first section of his speech, Ch'en discussed

---

[101] Chinese Communist Party, *op.cit.*, p. 40.

[102] See, for example, *Kuang-ming jih-pao*, April 7, 1961. For an official appraisal of the new emphasis in teaching, see *Hung-ch'i*, No. 17, September 1, 1961, pp. 25-29; *ibid.*, No. 20, October 16, 1961, pp. 33-35; *ibid.*, No. 21-22, November 10, 1961, pp. 48-51; and *ibid.*, No. 23, December 1, 1961, pp. 24-26.

[103] *Chung-kuo ch'ing-nien*, No. 17, September 1, 1961, pp. 2-5. As an indication of the importance of this speech, it is the only document directly on education reprinted in *Jen-min shou-ts'e* (People's Handbook), Peking, Ta-kung pao she, 1061, pp. 219-321. For a more recent discussion of "red and expert," see *Kuang-ming jih-pao*, June 12, 13, and 14, 1962.

the problem of being red or specialized. Since most of the "masses of the youth" now support the Communist Party and socialism, he said, the present need is to emphasize special training. It would still be necessary to study party documents and participate in some party and league activities, but "it is both unrealistic and unnecessary that one should be at once a technical specialist and a political specialist." A person's political consciousness should not be judged by his political activity, Ch'en continued, and people who "can accomplish things within their own fields and contribute to our socialist construction . . . should not be criticized even if they do not participate in a great deal of political activity."

One likely reason for this dramatic reversal of the 1957 "red and expert" line may be purely practical. Technical specialists offer the Communists their only reservoir of talent capable of meeting the objectives and demands of modern economic management, and the current economic crisis may have become too severe to permit political study by these specialists. However, this probably tells only part of the story. The separation of political and technical specialists still leaves the problem of what to do with the political cadres. Ch'en's solution assumes that youth with high achievement motivation will no longer seek party membership and cadre status and will be content to remain mere technicians under the political control of non-technical cadres. High achievement motivation may not be so easily compartmentalized, however, and the attraction of cadre positions in factories and communes may be difficult to confine to men trained in political techniques alone. Ch'en also stated that political specialization requires even more intensive "thought construction" for cadres. Presumably technicians who are now party members or cadres will require increased ideological education to retain their leadership posts.[104] For political recruits, party leaders have demanded more intensive indoctrination and more rigid adherence to the revolutionary mass line doctrine. Furthermore, Ch'en Yi indicated that se-

---

[104] *Chung-kuo ch'ing-nien pao*, June 30, 1962, in *SCMP*, No. 2,782, 1962, pp. 7-10, makes this point and derives the obvious conclusion that even greater stress must be placed on political training for party applicants. After this paper was written, the increased stress on mass line procedures and ideological training for political cadres culminated in the re-publication in the August 1, 1962 issues of *Red Flag* and *People's Daily* of Liu Shao-ch'i's 1939 *How To Be a Good Communist*. In 1963 and 1964 party leaders vacillated sharply on the "red and expert" policy. Apparently the Chinese were unable to abandon completely the hope of creating the generalist cadre or were unable to prevent young technicians from entering the party and undermining party values.

lection for the elite no longer depends on class background and admitted that "many leaders in our party Central Committee came from the upper and middle classes." All are regarded as "children of the party" more or less equally capable of becoming leaders of the new China. One by one class background, technical qualification, and political education in the lower school grades have been deleted as prerequisites for the cultivation of the Chinese Communist leadership elite.

Conclusion

Although comparisons of Ch'ing and Communist institutions and issues involve a level of generalization that must be highly qualified in application, these generalizations clarify crucial distinctions that would otherwise remain hopelessly muddled in the rapidly changing Chinese environment. This study has suggested a possible hypothesis to explain the role of general and elite education in Chinese political development. The hypothesis has yet to be proved, but the trend in Communist China appears to be toward an over-all system of socialization that is practically the reverse of the Ch'ing system. In the Ch'ing model, a group-centered, personalized, non-competitive social base underlay the individuated, impersonal, competitive political structure. The Communist model, on the other hand, may have fostered a competitive, individualist, self-reliant social structure as distinguished from a group-oriented elite drawing its norms from the mass line and from the principles of collective leadership and democratic centralism. Both the Ch'ing and Communist systems attempted to resolve the conflict of styles by intensive re-education and the imposition of external discipline. Both met crises by reappraisals of the educational process, and both retained as a fundamental premise the notion that "leaders" must be selected on the basis of their unique knowledge. When the clear standards for such knowledge deteriorated, the possibility that a competitive elite would emerge to threaten the Ch'ing officials and the cadres provoked a wave of ineffective stop-gap measures and contradictory policy shifts.

The answers to many questions raised in the discussion can only be conjectural. For example, it is probable that the elite will not be able to divert individuals with high achievement aspiration into subordinate technical posts supervised by technically unqualified political cadres without causing increasing dissatisfaction. The high "achievers" will probably be motivated at an early age to join party-sponsored youth organizations simply to get ahead. The symbols of activism—particularly the language and formal participation—are easily acquired when implanted from childhood. The two brightest refugee university students whom the author interviewed in Hong Kong were also the most thoroughly versed in Marxism-Leninism. At the same time, they could be surprisingly detached. They confirmed Mao Tse-tung's 1957 inference that many intelligent students find Communist politics trivial and boring.

Political socialization in Communist China thus stands at a crossroads. At this crossroads are fewer than four million party members and cadres steeled by war and revolution in the mass line style. They now face the passing relevancy of the militant revolutionary. This rapidly aging elite must now transfer power to a new generation trained to value science, technique, and individual contribution. Rudely shaken by three successive years of economic failure, the party leaders have attempted to maintain their self-confident ability to assess crises and impose tactical adjustments. One crucial adjustment may have been signalled by Ch'en Yi in August 1961. By establishing a clear line between child training practices and elite socialization, the Communists apparently expect to pass on intact their revolutionary values, their operational style, and their political priorities.

By acclaiming the "red and expert" man as their ideal heir until late 1961, however, party leaders fostered among their actual heirs a code of conduct derived more in keeping with the economic expert than the political revolutionary. Those technical specialists who are now formally deprived of access to the leadership elite, moreover, came to expect political posts and acquired a knowledge of political styles. The outcome of the tensions between achievement and massline styles will depend on how the current leadership views the importance of political purity and on the timing of its perception of the underlying developments which it may not now see. The potential for change is extremely high. Should the party elite perceive in that change a threat to all they have fought for during the past forty years, a wave of imposed discipline and more drastic educational changes might occur. On the other hand, the economic crisis might prove to be too serious to permit further controls on key technicians. Either way, we may be witnessing the end of revolutionary mass line leadership in China.

CHAPTER 13

EDUCATION OF MILITARY LEADERSHIP IN EMERGENT STATES

WILLIAM F. GUTTERIDGE, M.B.E., M.A.

I. Introduction

THAT there is often a connection between the composition and outlook of the military leadership and the course of political evolution in developing countries is now self-evident. Pakistan, the Sudan, Iraq, Egypt, and Indonesia, among other newly emerged states, all, in different ways, display the signs and effects of this relationship. Though a pattern is not easily discerned and any attempt at exact quantitative assessment of results is clearly impracticable, it is a reasonable assumption that the method and content of the education enjoyed by the officer corps in such territories have a bearing on their outlook and therefore some effect on political activities. It is the purpose of this chapter to attempt a description of the main educational systems which have been adopted and to discuss their implications. Reference is made to as wide a range of territories as possible, with armed forces and officer corps at different stages of development. A detailed examination, however, is attempted only of the position in the states of Commonwealth Africa. This is a group of countries, not all of them as yet completely independent, in which the military elite is still for the most part in its formative period. They have also shared in a common military tradition.

A number of factors must be borne in mind in an assessment of the influence of the education and training of officers on both their professional and political behavior. In the first place, education has to be regarded as an integral part of the social background. The extent to which formal education in schools and colleges tends to conflict in its character-building role with informal education resulting from life in the family, clan, or tribe cannot be disregarded and is, in fact, especially important when considered in relation to the long overseas courses in Britain, or elsewhere, which constitute the most significant aspect of officer training in some territories. In fact, success in transplanting and instilling an essentially alien professional tradition may depend upon the extent of this conflict.

Though access to educational opportunities is rapidly improving throughout the developing areas, economic factors, or, more simply, the capacity to pay school fees, are likely to have a profound influence on selection for officer training and on the subsequent ability fully to benefit from it. The general assumption that an officer requires as a minimum some sort of secondary or high school education puts a premium on its provision in all the many areas where such education is still in short supply. However democratic a state's intentions may be, its choice of army officers is likely to be to some extent predetermined by the efficiency of educational provision and the financial resources of family groups.

It is virtually unknown for new states entirely to eschew foreign aid for military training and development. In the first place, unless they have completely destroyed all formal ties with their former imperial rulers, they are likely to have inherited not only the form of a military administrative system, but some of the associated traditions and a training scheme which will remain largely unamended for some time. Thus, for the time being, the outlook of the military leadership in a new state, and its strength, is likely to depend on the nature of the colonial policy which resulted in the birth of that state, and, therefore, of its national army.

The frequency with which military coups are reported must not be taken as an indication that politically conscious and active armies are inevitable in new states. Nor is it simply as a force for change or alternatively for preservation of the constitutional status quo that the political contribution of an army may be made. In various ways, armed forces may become instruments for the achievement of national unity. The army itself may become a means of spreading education, especially technical training, and individual officers may emerge as diplomats and administrators. In order to understand the influence of officer education on the political role of armies and on politics generally in new states, it is essential first to appreciate the fact that nationalism in new states puts in a new light all national institutions, including the armed forces.

II. Armed Forces in New States

It is certainly true that, with the decline of the former imperial powers, the areas of potential instability in the world have been considerably extended. There are, in the main, two ways in which this potentiality can become a reality. Either internal order can break down for political reasons or because of an inherent fissiparous tendency, or new states may fight among themselves for reasons of rivalry or because of territorial claims or to divert attention from domestic difficulties. In any case, in present conditions of East-West rivalry, chaos capable of exploitation by external forces may be created, and it is here that effective, responsibly led security organizations become a prime requisite. There is, therefore, not anything necessarily disquieting or undesirable in the build-up of national defense forces after independence on the basis of the often exiguous organization left behind by the colonial power. New states may not be able to influence the major decisions of the great powers, but they expect to be influential in their own continents, and their effectiveness is likely to depend in the end on the size and efficiency of their security forces.

It is not surprising that no newly independent state has elected to dispense entirely with an army. The possibility of substituting a mobile body of armed police has been considered in some cases—in Tanganyika, for instance, and in Sierra Leone. But in each case the decision has been in favor of the retention of the conventional body, because armed forces are regarded as part of the essential equipment of a new state without which complete independence will not be seen to have been achieved. They are thus symbols of national prestige and of the need for a new state to assert its position in the world. It is likely that they will continue to perform their normal and accustomed duties without taking into account the full implications of independence.

Very few nationalist leaders have given evidence of serious constructive thought about the structure of armed forces in their countries until complete freedom was imminent. The provision and education of indigenous officer corps has been Western-oriented, following the pattern set by colonial administrations. Chief Obafemi Awolowo, who in his autobiography[1] gives his reasons why the Nigerian forces should not be expanded, and Julius Nyerere, who had shown a keen personal interest in the Tanganyika units of the King's African Rifles even before he had a proprietary interest in them, are rare exceptions to the rule of nationalist indifference, preoccupation, or apathy (the appropriate term varies from territory to territory). Thus not only have the armies of the successor states taken over from the colonial defense forces, but they are, in fact, largely the same armies: and,

---

[1] "Awo," London, Cambridge University Press, 1960, p. 307.

with the exception of specific Cold War treaty commitments which would destroy the image of neutralism, they have the same responsibilities.

Internal security and frontier defense are the main tasks of all armies: this is no less true at the moment of independence than at other times. An effective police force equipped with modern infantry weapons and organized in mobile columns, such as has been developed in British territories in Africa, of which Kenya and Northern Rhodesia are prime examples, does, however, mean that the army will not generally have to be employed on large-scale operations, short of a major emergency. Only if routine police measures are inadequate will the army be required to deliver the sudden and heavy shock necessary to restore order. In this way a differentiation between the army and the police by function is easily maintained and this can be an important political factor. It is worth noting here that of the Commonwealth territories in Africa and Asia, only in Southern Rhodesia is it customary to employ police and army similarly and simultaneously in times of civil order and that territory the police force is not only regarded as the senior service, but some of the army's senior officers originally served in it.

Frontier patrol and defense constitutes the main role of an army apart from the maintenance of internal order, with which it is often closely linked. Most countries have at least one uneasy frontier; Thailand, Burma, India, Persia, Somalia, and Nigeria all provide good examples. The longer the frontier, the greater the premium on mobility; though an armored car squadron may be effective, the need for mobility often combines with prestige to encourage the establishment of an air arm, which in a large country like Nigeria may also be desirable for communication purposes. There remain the comparatively rare cases where there is a long-term plan for deliberate aggression against immediate neighbors or for participation in international military adventures farther afield. Clearly countries which were really interested in the establishment of, for instance, an African High Command for the purpose of conducting actual operations against what they regard as the last outposts of colonialism would require armies of a somewhat different nature from those which they at present possess.

It is, therefore, appropriate to ask what sort of armies are likely to emerge in the new states of Asia and Africa and where they will stand in relation to the civil power, for this is the precise field in which the education of the officers could have its greatest impact. The Western democracies, for reasons of history and tradition, are generally suspicious of any development that tends to bring together the civil and military departments of state. They regard this as the ultimate calamity and Latin America has for long been in their eyes the proof of the veracity of their view. In Central and South America armies appear to have existed primarily to make and break governments and indeed to attempt to govern. Having been in many cases the instruments of independence, they have become the agents of oppression. The question is whether in the new countries, where the educated elite is small and forms a tightly knit social group, parallel dangers can be avoided.

The composition and education of the officer corps can affect the stability of a state, whether old or new, in one of two opposing ways. It is primarily this body of men which will determine whether the army is a unifying and stabilizing element in society or a factor tending to cause chaos and disintegration. The Congo, where there were no indigenous officers at the moment of independence, provides the classic extreme example of the latter. Inherent ethnic or religious divisions, as in Burma in relation to the Shan minority, in the Sudan as between north and south, and in West Africa as between the Moslem hinterland and the coastal region could provide the circumstances of disruption. Inter-regional antagonism may be generated by a lack of ethnic balance among officers. This in its turn might be due to the political prejudices of the government but it also can arise from an uneven distribution of opportunities for education within a large and varied country—for example, Nigeria—and thus seem to be directly attributable to the standard of education expected of potential officers accepted for training.

But there is the other side of the coin. The mere existence of a well-disciplined force, in which individuals from all corners of a country serve, tends to consolidate national unity. Narrow local loyalties are weakened and allegiance to the larger entity is encouraged. The citizen army has not had much opportunity, except in major wars, to show its value outside Switzerland, but Israel has given the concept a new sense of direction. In this small dynamic state the army has become not only a means of fusing Jews from North Africa, Eastern Europe, and America into one nation, but a chosen educational instrument. Here the officers are responsible virtually for a school for citizenship on a large scale, inculcating civic duties and a pioneering spirit, as well as teaching Hebrew to new immigrants. The army is literally an extension of the educational system; it publishes its own journals and textbooks and runs its own radio station, in addition to providing more conventional opportunities for vocational training. The object is to create a modern state by emphasizing peaceful service to the community while at the same time encouraging nationalist sentiment.

The unique circumstances of the emergence of Israel make any comparison with other new states more than usually dangerous. There are, however, signs that lessons have been learned from her experience. It is no coincidence that Ghana should have sought advice from Israel for the training of an air force, a merchant navy, and what is now the Workers' Brigade. This is not just the attraction felt by a former colony to a country with all the Western techniques, but without the usual colonialist taint; an admiration for Israel's nation-building methods is probably involved.

There is evidence that President Nkrumah sees the armed forces in Ghana as part of a comprehensive scheme to stimulate national consciousness and a sense of discipline, and thus to ward off the dangers of disintegration. The use made of the armed forces on ceremonial occasions tends to confirm this and to suggest to the observer a deliberate focussing of attention on the state and nation of Ghana through particular institutions. It is clearly the hope that military discipline and a sense of responsibility will in some way spread throughout the community. Similarly, there is an attempt to bring certain civil organizations into the orbit of the forces for either training or administration, or both. Of these, by far the most important is the Workers' Brigade, formerly the Builders' Brigade. This is a uniformed organization designed to solve the growing African problem of the young urban unemployed who have some education, but not the opportunities to realize their potentialities. Work, a uniform, some discipline in a community, are used as a substitute for the abandoned family and tribal restraints. The Workers' Brigade is much in evidence on ceremonial occasions for cordon duty and other relatively menial tasks as a kind of poor relative of the police and the army, but its relationship with the latter force is developing. Not only has a certain administrative coordination developed, but during 1961 a number of the Brigade's officers took a month's course in drill, current affairs, and other suitable subjects alongside cadets for the army, navy, and air force at the Military Academy at Teshie. An interchange of officers or the employment of service advisers is a future possibility.

Elsewhere in Africa and Asia, the nation-building function of the military has not been so deliberately cultivated, but it could still be, if the training of officers is such as to suggest its desirability, an important element in the political development of any heterogeneous state. The inculcation of a common language is an important factor in this process, which could be adversely affected if potential officers for one army receive their training in several foreign countries speaking different languages. Thus, Somali officers were educated either in Britain or Egypt, though in their homeland their principal second language is either English or Italian according to origin. But the situation in the ethnically homogeneous Horn of Africa is artificial compared with that of India. Thus to quote S. S. Harrison: "The Indian Army may not yet be in the strictest sense a 'truly national army.' But it is, actively speaking, insulated from regional pressures. The discipline of a military establishment properly permits a degree of linguistic indoctrination inappropriate to a university campus. Varying degrees of linguistic homogeneity of the enlisted ranks in Hindustani and of the officer corps in English reinforce all the other factors giving the army its obvious magnetism as an instrument of national control."[2] The same author comments in a footnote on the removal of "the automatic allocation of a disproportionate number of officers' commissions to Sikhs" as means of reducing "provincial bias." It is clear here that the officers' common knowledge of English will become more important as the number of other ranks who speak a mother tongue akin to Hindustani diminishes and they cease to predominate.

The importance of the armed forces in the struggle for stability, unity, and political control illustrates clearly the heavy responsibility resting upon officers and also upon those, often foreigners, who train and advise them. Many questions arise of principle and detail: for instance, should political questions be included in the syllabus for the education of such an influential class? This is a question which could be answered either way. Knowledge and, more specifically, interest may be dangerous, but how else are such men to be made aware of the need to organize institutions calculated to stimulate national effort without opening the door to arbitrary rule and oppression? An

[2] S. S. Harrison, *India: the Most Dangerous Decades,* Princeton University Press, 1960, p. 303.

examination of the existing provisions in some new nations is clearly the next requirement.

III. Provisions for Officer Education in New States: the General Position with Some Examples

In most countries the early education of those who eventually become officers in the armed forces, and those who intend to continue as civilians, is common to both groups. It is only at one of two main points that their educational paths diverge: these points are either immediately before the secondary or high school phase begins or soon after it ends. In the majority of cases, officer education, in the narrow sense, may be classified as one of a number of varieties of further education on which a promising student may embark as he approaches manhood: it may not, in its educational content, as distinct from the military instructional element, differ very considerably from other courses at a similar stage in a man's professional career. However, the type of educational experience which entitles a candidate to be considered for officer training is of great importance. Methods of selection, in which social considerations have a clear role, are also relevant. Nor is it only the procedure for selection which has to be taken into account; in addition, limitations on the field of choice arising from, for instance, officially prescribed ethnic quotas or perhaps preference for so-called military families must be considered.

The records of selection boards are largely confidential and only rarely available to the investigator, but, apart from occasional access to restricted material, a number of indications can be gleaned. There are few countries today in which there is not at least the pretense of scientific and unbiased selection from a wide range of social groups. In many cases, however, especially in South East Asia, and for obvious reasons, candidates are more likely to be successful, whatever their origins, if their adherence to the existing regime is reasonably self-evident: in such cases, nomination, in some form or another, whether officially recognized or not, is likely to play its part. Occasionally, as in Thailand, the financial security, good housing, and other perquisites which go with officer status, combined with a personal oath of loyalty—in this particular case to the king—may properly be regarded as a reasonably effective guarantee.

In most countries recently emerged to independence the range of social class from which the officer corps is drawn has been extended, with opportunities for education up to adolescence. This is fundamentally as true in the short life of South Vietnam as, for instance, it is with regard to Egypt. In Egypt, for example, the Army's revolutionary role is clear, but there were signs that this might prove so as long ago as 1882 when under Arabi it emerged as a weapon in the people's hands. The crucial event, however, was a Wafd government decree, following upon the Anglo-Egyptian Treaty of 1936, which opened the military academy deliberately to all suitable qualified young men regardless of class or wealth. There is no evidence that any particular responsibility for subsequent events can be attributed to the curriculum in force at the academy: it was the fact of lower class recruitment, from the sons of the smaller landed bourgeoisie and the less substantial civil servants, which was decisive in producing revolution. The class graduating in 1938, which included Colonel Nasser, subsequently revenged themselves on society by overthrowing the Farouk regime. Though some of the resentment felt was specifically against continued British occupation, the army remained trained and organized on the British pattern by a military mission until 1947.

Throughout the world the prevailing pattern of specific military education is that of an institute of higher education whose curriculum approximates, and in many cases is recognized as the equivalent of, a university course. Pre-military education can be compared to that of the British public school or secondary grammar school and the American high school. Within this over-all pattern there are, however, a good many variations due to the rapid pace of nationalization. It has proved necessary in many forces to appoint to officer rank directly a great many non-commissioned officers and men. Thus in Somalia, Somalization was virtually completed in six months from independence with only a handful of young officers trained at Sandhurst, in Egypt, and elsewhere. A number of former British territories have and are making extensive use of a short purely military training of sixteen weeks at Mons Officer Cadet School, Aldershot, of the type which was normally provided for conscript national service officers. The policy of Burma, on the other hand, is to commission only well-educated men and, though many of the more senior officers were trained abroad, she has consistently provided in the military academy, which is an affiliated college of the University of Rangoon, a university course leading to a degree in the arts, sciences, or a professional subject. Although promotion in the armies of new states is inevitably rapid, there is a premium on a sound educational background.

In the desire to boost the educational achievement of available officer material, extensive use has been made of the military school for boys as a substitute for the secondary, pre-college phase of education. These schools have been widely accepted as desirable in Commonwealth territories. They are highly organized and effective in India and Pakistan, where they have been in existence since before World War II. The Federation Military College in Malaya provides a pre-cadet course and also accepts potential civil servants and, for example, professional civil engineers. This use of such a military secondary school has been considered in Commonwealth African territories, like Ghana, Nigeria, and Kenya, where potential senior NCO's and military tradesmen are already included, but there is an obvious danger in confusing and complicating the objectives for which the schools exist. A shortage of educated adolescents does, however, make some form of pre-cadet coaching in the basic high school subjects, especially the language of instruction, desirable.

The source of assistance in officer training, whether it be an overseas college or a training mission at home, is obviously of paramount importance in considering the effect of the education received on political development. It should, however, be emphatically stated that there is little ground for claiming that it is possible to predict the political behavior of an officer corps simply from a knowledge of the source of its training advice. Although the Russians, Czechs, and East Germans may be expected to make an increasing bid for representation in the training structure of Afro-Asian armies, at the moment Great Britain and the United States have by far the greatest responsibilities, with France, Egypt, and certain Commonwealth countries a long way behind. Generally, however, the interchange of students at the cadet and staff college levels is increasingly widespread. Burma, for instance, apart from her own resources, has made use of officer training schools in Britain, USA, Australia, Pakistan, and India. Such a distribution, in spite of the common military traditions of Commonwealth countries, while it has its advantages, is liable to cause difficulties due to the absorption of different methods and attitudes. This will be accentuated where a desire to assert "positive neutralism" produces an officer corps partly trained in the West with a minority with Communist experience.

French influence on the training of foreign armies and their officers is still extensive although progressively diminishing. The Moroccan, Tunisian, and Cambodian forces, as well as those of the Brazzaville group of African states of the French community, reflect this influence. The St. Cyr-trained officer will be a feature in these areas for some time to come. Some of the newer contributors in this field are worthy of notice, before we make a more detailed analysis of the position of the USA and Britain. Sweden and Norway, for instance, have assisted Ethiopia with her air force and navy respectively. Israel has shown willingness in a number of directions, notably with the Ghana air force, where her instructors assumed responsibility for elementary flying training at a time when the force was under the command of an Indian officer. India with fairly large forces of her own has not only received Ghanaian cadets, as did Pakistan on one occasion, and potential officers of the Iraqi army, but has recently undertaken the retraining of the Imperial Bodyguard and the staffing of the Military Academy at Harar in Ethiopia. Syrian officers have been trained in Egypt, Sudanese officers in both Egypt and Italy as well as under British auspices, and Algerian FLN cadets in one or two Arab countries, including Jordan.

The contributions to the education of military leadership from the United States and Britain are so great that all others in the free world are small by comparison. With the growth of military and economic strength that of the USA has rapidly expanded. British aid has for some time been contracting but it has had a sufficiently long history for more than one generation of officers in new countries to have been influenced by its methods. In addition, independent Commonwealth countries have themselves propagated the methods as a result of inheriting a ready-made tradition.

Since 1945 U.S. training assistance has been extensively developed and rationalized. It is designed in such a way as ultimately to reduce dependence upon United States training support. The over-all scale of the operation can be gauged by the figures of over 1,000 U.S. officers who have annually attended courses at the Military Assistance Institute, Department of Defense, to fit them for instructional and advisory tasks, and 16,500 foreign officers and men who passed through American schools in a recent period of two years. The cadet and staff training of officers is the most important of a number of objectives. Two examples, one general and one particular, may be quoted. Latin America is a key sphere for American military activity. Progressively, and particularly since 1945, various European training missions have been replaced by those of the United States. The introduction of American training methods has had several effects. Attention has been diverted away from the kind of militarism characteristic of, for example, pre-war Germany and Spain. Gradually the contagion of politically involved officer groups has been checked. Armed forces formerly above the law have gradually been curbed, partly as a result of the ironic encouragement of professionalism among young officers by military dictators. It is a reasonable assumption that this would not have been possible without the inculcation by American missions, primarily by example rather than dogma, of the view that the army officer represents a full-time specialist occupation requiring the mastery of a number of highly developed skills. It has been suggested that the recent trend away from military government, for instance in Honduras in 1957 when the armed forces returned power to a civil administration, is largely attributable to the realization, consequent upon officer education at American hands, of the virtual impossibility of becoming an expert soldier and efficient civil administrator at the same time. Training at West Point and at Fort Leavenworth, involving prolonged absence from the social pressures of the home society, has played the most significant role. It must, however, be emphasized that if this process is in practice desirable, it does, in fact, amount to the superimposing of elements of one state's military tradition upon the institutions of another. This is the dilemma of military assistance, whatever its source: its agents are in no position to develop a military ethos other than their own because they have no experience of it and perhaps cannot visualize an alternative, but before an officer corps can become effective a code of behavior and standards have to be evolved. Foreign aid in this sphere, if it succeeds in reproducing the pattern of the army by which it is provided, may thus contrive to make the gulf between the officer corps and the civil structure of society in the new state wider than it sometimes is in highly developed countries. This could be not only a threat to the political stability of the emergent states, but in the long run a danger to relations between the two countries, if, for instance, the foreign power tends to become accidentally identified with an unpopular regime. One can ask, "Is military aid in the shape of education likely to encourage the growth of sound democracy?" Whatever the answer to this may be, an emphasis on greater professionalism should obviously be the main object of all officer education provided in this way.

Outside the American continent U.S. military education is less in evidence. But the Korean Military Academy, first planned in 1946, provides an excellent example. This academy, according to the annual yearbook, "was patterned after the U.S. Military Academy, West Point" and provides a four-year curriculum for two hundred cadets admitted annually. The object is a carefully balanced education up to the standard of that of graduates of leading American universities. Qualifications for entry are necessarily somewhat varied in a developing country, but they are determined by an academic board, and, like the cadet command, organization, and uniform, owe much to the example of West Point. The range of subjects extends from mathematics, English, and the pure sciences to military history, culture, politics, economics, and, whenever possible, a foreign language. Classes are small and there is daily recitation and grading, as well as a minimum of two hours of private study. The daily instructional system adopted from West Point has apparently no parallel at any school elsewhere in Korea or the Orient.

The British approach to officer education contrasts with that of the United States at a number of points. The norm in Britain for regular officer education has long been a two-year or eighteen-month course. Before 1939 this took place at either RMA Woolwich, for arms definitely requiring a scientific basis to education, and at RMC Sandhurst, for infantry and cavalry. Since 1947 all arms have been catered for at RMA Sandhurst and the course is now of two years' duration. Time is allotted roughly equally to military and academic studies, but the latter are concentrated in the middle four terms of a six-term course. The educational standard for entry is at minimum that of the ordinary level of the General Certificate in Education, with satisfactory completion of specified subjects plus the capacity to pass a special entrance examination at a rather higher level. An increasing number of British cadets, however, are exempt from this examination to the extent that nearly 50 per cent have the nominal qualifications for entry to a university. Courses within Sandhurst are planned to cope with different standards and needs from a university type of curriculum in either science, languages, or the arts, downwards.

Most overseas students so far have taken a general course which includes under the heading of international affairs a study of aspects of political institutions, Commonwealth Affairs, Middle Eastern problems, and a case study of the Emergency in Malaya in the context of Southeast Asia. Those officers who have been trained at Sandhurst for overseas armies since 1947 have generally enjoyed a wider education than was possible in the pre-1939 period. Although pre-1939 officer training was significant, but narrowly distributed, the scale on which the British type of officer education has been made available since 1947 is likely to prove ultimately more important. The following is an extract of the summary totals of Commonwealth and foreign cadets who passed through RMA Sandhurst since January 1947 or were (January-July 1962) in the process of passing through:

Ceylon	100	Nigeria	62
East Africa	19	Pakistan	15
Fiji	4	Sierra Leone	6
Ghana	47	Somalia	9
Malaya	178	West Indies	13

All the territories mentioned are within the Commonwealth, but the summary could be extended to include, apart from Europeans from the Federation of Rhodesia and Nyasaland, a substantial number of cadets from Burma, Thailand, Jordan, and Iraq as well as a few representatives of Turkey, Iran, Ethiopia, Saudi Arabia, Libya, and one or two of the smaller Arab states in the Persian Gulf area. It is not only the number of countries, about thirty in all, which have been represented at various times, but the individual totals which really matter. The blanket reference to Burma disguises the important contribution made to the present senior ranks of that army between 1948 and 1951. The figures for Malaya and Ceylon speak for themselves: the majority of their officers have been to Sandhurst over a period of fifteen years, though in the last few years, since localization of the officer corps was more or less completed, the flow has been reduced to a trickle. In the last five years the largest contingents have, in fact, been those of Ghana and Nigeria. In these cases, in particular, long-term officer production has been supplemented by extensive use of the short course facilities at Mons Officer Cadet School. Thus in many Commonwealth countries local officers fall into two main categories: those who have been trained and educated in Britain for a total of up to three years in all, and those who have had barely four months basic military training for sub-unit command. In addition there are a few commissioned in the early days of localization who have been on the one-year Staff College course at Camberley or to short specialist courses of a different nature. This then is the pattern of education, and an indication of the scale of its provision for proportions of the officer corps, of perhaps thirty of the newer armies, varying from the insignificant to the overwhelming.

IV. The Case of India

India provides us with the classic example of an army for which at first the imperial power provided places at its own military schools, then established a local institution and eventually on independence transferred complete responsibility to the new state. India, moreover, has subsequently modified the system to suit her own ideas on the integration of the three defense forces and in so doing has borrowed from other sources, including the United States. This evolutionary process is worthy of examination primarily because it tends to demonstrate the acceptance by an Asian state of the Western European/American concept of a professional army.

At the end of the First World War there were nine Indian officers commissioned in the army of India. In connection with the Montagu-Chelmsford constitutional reforms which followed, a decision was taken to reserve ten places annually at Sandhurst. There was in effect to be an Indian competitive examination for the places approximately of the same standard as that prescribed in Britain. The upper age limit had to be adjusted from 19 to 20 because of the different stages of educational development in the two countries, and in 1922 the Prince of Wales Royal Military College at Dehra Dun was opened to provide preliminary education for those desiring to qualify for Sandhurst. The whole scheme was linked in 1923 with a plan to Indianize eight units of the Indian Army by 1946. The plan was subsequently abandoned, as was temporarily a plan for a full-scale military college in India, but at the same time places at Sandhurst were doubled, and a few provided at Woolwich for engineers and at Cranwell for air force aspirants. This strictly British pattern of education along conventional lines produced the great majority of officers who have dominated India's armed forces since independence. Of the thirteen senior officers (general to major general), whose biographies were given in the Indian Armed Forces Year Book 1958, all but one attended either Sandhurst or Woolwich after a period at Occidental-style schools and two had been to public schools in England. A similar pattern, though less complete, is discernible in the air force after 1929. A feature here and in the Indian navy has been the way in which the specialized military education has apparently fitted Indian officers to transfer toward the end of their careers into such appointments as General Manager, Hindustan Aircraft (Private) Ltd.; General Manager, Indian Air Lines; or Managing Director, Hindustan Shipyard. This flexibility in the deployment of highly educated military personnel in fields in which their skills are at a premium is likely to be a widespread characteristic of administration in new states, even where the army is not in political control.

There were ninety-one Indian army officers, all educated in Britain, serving by 1929, but in 1932 the Indian Military Academy was opened at Dehra Dun on the pattern of Sandhurst and henceforward the majority did not leave India during their formative years. Nevertheless the education which they received changed only in conformity with trends in Britain even after independence, until the establishment first of the Joint Services Wing at Dehra Dun in 1949 and then of the National Defence Academy at Khadakvasla near Poona, which opened early in 1955. The Indian Military College at Dehra Dun continued for some years closely to examine changes in syllabus at Sandhurst and often followed them. It is, in fact, the case that Asian and African countries of the Commonwealth, who have inherited or established their own officer training schools—namely India, Pakistan, Malaya, Ghana, Nigeria, and the Federation of Rhodesia and Nyasaland—have all at one time or another invited advisory teams from Britain and employed a proportion of British instructors.

In spite of the British example and connection, India has devised her own organization which owes a good deal to the United States pattern. The committee appointed in 1945 (before independence) to plan a defense academy visited the USA and Canada as well as Britain. Their brief from the government was to initiate an institution "on the lines of the United States Military Academy at West Point." The academy, as finally established, provides for entry by merit, with pre-university matriculation qualification, at the age of between 15 and 17½ years of age, to a four-year course. Of this four years, three are actually spent with cadets of all three defense services at the academy and they then go on to their respective service colleges, in the case of the army, the Military College at Dehra Dun, for more specialist training. The official objectives are worth remarking. According to the Armed Forces Year Book: "What it [the academy] turns out is not 'educated wage earners in uniforms' but patriots with full realization of their duty as guardians of national freedom and the national way of life. . . . The portals of the academy are open to all young men. There is no distinction or discrimination on the grounds of class, creed or religion. The academy, in fact, is a meeting ground of young men from distant corners of the country, living and learning in utmost harmony despite the differences in class, creed or religion. Living together, cadets start on the same footing and grow up in an atmosphere of a healthy secular outlook."

In order to achieve these goals, a strict discipline is employed, which focuses on the Code of Honor. At the same time a wide range of cultural and athletic activities is encouraged. The emphasis in the academic curriculum is essentially conventional with the stress on science, mathematics, and English. Some attention is paid to social studies, to Hindi (the nationally recognized Indian language), and to practical engineering work in the workshop. Throughout, and especially in the last year, the officer cadets' mess prepares the students for regimental custom and tradition. Thus is the Honor Code on West Point lines blended with British methods of achieving and maintaining esprit de corps. It is perhaps the fusion of traditions, on the one hand strictly professional and the other rigorously apolitical, which has enabled the Indian army so far to play a proper and unobtrusive role and to be a genuine force for national unity. It has contrived to create an aura of integrity, which has so far thwarted attempts by individuals, in the Lok Sabha or lower house of parliament for instance, to interfere with selection and rejection procedure.

Four years of intensive training and reorientation may in itself be sufficient to guide the young man to an unswerving professional course from which he will not easily deviate. However, India and her neighbor Pakistan have both shown themselves enthusiastic for the idea of the preparatory military school. There is, for instance, the Rashtriya Indian Military College, with its roots in the British period, which exists "for the primary object of catching 'would be' officers of the Armed Forces at an impressionable age to be able easily to mould their character." At this boys' college great stress is placed on physical standards, self-reliance, and social training. There are also in India four King George's Schools at Ajmer, Belgaum, Bangalore, and Dagshai. One-half of the vacancies in each case are reserved for the sons of junior commissioned officers and OR's and the remainder for those of officers and civilians connected with the forces. Institutions with a similar purpose are Sainik School, Nabla, which admits boys aged 9 to 12 to a course along the lines of an English public boarding school and reserves 120 of its 200 places for the sons of ex-servicemen, and the Army Cadet College, Nowgong, opened in May 1960 to provide training for certain categories of youth to fit them to appear before the selection board.

This examination of the Indian officer training method and a comparison of the method with the result—namely an apolitical army which is nevertheless an important educational and stabilizing factor in the state—suggests that in a developing country a long period of careful adjustment to professional standards may be required if an officer corps is to resist political pressures and temptations. It should not, however, be forgotten that in Pakistan, a Muslim state divided physically by India, where similar traditions have been inherited and methods employed, an entirely different political result has ensued. Clearly officer education is not the final determinant of an army's political attitudes.

Both these countries were, however, exceptionally favored by the long pre-independence preparation of the armed forces and the measure of localization which had taken place by that time. The present senior officers of their forces were already well established in their careers in 1947 and their predecessors had reached ranks as high as brigadier in wartime. The India subcontinent represents a measure of military development not reflected elsewhere. Let us, therefore, examine in greater detail a group of countries where the professional foundations of the armed forces have been laid down not since 1920, but since 1950 at the earliest—the territories of Commonwealth West and East Africa.

V. Officer Education in the States of Commonwealth Africa

All the armies of Commonwealth territories in Africa derive from colonial defense forces established about sixty years ago. None of the territories became independent until Ghana did so in 1957, and it is thus not surprising that selection procedure and ideas on officer education bear a common stamp, although some variations have begun to appear.

The characteristic feature of African territories south of the Sahara is the shortage of men with at least a high school type education, at a moment in history when opportunities for their absorption into rewarding employment are probably as dramatic as they will ever be. The first effect of this is that, even in a country like Ghana, where educational facilities have been progressively extended, it is unlikely that the university graduate or even the holder of a Higher School

Certificate after a sixth-form course will consider the armed forces as a career. Primary education is in the process of becoming compulsory and universal in Ghana: in 1960-1961 the percentage of children actually receiving some education was near to 90 per cent, but of more than half a million in schools of all kinds only 11,000 were in secondary schools, of whom a little more than 9,000 were boys. In 1959-1960 a total of 975 obtained school certificates and 208 Higher School Certificates in a country with a total population of nearly seven million. The limiting factor on effective expansion is the availability of graduate teachers of whom it is estimated that an additional 1,100 will be needed between 1960 and 1965. It is against such a background that the education of the military leadership must be seen. The temptation to lower the standards of selection to admit more to training schools is always present, particularly when ambitious targets have been set.

The existing officer corps in the Ghana army has inevitably been trained on British lines. The criteria which have been applied in the selection of these men and most of the others who have been chosen for officer training have been essentially European. This is not the anomaly which it at first appears to be. The schools which they have attended have generally prepared them along these lines. For instance, two-thirds of all boys receiving secondary education in Ghana in February 1960, in schools under the control of the Ministry of Education, were attending residential schools. This has insulated them to some extent against the handicaps which poor homes might have imposed and, more positively, it has greatly increased their adaptability for training in what has so far been an essentially European style environment. Until recently about a dozen schools, with well-developed perfect systems on the English pattern and a high proportion of expatriate staff, dominated officer selection for the armed forces and they still make the most substantial contribution.

In line with British developments over the last fifty years, six of Ghana's leading secondary schools, including Achimota and two wholly government owned and maintained establishments, at Takoradi and Tamale respectively, have cadet forces inaugurated during the 1950's. Though not primarily regarded as sources of potential officers, they obviously play an important part in officer recruitment, particularly where they have been brought into contact with the Military Academy.

The educational background in the selection of potential officers is generally similar in Nigeria to that prevailing in Ghana. However, the problems, except in the Eastern Region, where there are a number of good secondary schools, are more acute. It is a striking commentary on the Nigerian scene that at the beginning of 1961 out of 81 African officers commissioned, nearly three-quarters were from the east and of these the majority had been educated at schools within a short radius of Onitsha on the Niger, notably at Government College, Umuahia. The political implications of such a concentration from one area with strong local affiliations are obvious. Educational development in the north has been slow. More than half of the 36 million population of Nigeria live in the latter region and the majority are Muslim. Attempts by Lord Lugard in the 1920's to introduce Western-style education in the area were resisted, with the result that there is now a clamor from the traditional rulers for steps to be taken to close the educational gap between the regions. The discrepancy in the total numbers of secondary school pupils in 1959 between the north (4,683) and the east (15,798), both figures representing a steep increase on those for 1955, serves to point the problem. Recently a regional quota system has been introduced to ensure a future ethnic balance proportionate to population among new officers. This is a dramatic example of the relationship which can exist in a developing country between the educational pattern and the political balance as far as the military leadership is concerned.

Shortage of secondary school places and of graduate staff to teach at that level is endemic throughout Africa. Sierra Leone, where there is some difficulty in finding suitably promising children to fill spaces, is an exception due to the uneven way in which education in the territory has been developed. On the east coast in Tanganyika, Kenya, and to a lesser extent in Uganda, the situation is serious. The education of the military leadership in these areas is hampered for lack of qualified candidates. So great are the opportunities for them in other government and commercial employment that few are willing to undertake the long, and to them apparently treacherous, path to a commission.

Methods of selection and subsequent education of officers in Commonwealth Africa vary only in detail from country to country. The procedure from the point where a candidate's educational qualifications are provisionally accepted to the point when he emerges as a young officer is in part concerned with selection and in part instructional and educational. However, selection procedures can in themselves be regarded as an integral part of the education of military leaders, especially when several phases are involved at each of which a candidate may be finally rejected. Here a seriatim description of the processes in three territories or groups of territories—namely, Ghana, Nigeria and Sierra Leone, and Tanganyika, Kenya and Uganda—may be useful.

GHANA

Before independence in 1957, potential officers in Ghana (at that time the Gold Coast) appeared before a selection board, were interviewed at various levels up to a personal meeting with the General Officer Commanding, British West Africa, and underwent a course of basic military training before proceeding to Britain for a long course at Sandhurst or a short course at one of the two officer cadet schools then in being. Since independence, adjustments have been made as Ghana has sought to pursue a distinctive course of her own. Until early in 1960 the basic training facilities at Teshie near Accra were common to all the countries of Commonwealth West Africa. This ceased with the establishment of the Ghana Military Academy in April 1960, but it should be remembered that the existing officer complement of the army was largely produced under the earlier scheme and that the senior officers were, in fact, more or less directly commissioned from the ranks in the period before 1954; a number of these had, however, had a secondary school education and had been warrant officers and NCO's in the education service. Candidates for cadetships, who are educationally qualified, have today first to appear before a selection board which includes both military and civilian members; this board applies individual and group leadership tests of a physical and intellectual nature. Each candidate is also required to address the board on a topic of his own selection. The application of this type of test to African conditions has not proved easy, but the net result appears to be just and, liberally interpreted, it avoids discrimination of any of the normal ethnic or religious kinds. The Ghana Military Academy, established with British advice and manned largely by British army officers in the early stages and by a proportion of Canadians since August 1961, provides initial training for officers of all three armed services for the first six months. The course is on the Sandhurst pattern, but the historical, geographical, and political element in the course have been adjusted to focus on the African scene. Some attempt has been made to introduce French into the curriculum, which in the situation of Ghana is obviously desirable, not only from the political point of view. Unfortunately, time and staffing problems have tended to frustrate this admirable intention. Nor were French courses initiated in 1960 for officers already commissioned a substantial success. It is, however, clear that progress in this field among such an influential body of public servants could quite quickly revolutionize relationships between the English-speaking and French-speaking areas of West Africa, between which, in spite of political devices, there is a gulf.

After the common course of six months, air force cadets proceed to a flying training school at Takoradi and naval candidates to an overseas course usually in the United Kingdom at Dartmouth. The majority of army cadets remain at the academy for a further year. Select groups continue their training either at the Indian Military College or at Sandhurst. The latter course involves a minimum further period of two years, but the prestige of an overseas course is such that there is no lack of those anxious to be trained in either Britain or India, in spite of the prolonging of the period between acceptance and commissioning. Reactions to Russian training made available in September 1961 and its consequences cannot yet be assessed.

An officer's education continues throughout his career. Places on signals and other specialist courses as well as company commanders' courses are in demand in Britain. One young officer attended the degree course at the Royal Military College of Science. One or two places annually are available on the Staff College Course at Camberley. Officers attend this course as majors and though their seniority varies a good deal, five or six years of commissioned service seems to be the requirement for nomination. This course includes not only consideration of advanced military problems but also the discussion of politico-strategic questions. Thus in general the training of the Ghana army officer is similar to that of the British officer, though his initial educational attainment varies more widely. The greater its breadth and depth, the more likely he is to be considered for preferment. Generally he ranks in society with senior civil servants and business executives as a member of Ghana's small and compact educated elite.

NIGERIA AND SIERRA LEONE

Since Ghana finally severed the military ties which linked the West African Commonwealth countries in the days of the Royal West African Frontier Force, Nigeria and Sierra Leone have continued to cooperate. It will be sufficient for the current purpose to describe the procedures of military education in Nigeria. This is in process of flux due to the creation of a defense academy mainly concerned with the manning of a new air force. However, it is likely that for some time cadets for the army will proceed to Britain for long or short courses according to age and qualifications. At present twenty-three is the age limit for Sandhurst candidates. The appeal of such a training, though it has not always produced an adequate flow of young men, appears to be second only to that of a university course, with the added advantage that it inevitably involves travel outside Nigeria. Selection takes place twice yearly and selection boards similar to those described in the case of Ghana are held at Kaduna and Ibadan. In this instance, however, they are purely military in composition and presided over by a Brigadier. The successful candidates have since 1960 gone, along with nominees from Sierra Leone, to the Nigerian Military Forces Training Centre at Kaduna for a period which is now rather less than six months. Some have failed to adjust to the rigors of the course and have been rejected at this stage; the remainder have finished their training in Britain on one of the two types of course available. The curriculum at the center includes basic military instruction and further academic education. It is specifically designed to bring the candidate weak in intellectual attainment but strong in personality up to a standard which enables him to perform adequately at Sandhurst. In this respect the center has been successful.

It is only in Nigeria, of the territories under discussion, that the concept of the military secondary school has been, to any marked degree, effective as a source of officer recruits. Such is the demand for secondary school places over the whole country that there is no difficulty in filling the annual list of sixty boys admitted to the Nigerian Military School at Zaria. The age for admission is about fourteen years and acceptances are on a quota basis for the whole country, including some attempt at an even distribution by provinces in the northern region. The course pursued, apart from elementary military subjects, leads in four years to a limited range of the options taken by British schoolboys for the General Certificate of Education, Ordinary level. There are, however, a number of difficulties. In the Nigerian environment, indeed in the African environment, leadership qualities are not at present easily discernible at such a comparatively early age, and the provision of a first-class secondary education, with all that that implies in the way of staff and range of subjects and activities, is a formidable task for the army in present conditions. The triple objective of training potential officers, NCO's and tradesmen in the same establishment tends to confusion. However, with all sections of the country represented, the school could before long make a substantial contribution to the maintenance of an ethnic balance in the officer corps.

TANGANYIKA, KENYA AND UGANDA

In spite of Tanganyika's achievement of independence, the three East African territories whose fortunes have been linked by British administrative practices and the accident of geography since 1918 have a common system for the provision of officers. They have, however, from time to time adopted different attitudes. Kenya with its substantial permanent Asian and European populations, who enjoyed better educational opportunities than the Africans, regarded these groups as potential sources of officers for the King's African Rifles. It is out of the units of this colonial force that the new national armies are likely to be built. By New Year's 1961 the Kenya battalions had a sprinkling of Europeans and Asians, but no African was yet at Sandhurst. Tanganyika's first indigenous officer was an Asian, but he was followed closely through Sandhurst by two Africans, one of whom planted the flag on Kilimanjaro to celebrate Tanganyika's independence. The first Uganda African "passed out" in August 1962. Otherwise all the Africans to achieve commissioned ranks in all three territories have had long service in the ranks and have mostly been educated under the army's own schemes. Once again, as in Nigeria, the structure of the incipient officer corps reflects the educational scene at large.

The situation in East Africa demonstrates the difficulties in sustaining a lengthy officer education procedure. The young man leaving school today who wants to embark on a military career will, in the normal way, take almost three years to become an effective officer. This is a long way to look ahead where African nationalism is strong. A long period of training may temper the steel of a man's character and greatly enhance his stature as an officer, but at the same time the delay in Africanization may raise tensions detrimental to the army.

In East Africa there are four main stages to final selection for officer training. A territorial selection board interviews educationally qualified candidates. Those who are successful join a unit for basic military training. After an interval they attend a special course at the

Outward Bound School at Loitokitok, the principal object of which is to enable the candidate and his sponsors to assess his mental and physical capabilities, often under adverse conditions, and to develop in him the idea of group cooperation. The report from this course combined with the results of the military initiation are then considered by a command selection board which makes the final decision. Thus there are several hurdles to overcome and East Africa has still to find a way around the obstacle to Africanization largely created by educational deficiencies.

VI. Conclusion

An examination of the influence of the education of the military leadership on the political scene in developing countries can serve only to indicate lines of thought for the assessment of new situations as they develop. It is apparent that the source of military assistance and the nature of the training provided are not in themselves decisive factors in the political role of the military. India and Pakistan, who divided an army between them, are a clear warning against the dangers of generalizations on this score. Subtle differences are already distinguishable as between Ghana, Nigeria and Sierra Leone in spite of the common colonial origin of their military forces. Nor does the content of the curriculum appear to be a principal determinant in settling the political significance of an officer corps.

Historical circumstances new or old are clearly important. The degree to which armed forces play a role in nationalist endeavors to secure a transfer of power is clearly more significant than the type of education which their officers receive. In countries like Egypt, however, where the internal social revolution has been more important than the struggle to throw off foreign rule, the provision of officer education for a wider class of individual than has normally enjoyed real power in the community has proved most important.

It is not easy to say whether the widening political awareness among officers is due to educational opportunities. The training courses have not shown a tendency to political indoctrination, nor even an exaggerated concern with the mechanics and purposes of political institutions. The education provided for the officers of emergent countries tends to be strictly conventional—a direct extension of what is done in school and widely accepted as reasonable and apolitical.

The education of the officer corps in most countries does, however, foster homogeneity, and this means that there is a certain harmony of values and objectives between the individuals concerned. The long overseas course, in particular, tends to create a sense of solidarity among those who experience it and firmly to align them with other elements in the state who have undergone further education up to university or quasi-university level. They become part of a national elite small in total numbers, but out of which a true national leadership may emerge. Out of a population of 36 million in Nigeria it is estimated that the elite may at present consist of 30,000. Army officers are of paramount importance, even though newcomers to the scene, because they represent one of the ultimate sources of power. Their educational background is such that if they become surplus to service requirements or simply ambitious they will find their way into other walks of life. It is probable that the military administrator and diplomat will become an even more common feature of the international scene than he is today. It is this more than the possibility of *coup d'état* which makes a full and balanced education for officers in new states essential to stability.

CHAPTER 14

African University Students:
a Presumptive Elite

DWAINE MARVICK

~~~~~~

Intellectuals and the Politics of Withdrawal

In recent years much attention has been paid to the role of intellectuals in the political development of new states. Edward Shils has described the syndrome of intense politicization, heroic phantasies, ambivalent populism, and frustrated oppositionalism which is generated by the circumstances in which intellectuals are likely to find themselves—a syndrome, he holds, that too often leads them to the "politics of withdrawal."

Intellectuals, meaning those with advanced educations who have been touched by Western culture and have largely adopted modern standards and Western ways, both have and expect to keep a distinctive social status. Yet it is often hard for them to gain the full confidence and acceptance of ordinary people. These intellectuals are deeply concerned with the poverty and illiteracy around them, and "they strenuously insist on rapid economic progress so that their own peoples will be able to approximate the level of the peoples of the advanced countries."[1] But they often couple an insistence on large-scale state action with an open contempt for practical politicians and the crass dealings of officialdom. They yearn for a respected place in the indigenous culture that reared them and praise the "wisdom of the simple and the humble" while they simultaneously show disrespect for the views of the uneducated, and are quite ready to order them about for their own good.[2]

As a new state comes to run its own affairs in large part, many of its intellectuals find their talents wasted, their qualifications questioned, their desire for an heroic role denied them. Thus they are likely to feel ambivalent not only toward the traditional order of society, but toward the new order also. Shils concludes that this in turn "has strengthened the 'anti-political politics,' the politics of withdrawal,

[1] Edward Shils, "Political Development in the New States," *Comparative Studies in Society and History*, Vol. II, The Hague, Mouton Co., 1960, p. 274.
[2] *Ibid.*, p. 275.

which has been growing among the intellectuals of the new states." [3]

Having made this diagnosis, he identifies two groups among the intellectual class whose perspectives toward public life are better suited to the emergence of a stable and progressive civil order. One is the technical and executive group. More specialized in their work and more contentedly commonplace in their ideas and tastes, they are the "philistines" who are committed to making professional rather than political contributions to progress; hence they are prepared to serve under any sort of modernizing regime. The second group, always small, is composed of "civic-spirited, realistic and responsible intellectuals, devoted to the public good, critical and yet sympathetic, interested in the political growth of their society and yet detached enough from immediate partisanship to constitute a corps of custodians of the public good in the present and the future."[4]

For the present generation, the competence and self-restraint of the African leaders and their intellectual critics who count in shaping policy are already being tested. In today's political arenas, appeals to tribal and religious loyalties contend with pleas for secular rationality and national unity. For the next generation, however, the calibre of African leaders will depend on the young people who are today busy acquiring their certificates of higher education, either overseas or in African universities. Tomorrow, they will be the professional men, the governmental and community leaders—whether politicized or philistine—of still "new states."

To be sure, their apprenticeships in public life will come only after they leave college. But something can be guessed of the contributions they will make or fail to make by examining their perspectives and interests while still students: by studying their attitudes toward traditional society, toward their careers and their academic preparation for careers, toward the student community and the communities to which they will soon return, toward the nation's symbolic political struggles and toward the substantive problems of modernization that await solution.

The Locus of Education and the Proximity of the Relevant World

African intellectuals trained in the West return to their countries with envied credentials; their baptism in modernity's waters has been by total immersion. For them, it has been perhaps easier to grasp the

[3] *Ibid.*, p. 276.
[4] *Ibid.*, pp. 276-277.

pervasive meaning of modernity, but harder upon return to fit in and use their knowledge and skills successfully.

Intellectuals trained in African universities also go out with much-desired credentials. Like the student who goes overseas, they are living away from the daily greetings of family members, the village talk about public events, the enforced conformity to communal expectations. But living in a West African university's residential blocks is only a half solution, not the complete shift to an educational environment which, however ivory-towered, is contextually in harmony with its own society.

At a British-modelled West African university, academic routines and scholarly habits are European artifacts. Life is a chain of days spent considering Western civilization; purpose is constrained to the narrow rituals of set examinations flown out from England. For these students, it is probably harder to grasp the full significance of what it means to live in a modern society. But when they leave it may well prove easier for them to turn their lessons to practical use. For in this West African college they have the considerable and constant advantage of knowing themselves to be in an artificial environment.

In the autumn of 1960, I spent the Michaelmas term at Fourah Bay College, the oldest university in West Africa. It is a small place with about 75 staff members, mostly English, and 300 students, half from Nigeria and half from Sierra Leone. For ten weeks, twelve students regularly took part in my weekly seminar. Our sessions focused on problems in the development of the next generation of African community and political leaders. Especially were we interested in the place of higher education. How are the college students selected? What problems have they in adjusting to university life? Which opportunities do they seize upon and which do they neglect? What yardsticks do they use to judge the value of their academic work? How worried are they about leaving college and adjusting again to African community life? How active will they be in community affairs and later in national politics? How involved are they with current African politics? What do they see as the top priority tasks facing their nation? These were some of the seminar questions we canvassed. Often a student would illustrate a point by candid discussion of his own experience; sometimes the thread of discussion was lost in partisan argument.

Out of the seminar a more ambitious venture grew. We decided to construct a questionnaire covering the same ground, and interview as many other students as possible. The interviews we got provide the empirical basis for the quantitative analysis presented in this report.[5] In analyzing these interviews, certain key questions are posed and the evidence on each point examined. First, what deference and loyalty do these students show toward the traditional social order in which they were reared and in which their parents still live? Second, how self-centered and individualized do their career perspectives become as they pursue Western knowledge in an African college? Third, what standards of critical judgment do they use to evaluate their academic work, especially as they enter its final stages? Fourth, living in a bi-national and multi-tribal environment, how consciously aware do they become of the importance of tolerance and mutual cooperation for successful leadership in any community? Fifth, how preoccupied with national and world politics are they, and how bent on political careers themselves? Sixth, committed as they are to the modernization of tradition-bound ways of life, how sensitive are they to "tribalism" as a national problem, and to their own "social adjustment" as a personal problem?

This small college was made up almost equally of Sierra Leoneans and Nigerians; nearly half the student body were questioned and our survey reflects the presence of these two nationality groups. Thus through a happy circumstance it provides data for probing the formative significance of an African university environment not only for some of its country's own future leaders, but also for students who will return to a sister nation.

Academically these students have considerable drive, much self-discipline, and a lot of intellectual curiosity for socially relevant knowledge. But they do not have systematic knowledge about their own country's institutions and problems. They lack the habit of asking why, the assumption that causal conditions can be identified, the

---

[5] In the 1959-1960 academic year, Dr. Arthur Porter conducted another survey of Fourah Bay College student opinions, in cooperation with the Bureau of Social Science Research, Inc., Washington, D.C. Only a code and a tabulation of results by nationality of respondents are available for this survey, in mimeographed form, as *BSSR Publication No. 345*. Some of its findings supplement those of our own survey, and will be noted in passing. Thus it was found in both surveys that Nigerian students were considerably less likely than Sierra Leoneans to read the local daily newspaper, though a very high proportion did read the main newspaper from their own country. And while two-thirds of the home-country students listened every day to the Sierra Leone Broadcasting Service, only two-fifths of the Nigerians did so. Yet both groups spoke with equal frequency about listening to Voice of America broadcasts (81 per cent did so at least occasionally) and Radio Moscow (50 per cent did so at least occasionally).

willingness to treat an event analytically, as an example or case study, rather than descriptively, for its own sake.[6] To be sure, the same could be said with justice about undergraduates in any Western university. But also, these deficiencies seem partly due to the particular variant of British university practice followed, and especially the emphasis on being prepared on "examinable" aspects of each academic subject. Moreover, in modern countries with advanced education generally available, these deficiencies are less costly.

The Student Body and the Sample

Because these were our research objectives, a basic decision was made to secure interviews with as many final-year students as possible, rather than aim at a sample that was "representative" of the entire student body. The seminar members undertook to interview all final-year students, including one another. The same survey schedule

[6] One possible consequence of the kind of academic diet they received at Fourah Bay College was their image of various foreign nations, including Britain. In the earlier survey (*BSSR Publication No. 354*), students were asked which country could give them the best liberal arts education. Only 38 per cent said Britain, while 53 per cent named America, 12 per cent Russia, and 10 per cent West Germany. Asked next where they could get the best technical education, only 7 per cent preferred Britain, 45 per cent America, 24 per cent Russia, and 36 per cent West Germany.

Another question asked them which aspects of British, American, Russian, Indian, and Chinese life they would like more information about, listing a dozen categories to be checked. Fifty-nine per cent wanted more English literature, compared with 25 per cent, 31 per cent, 21 per cent, and 19 per cent for the other four countries. Both Britain and America had educational systems interesting to 58 per cent, compared with 38 per cent in Russia's case and 19 per cent for India or China. Only 24 per cent wanted to know more about Britain's technical and industrial development, a figure similar to that for India and China, while 55 per cent wanted this knowledge about Russia and about America. In labor-management relations, the same patterns of interest were found, though slightly less intense for each country. And while 59 per cent wanted to know more about American business, only 28 per cent were curious about British business, compared with 33 per cent Russia, 15 per cent India, 16 per cent China. Only 24 per cent wanted more knowledge about British church and religious life, compared with figures of 41 per cent America, 39 per cent Russia, 37 per cent India, and 24 per cent China. And perhaps as surprising as any finding, desire to know more about Britain's political system (56 per cent) was not much greater than that for America's (49 per cent), and less than Russia's (61 per cent); India scored 21 per cent and China 29 per cent on this aspect.

Finally, the question was put: "All things considered, what are your general feelings about the following countries?" Fifty per cent answered "very good" for America, 29 per cent for England, 19 per cent for India, 14 per cent for Russia, and 0 per cent for China.

In our subsequent survey, the question was asked: "How important is the economic and social modernization of West Africa to the government of [list of countries]? Again it is instructive to note where Britain and other non-African governments stand in the estimation of these students. The percentages answering "very important" were 63 per çent for Israel, 42 per cent Britain, 33 per cent America and India, 31 per cent Russia, and 25 per cent China.

was then distributed as a paper-and-pencil questionnaire to all other students.

Fifty-eight two-hour interviews with final-year students, out of 68 enrolled in the college, were completed by the seminar students. This was an 85 per cent census of final-year men: 92 per cent of the arts majors, 88 per cent of the economics students, and 70 per cent of the science specialists.

Our interest is not in the college as such; rather it is in what we can learn by comparing the responses of Sierra Leoneans and Nigerians; of Creoles, Ibos, and Yorubas; of final-year and preliminary-stage students; or of majors in arts, economics, and science curricula. Most of our inquiry concentrates on differences in the response patterns of various sub-groups within the student body. As a preliminary step, the interpenetration of these groupings must be examined, and certain built-in disproportions explicitly noted:

(a) Not only are the Sierra Leoneans Creole by a two-to-one ratio, but two-thirds of the Creoles are in their final year.

(b) Similarly, although Ibo and Yoruba tribal representatives are equally common among the Nigerians, nearly three-fifths of the Yoruba and only one-third of the Ibo are final-year men.

(c) Thus, when interpreting differences between final-year and preliminary-stage students, it must be remembered that the former are mainly Creoles and Yorubas while the latter are mainly Sierra Leone "countrymen" and Ibos.

(d) The Sierra Leoneans are likely to over-represent views derived from the arts curriculum, which nearly two-fifths of them pursue. However, the Creoles are just as likely to reflect the preoccupations of economics and science as of arts.

(e) The Nigerians, on the other hand, are less likely to reflect the outlook of arts students, but insofar as they do, it would tend to be Yoruba arts majors. The Ibos, at the same time, are likely to be the source of any emphases among Nigerians which can be said to reflect the ideas of majors in economics or science.

(f) Finally, when an interesting frequency distribution is found for arts majors, it may actually reflect what is really a peculiarity of Sierra Leoneans, and especially non-Creoles, for they are over-represented in that curriculum. In the same way, when it is the economics majors or science students whose answer patterns are distinctive, it may be due to the over-representation of Nigerians, and especially Ibos, in both curricula.

Loyalty to Parental Traditions

Many of these young students came into the sheltered atmosphere of the college after a good part of their formative years had been spent in rural tribal communities. Among the Sierra Leone contingent, however, the Creoles were "western educated Africans whose status is rooted in the urban conditions prevalent in the coastal towns."[7] Given these diverse ethnic backgrounds, our first task is to estimate the influence of their cultural origins on the students we interviewed. The pride they display in describing the tribal and religious way of life of their parents, the candor with which they discuss the traditional authority structure or the prevalence of superstition and magical beliefs in their home communities, the respect they manifest for their parents' community position—these are important clues to their basic feelings of loyalty to and identification with the traditional societies in which they were raised and to which they will return.

To explore their attitudes toward ethnically distinctive practices, this question was posed late in each interview: "For your parents, how important was their tribe or cultural group in setting a pattern of life to be followed?" While only half the Creoles stressed the importance of a "cultural group" in setting the pattern of their parents' lives, at least 80 per cent of the Ibo, Yoruba, and other students with tribal backgrounds did so. No variations in this emphasis appear to be linked to the student's field of work or stage of academic preparation.

In Sierra Leone, the Creoles are descendants of freed slaves who settled in the Freetown area during the nineteenth century. They developed a distinctive language and culture, modelled not on tribal patterns but on British colonial example. Today they are not numerous enough to dominate the political life even of Freetown, much less of the country. But as a cultural group whose members for several generations have been literate, Christian, and detribalized, their significance as teachers, civil servants, and professional men far exceeds their electoral weight.

In many ways they are closer in type to the civic-minded elite of a small community in a Western nation than they are to a tribal society. This may explain why they do not see the formative influence of their ethnic environment as clearly as other students do. As a group, the Creoles have not always been liked by their fellow Sierra Le-

[7] A. T. Porter, "The Social Background of Political Decision-Makers in Sierra Leone," *Sierra Leone Studies*, June 1960, p. 4.

oneans, toward whom in the past they are said to have been rather condescending. On the other hand they often take pride in the pattern they have set for the hinterland tribes.

The history of Nigerian nationalism is closely related to the political competitiveness generated between the two major groups in the southern portion of the country: the Yoruba and the Ibo. Throughout Nigeria it is the primary group living together in a given locality —the lineage—that commands the greatest loyalty. So in many ways the attachments to parental ways of Ibo and Yoruba students are similar. When discussing their own tribal rearing experiences, scarcely any informants were hostile or contemptuous. Rather, their descriptions were deferential and uncritical. There were few notes of disdain toward tribal methods of instilling moral standards in the children. As a basis for community effort, too, tribal solidarity was often spoken of as demonstrably effective. Finally, the enforcement of tribal standards was accorded acceptance that was sometimes grudging but seldom skeptical.

Yet there are important differences in the scale of political organization, the history of Western influence, and the approach to Nigerian nationalism of Yorubas and Ibos. Among the Yoruba, the sub-chiefs were "either hereditary or were elected from among a limited number of royal families who ruled in turn."[8] Before the British came, considerable urban concentrations had grown up in Yorubaland, and an elaborate political superstructure, "essentially that of a constitutional monarchy," existed.[9] After the British came, the Yoruba enjoyed initial advantages in education, in business and civil service careers, and in modern political activity. During the postwar movement for Nigerian independence, Yoruba leaders were more receptive to largely autonomous regional governments sustained by inter-tribal alliances within a federal framework. Ibo receptivity, on the other hand, to the goal of national unity transcending tribal loyalties was partly a reflection of their efforts to catch up, as latecomers to Western education and modern urban-industrial life, and partly the result of the rudimentary character of their traditional political order, with authority dispersed among groups and age-grades instead of centralized in any one body or person.

Briefly, we explored also the touchy ground of African superstition,

[8] James S. Coleman, *Nigeria: Background to Nationalism*, Berkeley and Los Angeles, University of California Press, 1958, p. 33.
[9] *Loc.cit.*

[470]

asking, "How important in the day-to-day life of your family were magical beliefs?" There was an understandable reluctance from many students to admit that magic had much importance, and the fact that more than two-thirds said it had "no importance" can hardly be accepted uncritically. What is noteworthy, rather, is the candor of nearly 30 per cent in admitting and discussing their family's acceptance of magical interpretations of sickness, death, dreams, and so forth. Indeed, not all students were defensive; one simply said, "What you call magic is to us 'African science'; we believe it."

Objectively, too, the prevalence of magical beliefs varies by ethnic groups. Relatively few Creoles reported such practices; both Yoruba and Ibo students more often did so. Among the smaller, less Westernized tribal contingents, superstition was most readily mentioned. Twice as many arts majors spoke of such backgrounds as did others.

The incidence of Christianity in the family matrix from which these students came deserves special attention. All the Creoles came from Christian families; among non-Creole Sierra Leoneans, however, only 29 per cent did while nearly half of them claimed to come from Muslim households (47 per cent). Christianity was thought of as Western and Creole, while being pagans—"practicing animism" as it was called—was backward; accordingly many tribal families in Sierra Leone are said to espouse a nominal Islamic faith. Four-fifths of the Ibo and Yoruba students came from Christian families. Of those who did not, the Ibos said their families were pagan while the Yorubas said they came from Muslim homes.

In the not very distant past, the Christian mission schools were almost the only sources of Western education at the primary and secondary school levels in British West Africa. For the Creoles, Christianity was one hallmark of their detribalized status. But it is noteworthy that a large proportion of the students who grew up in the closed communal order of tribal villages came from *families* in which the parental example of espousing and practicing Christianity was found. In some cases, it was simply that high moral standards were maintained and passed on.

Our inquiry into family and community backgrounds and the respect and pride with which students spoke of tribal and religious practices also probed the importance of parental examples of civic-mindedness and community leadership. When we asked, "While you were growing up, how active were your family members in community affairs where they lived?" A marked difference was found between the three big ethnic groups (see Table 1). Thirty-eight per cent of the Creoles and fewer than one-tenth of the Nigerians said "not at all."

TABLE 1: "WHILE YOU WERE GROWING UP, HOW ACTIVE WERE YOUR FAMILY MEMBERS IN COMMUNITY AFFAIRS WHERE THEY LIVED?"

	NATIONALITY		ETHNIC GROUP			ACADEMIC GROUP		FIELD OF WORK		
	Sierra Leone %	Nigeria %	Creole %	Ibo %	Yoruba %	Final Year %	Prelim. Stage %	Arts %	Eco- nomics %	Science %
Tribal or village official	18	52	8	63	40	35	45	32	45	50
Voluntary civic leader	49	41	54	28	52	52	36	48	38	44
Only good citizens	33	7	38	9	8	13	19	20	17	6
	100	100	100	100	100	100	100	100	100	100
(Cases)	(39)	(71)	(24)	(32)	(25)	(52)	(58)	(50)	(42)	(18)

Quite different were the answers given by Nigerian students, and here also the Ibo differed considerably from the Yoruba. Fully 63 per cent of the former reported parents who held official positions in village or tribal authority structures; a majority of the Yoruba, on the other hand, described their parents' role in voluntary community affairs and sometimes added that they belonged to the "ruling class." Yoruba students came from families that "spearheaded the building of roads, markets and mission work through community labour," or "took charge of the cleaning of springs and cleaning the streets of the town." To be sure, they not infrequently spoke of a close relative who was a chief or an important figure in "our leading tribal secret societies." But this background of officialdom was most pronounced among the Ibo: "Up to now the tax collector is from my family," or "our grandfather's compound is the meeting place of the village," or "my father was the scribe for one chief house; he always presided over village affairs—cultural events and law cases."

As several authorities have noted, the possibilities within traditional Ibo communities are greater for political apprenticeship in responsible positions, when compared with the Yoruba system, where greater emphasis is placed on age and ascribed status: "The Ibo political system gave great latitude to youth. An enterprising talented young man who acquired wealth could attain political power, even over his elders. Ibo youths were organized into age-grade associations which not only had disciplinary power over their members but also played important political and judicial roles within the community."[10]

Our evidence, then, suggests that these students make no wholesale rejection of their cultural origins—far from it, and for at least two reasons: first, many features of their parents' way of life are not seen as in conflict with the modern order they seek to bring about; second, their parents have often been sufficiently enlightened to help them in their educational efforts, and sufficiently influential in their communities to provide models of whom their children can feel proud, even after becoming Western-educated intellectuals. Parents who identify with the aspirations of their children, in short, appear to be important supportive factors in the lives of many of these young African students.[11]

Individualization and the Growth of Critical Judgment

Despite Ibo and Yoruba differences, the Nigerian students have typically come from cultural and communal settings essentially alike in many ways, and often quite different from those of the Creoles. The difficulties in securing a college education, the personal meaning they attach to it, and the standards they use in evaluating their college work are quite different for Ibo, Yoruba, and Creole students. The effect of the college environment on all of them is apparently important as well in changing their personal perspectives.

Under British colonial practice during the last century the Creoles were encouraged to assume predominant roles not only in local business and commerce but also in administrative and advisory governmental posts. After 1900, the benighted period of colonialism re-

[10] James S. Coleman, *op.cit.*, p. 336 and *passim* for a full discussion.
[11] In the earlier survey, *BSSR Publication No. 345*, *op.cit.*, the distribution of occupations pursued by the fathers of Fourah Bay College students was ascertained. While 51 per cent of the Sierra Leoneans were employed in jobs requiring literacy (teacher, clerk, manager, clergyman), only 17 per cent of the Nigerians were; conversely, only 9 per cent of the former were chiefs or other tribal figures of importance, while 28 per cent of the latter were. One in five were traders or artisans in both groups. But nearly twice as many Nigerians were farmers (36 per cent compared with 19 per cent). Also from that earlier survey, we know that 54 per cent of the Nigerian students' fathers had no formal education and 29 per cent had only finished primary school. Compare this with the figures for Sierra Leonean students' fathers: 24 per cent and 15 per cent respectively.

versed these trends. Creoles were squeezed out of discretionary posts in government; foreign investors brought their own personnel to run such new industrial and commercial ventures as were begun.[12]

By then, however, the Westernization of Creole practices and aspirations had crystallized. Their children should become literate, Christian, and middle class; the preferred vocation for a shopkeeper's or an artisan's son was that of lawyer or medical doctor. Active civic work with voluntary associations, continuing interest in schoolboard matters, support for all church-supported projects: these were the proper roles for a Creole adult.[13]

More than the others, Creole students in our survey seemed to take their college careers for granted. They fully appreciated that college was an opportunity denied to many. But it was a long-established pattern for a diligent Creole youth with ability. Moreover, to them a college education was seen largely as a personal and private advantage to be won. Creoles seldom spoke of their nation or their community as benefitting from their education. In this as in other ways, Creole students appear less politically-minded than others. In part this probably reflects the disenchantment and privatization of a social elite never allowed under British rule to become the political elite, and now too small and too suspiciously regarded by other Sierra Leoneans to furnish political leaders for the country. In part perhaps it also reflects the manner in which their education is sponsored.

We asked each student to tell us how his college education had been subsidized: whether by his family, the government, or some other means. Rather remarkable differences were found. Fully 96 per cent of the Creoles answered "by government scholarship," while only 44 per cent of the Yoruba and no more than 24 per cent of the Ibo students reported such backing. On the other hand, nearly three-fourths (72 per cent) of the Ibo students said their education was sponsored largely by their families.

The struggle to secure educational credentials in both countries, when compared with America, is hard. When the average Fourah Bay student finishes his degree work he is twenty-seven years old. This means that as he starts his postgraduate life he is nearly six years older than his Western counterpart.[14] Moreover, his career is

[12] Cf. A. T. Porter, op.cit.

[13] Cf. Michael Banton, *West African City*, London, Oxford University Press, 1957.

[14] The average Sierra Leone student was 24, with Creoles averaging a year less and non-Creoles two years more than that. The mean age of Nigerians was 28, with the

substantially more likely to be cut short at its other end, by death or ill health. Repeatedly during our interviews, worry about health was expressed.

Further light is thrown on the difficulties confronting those who want higher education by the responses to the question, "Did you come to college right after you finished your earlier education, or did you do something else for a while?" Coming directly from secondary school was distinctly more common among Creoles (40 per cent) than among either Ibo or Yoruba students (10 per cent and 4 per cent). Among those who did work for a while, half the Creoles and Ibos but only a third of the Yorubas interrupted their education for five years or more. Economics majors were much more likely than others to have worked for a while, and, of those who had, nearly two-thirds had done so for at least five years.

These facts about age and work interims will help us to understand more clearly some of the later findings. It is not surprising that students, after having made great sacrifices and having waited so long, often seem to overstate the value of a college degree. They are not about to undervalue it, nor think critically of the status and opportunity it confers. On the other hand, often they have been part of the educated labor force for years since leaving secondary school. About half of those who worked for a while became teachers; thus they did not leave the classroom, but instead changed roles in it. Those who did not teach often worked as government clerks, especially those who subsequently pursued economics as their field of study (29 per cent), or as technicians in private industry and commerce. This last option was especially common among those who later majored in science (39 per cent). Many of them, then, had on-the-job awareness of the working milieu to which they would return, as college-educated teachers, executives, or specialists. Mundane familiarity with the actual requirements needed in key administrative or professional roles might be expected to produce quite critical evaluations of their academic fare, wherever those studies seemed imprac-

---

Ibos slightly older and the Yoruba and others slightly younger. Curiously, the result was that the final-year students averaged about half a year younger than preliminary-stage students, reflecting the recent influx of Ibo students. In the arts curriculum, Nigerians were about a year younger on average than their counterparts. Only in the economics field was the age difference startling, with Nigerians averaging 29 and Sierra Leoneans only 22. Among the science majors those from Sierra Leone on the average were nearly three years older than the Nigerians.

tical or unrealistic as preparation for the career posts to which they aspired. As we shall see, this was often the case. Their maturity and practical experience apparently enabled them to judge the social utility of their academic work, although it did not suffice to give them clear notions of how, by their own efforts, they could add to the social relevance or career value of their course work.

Early in each interview, the student was asked why he personally wanted a college education. Despite the question's wording, no more than half answered by talking *only* of the psychic or material advantages accruing to themselves. Moreover, the ethnic group scores are somewhat surprising. Ibo students, said to derive from a culture that is distinctively competitive and materialistic and that emphasizes achieved status, proved to be least self-centered (42 per cent), while Creole students, whose cultural background might be expected to prompt them to speak in civic-minded terms, were most self-centered (60 per cent). Yoruba students scored in-between, at 47 per cent.

It seems probable that this pattern reflects the impact of the college environment itself. If we analyze the responses by academic stage of work, the contrast is indeed greater. While 46 per cent of the final-year students gave self-centered responses, only 25 per cent of the less-advanced students did so. Individualization at the expense of social responsibility—at least on the verbal level—appears to be a measurable consequence of higher education of these students.

Another factor also has a differentiating effect—the field of academic work pursued. If we remember that the ratio of final preliminary stage students is virtually the same in all three curricula, it is noteworthy that half of the science majors responded in a self-centered way while only a third of the arts or economics students entirely ignored the vicarious beneficiaries of their personal achievements. Whether this reflects earlier propensities that led to the choice of a particular academic field or whether it is a result of preoccupation with that field's subject matter is a moot question.

When lengthy answers such as we obtained on this question are reduced to numbered codes and classified merely as "self-centered" or "reflecting social awareness," it is difficult to get an adequate picture of the subjective differences in outlook behind the statistical disparities reported. Although the flavor of each of the following quotations is unique, examples of the self-centered response pattern could be multiplied many times over:

"As a teacher without a degree, one is looked down upon. A

teacher must get to the top. Otherwise my students will come to pass me. I like mechanical things, which are despised by degree holders; fortunately I had science lessons when I was young, otherwise arts courses might have been my fate. To graduate, I needed £50. I laboured a long time to buy up to this class. An executive post and respect will surely be given me."

"A college education is a must. Without it, I will suffer some inferiority complex, some lack of anything detailed to take my attention in later life. I feel that if I do not get such an education I will become very lustful, a drunkard, and one without anything to keep him busy. I will grow nasty every day, and do no reading."

By way of contrast, consider these statements, which reveal a lively awareness of the social benefits that flow from one's personal educational attainments:

"I want a college education to enable me to be in a better position to serve my family. My family responsibilities are many and I need a good paying job which I can only get by college education. In a rising African race I wish to inspire my children by my attainment and enable my parents to be proud, too, of having a graduate son."

"In a young developing nation, the role of students in the upkeep of her economic, cultural, and scientific advancement cannot be overemphasized. It is needful that any able young man must avail himself of that opportunity where possible. Being able to think better, I will be able to influence my own society, where most people are now wallowing in ignorance. Hence if I acquire a college education, I am sure to be an asset to my people."

Our interviews dealt for some time with how students evaluated the academic subjects they were studying: what subject was most stimulating, which had the greatest social relevance, which called for most mental discipline, what subject influenced their choice of career most. Three rather different modes of student evaluation were commonly employed, often but not always in combination with one another and with other, less frequently cited criteria. All references to "social utility" were noted; wherever explicit reference was made to the "African content" or to the "career credentials" value of academic work, it was separately scored.

Nearly half the students—but almost twice as many among final-year men as among the rest—talked about their academic work in terms of its practical social relevance and utility. Latin was "a dead language." Greek and Roman culture was a "collection of battles, long names and dull poems." On the positive side, economics was "a modern subject, practical in outlook and touching every aspect of human life." However, many students were unprepared to make *any* critical comments on their work.

To about one-fourth, evaluating their studies meant asking about its African content. Often this criterion was passionately invoked: "We know too much about European history and virtually nothing about the Dark Continent"; "I will never support the idea of an African doing honors in a subject like Latin"; "I hate to read the very scanty remarks about Africa in a supposedly 'world' geography book, where the author wastes most of his time on the British Isles." It was, of course, often coupled with use of the social utility test, for instance, when economics was criticized for not dealing more explicitly with the problems of developing countries like Sierra Leone, or when zoology was said to give too little attention to tropical fauna. Asking that all work be judged by its concentration on African affairs often seemed to be prompted by a psychological hunger for a clarification of collective "identity"; sometimes it served to divert attention from the pressing need for a more instrumental, more analytical, more skill-conscious approach to higher learning.

Quite different again was the standard used by about one-third of the Sierra Leoneans and nearly half the Nigerians—the narrow question of how it added to the credentials needed for one's career. Those who were preoccupied with their career credentials were likely to ask for an academic diet that would establish them. The content of their college work seemed less important to them than the college degree.

As Table 2 shows, the three main criteria were used with quite different frequency by sub-groups in our student sample. When their use by students in different fields of academic work is examined, each discipline has a distinctive pattern. Science students are strongly inclined to stress the "career credentials" they are seeking, though they also give as much weight as arts students to the "social utility" of their studies. But they are distinctly less inclined to look for a specific African content or explicitly African points of application; no doubt this reflects the nature of their studies, though in zoology, botany, or geography the pertinence of African content is demonstrable.

Majors in economics presented the most balanced use of all three criteria. Surprisingly, "social utility" is least commonly invoked by them. One might have expected that learning the principles of administration, law, and economics, and gaining rudimentary skills in accounting, finance, and statistics would have quickened their appreciation of the practical applicability of their work. It is not unexpected, on the other hand, that students concentrating on these subjects commonly thought of the "career credentials" they were thus getting. What is distinctive, however, is the lively awareness they displayed that their studies had or should properly have an explicitly "African content."

TABLE 2: CRITERIA USED IN STUDENT EVALUATIONS OF
ACADEMIC WORK

| | NATIONALITY | | ETHNIC GROUP | | | ACADEMIC STAGE | | FIELD OF STUDY | | |
	Sierra Leone %	Nigeria %	Creole %	Ibo %	Yoruba %	Final Year %	Prelim. Stage %	Arts %	Eco- nomics %	Science %
Criteria										
Social utility	46	47	59	55	43	61	33	52	39	48
African content	19	33	23	29	37	35	24	27	42	13
Career credentials	32	47	23	61	37	42	43	25	52	65
Only other criteria	27	18	27	10	23	18	24	29	18	9
(Cases)	(37)*	(79)	(22)	(31)	(30)	(57)	(58)	(52)	(40)	(23)

* Columns do not add to 100 per cent because many students used more than one criterion in their evaluation.

What criteria might be expected from those whose academic program leads to a general degree in arts? Part of their work was typically in classical language and ancient history. The rest dealt either with Western philosophy and English literature or with British history and political institutions. In the final year it was possible to include the study of Europe's historical role in Africa. Apart from that option, there was little possibility within the scope of their syllabus to give explicit attention to African content. Nor was there any special stress on competence as a career asset for future teachers in secondary schools. What might have been expected, but did not appear, would have been a distinctively heavy emphasis on the social utility and practical significance of a "humanist" education.

It is not only the field of work that affects use of critical standards;

cultural background also has its influence. Both the Creoles and the Ibos outdistanced the Yoruba in their use of the test of social utility. With the Ibos, however, this was simultaneously linked to the question of how their academic work might be said to add to their career credentials; with the Creoles, no such test was common. As for the Yoruba, they were neither as career-minded nor as practically oriented as their Nigerian rivals, the Ibo; they were, however, more preoccupied with the question of the African content of their studies.

We can argue, then, that the critical standards of these West African students tend to reflect the cultural values and preoccupations of their ethnic backgrounds, while they also are affected by the field of academic work chosen at college. What remains to be examined is the effect of length of college residence. When this is done, what first emerges is that neither reliance on "career credentials" as a test nor preoccupation with "African content" as a basis for judging academic work appears to depend on how far along in college a student is. Apparently the choice of a career and the selection of a field of academic study in which one must qualify largely occur before coming to college, with the result that those who use this test are as likely to be at preliminary stages as in their final year at Fourah Bay College. Nor is concern with African content in one's studies greatly increased by length of stay in the university environment. In a West African college some of the factors are seemingly muted that, among African students sent overseas to American or British universities, tend to generate intense nationalism and militant cultural solidarity.

What also emerges from analysis of the criteria used at earlier and later academic stages is the marked increase among the more advanced students in their use of the "social utility" test. Fully 61 per cent of the final-year students and only 33 per cent of those less advanced in their work made their critical judgments on grounds of practical utility and social significance. It is difficult to view this finding as an artifact of the sample that is due to differences in the ethnic composition of the final-year and preliminary-stage groups. Rather it appears to be a product of the academic environment and the length of time spent in it.

Our evidence prompts a number of comments about the struggle for higher education in West Africa and its resulting individualization of outlook and development of critical judgment. First, it often depends initially on the support and encouragement of one's family;

students are not at the outset "on their own," either isolated or estranged from their background. Second, it frequently involves interrupting formal education for a period of years spent gaining practical experience as teachers, clerks, or technicians; it seems likely that in this pre-college period much of the later preoccupation with securing the formal credentials of an educated man is initially generated; this period, too, appears to foster a continuing concern with an education having an African content wherever possible. Third, individualization of outlook, in terms of a self-centered view of who benefits from one's own education, appears to increase substantially the longer one stays in college and the closer one gets to graduation. Fourth, the growth of critical judgment, in terms of the practical value of one's academic studies, also is found to coincide with the length of one's college experience.

Although at the verbal level it might seem that individualization is being achieved at the expense of social responsibility, the parallel finding that critical judgment increasingly invokes the test of social utility suggests a different view. Individualization is rather an index of a student's mature awareness that the benefits of his education do not automatically flow to others. Further exertions must be made in order to translate academic knowledge into a form that bears an instrumental relationship to his society's needs.

Self-Discipline and the Growth of Civility

The time spent at the college seems to have fostered in many students a greater individualization of perspective and a more instrumental attitude toward knowledge. Does it also contribute to self-discipline toward intellectual tasks? Does it further encourage the growth of civility—those attitudes of tolerance, conciliation, and a disposition to intermingle socially with people of quite different backgrounds and habits which are necessary for the maintenance of a harmonious civil order?

To inquire about these student attitudes, two sets of questions were put to each informant. One set dealt with his general impressions of Fourah Bay College, in light of his initial expectations and in terms of the advice he would give to new students. The other set called on him to discuss what he felt was his biggest personal problem, how he planned to cope with it, and what help his education would be in meeting it.

THE STUDENT IMAGE OF A WEST AFRICAN COLLEGE

Each interview began by asking about the circumstances that led the student to come to the college. Quite understandably, the Nigerians more often had been guided by newspaper advertisements (46 per cent compared with 13 per cent) while the Sierra Leone students had been urged by people at the secondary schools (52 per cent for Sierra Leone, 20 per cent for Nigeria). The high reputation of the college throughout West Africa is suggested, however, by those who reported being influenced in their choice by alumni of Fourah Bay College whom they had met (50 per cent of the Sierra Leone students, 40 per cent of the Nigerians).

Though both nationality groups therefore had rather a good basis for developing realistic expectations about what to expect, this was less so for the Nigerians. Moreover, there is the question of frustration in their desires to have gone elsewhere. Fully 61 per cent had wanted to go to Britain, and none talked of America. No Sierra Leone student talked of preferring a Nigerian college, but a third would have liked advanced education in England and the same proportion had wanted an American degree.

We next asked each student, "In what ways has life at Fourah Bay College turned out to be different from what you expected?" It is not surprising that most answers were tinged with criticism; to large portions of both nationalities, it was second choice, not first. The Nigerians especially were unhappy. Coming from a richer country whose handsome universities more closely approximated their English prototypes, they were unprepared for the poorer physical circumstances at Fourah Bay.

Sierra Leoneans and Nigerians alike voiced criticisms of the university's academic quality—its student-faculty relationships and its intellectual tone. A closer look, however, reveals that 53 per cent of the Creoles and 48 per cent of the Ibos voiced strictures on this ground, while only 32 per cent of the Yoruba students did so. Despite this (if we remember that 58 per cent of the Yoruba were final-year men) it is again true that the final-year students were significantly more vocal about academic inadequacies than were the less advanced students (58 per cent to 28 per cent). As to those in different curricula, science students were considerably more outspoken than others.

Sometimes the fault-finding about the academic environment was more general, less sensitive to staff performance or academic facilities than to the intellectual life of the campus. There was a third theme of disappointment—with the social life and student activities. The substantial difference lay between the disappointment of preliminary-stage students, 49 per cent of whom complained in this way, and the relative satisfaction of those in their final year, only one in five of whom criticized the college's social life.

The overwhelming mode of response to this question, then, was one of criticism, complaint, and disappointment. Quite different emphases were apparent when our student informants were next asked to outline a speech of advice they might give to new students. Nearly nine out of ten said they would recommend self-reliance and hard work. About half of our informants would counsel newcomers to enlarge their social lives by joining at least some student groups, though a few warned against having anything to do with "closed societies." In part, "social mixing" was urged as a necessary break from study. "Never force yourself to read after you have been at it all day," said one Nigerian arts major. More often, however, group participation was held to be essential if one hoped to learn many things not in books. Often these reasons were explicitly related to the bi-national character of the student body: "I would tell them to make use of the international contacts and exchange of opinions and thus equip themselves for the tasks of leadership tomorrow."

There is some slight evidence that the Creoles, as representatives of the host country, were less inclined to urge new students (46 per cent) toward social participation than were the Yoruba (62 per cent) or even the Ibo (53 per cent). At the same time, it was the Creoles who stressed the theme of tolerance and good will (31 per cent) while the Nigerian students slighted it. Only 10 per cent of the Yoruba and 20 per cent of the Ibo students would include such a plea in their advice. The frequency with which this theme was invoked appears also to be linked to academic pursuits, with 28 per cent of the economics majors and only 10 per cent of the science specialists voicing it. At times, tolerance was seen as a matter of duty and moral virtue. More often, and especially from final-year students, tolerance was presented as an instrumental policy, a "strategy for learning."

Almost all our informants, then, would give a speech heavy with advice to be self-reliant and to work hard. About half of them, especially the Nigerians, would urge newcomers to join in student activities, at least in moderation, while about one-fourth, and especially the Sierra Leoneans, spoke about tolerance of different cultures and the advantages of being open-minded.

Occasionally a speech outline would touch explicitly on the loneliness and strangeness of a college in a foreign culture. The candor of one Nigerian student reveals something of the exclusiveness and pride as well as the sensitivity associated with "nationalism": "This place is no bed of roses, I would tell them. Before relaxing, you should feel it out first. Know your stand before you go in for much social life, and don't come to the front in social clubs. It will take all your time. Don't always let people know the amount of knowledge you have; pretend to be ignorant. And don't be uncritical of what you are told. The attitude to life here is not like Nigeria. We look to our own background. Here it is all Western culture and European ways. Keep your own culture. Appreciate it!"

In several ways, then, Fourah Bay College was a distinctive kind of academic community which taught its students self-discipline and self-reliance and which was a laboratory preparing them for leadership in the communities where they would later live. Its staff was largely British, and perhaps understandably the faculty sought to create a facsimile of English faculty life; this erected a wall more of remoteness than of prejudice between themselves and the students. Thus the staff was removed from the extracurricular life of the college.[15] Even on the academic side, there was only an irregularly followed "group tutorial" system to sustain meaningful intellectual contact between staff and students, to supplement lectures with discussion of central questions, to give informed guidance for the private reading program of each student. It is not surprising that nearly 90 per cent of our informants said they would advise new students to "work hard and be self-reliant."

Second, the lack of "amenities" at the college kept the students from shutting out awareness of the absence of material well-being in the world for which they were preparing. The jumble of tribal, religious, and national contrasts made casual friendships as well as organized social intercourse both stimulating and disconcerting. No one could claim to feel "at home," graciously mingling with those to whom the environment was strange; even the Creoles could not play

[15] On the other hand, the staff included at least half a dozen Africans and a similar number of Englishmen to whose interest and encouragement their students responded quickly and warmly, and who were important to the student community as a whole.

the role of host the way American or British students on their home ground might welcome foreign students. It was not liberal theory but a mutual adjustment to an environment strange to all that prompted many to develop attitudes of tolerance and good will, that led them to make calculations that they would "learn something" by group participation, and that fanned impulses of camaraderie growing from the need to compensate for "a lonely life of much self-planning."

Other features need attention also. These students came from secondary schools where they were drilled and quizzed and kept under very close surveillance by their teachers. According to many informants, their lessons had been punctuated by floggings not only for poor deportment but also for ill-prepared or poorly-phrased lessons. They came, without expecting a change, into a system where, with conspicuously little encouragement or guidance, they were expected to read and ponder, search out new materials and make comparisons, learn to annotate, paraphrase, and summarize. There was the further difficulty that all of them had to make the transition in a foreign language, English, which none of them could call his mother tongue or even the language used in his home today.

Such a combination of circumstances was almost certain to make a student keenly aware of how much he put into the task of educating himself. As one informant put it succinctly, "there is too much self-help here." Knowing they must be prepared on the "examinable" aspects of their chosen subjects and that, as "external" students, they must cover the whole syllabus rather than those aspects featured in lectures, many of them, it is not surprising to note, tried to memorize not only factual details but the views and arguments of "authorities" on subject matter that often must have seemed all too arbitrary and esoteric.

PREPARING TO MEET PERSONAL PROBLEMS

Our survey was especially successful in interviewing final-year students; others too were preoccupied with the real world into which they would return. We asked each informant to tell us in his own words, "What is the biggest problem that people like yourself face in life?" It is not surprising that half the final-year students and nearly a third of the rest said they were worried primarily about how to adjust to their own society. This was the major problem for all, the various tribal and national sub-populations and those in all three curricula.

To more than one-third, and especially the preliminary-stage students and those training for executive and technical careers, the biggest personal problem was how to raise one's living standard—how to earn a good living. The intense "materialism" of modern Africa has often been noted; it is perhaps surprising that only about one-third of these students specifically spoke of poverty and poor living conditions. Creole students spoke of material conditions most frequently, more often than Ibos and even more so than Yorubas. Perhaps a frank preoccupation with one's living standard is too self-centered a pose to be adopted very often by young men reared in the mould of tribal reciprocity and who now find themselves far from home.

Often the concern about money and the desire for a better living standard is linked to family responsibilities. When we analyzed data in terms of explicit identification of family needs as the central problem, about one-fourth of our informants could be so classified. Among them, both Ibo and Yoruba students were especially prominent, and —what cannot be reduced to the same thing—economics and science students rather than arts majors. Clearly, their obligation often irked them, and sometimes they seemed ready to deny its basic legitimacy.

Next our informants were asked how they planned to cope with their personal problem. Those in economics and science were somewhat more likely to stress "earning money" as the key to their problem's solution; arts students tended to put the emphasis on "studying hard" while still in college. Apart from these relatively precise answers, students tended to respond in one of two rather clearly contrasting styles. On the one hand, for more than one-third (and especially for Yoruba students) the formula called for being sympathetic, sociable, outgoing, gregarious. Often these were the same people who saw their biggest problem as "the difficulty of coming down to the level of less fortunate counterparts at home after graduation." On the other hand, for about 60 per cent of the students (but least for Yorubas), the formula called for more aggressive solution, through taking the lead, giving advice, providing a working example.

A second probing question was next put, asking each informant, "In what ways do you feel that your work at Fourah Bay College has prepared you to help solve that problem?" Nearly every tenth student said it had not helped in any way. The most frequent benefit mentioned was the cultural and social broadening which living in daily contact with fellow students of varied backgrounds had given.

About one-third spoke of the intellectual insight and discipline they had gained for coping with life's problems. "The intellectual stimulation here is trying to undo the rust of ignorance that used to seal my mind," said one Nigerian arts student. "I am able to look rationally upon the problems of life," said another. "It has made me realize that the pursuit of knowledge with its ultimate results is in fact to be preferred to any other type of wealth," said a third.

Only about one-fourth confined their comments to the specific academic knowledge and skills they were acquiring, while slightly more stressed the status a college degree would give them, with concomitant job security and promotions.

Our inquiry has been concerned with self-discipline and the growth of civility. How far can it be said that these are encouraged by the college environment? The evidence is derived from the students' image of the college community and also from what they see as their biggest personal problem and how to meet it.

Living as a student for a period of years at Fourah Bay College is not a "prolonged period of adolescence," as some critics characterize American college life. It is an altogether more sobering and maturing process. Self-help is the motto, and the phrase has an urgent quality to young Africans accustomed to strict supervision in secondary school, now suddenly asked to prepare themselves for the awesome examinations of a British university scheme, while their relationships to the faculty seem strangely formal, distant, and imprecise.

Ambiguous too are the proper modes of conduct toward one another in a student community with different classes, tongues, cultures, and nationalities. Nor, in a college whose social life is intensely African and whose absence of creature comforts continues to irritate even final-year men, can these future leaders shut out the daily reminders that soon they must adapt themselves to larger communities where more than the "examinable" aspects of their studies will be tested.

One basic finding is the high frequency with which these students have manifested poise and confidence in their own intellectual self-discipline; another is the level of their awareness of how common interests are served when, despite cultural barriers, people who live together extend to each other not only mutual tolerance and respect, but reciprocal confidence and teamwork.

Still, one must add some reservations. These students have only tested their capacities for mental discipline and intellectual self-reliance by their performances in subject-matter examinations on foreign institutions, alien societies, and didactically rendered sciences. Similarly, what they have acquired of the tolerance and skill needed for effective participation in a civil society—their civility—has been subjected only to the strains of a kind of "laboratory community." We need next to consider what roles they see ahead of them, in the community life and public affairs of their fast-developing home countries.

Politicization and the Contributions of Public-Spirited Intellectuals

This brings us almost full circle, and raises again the problem posed by Edward Shils—the propensities of intellectuals in new states toward a "politics of withdrawal." How politicized are these fledgling intellectuals? How fascinated are they by the *symbolic* struggle on their country's political stage? How committed are they to making a professionalized contribution toward solution of their country's *substantive* public problems?

Doubtless much depends on the kind of apprenticeship these college students have in the immediate years ahead. But how they react to their experiences as junior figures in the functional institutions, tribal communities, and political arenas of the next few years seems likely to depend also on their current involvement in politics and their desire to have a future place in it. Moreover, it probably depends on what they see as the top-priority problems confronting their nations, and what options other than "politics" they recognize for contributing to their solution. Our interviews included questions on these points.

First, nearly two-thirds of all students told us they expected to become teachers in secondary schools. Most of the rest planned to enter their country's civil service, sometimes as diplomats but more often as administrators. Among the Creoles, there were nearly a dozen who wanted to go on to become lawyers, doctors, or scientists. Among the Ibos a comparable number talked of becoming entrepreneurs. But most arts majors and quite a few economics and science specialists planned to become teachers. Most of the rest would be absorbed by government.

Why did they want careers in teaching or government service? Often enough, the scholarships they held required a period of service in specified work after graduation. This coercive fact, of course, did not prevent students from being quite receptive to the future careers. Almost 60 per cent, asked why they chose their career fields, saw it as a way of making a real social contribution; "trained manpower is one of my country's most pressing needs" was a common remark. The nature of the teaching profession, however, led many to identify themselves with the next generation, through whom they could hope to gratify their private aspirations for leadership and power vicariously. With those planning civil *service* careers, however, they were the next generation, replacing expatriate Europeans. Although the tendency to explain one's choice of career as an opportunity to contribute to the nation's manpower resources did not vary by academic stage or field of studies, it mirrored ironically the extent to which government had sponsored the college education of Creoles, Ibos, and Yoruba. Nearly all Creoles were subsidized by their government; only 39 per cent of them spoke of contributing their talents to meet the nation's needs as reason for their career choice. Only 24 per cent of the Ibos came to Fourah Bay College under government subvention, but 65 per cent explained their career choice as essentially a desire to serve their country. Appropriately, on both counts, the Yoruba students registered in between.

How did these students see themselves fitting into the African communities in which their teaching or administrative assignments would take them? Part of the answer has been seen in how they planned to cope with their biggest personal problem. We also asked each student explicit questions about his plans for active participation in community life. Only 4 per cent of the Creoles had plans to enter local politics; 16 per cent of the Ibo and 38 per cent of the Yoruba students were aspiring politicians.

This did not mean, however, that the rest would be uninterested in public affairs. Only about one in every four or five would say that he expected to be simply a "good citizen," giving moral or financial support to "worthy causes." There was a middle ground, especially at the level of community affairs; one could be a "civic leader" without being a "politician." It was this role that appealed to two out of three Creole and Ibo students; among Yoruba, however, such a distinction was less meaningful. More than a third intended to be local politicians; only an additional third planned to be civic leaders.

Each student was asked what role in community affairs he hoped to play by the time he was forty-five years old. In this longer perspective, 21 per cent of the Creoles expected to be local political figures and 53 per cent to be civic leaders. Apparently in eschewing local politics in the immediate post-college years, many Creoles (whose education was made possible by government scholarship) were aware of official inhibitions on openly political activity by government employees. Yoruba students, on the other hand, showed no greater propensity for politics in later life than immediately upon leaving school, two-fifths in each case planning "political" activity in their communities. When Ibo students were asked these questions, fully 40 per cent expected by middle age to be political figures in their communities, though only 16 per cent would enter local politics (as distinguished from community service work) soon after leaving college. Perhaps the character of Ibo community life and the institutionalized opportunities it gives for younger men to be active in affairs appropriate to their age grade as well as through voluntary associations is part of the explanation.

TABLE 3: "BY THE TIME YOU ARE FORTY-FIVE, HOW ACTIVE ARE YOU LIKELY TO BE IN THE POLITICAL LIFE OF YOUR COUNTRY AS A WHOLE?"

| | NATIONALITY | | ETHNIC GROUP | | | ACADEMIC STAGE | | FIELD OF WORK | | |
	Sierra Leone %	Nigeria %	Creole %	Ibo %	Yoruba %	Final Year %	Prelim. Stage %	Arts %	Eco-nomics %	Science %
Ministerial role	11	24	12	19	24	20	22	30	19	5
Legislative role	4	25	6	26	28	20	18	16	27	10
Other central role	50	24	38	23	20	27	34	35	30	17
No significant role	35	27	44	32	28	33	26	19	24	68
	100	100	100	100	100	100	100	100	100	100
(Cases)	(28)	(71)	(16)	(31)	(25)	(49)	(50)	(43)	(37)	(19)

Next, we pursued the question beyond the level of community affairs, asking each informant, "By the time you are forty-five, how active are you likely to be in the political life of your country as a whole?" (See Table 3.) Nearly half of the Nigerian students openly aspired to places in the legislature (including one of the three regional legislatures) or to be ministers. Consider some of their confident statements: "I aspire to be nothing short of a prime minister," "I hope to be a front bench speaker in my country's government," "I will represent my constituency in the legislature," or "In my days of statesmanship, I will be a central figure by general consent, as my late father was in his lifetime."

Few Sierra Leone students, Creole or otherwise, entertained similar hopes; only 12 per cent thought they might hold ministerial rank and only 6 per cent saw themselves as legislators in later life. At least 44 per cent expected to play no significant role at all in national politics; even among those who did, it was common for them to think of being "behind-the-scenes." The picture of the popular leader openly championing the interests of his constituents had remarkably little appeal to them. It may be pertinent to note that this small nation secured its independence in a singularly painless way, after a period of apprentice-responsibility for running its own affairs but without the long years of agitation and militant demands for self-government which Nigeria and virtually every other ex-colonial nation of today has experienced. Sierra Leone's political history has featured few demagogues, few zealous nationalists, and few charismatic leaders: from the Creoles especially come the kind of middle class rejections of "politics" as dirty and immoral that are typically found in countries where politicians perform routinized activities seemingly divorced from the serious business of its communities.

Not only ethnic-group differences were found in student aspirations for national political roles. The distinctive lack of interest in politics found among science students, 68 per cent of whom wanted no significant role in it, is in sharp contrast with the others; at least three-fourths of either arts or economics majors nurtured long-run political aspirations.

A student's involvement in politics is measured not only by his long-range hopes for an active part in community or national affairs. It is also disclosed in his fascination with developments on the contemporary political scene.[16] Two-thirds of these African students said they frequently talked about African and world politics with fellow students (see Table 4). On this count, Creoles were least politicized (63 per cent) and Yorubas most (79 per cent); final-year

---

[16] Some further insight into their outlook on contemporary politics is provided by the answers given the year before to a question about how favorably disposed they were to political leaders from various countries (*BSSR Publication 345, op.cit.*). Thirty men were listed. Two-thirds knew nothing about 5 (Mohammed V, Olympio, Kasavubu, Senghor, and Bunche); only about half could venture an opinion on 4 more (Verwoerd, Houphouet-Boigny, Haile Selassie, and Bourguiba); another group of 10 were known by 66 per cent to 83 per cent of the students and of these only Welensky was viewed definitely unfavorably; a Gaitskell, Ahmadu Bello, Nasser, Khrushchev, and Wallace Johnson were seen with lukewarm favor, and Hammarskjöld, Hastings Banda, Kenyatta, and Mboya clearly tended to evoke enthusiasm. Finally, nearly all students had personal opinions on 11 political leaders. The percentages having a "very good opinion" of each were as follows: Azikiwe (66 per cent), Nkrumah (62 per cent), Eisenhower (53 per cent), Nehru (45 per cent), Sékou Touré (44 per cent), Tubman (33 per cent), Milton Margai (25 per cent), Macmillan (24 per cent), Awolowo (24 per cent), Balewa (20 per cent), and De Gaulle (2 per cent).

students were somewhat more likely to "talk politics" (72 per cent), although the level of frequent discussion among less-advanced students (59 per cent) was substantial enough. The same point can be made on a comparison between science majors, only half of whom frequently talked politics (54 per cent), and the economics students, more than three-fourths of whom did (77 per cent). Partly this contrast may reflect the character of their course work; partly it may be the result of looking forward to careers as executives rather than as technicians or teachers.

TABLE 4: *POLITICIZATION LEVEL:* "IN THE LAST SIX MONTHS, HOW OFTEN HAVE YOU DISCUSSED WORLD POLITICS WITH OTHER STUDENTS?"

| | NATIONALITY | | ETHNIC GROUP | | | ACADEMIC STAGE | | FIELD OF WORK | | |
	Sierra Leone %	*Nigeria* %	*Creole* %	*Ibo* %	*Yoruba* %	*Final Year* %	*Prelim. Stage* %	*Arts* %	*Eco- nomics* %	*Science* %
Very frequently discuss politics:	64	67	63	71	79	72	59	61	77	54
Frequently do so:	17	18	15	10	10	14	21	20	16	14
Not very frequently:	19	15	22	19	11	14	20	19	7	32
	100	100	100	100	100	100	100	100	100	100
(Cases)	(42)	(70)	(27)	(31)	(29)	(58)	(61)	(54)	(43)	(22)

It is not enough, however, to equate involvement in politics with either long-run desire for high office or willingness to discuss the party issues and daily maneuvers of political leaders. To do so is to treat "politicization" as a fascination *only* with the symbolic struggles that eventuate in governmental decisions. But what of the real struggle to implement those decisions? Our students identify economic development, mass literacy, minimum levels of hygiene and well-being, and inter-cultural tolerance and harmony as the top priority tasks facing their nation. It seems useful to distinguish the processes that legitimate or repudiate proposals for national action to meet these problems from the equally vital processes that realize or frustrate the actualization of policy and that make the difference between "words on paper" and "actual achievements."

When we consider the content of "substantive politicization," it is by learning the answers to such questions as "what is the biggest problem facing your country as a nation today?" and "what can people like yourself do to help solve this problem?" Important differences in the perspectives of different types of students emerge when this is done (see Table 5). Thus, while length of college residence has apparently little effect on one's interest in "symbolic politics," it is correlated directly with concern over "tribalism" as a nationally divisive force. Final-year men were substantially more likely than others to name it as the biggest problem. Are we entitled to feel that they better appreciate the strength of the underlying cultural traditions to which current political leaders must address themselves and that their political thinking is therefore more responsible? Again, science students seemingly care little about party struggles or legisla-

TABLE 5: "WHAT IS THE BIGGEST PROBLEM FACING YOUR COUNTRY AS A NATION TODAY?"

	NATIONALITY		ETHNIC GROUP			ACADEMIC STAGE		FIELD OF WORK		
	Sierra Leone %	Nigeria %	Creole %	Ibo %	Yoruba %	Final Year %	Prelim. Stage %	Arts %	Economics %	Science %
Tribalism	44	49	39	28	65	58	38	53	49	30
Economic development	33	28	44	41	23	21	38	30	30	30
Educational needs	41	14	39	22	6	21	24	25	13	40
Living conditions	8	17	4	22	13	11	17	8	19	20
(Cases)	(39)*	(81)	(23)	(32)	(31)	(57)	(63)	(53)	(47)	(20)

* Columns do not add to 100 per cent because of multiple responses.

tive actions. Their substantive concern with public affairs is distinguished, moreover, by a comparative indifference to tribalism as a problem. Recall also how comparatively slight are their intentions to take active part in community politics, either immediately after college or in middle age. It seems likely that many of them will spend quiet lives, making useful contributions to the modernization of their country either as technicians or teachers, almost irrespective of what kind of political regime or civic life flourishes around them.

Consider, finally, the three major ethnic groups in our sample. While involvement with the shadow problems of the political arena was relatively low for Creole students, it should be noted that they are much more concerned than others with their country's educational needs. Recall that most of them plan to become teachers. Also, more consistently than the Nigerians when asked about their place in community affairs both upon graduation and in middle life, the Creoles eschew active politics in favor of the role exemplified by their parents—voluntary group service. Coming from families where "third-generation literacy" is not uncommon, they give reasons for wanting college educations that are more individualized at the same time that their critical judgment of academic work more frequently invokes the test of social utility. Furthermore, they are distinctively more likely than others to speak of choosing their career to ensure their status in life or because they found the work personally gratifying. Given the impossibility of Creole political dominance in Sierra Leone, these Creole students in many ways have already developed attitudes that should contribute to their effectiveness as the educators of other Sierra Leone generations.

The Ibo student seemed to have a rather different kind of professionalized outlook toward his country and its problems. Almost as intensely politicized and bent on a role in politics, both local and national, as his Yoruba rival, the typical Ibo was singularly unconcerned with "tribalism" as a problem. Instead he emphasized economic development and the tasks of improving the living conditions of his countrymen. On this score, too, like the Creole student, he was likely to feel that he could best contribute by "educating others" and by "providing working examples," not by "practicing tolerance."

Unlike the Creoles, however, Ibo students were highly conscious that their education would benefit not only themselves but others. They often spoke of choosing their careers in order to contribute to the solution of their society's problems. More than others, they were consciously seeking "career credentials" at Fourah Bay College, although, like the Creoles, they were also concerned with the social utility of their academic work. Like the Creoles again, they saw the solution to their personal problems in taking the lead, giving advice, and providing examples. More than other students, they were unworried about how to adjust to their own society after leaving college. Public-spirited in terms of their personal receptivity to politics, as a group they were more prepared than others to assert their claims to leadership, on the grounds that they had the know-how and professional competence to implement government policies and community goals.

Finally, Yoruba students much more frequently than others voiced a concern at and sensitivity to tribalism as Nigeria's central problem. This finding must be considered in light of their equally distinctive emphasis on "practicing tolerance" as the way to help solve their country's problem. Tribalism is rooted in people's loyalty to some symbols and patterns and their simultaneous distrust of others. Practicing tolerance is the ordinary citizen's way of helping to confine cultural contentions within the corporate framework of a civil order. But our Yoruba students did not aim to be ordinary citizens. More involved than any of the other ethnic groups in current political developments, they were also more often bent on becoming ministers or legislators in later life and in being political figures in their own community.

We cannot know how long these Yoruba student attitudes will persist. The effort and ingenuity spent making a public career, in Africa as elsewhere, may dull their sensitivity and render them callous. Once in the seats of power, they may feel a sense of fruition, of having arrived, which could cause them to relax and settle in. But their attitudes run counter to the syndrome of forces underlying the "politics of withdrawal." Edward Shils has suggested that, in every group of intellectuals, a small but precious portion achieve a perspective of "civility" toward the public scene and their own responsibilities in it. For young intellectuals to leave college with the attitudes found so markedly among our Yoruba informants is surely an encouraging sign that some of them at least will contribute to the civility of politics in their nation. What must be put into the balance, however, is the fact that they enter the next stage of their careers after an educational experience that has given them few analytical skills, little knowledge of their country's political, economic, or cultural institutions, and only a common-sense appreciation of the dynamics of human psychology and historical change. Neither in content nor in intellectual method has their college education been addressed to the tasks they will face or the responsibilities they wish to assume. On our evidence, they are also the group to whom cynicism, bitterness, or resignation may well come in the next ten years; they are the likeliest *candidates* for the "politics of withdrawal."[17]

[17] From the earlier survey (*BSSR Publication 345, op.cit.*), it is possible to learn what "attributes and status qualification are most necessary for a successful West African politician," in the opinion of Sierra Leone and Nigerian students at Fourah Bay College, respectively: "Having organizing ability," 96 per cent and 94 per cent; "A dynamic personality," 86 per cent and 92 per cent; "Powers of oratory," 82 per cent and 82 per cent; "Having a gregarious personality (a good mixer)," 66 per cent and 70 per cent; "Having a magnetic personality," 54 per cent and 69 per cent. These were the most frequently checked options; they reveal how much the image of a successful politician is cast in charismatic terms, even to recruiting his own followers

Many serious observers in recent years have reluctantly concluded that, in the fast-modernizing countries of Africa and Asia, political enterprise and initiative seemingly *must* come from above—from the nation's top leaders and a handful of their rivals. The specific strains of high office in the "new states" are said to arise from this fact. Whenever a common problem is recognized, there is a pervasive demand that its solution must be an authoritative one, and that a governmental program must be launched to meet it. However concrete and specific the problem, it must first be politicized and seen in its rhetorical and symbolic relationship to a larger political movement, cause, or heroic struggle. It is argued that no solution can be justified because of the enthusiasm and example of a few public-spirited volunteers. Rather, what is done must be formulated on a scale and accompanied by a fanfare appropriate to a project legitimated "in the name of the people." A serious damper is thus placed on voluntary and public-spirited activity.

Too often, modest community and small group enterprises are delayed and transformed by these pressures toward political glamorization, official governmental implementation, and populist legitimization. Pervading the whole symbolic arena of politics is an atmosphere of mutual distrust and suspicion for any project launched by a rival faction. At the very least, the top leaders in such cramped quarters may opt for policies and modes of implementation that stifle political criticism. Equally serious in the long run, they may adopt policies which ignore the potential support and voluntary cooperation to be secured from public-spirited people in every community. In both cases, they are tempted to govern in ways that perpetuate the transitional fact, and that sequester all political enterprise and organized initiative in an ever more authoritarian regime.

It is for these reasons that inquiry into the perspectives of potential West African leaders, even while they are still in college, needs to consider their substantive politicization—the concern with the real problems of modernization and how to tackle them—as well as their symbolic politicization. This is why we have explored their loyalty

---

and organizing his own show. Consider the less frequently preferred options, with their scores, to see the downgrading of more ascriptive status qualifications: "High non-tribal status," 41 per cent and 63 per cent; "Overseas education," 52 per cent and 39 per cent; "Personal wealth," 37 per cent and 48 per cent; "High status in tribal society," 29 per cent and 19 per cent; "Training as a lawyer," 17 per cent and 21 per cent; "Unmarried," 12 per cent and 3 per cent; and "A reticent personality," 4 per cent and 4 per cent.

and respect for the traditional pattern of life in which they were reared, why we looked also for signs of their individualization and for growth in their critical judgment of academic work, why we tried to gauge the empirical warrant for saying that their college experience had maturing effects on them, by developing both self-reliance and mental discipline, and a conscious realization of the importance to any civil society of tolerance and open-mindedness.

CHAPTER 15

Toward a Modern Intellectual Community in the New States

EDWARD A. SHILS

~~~~~~

I

To be modern, a society requires at least a rational administration which extends its jurisdiction to the territorial boundaries of the state. It requires a rational outlook about economic matters and a rational organization of its economic activities. It requires a relatively rational legal system, and institutions of public political action. It requires a government concerned with more than the conduct of war, the maintenance of order and the prevention of sacrilege. A modern government operates the educational system, takes responsibility for communication and transportation and seeks to foster economic growth. It has policies which require implementation, not just decisions which require enforcement.

These are minimal requirements. They do not refer to the mass of population, but only to the elites of the major institutional sub-systems of the society—the economy and the polity. Each of these subsystems requires an elite appropriate to its tasks. Rational administration requires higher civil servants, lawyers, judges, scientists, and technologists. A rational economic system requires enterprisers and managers, economists, accountants, chemists, agronomists, lawyers, and experts in transportation and marketing. Public political life requires politicians, party officials, editors and reporters, professors and social research workers, radio engineers and producers. These professions can neither be staffed nor carried on without a modern intellectual system. By an intellectual system I do not mean a system of ideas but rather a set of intellectual institutions in which persons are trained for or perform intellectual roles.

The elites of any society that reaches this level of modernization are also bound, willy-nilly, to have and desire a modern intellectual system. They might, it is true, wish to use some of their intellectual apparatus to glorify their traditional culture, but this purpose will not be the sole ground for their aspiration. The elites' desire for a modern intellectual system will rest in part on the fact that they already possess to some extent a modern culture which they will not want to see eradicated; it will also come from the belief, widely shared by the elites of the new states, that a modern culture, and particularly its intellectual institutions, are technically, or functionally, necessary for the modernization of the polity and the economy. Finally, it will come from the belief that the elements in an institutional system of modern intellectual action—universities, scientific research institutions, learned bodies, literary publications, libraries, and the cultural productions that are generated by these institutions—are as essential to a modern sovereign state as an army equipped with up-to-date weapons, an airline, and a flag. They are part of the constellation of symbols that a state must have nowadays to merit the respect of those who have created and run it, and, as they think, of the outside world. The strength and direction of the desire for a modern intellectual system varies of course among the different sectors of the elite. Intellectuals have practical and ideal interests in expanding such elements of the system as already exist. The interests of practicing politicians might emphasize the practical and the national status aspects more. Nonetheless there is general agreement that intellectual institutions of many sorts are necessary.

Those who assert the necessity of such an institutional system are correct. Persons qualified through an elaborate educational experience are necessary. The technical knowledge prerequisite to the tasks of modernization does require systematic preliminary formation. Obviously scientists and technologists must have learned the rudiments of their subjects before they begin to work on them. Accountants and agronomists, lawyers and economists can scarcely learn on the job what they need to know to meet a moderate standard of proficiency. The higher educational system of a modern or a modernizing society must make provision for the preliminary formation of such skills. There must therefore be a body of persons capable of reproducing and transmitting this pattern of technical and specialized knowledge and skill. A body of persons, different in the substantive content of their intellectual culture but having parallel functions, is no less necessary for providing the education prerequisite to administration, public discussion, and even practical politics.

Alongside these institutions for the formation of skills, the guidance of dispositions, and the preliminary exercise of the capacity for judgment, there are also the institutions in which these skills, dispositions, and capacities are to be brought into serious operation. Scientific and technological research institutions, institutes of economic and social research, government scientific services, scientific advisory committees, professional and learned societies, universities and other institutions of higher learning, museums and libraries, the machinery of communications (i.e., radio, newspapers, and periodicals), the publication of books, the machinery of their distribution, conferences, clubs and exhibitions—the list tails away as it ranges from the more massively organized to the more informal and spontaneous collectivities through and in which the actual work of productive and reproductive culture is carried out.

It becomes manifest that, as we move from the central institutions of the cultural system out toward the peripheral ones, the intellectual culture of a society does not consist of universities and research institutes in which people are trained for and perform intellectual work. It becomes no less manifest that the peripheral institutions are as much an integral part of the complex as those closer to the center. Without the former, the latter make little sense. There must, in other words, be roles and institutions in which the skills, dispositions, and capacities formed in the central institutions can be used. There must likewise be roles and institutions which, although apparently only ancillary, are indispensable conditions for the effectiveness of the central institutions. Libraries, publishing enterprises, bookshops, learned societies, periodicals, and so on, must exist. Institutions which link the production and transmission of knowledge to its practical application are necessary. Otherwise the social system of intellectual life will be incomplete, and the need for completeness inherent in the system and in the exigencies of the life of the society as a whole will require supplementation by foreign institutions. Alternatively, the central institutions will languish or wither away.

Furthermore, the social system of intellectual life must have a culture of its own. I refer here not just to the articulated culture of specific propositions, the culture that consists of the contents of particular books, the knowledge and practice of the sciences and the arts. I refer to that stratum of culture which underlies and permeates the specific culture. This stratum belongs more in the sphere of generalized dispositions and deeper categories; it is more a matter of standards of judgment, of the unarticulated criteria which distinguish the essential from the unessential. At the bottom of this culture lies the motivation that impels intellectual action: above all, curiosity, the desire to learn something new, the self-confidence in one's right and capacity as an individual to know and experience. Here we should also list the pleasure in contemplation of reality at whatever level of concreteness, and the desire to go beyond any particular level of concreteness to a deeper or more general understanding. Also relevant is the experience of intellectual conviviality, of being in contact with other persons of similarly directed curiosity, together with solidarity with such persons in one's own sphere of action, both at home and abroad.

The new states have in varying degrees made substantial progress in the establishment of the central institutions of intellectual life. In the former colonial territories—and those which were never colonized —there are numerous universities and university colleges. Some were established before independence; others have been found or reformed since independence. Even the few affiliated with a metropolitan sponsor are full-fledged institutions, with a full complement of departments covering the major fields of interest to modern universities. Moreover, many of them conform to a respectable standard of administrative and intellectual performance.

Beyond these institutions, the intellectual systems of the new states are hardly adequate to the requirements of a modern intellectual system. Museums, libraries, publishing houses, periodicals and newspapers, the opportunities for meeting a wide range of colleagues in one's own or neighboring fields, through their publications or through face-to-face encounters, are few. The intellectual systems of the new states suffer not so much from isolation from their own societies—the most common complaint against them—as from their isolation from colleagues and like-minded persons, whether within or outside their own societies. Most of the new states lack an intellectual public outside the universities, the higher civil service, and the journalistic and broadcasting professions, and these categories are so small that they do not provide sufficient differentiation and diversity. The stimulation of a diversified intellectual environment scarcely exists. Moreover, the networks of intellectual communication are so slightly developed that what small productivity there is has no internal channels through which it might be transmitted. The number of persons available to stimulate and fortify the adherence to standards, either through competition or through fellow-feeling, is too small to be effective. The paucity of local writing and publishing, and the meagerness of the social-intellectual environment, either result in desultoriness and slackness of intellectual exertion, or force continued dependence on the intellectual life of the metropolis. In any event there would be a marked dependence on the metropolis, because in many areas of endeavor, metropolitan societies are presently exhibiting a high degree of creativity. The similarity of pattern of the institutions of higher learning and those of the metropolis, the paths of communication between metropolis and province, as well as the presence of many metropolitan expatriates in the local universities, all tend to focus attention on the continued intellectual output of the metropolis. Furthermore, it should be stressed that no country can ever be fully self-sufficient in its intellectual life; to aspire to be so is an aspiration to intellectual suicide. Nonetheless, the internal structure and the level of institutional development of intellectual life in the new states make for far-reaching dependence on the metropolis. Even efforts to break away, as in Ghana, only introduce other metropolitan centers of dominance. This close relationship inhibits the emergence of motivations for a high quality of local performance.

It might be argued that what I have been saying applies only to intellectual structures, and that it has little to do with the process of political modernization. After all, what a society needs for modernization is a good corps of civil servants, engineers, and technologists; all the rest is trimming. Colleges, universities, and higher technical institutes are sufficient, and the rest is just a highbrow demand. I do not share this view; I think that a creative intellectual stratum is an indispensable element which no society can forego on its path toward modernity. The very establishment of a society on a national scale, coterminous with the scope of sovereignty, requires a sense of national identity which, at least in part, focuses on a cultural activity concerned with the past, the present, and the future of its society. The existence of cultural monuments inherited from the past, either by physical survival or by traditional transmission, requires interpretation. To interpret them in a modern way, highly qualified persons, well trained in the techniques of modern humanistic scholarship, which are of universal validity regardless of the parochiality of the subject matter, must be available. The inherited culture is not rich enough in itself either to serve as the cultural complement of a modern society or to engender the self-respect demanded by modernity. Cultivation of folk arts and of traditional medicine will not satisfy the elites of the new states, however traditionalistically they wish to present themselves on ceremonial occasions. There must be creativity in specifically modern genres, in literary and artistic production, in scientific research, in the social sciences, in history, and in the study of literature, language, and art. Self-discovery on a large scale is an essential part of the formation of a trans-local or national society, and to this end humanistic and social research is necessary. It must be a self-discovery in which fictitious and mythical elements are treated dispassionately and sympathetically, for otherwise they will be despised by intelligent people, even by those who use them demagogically. The modern techniques of research are indispensable for this purpose.

So much for the value of modern cultural achievement in the creation of the symbolism of a modern society. If the standards in operation in universities and colleges are slack and the performance is poor, according to universal criteria, the quality of the graduates produced will be poor. Scientists, engineers, technologists, and civil servants will be agents of modernization more in name than in performance. Their works will decay too soon, and their moral and economic competitive power will be low vis-à-vis their counterparts in countries whose agriculture is more efficient, whose commercial procedures are more orderly, and whose public and private administration is more trustworthy. Journalists will be less knowledgeable than the standards of the profession require, and politicians will tend to be of poorer quality, being less well informed and less realistic in their judgments. (Knowledge and realism, of course, are not the sole prerequisites to the effectiveness of politicians.)

The political public, unattached to any standards of judgment other than those provided by ethnicity, locality, party, or passion, will lack the capacity to pass judgment on the merits of policies, both for the very immediate present or the very remote future, and will be useless to the political culture of a modern society. Their culture will be a political culture in the worst sense of the term. Political development requires some limitations on politics. Excessive politicization is a degenerate form of political development. The poorly educated, proud and sensitive about their singular status, will be a source of perpetual political disturbance. No group exhibits this tendency more clearly than politicized university (and sometimes secondary school) students. The hyper-excitability of these youths, although it may sometimes be valuable in helping to overthrow a tyranny, is more often expressed in political procedures and on behalf of political ends that are not conducive to the formation of a pragmatic point of view or to the nourishment of a political culture capable of growth. An excessively politicized political culture helps to demoralize intellectual institutions and dooms them in effectual mediocrity.

II

India is a case in point. No new state of Asia or Africa is so well situated as India with respect to the scale of higher education and, indeed, its entire institutional apparatus of intellectual activity. No other new country is so capable of providing its own academic and intellectual personnel to staff its many institutions. No other new state is so well able to get along without the services of expatriates. In no other new country is the number of university graduates large enough to meet the country's needs. No other new state can show so many persons capable of outstanding intellectual achievement.

The modern sector of Indian society is a powerful and impressive structure. Much of it is the creation of the Indian educated class, or at least its continuance is the work of that class. If the traditional sector of Indian society is like an ocean, broad and deep, the modern sector is like a well-settled coastal civilization, deeply affected by its oceanic environment but rich enough and ramified enough to lead, to some extent, a life of its own.

Whereas practically all other new states, such as those of Africa and the Middle East, arrived at independence with a flimsy or nonexistent modern intellectual system, India already possessed, at least quantitatively, a fairly well-elaborated system of intellectual institutions. India has had universities for more than a hundred years, and colleges for even longer. In the twentieth century, well before independence, India possessed many learned societies, research institutes in the natural and social sciences, a number of outstanding scholarly libraries, a dizzying proliferation of periodicals, a well-established and sober English language press, a few scientists and scholars who were honored the world over, and two Nobel prize winners.

Contemporary India, although its well-wishers and critics lament the state of affairs, has not marked time since independence insofar as its intellectual system is concerned. The country has a journalistic profession which is outstandingly good with respect to probity, freedom, and corporate spirit, although it is still deficient in such matters as reportorial curiosity and initiative. Owing to the inadequacy of resources, derived from the smallness of the reading public and the insufficiencies of private advertising, the press has structural defects.

A fair number of publishing houses issue books in English and in Indian languages. It is beginning to have a few which publish books in English of a decent standard, and a few are of comparable quality in the Indian languages. India has many bookshops with large stocks, and in this respect exceeds any country in Black Africa or the Middle East.

At the center of the Indian intellectual system stand the Indian universities—now numbering more than fifty—with more than a million students and more than 30,000 teachers. There are about thirty government scientific and technological research laboratories, a number of private research institutions in the natural and social sciences, and a very large output of scientific and scholarly publications. Indian research students are found in the major universities of Great Britain and America, where many of them do good work and some are outstanding. A growing number of Indian scientists hold posts as teachers and research workers in universities outside India. Many Indian research students abroad defer their return home indefinitely because they are able to obtain and hold appointments in research or industrial organizations. Most of these persons, acknowledged as competent by even the highest standards, have had their undergraduate training in India.

All these accomplishments notwithstanding, the Indian intellectual system is subject to severe criticism. One of the most common complaints is that the system is out of touch with India, that, having inherited the university from Great Britain, it has not adapted it to Indian needs. Its failure to do so is sometimes alleged to be damaging to India; it is also adduced to explain the public disorders in which Indian college and university students participate. Another criticism, less frequently voiced officially but often asserted privately, is that the quality of university education is poor.

Let us consider first the charge that Indian universities have not adapted themselves to the new conditions of independence. Presumably this criticism censures them for retaining too close an affiliation with the intellectual life of the former ruling power, for not teaching in Hindi or in the local Indian language, and for not paying due reverence to Indian traditional culture. It must be acknowledged that there is a certain xenophilia among Indian university teachers; indeed, it could hardly be otherwise when so much of their intellectual sustenance comes from abroad. Many textbooks used in Indian universities have been written by British authors, although Russian and

American textbooks are beginning to achieve recognition. The scientific and scholarly literature read by Indians, particularly the former, is written almost entirely in English. Non-technical books and periodicals are written mainly in English. A disproportionately high percentage of the best Indian research students receive their advanced training in Britain and America.

Yet Indian problems and Indian subject matter are not overlooked by Indian universities. In every university classical and modern Indian studies, linguistic, literary, and historical, have a prominent place in the curriculum. Science, engineering, agriculture, genetics— subjects claimed to be necessary for Indian economic development— are taught and investigated. The social sciences, too, are amply represented. And, although British and American textbooks are used more frequently than Indian textbooks, Indian material is by no means neglected, despite its relative mediocrity. In certain subjects, it is true, syllabi and required and recommended books contain much that is out of date, and out-of-date material tends to be more British than Indian. On the whole, Indian universities, which owe their origin mainly to British inspiration, gain far more than they lose from their factual and sentimental xenophilia. It would be better if they could be more independent, and could introduce innovations more conducive to their effectiveness. In view of the absence of initiative, xenophilia keeps standards higher than they would otherwise be.

Other aspects of the charge that Indian universities are not sufficiently Indianized have little merit. The demand for teaching in the Indian languages is diminishing in intensity simply because such instruction has not proved practicable; most of the efforts in that direction have proved to be more injurious than beneficial. The demand for a deeper reverence for the Indian cultural inheritance is superfluous, because it has already been met. Indeed, individual staff members have done more than the government, with its sparing financial provisions for research and publication on classical Indian subjects, to inculcate respect for cultural traditions.

It is ridiculous to assert that the Indian university is a rootless institution, a foreign establishment on Indian soil. One could as well say that the Indian administrative service, the Indian army, and the system of parliamentary government are foreign institutions. The proposition makes sense only if, by India, one means traditional India, and if one regards anything modern as a rootless intrusion. It is impossible to argue that India should be modernized while at the same time denying that the universities are right in pursuing a course that implies adherence to standards of universal validity.

Universities must, in order to be universities, teach and investigate what is of universal validity; they must also teach and investigate what is of parochial value, either because it is practical or because it cultivates the parochial (or national) cultural tradition. The Indian universities serve all these purposes; their great deficiency is that they do not serve them well. There are outstanding exceptions. For example, the impressive young people who are recruited for the Indian administrative service, and the handful of outstanding young scholars and scientists, have almost all had their undergraduate training in India. Yet, despite these exceptions, Indian universities are on the whole doing a poor job intellectually; to the extent of their failure, the quality of performance of their graduates is bound to suffer. The public life of India will suffer accordingly. There will always be enough gifted persons to staff the upper grades of the administrative service and to provide a few brilliant scientists. Nevertheless, India runs the danger of having too small a supply of that solid stratum of B+ persons so necessary for the efficient functioning of any complex organization, be it administrative, political, or intellectual.

It is not that Indian universities teach the wrong skills, or skills that are irrelevant to India's problems. There are perhaps more persons trained in law than are really necessary, or more than can earn a decent livelihood from the practice of law. India does not suffer from a pronounced shortage of scientists and engineers; in fact, there is scarcely enough employment, most of it very ill-paid, for those who are available. (For this reason many who have traveled overseas wish to remain overseas.) Nor is it that Indian university education is too old-fashioned, in the sense of being humanistic and literary to the exclusion of scientific and technical aspects. The distribution of Indian university students is fairly well balanced. Particularly in view of the higher costs of a scientific or technical education, as compared with a liberal arts education, and of Indian poverty, the balance is quite reasonable. Furthermore, the arts subjects have served India well in the education of civil servants, politicians, and journalists, and there is no reason to suppose that the arts curriculum (including, of course, the social sciences) should not continue to do equally well by India in the future.

The deficiencies of the Indian university are deficiencies of teaching and research and of intellectual morale. The dismal pedagogy of the universities and colleges of India is a result of the teachers' poverty, their distraction by routine, and their feeling that they cannot do their work well under the present conditions. They feel meanly treated by the leaders of Indian society and the top officials of their own institutions; they are ill-at-ease and unhappy. Yet higher salaries and lighter teaching schedules, the improvement of academic administration, and less interference by politicians in the internal life of universities and colleges, however desirable and imperative such reforms may be, would not necessarily remove one very important source of the present malaise. These improvements would not be sufficient to arouse the Indian universities from their intellectual doldrums.

At present, not enough teachers and research workers take intellectual work seriously; not enough of them do serious study of their own, either in research or in teaching. Too many of those who are engaged in research projects of their own do the work in a perfunctory and indifferent manner without real conviction as to its worthwhileness, or do it on "assignment." Many of those who once had an interest in research have given it up, though they may still go through the motions. It is common for teachers to have so little interest in their subjects that their classroom presentation has become boring to themselves and to their students. Few manage to keep up with new developments in their respective fields. The same antiquated lecture notes are used year after year. (Better preparation and the use of more up-to-date literature are not easy, given the poverty of the teachers and the deficiencies of most college libraries.)

A teacher who has no love of his subject matter cannot communicate any love to his students; the indifference of the students only increases the teacher's boredom. Teacher and student are caught in a vicious circle which, if it breaks at all, goes into a downward spiral because of the student's difficulties in understanding English lectures and textbooks. It has often been observed that the English of university students is not what it was before independence. True, but then there were only 100,000 students, the majority of whom came from urban, educated, and professional families, whereas today there are a million students, many of whom come from rural and uneducated families. The number of students who know English well must be as large now as it was thirty or forty years ago, but now they are in a minority and cannot set the tone of the college or university. The alternatives are lectures in a regional language and good textbooks in English, which consequently would be even less intelligible, or potboiled, paste-pot-and-scissors textbooks in the regional language, the number of which is increasing. Neither of these combinations would make for lively teaching or for a sympathetically responsive student audience.

The ineffectiveness of the teaching staff stems in part, of course, from overwork, anxiety about the economic situation of one's family, which is universal in the lower middle class, and the lack of adequate research facilities at home or in the college. Poor preparation, especially among some of the younger men in smaller colleges, contributes its share. Yet all these factors are insufficient to explain why brilliant and often promising young men, as many Indian college and university teachers were at the start of their careers, sink into boredom, intellectual dullness, and sterility.

It is by no means uncommon to encounter a tired and hopeless Indian university teacher in early middle age who, as a young man in an Indian or a British university, was full of enthusiasm for his work, impelled by bright and sometimes profound ideas, which he pursued with intense industry and even dedication. By early middle age he has accomplished practically nothing with his talent or his training. He has failed, as the years passed, to go forward with the line of inquiry he began as a research student, and he has undertaken no new study. If asked what has happened, he tells a melancholy tale. He began his career full of life but after a time his vitality faded. The head of his department was resentful of his qualifications and his intellectual vivacity. He could not get the books or the equipment he needed, or he got them so long after applying for them that he had lost interest. His colleagues, who had gone further in the process of stultification, offered neither the stimulation of their own ideas nor an understanding and responsive audience for his own. Bit by bit, under the weight of growing family responsibilities and the allures of college and university intrigue, his mind wandered away from the problems that had once fascinated him. The result is one more depressed, saddened, or embittered middle-aged teacher, who in his turn will lead other bright young men of the succeeding generation on the path to intellectual dullness and indifference, and who will bore the restless to distraction.

In India, the livelier young man, on joining a college or university staff, is thrust into isolation from the company of other interested research students and of inspiring, or at least exacting, supervisors. It is not that he is physically alone—in fact, he can hardly ever be alone. But the filament that binds minds together into an intellectual community has gone dead, or has been ruptured. The new teacher loses contact with minds interested in his field of research; he misses contact with superior minds in other fields, which, quite apart from any substantive interest, have the electrical quality of intellectual brilliance.

There are, of course, geniuses who will do the work of genius whatever the immediate environment. For gifted men, as many young Indian university and college lecturers are, or could be under more favorable circumstances, it is intellectual death to be a member of so depressed a class. To do competent work, a teacher should be a member of an Indian and an international intellectual community, a community of peers who share a devotion to high standards and a common tradition. As it is, the Indian college or university teacher is not a fullfledged member of either an Indian or an international intellectual community.

India hardly has an intellectual community. Regional parochialism operates in intellectual as it does in political affairs. People in the academic world of India are astonishingly cut off from one another. There is little intellectual interchange among them, except within small circles linked by personal ties or by common memories of Cambridge, Oxford, or another university. Such is the circle that helps to make the *Economic Weekly* so interesting and so rare. Circles marked by vivid intellectual interaction are rare. Workers in a given field of research are often surprisingly ill-informed about related work in other parts of India; sometimes they know more about what is being done in Britain or America. There is a tendency to disregard Indian work. The means of intellectual communication in India are poor, although they are improving. Most Indian scholars and scientists still prefer to see their work published in a foreign journal rather than in an Indian one. A scholar who does publish in India fears that his work will not be noticed by colleagues in India or abroad; Indian journals are not accorded respectful attentiveness because scholars do not expect to find first-class articles in them. This attitude is understandable, but, as long as it persists, the creation of a coherent all-Indian intellectual community in science and scholarship will be inhibited.

Moreover, there is no all-India market for intellectual manpower except in a few subjects, such as physics or anthropology. People tend to stay, and to find their contacts, in their regions of origin. Instruction in regional languages at the university level will simply stabilize, or even extend this situation. This intellectual Balkanization is pernicious because it obstructs the emergence of intellectual Indian leadership in science and scholarship. Without such leadership to set higher standards and instill confidence in Indian capabilities, intellectual endeavors in India will continue to be second-rate and derivative.

The University Grants Commission could adopt measures that would improve the situation. India would be well served by institutions like the Institute of Advanced Study at Princeton or the Center for Advanced Study in the Behavioral Sciences at Stanford in the United States, or by a system of research fellowships like those at British universities, which give able and promising young men a few years of free time in which to continue and deepen lines of inquiry first investigated in their work for advanced degrees in India or abroad. Indian institutions, conducted on a more modest scale, could be much less expensive than their counterparts abroad. A small beginning, on a restricted scale, has actually been made in India in the direction of research fellowships, in a desperate attempt to recall some of the able young men who have shown a preference to remain in foreign countries where there are little opportunities. It is absolutely necessary that the recipients of such awards be chosen by a highly qualified body from which the ordinary "stuffed shirts" of the Indian academic world are excluded, and that applications be rigorously scrutinized by the selection committee without regard to the caste or the religious or regional community of the applicant. It is necessary, above all, that applications be made without the approval of vice-chancellors, deans, or heads of departments of the institutions which employ the applicants. Otherwise, the same deadening hand of the mediocre middle-aged, which is already responsible for the sterility of much of India's university life, will be felt once more. India has already made a start in the Tata Institute of Fundamental Research in Bombay, the Gokhale Institute of Economics and Politics, and the Deccan College Research Institute in Poona. If suitable adaptations were made, these bodies could effectively contribute to the enlivening of Indian academic work.

Another helpful measure would be the establishment, on a restricted scale at first, of intensive refresher courses for college and university teachers in their thirties and forties. Such courses might be devoted to single subjects, such as mathematics or linguistics or sociology. Ideally, they would extend through an academic session. A program of lectures and seminars could be supplemented by reading, writing, and informal consultation. Outstanding workers in various fields, Indian and foreign, would bring a carefully selected group of Indian college and university teachers up to date in their respective subjects, and try to stimulate them to do creative and original work in the future. Such measures would also serve to bring younger men with enlivened minds into contact with each other. Intellectual amity would be formed which would stimulate the participants to continued exertion. The awareness that there are other persons in one's own generation with similar interests and high standards would strengthen intellectual resolution.

As a more radical measure, the University Grants Commission might concentrate its resources so that a few already somewhat better universities could be made much better than they are. The Commission has already started the commendable practice of concentrating on certain special subjects by developing a system of "centers of excellence" in various research fields. Under the present proposal it might go further, and concentrate its program on a few outstanding institutions, such as the University of Delhi, which has high standards in many fields and is independent of any state government, or the University of Poona, which is fairly free of state interference and possesses a number of distinguished constituent institutions. It would be politically difficult to take this step, but in the long run Indian intellectual and political life would probably benefit from it.

One major advantage of concentration would be that it would terminate, or at least lessen, the tragic waste of gifted human beings which is characteristic of Indian higher education. If the best young men and women in each field were brought together, they would interact upon one another and achieve more intellectual progress. In so doing they would prepare a seedbed which would cultivate individual talents and thus provide the personnel for other Indian institutions. In the course of time, intellectual standards would rise. Such university centers would perform the functions that Oxford, Cambridge, and London performed for the modern provincial universities in Britain, until the latter got under way. If these specially improved university centers were genuinely national institutions, drawing students and teachers from all over India, their chances for influencing the other universities throughout the country would be enhanced. They could supply high grade teachers in sufficient proportions to have a stiffening influence and this would also further the process of forming a genuinely all-Indian community in a variety of fields of research and scholarship.

This concentration would, above all, create within India itself institutional models for other Indian colleges and universities. They would become the centers of an Indian intellectual community, radiating the standards embodied in their research and in their graduates. The center of gravity of Indian intellectual life would be brought into India itself. If India is to assume full citizenship in the world-wide intellectual community, she must have an intellectual life of her own, centered within her own borders.

III

The really marked amelioration that would come about as a result of improving the quality of the Indian university would be in the sphere of civil culture. India is, of course, much better off than any other new state in this regard, but it is not so well off as it might be in view of its greater political experience and its richer institutional and cultural inheritance from the former ruler and its own ancestors. Within the Indian university population, political hopelessness and alienation are common among the staff, and rebelliousness is rife among the students. The student, of course, is not likely to remain rebellious when he ceases to be a student, except possibly during the period of unemployment encountered by at least ten per cent of India's new graduates. Among these unemployed graduates, rebelliousness might become more intense, and might even be lifelong. For the most part, however, it will fade, as adolescent turbulence fades everywhere else in the world. Furthermore, the center of gravity of Indian political opinion rests among adults. Unlike his counterpart in some other parts of the world, the Indian adolescent or youth does not get the upper hand over his elders in politics. For these reasons, the turmoil within the Indian student body, expressed in demonstrations, riots, strikes, and other types of collective insubordination, is quite unlikely to disturb Indian political development in a direct way.

Indirectly, however, Indian student indiscipline, through its propensity to demoralize the teaching staff, impairs the dignity and the effectiveness of Indian universities, which suffer accordingly in public esteem. This additional weight on the negative side of the scale further depresses the position of the university, and prevents the powers that rule Indian society from taking the university or its members seriously.

Yet for Indian society to strengthen and expand its modern sector, the universities must supply manpower, ideas, and judgment. They will, in any event, supply manpower, some of which is bound to be good, but to supply the ideas and the judgment that are needed to enliven political life, the universities must be respected and self-respecting. They cannot reach this goal without genuine improvement in the performance of their constructive tasks—the teaching and discovery of truths—both Indian and universal in their reference and validity.

The major task in the development of the Indian intellectual community is the promotion of its intellectual creativity. The emergence of a number of points of creativity in Indian intellectual life—scientific, technological, scholarly, literary and publicistic—would have the effect of providing models and forming circles around those models. This would "Indianize" Indian intellectual life in a profound way, much more profoundly than the deliberately and officially sponsored promotion of Indian subject matters. Once creative minds take hold of a subject matter or a problem and proffer a new solution or a new formulation, this will be bound to give it an Indian cast. Those who work on Indian history or Indian society or Indian economic and technological problems will make these subjects more fascinating, more engaging of the intellectual vitality of their co-evals and their juniors. Those who work on more abstract and universal subjects will "Indianize" them by freeing them from xenophilic motives. General theories in sociology, economics, and politics will acquire an Indian substance. When this happens, people, except for a few hyper-patriots, will cease to worry whether or not their intellectual life is "Indian."

The real question refers to how this enhancement of creativity so necessary for a self-esteeming, self-sustaining intellectual community can be achieved. The answer paradoxically is that it requires the prior existence of some sort of intellectual community, in which good minds can support and challenge each other, in which a fruitful spirit of competition can operate. The human resources are there in India. They must be brought into frequent and free contact, in an environment of adequate material and institutional resources.

The criticism that Indian intellectual life is remote from the people, if it has any rationale at all, arises from the undistinguished quality of so much of Indian intellectual performance. The xenophilia which it attacks is only a symptom; it is a symptom of a weak intellectual morale. That morale can be strengthened only by accomplishment which will make Indian intellectual life less dependent on its foreign sources and models, and less responsive to their foreignness. When Indian intellectual life becomes more creative, it will live without self-consciousness and simultaneously in a universal culture and in the context of immediately interesting Indian problems.

The formation of an effective intellectual community in India must, for the foreseeable future, be confined to the non-literary fields of activity. There is little prospect of a national literature, directed towards common models and studied and judged on a national scale, as long as novels, drama, and poetry are written primarily in the Indian regional languages. It might be better for India if it had a national literary language, but that is among those things about which nothing can be done at present. Yet as far as the other sectors of the intellectual community are concerned, the obstacles are not insuperable. They have the common language, they know they must acknowledge common standards, they can know each other's work and discuss it.

Moreover, the intellectual community is sufficiently internally differentiated and specialized that the absence of one major sector from the total community, although it is a disadvantage, need not paralyze intellectual life in other spheres. Science and scholarship are not directly dependent on *belles-lettres*. The "two cultures," or rather the complicated system of specialized branches of knowledge, creation, and discovery to which that simplification refers, exist in India as well as in the West. (It is a testimonial to India's membership, however subordinate, in the worldwide intellectual community that it does.) The specialized subcommunities are more dependent on their substantively neighboring subcommunities than they are on the remoter ones.

Thus, the separation of the humanistic and scientific-technological cultures is no more a problem for India than it is for other more advanced intellectual communities, although its situation is somewhat more complicated by virtue of the linguistic problem. There is, however, another line of cleavage in the structure of the Indian intellectual system which is more injurious and about which something can and should be done. I refer here to relative isolation of the universities from other sectors of the Indian scientific and technological institutional system.

Whereas in the more advanced countries, the universities are the major centers of research and have a close connection with industrial research—the two together producing the main bulk of the research output—the Indian arrangement is different. There university and industrial research provide relatively little and research in separate research institutes receives the lion's share of financial support and produce most of the research. This is injurious to the achievement of Indian research. The universities, by virtue of their training functions and their capacity to do fundamental research, should occupy a more central position in India. Until the position is rectified, the formation of an intellectual community will be hindered.

I say this not merely out of a prejudice in favor of universities as such. Universities must be central to a modern intellectual community, especially in the sectors concerned with natural and social science and technology, because everyone who later enters the intellectual community must pass through them for an extended sojourn. But more than that, they must be in vigorous multilateral contact with those who use their personal and intellectual products. A university system which is not integrated with the executive—economic and administrative—sectors of its society is bound to be a withered growth.

A new charter is needed for the intellectual community in India and in that charter the universities must come to occupy a more central position than they do at present.

IV

What are the paths which Africa should travel in order to benefit from what has happened in India? What are the problems with which the new states of Africa must cope in order to make their intellectual life fruitful?

The first feature of the African intellectual which strikes one, in contrast with India, is the sheer paucity of numbers. The African universities, unlike their Indian counterparts, are still unable to staff themselves indigenously, and the expatriates whom they engage cannot under present circumstances see themselves as having a lifelong career in Africa: expatriates on short-term appointments, however excellently qualified by talent and training, cannot really "Africanize" themselves intellectually, and, even if they do, it is hard for them to have a lasting influence. A rapid rotation of expatriate university teachers puts a greater burden on the still small number of African university teachers. Their rapid promotion to senior responsibilities in the process of Africanization might mean that promising young men, full of intellectual vigor, are burdened prematurely with administrative responsibilities which interfere withe their intellectual productivity. The growth of the civil service means too that the universities and other intellectual institutions must face severe competition for outstanding young graduates. The numerous tasks of government which fall on the shoulders of the civil service reduce the leisure for avocational intellectual activity. The situation is further aggravated by the present necessity for Africans who wish to do advanced work, to do it abroad, so that the stimulus which they might contribute is, at least for the time being, removed from Africa.

All this means that the sheer number of man-hours available for creative intellectual work in all the various fields is seriously limited. Political concerns further reduce the time and energy available. How are these to be husbanded to secure the maximum effect? How can able and well-trained men be enabled to use their talents in ways which will be intellectually productive at a high standard and which will be useful to their fellow countrymen?

Concentration of the sort which has been considered above for India is entirely out of the question for Africa. The political obstacles which are at once apparent within a single country like India are even greater in a continent with a multiplicity of sovereign states to which their universities are important evidence of progress towards modernization. Quite apart from such considerations, the universities have too many national obligations, even local obligations, to permit amalgamation into a smaller number. It is not as in India, where there are already so many universities and so many teachers that concentration involves only differentiation in the allocation of resources, not the loss of identity of individual, already existing institutions. The latter is unthinkable for Africa because it is not only impracticable; it is undesirable as well.

The alternative procedure for overcoming the isolating consequences of small numbers is to foster opportunities for regional and continental contact. Conferences, seminars, meetings of small groups with common substantive interests would present such opportunities. Intra-African intellectual association, initiated from within Africa by persons who wish not just to form an organization but to discuss the problems on which they are working or on which they wish to work, might have the effect of contributing to a sense of intellectual community in Africa and diminish the sense of intellectual isolation within Africa and intellectual dependence on the metropolis. Financial support from abroad might be necessary, metropolitan participation is desirable, but the initiative and the setting of the problems must be African.

Such meetings, which need not be elaborate conferences on a grand scale and which might involve only ten or twenty persons working on similar problems of African life—social, economic, medical, technological, etc.—do not, of course, preclude other forms of collaboration. The exchanges of teachers and students among the African universities, the conduct of joint research projects entailing collaboration of universities and of governments, of regional research institutions, continental and regional learned and scientific societies, are all desirable.

Africa has not yet reached the position of India in which the universities have become isolated from other intellectual activities. This is partly a result of the undeveloped condition of intellectual institutions outside the universities. Nonetheless, the problem must be faced in Africa as it must be faced in India. Non-university intellectual institutions exist in Africa and will become more numerous. Research in agriculture, medicine, engineering, social sciences, and social welfare is under way in Africa and must continue to grow if Africa is to develop economically and socially. The isolation of the "producers" of manpower and knowledge from the "users" of that manpower and knowledge will be as injurious to the growth of an African intellectual community as the isolation of the producers from each other. Unless there is close and mutually appreciative contact between "producers" and "users," the intellectual community, even if it overcomes the isolation of its constituent elements, will feel itself peripheral to the life of its own society. It might even attain considerable intellectual distinction, but its morale—and its capacity for creative intellectual work—will suffer. It will be susceptible to the painful self-accusation of not being a part of an ongoing and growing national life. It will also be subject to the charge by politicians and journalists of being a costly luxury, more a part of the outside world of metropolitan culture than an integral part of its own society. An intellectual community must be both. Its failure to be creative in either regard will hamper its creativity in the other.

The custodians of the intellectual communities of the new states must therefore bear constantly in mind that the precipitation of a new and indigenous intellectual center of gravity within their own countries requires simultaneously the cultivation of good relations with the intellectual community outside and with the authoritative, executive sectors of their own society.

Part IV:

Educational Planning and

Political Development

INTRODUCTION TO PART IV

JAMES S. COLEMAN

IN FOCUSING upon the political consequences of different educational traditions and different patterns of educational development, we confront the danger of regarding education solely as an independent variable.[1] In certain contexts and at certain times it may indeed be decisively determinative. The educational system, however, is very much the creature of the polity. It depends upon the polity for its funds, for a specification of kinds and levels of training and, frequently, for its policies. In modernizing countries education may achieve a central role precisely because it is one of the principal instruments for change available to the polity. It must respond to politically generated demands for its services, whether such demands originate among the masses or reflect the ideological presuppositions of the governing elites.[2] It may also be affected by the desire of elites in new states to "consummate freedom" by reducing or eliminating dependence upon foreign educational institutions and personnel,[3] the

[1] The tendency to exaggerate the determinative role of one particular variable among a number of interrelated variables is common in the social sciences, and is most marked in special efforts to give high visibility to a previously underemphasized variable. The recent "rediscovery" of education illuminates this propensity with great clarity. Thus, for example, ". . . [education] is a system whose major functions seem to be delegated to it by the other systems (i.e., political, economic, familial), and, to a degree, the effective functioning of the other systems depends directly on the effective functioning of the educational system. . . . In short, the educational system seems unique in the range of its functions and the centrality of its relationship, at least theoretically, to the other social institutions." (M. Herbert, A. Thelen, and Jacob W. Getzels, "The Social Sciences: Conceptual Framework for Education," *School Review*, Vol. LXV, Autumn 1957, p. 346.)

[2] C. Arnold Anderson ("Education and Political Development: Reactions to a Conference," memorandum circulated to the participants in the Conference on Education and Political Development held at Lake Arrowhead, California, June 24-29, 1962, pp. 18-19, hereafter referred to as "Reactions to a Conference") has noted that "premature dispersion of educational resources in actuality as often results from collectivist notions about equality held by the elite as from populist ideas." One might add that such dispersion may result as well from advice given by foreign educational missions and external advisory groups.

[3] "The most logical starting point [in a strategy of human-resource development in the underdeveloped countries] . . . is the formulation of a program of localization . . . since this is the area of greatest political consequence. In effect, this means the construction of a schedule for replacement of foreigners at least over a ten-year time span. . . . For political reasons it is necessary to localize the government services first." (Frederick Harbison and Charles A. Myers, *Education, Manpower, and Economic Growth*, New York, McGraw-Hill, 1964, pp. 62-63.)

nationalistic compulsion to "indigenize" or "nationalize" the curriculum, the imperatives of national defense, the struggle to raise national status in the global power or prestige system, or by other purely political considerations. The education-polity relationship, in short, is one of reciprocal dependence, of mutual stimulus and response.

The impact of education upon the polity, rather than the reverse, has received major emphasis herein because we are primarily concerned with the determinants of *political development*. We seek deeper insight into the education-polity relationship, in both historical and comparative perspectives, not only because of our theoretical interest in patterns of political change, but also because we have an immediate practical interest in the direction of political evolution in the developing countries of the contemporary world. And, as we have

TABLE 1: ASSISTANCE TO EDUCATION AS A PERCENTAGE OF
TOTAL UNITED STATES TECHNICAL COOPERATION PROGRAM
IN DEVELOPING COUNTRIES, BY MAJOR REGION

Year	Far East	Near East	South Asia	Africa	Latin America	World total
1959	19.8	14.9	16.1	17.5	14.1	14.2
1960	21.8	18.6	28.4	20.1	16.2	17.2
1961	17.4	14.1	23.2	13.2	14.6	13.8
1962	18.4	13.7	18.7	31.8	29.3	24.5

Source: U. S. International Cooperation Administration, *Operations Report,* Data as of June 30, 1959-June 30, 1961; U. S. Agency for International Development, *Operations* Report, Data as of June 30, 1962.

seen, education tends to be regarded by many as the prime determinant of the total development process, as the master instrument for changing attitudes, for transforming social structures, for sparking or accelerating economic growth, and for determining new political patterns. Among the many indicators of this faith in the determinative power of education are the figures in Table 1, which show the increased size in the educational component of technical assistance from the United States. Behind these figures is a philosophy of development, a philosophy once made explicit by Secretary of State Dean Rusk: ". . . today in this country we recognize that education has a variety of roles to play. Democratic institutions cannot exist without education, for democracy functions only when the people are informed and are aware, thirsting for knowledge and exchanging ideas.

Education makes possible the economic democracy that raises social mobility, for it is education that insures that classes are not frozen and that an elite of whatever kind does not perpetuate itself. And in the underdeveloped economies education itself stimulates development by . . . demonstrating that tomorrow need not be the same as yesterday, that change can take place, that the outlook is hopeful."[4]

Because of our overriding concern with the impact of education upon the course of political development, we have devoted special attention to the politically destabilizing consequences of particular educational patterns and inputs. The destabilization appears in (1) the frustrated elite aspirants victimized by the progressive devaluation of education; (2) the anomic potential of the unemployed primary school leavers and the revolutionary threat posed in situations of their political coalescence with disaffected intellectuals, and (3) the conflicts and tensions within and among elites, and among ethnic groups, resulting from different kinds and amounts of education. Wider knowledge about these consequences may have a sobering influence on those who entertain exaggerated hopes and expectations regarding the returns on an investment in education.

Deeper insight into the circumstances under which particular educational patterns lead to undesirable political consequences may also provide guidelines for development planning, for determining what educational "mix," what educational pyramid, what curricular content, what timing and spacing of educational inputs, will best support the interrelated development of society, the economy, and the polity. In Part IV of this book we are concerned with the problems of devising educational strategies aimed at the potentialities of education as a manipulable instrument for controlling and guiding change while at the same time minimizing political vulnerability. These problems are critically examined by Bert Hoselitz and William Platt in Chapters 16 and 17. In this introduction, therefore, we will confine our attention to a few of the issues involved in the minimization of destabilizing influences, and to a brief consideration of what educational content is most likely to aid political development.

Developing countries burdened with tensions created by educational imbalances are not necessarily destined for anarchy. Protracted political instability, as well as retrogression to authoritarian stagnation, is a clear possibility, and even, in some instances, a probability.

---

[4] "Economic Growth and Investment in Education," *Department of State Bulletin*, Vol. XLV, Nov. 13, 1961, pp. 821-822.

In limiting ourselves to only one or two historical models, however, we may overlook the astonishing variety in the institutional configurations and developmental sequences that have actually existed at critical points in the modernization of many countries of the world.[5] Moreover, there is merit in the suggestion that we begin to think about developing polities, not as pathological deviants, but as a particular type of polity with its own distinctive characteristics, possibly possessing a capacity to survive and adapt, despite all appearances to the contrary.[6]

Many societies are able to develop self-corrective mechanisms for such imbalances as "overproduction of the educated." Despite the virtually uncontrolled expansion of higher education in Japan and the Philippines, for example, adjustments have been made and protective mechanisms (such as absorption of the educated into the private sector or the downgrading of exaggerated notions about "a job appropriate to one's education") have come into play. And the problem of educational overproduction, though admittedly serious, may eventually be resolved: "An education system may very easily produce more educated people than the economic system can currently absorb in the types of job or at the rates of pay which the educated expect. This is a short-period phenomenon. In the long run the educated learn to expect different jobs and to accept lower rates of pay. . . . As the premium on education falls, the market for the educated may widen enormously. Jobs which were previously done by people with less education are now done by people with more education. The educated lower their sights, and employers raise their requirements. . . . As a result of this process an economy can ultimately absorb any number of educated people. . . . [It follows that one] ought to produce more educated people than can be absorbed at current prices, because the alteration in current prices which this brings about is a necessary part of the process of economic develop-

---

[5] For a discussion of different historical paths in political development see S. N. Eisenstadt, "Initial Institutional Patterns of Political Modernization," *Civilisations*, Vol. XII, 1962, pp. 461-472; Vol. XIII, 1963, pp. 15-26. The data in Mary Jean Bowman and C. Arnold Anderson, "Concerning the Role of Education in Development," in Clifford Geertz, ed., *Old Societies and New States*, New York, Free Press of Glencoe, 1963, p. 266, suggest "distinct stages in educational lead and lag: an early stage of education-economic breakthrough; a plateau in which diffusing education is still not sufficient to support a high-level economy; and a third stage in which another economic breakthrough is possible, built on a well-educated population."

[6] Fred W. Riggs, "Theory of Developing Polities," *World Politics*, Vol. XVI, Oct. 1963, pp. 147-157. See also S. N. Eisenstadt, "Social Change, Differentiation and Evolution," *American Sociological Review*, Vol. 29, No. 3, June 1964, pp. 375-386.

ment."[7] It is true, however, that "the long run may be very long," that the loss of privileges by the educated through the depreciation of education "not infrequently has political consequences," and that the process of adjustment "is painful, and fraught with political dangers."[8] In reality, the "only assurance of a [politically] healthy situation is a dynamic economy."[9]

This statement brings us at once to the Great Debate over the relationship between education and economic growth, discussed by Bert Hoselitz in Chapter 16.[10] Here we need only underscore the fact that in the past both educational planners and development economists have unrealistically tended to exclude political considerations from the dialogue as well as from their own plans. They may have been motivated by a compulsion for professional purity, deference to the hypersensitivity of the political elites whom they were advising, or sheer political ignorance. Political imperatives and constraints, however, as well as probable political consequences are integral parts of this extremely complex issue. They should be given explicit recognition and due weight in all development planning, whether the specific goal is educational advance or economic growth, or both. It serves no useful purpose to "suggest solutions to economic problems which are politically unfeasible. . . . The policy planner should identify not just the desirable or theoretically possible, but the realistic alternatives which exist in the light of known or expected pressures."[11]

---

[7] W. Arthur Lewis, "Education and Economic Development," *International Social Science Journal*, Vol. XIV, No. 4, 1962, pp. 686-688.

[8] *Ibid.*

[9] Anderson, "Reactions to a Conference," pp. 16-17.

[10] There is already a sizable literature on this controversy, although only recently have economists shown concern over "human resource development." The two poles of the argument are fairly represented by Bowman and Anderson (*op.cit.*, p. 247), who argue that the evidence that education is "one of the few sure roads to economic progress . . . remains slim and confused," and by Harbison and Myers (*op.cit.*, p. 14), who argue that human resource development is one of the necessary conditions "for all kinds of growth—social, political, cultural, or economic." Seymour Martin Lipset ("Research Problems in the Comparative Analysis of Mobility and Development," *International Social Science Journal*, Vol. XVI, No. 1, 1964, p. 41) cites the Great Debate over the relationships between education and economic growth and education and political stability as a particularly illuminating example of the difficulties social scientists confront in sustaining ad hoc generalizations about the development process.

[11] Harbison and Myers, *op.cit.*, p. 20. Cf. David E. Bell, "Allocating Development Resources: Some Observations Based on Pakistan Experience," in *Public Policy*, Cambridge, Harvard University Press, 1961, p. 86; and Charles Wolf, Jr., *Foreign Aid: Theory and Practice in Southern Asia*, Princeton, Princeton University Press, 1960, who notes (p. 315) that "an expansion of educational services may be a commitment

Three additional observations on development planning are in point. First, whether the planning objective is economic growth or the minimization of political vulnerability, there cannot be a single educational strategy. As both Hoselitz and Platt argue, the desired strategy is one that maximizes both goals, or at least does not seriously compromise either goal. A separate strategy must be devised for different *types* of developing countries, as well as for different *phases* in their development.[12] Second, because statism characterizes both the political culture and the political process in many developing countries, governing elites have an extraordinary opportunity to employ various stratagems to minimize the politically destabilizing aspects of educational development. To take full advantage of this opportunity they need not only the professional advice of politically sensitive development planners, but also political courage of their own.[13] Third, few guideposts for educational planning can be found in the historical experience of more highly developed countries. The findings of the few existing studies are ambiguous or inconclusive; and even if a comprehensive body of validated theory based on Western experience were available, its relevance would be questionable. Hoselitz makes this point forcefully in Chapter 16. Indeed, a recent empirical study of the relationship between education and social mobility in a developing country points up several social and historical features that are in striking contrast to Western experience.[14]

---

already explicitly made and publicized by a politically perceptive government in response to popular demands. It may thus be a constraint, rather than a variable, in development planning."

[12] The Harbison and Myers typology (*op.cit.*), which ranks seventy-five countries in terms of a composite human resource development index and classifies them at four levels (Level I, Underdeveloped; Level II, Partially developed; Level III, Semi-advanced; Level IV, Advanced), and Daniel Lerner's postulated three-phase sequence in the evolution of a participant society, cited by Hoselitz in Chapter 16, are excellent examples of how typologies and sequential modes of analysis assist in devising educational strategies for different categories of countries and different stages of development of a particular country.

[13] The statism of many developing countries is the result, among other things, of the weakness of the private sector and the fact that the government controls scholarships to institutions of higher learning and most employment in the modern sector. Thus, through development planning, a country's opportunity to manipulate the compensation structure, to control the disposition of students, and to regulate the output of the educational system in accordance with occupational opportunities and manpower needs is maximized. It could be argued with equal force, however, that the opportunity for manipulation created by statism is more than offset by the political vulnerability of already fragile governments in statist societies.

[14] Philip J. Foster, "Secondary Schooling and Social Mobility in a West African Nation," *Sociology of Education*, Vol. XXXVII, winter 1963, pp. 150-171. Elman R. Service has argued that "in some respects exactly opposite effects are created by the

Moreover, as C. Arnold Anderson has noted, in the West there was usually firm ground in either the economy or the polity from which to grapple with change in the other, whereas in the developing countries the simultaneity of institution building in all spheres demands more fundamental conceptions of just how educational, economic, and political developments intertwine in the absence of such an anchor base.[15]

The second problem requiring brief examination here concerns the content of education. Education is not politically dysfunctional solely because of the over-production of educated persons, but because of the over-production of persons whose education makes them unemployable, owing either to their psychic disposition or to their lack of the requisite knowledge and skills. The problem of excess capacity in absolute quantitative terms exists mainly in the case of unemployed primary-school leavers, whose education has been essentially homogeneous.[16] Educational content becomes differentiated and variable, and the resultant heterogeneity becomes politically consequential, mainly at secondary and higher levels of education. The type of post-primary educational content considered most productive of unemployable intellectuals and political instability, and most criticized by development planners, is that in which legal, literary, and humanistic studies predominate. Development economists in particular have a pronounced bias "towards subjects which appear to promote rational methods of thought, like mathematics and the natural sciences, towards subjects which break up accepted attitudes, like sociology and other social studies, and towards practical subjects—crafts and elementary agricultural skills which enable people to develop their capacity to earn their own living."[17]

---

evolution of an industrial system in the area of its birth as opposed to its propagation in a new land" ("The Law of Evolutionary Potential," in Marshall D. Sahlins and Elman R. Service, eds., *Evolution and Culture*, Ann Arbor, University of Michigan Press, 1960, p. 115).

[15] Anderson, "Reactions to a Conference," pp. 16-17.

[16] Lewis (*op.cit.*, pp. 688-689) minimizes the significance of the curriculum, at least at the primary level. He argues that the politically dangerous frustration among primary-school leavers is not due mainly to the "failure of rural schools to adapt their curricula in such a way as to orientate rural children to a rural life," as is frequently claimed, but to "the status which his immediate predecessors have enjoyed. . . . Any good primary school will widen a child's horizon and create expectations which primitive farming cannot fulfill. So even if rural schools concentrate on rural life, their products are bound to suffer frustration unless the whole fabric of agriculture is being modernized at the same time."

[17] John Vaizey, "Economics of Education," *International Social Science Journal*, Vol. XIV, No. 4, 1962, p. 627. Harbison and Myers (*op.cit.*, pp. 84-85) cite the

The debate over what curriculum content contributes most positively to development reveals an unfortunate tendency to regard development as a homogeneous process. By now it is abundantly evident that developmental requisites are not necessarily the same or even congruent in the different institutional spheres—educational, economic, and political; indeed, they may be and frequently are at variance, and sometimes even conflict with one another. Rapid educational expansion does not necessarily give rise to either economic growth or political development; economic growth has occurred without extensive educational development, and, in many instances, it has been politically destabilizing.[18] To be sure, these incongruities in development among the different spheres are regarded as transitional; it is assumed that in the long run some sort of adjustment or balance will be achieved. But the long run can prove to be very long indeed. In any event, the immediate point is that the subject matter emphasis in curriculum content required for rapid economic growth may not be compatible with stable and democratic political development.

Two interrelated issues affect the relationship between political development and curriculum content in post-primary education. One concerns the political consequences of a predominantly scientific and technological curriculum; the other, the role of the social sciences in political development. The proposition that a predominantly scientific and technological orientation in education is not only compatible with, but possibly supportive of, political authoritarianism has been argued very persuasively:

"Will not education produce a questioning spirit incompatible with autocratic rule? Can an educated society continue to be regimented?

"overemphasis on faculties of humanities, law, arts, and medicine and underemphasis on sciences and engineering" as one of the major problems in higher education in partially developed countries. The main reason for the heavy concentration in the former fields is not student preference or government policy, but the fact that "the law, arts, and humanities faculties provide cheap and poor education for large numbers of students, and thus satisfy in part the demand for numbers of places in the universities." Thus, their graduates could be unemployable not only because of the country's occupational structure or because of the content of their education, but also because they are not really educated.

[18] See J. L. Hammond, "The Industrial Revolution and Discontent," *Economic History Review*, Vol. II, Jan. 1930, pp. 215-228; Bert F. Hoselitz and Myron Weiner, "Economic Development and Political Stability in India," *Dissent*, Vol. VIII, spring 1961, pp. 172-179; Ronald G. Ridker, "Discontent and Economic Growth," *Economic Development and Cultural Change*, Vol. XI, Oct. 1962, pp. 1-15; and Mancur Olson, Jr., "Rapid Economic Growth as a Destabilizing Force," *Journal of Economic History*, Vol. XXIII, Dec. 1963, pp. 529-554.

There can be little doubt that compulsory, universal education has a profound impact. It is doubtful, however, whether it inevitably produces liberalization, first because the questioning spirit may not suffice to bring about liberalization, and second because education does not necessarily have to foster an attitude that is critical of political life. . . . Education is or can be made largely vocational. It can be made to repeat the specialization of an industrial society. And specialization is purchased at the price of considerable ignorance of most other fields. . . . Even in the field of science, the correlation between scientific and political freedom is far from absolute. Studying Hegel or Kant or Locke produces reflection and concern about the nature of authority and freedom. The study of physics and chemistry need not. It is true that the scientific spirit requires a willingness to accept whatever results research may reveal. But this presupposes the autonomy of the scientific sphere, not freedom as such. In science there is a certain manipulative element which in a different social context than ours may prove by no means inconsistent with 'forcing men to be free.' "[19]

The existence of a link between scientific and specialized education and authoritarian propensities has been stated far more categorically by Alfred Cobban: "There is little evidence that scientists are more scientific in their thought outside their own particular fields than the rest of the community, nor indeed is it to be expected. The scientist is dependent on the possession of a large body of scientifically ascertained evidence: where he has not done this he must either take refuge in agnosticism, or base his opinions on prejudice and guesswork. Now the mere labour that the acquiring and maintenance of his expertness in his own subject demands, by itself prohibits the specialist from devoting the time necessary to the study, either in theory or practice, of the problems of government. Unguarded either by belief in an ancient creed, or by a rational study of the problems of social

[19] Henry A. Kissinger, *The Necessity for Choice*, New York, Harper & Brothers, 1961, pp. 295-297. Cf. Pendleton Herring, "On Science and Polity," *Items*, Vol. 15, No. 1, March 1961, who (at p. 1) asserts that "scientific advancement and democratic governments are intimately related . . . they spring from the same human impulses, rely on many of the same social conditions, and suffer from some of the same limitations. . . . Science knows no authority but the idea, the thought, the theory that holds up under scrutiny, under testing, under the replication of experiment by different experimenters or under examination by different investigators. Democracy means an open society, the give and take of debate, a readiness to experiment, to throw out one group and bring in another. . . . Freedom of thought, trial and error, discarding theories or policies that have failed to work—this is the culture both of science and democracy."

TABLE 2: SUBJECT MATTER ORIENTATION OF HIGHER
EDUCATION IN SELECTED COUNTRIES[a]

COUNTRY	LEVEL OF HUMAN RESOURCE DEVELOP-MENT[e]	PER CENT ENROLLED BY SUBJECT MATTER[b]				
		Science and Tech-nology[d]	Humanities, Arts, Law, Social Sciences			
			Humanities, Arts, Law[e]	Social Sciences[f]	Total	Other[g]
NON-COMMUNIST						
Africa						
Ghana	II	30	27	26	53	17
Nigeria	I	40	31	14	44	16
Senegal	I	25	61	1	62	13
Tunisia	II	16	66	2[h]	68	16
Asia						
India	III	27	58	8	66	7
Indonesia	II	23	31	21[h]	52	25
Japan	IV	22	27	26	53	25
Philippines	. . .	21	6	48	54	25
Middle East						
Egypt	III	24	35	22	57	19
Iran	II	16	47	—	47	37
Iraq	II	26	29	27	56	18
Israel	IV	42	50	. . .[i]	50	8
Latin America						
Argentina	IV	15	36	17	53	32
Brazil	II	19	39	11	50	31
Mexico	III	18	8	5	13	69
Peru	II	31	42	19	61	8
Uruguay	III	5	51	11	62	33
COMMUNIST						
Communist						
China	II	55.7	. . .	. . .	. . .	. . .
Czechoslovakia	III	46	6	11	17	37
Hungary	III	46	20	6	26	28
Poland	III	52	15	8	23	25
USSR	IV	45	8	9	17	38
WESTERN						
Democratic						
Australia	IV	28	23	7	30	42
France	IV	32	46	. . .[j]	46	22
West Germany	IV	25	29	13	42	33
Sweden	IV	30	49	5	54	16
United Kingdom	IV	34	35	6[k]	41	25
United States	IV	23	18[l]	29[l]	47[l]	. . .
Authoritarian						
Portugal	III	17	56	7	60	23
Spain	III	25	36	4	43	32

[a] Based on figures for 1957, 1958, or 1959.

[b] Rounded.

[e] I, Underdeveloped; II, Partially developed; III, Semi-advanced; IV, Advanced.
Based on the composite index of Human Resource Development by Frederick Harbison

life, the expert is ready to fall a victim to any new heresy. He will seize on any gospel that has the appearance of providing a safe orthodoxy on which to base the crumbling state, so long as it is presented by demagogues sufficiently clever or by tyrants sufficiently powerful. . . . In these conditions it is not difficult to understand why the general acceptance of the principle of universal education, and the great advance of specialist studies, should have been accompanied by the rise of dictatorship and the development of the totalitarian state. . . . The really surprising development is the extent to which the new doctrines, however wild and irrational they may seem, have won the sincere adherence, not of the illiterate, poverty-stricken masses, but of the professional classes, the technicians, the lawyers, doctors, scientists, engineers, administrators—in short of the experts who tend the complicated machinery of modern civilization. It is the educated, not the uneducated masses, who form the real problem in the modern state. . . . [In the future] the ablest minds from all ranks will be drawn into the service of society as scientists, or technicians, or specialists in some form or other. In many ways this is an admirable development; but it has the result that education can no longer be regarded as a preparation for government."[20]

These two authorities have been quoted at some length because they state with pungent succinctness the essence of the proposition that a predominantly scientific-technological emphasis in education is not in conflict with—indeed, it possibly may be conducive to—a nondemocratic pattern of political development. Their thesis derives sup-

---

[20] Alfred Cobban, *Dictatorship: Its History and Theory*, New York; Charles Scribner's Sons, 1939, pp. 232, 235, 240-241. Cobban's important, but extravagant, assertions reflect two special concerns. One is increased specialization per se. In his

---

and Charles A. Myers, *Education, Manpower, and Economic Growth*, New York, McGraw-Hill, 1964, pp. 31-34.

d Include agriculture.

e Humanities include archaeology, psychology, and history; arts include architecture.

f Include banking and commerce.

g Includes education and medicine.

h 1956.

i Included with humanities.

j Included with law.

k Part of social sciences included with humanities.

l Per cent of degrees earned in 1958.

Sources: Frederick Harbison and Charles A. Myers, *Education, Manpower and Economic Growth*, New York, McGraw-Hill, 1964, pp. 46-48; UNESCO, *World Survey of Education, III, Secondary Education*, New York, 1961, pp. 28 and 42; UNESCO, *Basic Facts and Figures*, 1961, Paris, 1962, pp. 56-60.

port from various studies made in different cultural milieus.[21] The figures in Table 2 underscore the heavy emphasis placed upon science and technology, and the comparatively slight attention given to the humanities, law, the arts, and the social sciences in Communist totalitarian countries. Further evidence of a correlation between field specialization and political values is revealed by Dwaine Marvick's sample survey of students in an African university, reported in Chapter 14. He found, it will be recalled, that students concentrating in science (in contrast with liberal arts or economics) tended to be markedly less concerned with party politics and public affairs, seemed only slightly interested in taking an active part in community politics in later life, and appeared likely to "spend quiet lives, making useful contributions to the modernization of their country either as technicians or teachers, almost irrespective of what kind of political regime or civic life flourishes around them." It is a moot question, Marvick suggests, whether this orientation reflects earlier propensities that led to the choice of a scientific field, or is the result of the socializing impact of the students' preoccupation with purely scientific subject matter. Once again we are reminded, not only of the extraordinary complexity of the issue of causal relationships, but also of the limited number of systematic comparative studies which have been made of this phenomenon.

The crux of the issue is not whether educational content should be exclusively scientific and technological or exclusively humanistic and legal, but what is the best "mix." Most development economists in the Western liberal tradition, it is only fair to note, do not propose that the curriculum should be exclusively scientific and technological in character; rather, they press for curricular changes that will correct the present imbalance favoring the humanities, law, and the arts—a lopsidedness vividly brought out by the data in Table 2—and pre-

---

view, the authoritarian vulnerability and the parochialism of the specialist are not solely qualities of engineers and technicians, but of all specialists. He asserts (at p. 233) that "the student of nonscientific subjects is in just the same boat. His education, too, has been becoming increasingly that of the specialist. Even in literature, history, and philosophy, the cult of the expert has conquered." His second concern is the eclipse of the "older education" (presumably the Oxbridge tradition) which "helped to produce a governing class, an aristocracy which was not merely one of birth."

[21] Seymour Martin Lipset, "The Political Behavior of University Students in Developing Nations," paper prepared for presentation at the UNESCO Conference on Students and University Education in Latin America, Bogotá, Colombia, July 13-19, 1964, p. 6. Cf. Hanan Selvin and Warren O. Hagstrom, "Determinants of Support for Civil Liberties," *British Journal of Sociology*, Vol. xx, Jan. 1961, pp. 66-68, and Morris Rosenberg, *Occupations and Values*, Glencoe, Free Press, 1957.

sumably producing large numbers of unproductive and destabilizing unemployables.[22] A consideration of equal importance is that the most desirable mix is not one that turns out a certain percentage of persons trained exclusively in science and technology, and another percentage trained exclusively in the humanities and law; rather, the mix should be in the heads of all students without sacrificing, of course, "the rigorous standards of the discipline in depth which are the virtues of specialization."[23] The fact is, of course, that the dominant European educational traditions which have served as models for the developing countries have emphasized intensive specialization.

The "either-or" quality of the polemic over the relative developmental power of a scientific-technological versus a humanistic-literary-legal education has meant that the middle ground, occupied by the "modern" social sciences[24] (anthropology, economics, history, political science, psychology, and sociology), has suffered neglect.[25] The

---

[22] Harbison and Myers state (*op.cit.*, p. 68) "it is essential that mathematics and science be stressed *as well as* languages, history, literature, creative arts and national culture." Italics added.

[23] Eric Ashby, *African Universities and Western Tradition*, Cambridge: Harvard University Press, 1964, p. 9. Ashby notes that in the United Kingdom the shift from a university curriculum embracing a range of related subjects to one of intense specialization is a phenomenon of the last two generations, but that "at the time when Britain was exporting universities to tropical Africa [and presumably to other countries in the developing areas] the fashion of specialization was at its height."

The model of a curricular mix designed to provide a significant social science component in the education of students concentrating upon scientific and technological subjects is being pioneered at the Massachusetts Institute of Technology, one of America's leading centers of scientific-technological *and* social science research and training. MIT's imaginative program is based on the simple reasoning that if scientists and technologists are increasingly going to be the nation's policy makers it is crucial that they understand both the physical *and* the human environment that policy is designed to affect. Integrated planning requires integrated education.

[24] By "modern" social sciences, we refer mainly to the "behavioral sciences," that is, to those of the six social science disciplines, or to tendencies within those disciplines, in which "the scientific imperative is explicit and aimed at establishing generalizations about human behavior that are supported by empirical evidence collected in an impersonal and objective way . . . [in order better to] understand, explain, and predict human behavior." Bernard Berelson, "Introduction to the Behavioral Sciences," in Bernard Berelson, ed., *The Behavioral Sciences Today*, New York, Basic Books, 1963, p. 3.

[25] Harbison and Myers (*op.cit.*, p. 31), in constructing their composite index of levels of human resource development, explicitly excluded the social sciences (other than history and psychology) from their indicators of orientation in higher education. They contrast only scientific and technical faculties (natural sciences, engineering, and agriculture) and humanities, fine arts, and law faculties. Lewis (*op.cit.*, p. 686) is responsible for the same exclusion. Similarly, C. P. Snow, *The Two Cultures and the Scientific Revolution*, New York, Cambridge University Press, 1961, contrasts the literary intellectuals at one pole with the physical scientists at the other. The omission of the social sciences in all instances is possibly explained by their incoherence and

social sciences, although occupying a "strategic place in the intellectual spectrum, between the poles of physics and the arts and literature,"[26] are least solidly established as a coherent whole, and therefore are the least recognized among the four major branches of learning (physical sciences, biological sciences, social sciences, humanities). Their lack of coherence and the instability of their middle position are reflected in the fact that the subject matter, as well as the practitioners, of the six disciplines are classified differently in different academic traditions.[27] Moreover, within each discipline there are markedly divergent intellectual tendencies, of which the polar extremes are the philosophical-humanistic versus the empirical-scientific. A marked shift from the former to the latter is occurring in all of the social science disciplines, however, as a consequence of the impact of the scientific revolution. Nevertheless, except for economics, the relevance of social science knowledge and theory for understanding and guiding the development process is still not generally comprehended or appreciated, least of all in the developing countries themselves.

There are several reasons for the rudimentary state of understanding, and the limited utilization, of the social sciences in the developing areas. First, these disciplines were comparatively neglected by the major European academic traditions after which educational systems in the developing areas have been patterned.[28] The continuing obstacles to the introduction of the social sciences into the curricula of these systems include not only the inherent rigidities of established academic traditions, but also the fact that university faculties and research institutes in the new states are predominantly staffed either

---

internal ambivalences as a major field of learning, by the desire to dramatize a polarity (C. P. Snow says, at p. 10, that "attempts to divide anything into two ought to be regarded with much suspicion . . . [but, for purposes of demonstration] two cultures is about right"), or by the defensible assumption that the social sciences, insofar as they are reasonably scientific in their methods and approach, are implicitly included in the scientific pole. Cf. David E. Apter, "New Nations and the Scientific Revolution," *Bulletin of the Atomic Scientists*, Vol. XVII, Feb. 1961, pp. 60-64.

[26] Herring, *op.cit.*, p. 4.

[27] The lack of agreement as to what is or what is not a social science is illustrated by UNESCO, *World Survey of Education*, III, *Secondary Education*, New York, 1961, in which, for example, banking, commerce, diplomacy, home economics, journalism, and social welfare are classified as "social sciences," whereas archaeology, history, and psychology are in the humanities category.

[28] See Pierre de Bie et al., *The University Teaching of Social Sciences*, Paris, UNESCO, 1954; J. Ben-David and A. Zloczower, "Universities and Academic Systems in Modern Societies," *European Journal of Sociology*, Vol. III, 1962, pp. 45-85; and Joseph Ben-David, "Professions in the Class System of Present-Day Societies," *Current Sociology*, Vol. XII, No. 3, 1963-1964, pp. 265-272.

by expatriate scholars nourished in those traditions or by indigenous scholars trained in metropolitan institutions. Both groups have a vested interest in preserving the purity of the imported tradition. Significant changes are in progress, however, partly because the social sciences are being accepted or upgraded in most European universities,[29] partly because many returning indigenous scholars have been educated in American universities where the empirical social sciences are comparatively strong and well developed, and partly because the international educational activities of American universities and scholars are expanding.[30] Despite these encouraging signs, however, the empirical social sciences are a novelty in most developing countries, and have yet to become fully integrated into the indigenous educational pattern.

A second reason why the strategic elites in the developing countries are insensitive to the potential of social science knowledge—despite their pronounced instrumentalist stance toward science in general—is that its relevance to their problems has not been effectively communicated to them by social scientists. Insofar as there has been a social science component in their imported European academic traditions, it has tended to have a highly theoretical orientation, at least until recently. The problem of communicating the relevance of the social sciences has been further compounded by the culture-bound character of the findings of the overwhelmingly "applied" social science tradition in the United States—a tradition which presumably could have had a powerful demonstration effect.[31] The fact is that very few among the accumulated stock of behavioral science findings arrestingly obtrude themselves as immediately and obviously applicable to problems and situations in the developing areas, even though they may in fact be highly relevant. They appear culture-bound because they are derived almost exclusively from empirical studies of West-

[29] A. H. Halsey, "The Changing Functions of Universities," in A. H. Halsey, Jean Floud, and C. Arnold Anderson, eds., *Education, Economy and Society*, Glencoe, Free Press, 1962, pp. 456-465.

[30] Joseph LaPalombara, "American Higher Education and Political Development," in D. C. Piper and Taylor Cole, eds., *Post-Primary Education and Political and Economic Development*, Durham, Duke University Press, 1964, pp. 95-127.

[31] Cf. Nathan Glazer, "The Rise of Social Research in Europe," and Harry Alpert, "The Growth of Social Research in the United States," in Daniel Lerner, ed., *The Human Meaning of the Social Sciences*, New York, Meridian Books, 1959, pp. 43-88. As Herring observes (*op.cit.*, p. 5): "Science has always been close to the workaday world [in the United States]; indeed criticism has often been voiced of our unique emphasis upon applied research. . . . Scientific research bears a relationship to virtually all the major departments of government just as it bears on most segments of our national life."

ern phenomena, or because they have a pronounced bias toward the maintenance of stability rather than understanding and guiding change. The problem of communicating a belief in the "applied" potential of the social sciences has general applicability in the developing areas. Its essence is illuminated by the report by Bryce Wood and Charles Wagley on the state of the social sciences in Latin America: "Latin American universities and institutes, in trying to take advantage of the most recent work in sociology abroad, have found that many sociological propositions developed in the United States and Europe are culture-bound and are at best only partially valid in Latin America . . . examples are often based on Chicago, New York, or Los Angeles, and not Mexico City, Buenos Aires, or Rio de Janeiro. Rural sociological studies often refer to conditions in Iowa, New York State, Louisiana, etc. Efforts are under way, therefore, to develop teaching materials in sociology that are based on research in Latin America."[32]

These disabilities of the social sciences are correctable. A far more serious obstacle to their acceptance and integration into university curricula and research activities in the developing areas is the hostility directed toward them on political grounds. Social science education and research may have a politically destabilizing effect; the social science spirit of empiricism is inherently anti-authoritarian; and, to hypersensitive nationalists, social science evangelism may appear as a form of academic neo-imperialism. "The social sciences," Lipset has observed, "have been viewed as a threat in many societies because they are correctly perceived as being engaged in an activity which tends to erode public and private commitment to traditional values, an erosion that follows simply from the systematic questioning and objective analysis of these values. Moreover, since the jurisdiction of the social sciences involves areas of political relevance, social scientists are more likely than other groups of intellectuals to come into overt conflict with the ruling authorities. As the German sociologist Theodore Geiger has stated: 'Of all groups in the *intelligentsia,* the social scientists are most sensitive to the power dimension in society, and

[32] "The Social Sciences: Parochial or Cosmopolitan? Reflections on the Inter-American Conference on Research and Training in Sociology," *Items,* Vol. 15, Dec. 1961, p. 44. The findings of discrete "applied" empirical studies will inevitably be culture-bound to a degree; their generic character has to be sought and established through systematic comparative studies. Thus, the criticism that American applied social science is by nature culture-bound is misplaced; it should be directed at the failure of American social scientists to test their findings cross-culturally.

also the most exposed to the attacks on intellectual freedom by those in power. The loss of intellectual autonomy and freedom also endangers their professional work and calling.' "[33] The wide difference between the percentage of students enrolled in the social sciences in non-Communist countries and the percentage in Communist countries (see Table 2) points up the fundamental incongruity between totalitarian dictatorship and empirical social science.

The social sciences are distrusted not only because they may probe too closely into power relationships and popular attitudes, but also because most of their spokesmen and evangelists are Western—predominantly American—scholars. Although there is a growing number of well-trained modern social scientists in some developing countries, such as the Philippines and India, in most areas the expatriate social scientist is the highly visible agent of what all too frequently seems to be a new form of academic imperialism. Moreover, in many areas social scientists are the hapless victims of the indiscretions, the paternalism, the invasions of privacy, and the exploitative practices of predecessors, who ignored the canons of objective and respected social science inquiry. The unfavorable image the latter created, coupled with the extremely limited number of indigenous social science scholars and the reluctance to accept continued dependence upon foreign scholarship, aggravates nationalistic resentment. For these and other reasons the climate for the expansion and the development of the social sciences, both in the curricula of institutions of higher learning and as an urgently needed dimension of scholarly research, is generally not favorable. There are some notable exceptions, however, and much can be done to improve the situation.

If the social sciences are potentially destabilizing, possibly provocative, and probably suspected and unwanted, why do we stress the importance of their inclusion in the curricula and the research programs of the developing countries? Why should educational planners consider the social science component of educational content as seriously as they consider the engineering-technological component, or the quantitative output, or the shape of the educational pyramid? These queries are particularly in point when it is realized how recent, and how far from complete, has been the acceptance of the social

[33] *Op.cit.*, pp. 3-4. Lipset adds (at p. 38): "Fields such as the natural sciences, which generally require more concentrated study and work than the humanities or social sciences, will adversely affect student involvement in politics." The politically sensitive aspects of the social sciences are also noted by Wood and Wagley, *op.cit.*, pp. 42-43.

sciences by governments and the general public even in highly developed countries. This is not the place to detail the rationale for the modern social sciences; it is a subject that already commands a substantial literature.[34] The issue, however, is brought into particularly sharp focus for our purposes by Dwaine Marvick's observations regarding the extent to which the education of members of the presumptive political elites of the future prepares them for their task. One comment in Chapter 14 merits recall:

"Academically these students have considerable drive, much self-discipline, and a lot of intellectual curiosity for socially relevant knowledge. But . . . they lack the habit of asking why, the assumption that causal conditions can be identified, the willingness to treat an event analytically, as an example or case study, rather than descriptively, for its own sake. . . . [The fact is] that they enter the next stage of their careers after an educational experience that has given them few analytical skills, little knowledge of their country's political, economic or cultural institutions, and only a common sense appreciation of the dynamics of human psychology and historical change. Neither in content nor in intellectual method has their college education been addressed to the tasks they will face or the responsibilities they wish to assume."

The central purpose of the social sciences is to fill the foregoing lacunae: to prepare each individual to understand his social environment and his role in it; to recognize that his experiences and situations are not unique, but are in many respects related to similar phenomena elsewhere in space and time; to develop a critical posture toward generalizations about human behavior; and to give him "some familiarity and experience with the methods by which knowledge is gathered."[35]

In concentrating upon the selection of an educational strategy that would be most effective under a given set of circumstances in minimizing the politically dysfunctional consequences of education development, we find ourselves in the astonishing position of casting the

[34] See Lerner, *op.cit.*; Berelson, *op.cit.*; the statement by the Behavioral Sciences Subpanel, Life Sciences Panel of the President's Science Advisory Committee, *Strengthening the Behavioral Sciences*, Washington, U.S. Government Printing Office, 1962, the twelve-volume series, *Science, Technology and Development*, containing the United States papers prepared for the United Nations Conference on the Application of Science and Technology for the Benefit of the Less Developed Areas, Washington; U.S. Government Printing Office, 1961; and Ruth Gruber, *Science and the New Nations*, New York, Basic Books, 1961, especially pp. 201-257.

[35] Berelson, *op.cit.*, pp. 10-11.

relationship between education and political development in essentially negative terms. This stance is partly the result of our overriding concern for the short-run survival of fragile polities in order that the long-run potentialities of education may be realized. It is also partly owing, no doubt, to our assumption that the ultimate importance of education for any form of societal development is so obvious that it does not require discussion. Assuming that these considerations explain the imbalance in our emphasis, we find it nonetheless useful to make explicit the way in which education positively contributes to political capacity.

Political capacity does not depend solely upon the growth in organizational technology or efficiency in the highly differentiated administrative structures of a modern polity, although the ever-increasing bureaucratization of modern life obviously heightens their importance. What we are concerned with is the capacity of the total political system; and this capacity is not determined alone, or necessarily even mainly, by the efficacy of the authoritative structures. Capacity is also a function of the extent to which the society itself—the economic, social, and political infrastructure—can absorb, deflect, or respond to the enormous demands of a modernizing country, and thereby minimize or obviate explicit government involvement. It also depends upon the character of the political culture, particularly the extent to which it restrains, moderates, or postpones demands upon the government, or in other ways reduces the decisional load on formal administrative structures. We are concerned, in short, with the capacity of a whole system, which depends upon the functional load carried by and the functional performance of all parts and sectors of the society.

Education not only prepares the strategic elites for their roles; it also enlarges the capacity of all members of a society, and in this way maximizes the capacity of the whole polity. Platt points out that education releases talent and creativity and maximizes the dispersion of energy and initiative throughout the society on behalf of the total development process. But it is not education per se that does this; it is education that enables a citizen to understand both the physical and human environment of which he is a part. And, "the social sciences are one important means of advancing this essential self-knowledge. They provide the most articulate and systematic expression of this awareness."[86]

[86] Herring, *op.cit.*, p. 3.

Just as one must take the long view in planning and rationalizing investments in the quantitative expansion of education, so one must take a similar stance in planning and justifying a social science component in its content. Both threaten short-run instability. Which long view one takes depends upon one's ultimate values. As Daniel Lerner has put it:

"The real test of social science comes when the urban-industrial matrix begins to evolve those distinctively participant lifeways of modern society. For the unique function of social science—as a method of inquiry into the social process whereby its operations are continuously recorded and regulated—can only come into play after the psychopolitical die is cast. If the rulers prefer to govern by the tidy simplicity of coercion, avoiding the complex ambiguities of consensus, they will require nothing more than some rudimentary system of social auditing. If they opt for widespread participation under the rule of consensus, then the full conceptual and procedural range of social science—including attitude research—becomes relevant."[87]

In the general introduction to this book we endeavored to formulate a neutral, non-culture-bound concept of political development. It was suggested that the "modern participatory state" symbolized generic political modernity. Further specification of the traits of political modernity, however, leads one inescapably to two polar patterns of political development, one that derives its capacity through coercion and rests upon a subject political culture, and one that generates its capacity through consensus and a civic political culture. The long-run capacity of the latter is infinitely greater than the former. The basis of this belief is that "a democracy's potentiality is as great as the released intelligence of each individual member. . . . the ultimate justification for democracy as a political process lies in its capacity to liberate the spirit of man and to insure freedom of thought to the end that there may be an optimum release of human intelligence."[88] This is how education, the social sciences and democracy are conjoined.

[87] Lerner, *op.cit.*, p. 37.

[88] Herring, *op.cit.*, p. 3. See also Talcott Parsons, "Evolutionary Universals in Society," *American Sociological Review*, Vol. 29, No. 3, June 1964, pp. 353-356.

CHAPTER 16

INVESTMENT IN EDUCATION
AND ITS POLITICAL IMPACT[1]

BERT F. HOSELITZ

∼∼∼∼∼∼∼∼∼∼∼∼∼∼∼∼∼∼∼∼∼∼∼∼∼∼∼∼∼∼∼∼∼∼

I

IN THE last few years extensive attention has been given to the problem of the formation of human capital and its role in the process of economic development. Among the growing list of scholars who have contributed to this literature, substantial consensus has been reached on the proposition that education is one of the most important, if not the most important, variable in the determination of the rate and level of economic advancement. For example, in a recent paper T. W. Schultz has argued that "except for some pure rent (in earnings) for differences in inherited abilities, most of the differences in earnings are a consequence of differences in the amounts that have been invested in people."[2] Although investment in people consists of such other factors as improvement in health, information about jobs, on-the-job training, and migration from low-wage to higher-wage areas, the major component of investment in human beings is in the form of more and better education.

These views have had a strong impact upon the students of investment patterns and investment programs in developing countries. For example, the various papers and reports submitted at a Conference of African States on the Development of Education in Africa, which met at Addis Ababa from May 15 to 25, 1961, abound with citations of the achievements of education in the advanced countries and the admonition to the African countries to imitate this experience.[3] There is good reason to believe that these admonitions are, indeed, valuable,

---

[1] This study was written while I was the holder of a John Simon Guggenheim Memorial Fellowship. I wish to express my gratitude to the officers of the Foundation for having afforded me the required time for research and reflection to make this essay possible.

[2] See T. W. Schultz, "Reflections on Investment in Man," *Journal of Political Economy*, Vol. LXX, No. 5, Part 2, October 1962, pp. 1-8.

[3] United Nations, Economic Commission for Africa-UNESCO, Conference of African States on the Development of Education in Africa, *Final Report*, Document No. UNESCO/ED/181, Paris, 1961. (Cited hereinafter as *African Education Report*.)

though one may perhaps dispute the views expressed by some commentators and experts on the precise allocation of educational resources as between different kinds of training and the overall magnitude of financial contributions to educational as against other objectives.

Education presents a Janus-like appearance. It is a consumption good and a production good at the same time. Even those who never exercise any of the occupations for the performance of which they may have received an education probably have gained enormously by their educational experience in that they have access to more and different forms of consumption than they would have had without this education. But it should be noted that those who have stressed the productive aspects of education have, on the whole, drawn their examples and their empirical evidence from such countries as the United States or western European nations, i.e., countries which exhibit the following chacteristics:

The countries in which returns to investment in man were found to be high are endowed with a highly developed and quite rapidly growing economy in which a subsistence sector is absent for all practical purposes or has only a very small size, and in which resources, commodities and services are allocated overwhelmingly by the exchange sector or some complex alternative allocation mechanism in place of an exchange sector (as in some countries with a high degree of socialist planning). As a corollary of this, all these countries considered have a highly diversified occupational structure with a high degree of specialization in many occupations and hence with a substantial need for elaborate training programs for many of the skilled occupations. Thirdly, these countries have relatively full employment of human resources; they also have relatively efficient labor markets and usually well-functioning mechanisms providing information on available job opportunities and skill requirements for certain jobs. Finally, these countries have elaborate communication systems which are based upon the generally valid assumption of universal literacy. They also display a relatively high degree of social and occupational mobility and have only weak traditions by which access to certain occupations is limited to persons with special ethnic, religious, or kinship characteristics. In other words, recruitment to most occupations and jobs is based principally on achievement criteria rather than on ascriptive criteria. There exists in these countries a relatively high correlation between specific types of educational experience and future occupational careers, e.g., individuals trained as medical officers will actually practice medicine, and persons instructed in business education will actually perform managerial tasks in business enterprises.

These conditions apply only to a very limited extent in many developing countries, and in some of the economically least advanced nations; for example, in some of the new states of Africa, they apply hardly at all. Although some returns from investment in education may be expected at all stages of economic development, investment in educational facilities may produce much lower returns at certain earlier stages of economic growth than the application of equal amounts of investment in other forms of capital, especially capital constituting the material infrastructure of an economy. For example, the development of roads or the installation of basic power facilities may at some early stages of development yield substantially higher returns than equal amounts of investment in education.

Thus, from the purely economic point of view—i.e., in terms of net returns on various forms of investment outlay—we may distinguish different phases in a developing country. At certain periods investment in a given set of non-human resources and at other periods investment in human resources brings about a higher sustained rate of growth of average income. Moreover, we must distinguish not only between outlays on investment in human against non-human capital, but also outlays on investment in different forms of human capital. For example, it has become popular to emphasize outlays on the formation of what is called high-level manpower, and this concept has gained considerable popularity in developing countries, especially in Africa. Yet, it might be argued that—again in purely economic terms—large outlays on the formation of high-level manpower at a low level of economic performance may be a misplacement of funds devoted to education and to capital formation, in general.

It is the purpose of this chapter to explore various alternative patterns of investment in developing countries and to evaluate them, not in terms of economic returns as such—though these also form a significant consideration of the appropriateness of these investment patterns—but rather in terms of the probable political consequences of various investment policies. I shall stress particularly investment in education, i.e., investment in human capital, but, as was pointed out earlier, we must also consider societies in which the direct economic returns on investment in other facilities are likely to be greater. Many of the conclusions reached in this chapter are tentative and should be regarded primarily as suggestive and hypothetical, rather than as constituting well-supported findings or generalizations. But it is hoped that even the voicing of these suggestions may lead to some further research in a field which is as yet largely unexplored.

II

Much of the discussion on the economic effects of additional years of schooling and on the desirability of strengthening various forms of higher education has been concerned with alternative policies of secondary and higher or vocational training.[4] But the educational process, if taken in its widest meaning, begins much earlier. In fact, it begins as soon as a man is born. Since we are concerned here not so much with the net economic results of additional years of schooling but with political implications of various educational policies, I shall examine the educational process in its broadest form. We may then distinguish four stages or phases of education: (1) education by a person's family and kinship group from the time of birth; (2) primary education, in which the basic skills in reading, writing, and arithmetic are acquired; (3) secondary education, which leads to the development of certain of the minor managerial and technical skills; and (4) higher education, which is similar in content and objectives to the collegiate and university education in Western countries.

The first phase in this educational schema is provided in every culture almost always by the household or the kinship group into which a child is born, and consists essentially in equipping the individual with the skills enabling him to function effectively in his culture. In all societies, including those with elaborate formal school systems, this stage of education is completed at a relatively early age. To be sure, the old adage that we learn as long as we live is quite true, but most of our learning of the ways of our culture is acquired in childhood, especially in early childhood, and is gained without formal mobilization of resources by the society. Our teachers at this stage of our educational career are our parents or other relatives and in no society is any formal provision made—if we except orphanages and foundling homes—for the administration of this phase of the educational process.

[4] For example, T. W. Schultz considers primarily the costs of secondary and higher education, and includes the costs of primary education only to derive total national outlay on education, in his paper, "Capital Formation by Education," *Journal of Political Economy*, Vol. LXVIII, No. 6, December 1960, pp. 571-583.

Little attention has been paid to the resources applied by society to this phase of the educational career of a child. Yet it may be argued that the economic aspect of this non-formal education should receive more attention and, particularly, that its political implications should be considered more explicitly. For in this stage of the educational process more is inculcated in the child than merely the external ways and means of his culture. Psychologists of various theoretical persuasions are agreed that important personality characteristics are fashioned in early childhood—and even in later childhood through the continued impact of the family environment. Moreover, in many societies in which illiteracy rates are still high, the bulk of the educational experience of an individual is extended to him by members of his family or other near relatives. Clearly the external conditions under which the family exists and functions are determinants of the kind, amount, and degree of formalism of the educational experience. In addition the question of whether a person's education remains confined to what he can learn within his kinship or whether he will undergo more formal schooling is largely influenced by the external conditions of a family's existence.

Most important is the fact that many people in developing countries do not receive formal schooling. This fact affects the relations between political leaders and the masses they lead; it affects through differences in the class structure the relative distribution of power in a society; it affects the nature of political movements and the conditions under which leadership in political parties and other groups is attained; it affects the nature of demands made by the rank and file on its leaders and by the leaders on the political elite or the central political power.

Among the important factors that will affect the family, especially the farm family in developing countries, is the degree of access it has to information, to wider markets, and to centers of decision making. In developing countries by far the majority of the population is still dependent for its livelihood on agriculture and around 80 per cent or more of the population live in rural areas. A large part of the population lives in a subsistence or near-subsistence economy, and, on this account, is relatively far removed from the impact of modernizing trends underway in the society. One of the important factors influencing the whole pattern of economic development is the abolishment of this intellectual isolation and the bringing into closer contact with the national society as a whole those persons who still rely exclusively or predominantly on particularist group ties and economic self-sufficiency associated with them.

In many developing countries where the changeover from subsistence to market activities is very slow and where, therefore, employment opportunities in the exchange sector are greatly limited, the acquisition of even a modicum of education is considered a means of enabling young people to move out of the subsistence sector into the exchange sector. But any more intensive empirical analysis of these processes shows that the supply of educated persons grows in the short run at a much faster clip than the demand for them in new jobs in the exchange sector, and for this reason they either are forced to return to subsistence agriculture and traditional forms of farming, a development which they would consider a serious defeat of their endeavor to better their occupational career, or they experience long periods of urban unemployment or part unemployment, a condition which has serious political implications.[5]

These considerations lead to the following conclusions: it is possible that at a given state of the development of a country's resources, a rapid and farflung educational program may produce serious short-run misallocations of resources. These misallocations produce excess capacity, with the consequence that certain forms of human capital may be available in such relatively large amounts that they cannot be employed fully in the short run. But whereas the appearance of excess capacity in certain fields of non-human investment may have relatively unimportant political consequences, excess capacity in the realm of human capital formation is of great concern, especially if it can be expected that this excess capacity may be of some duration and may have a tendency of becoming worse—at least temporarily —rather than better. A corollary of this observation is that under these conditions several policy alternatives for a more "balanced" progress of a developing economy are possible. One would be the cutting down of expenses for formal education, the imposition of some selective process of school admissions, and the imposition of standards of educational performance that would eliminate many potential students at the outset, or at an early stage of the process of formal education. It is difficult to conceive that this solution would be widely acceptable, and even if it were it would easily lead to manifold

---

[5] For these points and several others raised in this chapter, see the paper by Archibald C. Callaway, "School Leavers in Nigeria," in *West Africa*, March 25, 1961, April 1, 1961, April 8, 1961, and April 15, 1961, pp. 325, 353, 371-372, and 409.

abuses. Another alternative would be the extension of primary education and the raising of the school leaving age, but this would merely provide a temporary breathing spell and might lead to a larger number of early drop-outs. The third and most logical alternative would be the stepping up of investment in areas other than education. For there is no doubt that, in the long run, the excess capacity which exists in the realm of human capital will disappear, but this requires two interrelated developments: on the one hand, the creation of additional non-human capital providing employment opportunities for the school-leavers; on the other hand, a change in outlook and probably also in values of the agricultural population.

Today in many developing countries the acquisition of even a modicum of formal education provides the school-leaver with a rationale for a job outside of farming. This is not surprising. In these societies, in the not too distant past, all persons who were uneducated and illiterate were farmers and artisans, and those who had acquired education were usually part of the political or social elite. To be sure, it was very rare that a farmer's son could ever attain an education, but in the folklore and even in actual fact there were some cases which could be appealed to and which showed that it was with education and learning (and often sheer luck) that a peasant's son became a politically powerful figure. Even under colonial rule this image of the relation between illiteracy and farming, or other forms of low-skilled work, on the one hand, and literacy and political power, on the other, was not dispelled. For the representatives of the metropolitan powers also attracted—to the extent to which they admitted indigenous personnel at all—educated persons to the bureaucracy and other governmental services, and in some instances established schools to train indigenous personnel for administrative and related positions.

It is no wonder, then, that in the minds of many people in developing countries the acquisition of education is equated with the aspiration to obtain a position outside farming. Yet, as long as a large portion of the national output of a country is produced in the agricultural sector, ways and means must be found to attract a more highly skilled labor force to agriculture, and hence a change in outlook and values of the agriculturalists of developing countries may be required. They must learn to accept the fact that education, especially primary education, and farming are compatible. But at the same time it is clear that the crude type of subsistence farming will not prove attractive to more highly educated persons, whereas a more modern, scientific, and economically attractive type of farming may produce change. Not only does this new type of farming make much greater intellectual demands upon the performer than the traditional simple, technologically backward methods, but it also establishes the expectation of yielding a higher income. But in order to make a more modern type of farming economically attractive it is important to allocate a substantial amount of new investment to the building of roads, marketing centers, communication and transport equipment, and related forms of social overhead capital.

What has been said about the relation between traditional agriculture and education also holds for many forms of traditional rural (and urban) handicrafts. The gradual development of small industry on modern technological and organizational lines is dependent upon the breakdown of pre-industrial attitudes, as well as upon the supply of skilled personnel. This change of attitudes, as well as the development of economically feasible patterns of investment in small- and medium-scale industry, depends not only upon the availability of better educated persons, but also on increased investment in various forms of social overhead capital particularly in small and medium-sized towns, market centers, and similar places.

It may seem that in this portion of this chapter I have strayed away from the problem I had posed at the beginning of this section—the discussion of the educational phase in the pre-school period and the impact of the educational services of the family or the wider kinship group. But if it is remembered that the educational services of the family are affected by changes in the environmental conditions under which it functions, then it will be understood that investment in social overhead capital, which draws the rural family into a wider circle of social interaction and which brings to it more information and knowledge on farming, as well as on personal relations and forms of social and political behavior, contains a heavy indirect educational component. From the purely economic point of view it does not matter whether this overhead capital is brought to the villages and small rural towns by planned public projects or by private initiative. It may make a good deal of difference, however, in the actual impact it has, whether it is transferred through community development projects or other means. There is no space here for a detailed discussion of the most appropriate mechanisms of application of social overhead capital, though this is an important and very relevant problem. What I have shown is that under certain circumstances the development of a country's economy can be fostered more fruitfully, in the short run, by investment in capital other than man, and that some of this investment, especially to the extent to which it affects attitudes towards productive activity in agriculture and handicrafts, has an important indirect educational component.

III

I now turn to the problem which is discussed much more extensively in the economic literature: the provision of formal education in schools and related institutions (training centers, on-the-job training, etc.). Because quite a few research results have been published on this problem, I need not repeat many of the economic considerations on how outlays may be allocated among the different phases of this process and what are the likely economic effects of each of these patterns of educational strategy.[6] But it may be useful to review a few simple data, since they will have some bearing on the subsequent discussion of the political implications of different educational programs.

First, let us consider an approximate measure of the resources devoted to various forms of education. In general, costs per pupil vary greatly and although the contents of education at different levels differ substantially and require quite different types of equipment, the costs, especially in developing countries, for education at different levels reveal the extent to which education may contribute to greater social and economic equality. For example, it is estimated that in Brazil in 1958 the annual cost of higher education was $1,150 per pupil, whereas in secondary education the corresponding per-pupil outlay was $165, and in primary education $25.[7] Similarly, according to the estimates published in the *African Education Report*, cost per pupil in Africa for 1961-1962 was $24.50 in the primary schools, $261 on the secondary level, and $1,471 on the higher education

[6] Perhaps the following are the most useful compendia on the economic aspects of education and investment in man in their relation to economic development: Mary Jean Bowman and C. Arnold Anderson, "The Role of Education in Development," in Brookings Institution, *Development of the Emerging Countries*, Washington, 1962; William J. Platt, *Towards Strategies of Education*, Menlo Park, SRI, 1961; T. W. Schultz, "Investment in Human Capital," *American Economic Review*, Vol. LI, No. 1 March 1961, pp. 1-17; John Vaizey, *The Economics of Education*, London, 1961; and the papers published in *Journal of Political Economy*, Vol. LXX, No. 4, Supplement, August, 1962.

[7] The data on Brazil were kindly supplied by my colleague Robert J. Havighurst.

level. The *Report* also provides several alternative estimates of the prospective costs of education in Africa. In one supporting memorandum recurring costs per pupil per year are estimated as follows: $20 per year on the primary level, $40 on the level of vocational training, and $150 on the general secondary level. Recurring annual costs per student in scientific and technical university faculties are estimated at $1,600 and in other university programs at $800.[8] On the other hand, direct outlays on higher education in the United States in 1956 were estimated to have been $524 per pupil in secondary schools and $1,168 per student on the college and university levels.[9]

From these data it can be seen that in Africa and Brazil, two regions with a much lower overall level of economic performance than the United States, outlays per student on the university level are roughly equal, whereas outlays on the lower school levels are substantially lower. In other words, outlays per student in the economically less highly developed countries are now more unequal between levels than in the more highly developed United States. At the same time, these findings suggest that the great difference in per student costs at different levels of education is correlated with differences of roughly similar magnitude in the potential earnings of persons with different years of schooling. This, in turn, appears to mirror the structuring of the society as a whole and the political problems implicit in this structure. I shall return to this point later.

A further corollary of this observation of differences in costs of education is the consideration that different educational programs may involve substantial differences in total costs. As was already pointed out earlier, there is a good deal of favorable sentiment expressed with regard to the need for creating high-level manpower skills in developing countries. This point is stressed, above all, by Frederick H. Harbison in a paper submitted to the Conference of African States on the Development of Education in Africa and in earlier writings.[10]

[8] See "Outline of a Plan for African Educational Development," in *African Education Report*, pp. 12-13; and "Report," *ibid.*, pp. 24-28.

[9] The figures for the United States are derived from Tables 5 and 6 (p. 580) in the paper by T. W. Schultz, "Capital Formation by Education," *op.cit.*

[10] See Frederick Harbison, "The Process of Education Planning," in *African Education Report*, Annex IV, pp. 47-55; and idem, "The Development of Human Resources in the Newly Developing Countries," in J. Douglas Brown and Frederick Harbison, *High-Talent Manpower for Science and Industry*, Princeton, 1957, pp. 61-90.

Harbison accepts the need for industrialization as an inalterable objective of developing countries and, focusing on the human agent in this process, comes to the conclusion that among the factors determining the course of industrial development, "the really critical factor is that of attracting, accumulating, and developing the high-level human resources which modern industrialization unconditionally demands." Harbison quite correctly argues that among the strategic factors in the industrialization process there is one composed of a number of persons—who often may form only a minority of the total population or total working force—who make up the "cadres" of the industrialization process. These are the entrepreneurs, managers, administrators, scientists, engineers, and other individuals with high technical competence. Importation of these strategic manpower resources is a transitional measure during early stages of industrial development. In the longer run each nation must generate its own strategic manpower resources through education. But since educational facilities are limited and total educational outlays more or less fixed, priority must be given to the development of scientists, managers, engineers, and administrators, if necessary at the cost of curtailing elementary education or other forms of higher education. The application of these general views to one developing country, Nigeria, are developed explicitly in the *Report on Higher Education* (Ashby Report), in which the summary recommendations—based perhaps on not too accurate primary data—are made that "Nigeria's most urgent need in the near future is for expansion of intermediate education," and "technical and scientific education, both at the university and intermediate level, needs to be given the highest priority."[11]

On the surface these counsels and the analysis on which they are based appear unassailable. But the particular targets and priorities for educational outlays must be geared to a general economic development program, for otherwise we would witness the same type of excess capacity in the form of high-power human capital as we witness in many developing countries on a lower level of skills. There are signs in not a few developing countries that such excess capacity already has developed in the humanities and arts and, though the need

[11] See Frederick Harbison, "High Level Manpower for Nigeria's Future," in Nigeria, Federal Ministry of Education, *Investment in Education, The Report of the Commission on Post-School Certificate and Higher Education in Nigeria*, Lagos, 1960, p. 64.

for scientifically and administratively trained people is as yet largely unfilled, the rapid development of these forms of high-level manpower without commensurate capital investment in fields in which they can find productive employment would be a serious misallocation of resources. Yet the enthusiastic reception of ideas on the need for highly skilled technically trained manpower in Africa and other less developed countries may lead to a more vigorous implementation of the programs of higher education without commensurate investment in non-human capital for the management and administration of which the high-level manpower supposedly is being trained.

The main issue suggested by this analysis is that in much of the current discussion on the economic impact of education and the need for educational planning in developing countries—especially in almost completely non-industrialized countries of sub-Saharan Africa —too flat a transference is made from the European past and present to the African and Asian future. The will to industrialize and the need for industrialization is taken to mean that it can actually be accomplished according to ambitious plans and that the bulk of industrial development will occur through application of Western technological and organizational prototypes to the economic activities of developing countries. It is often forgotten that the social, political, and cultural constellations at the initial stage of industrialization in Europe and in present non-Western developing countries differ profoundly. Even relatively superficial inspection of the facts should suggest that in all developing countries, but especially in those in which there already exists heavy population pressure and high population density in rural areas, patterns of economic growth must be found which are more attuned to the relative factor supplies existing in these counties than to those prevailing in Western countries. There is extensive discussion in India and elsewhere on whether more labor-intensive and yet modern, patterns of industrial production can be developed rather than merely adopting those currently employed in western Europe or in the United States. It may be argued with some force that the consistently high growth rate of Japan was made possible, in part, because in that country the pattern of industrial production was creatively adjusted to the prevailing forms of social interaction and factor supplies. The result was that as late as 1957, 52 per cent of the industrial labor force of Japan was working in plants employing fewer than 50 workers and the gross output of firms in the secondary and tertiary sector combined was distributed as follows: 59

per cent was produced in firms designated as "small business" (i.e., individual enterprises and corporations with less than 10 million capital), and 41 per cent in large firms.[12]

Though in a certain sense the Japanese experience is unique, it has some features which are of relevance for other developing countries. It shows that under conditions of serious backwardness, and in a society in which population pressure is mounting, significant economic progress can be made by developing small-scale enterprises in which employment opportunities for high-level manpower with certain technical skills would not be available. This experience also points to the utility and potential impact which a general education program on the primary level may have. It shows that there may be a different growth potential in a society in which literacy and schooling up to a minimum level is quite common and one in which there are still large islands of illiterate persons. Unfortunately, much less emphasis has been given to the economic and social impact of transforming a society from one with many illiterates into one with virtually full literacy than has been given to the economic aspects of higher and intermediate education. This is understandable since, in spite of the very free applications that have been made of the findings of Western scholars in this field to the problems of developing countries, most of the empirical data have been drawn from the experience of Western countries in which primary education is practically universal and in which, apart from some marginal individuals, 100 per cent of the adult population is literate.

One of the changes which has often been observed in developing countries is that the extension of primary education has led to changes in consumption and aspirations for consumption and in new career choices. I have referred to this last point earlier. Changes in consumption have primarily a development-retarding effect, since they foster a desire to increase the share of income applied to consumption and reduce the share applied to savings by persons with more education.

But when we consider the wider extension of elementary education in a country which in the past had rather sizeable sectors of formally uneducated persons and illiterates, we should consider the impact of the universalization of literacy over a relatively short period of time. It may be that the impact of widening the educational base of a population through providing primary education is a process which does not have significant effects on a *marginal* scale, but only a *total*

[12] Japan Productivity Center, *Small Business in Japan*, Tokyo, 1960, pp. 5 and 6.

scale. In other words, the increase of general literacy from, say, 30 per cent of the adult (or adult male) population to 35 per cent of that population may not have any important effect on general productivity in that society and may even put more strain on its resources because of a stepping up of consumption patterns. But the increase from 30 per cent literacy to 75 or 80 per cent in a relatively brief time may be of immense significance for the economic structure and general capacity for economic development of a society.

We may compare this difference between marginal and discontinuous large-scale changes in the number of persons with elementary education with Joseph Schumpeter's discussion of general economic development. Schumpeter distinguishes between small changes which occur in the productive processes of any society and which may be compared to routine innovations that have been found to occur in societies displaying little dynamism in their economies and genuine innovations which establish a harsh break with previously existing productive patterns and lead to genuine economic development.[13] If we translate this into ideas applicable to educational policies we may say that only a sizeable and discontinuous extension of the amount of primary education is likely to have an effect upon the productive performance of a society, whereas a small change in primary education probably is dissipated in the short and medium run as being primarily an addition to consumption rather than a basic change in production functions.

The reason for the powerful impact exerted by a discontinuous growth of the number of persons possessing an elementary education is the difference in patterns of communication made possible by the acquisition of general literacy. In some fictional accounts the difficulties of an illiterate person in a society in which it is assumed that everyone can read and write have been recounted. Even with access to radio and television, an illiterate person would not be able to secure a great deal of information. He would be unable to call on the telephone, for he could not dial; he would be unable to identify a building or an office within a building if the name of the building or the occupant of the office is lettered on the door. He would be unable to read the advertisements, the destination of buses, the names of train stations, etc. But

---

[13] Joseph Schumpeter, *The Theory of Economic Development*, New York, Oxford University Press, 1961, pp. 62 to 63 and ff. On routine innovation see the essay by Robert S. Merrill, "Routine Innovation," unpublished doctoral dissertation, Department of Anthropology, University of Chicago, December 1959.

more important than the experiences of daily life, the productive processes in a society in which everyone is literate are distinct from those in societies where illiteracy is common. In the former, job instructions are written or printed, directives, information bulletins, massive quantities of relevant information are distributed by means of written or printed communications, all of which are absent in societies with mass illiteracy.

Richard L. Meier has estimated the quantity and composition of information flow in a Western metropolitan area. He has computed the total amount of information "bits" transmitted in a metropolitan society of 5 million persons to come to 6×10^{14} bits. Of this, 3.6×10^{14} bits, or 60 per cent, is transmitted by reading, the rest by means of radio, television, lectures and discussions, films, observation of environment, and other miscellaneous means. In other words, the vast bulk of information in a major Western metropolitan area is transmitted by means of the written word. Meier also estimates that in San Francisco the amount of information transmitted is approximately 10^8 bits per person annually. In a city of similar size and importance in a developing country the corresponding quantity of information is around 10^6 bits per person annually. The quantity of information transmitted in an urban area in which the total population is assumed to be literate is a hundred times as large as in a similar area located in a country in which large proportions of the population are illiterate.[14] Not all the information that is transmitted in either of the two countries is information exclusively for productive purposes, or even information with indirect relevance for production. But since we have shown that a society with general literacy makes possible a basically different organization of economic activity, the greater intensity of information transfers in literate societies is even more important than the greater numerical quantity of such transfers. In a society with general primary education, the actual production processes which may be applied are of a different kind than those possible in a society with large islands of illiteracy and lack of primary education. The distinction is particularly pronounced in the realm of economic organization, since in societies in which written processes of communication are the rule types of bureaucracies and patterns of administration (in the economic as also in the political field) can be established which perform on a different and typically much more ele-

[14] See Richard L. Meier, "The Measurement of Social Change," in *Proceedings of the Western Joint Computer Conference*, San Francisco, 1959, pp. 327-331, esp. pp. 330-331.

vated level of productivity than corresponding entities in non-literate societies.

IV

I now turn to a brief examination of the importance of these different types of educational allocation for the political relations in developing societies. What are the probable political implications of the development of excess capacity of trained persons for whom appropriate occupational opportunities may not be available in the short run, i.e., for several years after they leave school? What are the likely political consequences of an educational program in which, because of the great differences in outlays between primary, secondary, and university education, many of the existing profound differences in social structure are maintained and possibly sharpened or placed on a new level? Finally, what might be the political implications of an educational program dedicated to the eradication of mass illiteracy and through which patterns of social communication could be changed profoundly in a relatively short time? Moreover, the question should also be asked whether these programs are realistic in terms of the political conditions and the social structures and the forces influencing these social structures prevailing in developing countries. In order to throw more light on these questions, we will examine in a general way the typical patterns of social structure and distribution of political power in developing countries and ask how different educational policies, particularly those discussed in this chapter, are influenced by, and in turn influence, the socio-political relations of these nations.

Some distinctive characteristics of socio-political structures of developing countries may be sketched as follows: many developing societies are currently engaged in the task of nation building, a process which requires above all the formation of a national elite with power over all parts of the country; the development of a uniform national ideology which is shared in its essentials by all persons inhabiting a national territory; and the evolution of political procedures adequate for successful interaction with other nations in the modern world. In this process of nation building it is important to destroy many still existing particularisms in the political sphere. In other words, the newly arising central elites must develop among the masses a level of political action and political commitment to an entity larger than the customary tribes, village communities, castes, lineages, or other small groups which in the past formed the major foci of the loyalty of the masses. In countries in which former colonial rule has been abolished, the new elite must, moreover, develop new symbols for national unity and objectives of common policy. Many of these objectives are in the economic sphere and their formulation from an overall national viewpoint differs from that of the large masses of principally rural dwellers. A hydro-electric power-dam project, for example, may have very different significance from the viewpoint of the national elite and that of the rank and file. The former consider primarily its potentialities for increasing production, the latter think chiefly of its contribution to consumption—if they are familiar with the uses of electricity at all. This contrast in attitudes may be generalized: the elite often looks at economic development from the standpoint of overall national interests, insisting on the growth-producing elements of economic policies. The rank and file looks at economic development from the standpoint of the consumer, i.e., it regards the comfort-providing elements of economic measures. This means that from the standpoint of the elite the savings-investment aspects of economic growth are paramount, whereas from the standpoint of the masses the consumption aspects stand out.

In addition to the need for national unification, the abolition of particularistic loyalties, and the differences in the image of the goals of economic policies between the political elite and the masses, two further general aspects of political relations in developing countries must be noted. The first is based on the findings of James S. Coleman. He suggests that there is some correlation between competitiveness in the political sphere and the degree of economic performance, but that even in highly competitive political systems there is a "tendency toward unitary government and heavy concentration of decision-making."[15]

My second general observation is a corollary of this proposition, that is, that one of the primary avenues towards the achievement of higher status in developing countries is through recruitment into the political elite or the administrative bureaucracy and that the attainment of education is the major alternative to various essentially ascriptive criteria for recruitment. In more concrete terms this may be stated as follows: in many developing countries the traditional

[15] See James S. Coleman, "The Political Systems of the Developing Areas," in Gabriel A. Almond and James S. Coleman, eds., *The Politics of the Developing Areas,* Princeton, Princeton University Press, 1960, pp. 532ff., esp. p. 544 and pp. 558-559.

method of recruitment to government service rested predominantly on the basis of ascription, i.e., only persons who because of their family connections or other relationships had close ties with those in positions of power could actually enter government service and ultimately attain positions of political leadership. There were some exceptions to this rule—at least ideally—and these permitted recruitment to political power positions on the basis of achievement criteria, i.e., on the basis of educational performance. For example, in traditional China an elaborate system of examinations was set up which constituted the "ideal" apparatus for the recruitment of the bureaucracy, though in fact persons belonging to the wealthiest and most powerful families had easier access to the examinations and even to positions within the administrative apparatus by means of direct appointment to their posts. In other societies positions in the bureaucracy could be attained by purchase, and here also access to power was effectively confined to persons who already formed part of the elite.[16] For in these societies the possession of wealth was closely associated with the control of power and attainment of higher levels of education.

But in all these systems, especially as they began to face more complex tasks internally and externally, a premium was placed on persons with special skills, which primarily could be attained by better education. In other words, quite apart from its contribution to the purely economic development objectives of a backward country, high-level manpower qualifications are increasingly useful in the process of attaining political power. We actually see that in organizations of various scope in developing societies positions of leadership, which actually do or may be expected to endow their holders with power, are held primarily by intellectuals. This is true of leadership in government and various government services; it is also true in labor unions, political parties, farmers' associations, and other interest groups. The outlook of these intellectuals may vary greatly: some may be Western-educated or at least oriented towards Western approaches; others may hold traditional attitudes and orientations, but they are distinguished from the rank-and-file they lead by having

[16] See on this problem my chapter, "Levels of Economic Performance and Bureaucratic Structure," in Joseph La Palombara, ed., *Bureaucracy and Political Development*, Princeton, Princeton University Press, 1963, pp. 193-194. On the Chinese bureaucracy see Chung-Li Chang, *The Chinese Gentry*, Seattle, University of Washington Press, 1955, pp. 21ff.

acquired a good deal more formal education than the ordinary citizen and by having legitimized their access to power (or potential power) through this educational achievement.

It is against this background of increasing political power of educated persons that we must evaluate the various educational policies which may be selected as instrumentalities of the economic development objectives of a developing country. To begin with, it is quite clear that a program designed to enhance high-level manpower training in developing countries is likely to perpetuate, and possibly even strengthen, the social inequalities and with them the political inequalities which exist today. A program which sacrifices the generalization of education on a lower level for concentration of educational outlays for higher education widens the gap which exists between those who possess education, wealth, and power, and those who do not. As we have seen before, unless a program of high-level manpower training is rigorously tied in with a general development plan, and unless the planned targets are met and positions are created into which the newly trained high-level manpower can actually step, problems of competition for high-level positions will ensue and may even result in a potential export of high-level talented manpower from the developing country. These developments are a consequence of the continued inequality in social structure and levels of income, the close tie-in between the acquisition of higher education and elevated positions in the power hierarchy, and the imbalance in the market for persons with elevated skills.

Examples of this situation may be found, among others, in such countries as Greece, where the supply of objectively well-qualified persons for many high-level manpower positions is greater than the demand. As a consequence many highly trained Greeks do not serve in their own country but become voluntary émigrés to more highly developed countries, where their talents can be used more fruitfully. This situation, moreover, establishes within the country a climate of excessive competition for jobs requiring high-level training, with the consequence that ascriptive orientations in the recruitment process are by no means abolished, and that the close correlation between wealth, educational achievement, and political power is maintained. These features tend to strengthen the persistent inequality in the society and to retard developments in democratization and the wider spread of participation in political decision-making processes. Another exam-

[559]

ple could be cited from India, where also, as a consequence of the excessive number of highly trained individuals in many fields of scholarship, there are numerous attempts to find appropriate employment abroad. This is true not so much for people trained in law, literature, and the arts, but rather in more highly technical fields, e.g., economics, physics, or even engineering. Hence, in these instances we encounter the strange inconsistency that developing countries, which on the one hand display important shortages in certain highly skilled professions at the same time come to be exporters of human capital of high quality. These inconsistencies are only in small part due to the malfunctioning of the market or some alternative allocation process: they are primarily the consequence of social structure and of the tieup between social status and political power in developing societies.

Alternative educational policies which have been suggested earlier may consist either in a concentration on the provision of mass literacy or in the expansion first of general community services and social overhead capital formation largely for the rural population coupled at a later stage with educational programs. I shall discuss these two alternatives in order.

Let me begin by citing a passage from a study by Daniel Lerner which is explicitly concerned with this problem. Lerner says: "The secular evolution of a participant society appears to involve a regular sequence of three phases. Urbanization comes first, for cities alone have developed the complex of skills and resources which characterize the modern industrial economy. Within this urban matrix develop both of the attributes which distinguish the next two phases—literacy and media growth. There is a close reciprocal relationship between these, for the literates develop the media which in turn spread literacy. But, historically, literacy performs the key function in the second phase. The capacity to read, at first acquired by relatively few people, equips them to perform the varied tasks required in the modernizing society. Not until the third phase, when the elaborate technology of industrial development is fairly well advanced, does a society begin to produce newspapers, radio networks, and motion pictures on a massive scale. This, in turn, accelerates the spread of literacy. Out of this interaction develop those institutions of participation (e.g., voting) which we find in all advanced modern societies. For countries in transition today, these high correlations suggest that literacy and media participation may be considered as a supply-and-demand reciprocal in a communication market whose locus, at least in its historical inception, can only be urban."[17]

Apart from pointing out the high intercorrelation between urbanization and the acquisition of literacy, Lerner stresses a phasing, according to which the establishment of a mass literacy program has the best effects at a time when industrialization and urbanization have already undergone a fair degree of development. Hence the large-scale elementary education programs of some of the least urbanized and least industrialized countries of Africa do produce a series of school leavers who roam the streets of cities in search of what they consider appropriate employment, and this excess capacity of human capital equipped with low-level skills cannot be absorbed quickly, except to the extent to which provision is made for complementary investment in industrial and modern agricultural facilities.

However, as we saw earlier, there is some point in considering a large-scale discontinuous increase in the number of persons with elementary education, since this makes possible the introduction of new and much more efficient production functions. To the extent to which modernization is pushed in the productive sector of a developing country and to the extent to which new methods of farming and industrial production are introduced, educational systems designed to spread primary education and, above all, literacy must be geared in to produce the manpower with the necessary skills of operating these new devices and of understanding and implementing the new productive patterns. But as we have seen from the plight of school-leavers in Nigeria and of the so-called "educated unemployed" in India, the supply of persons with the required skills is not lacking. What is lacking is the necessary non-human capital in new agricultural and industrial enterprises and the change in values and beliefs which makes traditionally or previously low-ranked occupations compatible with the acquisition of some education.

As long as these concomitant changes have not taken place, it is futile to expect the spread of elementary education to perform the wonders which some assign to it. Rather than a tool for an economic breakthrough, the excessive dispensation of elementary education may be a hindrance to it through its adverse impact upon political stability. For as I have pointed out earlier, in a society with large pockets of illiteracy the acquisition of primary education has chiefly

[17] Daniel Lerner, *The Passing of Traditional Society*, Glencoe, The Free Press, 1958, p. 60.

an impact on consumption and aspirations for higher levels of consumption by those who receive an education. They congregate in cities and there form a pool of relatively unskilled labor. They experience long periods of unemployment and some remain permanently without regular jobs. These basically hopeless educated unemployed become the members of the cadres of various messianic or revolutionary political movements. The leadership is provided usually by persons whose training and education has been even more extensive, but who have been unable to find suitable employment or have become disillusioned with the more regularized employment they might have secured. Whether and to what extent these socio-political movements exert an influence on the rate or direction of economic growth depends upon numerous factors, but from past experience they have, on the whole, produced a high degree of political instability and have, in this way, greatly impeded economic growth. Their existence and growth appears to depend upon the presence of at least a few highly trained and a rather larger number of less-well-trained persons, who form the leadership and the cadres of these movements. Without leadership and cadres, such movements of violent protest might be confined to momentary flareups, but no permanent political agitation and no long-run propagation of political views and action of a radical or subversive character could develop.[18]

These political movements are aggravated by the misdirection of planned investment activity, the sluggishness of capital accumulation in technologically new fields, and manifold resistances against innovating entrepreneurial activity. It is futile to argue that a big push in education by itself is an adequate means of promoting the developmental objectives of a new country. It is equally futile to point to the great contribution which education has made in the more highly developed countries. In the United States and western Europe the growth of mass education, as well as training for high-level manpower, had many of the spectacular results attributed to them because they took place in a setting in which such results could be achieved. Those who support the proposition that in the United States and elsewhere a large part of the "unexplained" increase in output (i.e.,

---

[18] The points expressed in this section have been influenced by a reading of the excellent essay by John H. Kautsky, "An Essay in the Politics of Development," in John H. Kautsky, ed., *Political Change in Underdeveloped Countries*, New York, John Wiley & Sons, 1962, pp. 3ff. I also owe a debt of gratitude to Myron Weiner of the Massachusetts Institute of Technology and David H. Bayley of the University of Denver for having provided information on radical movements and the sources of political violence in India.

that portion which is not directly attributable to corresponding increases in inputs) is due mainly to the greater investment in man, often forget to add that this investment in man is a *joint product attributable not only to the educational process as such, but also to the cultural, social, and material environment in which this new and larger amount of education is acquired.*

This means that European or United States policies relating to education—as also to other features of economic development—have very limited applicability to developing countries. Above all it changes the priorities according to which development outlays are to be ranked and it underlines the fact that certain allocations which may produce notable results in economically advanced countries may have virtually no impact on the rate of economic growth of newly developing countries and, in extreme cases, may even be conducive to a decline in the level of income. The applicability of a given set of policies depends upon the social, cultural, and material environment in which these policies are applied, and this holds for education as well as for other measures designed to lead to economic advancement. These are the main reasons education on all levels must be geared to a wider, integrated development program and must be planned in as precise correspondence as possible with this program. This may mean, as already suggested earlier, that at some phases of the development process investment in social overhead, in community development or related projects, and in development of agriculture and productivity in farming and small industry may have greater priority than large-scale educational projects. Once such projects, emphasizing overhead development, are initiated they must, in turn, be supported by providing additional education especially among the rural population. The educational component of these programs then becomes geared into the more general plan of overall development and the present illusion that by additional education all the sources of economic backwardness in developing countries can be eliminated, as if by a miracle, may be destroyed. This illusion is common to many simple farmers of the developing countries themselves and also to some well-known Western social scientists of our day. For example, however much P. T. Bauer and T. Balogh may disagree on other points, they are in full agreement on the almost miraculous impact of rural education.[19]

[19] See P. T. Bauer, *Indian Economic Policy and Development*, London, George Allen & Unwin, 1961, p. 125 and *passim*; and Thomas Balogh in *The New Statesman*, March 23, 1962, p. 412.

I have come full circle to the point at which I started. The needs of the developing countries consist above all in progress in industrialization and rationalization of agriculture. There is general agreement on the former but much less agreement on the latter. Yet, if any lesson can be learned from history, it is that economic development requires a reasonably well-functioning agricultural sector for taking root. This does not mean that invariably an "industrial revolution" must be preceded by an "agricultural" revolution, as allegedly was the case in Britain. But it does mean that unless a still largely agricultural country experiences an improvement in agricultural efficiency and a longer farm product which in part can be converted into investment in social overhead capital and industrial and industry-related plants, a genuine growth process supported mainly out of the developing country's own resources cannot take place. But with a large rural population whose attitudes and behavioral norms are still predominantly "traditional" and who rely on self-subsistence rather than on production of cash crops for the market, the production of a "surplus" is difficult and perhaps illusory. The change of these attitudes can, in part, be altered by education. But it can be altered decisively only by a planned investment program through which opportunities for greater integration of the agricultural sector in the national economy is assured and through which the farm population is brought into closer contact with markets, the centers of information, and the centers of political decision-making. It is not denied that such a program has Herculean dimensions, but economic development is a serious and overwhelmingly difficult task. All the talk about educational needs and the requirements for high-level manpower do not provide adequate substitutes. The most effective alternative is developmental planning on a realistic basis, taking account of the predominantly agricultural character of developing countries and the profound backwardness of the rural sector.

The political consequences of such a program of slow deliberate development of the major resources available in developing countries are likely to be more favorable than the insistence on large-scale primary education or on a crash program producing a large reservoir of high-level manpower. It is the only program which may gradually produce increased political participation by the ordinary members of the rank and file and which draws, step by step, an ever-increasing number of the members of the developing nations into the circle of politically aware citizens. It would be foolish to maintain that such a program could proceed without producing bottlenecks or encountering serious difficulties and possibly even temporary setbacks. But it is a program which would encounter fewer political impediments than any alternative program of development. Moreover, it is the only program which is likely to lead to political solutions compatible with a free and increasingly democratic society.

CHAPTER 17

CONFLICTS IN EDUCATIONAL PLANNING

WILLIAM J. PLATT

~~~~~~

The Educational Imperative

AN urge for development in many countries is now expressing itself increasingly in what might be called the educational imperative. In this sense, education, like malaria control, tends to be perceived as some sort of fundamental human right to which each person is entitled. Policy makers and social scientists need to cooperate in converting the mystique of this imperative into feasible and beneficial programs of development.

In developing countries the demand for education tends to exceed the supply. There is an almost universal wish on the part of parents for a better life for their children. This wish may have several motivations, only some of which may be "rational" in terms of whether or not the child is acquiring skills and knowledge with which to support himself. Other motivations may arise from parental regret over lost opportunities or lack of diligence. Another motive may be an undiscriminating faith in the power of education to automatically confer status and prestige, not only upon the child but upon the family.

Fortunately, there is something more tangible with which to build development programs than the motives just described. We are acquiring new insight into the relationships between education and economic and social development. Theory is moving quickly from professional journals to application in education budgets—perhaps too quickly for some who question the reliability of theory. However, the pressures of demography and technology will not wait. Failure to apply the new insights into the education process usually results in the perpetuation of educational practices and programs poorly geared to development needs.

With the spread of the educational imperative and its companion, the development urge, governments as a whole are having to become involved in educational policy. Policy makers are beginning to see the role of education in a context larger than the one in which it has been viewed traditionally. It is now an instrument for the development of people and of states. This role for education has been the subject of international policy conferences on economic growth and investment in education, including the following: May 1961, Addis Ababa, Ethiopia, 39 African countries; October 1961, Washington, D.C., 20 Western European and North American countries; March 1962, Santiago, Chile, 19 Latin American countries; April 1962, Tokyo, Japan, 18 Asian countries. These conferences were not only confrontations of delegates from one country with their counterparts from other countries; they were also, in effect, a dialogue between ministers of education and ministers of economics or finance, supported by professional educators, economists, and other social scientists. This kind of "educational summitry" within delegations and between delegations sets a new trend in which educational policy is determined as a part of over-all economic policy. For the first time there is beginning to be the opportunity to understand how investment allocations in all forms of development, including human capital formation, can enhance and support one another.

The World Bank is now entertaining loan applications for educational development, and has granted one or two. This step tends also to throw national educational issues into the arena of international politics. Education ministries thereby have a new prominence relative to other agencies of government. Issues of vocational education versus academic, of science versus humanities, of universal primary education versus education for high level manpower—all these issues that formerly were of primarily intra-education discussion can now become of national and international interest. Through this process a wider audience, including political elites at home and abroad, can be introduced to aspects of educational policy. What the wider audience will see in the country's education system is not only the society's means for regenerating itself, but also the curious pattern of influences that the former metropolitan power left behind. Some of these influences, such as the relative prestige accruing to various educational courses or certificates, are exceedingly persistent, thereby sometimes exercising a stronger influence upon the channeling of talent than do economic forces of demand, supply, and price.

Before the growing integration of education and economic development, education was viewed as an expenditure, not an investment. Under the new partnership of all those charged with policy making for development, including human resource development, the opportunity is emerging for education's claim on the budget to be determined and defended more systematically as part of a program of investment. These changes offer a new setting and a new set of playing rules in the arena of polity for statesman, educator, economist, and politician. The social scientists in each of their several disciplines will find something of interest in the emerging relationships wrought by education's new partnership in development.

While the confrontations taking place at the conferences are new, the insights now being applied to education are not. Most have been in the social science literature for a century and more. Take the elementary principle of "economizing." This term is used in the economics sense of the word—allocation of scarce resources to large needs. Another definition of economizing is maximizing output per unit of input. In few activities of society is there a greater gap between needs and resources than exists in education. Paradoxically, in few has there been less application of economizing than in education. Fortunately, the neglect of economics by education's policy makers and the reciprocal neglect of education by economists are both being corrected.[1]

Some readers may challenge the charge that little economizing is practiced in educational planning and operations. They will think of the intensive scrutiny to which budgets for education are subjected at every level of government in every society. Admitting that cost cutting is widely practiced in educational planning and operations, I still

[1] See, in addition to other works cited in this chapter, G. A. Almond and James S. Coleman, eds., *The Politics of the Developing Areas*, Princeton, Princeton University Press, 1961; C. Arnold Anderson, "The Impact of the Educational System on Technological Change and Modernization," North American Conference on the Social Implications of Industrialization and Technological Change, sponsored by UNESCO, at Comparative Education Center, University of Chicago, September 15-22, 1960; Gary S. Becker, "Underinvestment in College Education," *The American Economic Review*, Vol. L, No. 2, May 1960, p. 346; Mary Jean Bowman and C. Arnold Anderson, "Concerning the Role of Education in Economic Development," in Clifford Geertz, ed., *Old Societies and New States*, New York, Free Press of Glencoe, 1963, pp. 247-379; Philip H. Coombs, "Educational Planning in the Light of Economic Requirements," *Forecasting Manpower Needs for the Age of Science*, Office for Scientific and Technical Personnel, Organization for European Economic Cooperation, September 1960, pp. 25 and 31; H. S. Houthakker, "Education and Income," *Review of Economics and Statistics*, Vol. XLI, No. 1, Feb. 1959, p. 24; Herbert S. Parnes, ed., *Planning Education for Economic and Social Development*, The Mediterranean Regional Project, Organization for Economic Co-operation and Development, 1962; Herbert S. Parnes, *Forecasting Educational Needs for Economic and Social Development*, The Mediterranean Regional Project, Organization for Economic Co-operation and Development, October 1962; Edward F. Renshaw, "Estimating the Returns to Education," *Review of Economics and Statistics*, Vol. XLII, No. 3, Aug. 1960; and Theodore W. Schultz, "Education and Economic Growth," *Social Forces Influencing American Education*, National Society for the Study of Education Yearbook, Part II, 1961, p. 46.

submit that economizing in the technical sense is seldom practiced. I refer to the following systematic process: the identification of objectives of an education system or of an institution within a system; the formulation of feasible alternative courses of action that are most likely to achieve those objectives; the measurement of costs and benefits attending each alternative; the selection of the alternative that best meets objectives within all operative constraints; and, finally, the design and implementation of an evaluation process by which feedback will offer corrective signals for the cases in which estimates of costs or of benefits are in error.

Educational Planning and Politics

The application of economizing concepts in education planning results in certain complications and implications of a political nature. These are the focus of my chapter, which proposes the following: (1) All societies face the problem of economizing in allocating resources to and within education. (2) Legitimate centripetal forces tend to encourage allocation policies and instrumentalities that are efficient, investment-oriented, and centralized. Legitimate centrifugal forces in education tend to encourage allocation policies and instrumentalities that are decentralized, independent, and "liberal." (3) Each society must seek ways to resolve these conflicting, equally legitimate forces.

Before we describe the conflicts in education planning in detail, it will be useful to mention briefly why the process of allocation-planning-conflict resolution may be related to political development: (1) Education is almost inevitably an accelerating or perturbing force in society, e.g., its effects in the United States, the USSR, Philippines, Communist China. (2) Educational institutions themselves wield political power, e.g., university students and faculties in many Latin American countries. (3) The instrumentalities and institutions for planning educational policies and budgets and for carrying out such programs affect political development. Space does not permit development of the foregoing statements. Suffice it to say that education is far from inert politically.

Conflicts in Educational Planning

In the course of economizing—in the sense of planning to make the most effective use of scarce educational resources—there will inevitably be certain legitimate conflicts of policy choices. The resolution of these conflicts will determine the character and even the success of a significant part of a society's development program.

Consider the following five pairs of opposed forces:

Pair No.	Centripetal Force	Centrifugal Force
1	Integrated and investment-oriented education	Independent and consumption-oriented education
2	Modern and future-oriented education	Classical and parent-oriented education
3	Pragmatism	"Pure" learning
4	Concentrated centers, efficient organization, economies of scale	Uniform distribution, small classes, small schools
5	Protectionism to achieve a balanced foreign trade in talent	International free trade of talent

"Centripetal" is used here to denote centralizing tendencies, while "centrifugal" denotes dispersive tendencies toward spontaneous laissez-faire arrangements.

These pairs come into sharpest focus only under the conditions of rapid development and where national resources must be austerely "economized" to stretch them as far as possible. Societies content with only gradual development and already operating at a fairly advanced stage of development will not find these forces in nearly as clear opposition. In many cases, in fact, a relatively rich country can afford such redundancy in its education budget as to be able to be responsive to both polarities of the potential conflict. To some degree the United States enjoys this redundancy, although new international responsibilities may be mitigating factors.

INTEGRATED AND INVESTMENT-ORIENTED EDUCATION VS. INDEPENDENT AND CONSUMPTION-ORIENTED EDUCATION

Educational opportunities may be designed to offer all the varieties of education in which students and their parents are interested, at least up to some fiscal restraint. This is what is characterized as "consumption-oriented" in that the student's choice is guided by his own wishes and the community is obligated to provide the kind of educational opportunity that will permit him to indulge that choice. The choice may turn out to be investment-oriented in the sense of investing in a skill or talent that will have earning power for the individual, but the probability that the investment will fit feasible patterns of development is left entirely to chance. True, there is the student's own perception of the nature of the investment, and that of the student's parents.

Often the centrifugal, or "independent," force leads to the creation of the educated unemployed. J. B. Condliffe describes the following personal visit to an Indian graduation exercise in 1950: "We went along to the convocation. It was a very impressive affair. The bagpipers played the Colonel Bogey March to play in the President of India. He made us a long speech in Hindi urging that Hindi should be used as the medium of instruction. Most of the professors, in their red Oxford, Cambridge, and London doctors' gowns, had to read the English translation to understand what the President was saying in his capacity as Chancellor. This was sad enough but what was worse was to see the classes come up for graduation. As I recall, there were about 10 engineers. There were only 3 or 4 nurses. But when the lawyers came, they came in wave after wave. There must have been several hundreds of them that graduated that year. This was the easiest way to a degree in India. The teaching is at a very low standard, it has little relation to Indian problems, and it simply creates an unemployed intellectual litigious proletariat."[2] Since 1950, the Planning Commission of India has begun calculating manpower needs for the economy and has tried to persuade the universities to reorient themselves accordingly. India is still hunting for a proper resolution.

None will deny that completely independent individual choice in education is in the finest liberal tradition and an appropriate candidate among goals for education. Yet a legitimate case may also be made for the other pole of the pair of forces, namely, planning educational capacities, types of education, and incentives with an integrated investment orientation. "Integrated" here means made a part of or contributing to a total program of development. "Investment" is used in the usual economics sense of creating intellectual or skill capital whose productivity will be useful later.

In a newly developing country, an obvious way to economize on the too scarce resources available for education is to embark upon some kind of manpower planning. This proceeds from a decision not to waste expensive education on the development of skills and talents for which there will be little or no use in the economic or social

[2] J. B. Condliffe, "Industry as a Vehicle of Education," unpublished Stanford Research Institute (SRI) staff paper.

scheme of things. Making manpower projections and translating them in terms of the types and capacities of educational institutions most appropriate seems to be an obvious way to economize here.[3] This is the case for integrated investment-oriented education.

Clearly some middle ground must be sought. Can there not be attention to the manpower planning problem and also allowance for the exercise of individual choice within community-generated options? As will be pointed out later, public policy can establish many non-mandatory incentives and disincentives which will result in the kinds of student flows that will come closer to economizing than would a completely laissez-faire approach.

MODERN AND FUTURE-ORIENTED EDUCATION VS. CLASSICAL AND PARENT-ORIENTED EDUCATION

There is a tendency for education to transmit traditional culture (i.e., to be parent-oriented) rather than to stress modern and future-oriented curricula. A cultural heritage certainly contributes to a society's cohesiveness and motivates the members of the society toward the perpetuation and enhancement of the culture. Education is a key means of passing on this heritage from generation to generation.

In opposition, of course, are all the modern demands inherent in a complex interdependent world. Science, domestic language reform, the need to update obsolete standards, the need to communicate new economic and social concepts, and foreign languages—all these compete with one another and with other modern needs for the scarce supply of classroom hours. Contemporary forces cry for education to respond to social and economic needs of today and tomorrow.

Also, the classical demand is for specialization in well-bounded and "comfortable" expertise, often unrelated to modern needs. The countervailing modern demand is for versatility and the kind of education that will allow for easier mobility of graduates of all levels of education from obsolescing fields to emerging ones. At the sub-professional level, the traditional approach will favor vocational skills of wood and metal shop, while the modern demand is for stronger general education that will create versatile trainability and re-trainability to perform in a variety of vocational occupations. Finding a

---

[3] For further discussion, see my paper, "Education: Rich Problems and Poor Markets," *Management Science*, Vol. 8, No. 4, July 1962; and Frederick Harbison and Charles A. Myers, *Education, Manpower, and Economic Growth: Strategies of Human Resource Development*, New York, McGraw-Hill Book Company, 1964.

trade-off point at which equilibrium can be achieved in this conflict of classical and modern forces can be difficult, and extremely controversial when it comes to allocating resources to education.

PRAGMATISM VS. "PURE" LEARNING

Compilers of the educational budget will have to concern themselves with the trade-offs between pragmatic instruction and pure learning. Pragmatic education is oriented toward applications and problem solving, whereas pure learning is more concerned with erudition and scholarship, which, though attractive from a liberal point of view, are often extravagant in an austere budget.

There are degrees to which pure learning can be given utilitarian application. Pure learning in art or literature probably rates more as a luxury in the education budget than does "pure" learning in one of the physical or life sciences. The latter may bring a discovery or an unforeseen application within a sufficiently short leadtime to pay off, even in a capital-poor country.

CONCENTRATED CENTERS, EFFICIENT ORGANIZATION, ECONOMIES OF SCALE VS. UNIFORM DISTRIBUTION, SMALL CLASSES, SMALL SCHOOLS

The logistics of education tend to be grouped under one of two opposing policies. The centrifugal forces are represented by egalitarian efforts to achieve uniform geographical distribution of educational opportunity. Often associated with this is a desire for small classes and small schools. The latter tend to make for non-specialized and self-contained educational units. The opposing centripetal forces call for deliberately concentrating and rationally organizing educational resources. The objective of the latter is to exceed the threshold of minimal concentration and specialization and to realize economies of scale associated with fully utilizing specialized talent and facilities. The following examples illustrate activities feasible only under concentration: (1) quality in-service training of faculties in new content and techniques; (2) psychometry for identifying and encouraging student talent; (3) guidance; (4) language laboratories; (5) scientific laboratories.

The risk of concentrating educational opportunities is primarily that of losing widespread political support. More even distribution of educational opportunities may mean sacrifices in educational productivity—effectiveness per unit of resource input. Scarce resources in education, it must be remembered, are not just financial; they nearly always involve a shortage of teachers also. Teachers who are qualified should be employed in a logistic configuration that maximizes their effectiveness.

PROTECTIONISM TO ACHIEVE A BALANCED FOREIGN TRADE IN TALENT
VS. INTERNATIONAL FREE TRADE OF TALENT

There is a surprising number of international transactions in education and in the exchange of talented manpower; student and teacher exchanges are one example and the export and import of talented people is another. Frequently these result in permanent moves through emigration, immigration, and expatriation of exchange students.

The economic doctrine of comparative advantage would argue for mobility of talent within the free world such as has long been the case in the United States and is becoming the case in the European Common Market. One can speculate that in an international common market of talent, exports and imports of skill and talent could take place on a much larger scale. Under primogeniture, the second and later sons of educated British families in the nineteenth century frequently had to seek a career somewhere abroad. This was, in effect, an early form of technical assistance or export of talent.

In economically advanced nations technical assistance is generally thought of as the lending of skilled personnel to emerging countries for the purpose of giving advice on aspects of development. Because of the relative attractiveness in several advanced countries of higher education and of positions based on this education, a reverse form of technical assistance has inadvertently arisen. The exchange students from developing countries often voluntarily choose to become expatriates because there is as yet no adequate outlet for their talents at home. This represents an unsolicited form of the export of high talent from a developing to an advanced country. These flows are a great loss to the source country, where high talent is at a premium and where the best of scarce local educational resources has been devoted to educating the expatriating student. Nations seeking development progress can be expected to fashion policies that will husband their human resources in somewhat the same way they watch their balance of payments. This vigilance is only in small part chauvinistic. Reduced to fundamentals, it is a concern for the viability of the particular nationhood. Less developed nations may fear being relegated to permanent positions of economic inferiority by a constant draining off of some of their best human resources. It can be expected that policies aimed at protecting talent resources will arise in such countries. Hopefully these policies will reflect affirmative planning and incentives such as are discussed here rather than repressive measures such as the wall of East Berlin.

Perhaps regional groupings of countries with substantial common interests can lead to greater international mobility of talent and at the same time acceptable political consequences. If advanced countries continue their policies of technical assistance and achieve a true export of talent to needy countries, the latter can begin catching up in development and thus eliminate the gaps in opportunity that encourage political leaders to seek to imprison talent.

Resolving the Conflicts

Resolving the opposing centrifugal and centripetal forces that affect education planning is the art of human resource development in a constantly changing world. On the big canvas of this art, I can only hope to paint in a few small areas. My objective is to nominate some candidate principles that may be useful in the search for viable policy positions on education. Resolving these forces, as I mentioned earlier, tends to be agonizing only: (1) when there is an effective political demand for rapid economic, social, and technological development, and (2) when there is some austerity in the education budget. To the degree that either or both conditions can be relaxed, a laissez-faire solution to most of the education planning problems is possible.

The few principles for resolving conflicts in education planning covered by this chapter should be viewed as part of strategies[4] for human resource development. The formulation of balanced strategies for human resource development is probably in a primitive stage everywhere. This is because the relationship of education to economic development has only begun to be recognized. Few people have had

---

[4] Since publishing a paper in January 1961 entitled, "Toward Strategies of Education," I have received some criticism that the term "strategies" is too suggestive of the word's military connotation. I employed it in the economics and systems analysis sense. It still seems to be the most comprehensive word to suggest the need for unifying concepts of action that take account of the trade-offs inherent in the necessity for economizing.

experience in helping to develop planning of this kind. The need to create cadres with such experience is reiterated at each of the international educational policy conferences.

Three principles that may help to resolve conflicts in education planning are: (1) a philosophy of development in which the role of human capital formation is explicitly identified; (2) manpower programming; (3) the public policy "dial settings" that can encourage those flows through the education system that will be in keeping with the philosophy of development and with manpower opportunities.

A PHILOSOPHY OF DEVELOPMENT

A philosophy of development should naturally be something intimate to a particular society. The liberalist tradition, however, offers some common concepts that can run through these philosophies. Following are some re-statements of liberal concepts that may have application in conflict resolution:

1. A purpose of development and of education is to enable each individual to develop to his fullest capacity.

2. The individual should participate in the formulation and fulfillment of rules under which he lives and works. This is the concept of government by consent.

3. There should be equal access to education. Equality here must be determined by objective tests of potential skill and talent rather than by social status, political status, or racial or ethnic origin.

4. A guide for the content and methods of education should be the release of talent, meaning the stimulation of creativity and understanding. It is only thus that widely dispersed centers of initiative can begin to help the total development process. The engine of development operates fastest when entrepreneurship begins to spread widely.[5] In too many newly developing countries, education tends to be equated with the recital of facts and other sterile forms of scholarship. Sometimes this has come about through perpetuation of erudition for its own sake only, sometimes through borrowing only portions of the value system of education from an advanced society where these types of scholarship have served a more nearly legitimate role.

5. There should be a deliberate effort to modernize and reinter-

[5] Maurice Zinkin, "Entrepreneurs: Key to Growth," *SRI Journal*, Vol. 5, Second Quarter, 1961.

pret traditional practices in a culture so as to give them meaning and connection with needs of the day. Some societies have found ways in which to update ancient rituals and thereby enrich modern life. This principle can help to neutralize the polarities felt in the classic versus modern opposition.[6]

6. Various levels of a liberal training should be offered universally. Some attention must be given to the humanistic disciplines as a means of undergirding responsible citizenship and of creating a base for lifetime re-educability and retrainability. This principle is recognition that education can no longer be a one-time event in the career of a semi-skilled worker, a professional man, or a teacher. The pace of change in technology and in society is such that useful and responsible citizenship can come only with constant re-education. Re-education need not necessarily be through formal educational institutions; more flexibility is now available in the mass media of radio and television. In-service and on-the-job retraining will find its way into more and more places of gainful occupation.

7. Educational effort should be dispersed but not to the point of excessive dilution. Dispersion can be accomplished by decentralizing the educational effort geographically and offering incentives for local authorities to share a society's responsibilities. The expansibility inherent in a decentralization of educational effort is well described in a UNESCO paper prepared for the meeting of ministers of education of Asian member states in Tokyo, April 1962: "It is interesting to note that three of the economically well-developed countries (USA, UK, USSR) with very different economic systems relied heavily in establishing their primary education systems upon breaking down the

---

[6] J. B. Condliffe illustrates this principle in discussing Maori land tenure: ". . . the great Maori leader Sir Apirana Ngata found that he could not get anywhere with the scattered system, not so much of land ownership, as to rights to land usage. One man had a right to live on a piece of land or to cultivate it because his grandfather was buried there. Another man might have a right because he killed that man's grandfather there. There were all kinds of rights. By laborious discussion, Ngata worked out a system of consolidation of rights, not for individuals, but for sub-tribes, for extended families. Then Ngata incorporated the sub-tribes (*hapus*) under English limited liability law so that the land became the property not of the individual but of the group and on this corporate basis he organized cooperative institutions. All through, he wrote new words for the old songs and dances so that when you go down and see these Maori entertainers of Whakarewarewa and listen to them singing and dancing and miming, you will very often find that they are discussing the effect of the introduction of telephones or of the new system of butter factories. This appeals to them. The poetry has a long history and is full of allusions to history and tradition. It has been a very potent means of education. It links the old with the new." ("Industry as a Vehicle for Education," unpublished SRI paper.)

problem at the central level by drawing heavily upon local initiatives. During the year 1929-1930, for instance, only 4.6 per cent of the 53,647 schools in the USSR engaged on the eradication of illiteracy were paid for out of the state budget, whereas 74.4 per cent were supported by local municipal, district, and rural budgets, and 21 per cent were financed from extra-budgetary sources (trade unions, cooperatives, etc.). During the same financial year the number of schools in the USSR with paid teachers was 50,965, and with unpaid teachers 46,142 (the latter coming from 'anti-illiteracy societies,' factories and institutions of various kinds). In the case of the great expansion of the USA in the last century, the building of a school was one of the first charges on the resources of the newly established communities and voluntary teachers were widely used."[7]

8. Those who employ graduates of the educational system should cooperate in education planning and regeneration. Major employers must comprehend the principle that they should reimburse the education bank in some way for the talents they are drawing from it. They should practice conservation—talent conservation—and avoid the danger of exploiting and bankrupting the stock of human talent. Conservation can be practiced by supporting scholarships, by making educational materials available, by industry-school committees, and many other means.

The foregoing are a few of many concepts that need to be debated and adopted to help resolve opposing forces in education planning.

MANPOWER PROGRAMMING

When rapid development is sought, it is essential that manpower analysis be used to help education serve as an instrument for economic and social development. The steps in such an analysis include the identification of general economic development needs for future periods; the translation of these needs into the associated manpower requirements, particularly requirements for the various types of high talent and highly skilled manpower needed; and, finally, the analysis and design of the educational program that will provide graduates to match the manpower requirements.[8]

For manpower planning to be comprehensive it almost inevitably has to be integrated centrally. In keeping with some of the foregoing

[7] UNESCO, *The Economic Implications of the Plan of Educational Development in Asia*, UNESCO/MINEDAS/5, February 27, 1962.

[8] Some development may be found in Harbison and Myers, *op.cit.*

points of philosophy, however, there should be width and breadth of participation in the process. There is nothing inherently authoritarian in the act of education planning itself. Its purpose is to assist all those responsible for educational investments by increasing their understanding of the consequences of alternative patterns of allocation. "Consensus" planning as opposed to "command" planning is necessary in a pattern of government by consent.

In the manpower plan, special attention will have to be given to the supply of teachers. In every newly developing country the shortage of teachers is as great a bottleneck to the expansion of education as the shortage of funds. One untapped source of teachers may be the pool of the intellectual unemployed that is fairly common in Southeast Asia, in Muslim countries in the Middle East, and to a lesser extent in South America. This pool usually consists of graduates of an educational system whose curricula and values have been borrowed from an advanced country without adequate adaptation to local needs. If adequate incentives (both moral and material) can be designed, the educated unemployed or underemployed may be persuaded to help fill the teacher shortage by either serving as teachers or by training them. Vaizey reminds us that even this effort needs to be integrated into a manpower plan: "Clearly it would be preposterous to use intellectuals to train yet more intellectuals to be unemployed in their turn. Unless it takes place in a context of vigorous economic growth, and above all of a manpower plan, the development of education is merely an open invitation to revolution. Thus a manpower plan is a *sine qua non* for the use of education as a means of economic growth."[9]

PUBLIC POLICY DIAL SETTINGS

The final group of suggestions I have for resolving conflicts in education planning has to do with the design of a system of public policy "dial settings." The term "dial settings" was chosen to suggest the selection, by public officials, of the rates of flow that represent feasible performance for the education network as a whole. Feasibility, of course, is defined by the manpower opportunities and available resources for education. The policy options which educational authorities in a free society can use to encourage various patterns of student flow include incentives such as scholarships and fellowships; disincentives such as fees and charges; a mutually consistent set of admission,

[9] John Vaizey, *The Economics of Education*, Faber and Faber, 1962, p. 129.

retention, and graduation requirements; and counseling and guidance.

Once the manpower program has been translated into the approximate number, types, and levels of graduates needed, plans must be laid for acquiring the appropriate educational capacities. There still remains the question of whether consumer choice—which is usually made while an individual is still uneducated—will bear any resemblance to the needs determined from the manpower programming exercise. It is here that great skill in economics, psychology, and sociology must be brought to bear in the design of a mutually consistent and liberal set of public policy dial settings.

It is to be expected that the manpower program will identify shortages in some key areas of education that do not necessarily correspond with traditional perceptions of scholarship or career opportunity. It is these areas that should receive scholarships and fellowships. Teaching facilities, faculties, and teaching materials covering these areas must be given special attention and extra incentives. While supporting the type of graduates who are in short supply sounds so obvious as to be almost banal, it is surprising how often it is not done. There is a popular notion that any one curriculum deserves egalitarian attention in competition with all other curricula. This merely results in future imbalances in the pool of trained manpower and frustration for the surplus graduates.

Fees, tuitions, and charges can act as disincentives to discourage excessive enrollment in unneeded curricula. An extreme application of this policy would be to set fees that *more* than cover course costs, but this might be considered punitive. It is probably better to rely on the affirmative approach of offering scholarships in subject areas where shortages exist and none where they do not. Tuition charges equivalent to full costs would appear to be an equitable way to discourage the proliferation of course selections that are consumption-oriented.

A mutually consistent system of admission, retention, and graduation requirements needs to be designed as one of the dial settings that will encourage needed student flows. Of course the admission and retention requirements would not apply for levels of education that are compulsory or universal. For the higher levels that are discretionary—in some countries secondary and in some countries higher education—some guide-lines must be in effect to ration the amount of education that a society can afford. As we pointed out earlier, the demand for education almost always far exceeds supply. Thus, policy makers have no choice but to design some logical and equitable method of rationing the scarce supply of discretionary levels of education.

The entrance examination is a frequently used method of screening for potential ability. Superficially, the entrance exam would appear to be attractive on many counts: (1) It is objective in that it measures individual performance. (2) If carefully and honestly administered, it cannot be abused by the student and/or by the administering agency.

There are several direct and indirect disadvantages, however. They include: (1) To allow efficient grading, the examination must be constructed for objective, as opposed to creative, responses. (2) The able student may be taking the exam on a bad day, or he may perform below his ability under the environment of the exam. Unless the potential hazards can be carefully avoided, the system of entrance exams can have a negative effect.

The entrance exam tends to establish and dominate the pattern and emphasis of instruction in the next educational level below. If the entrance exam can be made truly comprehensive, or a reliable sample of the truly comprehensive, then preparation for it in lower grades is fine. Too often, though, it is a test of factual knowledge, with insufficient stress upon synthesis, understanding, and creativity. When this happens, the same emphasis appears in the curricula in the grades below, or there is parental pressure to change curricula to accommodate such tests.

It would appear that a more skillful blending of entrance examinations with retention and grading policy would be preferable to over-reliance on entrance examinations. In the first place, entrance examinations violate the useful principle of constant feedback of student performance to himself and his teachers. It is the "sudden death" approach to educational opportunity. Putting more reliance on day-to-day performance seems both psychologically more sound and more likely to encourage the kinds of creativity that will contribute to development.

Guidance and counseling practices are another extremely useful device in the system of encouraging needed flows. Through a network of guidance personnel, up-to-date information can be disseminated on career opportunities and on how these are changing with new developments. From the short view, specialists in guidance and counseling may appear to be a luxury in the education budget; but for long-range planning and for the welfare of the students being counselled, they are essential. If such counselors can be well informed on long-range education and manpower opportunities, they can save their own cost to society many times over by preventing maldistribution and wastage of talent.

Conclusion

In summary, I have sought to show: (1) Education has become an imperative. (2) For the first time governments as a whole are involved. (3) Educational planning requires economizing in the technical economic sense.

I have tried to fit educational planning into the environment of rapid development, where centripetal and centrifugal forces of considerable magnitude are at work. To spend money on education is to strike some implicit position in the range of options among conflicting forces. My efforts have been to make the choices and their legitimate rationales a little more explicit and to discuss some principles that might help in the resolution of conflicting forces.

Policy makers in or associated with education can rightly view their authority as an affirmative one. The wise public servant is the one who discharges his responsibilities to increase rather than restrict the range of options available to his fellow man, and this view is easily implemented in education policy making. The education policy maker enjoys unusual prerogatives for creating opportunities not previously available and for unlocking talent and skill. If this view pervades the work of those associated with education policy, they will enjoy the satisfaction that comes from contributing to a useful enterprise.

A Bibliographic Guide

to Education and Political Socialization

ATTITUDE, COMPETENCE, AND EDUCATION:

A Selective Bibliographic Guide to the Relation of Education to Political Socialization

KENNETH I. ROTHMAN

~·~

I. Introduction

This guide is a multi-disciplinary sampling of materials relevant to research into the relation of education and political socialization, with particular reference to the role of schools and schooling (of all types and levels) in nation building. It aims primarily to facilitate further inquiry, and only secondarily to provide a comprehensive catalog of past contributions. Disciplines and perspectives brought to bear are sociology, anthropology, social and clinical psychology, comparative education, and, to lesser extents, history, literature, and political science. The limited contributions from the latter discipline reflect a paucity of attention by political scientists to the interaction of the educational and political systems, as discussed by the editor in his introduction.

This guide aims to present references to studies which will indicate the *range of approaches* to the topics. It is intended primarily for use as a research tool by social scientists interested in political development. The attempt has been to select items which will not cause the non-specialist undue difficulty. Mainly English-language publications are cited. The guide is intended to supplement the citations provided in the various chapters of this volume. It is regretted that it has not been possible to bring the bibliography fully up to date during the lapse of time between submission and publication.

The underlying interest in political development results in our giving somewhat more attention to the consequences of educational processes for the polity than we give to the influence of political factors upon education. (The relation is of course seen as two-way, and as being rarely a simple one of cause-effect.) The use of terms such as "nation building" indicates a reluctance to coin new vocabulary rather than acceptance of a particular theoretical approach to development. Nor, in speaking of development, do we wish to equate it with the imitation of specific social or political forms or with "the desirable."

ANALYTIC CONTRIBUTIONS: METHODOLOGICAL AND THEORETICAL

II. Background Materials

A. DEFINITION AND SCOPE

G. Almond and J. S. Coleman, eds. *The Politics of the Developing Areas.* Princeton, Princeton University Press, 1960. Almond's theoretical introduction is followed by five sections treating major developing areas; Coleman furnishes a synoptic conclusion. The conceptual framework is essentially functional.[1]

D. Easton and R. D. Hess. "Youth and the Political System," in S. M. Lipset and L. Lowenthal, eds., *Culture and Social Character: The Work of David Riesman Reviewed*, New York, Free Press, 1961, pp. 226-251. A careful discussion of the concept of political socialization and its implications for empirical study.

M. J. Herskovits. *Man and His Works*. New York, Knopf, 1950. Some writers use "education," "schooling," and "enculturation" interchangeably. Herskovits, in his useful text, suggests that enculturation be defined as a life-long process of both spontaneous and directed learning. Education would then refer to directed learning only, while schooling would be directed learning carried on via specialists in teaching.

B. POLITICAL MODERNIZATION

R. E. Asher, et al. *Development of the Emerging Countries: An Agenda for Research*. Washington, D. C., The Brookings Institution, 1962. Interdisciplinary in scope and suggestions.

T. Coombe. "Education in the Building of Nations," Special Paper, Ph. D. in education program, Harvard University, May 1963. Excellent presentation and interdisciplinary synthesis of present knowledge about education as a factor in nation building and modernization; also discusses "social and political concomitants and consequences of educational expansion in developing countries." Excellent bibliography.

R. Emerson. *From Empire to Nation: The Rise to Self-Assertion of Asian and African Peoples*. Cambridge, Harvard University Press, 1960. Lucid and authoritative treatment of national development and political change.

E. S. Griffith, J. Plamenatz, and J. R. Pennock. "Cultural Prerequisites for Democracy," *American Political Science Review*, Vol. L, March 1956, pp. 101-137. Philosophical; based on consideration of five industrially developed nations.

J. H. Kautsky, ed. *Political Change in Underdeveloped Countries: Nationalism and Communism*. New York, Wiley, 1962. Scope of the twelve essays and extensive editorial explication is broader than the specifically political. Useful for amplifications of the notion of modernization. Contains, inter alia, E. Shils, "The Intellectuals in the Political Development of the New States," pp. 195-234, which was originally published in *World Politics*, Vol. XII, April 1960, pp. 329-368.

T. Parsons. *Structure and Process in Modern Societies*. Glencoe, Ill., Free Press, 1960. An attempt to conceptualize modern industrial society in terms of a sophisticated and somewhat complex post-Weberian theoretical scheme.

J. Plamenatz. *Alien Rule and Self-Government*. London, Longmans, Green, 1960. A basic statement by a philosophically oriented student of government.

L. Shannon, ed. *Underdeveloped Areas: A Book of Readings and Research*. New York; Harper, 1957. Contains many important selections which will not soon become outdated. Interdisciplinary.

[1] In this bibliography, "political socialization" subsumes Almond's "political socialization" and "political recruitment." Cf. pp. 26-33 in Almond and Coleman.

C. SOCIOLOGICAL AND ANTHROPOLOGICAL APPROACHES

1. Political Sociology

R. Bendix and S. M. Lipset. "Political Sociology—A Trend Report and Bibliography," *Current Sociology*, Vol.vi, 1957, pp. 79-169. Broad-ranging conception of the field. Integrative essay; classification of existing writings.

J. R. Gusfield. "The Sociology of Politics," in J. B. Gittler, ed., *Review of Sociology: Analysis of a Decade*, New York, Wiley, 1957, pp. 520-530. Annotated bibliography for the productive postwar decade.

2. Sociology, Anthropology, and Education

B. R. Clark. *Educating the Expert Society*. San Francisco, Chandler, 1962. Largely restricted to the U.S., but otherwise the best introduction to sociological analysis of education.

Jean Floud and A. H. Halsey. "Education and Social Structure," *Harvard Educational Review*, Vol. xxix, 1959, pp. 288-294. Brief, significant orientation for non-specialists.

————. "The Sociology of Education: A Trend Report and Bibliography," *Current Sociology*, Vol. vii, 1958, pp. 165-235. Useful classification of extensive list of bibliographic items; integrative essay.

C. W. Gordon. "The Sociology of Education," in Gittler, *Review of Sociology*, pp. 500-519. Annotated bibliography.

N. Gross. "The Sociology of Education," in R. K. Merton et al., eds., *Sociology Today: Problems and Prospects*, New York; Basic Books, 1959, pp. 128-152. Outline and critique.

F. C. Gruber, ed. *Anthropology and Education*. Philadelphia, University of Pennsylvania Press, 1961. Report of a conference, theoretically oriented but not overly technical.

A. H. Halsey, Jean Floud, and C. A. Anderson, eds. *Education, Economy and Society: A Reader in the Sociology of Education*. New York, Free Press, 1961. Not restricted in relevance to economic development. See especially: Floud and Halsey's "Introduction," pp. 1-14; H. S. Becker, "Schools and Systems of Stratification, pp. 93-104 (reprinted from "Schools and Systems of Social tatus," *Phylon*, Vol. xvi, 1955). R. J. Havighurst, "Education and Social Mobility in Four Societies," pp. 105-120 (reprinted from "Education, Social Mobility, and Social Change in Four Societies," *International Review of Education*, Vol. iv, 1958, pp. 167-185); R. H. Turner, "Modes of Social Ascent through Education: Sponsored and Contest Mobility," pp. 121-139 (reprinted from "Sponsored and Context Mobility and the School System," *American Sociological Review*, Vol. xxv, 1960, pp. 855-867); J. Nisbet, "Family Environment and Intelligence," pp. 273-287 (reprinted from "Family Environment and Intelligence," *Eugenics Review*, Vol. xL, 1953, pp. 31-42); Margaret Mead, "The School in American Culture," pp. 421-434 (reprinted from *The School in American Culture*, Cambridge, Harvard University Press, 1951); T. Parsons, "The School Class as a Social System: Some of Its Functions in American Society," pp. 434-445 (reprinted from "The School Class as a Social System: Some of its Functions in American Society," *Harvard Educational Review*, Vol. xxix, 1959, pp. 297-318); A. H. Halsey, "The Changing

Functions of Universities," pp. 456-465 (reprinted from "The Changing Functions of Universities in Advanced Industrial Societies," *Harvard Educational Review*, Vol. xxx, 1960, pp. 119-127).

R. J. Havighurst and B. L. Neugarten. *Society and Education*. Boston, Allyn and Bacon, 1957. Good standard text.

J. Henry. "A Cross-Cultural Outline of Education," *Current Anthropology*, Vol. 1, July 1960, pp. 267-305. Well-developed and very useful set of data categories for the observation, recording, and analysis of classroom interaction.

B. H. Junker. *Field Work*. Chicago, Chicago University Press, 1960. Good practical introduction to observation, with excellent bibliography. Developed from a seminar under Professor Everett C. Hughes; introduction by Hughes.

Elsa P. Kimball. *Sociology and Education: An Analysis of the Theories of Spencer and Ward*. New York, Columbia University Press, 1932. Education as agent of development and reform.

A. K. C. Ottaway. "The Educational Sociology of Emile Durkheim," *British Journal of Sociology*, Vol. vi, 1955, pp. 213-227. Concise and thorough presentation of the key ideas of a seminal thinker.

N. Sanford, ed. *Social Science and Higher Education: A Comprehensive Bibliography*. Boston, Researchers' Technical Bureau, 1958. Exceedingly thorough compilation; most studies done in U.S.

G. D. Spindler, ed. *Education and Anthropology*. Stanford, Calif., Stanford University Press, 1955. Papers and report from a conference attempting liaison between the two fields.

———. *Education and Culture: Anthropological Approaches*. New York, Holt, Rinehart and Winston, 1963. A valuable reader. Part I, "The Articulation of Anthropology and Education"; Part II, "Education in American Culture"; Part III, "Education Viewed Cross-Culturally." Noteworthy selections from Parts II and III will be listed below in the appropriate places. In Part I the writers attempt to bring anthropological theory and technique to bear upon inquiries into education in familiar and unfamiliar contexts.

D. SOCIAL-PSYCHOLOGICAL APPROACHES

1. Introductory Writings

G. W. Allport. "The Historical Background of Modern Social Psychology," in G. Lindzey, ed., *Handbook of Social Psychology*, Vol. 1, Reading, Mass., Addison-Wesley, 1954. Of great value to the behavior-oriented researcher in any discipline. Deals with theories of man and society in comprehensive but rigorous fashion; aims to eliminate the dangers of entering blind alleys which await the researcher who is shallowly grounded in basic aspects of behavior study.

J. H. S. Bossard. *The Sociology of Child Development*. Rev. ed. New York, Harper, 1954. Analyzes and interprets data from several societies.

H. Cantril. *Human Nature and Political Systems*. New Brunswick, N.J., Rutgers University Press, 1961. Brief and readable attempt to reach a "political psychology" relevant to national development.

Y. A. Cohen, ed., *Social Structure and Personality: A Casebook*. New York, Holt, Rinehart and Winston, 1961. Of particular value are the introduction and Section V, "Social Change, Acculturation, and Personality," pp. 387-455.

E. H. Erikson. *Childhood and Society.* New York, Norton, 1950. Perhaps this book should be called "Adolescence and Culture," but under any title the beautifully presented and documented discussion of identity and ideology, against a background of history and ethnography, is substantial and significant.

J. J. Honigmann. *Culture and Personality.* New York, Harper, 1954. Good standard text.

F. L. K. Hsu, ed. *Psychological Anthropology.* Homewood, Ill., Dorsey Press, 1961. Well-selected recent articles, some cited in appropriate sections below.

H. H. Hyman. *Political Socialization: A Study in the Psychology of Political Behavior.* Glencoe, Ill., Free Press, 1959. Analyses of data from opinion polls, in terms of a behavioristic socialization model.

A. Inkeles. "National Character and Modern Political Systems," in Hsu, *Psychological Anthropology*, pp. 172-208. An attempt to (1) clarify and operationalize "national character" and "political system," (2) review "systematic empirical studies"—particularly those of postwar vintage, (3) distinguish several politically relevant aspects of national character—"values about the self, orientation toward others, orientation toward authority, attitudes toward the community," and (4) summarize "problems and prospects" of a "comparative social psychology of the political process to support and suplement our traditional study of politics." Excellent bibliography.

C. Kluckhohn, H. A. Murray, and D. M. Schneider, eds. *Personality in Nature, Society, and Culture.* 2d ed., rev. and enl. New York, Knopf, 1956. A bit more technical than Honigmann, but the extensive editorial comments and syntheses provide what is still the best interdisciplinary introduction to the topic. Extensive and varied set of readings.

H. D. Lasswell. "Propaganda and Mass Insecurity," in A. H. Stanton and S. E. Perry, eds., *Personality and Political Crisis: New Perspectives from Social Science and Psychiatry for the Study of War and Politics*, Glencoe, Free Press, 1951, pp. 15-43. A link between psychopathology and politics.

————. *Power and Personality.* New York, Norton, 1948. An important statement on motivations and theoretical implications.

R. Linton. *The Cultural Background of Personality.* New York, Appleton-Century-Crofts, 1945. Brief, clear, and authoritative statement of relations of status and role, culture and personality.

M. Singer. "A Survey of Culture and Personality Theory and Research," in B. Kaplan, ed., *Studying Personality Cross-Culturally*, Evanston, Ill., Row, Peterson, 1961, pp. 9-92. Comprehensive historical and analytic presentation.

M. B. Smith, J. S. Bruner, and R. W. White. *Opinions and Personality.* New York, Wiley, 1956. Intensive study of the significance of political beliefs for the personalities of experimental subjects.

R. W. White. *Lives in Progress.* New York, Holt, 1952. Lucid and stimulating presentation of inter-disciplinary approaches to case materials.

2. More Advanced Works

H. J. Eysenck. *The Psychology of Politics.* London, Routledge and Kegan Paul, 1954. An attempt to force a variety of data into a formalistic and behavioristic framework.

J. C. Flugel. *The Psychoanalytic Study of the Family*. London, Hogarth Press, 1960. Chapter XII, "Family Influences in Social Development," pp. 117-132, is largely concerned, from a Freudian theoretical position, with the individual and social consequences of displacements of family-bred feelings upon home, clan, school, town, state, ruler, etc. Discusses variations in national orientations toward the state.

A. Inkeles. "Personality and Social Structure," in R. K. Merton et al., eds., *Sociology Today: Problems and Prospects*, New York; Basic Books, 1959, pp. 249-276. An attempt to explicate and codify various research approaches; good analyses of previous accomplishments—including an important elucidation of some writings of Fromm.

A Inkeles and D. J. Levinson. "National Character: The Study of Modal Personality and Sociocultural Systems," in G. Lindzey, ed., *Handbook of Social Psychology*, Vol. II, Reading, Mass., Addison-Wesley, 1954, pp. 977-1,020. Intensive analytic critique.

D. J. Levinson. "Role, Personality, and Social Structure in the Organizational Setting," *Journal of Abnormal and Social Psychology*, Vol. LVIII, 1959, pp. 170-180. Significant critique; proposal of a revised approach.

E. COMPARATIVE EDUCATION

1. Frame of Reference

C. A. Anderson. "Methodology of Comparative Education," *International Review of Education*, Vol. VII, 1961, pp. 1-23. Rather comprehensive discussion. Urges use of typologies, analysis of co-variation.

P. Foster, "Comparative Methodology and the Study of African Education," *Comparative Education Review*, Vol. IV, 1960, pp. 110-117. Well-documented, incisive handling of key issues in comparative education.

N. Hans. *Comparative Education*. London, Routledge and Kegan Paul, 1941. Takes a functionalist approach—rare in comparative education textbooks.

B. Holmes. "The Problem Approach in Comparative Education: Some Methodological Considerations," *Comparative Education Review*, Vol. II, 1958, pp. 3-8.

I. L. Kandel. "Problems of Comparative Education," *International Review of Education*, Vol. II, 1956, pp. 1-13. A non-functionalist approach.

————. *Studies in Comparative Education*. London, George G. Harrap, 1933. Outlines and describes interplay of national character, social and political institutions, and state systems of education.

L. J. Lewis. *Education Policy and Practice in British Tropical Areas*. London, Nelson, 1954. General discussion by a professional educator.

V. Mallison, ed. *An Introduction to the Study of Comparative Education*. New York, Macmillan, 1957. A more provocative collection of essays than is usually the case in comparative education readers.

Margaret Read. *Education and Social Change in Tropical Areas*. London, Nelson, 1955. General discussion from a somewhat sociological point of view.

E. H. Reisner. *Nationalism and Education Since 1789: A Social and Political History of Education*. New York, Macmillan, 1922. Useful for background reading.

R. Ulich. *The Education of Nations: A Comparison in Historical Perspective*.

Cambridge, Harvard University Press, 1961. Well-documented; sometimes insightful, but sometimes ingenuous.

W. E. F. Ward. *Educating Young Nations.* London, Allen and Unwin, 1959. Essays, some in the nature of memoirs, by a talented, experienced, and sophisticated educator.

2. Selected Studies

T. R. Batten. *School and Community in the Tropics.* London, Oxford University Press, 1959. On utilization of schools and teachers for community development.

C. S. Brembeck. "Education for National Development," *Comparative Education Review*, Vol. v, 1962, pp. 223-231. A general and somewhat hortative statement.

A. Curle. *Educational Strategy for Developing Societies: A Study of Educational and Social Factors in Relation to Economic Growth.* London, Tavistock, 1963. Based on comparative statistics and extensive first-hand experience.

R. A. Hodgkin. *Education and Change: A Book Mainly for Those Who Work in Countries Where Education is Part of a Process of Rapid Social Change.* London, Oxford University Press, 1957. Brief, cultivated, lucid synopsis of issues and problems in planning and enacting effective educational development.

W. I. Jennings. "Universities in the Colonies," in L. W. Shannon, ed., *Underdeveloped Areas*, New York, Harper, 1957, pp. 114-119. (Adapted and reprinted from *Political Quarterly*, Vol. xvii, 1940, pp. 228-244.) Discusses problems common among colonial universities.

Margaret Mead. "Professional Problems of Education in Dependent Countries," in Shannon, *Underdeveloped Areas*, pp. 340-350. (Adapted and reprinted from *Journal of Negro Education*, Vol. xv, 1946, pp. 346-357.) Insightful outlining of the needs for building of individual and cultural competence in underdeveloped areas.

A. Myrdal. "The Power of Education," in E. J. Hughes, ed., *Education in World Perspective*, New York; Harper and Row, 1962, pp. 137-159. Includes historical evidence for the importance of universal literacy for a social development "takeoff."

United Nations Economic Commission for Africa. *Final Report, Conference of African States on the Development of Education in Africa, Addis Ababa*, 15-25, May 1961. UNESCO, 1961. Many good papers in "Annex IV: Selected Background Papers," pp. 31-120.

A. F. C. Wallace. "Schools in Revolutionary and Conservative Societies," in F. C. Gruber, ed., *Anthropology and Education*, Philadelphia, University of Pennsylvania Press, 1961, pp. 25-54. Control and goals of education are seen to vary cyclically with societal type.

III. Theoretical Approaches

A. SOME ASPECTS OF SOCIOLOGICAL ANALYSIS

Francesca Cancian. "Functional Analysis of Change," *American Sociological Review*, Vol. xxv, 1960, pp. 818-827. Up-to-date review, critique, and contribution to the literature on functionalism. A functional approach is argued to be useful for analysis of structural change as well as static conditions.

D. Easton. "Function of Formal Education in a Political System," *School Review*, Vol. LXV, 1957, pp. 304-316. Elementary approach to functional analysis of schools.

H. Gerth and C. W. Mills. *Character and Social Structure*. New York, Harcourt, Brace, 1953. Somewhat heavy reading; examines political process and social structure from a Weberian standpoint.

J. W. Getzels. "Administration as a Social Process," in A. Halpin, ed., *Administrative Theory in Education*, Chicago, Midwestern Administration Center, University of Chicago, 1953, pp. 150-166. Useful model for structural-functional analysis of administration. Not overly technical.

N. Jacobsen. "Political Science and Political Education," *American Political Science Review*, Vol. LVII, Sept. 1963, pp. 561-569. Speculation on the instructional function of political theory; relevant to influence of political education in developing areas. Refers to its possible role in shaping of American constitutional and social history.

T. H. Marshall. *Citizenship and Social Class*. Cambridge University Press, 1960. Citizenship is divided into "civil, political, and social" elements in this masterful set of eclectic analytic essays, drawing upon the last 250 years of (mainly English) social and economic change. Social—particularly educational—legislation and opportunity are related to political involvement and social stratification and welfare. Integration of these factors amplified and continued in Marshall, *Class, Citizenship, and Social Development*, Garden City, New York, Doubleday, 1964.

R. K. Merton. *Social Theory and Social Structure*. Rev. and enl. ed. Glencoe, Ill., Free Press, 1957. Seminal discussions of function and functional analysis, relations of theory and empirical research, change and anomie, bureaucratic structure and personality, role of intellectual, reference group theory, influence patterns, etc. Well-written but somewhat technical.

T. Parsons. "The School Class as a Social System: Some of Its Functions in American Society," *Harvard Educational Review*, Vol. XXIX, 1959, pp. 297-318; also in A. H. Halsey, Jean Floud, and C. A. Anderson, eds. *Education, Economy, and Society: A Reader in the Sociology of Education*, New York, Free Press, 1961, pp. 434-455. Important functions are seen as socialization (generation of motives and capacities) and allocation (selection or sorting of individuals). Writing is somewhat technical.

F. Znaniecki. *The Social Role of the Man of Knowledge*. New York, Columbia University Press, 1940. Various roles and social patterns of intellectuals and quasi-intellectuals.

B. SOCIAL-PSYCHOLOGICAL MODELS

D. F. Aberle. "Culture and Socialization," in F. L. K. Hsu, ed., *Psychological Anthropology*, Homewood, Ill., Dorsey Press, 1961, pp. 381-399. "Socialization as a dependent variable" of several aspects of culture, including technology, economy, polity. Suggests direction of further inquiry.

L. W. Doob. *Becoming More Civilized: A Psychological Exploration*. New

Haven, Yale University Press, 1960. Excessively schematic in approach, but interesting neverthless. "The theme . . . remains hopelessly intriguing: the focus is not upon whether less civilized men learn to smoke cigarettes or put on pants, but upon what changes occur in their way of thinking, in beliefs, and in their personalities."

E. Fromm. *Escape From Freedom.* New York, Holt, Rinehart, and Winston, 1961. Personality, social structure, and political behavior in historical and psychoanalytic perspectives. Man's desire for authoritarian domination is seen as being at least as strong as his desire for creative freedom.

H. Goldhamer. "Public Opinion and Personality," *American Journal of Sociology*, Vol. LV, 1950, pp. 346-354. "This paper discusses certain constraints on *a priori* expectations that public, and more especially, political opinion is influenced by personality characteristics."

R. Lane. *Political Life: Why People Get Involved in Politics.* Glencoe, Ill., Free Press, 1959. Reviews and synthesizes psychological approaches to political behavior in the American setting.

L. W. Pye. "Personal Identity and Political Ideology," in D. Marvick ed., *Political Decision Makers*, New York, Free Press, 1961, pp. 290-313. Discussion of and reaction to E. H. Erikson, *Young Man Luther: A Study in Psychoanalysis and History.* New York, Norton, 1958. Marvick interprets political behavior in the light of, but does not reduce it to, psychic crisis.

T. Shibutani. "Reference Groups as Perspectives." *American Journal of Sociology*, Vol. L, 1955, pp. 562-570. Definition of reference group as "group whose perspective is used as a frame of reference by the actor."

F. L. Strodbeck. "Family Interaction, Values, and Achievement," in D. C. McClelland et al., *Talent and Society: New Perspectives in the Identification of Talent*, Princeton, Van Nostrand, 1958, pp. 135-194. Primarily of methodological interest to specialists, but of wider interest as a depiction of the inculcation of values and attitudes.

R. W. White. "Competence and the Psychosexual Stages of Development," *Nebraska Symposium on Motivation*, Vol. VIII, 1960, pp. 97-140. Highly relevant Neo-Freudian approach. Includes a readable critical review of other psychoanalytic orientations. Based on study of normal individuals.

J. W. M. Whiting. "Socialization Process and Personality," in Hsu, *Psychological Anthropology*, pp. 355-380. Comprehensive review and synthesis of "crosscultural studies which have used a large sample of societies. . . ." The studies deal with interrelation of child-rearing practices, personality variables, and social institutions.

C. SOCIAL AND BEHAVIORAL CHANGE

W. R. Bascom and M. J. Herskovits, eds. *Continuity and Change in African Cultures.* Chicago, University of Chicago Press, 1959. Especially S. Ottenberg, "Ibo Receptivity to Change," pp. 130-143, and H. K. Schneider, "Pakot Resistance to Change," pp. 144-167.

E. M. Bruner. "Cultural Transmission and Cultural Change," *Southwestern Journal of Anthropology*, Vol. XII, 1956, pp. 191-196. Various socializing agents and their roles as mediators of change.

S. N. Eisenstadt. "The Process of Absorption of New Immigrants in Israel," *Human Relations*, Vol. v, 1952, pp. 223-246. Cultural assimilation conceptualized in terms of learning.

L. Festinger. *A Theory of Cognitive Dissonance.* Evanston, Ill., Row, Peterson, 1957 An approach to attitude and behavior change which has been acclaimed.

M. J. Herskovits. *Acculturation: The Study of Culture Contact.* New York, J. J. Augustin, 1938. Somewhat dated; a comprehensive summary of research progress up to 1938.

A. Inkeles. "Social Change and Social Character: The Role of Parental Mediation," *Journal of Social Issues*, Vol. xi, 1955, pp. 12-23. Analysis of data from studies of USSR. Concepts of national character and socialization extended in applicability to conditions of rapid social change. Social change affects parent; parent socializes child differently than parent himself was socialized.

F. M. Keesing. *Culture Change: An Analysis and Bibliography of Anthropological Sources to 1952.* Stanford Anthropological Series, 1. Stanford, Calif., Stanford University Press, 1953.

H. C. Kelman. "Processes of Opinion Change," *Public Opinion Quarterly*, Vol. xxv, 1961, pp. 57-78. Describes three processes of social influence which can be distinguished according to motivational basis and which can be ordered according to relative strength of the influence: "compliance," "identification," and "internalization."

June Macklin. "Culture Change," in J. B. Gittler, ed., *Review of Sociology: Analysis of a Decade*, New York; Wiley, 1957, pp. 531-545. Annotated bibliography of works appearing during the fertile postwar period.

B. Malinowski. *The Dynamics of Cultural Change.* New Haven, Yale University Press, 1945. Most useful for its methodological sections.

Social Science Research Council Summer Seminar on Acculturation, 1953, "Acculturation: An Exploratory Formation," *American Anthropologist*, Vol. lvi, 1954, pp. 973-1002. Includes useful bibliographic material.

A. Southall, ed., *Social Change in Modern Africa.* London, Oxford University Press (International African Institute), 1961. Stimulating "Introductory Summary" of factors which may be seen as setting the stage for political modernization. Studies reported are from several countries; of particular interest: J. E. Goldthorpe, "Educated Africans: Some Conceptual and Terminological Problems," pp. 145-158; M. Banton, "The Restructuring of Social Relationships," pp. 113-125.

A. Strauss. *Mirrors and Masks: The Search for Identity.* Glencoe, Ill., Free Press, 1959. Changes in personal identity are seen as a function of changes in one's inter-personal relations. Approach is useful for studies of socialization by means of role transition in schools, training programs, etc.

F. Werner. "Acculturation and Milieu Therapy in Student Transition," in G. Spindler, ed., *Education and Culture—Anthropological Approaches.* New York, Holt, Rinehart and Winston, 1963, pp. 259-267. Presents and documents a typology of student response to a cultural environment dissonant with earlier experience.

D. E. Wilmott. *The Chinese of Semarang.* Ithaca, N.Y.; Cornell University Press, 1960. Includes an up-to-date review of the literature on social change, pp. 303-364.

G. and Monica Wilson. *The Analysis of Social Change*. London, Cambridge University Press, 1945. Based on field work.

DESCRIPTIVE LITERATURE: OBSERVATIONAL AND STATISTICAL
IV. Traditional and Quasi-Traditional Systems [2]

A. WESTERN HEMISPHERE

G. A. Pettit. "Primitive Education in North America," *University of California Publications in American Archaeology and Ethnology*. Vol. XLIII, 1946, pp. 1-182.

R. Redfield. "Culture and Education in the Midwestern Highlands of Guatemala," *American Journal of Sociology*, Vol. XLVIII, 1943, pp. 640-658. (In C. S. Johnson, ed., *Education and the Cultural Process*. Chicago, University of Chicago Press, 1943, pp. 12-20.)

B. AUSTRALIA, OCEANIA, SOUTH-EAST ASIA

C. W. M. Hart. "Some Contrasts Between Pre-Pubertal and Post-Pubertal Education." See full note in Section IV.E, below. Argument based on data from Australian tribes.

Margaret Mead. *Coming of Age in Samoa*. New York, William Morrow, 1928. Mead's first field study.

———. *Growing Up in New Guinea*. New York. William Morrow, 1939. A classic of culture-and-personality ethnography.

D. L. Oliver. *A Solomon Island Society: Kinship and Leadership Among the Siuai of Bougainville*. Cambridge, Harvard University Press, 1955. Meticulous description of education, pp. 191-194.

J. W. M. Whiting. *Becoming A Kwoma: Teaching and Learning in a New Guinea Tribe*. New Haven; Yale University Press, 1938.

H. A. Wyndham. *Native Education: Ceylon, Java, Formosa, Philippines, French Indo-China, and British Malaya*. London, Royal Institute of International Affairs, 1933.

C. NEAR EAST AND NORTHERN AFRICA

H. M. Ammar. *Growing Up in an Egyptian Village*. London, Routledge and Kegan Paul, 1954.

B. az-Zarnuji. *Ta'lim al-Muta'allim—Tariq at-Ta'allum. Instruction of the Student: The Method of Learning*. Translated, with an Introduction by G. E. von Grunebaum and Theodora M. Abel. New York, King's Crown, 1947. Fascinating description of education in medieval Islam, with introduction written "from the combined viewpoints of the Islamist and the psychologist." Illustrates and articulates practices and ethos of Islamic schooling ca. A.D. 1200.

[2] *Caveats:* (1) Particularly in traditional settings, child-rearing studies overlap with studies of education, and we do not presume to be able to make a rigorous distinction. (2) For convenience, breakdowns are by area. Of course, research relevant to problems studied on one area may have been done in other areas. (3) Particularly in traditional settings, separation of the political component of socialization is difficult or questionable.

D. SUB-SAHARAN AFRICA

J. C. DeGraft-Johnson, "African Traditional Education," *Présence Africaine*, n.s., No. 7, April–May 1956, pp. 51-55.

M. Fortes. *Social and Psychological Aspects of Education in Taleland.* Supplement to *Africa*, Vol. XI, 1938. London; Oxford University Press, 1938. A classic of description and insight. Depicts socialization differences between between strata of a tribe; explicates mode as well as content of learning.

G. Harley. "Notes on the Poro in Liberia," *Peabody Museum Papers*, Vol. XIX, No. 2, 1941; abr. and rep. in C. S. Coon ed., *A Reader in General Anthropology*, New York, Holt, 1948, pp. 347-369. A bit outdated; describes details of activity in secret initiation schools.

C. Laye. *The Dark Child.* New York, Noonday Press, 1954. Well-written autobiography of a Guinean childhood, shedding light on traditional education. Reprinted as *The African Child.*

K. L. Little. "The Role of the Secret Society in Cultural Specialization," *American Anthropologist*, Vol. XLI, 1949, pp. 199-212. Reprinted in S. and Phoebe Ottenberg, eds., *Cultures and Societies of Africa*, New York, Random House, 1960, pp. 199-213. The best article on traditional systems. Covers details thoroughly and concisely, classifies descriptive data in sophisticated fashion, and (most important) relates the secret societies to the wider social setting.

O. F. Raum. *Chagga Childhood.* Oxford; Oxford University Press, 1940.

Margaret Read. *Children of Their Fathers: Growing Up Among the Ngoni of Nyasaland.* London, Methuen, 1959.

Esther S. Warner. *Seven Days to Lomoland.* Boston, Houghton Mifflin, 1954. A novel of a journey into the Liberian interior, including descriptions of Poro rites and customs.

M. H. Watkins. "The West African 'Bush' School," *American Journal of Sociology*, Vol. XLVIII, May 1943, pp. 666-675. (Johnson, *Education and the Cultural Process*, pp. 38-47.) Reprinted in G. Spindler, ed., *Education and Culture—Anthropological Approaches*, New York, Holt, Rinehart and Winston, 1963, pp. 426-443. Social nature and function of indigenous schooling of adolescents.

E. GENERAL

W. D. Hambly. *Origins of Education Among Primitive Peoples.* London, Macmillan, 1926.

C. W. M. Hart. "Some Contrasts between Pre-Pubertal and Post Pubertal Education," in G. D. Spindler, ed., *Education and Anthropology*, Stanford, California, Stanford University Press, 1955, pp. 127-146. Also in Spindler, *Education and Culture*, pp. 400-425. Hart suggests that socializing processes change radically at the socially defined time of puberty, from indulgence to grim correction. The change marks the passing of the person from the family to the state, the private sphere to the public. Lore central to cherished tribal belief is taught in the later period; all initiates are treated alike; strangers rather than intimates teach and rebuke; training of mundane skills is eschewed.

Margaret Mead. "Our Educational Emphasis in Primitive Perspective," in Spindler, *Education and Culture*, pp. 309-320. Reprinted from *American*

Journal of Sociology, Vol. XLVIII, 1943, pp. 633-639. (Johnson, *Education and the Cultural Process*, pp. 5-11.) Ideal-typical differences between teaching and learning in modern and folk societies.

G. P. Murdock. *Our Primitive Contemporaries.* New York, Macmillan, 1934. Esp. pp. 384-435.

W. J. Ong, S.J. "Latin Language Study as a Renaissance Puberty Rite," in Spindler, *Education and Culture*, pp. 444-465. Reprinted from *Studies in Philology*, Vol. LVI, 1959, pp. 103-124. Well-documented; includes discussion of social and political implications.

V. Contexts of Transition

A. WESTERN HEMISPHERE

Dorothy Eggan. "Instruction and Affect in Hopi Cultural Continuity," in Spindler, *Education and Culture*, pp. 321-350. Reprinted from *Southwestern Journal of Anthropology*, Vol. XII, 1956, pp. 347-370.

R. B. Mac Vean and F. C. Nieves. "Educational Reorganization in Guatemala," *Comparative Education Review*, Vol. I, 1958, pp. 18-23.

G. D. Spindler. "Personality, Sociocultural System, and Education among the Menomini," in Spindler, *Education and Culture*, pp. 351-399.

B. AUSTRALIA, OCEANIA, SOUTH-EAST ASIA

J[ohn] L. Fischer. "The Japanese Schools for the Natives of Truk, Caroline Islands," in Spindler, *Education and Culture*, pp. 512-529. Interaction of influences from two cultures.

J[oseph] Fischer. "Universities and the Political Process in South-East Asia." Paper read in part at the Association of Asian Studies meeting, March 1961. Draft of work in progress. Analysis at several levels moves this research far ahead of existing contributions. Recruitment and allocation, at the "macro" level, internal organization and interethnic contact, at the social system level, and induction into political culture, at the micro level, are some aspects of this complex and comprehensive study. Portions have been published as "The Student Population of a Southeast Asian University: An Indonesian Example." *International Journal of Comparative Sociology*, Vol. II, 1961, pp. 224-233, and "Universities and the Political Process in Southeast Asia," *Pacific Affairs*, Vol. XXXVI, Spring 1963, pp. 3-15.

Margaret Mead. "Cultural Factors in Community-Education Programs," in Spindler, *Education and Culture*, pp. 480-511. Reprinted from N. B. Henry, ed., *Community Education*, National Society for the Study of Education, 58th Yearbook, Part I, 1960, pp. 66-96. Inducement of adult learning under conditions of rapid change. Includes discussion of three cases.

―――. *New Lives for Old. Cultural Transformation—Manus, 1928-1953.* New York; Morrow, 1956. Comparative re-study of the group described in *Growing up in New Guinea* (cf. Section IV.B above). Transformation at the global cultural level is parallelled by a transformation of interpersonal relations, bringing the Manus to the brink of politicization. Worth reading in its entirety.

B. Ryan. "The Dilemmas of Education in Ceylon," *Comparative Education Review*, Vol. IV, 1960, pp. 84-92.

V. Thompson and R. Adloff. *Cultural Institutions and Educational Policy in South-East Asia*. New York, Institute of Pacific Relations, 1948.

J. M. van der Kroef. "Educational Development and Social Change in Indonesia," *Harvard Educational Review*, Vol. XXIV, 1954, pp. 239-255.

C. INDIA AND THE ORIENT

B. T. McCully. *English Education and the Origins of Indian Nationalism*. New York, Columbia University Press, 1940. This book is history in the finest sense. Governmental documents, public decisions, reports of commissions, and statistics are utilized, but the special contribution is the sophisticated interpretation. Social classes and social change, the press and the public, administration and political mobilization, doctrine and action, are related so as to provide a valuable paradigm for analysis of social history in any area.

N. Patnaik. "Education in the Area of Bargali," in L. Shannon, ed., *Underdeveloped Areas*, New York, Harper, 1957, pp. 100-108. Reprinted from *Man in India*, Vol. XXXIV, 1954, pp. 20-38. A village schoolteacher does an excellent job of briefly and comprehensively describing his school and its problems, including general school conditions, background of teachers, attendance statistics, description and measurement of work done at home by students (farming, etc.), lack of interest in learning, endemic disease and malnutrition, distance from the school, etc. Used an opinion poll for some attitudinal data.

A. Peshkin. "Education, the Muslim Elite, and the Creation of Pakistan," *Comparative Education Review*, Vol. VI, 1958, pp. 305-324. Differential responses of Muslim and Hindu elites to British-style education.

D. NEAR EAST AND NORTHERN AFRICA

R. Arasteh. "Growth of Modern Education in Iran." *Comparative Education Review*, Vol. III, 1960, pp. 33-40. Modernization involves differentiation of the educational system from occupational as well as religious collectivities.

L. Binder. *Iran: Political Development in a Changing Society*. Berkeley and Los Angeles, University of California Press, 1962. Esp. pp. 269ff. on role of the faculty of the University of Teheran.

D. Lerner. *The Passing of Traditional Society: Modernizing the Middle East*. Glencoe, Ill., Free Press, 1958. Development of personal empathy and societal communications owes much to education, including education outside of schools. Modernization of individuals makes possible a "take-off" of societal mobilization. Both statistical and qualitative data are used. This book asks as many questions as it answers.

H. Reed. "Turkey's New Imam-Hatip Schools," *Die Welt Des Islams*, Vol. IV, 1955, pp. 150-163. Changes in training of Islamic functionaries.

E. SUB-SAHARAN AFRICA

J. S. Coleman. *Nigeria: Background to Nationalism*. Berkeley and Los Angeles, University of California Press, 1958. Esp. chapters 5 and 6, for statistical and descriptive presentation and interpretation of data on educational development and its consequences.

S. Collins. "The School Teacher in His Role as Leader in West Indian and African Societies," *Civilisations*, Vol. x, 1960, pp. 315-325. Case studies of careers of teachers, which often branch into politics.

V. D. Du Bois. "Guinea Educates a New Generation," *Africa Report*, Vol. vi, July 1961, pp. 3-4, 8, 12. General description; of particular importance for comparison of colonial period and post-Independence educated elites.

L. A. Fallers. "Ideology and Culture in Uganda Nationalism," *American Anthropologist*, Vol. lxiii, August 1961, pp. 677-686.

P. J. Foster. "Ethnicity and the Schools in Ghana," *Comparative Education Review*, Vol. vi, 1962, pp. 127-135.

———. "The Transfer of Educational Institutions: The Ghanaian Case Study." Unpublished Ph. D. dissertation. Department of Education, University of Chicago, 1962. A truly comprehensive study: historical, statistical, opinion polling, interviewing. Includes excellent discussions of functional methodology, comparative studies, institutional transfer. Refutes clichés re "adaptation" of education in Ghana.

A. W. Hoernle and Ellen Hellmann. "An Analysis of Social Change and Its Bearing on Education," *Race Relations Journal*, Vol. xx, 1953, pp. 33-44. Native education in South Africa.

G. Hunter. "Western Culture and the Advancing African: The Task of Adult Education," *Civilisations*, Vol. ix, 1959, pp. 313-328.

G. Jahoda. *White Man: A Study of the Attitudes of Africans to Europeans Before Independence*. London, Oxford University Press (Institute of Race Relations), 1961. Includes comparisons of attitudes of Ghanaian school children at different educational levels, and adults.

T. J. Jones, ed. *Education in Africa: A Study of West, South and Equatorial Africa by the African Education Commission, Under the Auspices of the Phelps-Stokes Fund and the Foreign Mission Societies of North America and Europe*. New York, Phelps-Stokes Foundation, 1922.

K. L. Little. "Mende Political Institutions in Transition," *Africa*, Vol. xvii, 1947, pp. 8-23. One of the implications: new skills needed in the bush.

E. G. Malherbe. "Training for Leadership in Africa," in Hildegarde Spottiswoode, ed., *South Africa, The Road Ahead*. London, Bailey Bros. and Swinfen, 1960, pp. 127-151. Influence of government education program on parties and other elites. Westernization in West and South Africa contrasted.

R. J. Mason. *British Education in Africa*. London, Oxford University Press, 1959. General description, including a chapter on the English educational system as a model for transfer.

C. A. McLaren. "Local Government Training in the Gold Coast," *Journal of African Administration*, Vol. ix, April 1957, pp. 63-71.

W. B. Mumford. *Africans Learn to be French: A Review of Educational Activities in the Seven Federated Colonies of French West Africa in 1935*. London, Edans, n.d.

A. V. Murray. *The School in the Bush: A Critical Study of the Theory and Practice of Native Education in Africa*. London, Longmans and Green, 1929.

Description and discussion of Western-style schooling throughout much of Africa, 1927-1928. An appendix attempts "to burst the bubble of that 'uniqueness' which is supposed to be characteristic of the African scene" by comparing the educational situation of the 1927 African native, the French medieval peasant, and the British working man of the early industrial revolution.

F. A. Musgrove. "Uganda Secondary School as a Field of Culture Change," *Africa*, Vol. XXII, 1952, pp. 234-249.

W. G. McD. Partridge. *Portrait of an African School*. London, London Missionary Society, 1961.

Margery Perham. "Education for Self-Government," *Foreign Affairs*, Vol. XXIV, 1945, pp. 130-143. Presents British viewpoint on tempo of attainment of independence; outlines goals for political education which should be attained before independence.

I. B. Tabata. *Education for Barbarism: Bantu Education in South Africa*. Durban, Prometheus, 1959. Hortative as well as descriptive, but enlightening. Deplores present Bantu education plan; outlines authoritarian ideologies which underly the plan.

F. GENERAL

C. S. Johnson, ed. *Education and the Cultural Process*. See below, section VI-B-2.

B. Kaye. "The Task of an Education Department in a Developing Area," *Universities Quarterly*, Vol. XV, 1961, pp. 84-90.

S. Tax. "The Education of Underprivileged Peoples in Dependent and Independent Territories," *Journal of Negro Education*, Vol. XV, summer 1946, pp. 336-345. In culturally mixed societies, "whose cultural tradition is to be transmitted?"

E. A. Tiryakian. "Educational Changes in Underdeveloped Areas; Consequences for the Social Structure." Paper presented to the American Sociological Association meetings, August 1960. Ramifications of the introduction of formal education.

VI. Modern Settings

A. SCHOOLING

1. Civic and Political Education

American Council of Learned Societies. *The Social Studies and the Social Sciences*. New York, Harcourt and Brace, 1962. Attempts to orient secondary school social studies curricula to the possibilities opened by advances in the social sciences.

G. Z. F. Bereday, ed. *The Politics of Soviet Education*. New York, Praeger, 1961. Essays on interaction of polity and schools.

U. Bronfenbrenner. "Soviet Methods of Character Education. Some Implications for Research," *Religious Education*, Vol. LVII, 1962 (4, Res. Suppl.), S45-S61. Reprinted in *American Psychologist*, Vol. XVII, 1962, pp. 550-564. Writings of Makarenko (the Soviet Spock) and teaching manuals are used to derive guiding principles and practices of the Soviet approach to behavior training.

The family is surpassed by the school as socializing agent; "group incentives" and "group criticism and self-criticism" underlie the socializing practices.

C. Ehrlich et al. "Social Studies at an African University College," *Universities Quarterly*, Vol. x, Nov. 1955, pp. 56-63.

F. I. Greenstein. "The Benevolent Leader: Children's Images of Political Authority," *American Political Science Review*, Vol. LIV, Dec. 1960, pp. 934-943.

I. L. Kandel. "Nationalism and Internationalism in Education," *Harvard Educational Review*, Vol. XXVII, spring 1957, pp. 75-84.

Penelope Leach. "Teaching Tolerance: the Role of the School in Furthering Constructive Inter-Group Relations," *International Review of Education*, Vol. x, 1964, pp. 190-201. Analytic review of the literature with reference to experiment and practice.

R. J. Lifton. "Thought Reform of Chinese Intellectuals: A Psychiatric Evaluation," *Journal of Social Issues*, Vol. XIII, 1957, pp. 5-20.

F. Lilge. "The Politicizing of Educational Theory," *Ethics*, Vol. LXVI, April 1956, pp. 188-208. Argues that even in democratic states values can be undermined through subservience of education to immediate political aims.

G. L. Lippitt, ed. "Training for Political Participation," *Journal of Social Issues*, Vol. XVI, 1960, entire number. Description and discussion of "some new political education endeavors"—including programs run by political parties, business organizations, labor unions, citizens' groups, and universities—all in U.S.A.

E. Litt. "Civic Education, Community Norms, and Political Indoctrination," *American Sociological Review*, Vol. XXVIII, Feb. 1963, pp. 69-75. Provocative and strategic study of social-class differences in "political themes in civic education texts, attitudes of community leaders, and effects of courses on student political attitudes." Well annotated.

W. J. M. MacKenzie. "Political Theory and Political Education," *Universities Quarterly*, Vol. IX, Aug. 1955, pp. 351-363. Critical commentary on Oakeshott (see below).

C. E. Merriam. *The Making of Citizens: A Comparative Study of the Methods of Civic Training*. Chicago, University of Chicago Press, 1931. Standard authority on civic education for at least a generation.

M. J. Oakeshott. *Political Education*. Cambridge, England; Bowes and Bowes, 1951. Philosophically based discussion.

A. Somit, et al. "The Effect of the Introductory Political Science Course on Student Attitudes toward Personal Political Participation," *American Political Science Review*, Vol. LII, Dec. 1958, pp. 1,129-1,132.

2. *Studies of Educational Organization, Role, Curriculum, and Attitude Change*

A. H. Barton. *Studying the Effects of College Education: A Methodological Examination of "Changing Values in College."* New Haven, Hazen Foundation, 1959. Problems of "evaluation studies." Behavior is seen as related to both predispositions and situations. Re-analysis of many of Jacob's (see below) pessimistic conclusions.

H. S. Becker. "Social-Class Variations in the Teacher-Pupil Relationship,"

Journal of Educational Sociology, Vol. xxv, April 1952, pp. 451-465. In Chicago public schools, perception of and behavior towards pupils is shown to be correlated with their class background. The study design and results are applicable to any setting in which membership is heterogeneous.

Daedalus. Journal of the American Academy of Arts and Sciences. "Education in the Age of Science," entire issue, Vol. LXXXVIII, winter 1959. Notable contributions from several disciplines.

S. M. Dornbusch. "The Military Academy as an Assimilating Institution," *Social Forces*, Vol. XXXIII, May 1955, pp. 316-321. Well-executed analysis of socializing functions and informal organizational structure, based on participant observation.

N. Hans. "Nationalism and Education in Asia," *Comparative Education Review*, Vol. II, Oct. 1958, pp. 4-11.

J. Henry. "Docility, or Giving Teacher What She Wants," *Journal of Social Issues*, Vol. II, 1955, pp. 33-41. Covert socialization in the classroom revealed by observers' analysis of interaction. Through subtle rewards and punishments, standardization of attitudes is accomplished. See also Henry, "Spontaneity, Initiative, and Creativity in Suburban Classrooms," in G. D. Spindler, ed., *Education and Culture*, New York, Holt, Rinehart and Winston, 1963, pp. 215-233 (reprinted from *American Journal of Orthopsychology*, Vol. XXIX, April 1959, pp. 266-279); and Henry, "Attitude Organization in Elementary School Classrooms," in Spindler, *Education and Culture*, pp. 192-214. The latter article is in part concerned with the role of unconscious needs in shaping the influences upon politically relevant attitudes of children.

P. E. Jacob. *Changing Values in College.* New York, Harper, 1957. This book sparked a proliferation of research (and despair) in colleges, when it announced that quantitative studies made in many colleges indicated a lack of impact of higher education on student values and attitudes. Unfortunately most of the studies were deficient in conception, design, and execution, and Jacob's naive interpretations of them enhanced their ambiguity. Barton, (above) takes issue with Jacob on technical matters; Riesman (below) questions Jacob's understanding of the significant issues confronting American higher education.

P. F. Lazarsfeld and W. Thielens, Jr. *The Academic Mind.* Glencoe, Ill., Free Press, 1958. Survey of professors' orientations to the political climate and pressures of the McCarthy years; correlation of their attitudes with characteristics of their colleges. Eight indices were used to describe political orientations of respondents; two described their colleges.

C. G. McClintock and H. A. Turner. "The Impact of College upon Political Knowledge, Participation, and Values," *Human Relations*, Vol. XV, 1962, pp. 163-176. Surveys of freshmen and seniors in several Southern California colleges.

T. M. Newcomb. *Personality and Social Change: Attitude Formation in a Student Community.* New York, Dryden, 1943. Pioneering study of political socialization—in this case, liberalization of political and economic attitudes of Bennington College students under the influence of peer group and faculty.

D. Riesman, et al. *Faces in the Crowd.* New Haven, Yale University Press, 1950. Highly stimulating use of case materials to delineate political and personality styles and their relation to socializing factors. Includes depictions of several varieties of schools and associated characteristics of students.

————. "Review Article: The 'Jacob Report.'" *American Sociological Review*, Vol. xxiii, Dec. 1958, pp. 732-738. See note on Jacob (above).

M. A. Rozanov. (N. Ognev, pseud.) *The Diary of a Communist Schoolboy*. Trans. by A. Wirth. London, Gollancz, 1928. Fiction based on first-hand observation.

N. Sanford, ed. "Personality Development During the College Years," *Journal of Social Issues*, Vol. xii, 1956, entire issue. Key variables of intensive study of Vassar students: "intellectual functioning and achievement," "authoritarianism and its opposites," "femininity and masculinity," "psychological and physical well-being." Expanded coverage of these and additional themes can be found in Sanford, ed., *The American College*, New York, Wiley, 1962.

H. Selvin and W. O. Hagstrom. "Sources of Support for Civil Liberties," *British Journal of Sociology*, Vol. xi, 1960, pp. 51-73. Differences in patterns of attitude change among different student groups.

M. E. Spiro. *Children of the Kibbutz*. Cambridge, Harvard University Press, 1958. Socialization for democratic living in a collective community. See also: Spiro, "Education in a Communal Village in Israel," in Spindler, *Education and Culture, op.cit.*, pp. 467-479.

C. H. Stember. *Education and Attitude Change*. New York, Institute of Human Relations Press, 1961. Analysis of data from Roper's survey of freshmen and seniors in a variety of colleges showed that although on the average there was little change in attitudes toward minorities, there were great variations when the sample was categorized according to field of study, living arrangements, etc.

G. G. Stern. "Environments for Learning," in N. Sanford, ed., *The American College*, New York, Wiley, 1962, pp. 690-730. Outlines ranges of variation of attitudinal climates.

S. A. Stouffer. *Communism, Conformity, and Civil Liberties*. New York, Doubleday, 1955. Level of education is correlated with political tolerance. Study is extremely interesting methodologically.

F. H. Werner. "Acculturation and Milieu Therapy in Student Transition." See note in Section iii.c (above).

L. Wylie. *Village in the Vaucluse*. Cambridge, Harvard University Press, 1960. Chapter 4, "School," is a perceptive and thorough description of French classrooms and schools, with explicit and implicit comparison to the U.S.A. This unusually acute piece of observation demolishes many clichés about French education.

3. Student Activities and Student Culture

C. Driver. "Undergraduate Politics," *Spectator*, Vol. cxciv, Feb. 18, 1955, p. 178. Union and clubs at Oxford.

D. Goldrich and E. W. Scott. "Developing Political Orientations of Panamanian Students," *Journal of Politics*, Vol. xxiii, Feb. 1961, pp. 84-107.

Rose Goldsen, R. Williams, and E. A. Suchman. *What College Students Think*. Princeton, Van Nostrand, 1960. Multi-campus survey.

Janine Hauser. "Notes sur Quelques Attitudes de la Collégienne Dakaroise." *Bulletin de l'Institut Français d'Afrique Noire*, Vol. xvii, Series B (1955), pp. 203-209. Compares essays written by Dakar and Brazzaville school girls according to degree of Westernization vs. attachment to tribal living, etc.

H. Hyman, et al., "The Values of Turkish College Youth," *Public Opinion Quarterly*, Vol. xxii, fall 1958, pp. 275-291.

M. L. Levin. "Social Climates and Political Socialization," *Public Opinion Quarterly*, Vol. xxv, winter 1961, pp. 596-606. High school opinion climates as related to students' political attitudes. In the same issue, see also D. L. Sills, "Three 'Climate of Opinion' Studies," pp. 571-574, and J. S. Coleman, "Comment on Three 'Climate of Opinion' Studies," p. 607-610. Key factors in opinion development: "political interest" (in specific issues) and "strength of attachment to a social system" (family, school, etc.). Amply annotated.

S. Spector. "Studies and Politics in Singapore," *Far East Survey*, Vol. xxv, May 1956, pp. 65-73.

S. W. Washington. "Student Politics in Latin America: The Venezeulan Example," *Foreign Affairs*, Vol. xxxviii, April 1959, pp. 463-473. Political sources, exploitation, and implications of student unrest. Well-documented presentation of a rather typical Latin American case.

Maria Yen. *The Umbrella Garden: A Picture of Student Life in Red China.* New York, Macmillan, 1954.

4. Cross-Cultural Education

J. W. Bennett, H. Passin, and P. K. McKnight. *In Search of Identity: The Japanese Scholar in America and Japan.* Minneapolis, University of Minnesota Press, 1958. Culture contact and conflict; acculturation.

Cora Dubois. *Foreign Students and Higher Education in the United States.* Washington, D.C., American Council in Education, 1958. Based on critical comments of 43,000 students.

Claire Seltiz, et al. *Attitudes and Social Relations of Foreign Students in the United States.* Minneapolis, Minnesota, University of Minnesota Press, 1963.

M. E. Spiro. "The Acculturation of American Ethnic Groups," *American Anthropologist*, Vol. LVII, 1955, pp. 1,240-1,252.

J. Useem and Ruth H. Useem. *The Western-Educated Man in India: A Study of His Social Roles and Influence.* New York, Dryden, 1955. Over one hundred students studied after their return to India.

Jeanne Watson and R. Lippett. *Learning Across Cultures.* Ann Arbor, Michigan, University of Michigan Press, 1955. Social-psychological study of foreign exchange.

B. POLITICAL CULTURE

1. Attitude Studies

H. Becker. *German Youth.* New York, Oxford University Press, 1946.

R. Centers. "Children of the New Deal: Social Stratification and Adolescent Attitudes," in R. Bendix and S. M. Lipset, eds., *Class, Status, and Power*, Glencoe, Ill., Free Press, 1953, pp. 359-370. Reprinted from *International*

Journal of Opinion and Attitude Research, Vol. IV, 1950, pp. 315-317; 322-335.

Françoise Giroud. *La Nouvelle ,Vague: Portraits de la Jeunesse.* Paris, Gallimard, 1958. *L'Express* poll of values and attitudes of French youth in 1957.

D. V. McGranahan. "A Comparison of Social Attitudes among American and German Youth,": *Journal of Abnormal and Social Psychology*, Vol. XLI, 1946, pp. 245-257.

H. Schelsky. *Die Skeptische Generation—Sociologie des Deutschen Jugend.* Dusseldorf, Diedrichs, 1957.

2. Case-Oriented Studies

E. C. Banfield. *The Moral Basis of a Backward Society.* Glencoe, Ill., Free Press, 1958. A Southern Italian community remains underdeveloped partly because of socialization patterns that produce negative "associational sentiments" which render individuals incapable of effective organizational participation.

Daedalus. Journal of the American Academy of Arts and Sciences. "Youth: Change and Challenge," entire issue, Vol. XCI, winter 1962. Provocative articles written from a variety of disciplinary viewpoints and employing, in some cases, materials from several cultures.

E. H. Erikson. *Young Man Luther: A Study in Psychoanalysis and History.* New York, Norton, 1958. Stirring and provocative, Erikson's study elucidates the dynamics and direction of leadership by relating Luther's personal identity crises to the needs and possibilities for action in Luther's world.

C. S. Johnson, ed. *Education and the Cultural Process.* Chicago: University of Chicago Press, 1943. Reprinted from *The American Journal of Sociology*, Vol. XLVIII, May 1943, entire issue. Case studies and essays concerning acculturation, of which one aspect is political socialization. Includes studies of influences on immigrants, minority groups, and traditional societies.

A. Kardiner and L. Ovesey. *The Mark of Oppression: A Psychosocial Study of the American Negro.* New York, Norton, 1951. Conditions of socialization, which themselves are related to the life-chances and cultural orientations of Negroes, starkly limit Negroes' capacity to behave in ways required for effective functioning of organizations. Parts I and III are of greatest relevance for political scientists.

R. Lane. "The Fear of Equality," *American Political Science Review*, Vol. LIII, March 1959, pp. 35-51. Lower-class whites in an Eastern city do not aspire to the political and social promises of the American Dream. A study of the dynamics of apathy.

M. B. Levin et al. *The Alienated Voter: Politics in Boston.* New York, Holt, Rinehart and Winston, 1960. Political scientists and a psychiatrist collaborate to examine the reactions of Boston voters following an electoral upset and to examine, in a more general framework, the causes and implications of "feelings of political frustration and powerlessness."

S. M. Lipset. *Political Man: The Social Bases of Politics.* New York, Doubleday, 1959. The characteristics of political man depend in various ways upon education. The clearest case of a relation is seen in Chapter IV, "Working-Class Authoritarianism," pp. 97-131; at the other extreme in some ways are the intellectuals, dealt with in Chapter x.

Eleanor E. Maccoby, R. E. Matthews, and A. S. Morton. "Youth and Political Change," *Public Opinion Quarterly*, Vol. XVIII, spring 1954, pp. 23-29.

S. E. Perry. "Notes on the Role of the National," *Conflict Resolution*, Vol. I, Dec. 1957, pp. 346-363. Social-psychological conceptualization of cross-national interaction.

D. Riesman, et al. *The Lonely Crowd*. New Haven, Yale University Press, 1950.

————. "The Lonely Crowd: A Reconsideration in 1960," in S. M. Lipset and L. Lowenthal, eds., *Culture and Social Character: The Work of David Riesman Reviewed*, New York, Free Press, 1961, pp. 419-458. Insightful dissection of American character and political style. Riesman traces the parallels and dissonances of child-rearing, education, and adult behavior in terms of styles of action. Historical sequences presented may be valid for many societies.

VII. ELITES AND CADRES

A. MILITARY

M. Berger. *Military Elite and Social Change: Egypt Since Napoleon*. Princeton Center of International Studies, Research Monograph No. 6, Princeton University, 1960.

S. M. Dornbusch. "The Military Academy as an Assimilating Institution." See note above, in Section VI.A.2.

W. Gutteridge. *Armed Forces in New States*. London, Oxford University Press (Institute of Race Relations), 1962. Includes descriptions of recruitment and training.

M. Janowitz. *Sociology and the Military Establishment*. New York, Russell Sage Foundation, 1959. Chapter III, "Assimilation of Military Roles," reviews and integrates a broad range of studies of recruitment, selection, training, and career development as aspects of socialization into the professional military, rather than the political, facets of the role. Most data from U.U.S. Useful for consideration of effects of military socialization upon political orientations.

J. W. Masland and L. I. Radway. *Soldiers and Scholars: Military Education and National Policy*. Princeton, Princeton University Press, 1957. An authoritative study.

L. Pye. *Armies in the Process of Political Modernization*. Cambridge, Massachusetts Institute of Technology, 1959.

B. GOVERNMENT: POLITICAL LEADERSHIP

H. J. Benda. "Non-Western Intelligentsias as Political Elites," in J. H. Kautsky, ed., *Political Change in Underdeveloped Countries: Nationalism and Communism*, New York, Wiley, 1962, pp. 235-251. Of particular interest: "The Military Intelligentsia." Reprinted from *Australian Journal of Politics and History*, Vol. VI, Nov. 1960, pp. 205-218.

R. Bendix. *Higher Civil Servants in American Society*. Boulder, Colorado, University of Colorado Press, 1949. Compares data from different periods.

G. I. Blanksten. "Political Groups in Latin America," in Kautsky, *Political*

Change in Underdeveloped Countries, pp. 140-166. Reprinted from *American Political Science Review*, Vol. LIII, March 1959, pp. 106-127.

J. C. Brown. "Education of the French Administrative Class," *Public Personnel Review*, Vol. XVI, Jan. 1955, pp. 17-27.

L. W. Dobb. "Ganda Leaders, Followers, and Attitudes toward Leadership," in L. A. Fallers and Audrey I. Richards, eds., *Studies in Leadership in Modern Buganda*, London, Oxford University Press, 1961.

G. Fitzgerald. "Training Public Servants for National Development," *Administration*, Vol. VII, winter 1959-1960, pp. 337-348.

P. Garigue. "Changing Political Leadership in West Africa." *Africa*, Vol. XXIV, July 1954, pp. 220-232. After a synopsis of methods of attaining political leadership among Yoruba, Ashanti, and Dahomean peoples, Garigue concludes that "the political systems of the three colonies . . . today give predominant influence to those persons who are characterized by being 'manipulators' of slogans and associations."

C. Geertz. *The Bureaucracy Sector: The Development of the Civil Servant Elite In the Social Context of Economic Change: An Indonesian Case Study.* Cambridge, Massachusetts Institute of Technology, 1956.

R. Heussler. *Yesterday's Rulers: The Making of the British Colonial Service.* Syracuse, N.Y., Syracuse University Press, 1963. Recruitment and training through 1947.

R. K. Kelsall. *Higher Civil Servants in Britain.* London, Routledge and Kegan Paul, 1956.

H. D. Lasswell, D. Lerner, and C. E. Rothwell. *The Comparative Study of Elites.* Stanford, Calif., Stanford University Press, 1952. Authoritative approach to research into political elites; uses case histories, power structure analyses, etc.

D. Marvick, ed. *Political Decision Makers.* New York, Free Press of Glencoe, 1961. Collection of studies of influentials in a variety of settings. Orientation is that of "political behavior" rather than "institutional analysis."

D. R. Matthews. *The Social Background of Political Decision Makers.* New York, Doubleday Short Studies in Political Science, 1954. Includes a background discussion of theoretical points relevant to recruitment studies; uses data from several nations.

J. W. Price. "Education and the Public Service in Europe," *Western Political Quarterly*, Vol. X, Dec. 1957, pp. 817-832.

R. Wilkinson. "Political Leadership and the Late Victorian Public School," *British Journal of Sociology*, Vol. XIII, Dec. 1962, pp. 320-330. Effects of public school experience on leadership style. Developed in greater detail in Wilkinson, *Gentlemanly Power: British Leadership and the Public School Tradition*, London and New York, Oxford University Press, 1964, which stresses the congruence between the school and imperial society.

C. GENERAL: BUSINESS, INTELLECTUALS, ETC.

E. D. Baltzell. *Philadelphia Gentlemen: The Making of a National Upper Class.* Glencoe, Ill., Free Press, 1958. The upper class is seen as functioning to integrate the activities of various occupational elites. See especially: Chapter IV,

"The Structure and Function of an Upper Class"; Chapter XII, "Education and Status Ascription"; and Chapter XIV, "A Primary Group of Prestige and Power."

J. E. Goldthorpe. "Educated Africans: Some Conceptual and Terminological Problems," in A. Southall, ed., *Social Change in Modern Africa*, London; Oxford University Press, International African Institute, 1961, pp. 145-158. Asks about the nature of the classification of educated African—is it a group, an elite, a social class, or merely a category?

G. E. Lichtblau. "The Politics of Trade Union Leadership in Southern Asia," in J. H. Kautsky, ed., *Political Change in Underdeveloped Countries: Nationalism and Communism*, New York, Wiley, 1962, pp. 265-281. Reprinted from *World Politics*, Vol. VII, Oct. 1954, pp. 84-101. Relation of intellectuals to trade union movements.

S. M. Lipset and R. Bendix. *Social Mobility in Industrial Society*. Berkeley and Los Angeles, University of California Press, 1960. Comparative statistical analysis of occupational mobility in U.S. and several European nations: includes data on role of education, ideology; re-analyses data on American business leaders.

C. McArthur. "Personality Differences between Middle and Upper Classes," *Journal of Abnormal and Social Psychology*, Vol. L, 1955, pp. 247-257. Provocative hypotheses are raised, but later studies (as yet unpublished) have not confirmed McArthur's conclusions—perhaps because of changes in the upper class.

M. Maung Gyi. "An Analysis of the Social and Political Foundations of the Burmese Executive, 1948-1956." Unpublished Ph. D. dissertation, Yale University, 1958. Includes analysis of certain traditional Burmese attitudes which are dysfunctional for cooperation with government.

C. W. Mills. *The Power Elite*. New York, Oxford University Press, 1956. Advances thesis of increasing secrecy and centralization of control in the U.S. Tone is quasi-Veblenian.

E. Shils. "Influence and Withdrawal: The Intellectuals in Indian Political Development," in D. Marvick, ed., *Political Decision Makers*, New York, Free Press of Glencoe, 1961, pp. 29-56.

————. "The Intellectuals in the Political Development of the New States," in Kautsky, *Political Change in Underdeveloped Countries*, pp. 195-234. Reprinted from *World Politics*, Vol. XII, April 1960, pp. 329-368. Changes in the role of the intellectual are related to the progress of political development.

H. H. Smythe and Mable M. Smythe. *The New Nigerian Elite*. Stanford California, Stanford University Press, 1960. Education, life style, etc., of upper strata.

R. Van Niel. *The Emergence of Modern Indonesian Elite*. Chicago, Quadrangle, 1960. University training and elite careers.

CONTRIBUTORS

~~~~~~

JEREMY R. AZRAEL, born in Baltimore, Maryland in 1935, is Assistant Professor of Political Science at the University of Chicago. He spent the year 1958-1959 in the USSR as a participant in the US-USSR academic exchange program and the year 1962-1963 as a fellow of the Russian Research Center of Harvard University. He has written on various aspects of Soviet politics for such journals as *Survey*, *Problems of Communism*, and *Social Forces*, and is currently completing a study of the Soviet managerial elite.

FRANK BONILLA, born in New York City in 1925, is Associate Professor in the Department of Economics and Social Science of the Massachusetts Institute of Technology and a member of the Senior Staff of MIT's Center for International Studies. As Director of Communications Research for International Research Associates, Inc., he planned and directed large-scale opinion and attitude surveys in many Latin American countries as well as India, Singapore-Malaya, and Japan between 1950 and 1960. In 1960 he joined the American Universities Field Staff to collaborate on a four-country study of education and social development. As an AUFS Associate he also wrote and lectured on Brazil and other Latin American countries. He has contributed chapters to recent volumes on nationalism, social change in Latin America, and cross-national political research.

LEON CARL BROWN, born in Mayfield, Kentucky, in 1928, is Assistant Professor of Middle Eastern Studies at Harvard University. He has travelled and worked both in the Arab East and in North Africa. For the past few years he has been concentrating his attention on North Africa and is presently engaged in research on the modern history of that area. He is co-author of *Tunisia: The Politics of Modernization*.

JAMES S. COLEMAN, born in Provo, Utah, in 1919, is Professor of Political Science and Director of the African Studies Center, University of California, Los Angeles. He has engaged in research in Tropical Africa and is author of articles on political developments in that area. In 1963-1964 he was a Fellow at the Center for Advanced Study in the Behavioral Sciences. He is a past president (1962-1963) of the African Studies Association and a vice president and member of the Bureau of the International Congress of Africanists. He is author of *Nigeria: Background to Nationalism*, and co-author and co-editor of *Politics of the Developing Areas* and of *Political Parties and National Integration in Tropical Africa*.

MICHEL DEBEAUVAIS, born in 1922, is Professor of Economics of Education at the Institut d'Etude du Développement Economique et Social, University of Paris, where he also conducts interdisciplinary research in the field of educational planning in developing countries. He has previously been employed by the French Ministry of Foreign Affairs as assistant director of the Technical Assistance Division. Among other countries he has visited Tunisia, Brazil, Mexico, Lebanon as a consultant to UNESCO, the Organization of American States, and other international organizations. He has contributed to various journals of Economics, Social Science and Education. He is co-editor of the quarterly *Tiers-Monde*, co-author of *Some Economic Aspects of Education in Europe*, author of *L'Assistance technique en matière d'administration publique*. He has conducted research activities on educational development prospects in Latin America, world literacy, quantitative and qualitative analysis of education in Africa, quantitative history of education in France, administrative aspects of national development planning, and problems of university admissions in France.

JOSEPH FISCHER, born in New York City in 1926, is presently Lecturer in Comparative Education at the School of Education, University of California, Berkeley. He has held the posts of Lecturer and Researcher at Rangoon University, Burma (1954-1956), and Lecturer at Madjah Mada University, Jogjakarta, Indonesia (1956-1958). He has done field research in Indonesia and Southeast Asia (1960, 1962). His major interest is the role of education (particularly of universities) in the political and economic development of Asian and African countries. He has published several articles on students and universities in Asia, and is the author of *Universities in Southeast Asia*.

WILLIAM F. GUTTERIDGE, born in Surrey, England, in 1919, is Head of the Department of Languages and Social Science, Lanchester College of Technology, Coventry, England. From 1949 to 1963 he was Senior Lecturer in Modern Subjects, Royal Military Academy, Sandhurst. His particular interests are political relationships in the Commonwealth, especially in Africa. Recently he held a Nuffield Foundation Home Civil Service Travelling Fellowship in Africa to study the role of the armed forces. He is author of *Armed Forces in New States* and numerous articles, and is engaged in further writing on the military leadership in relation to society, including a full length study entitled *Military Institutions and Power in the New States*.

BERT F. HOSELITZ, born in Vienna in 1913, is an economist and a member of the Research Center in Economic Development and Cultural Change at the University of Chicago. His work in the past has involved him as a consultant to the government of India, to UNESCO, and to other agencies of the United Nations Organization. In 1955-1956 he was a Fellow at the Center for Advanced Study in the Behavioral Sciences. His primary research and teaching interests include the fields of economic growth and history and the history of economic thought. He is editor of *The Progress of Underdeveloped Areas* and *Economic Development and Cultural Change*, and author of *Sociological Aspects of Economic Development*.

MALCOLM H. KERR, born in Beirut, Lebanon, in 1931, is Associate Professor of Political Science at the University of California, Los Angeles. He taught at the American University of Beirut from 1958 to 1961 and was a research visitor at the Middle East Studies Centre of St. Antony's College, Oxford, in 1961-1962. His publications include *Lebanon in the Last Years of Feudalism, 1840-1868*, a number of articles on Arab ideological problems, and the forthcoming *Muhammad Abduh and Rashid Rida: Reinterpreting Islamic Political and Legal Theory.*

ANTHONY H. M. KIRK-GREENE, born in England in 1925, is Head of the Department of Languages, Ahmadu Bello University, Northern Nigeria. He joined the Nigerian Administrative Service in 1950 and after seven years as a district officer in the field, he was selected to organize the first Administrative Service training course for African civil servants. In 1958 he was a Harkness Fellow at Northwestern University, and between 1961 and 1963 was Visiting Professor in African Studies at the University of California, Los Angeles, and at Syracuse University. He is editorial adviser to the *Journal of Local Administration Overseas* and author of many publications on African affairs, including *The New African Civil Service: Recruitment and Resources.*

CARL H. LANDÉ, born in Tübingen, Germany, is Assistant Professor of Political Science at Yale University. In the past he has taught at the University of Kansas and the Ateneo de Manila. He has spent four years in the Philippines, engaged in research on Philippine politics. He has written a monograph, *Leaders, Factions and Parties: The Structure of Philippine Politics*, which will be published early in 1965, and is presently preparing a book to be entitled *Philippine Democracy.*

JOHN WILSON LEWIS, born in Seattle, Washington, in 1930, is Associate Professor of Government at Cornell University. He has lived and conducted research in the Far East and was a Ford Foundation Fellow in Taiwan and Hong Kong from 1959 to 1961. His primary field of research is comparative politics with particular emphasis on problems of leadership organization and control in China. He is author of *Leadership in Communist China* and *Major Doctrines of Communist China* and is presently engaged in a study of urban political development in China.

DWAINE MARVICK is Professor of Political Science at the University of California, Los Angeles. He has held teaching positions at the City College of New York, Rutgers University, and the University of Michigan. During the academic years 1951-1953, he was a Fellow at the Survey Research Center of the University of Michigan. He has previously published *Career Perspectives in a Bureaucratic Setting, Competitive Pressure and Democratic Consent* (co-author) and *Political Decision Makers* (editor). He has written studies in the fields of political recruitment and legislative behavior.

AYO OGUNSHEYE, born in Ile-Oluji, Nigeria, in 1923, is an economist and has been Director of Extra-Mural Studies at the University of Ibadan since 1957. He has served as a consultant to UNESCO and was Visiting Professor at the Sorbonne in 1959. He has travelled widely in Europe, North America, Asia and West Africa. His primary research interests include planning—economic and educational—and he has served on government planning bodies and corporations in Nigeria. He is co-author of *Problems of Economic Growth* and *Africa: The Dynamics of Change,* and editor of *Report on the Press in West Africa.*

HERBERT PASSIN, born in Chicago in 1916, is Professor of Sociology in the East Asian Institute of Columbia University. He has lived and travelled for long periods in Asia, Africa, and Mexico. He is co-author of *In Search of Identity, The Japanese Village in Transition,* and *Africa: The Dynamics of Change;* and author of *Education and Society in Japan.*

WILLIAM J. PLATT, born in Colorado in 1916, is Director of the Economic Development Division at Stanford Research Institute and Lecturer at Stanford University. On the Institute staff since 1949, he has directed research in economic development and management sciences. During the last several years his own specialization and publications have been in the economics of education and manpower development, based upon project studies in Taiwan, Thailand, Chile, and the United States. He is author of papers in *Management Science, Harvard Business Review, International Development Review,* and *Operations Research,* of which he is Associate Editor.

EDWARD A. SHILS, born in Philadelphia in 1915, is Professor of Sociology and Social Thought in the Committee on Social Thought at the University of Chicago, and a Fellow of King's College, Cambridge. He has also taught at Harvard University and at the Universities of Paris, London, and Manchester. He is the translator of works by Max Weber and Karl Mannheim, co-editor of *Toward a General Theory of Action* and *Theories of Society,* and the author of *The Torment of Secrecy: The Background and Consequences of American Security Policies; The Intellectual between Tradition and Modernity: The Indian Situation; Political Development in the New States* and of numerous articles in sociology and on the politics of underdevelopment. He is also editor of *Minerva: a Review of Science, Learning, and Policy.*

FRANCIS X. SUTTON, born in Oneida, Pennsylvania, in 1917, is Representative for East and Central Africa, The Ford Foundation, Nairobi. From 1954 to 1963 he held the posts of Program Associate, Behavioral Sciences Program and Program Associate, Overseas Development Program (Middle East and Africa), The Ford Foundation. He has taught sociology and general education at Harvard University (1949-1954), has served as Visiting Professor at Columbia University and the Massachusetts Institute of Technology and as Lecturer at Lowell Institute, Boston, the Salzburg Seminar in American Studies and the University of California, Los Angeles. He is co-author of *The Behavioral Sciences at Harvard,* and of *The American Business Creed,* and has contributed many papers on political and cultural change in Africa to several volumes and various scholarly journals.